MANAGEMENT

IN THE MODERN

ORGANIZATION

MANAGEMENT IN THE

SECOND EDITION

MODERN ORGANIZATION

Theo Haimann
Saint Louis University

William G. Scott
University of Washington

HOUGHTON MIFFLIN COMPANY Boston
Atlanta Dallas Geneva, Illinois Hopewell, New Jersey
Palo Alto London

Contents

CASES

IV STAFFING

CASES

Preface

Systems, processes, and functions form the backbone of management theory and practice. The previous edition of our book was built around these concepts, and the new edition continues this orientation. Our objective is still to integrate the proven, traditional, functional approach to management with contemporary developments from systems theory and the behavioral sciences. This framework permits us to discuss management in systems terms, which involve inputs and outputs of various processes connected by feedback loops. The relationship between the planning and controlling functions is one example of the use of this kind of analysis in our book. Another example is the relationship between planning and organizational design, which we discuss in the context of decision-making.

We consider management to be a system-facilitating process that through various social and technological activities utilizes resources, influences human action, and plans change in order to accomplish rationally conceived goals. Management consists not just of one activity, but of several distinct, though interrelated, processes — planning, organizing, staffing, influencing, and controlling. The systems approach helps the student to comprehend the intricate relationships among these five functions and to picture managing as a dynamic and unified activity.

The functional systems approach enables us to incorporate in this book current developments in management and in the behavioral sciences. Attention is given to sociology and to psychology as they bear upon the management of human resources. Thus, leadership, group dynamics, and motivation are all appropriate subjects to be treated within the framework we have selected. Moreover, quantitative tools and techniques can be included. We discuss quantitatively focused subjects such as operations research, PERT, rational decision-making, and financial controls. However, the level of our consideration is elementary, requiring a minimum of mathematical preparation.

We must stress that this edition of *Management in the Modern Organization* retains its emphasis on the five basic managerial functions. These functions represent the essential elements of management: They are what managers do. By weaving the functional approach into a systems framework, we strive to make management pertinent to the student of the mid-1970's. One overwhelming fact of our culture is that we live in a society dominated by professional managers in organizations such as business firms, universities, hospitals, government departments, and social agencies. Our approach is intended to portray management as a discipline in applied science and to reinforce the professional nature of the management field.

Many important changes have been made in the new edition of *Management in the Modern Organization*. Beyond a general updating of content and reorganization of topics, we have introduced a number of new features, which will improve the teaching and learning qualities of the book. While presenting approximately the same amount of textual material as was in the previous edition, we have included new information on the social responsibilities of management and the social audit of organizations. Our discussion of the latter subject is in the completely revised, tightly integrated Part VI, on the controlling function. The chapter on decision-making has been changed extensively. Quantitative decision-making is deemphasized in this edition, and more attention is given to decision-making as a management activity having both quantitative and qualitative dimensions.

In Part V, on influencing, several new subjects reflect the rapid evolution of knowledge and practice in the areas of motivation and group dynamics. The topic of communication introduces this section, in acknowledgment of the fact that communication is central to management in organizations. Other topics receiving attention are emerging patterns of influence and various kinds of behavioral intervention such as organizational development.

These and many other improvements ensure that the total focus of contemporary information is on basic management subjects. Our aim is to give beginning students of management the foundation necessary for additional work in advanced courses in management.

Theory, concepts, and principles are fine starting points for building an understanding of management. But they are not full reflections of the everyday organizational world. Organizations have ways of taking jumps and turns that cannot be foreseen through abstractions alone. Very likely the sharpest insights into the challenges management faces come from the analysis of case studies based on organizational experiences.

This edition has many more cases than the previous one had. Many of our colleagues who used the first edition of this book expressed a need for brief cases involving each process of management individually. Thus, at the end of each discussion of a process are several short cases, which enable students to apply the concepts in each part of the book to real situations. Concluding the book are fourteen comprehensive cases describing complex situations and showing the interaction of the managerial functions. They are good indicators of the importance of an integrated systems approach to management.

The cases reveal the interdisciplinary nature of management. In their details are many contributions of the behavioral sciences as well as many of the theoretical concepts discussed in the book. Close study of the case studies will demonstrate both the relevance and the limitations of theory. It will also reaffirm the importance of the human factor in management and reemphasize the need for managers to utilize human resources effectively.

Two problems of language that we faced when writing the first edition continued to bother us as we prepared this one. Throughout the text we use the term "subordinate" to designate a person who is below a manager in an organization's hierarchy. We make no qualitative judgment by our use of this word and certainly do not want to disparage nonmanagerial people. The term should be understood to denote position, not worth. The other problem results from the lack of a pronoun in English that unambiguously refers to men and women together, making awkward "his or her" and "he or she" locutions unnecessary. Current authoritative publications, including those issued by the federal government, use the masculine pronoun even when a reference is to men and women, and we have for the most part done so too. Such usage is unfortunate, though concise, and should not be interpreted as a sign of belittlement or ignorance of the important managerial roles played by women.

A book of readings and a Study Guide are available for use with the new edition of *Management in the Modern Organization*. Patrick E. Connor of Oregon State University has compiled and introduced a collection of articles drawn from current literature on management. The anthology, *Dimensions in Modern Management*, is coordinated chapter by chapter with the textbook. Professor Connor has also prepared the Study Guide, which summarizes the key points of each chapter of *Management in the Modern Organization* and provides objective questions for review and discussion questions for individual and class use. The aim of the Study Guide is to maximize students' comprehension of and involvement in the subject of the textbook. *Dimensions in Modern Management* and the Study Guide, used in conjunction with *Management in the Modern Organization*, compose a set of complementary materials designed to maximize the teaching and learning effectiveness of our book.

For teachers, Michael J. Jedel of Georgia State University has prepared an excellent manual, which should be gratefully received by busy instructors and those new to the teaching of management. Professor Jedel has worked closely with us and with Professor Connor to provide a helpful and informative manual.

Our revision of the text has benefited from suggestions made by many individuals. Detailed analyses and reviews of the manuscript were prepared by Gaber Abou El Enein (Mankato State College, Minn.) and William C. Pavord (University of Cincinnati, Ohio). Some users of the first edition kindly took the time to suggest ways to improve the second edition. They are A. J. Dirksen (Northern Illinois University), Leo Erlon (Rockland Community College, N.Y.), C. R. Hitchcock (Armstrong College, Calif.), Jason Kesler (Bellarmine-Ursaline College, Ky.), George E. Maddox (Georgia Institute of Technology), John J. Murphy (Indiana State University, Terre Haute), Paul H. Pietri and Dennis F. Ray (Mississippi State University), and William Rodgers (Moor Park College, Calif.). The ideas and comments of all these people helped us to prepare this book. We also want to acknowledge the assistance we received from our editors at Houghton Mifflin. Their contributions are beyond counting.

Theo Haimann

William G. Scott

MANAGEMENT

IN THE MODERN

ORGANIZATION

I MANAGEMENT AND SYSTEMS

THE FUNCTIONAL APPROACH TO MANAGEMENT SYSTEMS. The diagram shows the approach and organization of this book. The sequence in which the functions of management are discussed and their interdependence reflect the essence of the management process.

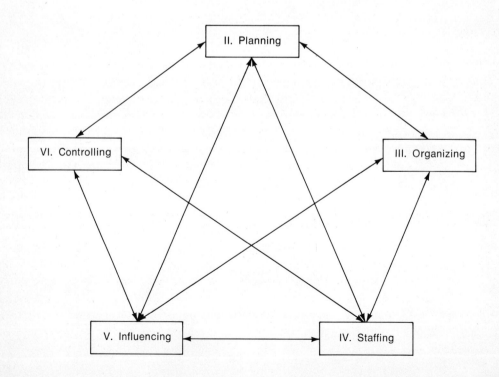

Systems abound everywhere. They pervade the skies, from our great solar system to the galaxies beyond. On a far more minute scale, finely wrought gears, levers, pins, and springs compose the system of a watch. Vast or microcosmic, all systems have something in common. They are sets of interrelated, interdependent elements in which the function of each part fully depends on the other parts, which in turn rely on the element initially singled out.

The complexity of most systems necessitates some sort of management to assure that the parts perform for the benefit of the whole. Management is a process by which all systems are administered. Managers are concerned with the elements of organization, how they relate to one another and how they may be regulated in order to achieve the system's objectives. Of course, in this book we are particularly interested in the management of a man-made system known as an organization.

Often a system is arbitrarily defined; that is, its limits are whatever they have been defined to be. We may say, for example, that General Motors is a system, but so is the Chevrolet division of GM and so are its industrial relations department, assembly lines, research and development arm, and sales promotion program. The problem of defining systems is somewhat eased by the concept of *subsystems* within a system. We may speak of the various divisions of GM as subsystems. However, we must recognize that GM is a subsystem of the environment in which it operates. Again, what constitutes a system is a matter of definition.

Definitions that say everything really say nothing. They obscure the variations and subtleties that are important to layman and scientist alike. Our broad definition of systems makes no explicit provision for the feedback in all living and some nonliving systems. Feedback regulates a system's

activities by detecting variations in performance. Without it, life itself could not go on, for biological feedback regulates body temperatures, blood sugar, and many bodily functions. For example, when we are hot, we perspire; when we are cold, we shiver. Thus our internal thermostat maintains our average bodily temperature at 98.6 degrees Fahrenheit. Feedback also keeps us comfortable in our homes; the thermostat that controls room temperature represents the feedback principle at work. In like manner, other kinds of feedback control electronic, mechanical, and even business systems.

Keeping the business system and its feedback in line so that the system performs smoothly calls for an administrative procedure that is part active and part intellectual. Enlightened by feedback, management pulls together the various components of a system to make it work efficiently. Some managers consider management an agent of change that adapts an organization to its environment. In the view of others, management allocates and controls resources so that objectives are met.

Traditionally, management has been defined in terms of what managers do. Although this approach has limitations, it has not been improved upon. The management process involves a group of functions performed by managers regardless of the type of organization they are in. The functions are planning, organizing, staffing, influencing, and controlling. Interrelated and interdependent activities, they proceed without beginning or end. They exist and apply in all administrative organizations regardless of the limits placed on the system or subsystem. In this book we examine the functions that help an organization to reach its objectives.

Management is not impersonal, though it might at first seem to be so. Management is a human force. It is vital in a society dominated by organizations — hospitals, schools, government agencies, unions, as well as businesses. All organizations are run by managers who are responsible for policies that affect millions of people who consume products, use services, and work for and own businesses. The manager is one of the most strategically placed persons in our society. He has not always been so important. His present status results from modern social and technological changes. In other nations, the dominant class may be capitalist entrepreneurs, politicians, churchmen, or soldiers. These groups are still important in our society, but their power is shared by managers who pursue their own careers in administrative positions.

Of the many forces responsible for the appearance of career managers, technology, specialization, and complexity of organization are among the most important. Modern manufacturing methods and an abundance of products are signs of technological advances in applied science and engineering. Increased specialization through the education and experience of employers accompanies technological sophistication. Finally, the growth in the size and complexity of organizations creates a variety of skills and combinations of specialties absent from small enterprises.

Historically, these forces widened management's role. Around the turn of the century, managers were concerned with the coordination of machines, raw materials, and production processes. Employees were not ignored but were considered things — economic factors of production. Today they are viewed by management as people with a full range of social and psychological needs. In light of this development, it has become fashionable to talk about sociotechnical systems. These are systems that permit machines, men, groups, tasks, and technology to interact effectively. To design interactional systems that account for all the resource inputs of an organization is one of the most important challenges facing professional management. Effective organizational design is not static but must include the ability to adapt to change.

Fortunately, the enlarged responsibilities have been met by new techniques. The computer revolution and the applied behavioral sciences help managers do their job. Additionally, information is increasing at an exploding rate. Managers know more; they can therefore manage with a surer hand and are in a better position to plan. Improved techniques increase management's confidence that it can wisely shape an organization's destiny. Nevertheless, management still deals with uncertainty. The impression that managers can predict with assurance is false, and history tells us that they are endlessly "questing the one best way," constantly searching for rational and appropriate methods to achieve a particular end and trying to improve the techniques for organizing, producing, and distributing goods and services.

The burden of modern management is awesome. Managers are responsible for (1) the design of interactions in a sociotechnical system, (2) change and organizational flexibility, (3) the allocation and flow of material and human resources, (4) processes affecting the production, distribution, and financing of goods and services, and (5) the relationship of the organizational system to its environment. In short, management seems to do everything.

Establishing contact with such vast responsibilities is difficult, though not impossible. For this purpose, we have chosen the functional approach. Management functions describe management's role; they are uniquely managerial forms of behavior. If

one is asked what managers do, a reasonable
answer is: They plan, organize, staff, influence, and control.

The professionalization of management,
the historical evolution of management, the
contemporary status of management, and
management decision-making are discussed
in Part I. Our observations in this part are
intended to be general, providing perspective
for the functional areas examined later.

CHAPTER 1

Management: A Point of View

Sometimes "management" identifies the executive personnel in an organization — all those having supervisory responsibility, from the chief executive down to the first-line supervisor. At other times, the term refers to planning, organizing, staffing, influencing, and controlling. "Management" also designates a body of knowledge, a practice, a discipline. David Lilienthal used it this way when he wrote, "In creating the Tennessee Valley Authority, Congress adopted and carefully wrote into law the basic principles and practices of modern management."[1] Clearly, "management" means different things to different people —a condition not unusual in so young a discipline.

Our definition stresses management as a process: *Management is a social and technical process that utilizes resources, influences human action, and facilitates changes in order to accomplish an organization's goals.* While emphasizing processes, however, we do not ignore the personal side of managerial behavior or the general side of management as a discipline. Managers and management are found in all institutions. Like mathematics, the management activity is cross-cultural. A major characteristic of modern nations is management in organizations.

WHO ARE THE MANAGERS IN AMERICA?

Managers have the right to order with authority action from others: They are hospital administrators, generals, college deans, heads of government agencies, chiefs of subdivisions, school superintendents, labor leaders, bishops, charity fund administrators, business executives. The administrative or managerial group is composed not only of top-level men and women but also of subordinate executives. All are managers. Our attention in this chapter is directed mainly to business executives and to the extensive research made into their family backgrounds, education, and motivations.

Social Background

In earlier years, business leaders tended to come from wealthy families of independent businessmen. Most leaders of industry now assert that they come from poor

---

[1] David E. Lilienthal, *TVA: Democracy on the March* (New York: Harper and Row, 1944), p. 167.

Figure 1-1. Family Background of Big Business Executives, 1900–1964

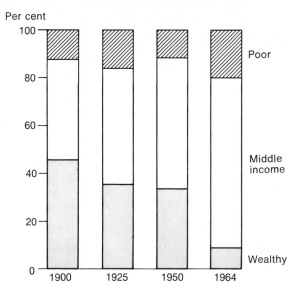

Increasing numbers of top executives in industry have been coming from poor or middle-income families.

Source: Adapted from the *Scientific American* Research Study *The Big Business Executive, 1964.* Copyright © 1965 by Scientific American, Inc. All rights reserved.

and middle-class homes, and there is little doubt that today's executives are drawn from wider socioeconomic classes than ever before (see Figure 1-1). The reason for this democratization is education. The greater relative availability of education makes it possible for individuals of all classes, as Figure 1-2 indicates, to qualify for employment in large business firms. This opportunity together with the stress on science in higher education has increased vertical mobility in business regardless of employees' social backgrounds.[2]

Of course, a successful business career depends on more than education. Business leaders tend to come from big cities rather than from small towns or farms. They frequently move around the country during their business careers, often transferring within their company but changing companies as well. Geographic mobility seems to be directly related to a successful business career.[3] Large companies seem generally to offer more opportunity for rapid advancement than do smaller companies. However, many small science-based firms that create and produce space-age products provide unusual opportunities, and scientists with an administrative bent and managers with a science background frequently find that such small firms provide

[2] See Mabel Newcomer, *The Big Business Executive: The Factors That Made Him* (New York: Columbia University Press, 1955).

[3] W. Lloyd Warner and James C. Abeglen, *Occupational Mobility* (Minneapolis: University of Minnesota Press, 1955), ch. 1.

Figure 1-2. Family Background and Education of Big Business Executives, 1900–1964

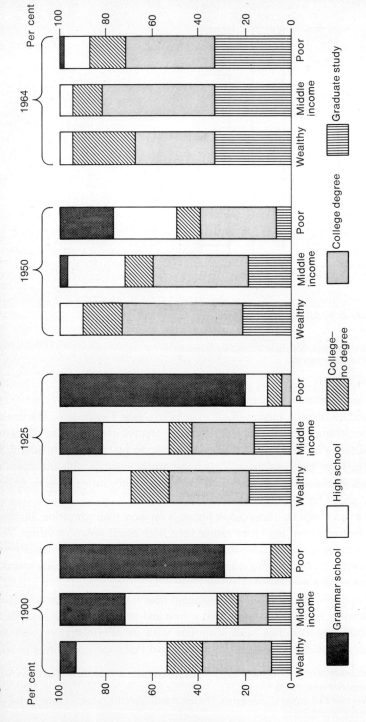

In 1964, the percentage of executives from poor homes who were qualified by under-graduate degrees and by graduate study was just about equal to corresponding per-centages for executives from wealthy homes. This contrasts sharply with the situation in 1900.

Source: Adapted from the *Scientific American* Research Study *The Big Business Executive*, *1964*. Copyright © 1965 by Scientific American, Inc. All rights reserved.

an excellent setting for a career. For example, Route 128, which circles Boston, is lined with many small science-oriented businesses employing bright young scientists and administrators.

For those in the middle and lower managerial levels the opportunities also seem great. Individuals who lack "connections," who came from small towns, who grew up in laboring and farm families, who have not attended prestigious schools, may find their way into management. Young men and women can expect to equal or exceed their fathers' social and economic status through advancement in management.

The Need for Achievement

Being a manager may satisfy an individual's need for achievement. David C. McClelland calls it n(achievement), which is present in each individual's personality.[4] It is a learned need, conditioned by family life, religion, education, and indeed the whole process of growing up in a competitive culture. McClelland believes that the level of a society's n(achievement) determines the extent and speed of its economic growth and development. This need impels a person to advance in an organization. Achievement underlies business drive and motivation. McClelland shows, for example, that in small firms the president's n(achievement) is higher than that of his subordinate managers. In other cases, less successful managers do not score so high in n(achievement) as successful ones. Managers in large companies in the $20,000 to $25,000 salary bracket are most concerned about achievement, and managers in general are more highly motivated to achieve than other professional or technical specialists are.

As a result of their motivations, education, background, aspirations, and identification with administrative specialization, managers seem to be emerging as an elite group. This contention may be disputed, but a trend toward a managerial elite has been identified by several writers.[5] The rise of a managerial class brings up the issue of professionalization.

MANAGEMENT AND PROFESSIONALISM

In the past, "professional" was narrowly applied to three groups — lawyers, doctors, and clergymen — and professionalism carried a precise meaning when applied to them. Five elements characterize a profession:

1. definite standards of entry and practice
2. a body of knowledge pertaining to the discipline

---

[4] David C. McClelland, "Business Drive and National Achievement," *Harvard Business Review* 40 (July–August 1962): 99–112.

[5] For example, James Burnham, *The Managerial Revolution* (New York: Day, 1941); John Kenneth Galbraith, *The New Industrial State* (Boston: Houghton Mifflin, 1967); Suzanne Keller, *Beyond the Ruling Class* (New York: Random House, 1963); and C. Wright Mills, *The Power Elite* (New York: Oxford University Press, 1956).

3. a code of ethics
4. prescribed course training
5. privileged testimony in a court of law

Viewed from the standpoint of these criteria, management does *not* qualify as a profession. Nevertheless, the term "professional management" is widely used, and what it means must be investigated, especially in light of the emergence of a managerial class and the growth of the influence of managers.

The scope of management interests is wide. Managers must balance the expectations of all their clients — of all those who have contacts with modern business organizations. In addition to customers, clients include employees, who are often represented by large national unions having managers of their own. Business management must relate to independent groups, such as union managers, who are not subordinate to them and with whom they must bargain as peers. Business management must be involved with owners, suppliers of raw materials and capital, and with independent but related firms that form a network of manufacturing, service, and distribution facilities. Moreover, the government must also be dealt with, for it has a stake in business as a producer of tax revenue, a supplier of goods, and an object of regulation.

Management has faced particularly difficult challenges. Government controls, especially those imposed since 1950, have complicated managers' jobs. Government regulations affect wages and hours and collective bargaining. Government action influencing the determination of company policy has become increasingly important, particularly in the forms of legislation and the enforcement of anti-monopoly regulations by the Anti-Trust Division of the Justice Department. Management must frequently consider how prevailing anti-trust legislation might affect a contemplated expansion move. Current legislation on Fair Employment Practices to end discrimination is another example of government influence on company policy. Not only do managers have to be concerned with the interests of government, employees, and owners; they must also pay attention to public opinion. The public expects business transactions to be conducted ethically, in a spirit of social responsibility. Finally, many businesses have expanded internationally. This growth has placed cross-cultural demands on firms operating in foreign countries. Management must balance all these interests; it cannot maximize one to the exclusion of the others.

Management's responsibilities for ensuring the health of the enterprise increase as the complexity of the environment in which it operates grows. Adjusting to change and to new business demands used to be relatively simple for the owner-manager. But the modern manager, who usually is not the owner, must consider not only the owners' welfare but also technical factors. These factors vary with the complexities of production techniques, distribution, location, and employees' skill. The trend toward industrial complexity, which began before World War I and rapidly grew during World War II, has become increasingly apparent.

The professional manager must be an expert, not only in his job and in his company but also in his use of principles, concepts, and practices peculiar to management. He must be both a specialist and a generalist in order to cope successfully with the complex business environment.[6] This professionalization of management's role has paralleled the development of general environment changes that have been at work since the turn of the century.

The Separation of Ownership from Control

In an earlier era of business, even the greatest companies were commonly controlled and managed directly by the owner. Andrew Carnegie headed the nation's largest steel company before it was merged with other firms to form United States Steel Corporation in 1905. As businesses grew, it became apparent that conventional ways of obtaining capital had to be replaced by new methods of financing. Encouraged by favorable state legislation, firms increasingly turned to incorporation. From the sale of stock to the public, vast amounts of capital were available for financing business expansion, and the positions of owners and managers were transformed.

The widespread sale of stock meant that the ownership of America's major corporations was distributed broadly throughout society. Frequently no one person, group, or trust owned as much as one per cent of the outstanding shares. For all practical purposes, owners could no longer directly control the policies of the corporation. Although the *legal* right of control was retained by the stockholders, *actual* control of the corporation fell to management.

The separation of ownership from control created a stewardship role for management. Like the stewards of biblical times, managers are responsible for the property of others. Management must protect the owners' property and assure that it yields a reasonable return and grows in value. However, in doing so, managers are confronted with more conflicting demands than were faced by the biblical stewards, demands emanating from the many clients of a business organization.

One of the reasons managers claim the designation "professional" stems from this unique stewardship role: Managers run corporations in the interest of owners (paying considerable attention to other interests as well), though they do not have controlling ownership interests.

Technology

American science and technology are constantly challenged by consumer demands, by nuclear and space research, by the need for sophisticated military weapons systems, and by international competition for markets. Whether the challenge is met successfully depends on American industry and management. The response of management has been to recruit great numbers of scientists, engineers, and technicians, who are employed to create advanced products, manufacturing systems, and distribution schemes.

[6] Mabel Newcomer, in *The Big Business Executive*, traces the rise of professional management over a fifty-year period. She discusses the changing social, cultural, and educational backgrounds of top executives.

Like the separation of ownership from control, this change in the industrial scene seems to have contributed to the professionalization of management. Managers must be concerned about the work environment of these intensively educated persons so that they can effectively use their special talents. Creative initiative flourishes best when encouraged and suitably rewarded, and it requires freedom from direct control. Management can meet these needs only by revising its style of leadership.

The training of management is changing. According to one study, "As of 1964, 38 per cent of America's big business executives had a technical background." Of executives holding academic degrees in 1964, 33 per cent received theirs in engineering, science, and technology. This compares with 7 per cent in 1900. Not only are more executives getting degrees (28 per cent in 1900, 74 per cent in 1964), they are also getting more degrees in technical subjects.[7] These changes in education are bound to influence management. As Warren G. Bennis says, managers will increasingly draw "their rewards from inward standards of excellence, from their professional societies, and from the intrinsic satisfaction of their task."[8]

Professional Management Beyond Business

The growth of organizations in nonbusiness fields has increased the number of managerial positions and the demand for people trained in management areas. Local, state, and federal government employs many executives to fulfill diverse functions in various agencies. Each federal agency alone requires a cadre of managers to oversee the execution of the agency's responsibility. Public administration programs that train people for government service are popular in universities around the country; more and more of them stress management theory and practice. Education, health care, and social service organizations also require the talents of people in management jobs. Reflecting this need, large universities offer administrative programs in nursing, hospital administration, social welfare, education, natural resources, and library science. These programs all draw from a common store of management theory and concepts. Although we cannot call management a profession, the emergence of a literature pertaining to a body of knowledge and practice is an important first step toward so terming it.

MANAGEMENT: ART OR SCIENCE?

Management cannot be considered a science like the natural and physical sciences. The experimentation characteristic of them is impossible in management, which is not able to control all factors. However, managers can define, analyze, and measure phenomena, and they can use some of the techniques that enable scientists to experiment and obtain proof.

[7] The Big Business Executive, 1964, Scientific American (Special Report, 1965), pp. 1, 9.
[8] Warren G. Bennis, Changing Organizations (New York: McGraw-Hill, 1966), p. 25.

In *The Principles of Scientific Management,* Frederick W. Taylor, an early major contributor to management theory, directed his attention to science and management.[9] While considering the best way to make a cut of specified dimensions in a piece of metal of a particular size and hardness, he realized that an operation could be repeated but that experiment and proof were less applicable to dealings with people. Nevertheless, he proposed to standardize motivation through financial incentive systems and the selection of employees according to specific job requirements. Taylor applied "scientific" techniques to studies of planning, organization, routing, and costing. He used a scientific approach to derive new techniques for action.

Taylor believed that the science of management, like political science and military science, was concerned with human beings, and he realized that the principles of these "sciences" cannot be subjected to rigorous experimentation as can those of the exact sciences. According to Luther Gulick, "The contention that free will, built into man's heredity, removes his behavior and institutions from scientific analysis arises from a limited definition of the term 'science' which mankind cannot accept."[10] He maintains that management is a science dealing with a field of knowledge that has been defined and made public. Because it has been "pursued for some time, organized into an elaborate system of explicit primary and secondary theories, which have been or are being tested by logic and the realities of the universe, so that past and current changes in the system can be explained and future changes predicted or produced," it may be termed a science.[11]

What can be said about management as an art? Art is the systematic application of knowledge and skill to achieve an objective. This definition applies not only to the creation of a work of art such as a painting or a symphony but to a mundane managerial undertaking such as organizing a sales promotion program for a new product. The key word in the definition of art is "application." Management is an activity applying knowledge and skill to achieve objectives and is an art as well as a science. Chester I. Barnard, an eminent contributor to management theory, has pointed out that the function of the sciences is to explain the phenomena, the events, the situations of the past. Their aim is not to produce specific events, effects, or situations, but rather to produce explanations, which are termed knowledge. However, Barnard wrote, "It is the function of the arts to accomplish concrete ends, effect results, produce situations, that would not come about without the deliberate effort to secure them. These arts must be mastered and applied by those who deal in the concrete."[12] This know-how is indispensable to the manager, who learns it mainly through practice and experience.

---

[9] Frederick W. Taylor, *The Principles of Scientific Management* (New York: Harper and Row, 1911).

[10] Luther Gulick, "Management Is a Science," *Journal of the Academy of Management* 8, no. 1 (March 1965): 7–13.

[11] *Ibid.,* p. 10.

[12] Chester I. Barnard, *The Functions of the Executive* (Cambridge, Mass.: Harvard University Press, 1938), p. 290.

MANAGERIAL SKILLS

Managers need human, conceptual, specialized, and general skills. Regardless of the level of their authority, they must have human and conceptual skills: They must be able to influence, motivate, and induce people to accomplish organizational objectives while creating a climate for the satisfaction of individual needs. Conceptual skills permit an executive to generalize solutions of business problems and apply them to specific situations. Specialized and general managerial skills vary according to an executive's position in the organization. Most managers at lower levels use specialized skills extensively in their work. As they advance, specialized techniques become less important and the application of general skill grows. There is a saying that in any given position in an organization everyone above the individual seems to be a generalist and everyone below a specialist.

Clearly, the chief executive of an organization exercises far fewer technical skills than his subordinates do. However, because of his general skills he will be aware of the kinds of specialists needed by his organization. Generalists must know what specialized talents are needed by the organization. When specialties have been determined, according to the requirements of the tasks to be performed, the generalist's job becomes one of coordinating activities.

Joan Woodward has shown that technology shapes the role of management and the structure of the organization.[13] She stresses that the nature of work determines the behavior of people on the job, the relationships among them, and the work they do. For example, work in a gravel pit is unskilled, and the structure of the organization is likely to be rigid. Work in a research laboratory requires considerable education and skill, and the structure of the organization will probably be loose. The managerial generalist should be aware of such differences in task and technology. They affect the design of the organization and management's role in it.

THE NEED FOR A MANAGEMENT THEORY

The development of managerial skills requires a theory of management. Theory cannot give managers complete and detailed answers for every situation in which they find themselves, but it can supply guides for action; it enables managers to approach problems systematically. According to a familiar saying: "It's a good theory but it doesn't work in practice." This is nonsense. Theories that do not work when applied are not good theories. The tests of a theory are predictability and generality. A "good" management theory predicts events reliably and encompasses a wide number of situations. The functional theory of management meets these tests well. Managers perform the planning, organizing, staffing, influencing, and controlling functions in a large variety of organizational situations.

The statement is often made that management is universal, that management skills and functions are transferable to different settings. The implication of this is

[13] Joan Woodward, *Industrial Organization: Theory and Practice* (London: Oxford University Press, 1965).

that a top executive of a transcontinental trucking firm could effectively manage a religious order. Recently, however, the transferability of management skills has been questioned. Woodward says:

There is a fairly widespread belief that at certain levels of responsibility managers and administrators are interchangeable between one industry and another and even between industry and other institutions. It is true, of course, that some people can and do move around successfully in this way, but the fact that they tend to be the exceptionally able people with a wide range of knowledge and skill may obscure any difficulties inherent in the interchange.[14]

Also doubtful is the universality of management principles.[15] Span of control, unity of command, and other principles of organization do not apply when an organization exceeds certain limits of size and technological complexity. Current research and theory also make the universality notion difficult to defend.

The picture changes for management functions; they are more nearly universal. Regardless of the managerial level or the type of organization, planning, organizing, staffing, influencing, and controlling are apparent.[16] Perhaps this is why the functional approach to management has been durable, although it has come under attack from those who maintain that it oversimplifies the manager's role. The functional approach is a valuable first approximation of the management process for two reasons: It describes what managers do, and it is a system of classification that is useful for organizing the contributions of many disciplines to management.

THE MANAGEMENT FUNCTIONS

Management is defined by the work it performs. It is a system of behavior composed of processes conventionally called functions. Each function embraces events that move the organization toward the attainment of its goals.

Planning

Planning is selecting objectives, policies, programs, and procedures. An intellectual activity, planning involves looking ahead and preparing for the future. Logically, it precedes any of the other managerial functions, though it cannot be said that when the other functions have been performed, the manager begins planning again. At the start, nothing can be done without a plan. As a manager carries out his functions, he continues to plan, revising his ideas and choosing alternatives when necessary.

[14] *Ibid.*, p. 79.
[15] For example, Herbert Simon, *Administrative Behavior* (New York: Macmillan, 1957), ch. 2.
[16] For a discussion of systems and processes see Wendell French, "Processes Vis-à-Vis Systems: Toward a Model of the Enterprise and Administration," *Journal of the Academy of Management* 6 (March 1963): 46–57.

Thus, although planning is the primary function, it is also a continuing one, carried out simultaneously with the other principal functions.

Organizing

The organizing process establishes the work to be done and decides the relationships among the tasks required to achieve the organization's objectives. Work elements are grouped and assigned to appropriate departments. When the manager organizes, he assigns activities, divides work into individual jobs, and defines the relationships among them. He also delegates the authority necessary to complete the task. Authority is the key to the manager's job; its delegation is the key to organization.

Staffing

Management is responsible for recruiting and making certain that people are available to fill positions. Staffing involves the selection and training of future managers. It also includes establishing procedures for manning executive posts, replacing and promoting employees and appraising their performance, and devising a system of compensation.

Influencing

People must be motivated to achieve the objectives of the job for which they are responsible. Influencing has many dimensions — morale, employees' satisfaction and productivity, leadership, communication. Management's goal is to create an environment that workers find agreeable and that promotes the objectives of the organization. In addition, influencing has important effects on a firm's flexibility and adaptability.

Controlling

The control process involves activities essential to ensuring that events proceed as planned. Through control, management determines whether objectives are being achieved and takes corrective action when they are not. Here again, we see the significance of planning as a primary managerial function. A manager could not determine whether work was proceeding properly if there were no plan to check against.

Interrelationship of Functions

Management sets standards for controlling in the planning process; staffs are organized and influenced; organizational designs must account for influencing and controlling staff members. These interrelationships could be multiplied endlessly. Even though *conceptually* we can separate managerial functions for analysis, *empirically* in the day-to-day job of the manager the activities are inseparable.

Clearly, the management cycle is a system of interdependent activities. The sequence in which they are performed and the amount of time spent on each are not relevant. Each blends into another and each mutually affects the performance of the others. The output of one activity provides the input for another.

The view of management as a system did not emerge suddenly. It evolved over nearly eighty years. Chapter 2 is an examination of that evolution, a consideration of some of the antecedents of contemporary management.

Discussion Questions

1. Is education a democratizing force in our society, especially as it is related to the selection of people for management careers?

2. In a six-month period, how many professional managers do you come into contact with? When your parents and grandparents were your age, did they have fewer or more such contacts? What reasons can you give for your answers?

Supplementary Readings

Blau, Peter M., and W. Richard Scott. "The Concept of Formal Organization." In *Dimensions in Modern Management*, edited by Patrick E. Connor. Boston: Houghton Mifflin, 1974.

Dale, Ernest. "The Functional Approach to Management." In *Toward a Unified Theory of Management*, edited by Harold Koontz. New York: McGraw-Hill, 1964.

Gooding, Judson. *The Job Revolution*. New York: Walker, 1972.

McGregor, Douglas. *The Professional Manager*. New York: McGraw-Hill, 1967.

Vollmer, Howard M., and Donald L. Mills. *Professionalization*. Englewood Cliffs, N.J.: Prentice-Hall, 1966. See chapter 8.

CHAPTER 2

Landmarks in Management History

Ever since man has engaged in group effort, there has been a need for the effective coordination of collective enterprises. Because management has a history as long as that of human cooperation, it would be reasonable to expect an accumulation of writings on management dating back many years. However, works by Andrew Ure and Charles Babbage, from the 1830's, mark the beginning of the study of management.[1] There were other writers on the subject later in the nineteenth century, but not until the start of the twentieth century did a body of literature about management develop.

MANAGEMENT IN PRE-MODERN TIMES

The great structures of antiquity must have required a high order of managerial skill. We tend to think that the pyramids of Egypt were constructed by a corps of slaves under the lash of the Pharaoh's overseers. Actually they were a sort of public works project built for the most part by the freemen of villages. The stone in the pyramids was quarried many miles up the Nile River from the construction site and was cut to size so that it could be fitted into place with slight adjustment. Each piece was moved by barge to the place of construction according to a well-synchronized schedule. Architects and engineers had important jobs to do. Orders and reports had to be passed up and down the line of command so that various activities could be coordinated. Indeed, the Egyptians had to know some basic principles of management.

The Greeks also had managerial knowledge. Socrates, in his discourse with Nicomachides, answers a question about whether one individual could manage a chorus as well as an army. He expresses his understanding and opinion of management: "Over whatever a man may preside, he will, if he knows what he needs and is able to provide it, be a good president, whether he have the direction of a chorus, a family, a city or an army." He goes on to say that one ought not

despise men skillful in managing a household; for the conduct of private affairs differs from that of public concerns only in magnitude; in other respects they are

[1] Andrew Ure, *The Philosophy of Manufacturers* (London: Charles Knight, 1835); Charles Babbage, *The Economy of Machinery and Manufacturers*, 3d ed. (London: Charles Knight, 1833).

similar; but what is most to be observed, is, that neither of them are managed with-
out men, and that private matters are not managed by one species of men, and
public matters by another; for those who conduct public business make use of
men not at all differing in nature from those whom the managers of private affairs
employ; and those who know how to employ them, conduct either private or public
affairs judiciously, while those who do not know, will err in the management of
both.[2]

In ancient Rome, an unwritten law stated that soldiers, administrators, and judges
had to take counsel before action, even though the advice was not followed.[3] This
is one of the first instances of the principle of compulsory staff advice. As the
Roman Empire grew, the bureaucracy of government also expanded. Government
agencies proliferated. Official control was felt in important areas of government
activity — tax collection, public works, food supply, administration of territories,
entertainment, accounting for the fiscal affairs of the state. The chief accountant, in
fact, had the title *a rationibus,* denoting the rational management of financial affairs,
one of the earliest applications of rationality to administration.

In spite of such indications of managerial efforts, no systematic treatise on
management and organizational problems was written in pre-modern times. The
government, the military, and the Catholic Church were the major administrative
organizations in pre-industrial society. They were run in accordance with "rules,"
which more recently have come to be called principles, and demanded from the
people associated with them a commitment to their purposes. The objectives of each
were rather uncomplicated. The Church and the military used chains of command,
coordination, unity of command, and staff.

From the military in particular came numerous applications of many of the
principles that modern businesses later adopted. The military chain of command
originated in the armies of antiquity and medieval times. The scalar principle —
the grading of duties according to the amount of authority and responsibility involved in them — was the backbone of early military organizations and remains
important in organizing activities. In the military, the chain is longer than in other
organizations, originating with the supreme commander and extending to squad
leader. Lengthening the chain of command requires lengthening the chain of delegated authority. This became necessary in Napoleon's time, though the commander
in chief was still able to survey the entire field of battle. Later, when the military
faced larger and even worldwide battlefields, the conduct of warfare involved no
new principles of organization but merely an extension of the old ones. Thus
centralized control and decentralized operations, or centralization of command and
decentralization of execution, evolved.

The staff concept also originated with the military. Use of the staff principle is
probably as old as war itself because of an army's ever-present need for quarters.

[2] Plato and Xenophon, *Socratic Discourses,* trans. J. S. Watson (New York: Dutton, 1910),
book III, ch. IV, pp. 80–81.
[3] H. Stuart Jones, "Administration," in *The Legacy of Rome,* ed. Cyril Bailey (Oxford:
Clarendon Press, 1923), pp. 98–99.

However, the formal function of a quartermaster, who is a staff officer, did not emerge until 1655 in the army of the margrave of Brandenburg, the precursor of the Prussian army. The evolution of a staff and the idea of a general staff were Prussia's contributions to modern military organization, the former beginning in the early part and the latter being developed toward the end of the nineteenth century. The Prussian army included in its system of staff training the periodic return of staff officers to line duty. General Scharnhorst, concerned that line and staff officers might become segregated, insisted on the rotation of duties.

In addition to the concepts of line and staff organization, management has learned other things from the military. For a long time the military has been aware of the necessity of not only telling the soldier what was expected of him but also telling him why. According to James D. Mooney: "It is recorded of Napoleon, the most autocratic of men, that he never gave an order without explaining its purpose, and making sure that this purpose was understood. He knew that blind obedience could never ensure the intelligent execution of any order."[4]

THE INDUSTRIAL REVOLUTION

The industrial revolution, which occurred in Europe at the end of the eighteenth century, brought great changes to business life and social structure. Its essential characteristic — the transfer of human skill and energy to machines — had profound consequences for management. Artisans who could not afford to purchase their own machinery were obliged to work on the premises of an artisan who possessed the necessary equipment. For the first time salaried employees worked in the employer's home or workshop. At the same time we see the start of the putting-out system. An entrepreneur of means who could not perform the functions of the artisan might purchase machinery and raw material, put them into the homes of artisans or workers, and at regular intervals collect the finished product. The entrepreneur had to manage workers, materials, and machinery; he had to coordinate the efforts of people toward a common objective.

The use of power, first from water and then from steam, together with concentrations of capital in the form of machinery, brought people together in a central location, from which emerged the city as well as the complex manufacturing organization. Eventually, the "managerial revolution" followed from these beginnings, for it was only natural that with the increase of business activities came a corresponding increase of managerial problems. However, there was a time lag before managerial problems were recognized. Logically, some attempt to produce a "science" of management should have been undertaken during the industrial revolution or shortly thereafter. But such an effort did not materialize. Management was the most neglected element of the industrial revolution; it was superseded by mechanical and technological improvements to create a mass production, mass consumption economy.

[4] James D. Mooney, *The Principles of Organization,* rev. ed. (New York: Harper and Row, 1947), p. 131.

Because the industrial revolution did not bring about managerial enlightenment, managers had to meet the demands of a growing economy and the necessity for specialization as best they could with whatever their knowledge and experience suggested. Some took clues from the military and church organizations, which had successfully applied principles of management for hundreds of years. These institutions provided "effective examples of the application of the principles to a single industrial unit for its internal operating necessities."[5]

THE SCIENTIFIC MANAGEMENT MOVEMENT

Although Charles Babbage and a few other early nineteenth-century British writers were concerned with management in a limited way, the real beginnings of a science of management did not emerge until nearly a hundred years later. Some remarkable Americans — mostly engineers such as Frederick Winslow Taylor, Henry Lawrence Gantt, Harrington Emerson, Carl Barth, Frank Bunker Gilbreth, and Lillian Moller Gilbreth — are credited with laying the foundation of the management movement, which became known as scientific management. Some credit must also be given to progressive American manufacturers such as Henry R. Towne and William Sellers, the latter for a long time Taylor's employer.

The Start of Scientific Management and the ASME

Industrialization created technological and human problems for management. Neither problem could be ignored; however, management was better prepared to cope with the first than with the second. Virtually nothing had been written about how to coordinate and motivate human effort in a business operation. Furthermore, there was no way for managers who were engaged in the daily running of their businesses and shops to exchange experiences. In this vacuum Henry R. Towne in 1886 made an appeal for writings about management theory and practice.

He did this mainly through the American Society of Mechanical Engineers (ASME), whose members were men in the theoretical and practical sides of mechanical engineering. Among them were managers and owners of businesses, such as Towne, who was the founder of the Yale and Towne Lock Company. The ASME provided a kind of professional association for shop managers. When Towne was elected president of the society in 1886, his inaugural address was an appeal to people in management to contribute articles on this subject to *Transactions*, the group's official magazine.

Frederick W. Taylor

At first the response to Towne's appeal was not overwhelming. However, in 1895 an article by Frederick W. Taylor appeared. His contribution was entitled "Piece

[5] *Ibid.*, p. 169.

Work System" and included two revolutionary proposals. He first urged the establishment of performance standards based on the scientific determination of how long a job should take. Workers who exceeded the standard were to be paid more than those who did not. The standard speed for a job might be 30 pieces per hour and the rate for each of the first 30 pieces might be 5 cents. A worker making 30 pieces an hour would receive a wage of $1.50. For the thirty-first piece produced the rate jumps to 8 cents and the hourly wage increases to $2.40. The strong financial incentive that this system provides is obvious. The scheme was in line with Taylor's philosophy of rewarding "first-class" men amply and punishing those who did not meet productivity goals. The *differential rate* became the basic ingredient of modern incentive systems.

Taylor's second proposal was that people responsible for making time measurements and setting job standards should concentrate on this task and be removed from those who supervised production activities. The notion of separating "planning from doing," as Taylor viewed it, was the beginning of the idea of *functional staff* organization. Taylor expanded on the functional concept in later years.

Taylor's article was the first intellectual foray into the hitherto uncharted management field. The time was right for the experimentation Taylor carried on. An engineer, he was trained in the basic physical sciences and was accustomed to applying the analytical tools of a scientist to problems of all kinds. Taylor founded the scientific management movement, though he did not coin the term scientific management.[6]

Before 1895, the foreman was responsible for setting standards for a job. The worker did not know how much management could and should expect of him, and in his concern for his livelihood he tended to make a job last as long as he could. In various experiments Taylor applied scientific methods to learn how much a worker should do. Not surprisingly, his efforts met with objections. Workers feared that his purpose was to force them to work faster. However, his intention was not only to increase production; he was also interested in increasing rates of pay as workers produced more.

Taylor's efforts marked the first time that scientific principles were applied to the problems of management. Taylor tried to determine how much workers could do, given the proper tools and instruction in their use. He was the first to state that management's duty was to tell workers what is expected of them and to specify the way in which the job is to be done. In all his experiments, Taylor strove to be fair. He thought scientific management could not exist in an establishment unless "both

[6] In 1910 and 1911, following the request of railroads in the East, the Interstate Commerce Commission held hearings to increase freight charges. Shippers opposed to the rate increase hired as their attorney Louis Brandeis, who later became a justice of the U.S. Supreme Court. Brandeis in turn engaged the services of general management experts, among them Harrington Emerson, a man with years of experience in improving business and personnel efficiency by scientific methods. During the hearings Emerson stated that if railroads used modern management techniques they could probably save great amounts of money. In these discussions the expression scientific management was used. Taylor and his colleagues adopted it when he published his book *The Principles of Scientific Management* in 1911.

sides . . . recognize as essential the substitution of exact scientific investigation and knowledge for the old individual judgment or opinion, either of the workman or the boss, in all matters relating to the work done in the establishment."[7] Whenever output increased, he raised wages. Most of his experiments were carried on between 1880 and 1890, while he was superintendent at the Midvale Steel Company in Philadelphia. After several years as a management consultant and another period of employment with the Bethlehem Steel Company, Taylor finally settled down to record his findings and theories. In general, he and other early contributors to management whose writings appeared in the pages of the ASME *Transactions* focused on one question: How can we devise better financial incentives to motivate workers to produce more?

The Emergent Philosophy of Scientific Management

Management interests hesitatingly expressed in the ASME *Transactions* in the late 1800's became the basis of a lively movement after the turn of the century. Exponents of scientific management sought no less than a "mental revolution" on the part of workers and management to change human relationships in industry and reduce conflict.

The heart of the movement and the way to industrial peace rested in mutuality of interests, which in turn was largely dependent on expanding productivity. People reasoned that the objectives of workers and managers were compatible: Workers wanted wages, managers desired profit, and greater wages and profits depended on increasing productivity. Therefore, workers and managers had a mutual interest in making sure productivity increased. Scientific management was supposed to stimulate the mental revolution, causing managers to manage better and workers to work harder.

In addition to Taylor, the movement was given momentum by other notable individuals. Henry Gantt, a student of Taylor's, is best known for his contribution to the techniques of production control. The Gantt Chart is still used to keep track of production schedules in manufacturing firms. Later in his career, Gantt became interested in industrial leadership and the role of scientific management in building national power.

Frank and Lillian Gilbreth were also important early in the movement. Their slogan was "the one best way." To find the best way to do a job, they used motion study, which reduced each task to its component movements. They believed that from motion and time studies more accurate job standards could be developed. Motion studies were also used to eliminate unnecessary movements from work. Lillian Gilbreth pioneered in personnel management; she was interested in the scientific selection, placement, and training of personnel.

Others active from the turn of the century until 1925 included Morris L. Cooke, known for his application of scientific management to public administration, and

---

[7] Frederick W. Taylor, "Testimony Before the Special House Committee," *The Principles of Scientific Management* (New York: Harper and Row, 1911), p. 31.

Carl Barth, an early associate of Taylor. Mary Parker Follett's contributions in the 1920's and 1930's were the foundation for a truly modern conceptualization of management and the administrative organization.

The Work of Henri Fayol

At the time of Taylor's activity in the United States, Henri Fayol, a French mining engineer, was making a great contribution to the science of management in Europe. Born in 1841 and graduated as a mining engineer in 1860, Fayol was employed by a French coal mine combine. He became its chief executive and remained in that position until he retired in 1918, to devote his time to the study of management. From 1918 until his death in 1925, Fayol sought to popularize his theory of administration. He was instrumental in starting in Paris a center of administrative studies, at which weekly meetings were held and from which came a considerable amount of management literature. There too a series of lectures described as "Fayolism at the School of Higher Commercial Studies" was given. In addition to his interest in popularizing his own administrative theories, Fayol set himself another goal: "trying to persuade government to pay some attention to principles of administration."[8]

Fayol tried continuously to apply managerial principles to managerial functions. In 1900 and 1908 he delivered two papers indicating his thinking about management. In 1916 his book *Administration Industrielle et Générale* was published. It was not available in English until 1929, and even then only a few hundred copies were distributed; not until 1949 was an English edition (retitled *General and Industrial Management*) widely distributed in the United States.

In *General and Industrial Management,* Fayol looks at management activities from the point of view of top management. In his preface he states: "Management plays a very important part in the government of undertakings: of all undertakings, large or small, industrial, commercial, political, religious or any other. I intend to set forth my ideas here on the way in which that part should be played."[9] He proposed to divide his work into four parts. The first deals with the necessity and possibility of teaching management. The second contains the principles and elements of management. In the third part, Fayol intended to write about his personal observations and experience, and in the fourth he planned to add the lessons of the war. The last two parts, however, were never written. Apparently he was going to present in them the practical application of the principles he sets forth in the first two. Lyndall F. Urwick, a British authority on management, points out in his introduction to Fayol's book that the essence of Fayol's views can be found in an interview published in 1925.[10]

In dealing with principles and elements of management, Fayol divides activities into six groups — technical, commercial, financial, security, accounting, and managerial. He dwells on the last group and distinguishes between "general prin-

[8] Lyndall F. Urwick, foreword to *General and Industrial Management*, by Henri Fayol, trans. Constance Storrs (London: Pitman, 1949), p. viii.

[9] Henri Fayol, *General and Industrial Management*, p. xxi.

[10] Urwick, foreword, p. x.

ciples of management" and "elements of management." Some of what he includes in the former category would today properly be considered policies, rules, and guides. Moreover, we would label Fayol's "elements of management" as "the functions of management." Fayol divides managerial functions into five broad categories — planning, organizing, command, coordination, and control.

Many concepts that have become traditional — universality of management, unity of command, the scalar chain, authority and responsibility — were originally applied to management by Fayol. His contribution to the theory of management is probably the most revolutionary and constructive ever made. His short book is the culmination of an outstandingly effective managerial career.

An Appraisal of Scientific Management

Taylor looked at management principles primarily from the bottom up, starting on the shop level. Fayol's observations were made on the management level, directed from the top down. Fayol was a high-ranking manager of his corporation, and his observations reflected his position. He was in a better position than Taylor to observe the functions of a manager. Taylor had begun at the bottom of the industrial hierarchy and had worked upward. Nevertheless, any evaluation of their contributions must recognize that to Taylor scientific management had two levels — one of philosophy and the other of mechanisms. The aims he sought on the level of philosophy were not realized because his hope that enlightened workers and managers would cooperate as partners in expanding productivity failed to materialize — at least not in the way he had anticipated. The assumption of mutual interest in the successful performance of an organization was not sufficient grounds for the establishment of industrial harmony.

On the level of mechanisms, in contrast, Taylor's scientific management found acceptance and widespread use. Various wage incentives, time study, motion study, work simplification, efficiency systems, and other devices were adopted and applied in both business and government organizations. That some of these were misused to exploit employees and deprive them of their share of increased productivity is a matter of record.

Taylor would have deplored the abuses. He felt that the fruits of efficiency had to be distributed equitably for the goals of scientific management to be attained. The scientific management movement failed to achieve this, but it did leave a legacy from which management continues to benefit. It opened the door to scientific methods and techniques. It freed management from reliance on tradition and rule of thumb methods to solve problems. To this extent then, management science is a direct outgrowth of Taylor's efforts at scientific management.

THE HUMAN RELATIONS MOVEMENT

Supporters of scientific management were responsible for establishing one of the major currents in management thought. Participants in the human relations movement were responsible for the other. Scientific management sought higher productivity based on the premise that man was rational and economically motivated to work. The human relations movement added another dimension to the understanding of motivation. It began at Harvard University, where a group of scholars led by the eminent psychologist Elton Mayo designed a research project to measure the effect on productivity of conditions in the work environment such as light, noise, and rest periods. The project started as a straightforward series of experiments in industrial psychology based on the hypothesis that a direct relationship existed between workers' productivity and the physical condition of the work environment. The experiments were conducted in 1927 at the Hawthorne plant of the Western Electric Company in Cicero, Illinois. F. J. Roethlisberger and William J. Dickson along with other researchers were responsible for the field work. The research came to be known as the Hawthorne Studies.[11]

The researchers were not far into their project when they realized something was wrong. They were not getting the results they expected. When the light in the one experimental room was reduced, for example, productivity went up instead of down. Something was indeed peculiar about the way the experiments were turning out. The researchers suspended activities and reviewed their initial findings, assumptions, and research design. They concluded that their basic assumption was wrong. Much more than the physical surroundings of the work environment affected productivity. Workers reacted to psychological and social conditions by producing at greater or lesser rates. Informal groups affected productivity; so did participation in decision-making and recognition of the individual employee, both of which had a favorable effect. Clearly, the giving or withholding of social and psychological satisfactions could influence employees' morale. It was only a step from this realization to the deduction that morale and productivity were directly related: High morale leads to high productivity and vice versa.

Experiments using the behavioral sciences to test these preliminary observations were devised. This was the first time that behavioral sciences such as sociology and social psychology were used together, systematically, in the service of management. If the Hawthorne Studies did nothing else, they contributed the introduction of the behavioral sciences to management. But they actually did much more than this. They demonstrated that workers are motivated by more than the satisfaction of economic needs and that they seek to fulfill social and psychological needs, which cannot be met entirely by money. They showed that an organization is a social system and not just a logical arrangement of work functions. Although tasks are important, so are the interactions of individuals and small groups with the tasks and with each other. The Hawthorne Studies also provided management with tools and skills to run organizations better by taking into account human factors.

With the development of the human relations movement in the 1930's, management thought divided into two main streams — the industrial management approach, following the traditions of scientific management, and the human factors

---

[11] See F. J. Roethlisberger and William J. Dickson, *Management and the Worker* (Cambridge, Mass.: Harvard University Press, 1956).

approach, following the lead set by the Hawthorne Studies. This division still exists, and current developments such as management science and industrial humanism reflect the quantitative and humanistic aspects of early management theory.

OTHER ADVANCES IN THE 1930's

The 1930's was a fruitful period for management. During the decade numerous individuals made distinguished contributions to the field. James D. Mooney and Alan C. Reiley attempted to systematize a theory of formal organization into a body of laws and principles.[12] They considered unity of action the principle underlying all organizational efforts, and from it they derived three subordinate principles:

1. the *scalar principle*, based on delegation that created the chain of command coupled with unity of command
2. the *functional principle*, based on specialization of work
3. *line and staff*, which introduced the idea of support and advisory activities for the main functions of an organization

The work of Mooney and Reiley was influential in shaping management thought about organizing.

In a work of broader scope, Ralph C. Davis developed the notion of the business plan.[13] This concept, similar to Fayol's, was a comprehensive model of business and management functions. Emphasizing business objectives as the starting point, Davis identified them as profit, service, and social. To achieve these objectives, management must plan, organize, and control. The functional approach to management was widely accepted and provides the basis for most elementary treatments of the subject.

One of the most distinguished collections of articles dealing with management was assembled by Luther Gulick and Lyndall Urwick in 1937.[14] The anthology does not represent a single theory or model of management practice; rather it is a collection of essays on a number of topics by the foremost management thinkers of the day. It was a milestone in management thought because it demonstrated the progress management had made in a relatively short period of time. Further, it firmly established the direction of research and speculation for the future. For example, one article brought the problem of span of control into focus. The problem and issues dealt with in the papers indicated that management had emerged as a discipline in its own right. Not only were management problems on the shop floor receiving attention; so too were issues vital to general management and administration.

[12] James D. Mooney and Alan C. Reiley, *Onward Industry* (New York: Harper and Row, 1931).
[13] Ralph C. Davis, *Industrial Organization and Management* (New York: Harper and Row, 1939).
[14] Luther Gulick and Lyndall F. Urwick, *Papers on the Science of Administration* (New York: Columbia University Press, 1937).

THE SYNTHESIS

Late in the 1930's, Chester I. Barnard, wanting to show that human factors and industrial management approaches were complimentary, published *The Functions of the Executive*.[15] Barnard, who for years was vice-president of the New Jersey Bell Telephone Company, anticipated and inspired some of the directions taken by management thought after the Second World War. His views on leadership, authority, and decision-making were influential.

Barnard suggested that management's responsibility was to create a cooperative system capable of satisfying the personal objectives of employees while meeting the impersonal objectives of the business. He said that business could exist by satisfying one or the other objectives but a cooperative system would meet both. Thus management has to be proficient in both human and technical skills; there should be no inconsistency between these skills when the total organizational needs of a business are considered.

This is approximately where management theory stood in 1940 at the beginning of the Second World War. Considerable progress had been made in understanding the management process and its functions. Through the Hawthorne Studies there had been an effort to introduce the behavioral sciences into management practice. An attempt had been made to reconcile the human and nonhuman elements in management. The concept of *system* was also introduced in this period, but it was not exploited. We shall see how contemporary developments are elaborations of these directions.

Discussion Questions

1. Why have unions never been particularly excited about the concept of mutuality of interests? What forces in the employment relationship make this concept viable? What forces work against its viability?

2. At the turn of the century, management confronted two major types of problems — human and technological. Such problems exist today. Which type do you think is the most pressing? Why?

Supplementary Readings

George, Claude S., Jr. *The History of Management Thought*. Englewood Cliffs, N.J.: Prentice-Hall, 1968.

Koontz, Harold. "The Management Theory Jungle." In *Dimensions in Modern Management*, edited by Patrick E. Connor. Boston: Houghton Mifflin, 1974.

Mee, John F. *Management Thought in a Dynamic Economy*. New York: New York University Press, 1963.

---

[15] Chester I. Barnard, *The Functions of the Executive* (Cambridge, Mass.: Harvard University Press, 1938).

Scott, William G., and Terence R. Mitchell. *Organization Theory*. Homewood, Ill.: Irwin, 1972.

Urwick, Lyndall F. "Major Concepts of Management." In *Readings in Management*, edited by Ernest Dale. New York: McGraw-Hill, 1965. See pp. 115–17.

Wren, Daniel A. *The Evolution of Management Thought*. New York: Ronald Press, 1972.

CHAPTER 3

Contemporary Management:
Status and Issues

By the early 1940's management theory was firmly based on the ideas and contributions of Taylor, Fayol, and others. After the Second World War traditional theory was infused with new ideas concerning universality, transferability of managerial skills, and general principles of management that had gained wide acceptance. Even with such infusion, however, traditional management theory remained intact until the 1950's, when an explosion of knowledge suddenly shook the foundations of management. Old ideas toppled and along with them fell the vested interests of some management specialists who either did not understand or would not accept innovations. By 1960, certain scholars believed the field of management to be in complete disarray.[1] Let us see how this startling development came about.

TRADITIONAL MANAGEMENT THEORY

The management theory that had evolved by the 1940's may be compared to a well-charted plain. Its landmarks stand out distinctly against a background of economic and rational assumptions about the business enterprise, its organization, and the behavior appropriate to it. Harold Koontz attributes the following seven features to traditional theory:

1. Management is a process composed of functions. What management is can be deduced by analyzing what managers do.
2. The principles of management have an empirical foundation; they are based upon the experience of those who developed and used them and thus have value for clarifying and improving management practice.
3. Management principles provide a take-off point for research to prove their validity and improve their applications to practice.
4. Management principles are valuable, practical, a priori elements of managerial theory and stand as universal truths until disproved.

[1] Harold Koontz, "The Management Theory Jungle," *Journal of the Academy of Management* 4 (December 1961): 174–99.

5. The practice of management is an art that relies on principles.

6. Even if in a given situation a manager ignores a principle (but incurs an added cost) in achieving an objective, the principle is in no way invalidated.

7. Management encompasses a unique and definable body of knowledge. It is not so broad that it includes everything, nor is it so narrow that it excludes the possibility of making some generalizations.[2]

This list shows the heavy emphasis traditional theory gives to principles (items 2 through 6). The theory says that managers should rely on principles when laying out a course of action, executing functions, and following up on results. From the standpoint of traditional theory, principles are *prescriptive*.

This view has brought forth much criticism. Critics charge that principles do not generally prescribe good management practice. Rather they describe certain situations and hence do not apply in all cases; indeed, in some cases they may be misleading. One prominent critic, Joan Woodward, who has written extensively on the influence of technology on a firm's organizational structure, observes:

One interesting characteristic of classical management theory . . . is that it was developed in a technical setting but independently of technology. In general the formulas are closely linked with the personalities of those who worked and wrote in this field. . . . The expedients they found effective in practice were often given the status of fundamental truths or general laws by those attracted to their ideas.[3]

In her own work, Woodward has shown that some traditional ideas on organizational structure pertain to firms with a particular kind of technology and are less relevant for firms with other technologies. The differences between two manufacturing operations illustrate this point. An assembly activity like that for the mass production of television sets uses a technology different from that of a continuous process activity like the petrochemical industry. These diverse technologies require organizational variations relating to span of management, levels of authority, direct versus indirect labor costs, the ratio of capital equipment to labor.

The relationship of technology to organizational structure is a recent source of dissatisfaction with traditional management theory. Previously, individuals in the behavioral sciences and in the quantitative management sciences voiced objections to the principles approach. Such dissatisfactions have helped to lead management from the plains of traditional theory to the forests of new ideas. The transformation has been due in part to contributions from fields outside but allied to management and in part to changes in the environment in which management operates.

The move from the plains to the forest has proved beneficial to both theory and practice. New ideas supplied by the behavioral sciences illuminate human motiva-

[2] *Ibid.*, p. 176.

[3] Joan Woodward, *Industrial Organization: Theory and Practice* (London: Oxford University Press, 1965), p. 35.

tion and organizational behavior. Management science permits a precision never before possible in areas such as inventory control and production planning. It has also enlarged managerial concepts through operations research. New opportunities for foreign investment in conjunction with improved communication and transportation have heightened managers' interest in cross-cultural understanding. Meanwhile, at home, faced by changes in the work force and in products and technology, managers have been obliged to rethink long accepted standards for leadership and organizational systems. Finally, the pressing issues of environment and social responsibility have caused management and the public to begin to reconsider industry's role in society.

CONTRIBUTIONS OF THE BEHAVIORAL SCIENCES

The Social System Concept

Very likely the major contribution of the behavioral sciences to management is the concept of *social systems*. Such a concept views an organization as more than an economic entity that rationally uses men, machines, and materials to advance the causes of efficiency and profit. It regards organizations as a fusion of *parts, processes,* and *goals,* which comprise a living, growing, changing system.

The parts consist of people, machines, and material resources, as well as tasks, formal structures of authority and power, and small groups also possessing some authority and power. Depending upon and influencing one another, the parts are tied together by processes such as communication and decision-making, which in turn link the parts and aim them squarely at organizational goals.

The communication network is the central nervous system of an organization. Through it flows information that supplies the parts with the data upon which decisions are based. Decision-making activates the system. It consists of five steps:

1. identification and definition of the problem or decision area
2. search for alternative courses of action based on the collection of data
3. selection of the most suitable alternative
4. execution or taking action
5. comparison of results with initial expectations

Decision-making cannot occur without communication, and communication has no purpose if it is not used for making decisions. Decision-making shapes and directs the parts of the organization and helps coordinate them for achieving the organization's goals and objectives.

The social system concept frees management from a narrow, efficiency view of the organization; it incorporates many variables that affect the system and influence the actions of management. The concept gives the manager more leverage for adjusting the system and a more realistic picture of his place in it and his impact on it.

Psychology

Of all the behavioral sciences, psychology has been the greatest shaper of management thought. Managers are continually influencing and motivating people, and they must know how to do it effectively. Tactics such as pay increases and threats of punishment may improve productivity, but they may also raise costs.

Psychologists have shown that people hope to satisfy a wide range of needs at work — not only economic needs but also social and personal ones. To the extent that people find at least partial fulfillment of their needs in the work environment, they can be influenced to work willingly, productively, and cooperatively. In other words, employees' morale appears to depend on how well the work environment satisfies their needs. One objective of management development is to train managers to create a work climate that provides a wide range of satisfaction for the individual. This can be done through providing opportunities for employees to participate in decision-making, communicating with employees so that they know what is going on and how it affects them and their job, and giving employees recognition so that they feel a sense of worth and believe they are important to the over-all operation of the enterprise. Much organizationally oriented psychology is concerned with how the satisfaction of participation, communication, and recognition needs influences morale and productivity.

A recent development in this area (mentioned in Chapter 1) is McClelland's use of the concept of n(achievement). The need for achievement is the individual's and, collectively, the nation's drive for fullfillment.[4] The concept has many implications for management: It can be used to select managers by identifying those who are high in n(achievement); training programs may be built around it to raise the level of n(achievement) of managers; and it is helpful for motivating people in emerging nations to assist in the economic development of their countries.

Sociology

Two major contributions to management have come from sociology. The first is focus on small groups, often treated in management literature as the informal components of organization. Much has been learned and conveyed to management about the behavior of small groups, their influence on members, and their impact on the formal structure. For example, the small group is frequently the focus of team effort in many situations. At one extreme, a biller and a packer may form a two-person group that processes customers' orders in a mail-order house. At the other extreme, a team of eight or more scientists may work together on a firm's research and development projects. In an entirely different context, small groups may arise in the work setting for social purposes having little to do with the tasks of the enterprise. The other major contribution of sociology is its study of complex formal organizations.

[4] David C. McClelland, *The Achieving Society* (Princeton: Van Nostrand, 1962).

In addition to those two contributions, sociology has improved management's understanding of the roles played by leaders and followers and an organization's patterns of authority, power, and influence. Other contributions of sociology are closely related to psychology and may be classified as the fruit of the rapid growth of social psychology.

Social Psychology

Social psychologists study the interactions of individuals and the groups with which they associate. They examine how groups and individuals influence and modify each other's behavior. Significant work using this approach has been done on communication, leadership, and decision-making. Most recently problems of conflict and its resolution have been examined. Because of its interactional nature, social psychology has many applications in business. In fact, it is difficult to find much current work of importance that does not in some way involve the elements of individual and group behavior.

Other Behavioral Sciences

Psychology, sociology, and social psychology are the key behavioral sciences shaping management thought and practice today. However, anthropology has also made a significant contribution by revealing the impact of culture on organizations. Culture gives an organization its identity. It provides objectives and means for achieving them and is a unifying force.

Political science, another social science, has not yet been a major contributor to management. Increasingly, however, students of management are becoming aware that organizations are systems of government. Political science eventually should be able to provide valuable insights in this direction.

New Applications of the Behavioral Sciences

Most contributions of the behavioral sciences to management have been in applied areas such as psychological testing for selection and placement of personnel, training and development, leadership, communication, organization theory, and organizational change. The net effect of the behavioral sciences has been to help management create a cooperative system — a system that is both effective and efficient, like Barnard's cooperative ideal (mentioned Chapter 2).

Recently, the behavioral sciences have gone beyond the cooperative-system philosophy. Today, we are hearing more about organizational health and its main criterion, flexibility — that is, the ability of an organization to adapt in the face of change. Warren Bennis points out that a cooperative system shows the health of an organization at a particular point in time, whereas flexibility is evidence of health over time.[5] Thus the planning of change, an important part of organizational flex-

[5] Warren G. Bennis, *Changing Organizations* (New York: McGraw-Hill, 1966), ch. 3.

ibility, is rapidly becoming a major area for new applications of the behavioral sciences.

OPERATIONS RESEARCH: CONTRIBUTION OF MANAGEMENT SCIENCE

The reorientation of management thought resulting from interaction with the behavioral sciences is paralleled by changes brought about by borrowings from management science. The best known and most widely accepted branch of management science is operations research, a technique that works best in narrow decision areas that can be clearly defined and quantified.

There are many definitions of operations research. According to one: "In simplest terms, operations research can be defined as research into the relationships and functions of an organized activity. The purpose, when applied to business problems, is generally how to use the resources on hand so as to achieve optimum results."[6] Operations research is thus analytical, experimental, and quantitative. It appraises and evaluates the over-all implications of various courses of action and provides the manager with an improved basis for his decisions.

Operations research has been applied to many organizational problems, but more has been directed toward inventory control than toward any other problem in industry.[7] However, other areas such as production scheduling, sales policies, effect of night openings on department-store sales, improved rail replacement programs, more effective use of existing equipment, traffic delay at toll booths, and servicing customers have also received attention. Operations research may be applied to a specific business problem in this way:

A manufacturer of chemical products, with a wide and varied line, sought more rational or logical bases than the customary percentage of sales for distributing his limited advertising budget among products, some of which were growing, some stable, and others declining. An operations research study showed that advertising effectiveness was related to three simple characteristics, each of which could be estimated from existing sales data with satisfactory reliability: (a) the total market potential; (b) the rate of growth of sales; (c) the customer loss rate. A mathematical formulation of these characteristics provided a rational basis for distributing advertising and promotional effort.[8]

In summary, operations research theories and techniques are decision-making and control tools. Operations research models as they are related to decision-making are examined in Chapter 4.

---

[6] *Operations Research: Studies in Business Policy*, no. 82 (New York: National Industrial Conference Board, 1957), p. 9.

[7] C. West Churchman, Russel L. Ackoff, and E. Leonard Arnoff, *Introduction to Operations Research* (New York: Wiley, 1957), p. 195.

[8] Cyril C. Herrmann and John F. Magee, "Operations Research for Management," *Harvard Business Review* 31, no. 4 (July–August 1953): 102.

INTERNATIONAL MANAGEMENT

Clearly, the behavioral and management sciences are the two major sources of new managerial knowledge and the basic inspirations for the division of management thought into industrial management and human relations. However, progress in management theory and practice is not only a response to internal organization demands; it is also the product of a complex mingling of external pressures. One pressure is the increased importance of international management.

The Rise of International Management

Since the end of the Second World War, six factors have stimulated interest in international management. Increased prosperity, mainly in Western Europe and Japan, has made overseas trade and investment attractive to American businessmen. Reciprocally, there has been an increase of foreign operations in the United States but not to so great an extent.

The economic and business development of the world's emerging nations has clearly revealed the need of these countries for management expertise. Major American business schools have responded to this need by training some foreign executives both in the United States and abroad. Continuing executive development programs have also been established in Switzerland, France, and most recently in Norway as a center of management education for Scandinavian countries.

The size and technological growth of some companies, particularly in Asia, have outrun the ability of family owners to manage them successfully. The traditional pattern of family enterprise is breaking down, and more and more family-owned firms are developing a professional management cadre. The necessity for this particular turn of events was emphasized by J.-J. Servan-Schreiber in his influential book *The American Challenge*.[9]

International management associations are arising to facilitate communication between scholars and practitioners in a number of nations. Examples of such groups are the IUC (International University Contact for Management Education) and CIOS (Comité International de l'Organisation Scientifique). *Management International* is a multi-lingual journal published in West Germany as a joint venture by these groups and others.

The growth of multi-national firms is complicating the problem of management. Some people are saying that three hundred multi-national corporations will control 90 per cent of world trade by the year 2000.[10] Complex international joint ownership and franchise arrangements are emerging in many industrial sectors. For example, Japanese suppliers of some electrical components for radio and television are partially owned by American firms that use the parts for final assembly. A major food processor in America has franchises in Japanese doughnut shops. Arrangements

---

[9] J.-J. Servan-Schreiber, *The American Challenge* (New York: Atheneum, 1969).
[10] Yair Aharoni, "On the Definition of a Multinational Corporation," in *The Multination Enterprise in Transition,* ed. A. Kapoor and Phillip D. Grub (Princeton: Darwin Press, 1972), p. 3.

such as these have existed for a long time with giants like Shell and Lever Brothers. Multi-national firms are increasing at a great rate, drawing the world's nations closer together along trade and economic lines. However, the enormous problems of international management posed by these changes are not yet appreciated. Intraorganizational relationships need to be investigated, and examinations of the problems of corporate headquarters' relations with foreign subsidiaries, centralization and decentralization of operations, and organizational flexibility and change are essential.[11]

Finally, a likely result of the U.S. government's recent contacts with the People's Republic of China, in addition to diplomatic relations, is Sino-American trade. Negotiations between China and the Boeing Company are already under way. How these developments will proceed cannot be predicted, but America certainly cannot enter an era of new relationships with the Chinese while holding on to the predilections that bankrupted earlier ventures. American managers understand next to nothing about Chinese values and culture.[12]

Problems of International Management

International management brings certain problems into focus. Paramount among them is achieving cross-cultural understanding. This in turn requires cross-cultural communication. More is involved than language barriers. Intercultural communication goes beyond language to meanings attached to behavior such as friendliness, politeness, outgoingness, and efficiency. For example, in some countries promptness is not desirable behavior. Businessmen are expected to be late for appointments, conferences, and other meetings.[13]

Americans must adjust their behavior to foreign business practices. Unfortunately, American executives seem much less adaptive to foreign environments than do their European counterparts.[14] Research and theory in cultural anthropology and ecology show considerable promise of overcoming such problems and furthering the cause of international management.

TECHNOLOGICAL CHANGE AND THE LABOR FORCE

Technology has two minimum requirements: (1) "the systematic application of scientific or other organized knowledge to practical tasks," and (2) a division of

---

[11] For an example of this type of research, see Hans Schollhammer, "Organization Structures of Multinational Corporations," *Academy of Management Journal* (September 1971): 345–66.

[12] Two works describing earlier Sino-American dealings and the Confucian influence are Barbara W. Tuchman, *Stillwell and the American Experience in China, 1911–1945* (New York: Macmillan, 1970), and Chan K. Hahn and Warren C. Waterhouse, "Confucian Theories of Man and Organization," *Academy of Management Journal* (September 1972): 355–63.

[13] Edward T. Hall and William Foote Whyte, "Intercultural Communication: A Guide to Men of Action," *Human Organization* 19 (Spring 1960): 5–12.

[14] This is the view of one European observer. See Jean-Luc Rocour, "Management of European Subsidiaries in the United States," *Management International* 1, no. 1 (1966): 27.

labor so that this knowledge can be focused on a well-defined segment of work.[15] Technological advancement is the progressive use of applied science and continuous specialization. For example, William Boeing and a few mechanics built their first airplane in a converted shed on the shores of Lake Union in Seattle. It was a crude vehicle in comparison with the modern 747 aircraft. Behind the 747 and other jet-age products are dramatic changes in aircraft manufacturing techniques that required work specialization of a sort not anticipated in the early days of the Boeing Company.

John Kenneth Galbraith points out that the application of science and specialization generates six additional effects, which when combined cast industry in its modern technological mold. They are:

1. a lengthening span of time separating the start and finish of a production process
2. an increase in the amount of capital required for running an enterprise
3. a tendency toward inflexibility in task performance, meaning that capital

Figure 3-1. Percentage of Labor Force Employed, by Level of Skill, 1900–1963

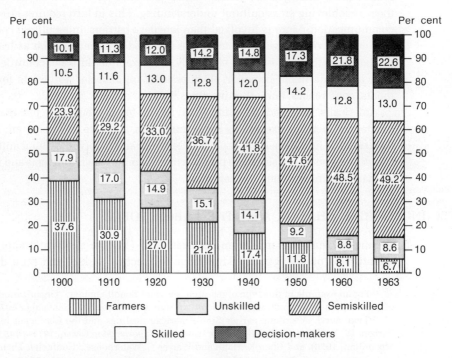

Source: Adapted from Daniel R. Fusfeld, "The Manpower Revolution," *Michigan Business Review* 18 (July 1966): 15. Used with permission.

[15] John Kenneth Galbraith, *The New Industrial State* (Boston: Houghton Mifflin, 1967), p. 12.

invested and time required to make changes slows down the rapidity with which a technology can be altered for any particular job

4. a growth of specialists in the labor force
5. increased intensity of organization
6. growing importance of planning to be sure that the most effective allocation of time, capital, and manpower is achieved within the constraints of the current state of the planning "art"[16]

In response to these changes the general work force and management have been upgraded. Throughout the labor market higher levels of skill are needed — among white-collar workers, employees in service industries, and manual workers in production jobs. Since 1900, the proportion of the labor force employed in professional and technical jobs has been growing.

These changes are portrayed in graphic form by Daniel Fusfeld. Figure 3-1 demonstrates that the percentage of "decision-makers"— managers, professional and technical employees, and proprietors — in the work force has grown larger. In 1900 it was 10.1 per cent; by 1963 it had grown to 22.6 per cent. During the same period the percentage of unskilled workers and farm labor declined. Fusfeld concludes:

Even though the trends in the middle echelon of skills may not be clear, there can be no doubt about what is happening at the two ends. There is a steadily rising demand for men and women with skill, education, and ability, and less and less place for the unskilled. This aspect of the manpower revolution has not developed overnight, or even in the last generation. The shift in skills to the top of the scale has been continuous throughout this century.[17]

EMERGING ISSUES IN MANAGEMENT

What will management be like in the year 2000? Forecasting events and trends is risky, but recent developments do point to several issues that are likely to occupy managements' attention in the years to come.

The Physical Environment

In 1967 an executive of a large manufacturing business was requested to address a group of students on the subject of social responsibility. After his talk, a student asked what his firm was doing about air and water pollution. His company was allegedly the cause of considerable water and air contamination, and the executive became quite upset by this question and answered, "I came here to talk about social responsibility, not pollution." It is hard to imagine an executive of a major corporation publicly expressing such an attitude today. Concern for the environment has

---

[16] *Ibid.*, pp. 13–17.

[17] Daniel R. Fusfeld, "The Manpower Revolution," *Michigan Business Review* 18 (July 1966): 18.

grown appreciably since the publication of Rachel Carson's book *Silent Spring* in 1962. As a result of her attack on DDT and insecticides, numerous threats to the quality of life have been exposed — nuclear contamination, garbage accumulation, intolerable noise levels in cities, oil pipelines in Alaska, oil spills, industrial waste disposal in the air and water, automobile exhaust.

Heightened sensitivity to environmental matters has induced private and government organizations to seek to regulate and control industry. Management must work with regulatory agencies that promulgate and enforce standards of environmental quality.

Air quality standards, for instance, cause many difficulties. A firm may install a condenser to remove pollutants before the exhaust of a manufacturing activity is expelled. The condenser is engineered to conform with existing standards, but the agency suddenly changes them, immediately making the control equipment obsolete. Many similar problems might be cited. Friends of the Earth and the Sierra Club were in the vanguard of the fight to prevent the building of the Alaska oil pipeline, claiming that it would do irreparable damage to the ecology of the north. Because of continuing pressure for economic development and the depletion of resources, management will be considering the environment and the quality of life.

The Professional

Changes in manpower and technology have consequences for management in the areas of leadership and organizational design. One of the most significant is technology's effect on an organization's structure. Structural modifications will be induced by increases in the complexity and size of certain companies. Some managers are becoming concerned with structural innovations.

A second important consequence is that more highly skilled and well-educated employees are making more demands on management than ever before. In response, management must develop organizational leadership and a work climate that will provide satisfaction for these people; otherwise, they will leave and find jobs elsewhere. Management has to learn to use the technical and educational resources brought to the company by these people. Simple economic incentives will not motivate skilled employees to the highest level of performance and achievement.

Society

In the future managers will be confronted by many issues of social responsibility — obligations beyond the traditional ones of rationality, profit, and efficiency: Equal opportunity, for example, includes not only the elimination of discrimination but also the effort to provide job training. All members of the organization should have the chance to achieve job satisfaction and to grow and develop in their jobs. This opportunity is essential in the face of the rapid obsolescence of human skills resulting from technological change. Managers will also have to pay attention to interface relationships among autonomous but interdependent organizations such as firms in electric power networks, business and government relations, and contractors and subcontractors. Technological progress and change and organizational reaction to and influence on them must also concern management.

MANAGEMENT: AN EMERGENT DISCIPLINE

The behavioral sciences, management science, international management, work-force changes, and technological advancement are only the broadest categorizations of the forces causing the revolution in contemporary management. Related to them are developments in decision theory, organization theory, communication theory, motivation theory, and quantitative methods, all of which are influencing management theory and practice.

Servan-Schreiber described the issue most clearly when he implied that the future belongs to the nations that can successfully weld their scientists, engineers, and technicians into viable administrative systems. Over such systems will preside the supramanagerial types capable of coordinating the whole in a rational, efficient, and effective pursuit of the organizational mission.

In 1940 James Burnham predicted a managerial revolution. Today that revolution is nearly over. By the year 2000, scientist-managers will most likely constitute the key social class. At present, they are consolidating their position in society, supported by the behavioral sciences, the natural sciences, and quantitative methods. Underlying this development, of course, is the predominant thrust of "management science."

Management has come quite a distance since Henry Gantt wrote, "The greatest problem before engineers and managers today is the economic utilization of labor." If modern management were faced with any one such problem, its job would be comparatively simple. Instead, the modern manager is confronted with so many great challenges that to isolate one or two of them is a dangerous oversimplification.

Fortunately for management, the increase in problems has been paralleled by improvement in techniques for solving them. The behavioral, quantitative, and natural sciences have contributed greatly to management theory and practice. Hence, management is neither desperate nor groping for answers. The basic tools of research and analysis are available. Although they may be crude, there is constant pressure to refine them into more precise instruments.

How should managers handle the new ideas so that they may be seen in perspective? What framework provides some order for analysis and at the same time has practical value for management? Management is an emergent discipline as well as a practicing art. It is evolving and therefore should be receptive to the contributions of all fields bearing upon it, while remaining mindful of contributions made in the past by traditional theory. The functional approach should be integrated with current work from fields surrounding management.

Table 3-1 lists some recent developments to be treated in a functional context. The list is not exhaustive, nor does it indicate the overlapping of functions.

Table 3-1. Traditional Management Functions and Recent Developments

Functions	Development
Planning	PERT, decision-making, quantitative methods, information theory
Organizing	Matrix (project) organization, lateral relationships, technological impact on structural relations, systems theory, organization change
Staffing	Management by results, executive personnel planning
Influencing	Leadership, communication theory, motivation, democracy in organizations, ecology, sensitivity training and management development
Controlling	PERT, CPM, cybernetics, feedback, and self-regulation

Discussion Questions

1. Social responsibility is not a "free good." Some trade-offs have to be made between exploiting the environment to increase productivity and conserving the environment to improve the quality of life. What are some of these trade-offs? What sacrifices are you willing to make? For example, would you voluntarily limit the use of your automobile and rely on public transportation?

2. Given the current status of management and future issues concerning it, would you want a managerial job? Consider the pros and cons. What are your alternatives?

Supplementary Readings

American Institute of Management. "What Is Management?" In *Dimensions in Modern Management,* edited by Patrick E. Connor. Boston: Houghton Mifflin, 1974.

Falk, Richard A. *This Endangered Planet.* New York: Vintage Books, 1971.

Johnson, Richard A., Fremont E. Kast, and James E. Rosenzweig. "Designing Management Systems." In *Dimensions in Modern Management.*

Martyn, Howe. *Multinational Business Management.* Lexington, Mass.: Heath, 1970.

Newman, William H., Charles E. Summer, and E. Kirby Warren. *The Process of Management.* Englewood Cliffs, N.J.: Prentice-Hall, 1972. See chapter 29.

CHAPTER 4

Managers as Decision-Makers

Stewardship is a chief characteristic of professional management. Managers are responsible for the property of others regardless of whether they are employed as hospital administrators, executives in the federal government, or business executives. How the property is used, how resources are spent, is managers' main responsibility.

Managerial performance is judged on the basis of how many resources are used to accomplish an organization's objectives. A wise investment broker has said that a person buys stock not in a company but in the ability of a firm's managers. The purchase or sale of shares is an expression of confidence in management. In a general way, the performance of executives is appraised by their success in managing the resources owned by other people.

Preliminary to the use or withholding of resources is the managerial act of choosing among alternative courses of action. Decision-making is conscious deliberation about alternative ways to use resources. Because resources are limited, the capacity of managers to exploit opportunities is limited; everything cannot be tried randomly or haphazardly. Decisions are made to discriminate rationally among available alternatives. Discrimination among alternatives is crucial in management.

Managers at all levels of organization and in all functions within organizations deliberate among alternative actions. Decision-making runs vertically from top management to first-line supervision, and cuts horizontally across areas of specialization such as industrial relations, sales, budgeting, and production. Decision-making is dynamically involved as a linking process, for it ties one function to another. The decisions of one manager or organizational unit are never made in isolation. Their implications and outcomes are related to other decisions throughout the organizational system.

Decision-making is an indispensable part of a systems approach to management. It is basic to every function of management; the job of management cannot be understood unless the nature of decision-making is appreciated.

ELEMENTS OF THE DECISION PROCESS

Decision-making is in the immediate experience of all people. It begins in early childhood when a person is first able to discriminate and select alternatives from competing stimuli. Choosing among alternatives continues until the individual dies. What piece of candy should I buy with my dime? Should I go out for soccer or basketball? What should be my college major? Whom will I marry? What job should I take? Where will I go on vacation? Common decisions in one sense differ little from managerial decisions.

All decision-makers must consider five elements:

1. the objective sought
2. alternative courses of action to achieve the objective
3. a prediction of the outcomes (consequences) for each alternative
4. a choice procedure (decision criteria) by which an alternative is selected
5. an evaluation of the choice of the alternative

Closely related to this process are the implementation of the decision and an appraisal of the effectiveness of the decision in achieving a goal. These two aspects of decision-making can be "intellectually" separated from the choice process, but in reality they are indispensable to it. Action is the reason for making a decision. Appraisal is feedback, and it becomes *data* for further deliberations. For example, if you decide to buy one make of car and have trouble with it, this experience will color your thinking when you are ready to buy again.

Decision-making has been studied extensively; it is so critical in management that not only have greater insights into it been sought, but some attempts have been made to create "decision rules." Based on decision rules, techniques of operations research have been discovered to ease decision-making in limited areas.

THE RATIONAL MODEL OF DECISION-MAKING

According to classical economic theory, rational man makes optimal choices in completely specified, narrowly defined decision situations. The rational man *maximizes* the values he seeks by selecting alternatives that have optimal outcomes for the goals he wants to achieve. How is rational man able to optimize in such a wondrous way? Rational man has set out before him a complete array of all the options open to him in a situation. Alternatives, thus, are givens. He knows the consequences of each alternative. In addition, rational man has a list on which the outcomes are ordered in terms of his preferences. He selects the alternative leading to the most desired outcome, which, according to the model, is the optimal solution to the decision problem. Decision-making for rational man is complicated somewhat when multiple consequences flow from a single alternative.

CHOICE UNDER CONDITIONS OF RISK AND UNCERTAINTY

When the outcomes of an alternative are known and under the control of a decision-maker, the choice procedure is unambiguous, and a condition of certainty is said to exist. However, under conditions of *risk* and *uncertainty,* a different choice procedure must be used to produce a rational decision.

Problems under risk and uncertainty involve an interaction between the decision-maker's choice of an alternative and the state of nature. The state of nature is the existence of a variable not under the control of the decision-maker, which affects the outcome of a particular alternative. For each decision alternative there are as many outcomes as there are states of nature. Because of the multiplicity of outcomes, choice is more complex under risk and uncertainty than under certainty. Risk exists when the probabilities of occurrence of each of the states of nature are known. Uncertainty exists when the probabilities are unknown.

What is the likely choice procedure when there is risk? Let us assume that cost is the appropriate measure of the outcome. The logical choice procedure then seems to be to select the alternative that yields the minimum expected value of cost. If the decision is repeated many times, this procedure would minimize the sum of costs of the individual decisions. But what if the decision is made just once? The decision-maker is likely not to incur the expected value of costs but something better or worse. The problem of the decision-maker is thus one of uncertainty rather than risk. There is no long period over which to "average out" the results.

Probability and Probability Distributions

Calculating costs for each alternative requires knowledge of the probabilities of the various states of nature. These probabilities can be determined in some cases by intuition; in other cases they must be determined empirically. Knowledge of them makes the calculation of expected values conceptually simple, but when the number of alternatives and outcomes becomes large, the problem is difficult in practice. In these cases, by expressing the probabilities in terms of mathematical equations, the theory of probability along with the methods of mathematical analysis can be used to solve the decision problem.

The Value of Information About the State of Nature

Information about the state of nature is an important element in any decision problem under risk. If the decision-maker can perfectly forecast the state of nature, he will be operating as if certainty existed. He will no longer choose the same alternative each time but will vary his decision with the predicted state of nature. The difference between the expected cost with and without forecasting is the value of the forecasting information. Obviously a knowledge of this value can mean a great deal to the decision-maker.

Objective and Subjective Probabilities and the Importance of Risk Analysis

In most practical problems, the probabilities of the states of nature are not known. This could mean that the decision-making problem under risk is virtually non-existent. The fact is, however, that although accurate probabilities are usually not known, some knowledge of them is generally available through existing data and experience. Such knowledge makes an analysis under risk a convenient approximation of the intermediate case.

How are probabilities measured? Objectivists believe that probability is relative frequency and that if data do not exist, probability cannot be measured. Subjectivists believe that probability is a state of mind measuring one's belief in the occurrence of a certain event and it can be applied with a meager amount of data consisting of experiences and impressions.

The importance of risk analysis is closely tied to the concept of the value of information. If estimated probabilities are used as though they were in fact true, the analysis can lead to reasonably good decisions. The reasonableness of the decision can be measured by the value of the information about the true probabilities. If we are led to virtually the same decision no matter what the probabilities, then the analysis under risk, even though not perfect, is worthwhile.

Decisions Under Uncertainty

In uncertainty the possible states of nature are known, but the probabilities of the occurrence of each of them is not. This polar case is rather unlikely. But what if it did exist? If we know nothing about the probabilities, how can a choice of alternatives be made?

The consensus in risk analysis, at least for repetitive problems, is to choose the alternative that minimizes (or maximizes) the expected values. In uncertainty no such consensus exists. Many procedures have been proposed, among them minimax (or maximin), minimax regret, and Bayesian procedures.

The minimax procedure is the pessimist's approach to decisions under uncertainty. The decision-maker determines for each alternative the worst outcome that could possibly occur. If outcomes are measured in cost, he determines the maximum cost for each alternative. He then selects the alternative that has the smallest value of maximum cost — the minimax. In this way, he is guaranteed a cost that is no higher than the minimax.

In the minimax regret procedure, regret is defined as the difference in cost between the outcome of the selected alternative and the outcome of the alternative that would have been selected had the decision-maker known the state of nature. It is the opportunity cost of an incorrect decision. The minimax regret procedure states that one should choose the alternative that minimizes the maximum regret.

Bayesian procedure reverts to the expected value concept in the following way: If no knowledge of the relative probabilities of the states of nature is available, one should act under the assumption that they are equally likely. The expected value choice procedure would then follow.

Rational decision-making is possible, of course, even under conditions where the lack of information or the state of nature create a situation of either risk or uncertainty. However, one problem is knowing which choice procedure is rational in a state of uncertainty. So far the science of decision-making has not provided a solution to this problem.

THE DECISION-MAKER

Rational decision-making consists of sequential stages that may overlap but are nevertheless relatively discrete. A conventional view of the process is illustrated in Figure 4-1. The decision-maker starts with the identification of a goal to be achieved. In this case the decision-maker has three alternatives (A_1, A_2, A_3), from which he will select the one that will give him the best solution to the decision problem — for example, how to achieve the goal in the most effective way. Each alternative has an outcome (O_1, O_2, O_3). Outcomes are the consequences that the decision-maker forecasts will result if a particular course of action (alternative) is followed. Associated with each outcome are two conditions that are crucial to the decision-maker's selection of an alternative. The first is the estimation of each alternative's probability for accomplishing the goal. The second is the value or utility that the decision-maker assigns to the outcome of each alternative. For example, if the value of O_1 is high but the probability that A_1 will accomplish the goal is low relative to the probability of other alternatives, then the decision-maker may select another alternative having a greater probability of success even though it might have a lower payoff.

The choice procedure used to evaluate the alternatives and their outcomes depends on whether the decision situation is one of certainty, risk, or uncertainty. Any of these analyses would be appropriate in the situation just described. However, in a situation of risk or uncertainty we need to add multiple outcomes to the process shown in Figure 4-1. Thus for A_1 we would have O_{1a}, O_{1b}, O_{1c}, and so on. The choice procedure will fall into risk analysis if we know the probabilities of these outcomes. The analysis will be one of uncertainty if we do not know the probabilities.

Figure 4-1. Steps in the Decision Process

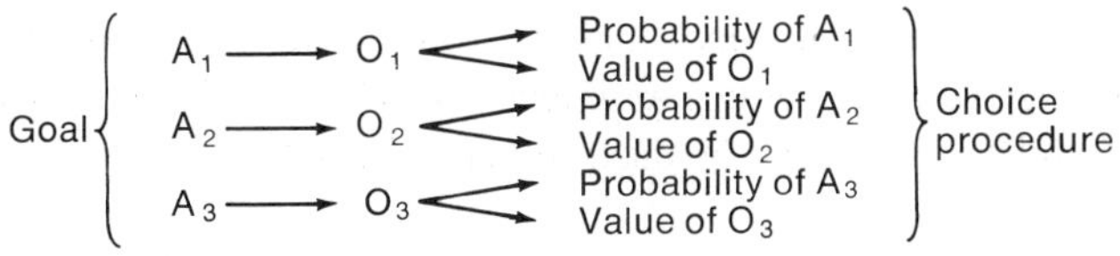

Irwin Bross, in *Design for Decision*, presents another way of looking at the decision-maker. This approach is shown in Figure 4-2. Bross' decision-maker directs attention to aspects of the decision process not emphasized in the conventional description. Lying beyond the decision-maker, but necessary to decision-making, are data, which Bross terms the "fuel of the Decision Maker."

Data

In some respects goals or objectives are data, but not in the usual sense. Data are the information, in various states of refinement, available to the decision-maker. Data

Figure 4-2. The Decision-Maker

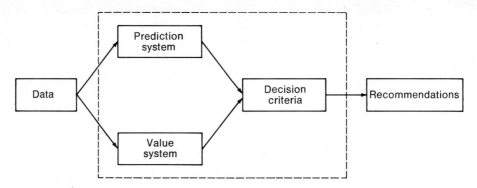

Source: Irwin D. J. Bross, *Design for Decision* (New York: Macmillan, 1953), p. 29. Copyright © 1953 by Macmillan Publishing Co., Inc. Used with permission.

generate alternatives, determine their outcomes, and find their probabilities and values.

Data are obtained from many sources. A sales manager needing information to make a decision about introducing a new product has four obvious ones: (1) Historical sources include sales records for existing and comparable products marketed by the company. (2) From observations of the performance of similar products of competing companies, useful information could be obtained. (3) Controlled tests in pilot markets may be valuable for getting data on consumer acceptance. (4) Consumer attitude surveys may indicate how the new product will be accepted.

Prediction Systems

A prediction system is used to help the decision-maker determine the likelihood that a given alternative will produce an effect that will accomplish a goal. Systems other than probability theory can be used to make these forecasts:

1. *Persistence prediction:* Present conditions will continue. Tomorrow's weather will be like today's. A new product line will have as much success as the old line did when it was introduced.

2. *Trajectory prediction:* Change will occur at a stable rate. According to this technique, a hospital that experienced a 2 per cent increase per year in the number of patients cared for in the past three years could expect a 2 per cent increase in the next year.

3. *Cyclic prediction:* Events will recur periodically. The seasonal popularity of different types of clothing enables designers, manufacturers, and buyers to plan their activities for a year.

4. *Associative prediction:* The occurrence of one event will produce another event because the relationship of events is stable. The training of animals is an example. Reward and punishment establishes a set of stable conditioning relation-

ships that reinforce the behavior sought by the trainer. Piece rate pay systems assume that rate of output is associated with money rewards. So a worker economically motivated will produce more if he can expect to receive more pay.

Value System

The value system is the utility a decision-maker assigns to an outcome. Utility is sometimes difficult to determine because many values cannot be quantified. Wherever possible, decision-makers express values in dollars and cents, recognizing that this expression is often only a rough approximation of an outcome's utility. However, the assignment of relative values to outcome is essential for developing a preference scale that helps a decision-maker discriminate among alternatives.

Decision Criteria

Decision criteria have two aspects. One is the kind of analysis to use in a decision situation — certainty, risk, or uncertainty analysis. The other aspect considers whether a decision-maker seeks an optimum or a satisfactory solution to a problem.

PROBLEMS WITH THE RATIONAL MODEL

The rational decision model is still haunted by the ghost of economic man, who tries to maximize his gains by seeking optimum solutions to decision problems. The model requires that all alternatives be given, their consequences known, and a complete preference scale established. The minimum requirement to enable management to make optimum choices is perfect information. This requirement, of course, cannot be met in practical circumstances, and so optimal solutions are unobtainable. Decision-makers, especially those confronting complex choices, have to be content with less than optimal standards. These observations prompted James March and Herbert Simon to suggest the concept of satisfactory standards, as opposed to optimal standards, for decision criteria. They say:

An alternative is optimal *if: (1) there exists a set of criteria that permits all alternatives to be compared, and (2) the alternative in question is preferred, by these criteria, to all other alternatives. An alternative is* satisfactory *if: (1) there exists a set of criteria that describes minimally satisfactory alternatives, and (2) the alternative in question meets or exceeds all these criteria.*

Most human decision-making, whether individual or organization, is concerned with the discovery and selection of satisfactory alternatives; only in exceptional cases is it concerned with the discovery and selection of optimal alternatives.[1]

This approach should not be considered nonrational. Indeed, rationality enters in regardless of whether the decision-maker is trying to optimize or to satisfice.

[1] James G. March and Herbert A. Simon, *Organizations* (New York: Wiley, 1958), pp. 140–41. Emphasis in original.

The notion of satisficing is, however, much closer to the "real world" of decision-making, where the manager cannot completely specify the decision situation or hope to gain complete information about it.

Boundaries of Rationality

Optimization presumes unlimited flexibility on the part of the manager to vary the organization to suit the actions he must take in order to maximize. Bounded rationality gives another picture of the limits to which maximization efforts can be carried. Boundaries of rationality are elements of the decision situation that are taken as given and do not enter the rational calculations of the decision-maker. Such boundaries are many and are found in the goals sought by the organization or the individual. Boundaries also arise in the organizational structure that needs to be maintained and in the premises used by decision-makers in planning. The research methodology used to generate data provides boundaries of rationality.

The use of the submarine by the Japanese navy during World War II is an interesting example of bounded rationality. The Japanese used submarines primarily as fleet-support weapons. They did not deploy them as attack weapons against shipping as did the Germans and Americans. The Japanese navy formulated its strategy on the premise that the primary goal of submarines was to defend major fleet units. This premise limited the military decision-makers to alternatives within the boundaries of defensive strategy. This faulty assumption resulted in the underutilization of the Japanese submarine fleet, although the decisions made within the framework of it were rationally formulated and executed.

The submarine example shows that a decision-maker can be rationally consistent but consistently wrong. Errors arise from faulty premises, irrelevant goals, and so on. The boundaries to rationality may be so blemished that effective managerial action is prevented.

On the positive side, bounded rationality maintains stability in decision situations. Everything in organizations cannot change at once. Change in some parts of an organization is predicated upon stability in other parts. Decision-making could not be effective if all the elements of a decision situation were varying wildly. For example, a college student would find it difficult to graduate if course offerings and curriculum requirements were constantly changing. The catalog of course requirements provides boundaries that help the student plan a program.

Boundaries of Bounded Rationality

The major issue that pertains to bounded rationality is the balance between stability and flexibility. From the administrative standpoint, both stability and flexibility are desirable qualities, though too much of either could stifle the organization or unhinge the decision process. But the problem in the final analysis seems weighted toward stability. In actual decision situations managers have to overcome considerable inertia in order to produce organizational change and create an environment favoring adaptability.

Part of this inertia arises from the goals, objectives, policies, and premises that are taken as givens in the decision process. It is the nature of rational boundaries that they go unexamined. Adaptation to change through continuous reappraisal of the givens is essential to innovation in decision-making. How can the system be opened to an examination of its basic premises? Probably the most elementary requirement is an improvement in the flow of information to strategic decision-makers. Questioning basic premises is all right, but to do so without adequate information is irresponsible. Beyond this requirement is another, somewhat more intangible because it consists of a change in management's attitude.

The examination of fundamental decision premises cannot occur without a commitment from management to an organizational design that stresses openness and freedom to explore. Conventional organizations place a premium on routine, mechanistic approaches to problem-solving. Negative rewards are likely to result if an individual questions organizational givens. These kinds of constraints have to be overcome in order to establish a creative atmosphere for decision-making.

DECISION-MAKING AND ORGANIZATIONAL DESIGN

Two organizational variables affect decision-making — the kind of job performed and the manager's level in the organization structure. As a rule, the higher the manager is in the organization, the greater is his authority and discretion. As the managerial hierarchy is ascended, broad, complex problems that defy routine or detailed solutions are encountered. Decision criteria are vague, and solutions to decision problems are ordinarily given in terms of policy guidelines. Under these circumstances, the boundaries of rationality are fewer and looser for upper management. Consequently there is opportunity for creativity and innovation in the decision process. Decisions made in these situations are said to be "unprogrammed."

Opposite conditions are found as the hierarchy of an organization is descended. Lower levels of management find greater and more precisely defined boundaries to rationality. Since their jobs are heavily involved with the implementation of basic decisions, their activities become routine. The decision process at these levels requires managers mainly to select the program out of several established programs best fitted to a given decision situation. Such decisions are called "programmed."

This analysis of the decision process assumes a conventional organization design. The structure of the organization is based on the specialization of work and a chain of command. For most real-world organizations, this is a fairly accurate first approximation of the decision setting. However, the fact that this analysis is a first approximation must be emphasized. Many modern organizations are far too complex to divide neatly the decisions of managers into programmed and unprogrammed categories.

For example, higher levels of management depend on managers at lower levels for information, advice, counsel, and assistance in formulating unprogrammed decisions. Therefore, lower managers can and do have a hand in shaping innovative decisions. The size of the hand depends on the expertise of lower management, the technology used by the organization to achieve its goals, and the organizational design. In turn, organizational design is a function of both technology and the level of managerial skill. The conventional model of the decision process is more closely approached by the organizational design of a firm quarrying limestone than it is by the aerospace division of an aircraft company.

The type of structure has a great deal to do with who participates in what kinds of decisions. Even factors such as management's leadership style encourage or discourage participation in innovative decision activities. A great deal of work has been done to improve understanding of the decision process. Operations research has supplied management with certain quantitative tools to help it make better decisions.

OPERATIONS RESEARCH

Methods

Operations research involves a particular view of management operations and a particular kind of research: "Operations are considered as an entity. The subject matter studied is not the equipment used, nor the morale of the participants, nor the physical properties of the output; it is the combination of these in total, as an economic process."[2] Operations viewed in this manner are subject to analysis by the thought processes and methods normally associated with the research work of natural scientists, physicists, and chemists. Because it makes use of general scientific methods, operations research is applicable to the study of operations in many types of organizations, including business, government, and the military.

Operations research uses a team or task force to approach a problem. This technique evolved during the Second World War when scholars from a variety of disciplines — natural sciences, economics, sociology, cultural anthropology, statistics, mathematics — found they could work together to solve related problems. Two early applications of operations research were the development of an anti-aircraft fire-control system to defend England against German bombers and a logistical system to coordinate the movement of convoys across the North Atlantic.

Because of their varied backgrounds and training, the members of task forces do not have a common technical vocabulary and are thus forced to use the universal medium of mathematics, which is abstract enough to permit mutual understanding. Although no approach has been firmly established, mathematics is essential to operations research. However, businessmen are rarely well trained in this field, and they are often at a loss when confronted with its symbols. They need not completely learn the language of mathematics in order to understand the place or use of operations research, but they must develop at least an awareness of its nature and applicability to business problems. Because the technique is still so new, some businessmen are reluctant to incorporate it into their own managerial skills, preferring to leave their problems to operations research specialists. They may continue to avoid the technicalities of operations research while accepting its methods on faith and proven results.

[2] Cyril C. Herrmann and John F. Magee, "Operations Research for Management," *Harvard Business Review* 31, no. 4 (July–August 1953): 101.

Presentation of Alternative Solutions

Operations research has two other major characteristics differentiating it further from customary business or organization research. First, the operations research team usually attempts to investigate and study the relationship of the activity under consideration to all other pertinent elements of the business. Second, the team makes an effort to uncover, catalog, and evaluate all courses of action that might be taken. The aim is not necessarily to find one definite answer, for in many cases there is no single "right answer." The final choice "is the one that will lessen or mitigate a problem or the one that will give the most beneficial results."[3] In other words, operations research presents management with an array of solutions to a given problem, the solutions being arranged in the order of their desirability and probability of success. If there is no clear evidence that one solution is more advantageous than another, the answer will most likely read: "Solution A should reduce absenteeism 20 per cent but may increase personnel administration costs 6 per cent. Solution B will reduce absenteeism 17 per cent but will raise personnel administration costs 3 per cent." This presentation of alternative solutions and costs represents the most important contribution of operations research to business management. It certainly helps the executive make decisions, but it will not make up his mind for him.

Models

A common method of applying mathematics to operations research is through the construction and study of mathematical models. Probably the best known of these is the accounting model: "Assets minus liabilities equals proprietorship." This is essentially "a simplified representation on paper, in the form of accounts and ledgers, of the flow of goods and services through a business enterprise."[4] Also familiar are the various models used in physics, such as three-dimensional representations of complex molecules and the many sets of mathematical equations.

In operations research, a distinction is made between descriptive models, which describe the facts and relationships of various problems, and policy models, which are useful for planning and selecting an optimum course of action. Operations research models can also be distinguished as exact or probabilistic, depending on the degree of chance involved. A major goal of the operations research analyst is the construction of a model constituting the most faithful representation of the operation. The mathematical model is particularly convenient because it can be manipulated to test the probable effect of contemplated changes without disturbing the existing order of things. The ability to manipulate prevents costly failures that could result from experimenting with the actual operation of a business.

Model-building can be considered a three-stage procedure. The first stage describes the situation under study in the terms of the symbolism adopted. The second stage introduces the motivational, behavioral, and technological assumptions. The third stage quantifies the process by assigning different sets of numerical values to

---

[3] *Ibid.*
[4] *Ibid.*, p. 103.

the parameters of the model.[5] These values make it possible for the operations research team to manipulate the model so that it will yield quantitative information showing the results the different values will produce. Much of this work has been made possible by the development of rapid computing machines.

Large segments of the business process are susceptible to such numerical treatment. Quantifiable data that can be used with considerable accuracy are readily available for most aspects of finance, shipping, production, and employment. However, when attitudes or emotional reactions are involved — particularly those relating to consumer responses, advertising, marketing, and collective bargaining — quantification is much more difficult and will probably be highly arbitrary. The calculations will not necessarily be valid because in these instances they are made on the basis of someone's own idea of the numerical value to be assigned to a feeling or attitude. In such matters, judgments vary considerably.

TECHNIQUES OF OPERATIONS RESEARCH

In analyzing such specific business problems, operations research scientists make use of techniques such as probability theory, game theory, queuing or waiting line theory, and linear programming. These are tools developed by mathematicians and statisticians.

Probability Theory

When risk or uncertainty is present in a business decision, probability theory can be called upon. According to probability theory, certain things are likely to happen in accordance with a predictable pattern. For instance, if a person tosses a coin one hundred times, the probability is that it will show heads fifty times and tails fifty times. The deviations can be set within a predictable margin.

Game Theory

Game theory introduces a competitive note. It brings into a simulated decision-making situation the actions of an opponent. Both competitors are presumed to be similarly motivated: The manager is interested in maximizing his gains and minimizing his losses, and so is his rival. Game theory will show the highest gains with the smallest amount of losses, regardless of what the competitor does.

Queuing Theory

Queuing theory develops the relationships that are involved in waiting in line. Customers awaiting service, cars at a toll gate, planes waiting to land, work in a production line awaiting inspection — each is typical of the problems that may be approached by the methods of queuing theory. The theory in effect balances the cost of waiting lines against the cost of preventing them by increasing facilities. The

---

[5] Robert Dorfman, "Operations Research," American Economic Review 50 (September 1960): 579.

problem is figuring out the cost of total waiting — that is, the cost of tolerating the queue — and weighing it against the expense of building enough service facilities to lessen the need for the queue. Sometimes it is more costly to eliminate all delay than to keep some of it.

Linear Programming

Linear programming is often applied when it is necessary to find an optimum combination or allocation of limited resources to obtain a desired objective. The resources may be the money a company has available for use, the capacity of its plant or individual machines, or its advertising budget. The objective may be the lowest cost or highest profit possible from the given resources. Linear programming must be considered in the light of the limitations on its use. A general prerequisite for utilizing it is that there must be a linear (straight line) relation among the factors involved. The limits of variation must be fairly well established. The volume of calculations required is often so great that a computer is essential. Linear programming has been commonly applied to transportation problems, such as that posed when a standardized commodity is to be shipped from a variety of sources to many destinations.[6]

Discussion Questions

1. When you decide how much time to devote to studying for each course you are taking, do you try to optimize or to satisfice? What decision criteria do you use to allocate your study time?

2. Eventually you will have to select a major field, if you have not done so already. Can you identify the boundaries of rationality in your choosing a major? (Example: My father has a CPA firm; therefore, I am majoring in accounting.)

Supplementary Readings

Bross, Irwin D. J. *Design for Decision.* New York: Macmillan, 1953.

Heilbroner, Robert L. "How to Make an Intelligent Decision." In *Dimensions in Modern Management,* edited by Patrick E. Connor. Boston: Houghton Mifflin, 1974.

Miller, David W., and Martin K. Starr. *The Structure of Human Decisions.* Englewood Cliffs, N.J.: Prentice-Hall, 1967.

Simon, Herbert A. *The New Science of Management Decision.* New York: Harper and Row, 1960.

Simon, Herbert A. "Administrative Decision Making." In *Dimensions in Modern Management.*

Wilson, Charles Z., and M. Alexis. "Basic Frameworks for Decisions." *Academy of Management Journal.* August 1962, pp. 150–64.

[6] Andrew Vazsonyi, *Scientific Programming in Business and Industry* (New York: Wiley, 1958), pp. 26ff.

II PLANNING

THE PLANNING FUNCTION.
Planning is a primary task of man-
agement, providing the framework
for all other managerial functions.

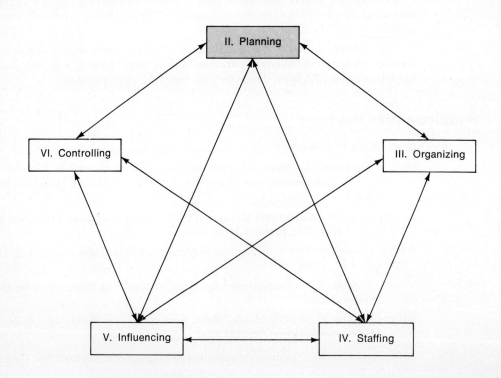

Through planning, information determining objectives and policies is gathered, strategies are laid, and tactics decided. Although planning is a key activity, we know little about it.

In developing plans, managers act in accordance with their firm's objectives. They are constantly aware of the need to perform efficiently, provide a service, satisfy social obligations, and cater to personal aspirations. Some years ago a debate raged over which one of these objectives was of primary importance. More recently, the discussion of objectives has taken a new turn. Management is influenced by many interest groups — owners, customers, employees, and the public (through the government). How can management balance its objectives so that each group receives an equitable share of the values created by the organization?

The word "values" is crucial. For business management, value is money. Two research studies presented in Chapter 5 reflect this. Their findings should not be surprising, for the managers of any economic institution should be interested mainly in technological and economic results. However, other values may enter management's planning and decision-making. That is why we ask, "How does management balance all its obligations (objectives) so that the organization can continually improve technologically and increase its value to society?"

The relationship of decision-making to objectives and of objectives to the management process orients planning. Information is assembled, planning premises are established, and courses of action are designed to fit objectives. However, management always gambles when looking into the future. Managers have fewer planning techniques and less information available to them than does a horse-racing fan who relies on a tout sheet. For this reason, planning has always

been the least reliable of the managerial functions. However, before the middle of the 1970's, this situation is expected to change. Hints of what may lie ahead can now be seen in computer simulation, PERT, game theory, probability theory, and behavioral techniques that prepare managers to make better decisions in uncertain environments. Moreover, a whole new area of planning devoted to forecasting technological change is also emerging. These developments should make not only planning activities but the four other managerial functions more efficient, providing them with objectives and standards of performance.

CHAPTER 5

Business Objectives, Policies, and Social Responsibility

Formulating objectives is foremost among management's responsibilities. Policies, procedures, methods, and performance standards are derived from objectives. Organizational structure, staffing, and influencing also depend to a large extent upon them. Controlling is meaningless without objectives as guidelines.

An organization should state its objectives as clearly and simply as possible in order to clarify the targets people are to reach. This is especially important since objectives are usually multiple, encompassing the long-run, necessarily broad objectives of organization-wide activities and the short-run, narrower objectives of divisions and departments. If these specific guides for subordinate units operating within the limits of over-all company policy do not exist, haphazard activities can result. For example, capital funds might be committed uneconomically. People might be poorly utilized, with disappointing operating results over the long term.

A MULTITUDE OF OBJECTIVES

Profit as an Objective

Profit is the net surplus earned by an enterprise after all legitimate operating costs, fixed charges, depreciation, and other expenses have been met. Although necessary for survival, profit is residual — the result of other endeavors such as making and distributing a product or service needed by the community. It has often been stated that the major goal of private business is profit. Without profits an enterprise cannot survive for any length of time.

Even most nonprofit organizations aim to operate within their budget of available financial resources. For example, a hospital, school, or welfare agency applies the same kind of logic to its efforts to balance a pre-established budget as does the business manager. Demands for fiscal solvency and even a profit are also often imposed on publicly owned industrial operations such as utilities.

No fixed rate of profit is generally considered right, just, or socially defensible. Rather, the rate of profit varies greatly from one enterprise to another and from year to year. However, profit-making is not the only goal of business; it is at best a limited objective. In the words of Ordway Tead: "To lay it down as an unassailable dogma that considerations of profit-making constitute the all-controlling and simon-pure aim of administration is just not the truth. Motivations are far more complex and plural."[1]

Other Objectives

Management is in fact motivated to achieve a number of other objectives because, as we already know, it is responsible for satisfying the desires of many interest groups. Peter Drucker points out that, in spite of the different nature of various enterprises, "objectives are needed in every area where performance and results directly and vitally affect the survival and prosperity of the business."[2] He discusses eight key areas in which objectives of performance and results have to be set: (1) market standing, (2) innovation, (3) productivity, (4) physical and financial resources, (5) profitability, (6) workers' performance and development, (7) work performance and attitude, and (8) public responsibility. It is conceivable that these areas require varying emphasis in different enterprises, but, as Figure 5-1 shows, they are all focused on the main objective of creating and distributing utilities that society determines to be useful.

Figure 5-1. Business Objectives

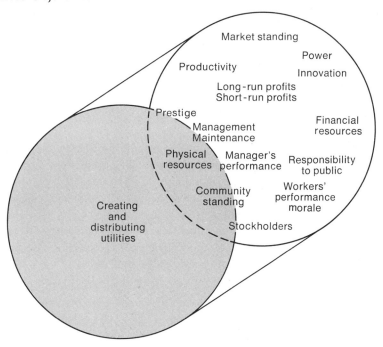

[1] Ordway Tead, *The Art of Administration* (New York: McGraw-Hill, 1951), p. 16.
[2] Peter F. Drucker, *The Practice of Management* (New York: Harper and Row, 1954), p. 63.

Balancing the Various Objectives

Management's real problem is not so much in selecting objectives as in deciding how to balance them. Quantifiable values are available for some objectives; for others they are not. Objectives concerning market standing as it compares to market potential can be established. Productivity goals can also be stated relatively clearly as can the goals concerning physical and financial resources. However, stating objectives in the area of innovation becomes more difficult. The same is true of objectives in the area of profitability Shall we use profit as a percentage of sales, as a return on invested capital, or shall we turn to some other formula? And, of course, there is also the question of what is considered a reasonable profit. Other objectives mentioned by Drucker are even less tangible. Workers' performance, morale, etc. are hard to objectify. In addition, it is difficult for a manager to set objectives in such areas as public responsibility and social obligation.[3] Nevertheless, in recent years management has become more aware of its social responsibility to the community, its employees, stockholders, and the public in general. By striving to incorporate objectives of this nature, the enterprise does not, however, abandon profit to philanthropy. As a matter of fact, conducting a business on the basis of its social responsibilities might even be essential to attaining profits.

In balancing various objectives, managers must establish a proper mix between immediate, short-term, and long-term goals. Moreover, they must balance all objectives with each other. They must decide whether to get a larger share of the market or to forgo this and improve manufacturing productivity. They must balance lower profitability against more innovation. Emphasizing any one of the objectives to the exclusion of the rest will lead to unpleasant consequences. Performance in balancing objectives will reveal the competence of management.

The Magnitude of Objectives

Business goals vary significantly in magnitude. Market domination, public acclaim, social prestige, and empire building are the objectives of some managements. Other managements want their enterprises to remain small and simple. Still others wish to keep their companies at the existing or a moderately increasing level of operation. This attitude is probably more widespread than commonly thought, though, understandably, it is seldom admitted. Many managers feel that by keeping the company on the same path, they are more likely to maintain their own position. This kind of thinking is probably more prevalent in small, closely held, family businesses and in small businesses engaged in nontechnological activities.

Reappraisal of Objectives

Objectives must also retain their validity under changing circumstances — technological advances, changes within the industry, and all other factors that are

[3] *Ibid.*, pp. 64–84.

essential to the success of the firm. It is an indication of management's perspicacity to know when to reappraise their objectives and, if need be, modify them. If management is constantly on the alert, evolutionary not radical change can occur. Reappraisal and adaptation of organizational objectives are essential to the maintenance of a firm's health.

RESEARCH ON BUSINESS OBJECTIVES

The general objectives of business are to make a profit, to provide goods and services of value to the consumer, to promote employees' well-being, and to contribute to public welfare. These primary aims are affected by additional considerations such as returns to stockholders, efficient and economic performance of the business, flexibility, and growth. All these objectives motivate managerial behavior and generate directions of action.

In what way do managers view the objectives of their business? What determines the emphasis they give to some objectives as compared to others? Research has provided some tentative answers to these questions.

Dent's Study

In one study James K. Dent[4] asked 145 chief executives in five cities, "What are the aims of top management in your company?" Table 5-1 shows the responses. It indicates that the goals most often mentioned by managers are profit, employees' well-being, and public service through good products. These findings are consistent with the objectives most writers over the years have attributed to management. However, the interesting part of Dent's study is the relationship he found between objectives and organizational characteristics.

He observed that managers of large companies express concern for good products and public service more often than managers of small companies do. However, managers of large companies are not uninterested in profits. Rather, managers of both large and small firms mention the importance of profits with equal frequency.

The interrelationship of size, unionization, and employee welfare is interesting. Managers of large unionized firms mention employee welfare as an important objective, whereas large nonunionized firms mention this objective much less frequently. This situation is exactly reversed for small unionized and nonunionized firms.

The managers of firms with a higher proportion of white-collar workers list growth as an objective more often than do the managers of firms having a high percentage of blue-collar workers. The only apparent reason for this is the cultural differences prevailing in the two types of firms. Management emphasis on growth in a predominantly white-collar firm takes on added significance when we recall the changing character of the work force discussed in Chapters 1 and 3. It is possible that

[4] James K. Dent, "Organizational Correlates of the Goals of Business Managements," *Personnel Psychology* 12 (Autumn 1959): 365–94.

Table 5-1. Aims of Managements in Five Cities and for Three Cities Separately

| | Percentage of managers giving various aims | | | | |
| | All 5 cities | | First 3 aims | | |
Aim	First aim	First 3 aims	City A	City B	City C
To make money, profits, or a living	36	52	49	75	39
To pay dividends to stockholders	1	9	9	12	2
To grow	12	17	14	5	22
To be efficient, economical	4	12	16	15	—
To meet or stay ahead of competitors	5	13	12	5	15
To operate or develop the organization	9	14	7	15	17
To provide a good product; public service	21	39	47	20	49
To contribute to the community relations	—	3	5	—	2
To provide for the welfare of employees: a good living, security, happiness, good working conditions	5	39	51	22	32
Miscellaneous other aims	7	18			
Total	100	a	a	a	a

Source: Adapted from James K. Dent, "Organizational Correlates of the Goals of Business Managements," *Personnel Psychology* 12 (Autumn 1959): 369. Used with permission.

[a] Adds to more than 100% because many executives gave more than one goal.

growth orientation is a response to the increasingly professional character of employees; growth provides opportunities for advancement in the organization.

Top executives of growing businesses also stress good products more strongly than do their counterparts in declining businesses. Finally, Dent observed that management's interest in broad social responsibilities such as community and employee welfare does not enhance the growth of a business.

England's Study

Although Dent found important relationships between certain organizational characteristics and the goals emphasized by management, he stressed that managers mentioned one objective more than any other — profitability. Similarly, George W. England[5] in a study of 1,072 managers observed a cluster of objectives, which he calls "maximization criteria," as the most influential in shaping managerial action. This cluster includes goals such as organizational efficiency, high productivity, and maximization of profit.

[5] George W. England, "Organizational Goals and Expected Behavior of American Managers," *Academy of Management Journal* 10 (June 1967): 107–17.

Another cluster of goals, which England found of secondary importance to managers, consists of organizational growth, industry leadership, and organizational stability. These goals are sought not for themselves but as tests for the maximization of alternatives. For example, management may ask what effect an equipment replacement policy will have on capital availability for future expansion.

Employee welfare is of tertiary importance. Although named by a large percentage of managers, it does not compare with either of the first two clusters as a source for the generation or testing of alternatives. This indicates that the welfare of employees does not motivate executive behavior as strongly as do other goals. It is not viewed as a major contribution to organizational success. Likewise, England found the last goal cluster, social welfare or community relations, to be very low as a motivator. Few managers see it as either important or necessary to organizational success. However, as problems of community relations assume greater and greater importance in American life, managers might have to give this goal more attention.

The similarities in Dent's and England's studies are striking. Both show high managerial interest in profit and comparatively low interest in employee and social welfare. Between these extremes, customer service, growth, and organizational stability seem to be goals that either stem from or contribute to the first cluster of objectives.

PROFITS AND SOCIAL RESPONSIBILITY

The multitude of objectives confronting management raises the problem of priorities. The Dent and England studies show rather conclusively that managers generally rank profit-making or organizational efficiency high on their scale of values. However, cries for social responsibility can be heard not only from social reformers, radical activists, and liberal university professors; they are heard also from executives in the business community.

There is a feeling among some that the pursuit of profit and organizational efficiency is tainted, that it has less social legitimacy than, say, employing the handicapped, training the hardcore unemployed, eliminating discrimination, or reducing pollution. On the other hand, others believe that business corporations, while remaining efficient, should direct their resources to the relief of social ills. Some call this the corporate reaction to its "social conscience."

Still others argue strongly against the notion of corporate social responsibility. Milton Friedman, a professor of economics, asks if it is appropriate to give the attributes of a conscience to an entity that is at best an artificial person.[6]

As we have said, professional managers are the stewards of the property owned by others. Their obligation is to manage this property in the interest of the owner. In a business corporation, this usually means maintaining and increasing corporate

---

[6] A popular statement of his position is in Milton Friedman, "The Social Responsibility of Business to Increase Its Profits," *New York Times Magazine* (September 13, 1970), pp. 32–33, 124–25.

earnings, and this in turn means maintaining or increasing the value of corporate property.

Friedman points out that if management unilaterally decides to reduce corporate earnings or wealth by contributing to social causes, it is in fact taxing the owners of the corporation. He argues that such a taxation is unjust and that managers who engage in it are not fulfilling their primary obligations — to provide goods and services and make profits in conformance with the basic rules of society.

In practice, conflict often arises between the broader goals of the public at large and the narrower objectives of a business organization. The problem management faces is balancing these interests in the face of conflicting evidence. For example, conservationists are presently concerned by the number of wild ducks that die from eating lead shot. This number is estimated at 2 or 3 per cent of the total yearly hatch. Therefore, they have pressured the makers of sporting ammunition to develop alternative loads using soft iron shot. However, it is not clear that this would solve the problem, because the use of iron shot would reduce the ammunition's speed and would result in more crippled and lost birds. Clearly, research on both issues would have to be conducted at the expense of the manufacturing firms. The cost of this research would be, in Friedman's terms, a tax against the owners. So again, what is the public interest, and how is the conflict of interest between the public and business to be resolved?

Social responsibility, here called public welfare, is often imposed by the federal government's regulation of interstate commerce. In this century we have seen the concept of interstate commerce extended to provide some form of government regulation in all but a few areas of business activity. The extension has resulted chiefly in the government's perception of the tension between social responsibility and the maximizing behavior of businessmen. Consider, for instance, government regulation of automobile safety features.[7] Industry argues that the public is interested mainly in style and power, that safety features do not sell cars. However, the mounting toll of highway accidents indicates that steps must be taken to improve automobile safety in spite of their cost.

Less publicized is the dilemma of fire insurance companies. As they grew increasingly reluctant to insure buildings in slum areas, landlords, finding insurance to be unavailable or extremely costly, refused to invest in major property improvements and thus contributed to the further decline of the neighborhoods. The public image of the insurance companies became tarnished; a threat of political reprisal arose; and soon state insurance commissioners began to apply pressure.[8] Eventually, under a pooling plan, the problem in some cities was alleviated.

Although many more specific examples could be cited, social responsibility cannot be understood solely on this basis. Ultimately, the values that underlie the various positions have to be exposed. Clearly Friedman supports the inviolability of private property. Thus, the responsible manager works in harmony with Fried-

---

[7] Considerable public and government attention was focused on this problem as the result of Ralph Nader's book *Unsafe at Any Speed* (New York: Grossman, 1965).

[8] *Wall Street Journal* (September 9, 1966), p. 8.

man's values and, theoretically, serves the collective well-being of society by doing so. However, other theoreticians feel that private property is not as sacred as previously supposed, that collective interests are not served by the pursuit of private interests. Their theories lead to government regulation and, at the extreme, nationalization of large segments of the private sector.

Such are some of the dilemmas raised by the issue of social responsibility. We cannot resolve them here, but at least we can now relate them to the concepts of objectives. Given objectives, implementation follows. Implementation requires the translation of objectives into specific guidelines for action. These guidelines take the form of policies, procedures, methods, rules, and standards.

POLICIES

Policies are the broad guides to thinking that lead to effective action. Although broad, policy guides do set up definite limitations. As we saw in Chapter 4, policies are rational boundaries for managerial decision-makers.

Major policies are important enough to be made only by the board of directors. The choice of industry, one of the most fundamental of company policies, is written into a firm's charter, but it is the board's prerogative to make policies within that industry's broad limits. For example, the board might decide to seek out the quality market. Every department must then make its plans in accordance with this major policy. The purchasing department would buy only good materials from the most dependable sources; the personnel department would obtain workmen capable of producing only quality products; the engineering department would demand close tolerances and fine finishes; the sales department would emphasize quality; and the advertising department would develop a quality appeal.

Characteristics

A certain amount of flexibility is necessary to policy-making. Some policy statements have flexibility built in, because of words such as "whenever possible," "whenever feasible," and "under usual conditions." If these expressions are not included, then the manner in which the executive applies the policy will determine the degree of flexibility. He must intelligently adapt the policy to a given set of circumstances. His flexibility, of course, must not be extreme or inconsistent. If policies are clear and provide a uniform guide for thinking, they will inspire confidence in the plans and goals that they reflect. If they are not clear, sooner or later widespread dissatisfactions and irritations will develop and employees will be less effective than they should be.

The areas of policy formulation are as varied as the activities of an enterprise. One broad group of policies pertains to the management of the company — planning, organizing, staffing, influencing, and controlling. Another is directed toward its functions — sales, finance, production, personnel relations, and public relations. Specifically, a company's policy might be to promote from within (staffing), to accept

that the customer is always right (public relations), to initiate a fixed price, to under-
price the competition (sales), to require preventive maintenance of equipment, to
decide to buy goods or make them (production), to own or to lease capital equipment
(finance), to adhere to high moral and ethical standards in performing the business
activities (planning). Policies also govern the scope of research activities, cover
distribution and procurement, and much more.

Origin

Obviously policies do not come about by chance but instead are determined by
management or at times by outside forces. Policies can emerge in several ways. They
may be management-originated, appealed, or imposed.

Originated Policy

The originated or management-created policy is no doubt the most significant. Top
management is in a position to see the types of over-all policies required to guide
the thinking of subordinates so that the enterprise's objectives can be achieved. For
example, a firm may have a policy requiring division managers to purchase all
available components of an assembly process from other divisions of the firm.
Although a division manager might find a less expensive source of supply, he would
realize that the purpose of the policy is to maximize the total profit picture of the
corporation, not merely that of his division.

Once broad policy has been created by top management, it becomes the guide for
policy-making by various managers lower down in the managerial hierarchy. Of
course, all these lower managerial decisions will implement the broader policy
originated by top management.

At times, instead of originating at the top and flowing downward, policy may
originate at or near the bottom of an organization and flow upward. "In a sense,
policies are sometimes generated at the operating and first-line supervisory levels and
imposed upward. If certain matters are not recognized or provided for by the set of
policies adopted, or if regularly adopted policies are not enforced, customs may
gradually emerge and achieve the generality, permanence, and authority of true
policies."[9] The extent to which this flow contributes to the success of the organization will largely depend upon whether the enterprise operates under the principles
of free and democratic supervision and whether subordinates can freely express
themselves.

At times policy may also be formulated simultaneously from both directions.
Such policy will incorporate top management's point of view, but at the same time
it will give ample consideration to the opinion of people on lower levels of the
organization.

[9] Billy E. Goetz, *Management Planning and Control* (New York: McGraw-Hill, 1949), p. 65.

Appealed Policy

An appealed policy has a different origin. It is most often formulated in order to cope with some exceptional and usually current problem. A manager will appeal to his superior for a decision because he does not know how to resolve a particular problem or because he disagrees with a previous decision and wants the question reviewed. The decision handed down by the superior then sets what is known as an appealed policy. Appealed policies can also occur in a slightly different manner: A subordinate might not know if a decision is within his jurisdiction or within the frame of broad policy, and he therefore appeals to his superior.

There is a danger in having too many policies formulated by appeal. Individual appealed policies are often inconsistent, uncoordinated, and confusing. Therefore, a manager who must frequently make policy decisions by appeal had better check into originated policies in the areas where questions are arising. He may find that too wide an area has been left without coverage or that the coverage needs updating or clarification. Additional policies may be required to fill the gaps. In this event, originated policies should predominate.

Imposed Policy

A third kind of policy originates externally. Here, policy is imposed upon an enterprise by external forces such as government, labor unions, and trade associations. The word "imposed" indicates that compliance cannot be avoided. Thus, policy formulation is imposed when a federal, state, or local law is passed, and to conform, management must translate it into company policy. Labor policies resulting from collective bargaining and union contracts are imposed as are the responsibilities expressed in labor laws and fair employment policies dictated by federal and state laws. Policy may also be imposed by trade associations or other groups seeking to eliminate trade abuses and to protect their members from destructive practices and competition. The legal status of such directives is sometimes difficult to determine.

Communication

Written and Unwritten Policies

Once formulated, it is essential that policies be carefully and explicitly stated and communicated so that they will be fully understood. This is no easy task. Since different meanings can be attached to words, it is difficult to avoid ambiguity. However, although there is no guarantee that even the written word will be properly understood, it seems desirable that policies be given in a written statement. Nevertheless, not many organizations write down all their policies. Some never get around to it, and others purposely do not do so.

There are several distinct advantages, however, to having written statements of policy. When a manager forces himself to sit down and write, the very act of writing will probably reveal discrepancies, conflicts, and omissions. Written policies are beneficial to all managers, whatever their level. Once written, they are readily accessible, their meaning cannot be changed by word of mouth, and the chance that they will be misinterpreted is small. If a misunderstanding occurs, it can be settled by recourse to a few written words. Moreover, written policy statements can be sent readily to all those affected by them, and new managers can speedily orient and acquaint themselves by reading them.

A disadvantage of written policies is management's reluctance to change them, even when they are outdated and outmoded. This, however, is not a disadvantage of written policy per se. Oral policies can likewise become outmoded. In such instances, the thoughtful subordinate should appeal for a revision.

The advantages of having a written policy far outweigh the disadvantages. But many organizations seem to prefer policies handed down by word of mouth. Oral policies are flexible and can be adjusted to changed circumstances with ease. However, since their exact interpretation might not be known, oral policies become less desirable than written ones.

Implied Policies

Policies that are neither written nor stated are said to be implied. Their presence can be ascertained only by watching the behavior of managers. Many organizations, for example, state that they have no upper age limit in their hiring policy. However, examination of the ages of the individuals hired during a given year might reveal that no one over fifty was employed. Another implied policy can often be observed in the failure to employ women and members of racial minorities.

At times managers justify the existence of implied policies by pointing out that in some areas policies are too difficult to state. They also say that they do not want to limit employees' freedom too drastically or that the enterprise is too dynamic for policies to be set in certain areas. Although such explanations are expedient, implication often leaves large areas open to misinterpretation.

Periodic Review

The dynamic nature of business and nonbusiness organizations makes it probable that policies will sooner or later become outmoded. Similarly, conditions may change so that the over-all thrust of an organization is no longer the same. Therefore, periodic policy review and appraisal are essential. Such a review might uncover practices that are in complete contradiction to stated policies. It might also show that the policies lack integration. In all probability, a periodic review will show the necessity for some changes and adjustments.

To say the least, it is undesirable to keep policies that have become ignored and outdated. As long as they exist, the individual must judge which policies remain current and which are not to be observed. Such decisions are really management's job. Regardless of how well conceived the policies were when originated, the dynamics of the organizational environment make periodic review and adjustment necessary.

PROCEDURES

Procedures are more specific than policies. Billy E. Goetz has written:

Procedures, in common with other forms of planning, seek to avoid the chaos of random activity by directing, coordinating, and articulating the operations of an enterprise. They help direct all enterprise activities toward common goals, they help impose consistency across the organization and through time, and they seek economy by enabling management to avoid the costs of recurrent investigations and to delegate authority to subordinates to make decisions within a frame of policies and procedures devised by management.[10]

Figure 5-2. The Relationship of Policies, Procedures, and Methods

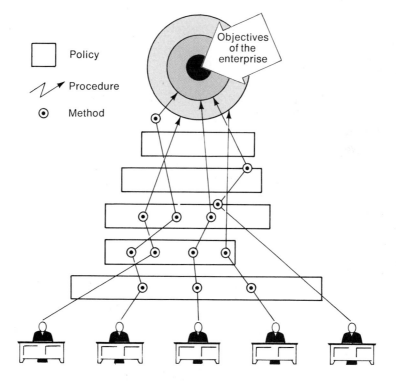

[10] *Ibid.*, p. 83.

Relationship to Policies

Policies define a broad field whose area is determined and limited by the objectives of the enterprise. Procedures show the sequence of concrete acts. As illustrated in Figure 5-2, they chart a path through the area of policy; they present the chronological order of acts to be performed. "Policy always sets an objective or delimits an area of action, while procedures fix a path toward the objective or through the area. Sequence is the *sine qua non* of procedure."[11]

Consider, for example, the statement that the customer is always right. This is *policy*. *Procedure* will specify the steps to be taken to ensure that policy. In the case of a department store, the procedure might be to send a complaining customer first to the buyer, then to the department manager or the floor walker or someone else, and finally to the adjustment office. Whatever decision these various managers make will be within the broad guide of thinking that the customer is right. Although the managers might not believe in a particular instance that the customer is justified, the complaint will be handled according to a prescribed procedure derived from the policy of the store.

There is no doubt that procedures have many advantages. The mere process of preparing a procedure necessitates analysis and study of the matter in question. Once a procedure is established, it assures uniformity of performance. It also gives the manager a standard for appraising work done by his subordinates. Inasmuch as a procedure specifies a sequence of how work is to be done, it decreases the need for further decision-making. Procedures, moreover, permit better coordination. There is, however, the danger that the existence of the procedures will stifle innovation and the development of new ways of doing the work. But this disadvantage can be overcome by periodic procedural review.

Methods

A method is even more detailed than a procedure. Whereas the latter shows a series of steps to be taken, a method is concerned only with one step and explains exactly how this step is to be performed (see Figure 5-2). Methods are most pertinent to production and in this connection mean the best way of performing the job.

Rules

A rule is different from a policy, procedure, or method. It differs from a policy because it does not provide a guide to thinking nor does it leave any discretion to the party involved. It is, however, related to a procedure insofar as it guides actions and states what must or must not be done. However, a rule does not specify a time sequence for a particular action. No smoking, for instance, is one of a long list of safety rules. There is no order of action involved as there is with a procedure; no smoking pertains whenever and wherever the rule is in effect. Such a rule is not to

[11] *Ibid.*, p. 84.

be confused with company safety policy, which might state, for example, that the company intends to carry on a continuous educational campaign about the danger of smoking. The company's safety policy provides the guiding thoughts for safety rules, but the two are clearly distinguished.

Single-Use Plans

Objectives, policies, procedures, and methods require planning by management. In a sense, policy formulation is a kind of planning; policies are made with an eye to repeated use over extended periods of time. Much the same may be said for procedures and methods. However, some plans are devised for a single use. These include programs, projects, and budgets. More is said about these plans in subsequent chapters. Clearly, both repeated-use and single-use organizational guidelines are formulated within the decision-making and planning processes.

Discussion Questions

1. We often hear the argument that social responsibility is good business. What do you think is meant by this statement? What kinds of problems will be created if corporate management seriously believes it?

2. Many organizations have a policy that calls for equal pay for equal work. What sort of objective do you think this policy is trying to achieve? Where do you suppose such a policy would originate? What kinds of procedures, methods, and rules are appropriate for the implementation of this policy?

Supplementary Readings

Business Week. "The War That Business Must Win." In *Dimensions in Modern Management,* edited by Patrick E. Connor. Boston: Houghton Mifflin, 1974.

Davis, Keith, and Robert L. Blomstrom. *Business and Its Environment.* New York: McGraw-Hill, 1966.

Perrow, Charles. "Tidying Up the Stables." In *Dimensions in Modern Management.*

Phillips, Charles F., Jr. "What Is Wrong with Profit Maximization?" In *Dimensions in Modern Management.*

Tosi, Henry L., John R. Rizzo, and Stephen J. Carroll. "Setting Goals in Management by Objectives." In *Dimensions in Modern Management.*

CHAPTER 6

The Nature of the Planning Process

Management planners chart a course of action for the future. Their aim is to achieve a consistent, coordinated set of operations relating action to objectives. Yet their plans alone are not enough; they must be acted upon.[1]

In the early 1900's, Fayol, remarking that planning was manifested on many occasions and in a variety of ways, called the plan of action the chief evidence of planning effort. "The plan of action," he said, "is, at one and the same time, the result envisaged, the line of action to be followed, the stages to go through, and methods to use. It is a kind of future picture wherein proximate events are outlined with some distinctness, whilst remote events appear progressively less distinct, and it entails the running of the business as foreseen and provided against over a definite period."[2]

Without planning, random activities prevail. Therefore, management must plan constantly. By planning, management realistically anticipates problems, analyzes them, foresees their probable effect on the activities of the enterprise, and decides on action that will lead to the desired result. As Ross Webber points out, "The critical aspect of planning is knowing where you want to be and how you want the future to turn out."[3] This statement underscores the necessity of defining goals and objectives before beginning the planning activity. Therefore, management's desires must be known and articulated.

PLANNING AS AN INTELLECTUAL PROCESS AND A PRIMARY FUNCTION

Planning is a process that involves decision-making. It requires a mental predisposition to think before acting, to act in the light of facts rather than guesses, and to order events logically. It requires the manipulation of abstract ideas and the anticipation of the impact of the many possible outcomes on the enterprise as a whole. There is no substitute for the intellectual exercise that planning demands. As Marshall Dimock says, planning is not the work of a theorist locked up in an

---

[1] Billy E. Goetz, *Management Planning and Control* (New York: McGraw-Hill, 1949), p. 63.
[2] Henri Fayol, *General and Industrial Management*, trans. Constance Storrs (London: Pitman, 1949), p. 43.
[3] Ross A. Webber, *Time and Management* (New York: Van Nostrand Reinhold, 1972), p. 127.

office and handing out blueprints through a crack in the door. "It is planning that makes it possible for him [a manager] effectively to combine knowledge with power in order to achieve the objectives of his enterprise."[4]

Relationship to the Other Managerial Functions

Planning is a primary function. Managers must plan before they can intelligently perform any other functions. How could they effectively set up an organization without having a plan in mind? How could they staff and influence subordinates? How could they possibly control? After all, one of the main consequences of planning is setting the standards by which control is accomplished and results are checked. Thus, it is safe to say that planning is a function managers have to perform before they can organize, staff, influence, and control.

This does not imply that once managers have gone through the planning stage, they will not need to plan again for some time. Although a manager must plan before he can organize, staff, influence, or control, it is conceivable that because of overlap he can begin performing a later function before completing the prior one. Additional planning, planning of details, and the revision of plans will take place continuously. Of course, planning must be finished before any and all the other functions can be completed, as illustrated in Figure 6-1.

Figure 6-1. Primary Importance of the Planning Function

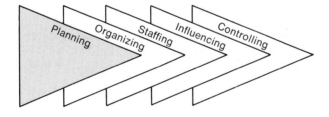

Control and Feedback

In practice, planning is a bit more complicated than theory would indicate. The controlling functions, in particular, constantly create planning problems. These problems could force a manager to change plans, and the change might necessitate alternative organizing, staffing, and influencing decisions. After having made his adjustments, the manager should again turn to controlling to learn whether the results occurred as planned. If they did not, it may become necessary for him to return to the planning stage. In other words, as shown in Figure 6-2, feedback from the controlling process indicates whether changes in plans are needed and whether such

[4] Marshall E. Dimock, *The Executive in Action* (New York: Harper and Row, 1945), p. 123.

changes are effective. Because of the system character of management functions, many adjustments are often required before objectives are realized. For example, if it appears that an annual sales quota may not be met, a firm will have to readjust its plans and take necessary steps in organization, staff, and motivation to stimulate performance or, if the situation dictates, cut back altogether.

Figure 6-2. The Relationship of Planning and Controlling

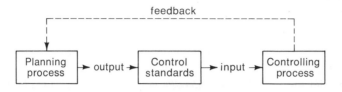

THE MANAGER PLANS

Who does the planning? By our definition of management, it is the manager who plans — every manager, whether he is the chairman of the board, the president of the company, or the first-line supervisor. However, the importance and magnitude of planning vary with the level on which it is performed. The scope tends to decrease in lower levels of management and near the point of execution of the plan.

Compare this situation to that of a mountain climber. At the base of the trail, all he can see are the trees around him; his view is not extensive. After an hour's climb, he may reach a clearing and can look off into the distance and study the surrounding countryside. Finally, when he reaches the summit, he commands a panoramic view of the landscape and can spot details many miles off. The analogy is clear. All managers plan, but the higher up the individual finds himself on the managerial scale, the broader will be his planning responsibility. In this respect, planning bears a close resemblance to decision-making.

Time-Span

George Orwell in his book *Animal Farm* said "all animals are equal, but some are more equal than others." Similarly, while all managers plan, some managers plan more and for longer periods than others. The time-span of managerial planning is also linked to managerial level. Top executives may plan for as long as five years, whereas the foreman plans for no longer than one month and frequently less.[5]

The nature of intermediate- and long-range planning introduces great uncertainty into the top executive's role. Consequently, planning resources are concentrated at this level. It is here that maximum staff support is required to gather information and intelligence so that strategies for the future can be laid.

---

[5] Norman H. Martin, "Differential Decision in the Management of an Industrial Plant," *Journal of Business* 24 (October 1956): 251–52.

Planning Participation

Research in the behavioral sciences indicates that as many managers as possible should participate in planning.[6] The more active the managers are, the more enthusiastic they will be in carrying out the various plans and the higher will be the quality of the plans. In addition, a manager can often contribute his intimate knowledge of operating conditions to the planning process. Also, extensive participation in planning will frequently expose those individuals in the enterprise who have good judgment, initiative, and originality.

The executive often requests staff assistance in his planning responsibilities. He may feel that certain areas call for special knowledge; he may wish to evolve a consistent policy in all-pervasive areas such as personnel and financial procedures. Staff members can thus greatly help managers in their planning tasks.

Another means of achieving participation in planning is through planning committees. Although there is much to be said for and against the use of such committees,[7] generally speaking they can be helpful if properly utilized. Management at all levels may participate in the planning process through regularly scheduled meetings such as supervisory conferences and management clubs. Top management may also stimulate participation by requesting lower levels of management to submit plans from the bottom up. Some type of joint participation is so beneficial and vital to sound planning that it has become second nature to many executives.

CHARACTERISTICS OF PLANNING

Because planning is concerned with the future, it is never completely finished. In some organizations, however, the future is more discernible than in others. Also, the future for a certain product or service can be predicted more reliably at certain times than at others. The manufacture of horsewhips provides an example. With the advent of the automobile, the dim future of the horsewhip could easily be foreseen and plans made accordingly. Another example is found in the industry that produces wooden crossties for railroads. In 1900, when railroads offered the only means of effective mass transportation, approximately 100 million crossties were needed, whereas in recent years only about 20 million crossties are laid annually. Although this decrease was partially caused by now-stabilized factors such as improvements in the treatment of lumber, the relationship of decreasing rail mileage to tie use can easily be seen. Hence, management must make plans to seek new products, new outlets, new things to do; it must plan for diversification.

Economic Aspects

Planning is rational in that it helps reduce the use of resources. This becomes evident if we digress for one moment into the area of planning for production, using as our

---

[6] Rensis Likert, *New Patterns of Management* (New York: McGraw-Hill, 1961).
[7] See Chapter 15.

example the production and assembly of an automobile. If this intricate product were not planned, it would be impossible to produce with such speed and at a relatively reasonable cost. But not only in production is planning economic; it is also economic in the general managerial arena. Planning yields purposeful and orderly activity. All efforts are directed toward a desired result; haphazard approaches are minimized; activities are coordinated; and duplications are avoided. Facilities are used to their best advantage, and guesswork is eliminated. Failure to plan may cause the loss of important resources.

The Planning Period

Short-run planning can be defined as that which covers a period of from six to twelve months. Long-term planning usually involves a considerably longer interval. In recent years, there has been an increasing trend for firms to plan ahead for five, ten, or even twenty years. Thus one-to-five-year plans have come to be considered intermediate range, whereas anything from five years upward is considered long range.

How long should the planning period be?[8] Organizations vary considerably in the length of the period for which they plan.[9] The type of enterprise, the kind of industry, the production cycle, the quality of managerial practice, and many other factors all figure in the decision. In general, the longer range the plan, the less flexible the organization will be in adapting to change.

Commitments

The length of the planning cycle should be linked to a firm's commitments. Koontz speaks of the "commitment principle" in pointing out that the planning period should cover at least the term for which the manager has committed the firm.[10] For example, a mail order house commits itself for approximately six months when it sends out a catalogue. Where commitments have been made in buildings and machinery, planning periods should extend far enough into the future to enable the recovery of the capital outlay. Considerations of this sort justify long-range planning of from ten to twenty years.

The nature of the organization has a bearing on the length of the planning period. If a firm manufactures a product whose cycle of production takes twelve months, it cannot plan for less than that period of time. If, however, the production cycle is shorter, planning can easily be done for six months or less. In an enterprise producing high-styled fashions, a three- to six-month plan might be considered long range. In other cases, for example in the building of a large generator that might take

[8] See Webber, *Time and Management*, pp. 130–33.

[9] "Industry Plans for the Future," *The Conference Board Business Record* 9, no. 8 (August 1952): 325; "In Business Everyone's Looking Ahead," *Business Week* (January 5, 1957), pp. 113–18.

[10] Harold Koontz and Cyril O'Donnell, *Principles of Management*, 3d ed. (New York: McGraw-Hill, 1964), p. 87.

several years to complete, three to five years is short range. Paper-making companies plant trees today in order to be able to harvest them in fifty or more years.

It does not follow that small enterprises usually make short-term plans and that only large enterprises make long-range ones. Many small enterprises achieved larger size only because they had long-range plans. However, long-range plans seem to predominate in large organizations. Frequently, the larger the organization, the greater is the control it has over its environment. By having at its disposal the means to exert economic, political, and social dominance, it often can make its plans become self-fulfilling prophecies.

The Trend Toward Long-Range Planning

Although long-range planning is heralded as one of the significant management developments of this century, it is interesting to note that Fayol spoke of it as "the precious managerial instrument" and devised for his firm a master plan made up of a series of yearly, ten-year, and special "forecasts."[11] In the larger economic setting, there is an increased need today for long-range planning. David W. Ewing has presented testimony on this need.[12] In his book *Long Range Planning for Management* representative heads of leading corporations discuss their methods for long-range planning and the ensuing benefits. As Ewing points out, long-range planning means many things to many people: "Some will find it visionary and impractical. Some who latch on to it will find they have a 'bear by the tail.' Others will make a fad out of it. But it should become for most companies — and for the economy — one of the really significant business developments of the century."[13]

The concept of long-range planning has far-reaching implications for the practice of management, for it necessitates looking analytically at a company's operations. Long-range planning produces a vast network of plans connecting the many functions of the enterprise. Therefore, the manager needs increased conceptual skills "as opposed to technical and human relations skills" to find his way through the maze. In long-range planning, top management takes into consideration the perpetual nature of the organization, the need to build institutions for generations to come. This approach often influences management to forgo short-term profits if they interfere with long-range plans. Long-range planning puts a premium on research and development, expansion and diversification, executive training programs, and many other items that represent a current expense but constitute future investment.

Integration of Short-Range and Long-Range Plans

Long-range and short-range planning must be integrated and coordinated. It is misleading to view long-range planning as an activity separate from and independent

---

[11] Henri Fayol, *General and Industrial Management*, pp. 43–52.

[12] David W. Ewing, *Long-Range Planning for Management* (New York: Harper and Row, 1958).

[13] *Ibid.*, pp. 3–4.

of short-range planning. No short-run plan should be made unless it contributes to the goals set out in the long-range plan. Therefore, top management must ensure that all other managers understand the long-range plans and objectives of the company and also must ascertain whether the short-range plans conform to long-range plans. Doing this initially is less difficult than correcting inconsistencies later on.

The Good Plan

Every good plan should have certain basic characteristics.[14] The plan must be based on a clearly defined objective, stated in a clear, concise, and accurate manner. Objectives should be quantified as much as possible so that accomplishments can be compared with goals. A good plan also requires operational clarity and should adequately cover all action required for satisfactory fulfillment of the objective. There is usually a hierarchy of plans, each suiting a level of authority and conforming to a portion of the plan's time-span. Naturally, the various plans must fit into a consistent pattern. The parts of the plan — its purpose, nature, and timing — must also be integrated so that coordination results. Furthermore, plans should be reasonably economical and should consider the resources available.

Another important characteristic of a good plan is flexibility. A flexible plan can be adjusted smoothly and without delay or serious loss of economy or effectiveness to the requirements of changing conditions. In order to permit such adjustment, a plan must be broad, containing alternative courses of action to meet possible changes as they arise. Management has to check the feasibility of plans regularly. Planning does not freeze action; at least it should not. If management learns that a plan does not lead to the required objective or that underlying conditions have changed, it then has to select an alternate plan. It is much wiser to be right than consistent.

Dissemination

It is essential that plans be properly and effectively communicated to the managers concerned with their implementation. This, of course, is not always necessary if all managers have participated in the planning. Where such participation is not possible, however, it is the duty of top management to communicate properly to all. An uninformed manager is an ineffective manager. The better informed a manager is, the better will he do his job and the more will he contribute to the objectives of the enterprise.

Often there is a gap in knowledge of plans between top-level and second-level management. This is frequently excused by the claim that many of the plans are confidential. Practitioners, however, know that little can be kept secret in any organization. Therefore, internal security cannot generally be used as an excuse. Managers, of course, appreciate the fact that some limitations to the communication

---

[14] Lyndall F. Urwick, *The Elements of Administration* (New York: Harper and Row, 1943), cites a number of these characteristics on p. 34.

of plans do exist, but nonetheless they must be well informed about the plans that will influence their particular activities.

The essence of planning, as we have said, is informed anticipation of the future. Planning takes place against a background of information, premises, and assumptions regarding all future conditions that will have a bearing on the organization. In addition to purely economic concerns, planning must take into account social, political, and technological change.

Discussion Questions

1. Few doubt that decision-making and planning are closely related. What, however, constitutes the principal distinctions between them?

2. It is popular today to speak of "planning for the year 2000." In light of this statement, consider the following quotation: "Long-range planning produces long-range commitments that reduce the flexibility of the organization."

Supplementary Readings

Fayol, Henri. *General and Industrial Management.* Translated by Constance Storrs. London: Pitman, 1949.

LeBreton, Preston P. *Administrative Intelligence-Information Systems.* Boston: Houghton Mifflin, 1969.

Thompson, Stewart. "What Planning Involves." In *Dimensions in Modern Management,* edited by Patrick E. Connor. Boston: Houghton Mifflin, 1974.

Webber, Ross A. *Time and Management.* New York: Van Nostrand Reinhold, 1972. See chapter 12.

CHAPTER 7

Planning Information: Forecasts

Planning is deciding what is to be done in the future. Such decisions, however, can be made only on the basis of sound planning information, information that includes knowledgeable estimates of future conditions. Thus, although the future is full of uncertainties, management must make certain assumptions about it in order to plan properly. These assumptions are based on forecasts.

THE PLACE OF FORECASTING IN MODERN ORGANIZATIONS

Forecasting as a major source of planning information is in its infancy, but it is growing rapidly. An interesting example of relatively advanced forecasting techniques is demonstrated in *The Year 2000*,[1] a book based on data developed by the Hudson Institute, one of the better known think tanks in the United States. In his introduction to this book, Daniel Bell states: "Machiavelli argued that half of men's actions are ruled by chance, the other half are governed by men themselves. This volume, and the work of the Commission on the Year 2000, is an effort to change that balance." Such an observation is appropriate to the entire planning area. Planning information and forecasts help management move from chance and the uncontrollable to prediction and improved control.

Forecasting is involved to some extent in every conceivable organization decision. Lyndall Urwick has written: "The man who starts a business is making an assessment of a future demand for its products. The man who determines a production programme for the next six months or twelve months is usually also basing it on some calculation of future demand. The man who engages staff, and particularly young staff, usually has an eye to future organizational requirements."[2] An appraisal of future prospects is inherent in all planning. In fact, the success of a business depends in large measure upon the skill of management in foreseeing and preparing for future conditions.

[1] Herman Kahn and Anthony J. Wiener, *The Year 2000* (New York: Macmillan, 1967).
[2] Lyndall F. Urwick, *The Elements of Administration* (New York: Harper and Row, 1943), p. 21.

Economic Variables and Control

Such preparation for the future involves consideration of an adjustment to four basic economic variables: the international climate, the national climate, industry conditions, and the status of the enterprise itself. An organization has seemingly little control over the first two. However, the military-industrial complex appears to provide an exception to this statement. The extent of control over the third variable seems to depend on the size of the organization. For example, General Motors has more control over events in the automobile industry than, say, a dressmaker would have in the ladies garment industry. Of course, a firm has its greatest control in its home territory — that is, within its own enterprise. In order to achieve this control, however, management must be informed; it must recognize industry, national, and sometimes international economic trends. Management must indeed forecast business conditions.

The use of forecasting did not become widespread until the depression of the 1930's caused businessmen to become acutely aware of business cycles. More and more organizations then began to analyze business conditions in order to anticipate economic trends and to estimate trends' probable effect on their own operations. By forecasting, a business gains time to formulate plans so that it may obtain maximum benefits from periods of expanding economy and minimize adverse effects when business activity slackens. A management that forecasts becomes aware of the difficulty of bucking the trend of general business conditions, especially as the company grows larger. Management forecasters also realize the possibility of serious losses when economic factors are not given sufficient weight. Evaluating those factors and basing forecasts upon them has been facilitated by the availability of more reliable and detailed information about the nation's economy.

Organization for Forecasting

The practice of forecasting among organizations varies from the reading of newspapers to the use of staff experts to interpret and analyze the relationship of current and future conditions to company operations. In all organizations, executives are expected to keep abreast of current economic developments through reading, contacts, and discussions. It is common practice for organizations to place staff forecasters close to top management. In some firms, one executive is responsible for the preparation of forecasts, and the staff of trained forecasting specialists usually works with him.[3] Staff members, mostly economists and statisticians, are regarded by the firm as professionals. This is indicated by the fact that the person in charge of forecasting is usually said to be an economist.

The American Management Association (AMA) reports that most business firms with their own forecasting staffs separate over-all economic forecasting from special-

---

[3] *Company Organization for Economic Forecasting*, Research Report No. 28 (New York: American Management Association, 1957), p. 21.

ized sales forecasting. If an organization does not employ its own forecasting staff, it will frequently hire economic consultants to analyze and interpret economic developments and forecasts. Some managements feel that in this way they can obtain expert advice at a lower cost than by maintaining their own staff of specialists. Sometimes a company that has its own staff of forecasters will also employ the services of outside research consultants in order to get a reliable check on their predictions and to obtain other viewpoints. This, of course, helps to improve the quality of the forecasts.

Some executives encourage discussion of the rationale, assumptions, and implications of their organization's forecasts, regardless of whether a company forecasting staff exists. In certain instances, periodic economic reports are circulated to familiarize managers with the outlook for business. It is of great importance to management that these forecasts be understood by all managers, for they form the basis for planning and other managerial functions.

Forecasts as Planning Premises

When assumptions about the future are used in a planning context, they are called *planning premises.* Such premises, or the assumptions from which they are derived, may be considered building stones forming the foundation of planning, and forecasts may be considered the prerequisites of the entire planning structure — or, in other words, the quarry rock from which the building stones for planning are cut.

Forecasts are possible in a multitude of areas. However, the manager selects and uses as planning premises or assumptions only forecasts that are strategically important and have material bearing on his organization. Forecasts important to one enterprise might not be of any significance to another; with time management learns which bears on its planning and which it can neglect. Some assumptions that were once important may become insignificant and can be eliminated. Others will be added as time goes on. Therefore, management must remain fully aware of the shifting requirements for some of its strategic assumptions.

The 1957 findings of the American Management Association indicate that the type of industry in which the enterprise is engaged influences the amount of effort devoted to forecasting. Additionally, the more a company is removed from the ultimate consumer, the more difficult forecasting becomes. Therefore, manufacturers of heavy industrial equipment and producers of primary products such as steel are likely to make widespread use of forecasting departments in order to overcome this difficulty.

Tangibility

Although most forecasts and the planning premises that result from them are tangible, management must not overlook intangible factors such as the company's reputation. For example, when deciding whether to produce a new product, management may look as closely at its compatibility with the company's image as it will at its suitability to the production and profit scheme. Such factors are important and must be taken into consideration, even though they cannot be quantified.

Foreseeability

Likewise, not all events — acts of God, wars, or strikes, for instance — can be foreseen and incorporated into planning premises. In the short run it might be possible to anticipate them, but in the longer run these occurrences cannot be predicted with any degree of exactitude. We therefore have to distinguish between foreseeable and unforeseeable premises.

Controllability

Another way to differentiate planning premises is to look at them from the point of view of controllability. Certain premises are controllable, others are semi-controllable, and still others are noncontrollable. Controllable planning premises might include policies, programs, and activities that are entirely regulated by management. Semi-controllable premises can be partially regulated; an organization's share of the market is an example of a semi-controllable premise. Management can do its part to obtain as much of the industry's total as possible, but the activities of competitors are a limiting factor. Of the premises that are noncontrollable, the most important is the general business cycle. All firms are affected by it, but there is relatively little an individual firm can do to stave off its effects. However, acknowledging the business cycle and gearing company activities to a similar cycle can be a great help to management. Like the business cycle, population trends are based on factors beyond the control of management. Government action such as the issuance of a report linking cigarette smoking to cancer and other health problems is yet another basis for a noncontrollable premise. Although the events themselves are noncontrollable, their effects on the firm are foreseeable to a large extent.

EXTERNAL PLANNING PREMISES AND FORECASTS

Perhaps the best way to classify planning premises is to distinguish between those that are external to the enterprise and those that are internal to it. External premises primarily refer to the general business climate and to industry conditions; internal premises refer to the firm's own climate.

The General Business Climate

Many management decisions are affected by the general business climate, but some are affected more than others. Plans for growth and expansion are particularly closely related to business conditions, as are plans for capital equipment purchases. Budgets, production scheduling, inventory levels, financial programming, market expansion, product design, and investments are also closely allied.

The scope of these decision areas emphasizes the importance of acknowledging the general business climate in forecasts and planning premises. Let us now look at some of the specific components of this climate and how they affect particular areas of managerial planning.

Government Policies

The job of forecasting general business conditions and formulating external premises has in some respects become more difficult and in others simpler because of the influence of government policies on economic conditions.

Fiscal Policy. Management has to make assumptions about the direction of governmental fiscal policy regardless of how difficult this may be. It must first know what to expect in regard to taxation. Managerial planning strongly depends on assumptions about the rate of corporate income taxes and will change if forecasts indicate that the 52 per cent corporation income tax will remain or will be raised or lowered. Excess-profits tax rates also affect managerial planning; if rates are high, management is likely to increase advertising and publicity budgets. Another impact of taxes upon planning results from the possibility of accelerated amortization, because if it occurs, management will surely want to make investment in new plants and equipment one of its prime planning premises.

Taxation is not the only area in which government fiscal policies form the basis for necessary planning assumptions. Another important area is federal government spending, which currently runs into billions of dollars and takes a large portion of the U.S. gross national product. An increase or decrease in such expenditures will certainly have a considerable impact on the economy. Management, therefore, must forecast what future government expenditures will be. Because of the indirect impact of government spending, this is necessary not only for enterprises that have the government as an important customer but also for those that do little or no government business.

Monetary Policy. Management must also forecast the monetary policy of the Federal Reserve Board — whether it will pursue a policy of loose or tight money and whether that policy will continue in the short run or in the long run. Forecasts on such matters will greatly influence financial planning. For example, if management thinks that money rates will remain high in the short run, it will probably assume that in the long run there will be periods during which the rates of interest will be lower, and it will postpone floating certificates of indebtedness. However, if management can see only higher interest rates for the long run, then it will make the opposite decision.

Anti-Trust Policy. Planning must take into account the enforcement of anti-trust laws. Management needs to appraise whether the Anti-Trust Division of the Justice Department intends to enforce the anti-monopoly laws vigorously or to sidestep some of the issues. Forecasts of this nature are particularly important when management is considering expansion by mergers and consolidations. If the assumption is that the Justice Department will not look kindly upon such mergers, management's expansion plans will probably be directed into other channels. If, however, enforcement has not been too vigorous, management will feel freer to pursue expansion plans.

Other Government Controls. Naturally, management will be influenced by other government controls and restrictions — tariffs, capital inflows and outflows, licensing. Sometimes planners can forecast the nature of controls by knowing factors such as the political party in power. But, whatever the foundation for its assumptions, management's planning will reflect its forecast of the trend in government control. These factors are of special concern to industries where regulatory agencies such as the Federal Communications Commission and the Federal Aviation Administration are important.

Space, Communication, and Defense Policies. Government influence on fiscal, monetary, and anti-trust matters has been substantial for many years. However, government influence in space, communication, and defense — a result of cold war tensions — has added a new dimension to government-business relationships. Space exploration, communication satellites, and missile defense systems are examples of technological achievements which would never have been realized without

Figure 7-1. Per Cent Distribution of Population by Age, 1972 and 2000

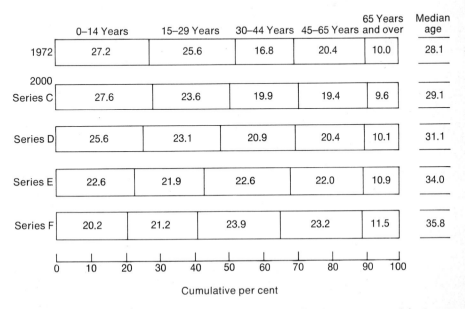

	0–14 Years	15–29 Years	30–44 Years	45–65 Years	65 Years and over	Median age
1972	27.2	25.6	16.8	20.4	10.0	28.1
2000 Series C	27.6	23.6	19.9	19.4	9.6	29.1
Series D	25.6	23.1	20.9	20.4	10.1	31.1
Series E	22.6	21.9	22.6	22.0	10.9	34.0
Series F	20.2	21.2	23.9	23.2	11.5	35.8

Cumulative per cent

Source: U.S. Dept. of Commerce, Social and Economic Statistics Administration, Bureau of the Census, *Population Estimates and Projections,* Current Population Reports, Series P-25, no. 493 (December 1972).

government sponsorship. Naturally, private enterprise is intimately involved in these projects through research, development, and often operations.

As contractors and subcontractors on such projects, business firms are subject to many additional regulations. Some of these are obvious; for example, a firm contracting to develop and manufacture a specialized missile system for the Air Force must naturally meet Air Force specifications for design, performance, and capability. But government contracts frequently regulate more than the character of the finished product. Some contracts require that management employ techniques such as cost effectiveness, PERT, and zero defects. Additionally, contracts now specify that the firm must offer equal-opportunity employment to overcome racial bias. These are just a few examples of the regulatory influence that has emerged as the government has become one of industry's main customers.

Population Trends

Recent reversal of the birth rate has caused the downward revision of over-all population growth projections (see Figure 7-1). The impact of the declining birth

Figure 7-2. Projections of Total Population, 1972–2020

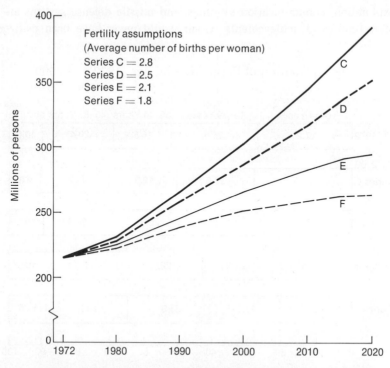

Source: U.S. Dept. of Commerce, Social and Economic Statistics Administration, Bureau of the Census, *Population Estimates and Projections,* Current Population Reports, Series P-25, no. 493 (December 1972).

Table 7-1. Summary of Projections of Total Population, 1960–2020

Year (July 1)	Series C	Series D	Series E	Series F
Estimates				
1960			180,671	
1965			194,303	
1970			204,879	
1972			208,837	
Projections				
1975	215,872	215,324	213,925	213,378
1980	230,955	228,676	224,132	221,848
1985	248,711	243,935	235,701	230,913
1990	266,238	258,692	246,639	239,084
1995	282,766	272,211	256,015	245,591
2000	300,406	285,969	264,430	250,686
2005	321,025	301,397	273,053	255,209
2010	344,094	318,156	281,968	259,332
2015	367,977	335,028	290,432	262,631
2020	392,030	351,368	297,746	264,564

Source: U.S. Dept. of Commerce, Social and Economic Statistics Administration, Bureau of the Census. *Population Estimates and Projections,* Current Population Reports, Series P-25, no. 493 (December 1972). NOTE: Figures are in thousands and are for total population, including Armed Forces abroad.

rate has already been felt in education, a field formerly geared to a policy of expansion and growth. However, few organizations are unaffected by population trends; therefore, estimates of future population must become a planning premise. The trend of the population is a major determinant of the production of products and services. Specifically, organizations catering to markets for the young will have to change their strategies. Figure 7-2 shows that recent population projections for the United States to the year 2020 depend upon fertility assumptions about the average number of births per woman. Table 7-1 summarizes these population projections on the basis of the four assumptions.

Economic Activities

Management also needs planning premises in the area of general economic activity — on employment figures, productivity, price levels, and national income. Through the development of comprehensive and accurate statistics, we are now able to analyze the composition and distribution of national income, one of the most widely used indicators of general business health. Basically, one must view the workings of the national economy as a sort of giant double-entry bookkeeping system. One side of the ledger indicates the income; the other side the expenditures.

Gross national product (GNP) is the essential element of this national accounting system. The expenditure side of the GNP consists of three major accounts: personal consumption expenditures (consumer spending), private investment expenditures (business spending), and government purchases of goods and services. It represents the total value at market prices of all goods and services produced by the nation's economy in a given period. Each of these accounts can be broken down into finer detail. Personal consumption expenditures, for instance, consist of expenditures for durable goods, for nondurable goods, and for services. Data for the various components of these subdivisions are also available.

The income side of the GNP ledger shows the net value of all final goods and services at factor cost of production rather than at market prices. From this side we can draw conclusions and assumptions as to the trend of income, savings, and so on. These data, of course, are related to the data on employment and working hours.

Forecasts on productivity and price levels — more realistically, the inflationary trend — also serve as valuable planning premises for management. History shows the erosion of the purchasing value of the dollar and management cannot afford to plan for the future without making assumptions about the rate of further erosion.

Technological Changes[4]

The activities of many companies are so closely related to rapid changes in technology that a need for technological forecasting has arisen. In many enterprises, a lot of the goods and services produced today were unknown a few years ago. Therefore, management is making efforts to forecast technological developments and to set a timetable for when blue-sky ideas will become realities.

Technological forecasting, however, is still in its early stages, and many years will pass before its techniques are as reliable as those of general economic forecasting. Economists are testing a number of different methods, but three main forecasting approaches stand out. The first is graphical charting, widely used in aerospace, electronics, and computer industries. It is based on the principle that most engineering developments, such as increasing the speed of an aircraft, tend to follow a straight line when plotted on a logarithmic scale. As confirmation, speeds of new aircraft have fallen on this line as anticipated and so will those of the supersonic transports. Another approach to technological forecasting was developed by the Rand Corporation and is known as the Delphi method. Here, anonymous questionnaires are issued to experts in a field and, from them, individual forecasts are compiled. These are then passed around for written criticism by other participants until a consensus on development and timing is reached. Some companies apply variations of the Delphi method but give them different names. The third major approach to technological forecasting is the matrix method. This lists technological developments down one side of a chart and product functions up the other side. The time factor can be added to the matrix as a third dimension. There is little doubt that these approaches leave much to be desired. With time and experience, the techniques will change and accuracy will be improved.

[4] Based on "New Products, Setting a Timetable," *Business Week* (May 27, 1967), pp. 52–61. Also see Harper Q. North and Donald L. Pyke, " 'Probes' of the Technological Future," *Harvard Business Review* 47 (May–June 1969): 68–82.

The Industry Climate

After having made planning assumptions regarding the general business climate, management needs a set of assumptions that refer to the climate of the industry in which the enterprise is engaged. Two of the most important assumptions are based on forecasts of the total volumes of domestic industry and of foreign imports. If the enterprise is in an industry that has had to face increasing foreign competition, assumptions about future imports will be significant. They will help to indicate whether management should plan to establish branches in foreign countries and thereby import its own products. Other planning premises specific for the industry should also be made — assumptions on the industry's expansion or contraction, on the extent of research and development, on the significance of new technology.

In projecting sales, the automobile industry, for example, is concerned with general assumptions regarding gross national product, industrial production, personal income, wholesale prices, consumer prices, and other matters. It is also concerned with numerous specific industry factors for which special assumptions must be made. Some of these are: the level of automobile prices in relation to industrial prices, used car prices versus new car prices, new car registrations as a percentage of cars on the road, installment debt repayments as a percentage of disposable income, the make-up of the car-buying population, and many more. Similarly, each industry will have its own set of specific factors for which it will want to obtain future forecasts.

Availability of Information

Information and data are readily available on the many subjects for which forecasts and external planning premises are needed. Beginning with the National Recovery Administration in 1933, numerous agencies of the federal government have collected great quantities of basic economic information. Private industry, in addition, has gradually become more willing to make available to government and other research agencies company data that might aid competitors. Moreover, World War II gave added impetus to the collection of economic data.

Current and expected business trends are the subject of considerable interest and study. There is a constant flow of articles, reports, analyses, and forecasts circulated not only by government agencies but also by such sources as trade associations, consultants, banks, brokerage houses, and research firms. Management is able to obtain a wide variety of estimates and information by merely reading the publications of these sources (many of which are free). Much can also be gleaned from newspapers and business weeklies. Although this is an easy way of gauging general business sentiment and of comparing management thinking with other opinions, the reader is usually unable to check the accuracy of the information. Sometimes the forecasts which appear in the business or mass media are merely public propaganda. Furthermore, the reader may find serious conflict between various published reports, and also the reports might not appear at a time when he really needs them most.

As we have noted, government agencies and trade associations make available many statistical surveys and interpretations. The United States Department of Commerce *Survey of Current Business* is one of the most widely used of the thousands of publications available. Other publications, to cite only a few, are: *Economic Indicators,* prepared for the Joint Economic Committee by the Council of Economic Advisers; the *Federal Reserve Bulletin;* and reports published by the National Industrial Conference Board. The advantage of the statistical information found in such publications is that it represents facts rather than opinions. It gives management a basis for evaluating outside opinion on the business outlook before establishing its planning premises.

Techniques

Much has been written about the techniques available for forecasting general business and industry trends. *Business Week* classifies these as "loaded deck," "oaks from acorns," and "test tube" techniques.[5] In the first, the forecaster is working from known data — inside information. He knows what has happened and what is happening before anyone else finds out. The second technique reasons that the future grows out of the present, though it is not identical with the past. The third strategy refers to theoretical economic models.

A. G. Abramson classifies four different groups of forecasting techniques. The first technique is purely mechanical. In it, recurrent cycles, lead series, and data are classified, and conclusions are drawn on the basis of past experience without any examination of past and current causal forces. Abramson's second technique is labeled "plans for future action."[6] The underlying idea of this technique is that at any moment there exist plans at various stages of completion, and if these plans can be uncovered in the early stages it is possible to predict what will happen in later ones. The third approach uses the opinions and expectations of others. In this technique the forecast is based on what businessmen expect their sales to be, on what consumers expect to spend, or even on what other forecasters believe will happen. This approach involves neither cause nor history. Abramson's fourth group of forecasting techniques is called "causal." In this technique an attempt is made to determine the causes of fluctuations in the series to be forecast, and then these causes are measured and evaluated.

In an actual forecast it is conceivable and even probable that a number of techniques may be combined.[7] "The identification of specific methods does not mean they should or must be used alone. In fact, as will be evident, it is sometimes difficult

[5] "Business Forecasting," *Business Week* (September 24, 1955), pp. 90–122.

[6] Adolph G. Abramson and Russell H. Mack, *Business Forecasting in Practice* (New York: Wiley, 1956), p. 71.

[7] For those who are interested in learning how one large concern forecasts the general business activity, the writers call attention to the very interesting article by Donald J. Watson in Abramson and Mack, *Business Forecasting in Practice,* pp. 224–69. In 1956, when the article was written, Mr. Watson held the position of Economist, Economic Research and Forecasting Operation, General Electric Company, at headquarters in Schenectady, New York.

to separate one method from another, and there are numerous conceivable classifications."[8]

INTERNAL PLANNING PREMISES AND FORECASTS

The Sales Forecast

Of the various internal planning premises which are used by a firm we shall devote
a large part of our attention to the most important one, the sales forecast. The sales
forecast is basic to internal planning, serving as both a forecast and a guide. The
sales forecast is a projection of expected sales — an estimate of anticipated sales
volume extending into the future for six months, a year, or an even longer period.
It is also a forecast of the revenue side of the income statement. In making a sales
forecast, management is concerned with the expectations of a single enterprise
within an industry after having determined the outlook for the entire industry. A
sales forecast is narrower in scope than is a general business or an industry forecast,
although those two often provide important elements in developing it.

Since the end of World War II, an increasing number of firms have made and
utilized sales forecasts. Whereas they used to serve only occasionally as a basis for
sales quotas and for other marketing division purposes, sales forecasts have now
become the backbone of financial and production planning.[9]

In most cases, however, sales forecasts are rather difficult to make. It is possible,
for instance, to make better forecasts of industry volume than of company volume,
for the individual company's share of industry production constantly shifts. In
forecasting sales, management must work with one influential variable which is
usually uncontrollable: competition from the other members of the industry. In
the past, for example, aggressive expansion by one automobile competitor has easily
depressed the volume and competitive shares of all the other firms in that industry.

In order to do an effective sales forecasting job, management needs a thorough
knowledge of company and industry problems, an awareness of general business
conditions, and the ability to see the significance of factors affecting sales. In addition, the sales forecaster must have the confidence and cooperation of the company's
executives.

Methods

A report of the National Industrial Conference Board, *Forecasting in Industry*, points
to the conclusion that no single forecasting method presently known gives uniformly
accurate results.[10] One of the surest aids to sound sales forecasting is to approach
the same goal by several methods, with each forecasting method acting as a check

[8] Abramson and Mack, *Business Forecasting in Practice*, p. 45.
[9] *Sales Forecasting: Uses, Techniques, and Trends,* Special Report No. 16 (New York:
American Management Association, 1956), p. 8.
[10] *Forecasting in Industry,* Studies in Business Policy No. 77 (New York: National Industrial
Conference Board, 1956).

on the others. Four different methods of sales forecasting are primarily used: the jury of executive opinion method; sales force composite method; users' expectation method; and statistical methods.[11]

Jury of Executive Opinion Method. This is probably the oldest and simplest method of making sales forecasts. As its name implies, it assembles and averages the opinions of the top management of various divisions in order to obtain a sounder forecast than could be made by a single estimator. Undoubtedly one advantage of this approach is that it is quick, and it does not require elaborate statistics. However, this method also has serious drawbacks. It is based entirely on opinion rather than on facts and analyses. Furthermore, averaging opinions reduces and disperses the responsibility for accuracy.

Sales Force Composite Method. This widely used method combines the views of the salesmen and sales managers concerning expectations of future sales. Each salesman is requested to estimate the future sales in his territory. His estimate is usually reviewed by regional sales managers, and then by the general sales manager. One obvious advantage is that those closest to the sales — those with a specialized knowledge of the market — do the forecasting. The salesman, moreover, is the one who has to make good on his forecast.

Yet, this method has many disadvantages. Although his proximity to the market enables the salesman to forecast for the immediate future, he is usually not a good long-term forecaster. Some salesmen tend to be too optimistic, whereas others play it safe, thereby inviting underachievement. Partly because of such disadvantages, there seems to be a trend away from the use of the sales organization as an integral part of the sales forecasting process. A few organizations, however, have worked out ways of using the sales force composite method more effectively.

Users' Expectations Method. Some companies ask their customers how much they expect to buy from them and base their sales forecast directly on this information obtained from those whose purchases will actually determine sales. This method is especially meaningful if the manufacturer serves an industry consisting of few companies. Another advantage of this method is that the cost of obtaining the information — by mail, phone, or personal interview — is negligible, thus enabling a small company with limited resources to make reliable forecasts. Furthermore, the users' expectations method generally provides more current and more complete information than is available from published sources. It is particularly useful in making a forecast on a new industrial product for which there is no previous experience or data.

However, the forecasts obtained by this method are based on expectations subject to change; that is, they rely on estimates of needs and not on commitments. Making such forecasts also requires considerable time and effort.

[11] All these methods except the users' expectation method are cited *ibid.* The users' expectation method is cited in *Forecasting Sales,* Studies in Business Policy No. 106 (New York: National Industrial Conference Board, 1963), pp. 30–32.

Statistical Methods. Many firms rely on several different statistical approaches to supplement personal judgment and increase sales forecasting accuracy. Correlation analysis and trend-and-cycle projections are the most frequently used statistical methods. They are applied by trained specialists who are usually attached to the staff of the market research or a similar department.

Correlation analysis is a method of measuring the relationship between two or more factors. In a sales forecasting context, it is used to discover whether a relationship exists between the company's sales and some other measurable series, then to determine what this relationship is and also its reliability. By using correlation analysis, the statistician is able to forecast the company's own sales on the basis of other series whose fluctuations precede those in sales, or to supplement judgment by relating the firm's sales to a well-known series which is being forecast by many others. The National Industrial Conference Board summarizes the advantages and disadvantages of correlation analysis as follows:

It describes in measurable objective terms the relationships influencing the course of sales. It indicates the degree of reliability which can be attached to such relationships; it forces the forecaster to qualify the assumptions underlying his estimates, making it easier for management to check his results. The great disadvantage is the danger of relying too heavily upon such relationships and of abandoning independent appraisal of future events. Even the best correlations are subject to chance variations and one serious variation may be enough to bring severe losses to a company.[12]

Trend-and-cycle analysis defines and measures three basic factors which influence a firm's sales: long-term growth trends, cyclical business fluctuations, and seasonal variations. For most industries this method is useful only in the long-range forecasting of their sales.

In addition to these two methods, some companies have developed mathematical models and computer simulation techniques in order to forecast sales. Such models can be constructed when the sale of the product depends upon several factors, each having a certain known effect on the sale. Thus, the tire industry, for instance, has been able to develop a mathematical model based on the fact that the demand for tires is affected by new car production, the number of cars in operation, the tires' wearing qualities, and the amount of service tires receive.[13]

Use

It is interesting to note that the sales forecast is used for a wide variety of purposes. Indeed, a survey of sales forecasting practices made by the AMA in 1956 indicated that most companies have, on the average, five or six specific uses for their sales forecasts. Of the 297 representative companies surveyed, nearly all listed production planning as the single most general application. Almost the same number also used

[12] *Forecasting in Industry*, p. 1.
[13] *Ibid.*, pp. 33–35.

the sales forecast for budget preparation. Other specific uses included: earnings forecasting, equipment and facilities planning, determining sales quotas, manpower planning, raw material stockpiling, promotion planning, inventory planning, and estimating cash requirements. Consumer goods industries use the sales forecast primarily to set sales quotas, whereas the service organizations use it primarily for budget preparation.

Time-Span

Most sales forecasts cover a period of at least one year, but many companies supplement them with additional forecasts both of shorter and longer duration. Four out of five companies review and adjust their forecasts at regular intervals, typically every three months. Logically, the larger the company the more likely it is to try to see far ahead; conversely, the smaller the company, the more it emphasizes short-range forecasts. Though almost all firms make annual sales forecasts, the vast majority of those that also undertake long-range forecasts project their sales five years ahead. These five-year forecasts are usually prepared every year and the annual forecasts are then adjusted every three months.

Accuracy

The degree of accuracy achieved by the sales forecast tends to increase with the duration of the company's forecasting program. This, in fact, applies to all types of forecasts. Thus, although the first forecast may be in error, a review of the sources of error will lead to increased accuracy in subsequent sales forecasts.

The American Management Association's survey gives us some indication of how close a forecast can be. For the 248 companies included in the survey, the deviation between the sales forecast and actual performance averaged 8 per cent. It is interesting to note that producers of consumer nondurable goods came within 4.2 per cent, producers of accessory equipment for industry within 5.9 per cent, whereas manufacturers of industrial components used as parts of finished products reported the greatest deviation — 11 per cent. This is not too surprising, because this group has to forecast from a point two or three times removed from its final customer.[14]

Other Internal Planning Premises

In addition to the sales forecast, firms have many other internal planning premises. For instance, the capital to be invested in the enterprise is an internal planning premise, and decisions and assumptions regarding it have significant bearing on future plans. Capital invested in fixed assets will be a particularly important factor in a firm's future direction.

The various basic policies of management regarding products, prices, labor, financing, and such also involve internal planning premises. They constitute bound-

[14] *Sales Forecasting: Uses, Techniques, and Trends*, p. 149. For an interesting description of how the Corning Glass Works prepares and coordinates its sales forecasts, see the article by Richard L. Patey in *Sales Forecasting*, p. 111.

aries to effective planning in the enterprise and define the nature and character of the company. If needed, policies can be changed; nevertheless, management must include them in its forecasts and planning premises.

FORECASTS IN GENERAL

Shortcomings

At the base of all forecasts lie certain assumptions, approximations, and averages that must conform to existing conditions. Management may become so entranced with the mechanism of the forecasting system that it fails to question its logic. Or it may become so intrigued with the forecasting system's record of accuracy, proved perhaps on a trial application of the formula to past operations, that it is not prepared for the unexpected and large deviations that sometimes appear suddenly. There is also a danger that the process of formulating ideas concerning the future outlook may produce an inbred conformity of opinion. Some of the forecasts which emanate from informed sources may not represent the sources' real prediction of the future but may have been uttered to achieve desired effects.

Nevertheless, this critical examination should not discourage forecasting attempts. No manager can afford not to forecast. However, forecasting is an art and not a science; there is no infallible way of predicting the future. Forecasting accuracy increases with experience; good results can rarely be achieved immediately after introducing a formal forecasting system. The original method of forecasting is invariably subjected to continuous refinements necessitated by the particular characteristics of the organization.

Length of the Forecast Period

The length of the forecast period is of significance in assessing accuracy. Short-term forecasts are generally more accurate than longer-term ones. However, some of the respondents to the 1957 AMA survey asserted that predicting the future on a long-term basis is easier than short-term forecasting. This statement is more understandable when, for instance, "the difficulty of predicting typical minor fluctuations in commodity prices or common stock prices is considered."[15] Many experts agree that it is less difficult to predict commodity prices and common stock prices a year ahead than to forecast them a few weeks or a month in advance. Old established product lines can, of course, be forecast more accurately than new products with little or no sales history. Over-all company forecasts are also probably more accurate than forecasts of a specific product or territory.

Expense

Management often pleads that it cannot afford the expense of forecasting. This plea frequently comes from smaller companies that have less money to spend on staff

[15] *Company Organization for Economic Forecasting*, p. 20.

activities. At best, however, theirs is a narrow point of view, for much forecasting information is available just for the asking. It should be possible at little or no cost for even the smallest firm to utilize some of the economic data readily available from external sources — data also used by the largest firms. The management of small enterprises should also bear in mind that a dollar saved or earned through forecasting usually means more to them than it does to a large enterprise.

When deciding how much should be spent for forecasting, management should consider factors such as its production schedules and the stability and complexity of its markets. If, for instance, the firm is engaged in a cyclical or seasonal industry, it will need forecasts especially designed for its circumstances. Firms producing goods which take a long time from production order to the point of sales will also be more vitally concerned with forecasting and probably more willing to incur additional forecasting expense. Moreover, suppliers selling small quantities to large numbers of customers have a more difficult and probably more expensive forecasting problem than industrial suppliers selling to only a few large customers.

All this points to the fact that the cost of forecasting varies greatly from industry to industry and from enterprise to enterprise. But no matter what the cost, utilization of forecasting information must be taken into consideration. The information must reach those people who are able and willing to act upon it. Unless properly utilized, even the most carefully made forecasts and the best planning information are wasted. This is why we must now consider the action phase of planning.

Discussion Questions

1. About six years ago, a state projected that its population would nearly double by 1990, increasing from 3½ million to 6 million. Recently the projection was revised downward to 4 million. From the standpoint of state government planning, what major areas would be most affected by the new forecast?

2. One recent trend in large business has been the movement toward conglomerates. Discuss how this will affect the data top management needs for forecasting. Do you suppose that the conglomerate movement makes forecasting more difficult? Less difficult?

Supplementary Readings

Bross, Irwin D. J. *Design for Decision*. New York: Macmillan, 1953. See chapter 9.

Quinn, James Brian. "Technological Forecasting." *Harvard Business Review* 45, no. 2 (March–April 1967): 89–106.

Redfield, J. W. "Elements of Forecasting." In *Dimensions in Modern Management*, edited by Patrick E. Connor. Boston: Houghton Mifflin, 1974.

Steiner, George A. *Top Management Planning*. New York: Macmillan, 1969. See chapter 8.

CHAPTER 8

Planning: The Action Phase

The ancient Chinese military writer Sun Tzu was the earliest to recognize the nature of strategy and to deal with it systematically: "What is of supreme importance in war is to attack the enemy's strategy."[1] A marvelous passage in his book reflects his view:

> In the later Han, K'ou Hsün surrounded Kao Chun. Chun sent his Planning Officer, Huang-fu Wen, to parley. Huang-fu Wen was stubborn and rude and K'ou Hsün beheaded him, and informed Kao Chun: "Your staff officer was without propriety. I have beheaded him. If you wish to submit, do so immediately. Otherwise defend yourself." On the same day Chun threw open his fortifications and surrendered.
>
> All K'ou Hsün's generals said, "May we ask, you killed his envoy, but yet forced him to surrender his city. How is this?"
>
> K'ou Hsün said: "Huang-fu Wen was Kao Chun's heart and guts, his intimate counsellor. If I had spared Huang-fu Wen's life, he would have accomplished his schemes, but when I killed him, Kao Chun lost his guts. It is said: 'The supreme excellence in war is to attack the enemy's plans.'"
>
> All the generals said: "This is beyond our comprehension."[2]

In this incident Kao Chun's staff officer was the center of intelligence and the source of strategy. That he was also rude, stubborn, and without propriety indicates that staff has not changed much in 2,500 years. Undoubtedly many modern line executives share K'ou Hsün's sentiments about staff decapitation. Nonetheless, Sun Tzu shows us that strategy is the key element in the implementation of plans.

STRATEGY AND LONG-RANGE PLANNING

The concept of strategy has more than military application. Strategy is the means for carrying out any policy. Its primary concern is effect.[3] What plan will produce the effect of achieving policy? From this definition we can see that objectives and policies must always precede strategy.

[1] Sun Tzu, *The Art of War*, trans. Samuel B. Griffith (New York: Oxford University Press, 1963), pp. 77.
[2] *Ibid.*, pp. 77–78.
[3] B. H. Liddell Hart, *Strategy* (New York: Praeger, 1954), pp. 333–35.

A number of years ago a major distiller embarked on a program of diversification, moving into areas quite apart from the liquor business. Its policy was to diversify activities, to get a wider base of operation and a better opportunity for growth. Management's *strategy* included pinpointing the industries in which to acquire firms. Its tactics included actual acquisition. In other words, high-level strategy became, in Liddell Hart's words, "the policy in action."[4]

Long-range planning requires that management apply a systems approach to the organization. By developing strategies based upon plans, management is forced to account for as many organizational elements and inputs as possible. Beyond this, planning and strategy force management to visualize the implication of the inter-relationships that exist among the elements of an organization. In this respect we emphasize the dictum of the systems approach, that nothing happens alone, every act affects every other act in a system of interrelationships. As George Steiner says, "[Planning] does not deal with each separate element of the business alone, by itself, but rather permits the manager to see things as parts of a whole."[5] Planning to build new buildings in an urban renewal program is not in itself sufficient. Thought must be given to the impact of these buildings on community services, shopping, schools, even the cultural values of the people living in them. Some city managers have learned to their dismay that new high rise apartments generate more social problems than existed in the substandard housing they replaced. Thus, the long-range plans to renew the central areas of cities and their resulting strategies must take into account the physical as well as the social dislocations that they will create.

Figure 8-1. The Relationship of Strategy, Tactics, and Time-Span of Planning to Management Levels

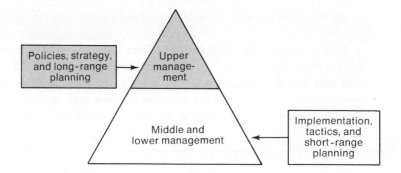

Strategy Compared with Tactics

If a department store has a policy of competing on the basis of price, its strategy is to avoid being undersold. This strategy pervades all its tactical devices — determining mark-up and profit margins, and obtaining intelligence information on the

---

[4] *Ibid.*, p. 335.

[5] George A. Steiner, *Top Management Planning* (New York: Macmillan, 1969), p. 66.

pricing activities of competitors. Notice that basic policy and strategy are formulated and implemented on higher managerial levels; the tactics of carrying out the policy occur on the lower levels and include salesperson and customer interaction.

As the foregoing indicates, strategy implies the formulation of plans with longer-range implications than those of tactics. The relationships of strategy, tactics, planning span, and management levels are shown in Figure 8-1.

Although vital to management, long-range planning is not nearly as susceptible to "scientific" treatment as short-range planning. Intimately connected with policy and strategy, long-range planning derives its data as much from hunch, intuition, and values as from concrete information. Part of the problem rests, of course, in the imprecision of forecasting and planning information. But a further part rests in the irrationality of the motives of the planners themselves. How, for example, does one quantify the power needs of executives or their feelings of social responsibility?

New Long-Range Planning Processes

Despite the difficulty of quantification, management does make long-range plans. Eugene Benge notes five steps in their planning process:

1. Realistically appraise the present strengths and weaknesses of the company.
2. Involve the company's key personnel in planning.
3. Base the plan on the consumer; give it a marketing orientation.
4. Establish a five-year plan, subdivide it, delegate responsibilities.
5. Set up a schedule for key events and try to keep it.[6]

The long-range plan, if executed properly, will produce guidelines for lower-level managerial, short-range planning. Points 4 and 5 in Benge's list suggest this. For instance, the division of a five-year plan into areas of separate responsibility such as research, marketing, manufacturing, objectifies the plan so that managers can clearly see the elements for which they must be concerned. Along with this must go the necessary delegation of authority to enable the subordinate managers to carry out their short-range planning activities. Scheduling of key events ties the accomplishment of goals to a time dimension. This allows the long-range plan to be tested during shorter time periods.

Fremont Kast points out a major dilemma in long-range planning.[7] On the one hand, management must decide upon the commitment of resources over a long planning period. On the other hand, faced with changing technologies and market conditions, it may find that during the planning period a better allocation of resources can be made. How can an organization commit its resources rationally over a long period of time while acknowledging increasing uncertainty in the environment? Part of the answer lies in working organizational flexibility into long-range

[6] Eugene J. Benge, "The Common Sense of Long-Range Planning," in *Management in Perspective,* ed. William G. Schlender, William G. Scott, and Alan C. Filley (Boston: Houghton Mifflin, 1965), pp. 203–04.
[7] Fremont E. Kast, "A Dynamic Planning Model," *Business Horizons* 11 (June 1968): 63–64.

plans. Essentially this amounts to designing organizations and developing managerial attitudes which stress adaptation rather than rigidity.

With constant feedback from the points of implementation, short-range planning adjustments in the long-range plan can compensate for actual experience. The problem of the Boeing Company in the SST design is a case in point. Obviously the long-range plan to produce a supersonic commercial aircraft involved commitment of immense resources by Boeing and the government. When the contract was awarded, it was based upon a swing-wing design. Further study indicated, however, that this feature added enormously to the weight of the plane. Short-range adjustments in the initial plan then provided for a fixed-wing design. Long-range plans have been imperiled as well. Citing a lack of economic justification and environment danger, Congress has refused to supply Boeing with further funds. Therefore, as of this writing, the project is still alive in the planners' minds, but until funding is available major work has ceased.

The Role of the Planning Staff

Around 1800 the Prussian military created the modern concept and the organization of the "general staff."[8] Basically, the staff had two major responsibilities — the creation of military plans and strategies and the coordination of field units in ways consistent with the implementation of those plans and strategies. The German general staff became a highly refined and effective military instrument, and it became in a sense a model for planning staffs in nonmilitary organizations.

Very early in management history, Frederick W. Taylor noted that planning must be separated from doing. He reasoned that specialized planning staffs should be used to support the line organization in generating information, providing alternate strategies, and facilitating top management's coordination of operations. He believed that this staff work required considerable skill and specialized knowledge and should be centralized in order to obtain maximum efficiency.

Taylor, perhaps, was ahead of his time. Not until organizations grew moderately large and began to utilize more complex technologies did planning staffs begin to be widely used by management. Their major responsibilities have been listed by Steiner:

1. developing long-range objectives in conjunction with top management
2. coordinating plans at various levels of the organization
3. assisting departmental and divisional segments of the organization with planning
4. reviewing and evaluating plans submitted by subunits of the organization
5. preparing specific studies on subjects of interests to top management
6. aiding management in planning for diversification, new product research, and new market development[9]

[8] Walter Goerlitz, *History of the German General Staff* (New York: Praeger, 1959).
[9] Steiner, *Top Management Planning*, pp. 116–21.

As we see from this list, a planning staff provides an information service for management; it collects data, analyzes information, and provides reports. In some instances, a centralized planning staff may also play an important role in coordinating the plans and activities of segments of an organization.

SHORT-RANGE PLANNING

Lower levels of management are concerned with the implementation of policies and objectives that result from long-range planning. Their activities require shorter planning periods and necessitate an understanding of technique and procedure.

During this phase of the planning process plans must be translated into more specific terms, financial or numerical, if this is possible. Some plans, however, cannot and need not be translated into such terms, for instance, the initial structuring of an organization. Instead, this type of organizational planning requires delineating, defining, and grouping the different activities of the enterprise in such a way that they may be most logically assigned and effectively executed, and it is concerned with the establishment of authority relationships.

In other cases, however, finances play an important role in business planning. At the end of the fiscal year, the balance sheet, the profit and loss statement, and many other records are reviewed by the chief executive, the board of directors, stockholders, the owners, and possibly the public at large.

Expense and Revenue Forecast

The expense and revenue forecast is one of the short-range plans which can be translated into dollars and cents. To do so, management estimates the future revenues and expenses of the company during a stated planning period of, say, one year. It is relatively simple to forecast financial revenues. Management needs only to base its figure on the sales forecast and multiply the various units to be sold by the price at which they will be sold. This naturally becomes more complicated if different products are involved.

On the expense side, management will have to anticipate the various costs involved in the creation and distribution of a good or service. In anticipating these costs, management is fully aware that it is looking into the future and that it will have to base its various estimates on prior planning premises. If one such premise assumes further wage increases, management accordingly must figure its costs to be higher. If a planning premise anticipates higher interest rates, the expenses for interest must likewise be figured higher. This is where various intermediate forecasts will help, enabling management to establish a realistic picture of the expense side of the expense and revenue forecast. Comparing both sides of the forecast, then, management can quickly see the estimated profit or loss of the operations during the planning period.

Cash Forecast

Another significant short-range financial plan is what is commonly known as a cash forecast. Everyone knows how important it is to have enough ready cash available to meet obligations. The failure of management to provide adequate amounts of cash at the proper times will, to say the least, interfere with the smooth flow of the enterprise's operations. The cash forecast will show whether or not there will be an adequate supply of cash on hand when it is needed to pay operating expenses and meet all other liabilities.

Understandably, in most enterprises cash inflow is closely related to the volume of sales. Cash outflow requirements also relate closely to the volume of sales. However, management cannot forecast the year's inflows and outflows of cash from the anticipated level of sales because such a forecast would tell little about sales timing. Cash inflows and outflows must be coordinated, and it is not enough that the annual total cash receipts exceed the annual total cash disbursements. Thus, the cash forecast must normally relate to monthly operations within the yearly period. This will enable management to judge rather closely how much cash will be coming in and going out from month to month. Based on this forecast, management can anticipate a need to borrow during some period or periods when cash inflow will be insufficient to meet cash requirements. Such a situation is likely to occur in a business that needs to build up its inventories during the first six months of the year and does not begin to sell its goods until the latter part of the year. The cash forecast will enable management to determine how much cash will be available during the months of inventory build-up.

There is another important aspect of cash forecasting, namely idle cash. Ordinarily, management uses a cash forecast merely to ascertain whether there is enough cash available at the right moment. However, what if too much cash is lying idle for two, three, and four months? Management should then make plans for its temporary investment. However, it definitely takes expert managerial planning to decide what to do with cash. Knowing that a certain amount of money will be idle at a certain time, management must formulate alternative plans for investing it. It must keep itself informed of interest rates on short-term treasury notes, government bonds, or other suitable investments. At the proper time it must decide which short-term investments to make. A cash forecast, therefore, is not only a plan to ensure that there is enough cash available to meet the obligations, but also a plan to make certain that idle funds are used advantageously.

Pro Forma Statements

Many firms also translate their short-term planning into a pro forma balance sheet or future income statement based on the information contained in sales, materials, direct labor, and other operating plans. Such a detailed projection will give management additional financial information for the planning period. These pro forma statements, as they are called, have significant use. Whereas a cash forecast for the coming year may show that the cash balance at the end of the year will be larger than the opening balance, a pro forma statement of profit and loss may indicate that if the planned operations are carried through, a net loss will result. The prospect of such a loss might lead to considerable changes in operating plans.

Budgets

A budget is a detailed plan covering some phase of activity in some future period. Budgets are prepared and expressed in numerical terms — usually in financial terms. As we noted in an earlier chapter, budget-making is planning and budget operation is controlling. Financial forecasts often become the basis for budget planning. For instance, the cash forecast can easily become the cash budget and the expense and revenue forecast can often furnish the basis for the expense and revenue budget. However, these forecasts can become the basis of budgets only if they are properly prepared, if they are estimates of what is reasonably attainable — not of what could be obtained under the best possible conditions.

At times some managerial practices result in more liberal financial forecasts than budgets. In order to enhance their chances for obtaining a bank loan, for example, management might be somewhat more optimistic in predicting their cash forecasts than they have a right to be. However, their budgets must still be based on a much tighter plan and are more conservative. But this divergence is not advisable; the financial forecast should be as realistic as the budget given to the various managers of the organization. If a variation does exist, it will soon become known and managers will be guided accordingly. They will feel that top management does not expect them to come up to the budget figures or to stay within them, whichever the case may be. If the divergence continues for any length of time, managers will know that budgets are unrealistic and that they are not bound by them. This, of course, defeats the purpose of a budget. Sound financial plans should be drawn up so realistically that they can automatically become the basis for budgets.

PERT

Up to this point we have discussed primarily the short-range planning of financial matters. However, current developments in planning have brought about short-range activity planning techniques, one of which is called PERT. This technique is so important in some modern planning efforts that much of the remainder of this chapter will be devoted to it.

PERT (Program Evaluation and Review Technique) is a technique developed in 1958 through the combined efforts of the U.S. Navy Special Projects Office and Booz-Allen and Hamilton, a management consulting firm. The objective of the PERT research team was to design a planning and control system for developing the Polaris missile system, a project that was subject to a great degree of uncertainty in the performance times of its activities. PERT dealt particularly with this uncertainty. The PERT system is based on three estimates of the performance time for each activity. It distinguishes itself from other planning techniques by the use of a network monitored by statistics and computers to dovetail complex parallel and sequential job combinations.

Managers involved in the planning function warmly accepted PERT because it enabled them to cope better with the increasingly rapid pace at which technological changes are introduced. Previously, management could afford pauses between various stages of research, design, and engineering; but today technology and the rapid introduction of new methods and processes make it necessary for these different stages to overlap. PERT has given management the tool with which to coordinate and control this. It enables management to plan complex programs and to evaluate their progress continuously. Management groups who use PERT quickly see potential and actual problems, because the system constantly gives status reports and determines the shortest time in which a project can be completed.

At about the same time PERT came into existence, another planning technique known as CPM (Critical Path Method) was developed by the Du Pont Company in connection with a construction program. The approaches of PERT and CPM are similar, although one originated within the military and the other within private industry. In contrast to PERT, CPM was developed for programs consisting largely of deterministic activities such as construction and maintenance projects. CPM omits statistical considerations and is based on a single estimate of the average time required to perform the activities in question. Although these distinctions between CPM and PERT are historically correct, with the passing of time the two techniques have merged, and the result is usually referred to as a PERT-type system.

Development of the PERT Network

The basis of both CPM and PERT is the project network diagram. A simple example is shown in Figure 8-2. The two major components of this type of diagram are events and activities. The diagram is therefore a pictorial representation of the interrelationships among all required events and activities in a particular project. An event, usually depicted by a circle, is the instant of time marking either the start or the accomplishment of a plan. An event can be the product of one or several activities. It must, however, occur at a specific instant of time. An event cannot be considered accomplished until all activities leading to it have been completed.

An activity, usually depicted by an arrow, is the time-consuming element of a network. An activity is the work required to accomplish an event, and it cannot start until all preceding activities have been completed. A network begins with a single event and finishes with a single event and is made up of many intermediate events related to one another by activities. Events must take place in the proper sequence — for instance, the frame of a house cannot be constructed before the foundation is laid, and none of the other work can be started before the frame is finished.

The network is essentially an outgrowth of the Gantt or bar chart developed by Henry L. Gantt in the beginning of this century. Gantt designed this chart primarily so that he could visualize the time element of a program in relation to the progress

Figure 8-2. Project Network Diagram

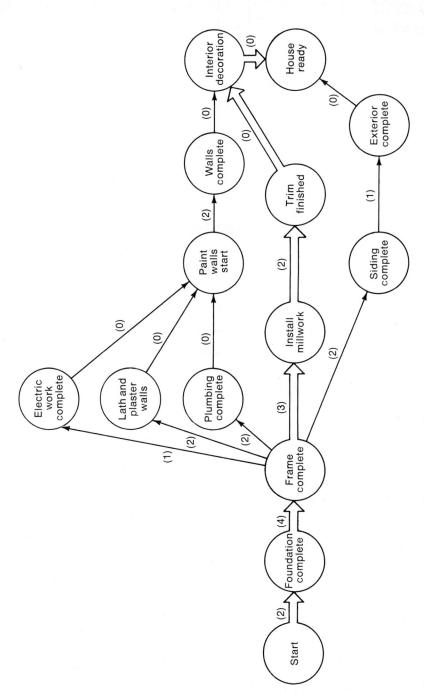

Source: K. L. Dean, *Fundamentals of Network Planning and Analysis* (St. Paul, Minn.: Univac Division, Sperry Rand, 1962), p. 68. Reprinted by permission of the Univac Division of the Sperry Rand Corporation.

Figure 8-3. Bar Chart

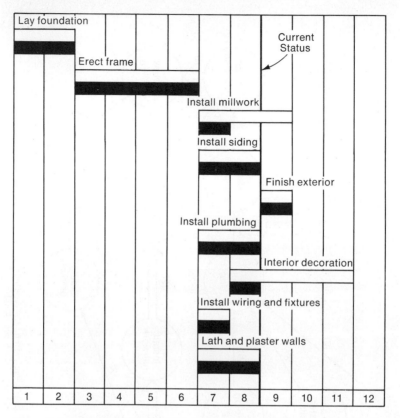

Source: K. L. Dean, *Fundamentals of Network Planning and Analysis* (St. Paul, Minn.: Univac Division, Sperry Rand, 1962), p. 67. Reprinted by permission of the Univac Division of the Sperry Rand Corporation.

of the work. The bar chart depicts graphically the activities of the project and the sequences of occurrence of the various activities. Figure 8-3 is a bar chart for the construction of a house. The plain bars are the plan, whereas the black bars show the progress in relationship to the plan at the end of the eighth week. The most serious shortcoming of bar charts is that they do not indicate the interdependence of various activities. The mere fact that activities are scheduled for simultaneous or overlapping time periods does not make them necessarily related or interdependent.

This same shortcoming was found in the milestone chart, the next step in the evolution of PERT. The milestone chart breaks up the long bars into shorter periods of time, each of which represents the accomplishment of an event within the long-term job (see Figure 8-4). Although the milestone chart improved upon the bar chart, it still did not show interdependencies. However, these interdependencies were clarified in the PERT network by the use of arrows between milestones. Thus, the

Figure 8-4. The Evolution of PERT

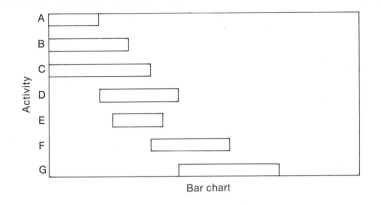

Bar chart

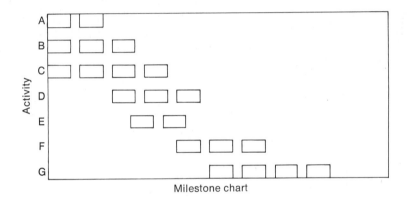

Milestone chart

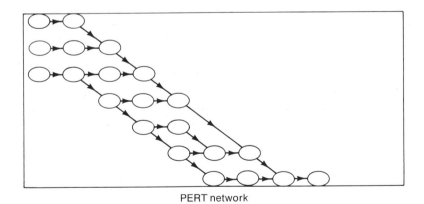

PERT network

Source: Harry F. Evarts, *Introduction to PERT* (Boston: Allyn and Bacon), pp. 16–17.
Copyright © 1964 by Allyn and Bacon, Inc.; reprinted by permission of the publisher.

milestones became events and the arrows became activities (see the third step in Figure 8-4).

Limitations

Although PERT can be applied in many management situations to reduce project time and achieve manpower needs, it has certain practical limitations. Therefore, PERT is primarily used by management when it is faced with projects which are not routine or repetitive and which must be conducted only once or twice. The project also should be complex, containing many tasks, interdependencies, and interrelationships within it. The key to whether to use the PERT technique lies in the uncertainty and complexity of the project.

Although initially developed for military purposes, PERT is now widely used by industry. Successful uses include computer programming and installation; shutting down and restarting of chemical plants, blast furnaces, oil refineries, and similar installations; installing production control systems; running pilot projects; and formulating research, development, and heavy construction programs. PERT is also potentially useful in coordinating advertising programs, securities issues, introduction of new products, and marketing plans. It should be borne in mind, however, that the PERT system is concerned only with time and does not of itself include other considerations such as costs, quantity, and quality. However, efforts have been made to integrate these constraints into PERT in order to make the technique an even more powerful tool for over-all management control.

Value

As we have suggested, PERT has its weaknesses. It is not a panacea for all management problems, but it does give them some relative magnitude. The usual management planning meetings illustrate this point. From four to twenty-four high-priced executives sit around a table and try to determine the status of a program: Will the delivery schedule be met, or won't it? What seem to be the problems? The group is surrounded by fires that PERT cannot extinguish. However, it can give them magnitude so that management at least knows which to quench first. In addition, the PERT technique assists in predicting where fires are likely to break out, permitting managers to take normal preventive action.[10]

Another important advantage of PERT is that daily status reports are easily obtainable through it. These reports describe the current status of a project, predict future performance, and point out potential trouble spots, thereby focusing the manager's attention on those parts of the project that are most likely to prevent its completion on time. The speed and accuracy of simulation with PERT are far superior to those of any other planning techniques.

---

[10] K. L. Dean, *Fundamentals of Network Planning and Analysis* (St. Paul, Minn.: Univac Division of Sperry Rand, 1962), p. 12.

Designing the Network

PERT methodology requires complete project planning: full consideration and detailed specification of all activities and their interrelationships. Failure to plan completely would lead to an incorrect solution.

In order to design a PERT network, one must first prepare a list of all activities necessary to complete the project. After the network has been designed, the next step is to make estimates of the time required to complete each activity. In order to achieve accuracy, those persons who are most familiar with the activity are generally requested to make three estimates: (1) an optimistic time (t_o), the length of time required if no complications or unforeseen difficulties arise in performing the activity; (2) a pessimistic time (t_p), the length of time required if unusual and unforeseen complications arise in carrying out the activity; and (3) a most likely time (t_m), the length of time in which the activity is most likely to be completed. These three time estimates are used to arrive at a statistically weighted average time, the expected time or elapsed time, (t_e), for the activity.

The expected time is calculated by the formula $t_e = (t_o + 4t_m + t_p)/6$. Logically, the expected or elapsed times, t_e, for the various activities can be used to calculate the earliest expected time (T_E) that an event can be expected to occur. T_E is equal to the summation of activity times from the beginning event to a given event. Step 1 in Figure 8-5 shows the three time estimates, t_e, and T_E. In this case, the earliest expected completion time (T_E) of the objective event (event 10) is 25 weeks.

Working backward from the objective event 10 through the network, we can determine the latest allowable time (T_L) for the events by deducting t_e. The latest allowable time is the latest time an event can occur without affecting completion of the objective event. In Step 2 of Figure 8-5, T_L is placed alongside T_E, and a study of the figure shows that for certain events T_L is larger than T_E, whereas in other events there is no difference between T_L and T_E. Wherever T_L is greater than T_E, that event can be delayed for the amount of the difference without affecting the outcome of the objective event. If, for instance, event 3 should be delayed by four weeks, the completion of the objective event 10 would not be affected. This difference is called slack, and the ability to determine it is one of the outstanding characteristics of PERT. The path with the least slack is the longest one between the beginning event and the objective (ending) event. The longest path, having zero slack, is the critical path as shown in Step 3 of Figure 8-5. The critical path is that sequence of activities linking the starting event with the objective event which requires the greatest expenditure of time to accomplish.

Other Uses

The foregoing discussion should have clarified our earlier point that PERT is not only a significant planning tool but also a powerful controlling one. Having a PERT program enables management to concentrate its attention on critical activities. With the help of the information it receives on slack time and the critical path, manage-

Figure 8-5. Designing the PERT Network

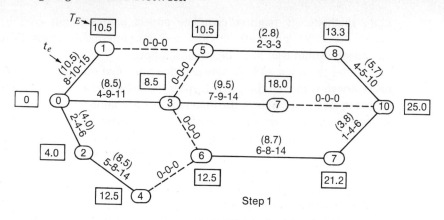

Step 1

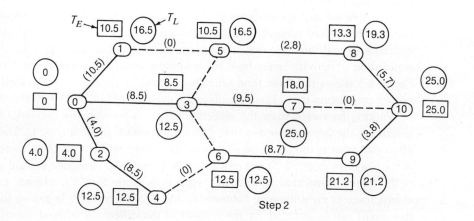

Step 2

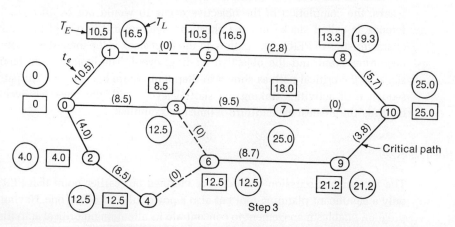

Step 3

Source: K. L. Dean, *Fundamentals of Network Planning and Analysis* (St. Paul, Minn.: Univac Division, Sperry Rand, 1962), pp. 38–39. Reprinted by permission of the Univac Division of the Sperry Rand Corporation.

ment can direct its attention to those aspects which require corrective action. Management will know precisely which item is out of control and what to do about it and it alone. If the item is on the slack path, then possibly no action is necessary. If an item on the critical path is not on time, however, then management may marshal resources from the slack path to aid those activities on the critical path in need of help and correction. PERT clearly provides management with a wealth of information that normally is not easily accessible. By isolating critical areas and enabling management to concentrate on them, PERT in itself is an application of the principle of management by exception.

The advantage of PERT can be more clearly seen by considering that when a program not on PERT is behind schedule, the whole program may require overtime. PERT, however, will enable management to decide exactly where the overtime would do the most good. Assuming that manpower is completely interchangeable and that the job's elapsed time is in direct ratio to the number of men assigned to it, labor trade-offs can take place among activities so that ultimately a reduction of project time is achieved without additional personnel.

LIMITATIONS OF PLANNING

While considering the specific limitations of PERT and other short-range planning techniques, management must also bear in mind the more general limitations on the over-all planning process that exist in spite of the thoroughness with which management may have established its premises, chosen its techniques, and gone about its planning. Planning is looking into the future. The accuracy of forecasts and the premises derived from them is one of planning's limitations. As long as management recognizes this limitation, it will plan flexibly and will provide for enough alternatives to enable it to switch plans if need be. Management must also know that the further in the future its plans are, the less reliable they will become. The nature of the enterprise may also limit planning. As we have demonstrated, the dynamic rate of change in industries such as electronics might play havoc with plans.

Internal Limitations

Philosophy

In addition, other internal and external planning limitations exist. Often a certain philosophy of management has become so ingrained in an enterprise that it limits planning. For example, a company that has been manufacturing a high cost, high quality product for many years may find its quality concepts to be so deeply embedded in the minds of management and employees that it cannot plan and carry out successfully the manufacture of a cheaper product. Or if a company has been working on the philosophy of cost-plus, it will be difficult to change this basic attitude. Again, companies that have grown very rapidly may not have made the necessary transition to large-scale thinking. In contrast, companies that have expanded greatly to meet wartime production conditions often find retrenchment and planning difficult at war's end.

Previous Decisions

Another serious internal limitation on planning is caused by previous decisions and actions. Once capital has been invested in equipment, future planning is limited. In some planning situations management might be wise to disregard completely an ill-advised sunken cost but in practice this is difficult. To this extent, then, capital already invested puts limits on the flexibility of planning.

Expenses and Time

Expenses and time are also real limitations to planning. No more expense should be incurred in planning than will be recovered from ensuing benefits. For all practical purposes, a large company can afford a greater amount of planning than a small company. However, even a small company can sometimes afford substantial plans, especially when they cover repetitive operations that, if properly planned and executed, can provide a great amount of saving. In such circumstances, planning involves expense but it will still pay off. The more detailed the plan, the more expenses will be involved. Likewise, the longer the plan runs into the future, the costlier it will be. Wise managerial judgment is necessary to balance the expense of preparing plans against the benefits derived from them.

Time itself sometimes seriously limits planning if there is not enough time available to go through the entire planning procedure. Planning is time-consuming, and when time is important, the span available will necessarily dictate the thoroughness and pervasiveness of the planning. In most organizations with a good record of planning, conditions of this sort do not occur too often, but they may occasionally happen. In such circumstances prompt action is sometimes more important than the advantages of thorough planning.

External Limitations

A number of external planning limitations — conditions of the external environment over which management has little or no control — also exist. Over-all national and international climates are examples of such external conditions as are the policies of large unions. Each of these can place serious limitations on management's planning. Consider, for example, the tension between labor contracts and the steel industry's plan for further mechanization and automation. According to industry, further mechanization will call for changes in certain working conditions and will be outlined in future contracts. If the union is not willing to agree to them, revision — often resulting in significant planning limitations — may result. Management simply will not be able to plan on as much mechanization and automation as it would like because of such limitations. Although these are only a few examples of the real limitations on planning, management should bear them in mind as it ponders how far to extend a planning concept in any particular undertaking.

This completes our discussion of the planning function, which, by any measure, is in its infancy compared to the other managerial functions. The contrast is particularly striking when one compares planning with the organizing function, described in Part III. Indeed, the subject of organizing and organization is the most developed of all the managerial functions. This is reflected by the large segment of the book given over to the discussion of organizing activities.

Discussion Questions

1. Suppose you are a football coach. What parts of your job would you consider strategy? Long-range planning? Tactics?

2. Planning has many limitations. To what extent do these limitations arise from bounded rationality?

Supplementary Readings

Dooley, Arch R. "Interpretations of PERT." *Harvard Business Review* 42, no. 2 (March–April 1964): 160–72.

Evarts, Harry F. *Introduction to PERT*. Boston: Allyn and Bacon, 1964.

Kast, Fremont E. "A Dynamic Planning Model." In *Dimensions in Modern Management*, edited by Patrick E. Connor. Boston: Houghton Mifflin, 1974.

March, James G., and Herbert A. Simon. *Organizations*. New York: Wiley, 1958. See chapter 7.

Mason, R. Hal. "Use of Corporate Planning Groups in the Analysis of Corporate Acquisitions." In *Long-Range Planning for Management*, edited by David W. Ewing. New York: Harper and Row, 1972. See pp. 285–300.

Steiner, George A. *Top Management Planning*. New York: Macmillan, 1969. See chapter 11.

CASES

II | 1

The Optico Company

The Optico Company, located near Boston, Massachusetts, manufactures sophisticated optical and photographic equipment used by the U.S. Air Force and NASA. The company was founded early in 1960 by two young scientists, an engineer and a physicist. Ever since its inception, the sales of the company have been primarily to government agencies. By 1970, 98 per cent of all sales were to the U.S. government.

However, in recent years, management has become greatly concerned about its over-reliance on government business. The board of directors urged the executives to diversify production so that half of the sales would be to the private sector of the economy and the other half to the public sector. Thus, early in 1972, Optico introduced a version of an instant camera that incorporated a few of the already patented features of its military and space products. The camera was a success; orders began arriving at an unexpected rate, and soon the backlog of orders amounted to millions of dollars. The managers quickly realized that within one year the company's civilian business could amount to $20 million in sales. Because their current volume of government orders was of the same magnitude, they had apparently succeeded in achieving their fifty-fifty objective.

In the middle of 1972, a large national mail order house proposed that Optico produce a special version of its camera for them under one of their brand names. The catalogue house was willing to guarantee annual orders amounting to $15 million. This, of course, would significantly change the character of Optico, from a military supplier to one primarily concerned with consumer goods. Because such a change would drastically alter the objectives of the company and would involve it in all the problems of producing and merchandising, the proposal was submitted to the board of directors, a group consisting of the two scientist-founders and five men from banking and leading industrial concerns in the Boston area.

Questions

1. If you were on the board, how would you decide?
2. What considerations would sway your decision?
3. What new planning premises would have to be considered if the company made the switch?

II | 2

The Elbert Manufacturing Company

Jack Elbert is the president and majority stockholder of the Elbert Manufacturing Company, a small but rapidly expanding enterprise producing machinery for the metalworking industry. He started the business in 1961 with only a few employees but by 1972 had seventy-five employees on the payroll. Annual sales increased from $60,000 during the first year to nearly $1 million in 1972.

Mr. Elbert realizes that because of this rapid growth he cannot devote enough attention to organizational arrangements, company policies, objectives, and goals. Nevertheless, he wants to pursue his original goal of providing machinery for the metalworking industry, though he has hardly begun to make a niche for his company in this apparently large market and he realizes that in a few years he may branch out into manufacturing machinery for plastics and other industries.

Not surprisingly, the company is a one-man organization. Mr. Elbert knows he is trying to do too much, but before he delegates authority and creates new departments, he wants to establish policies that will guide the decision-making of the managers he plans to appoint. He expressed his intentions to formulate policy and met with his three key men — Mr. Powers of the production department, Mr. Seeger from sales, and Mr. Fingert, who has been handling the accounting and financial parts of the business. It would not be correct to call these three men the managers, for they had been deciding very little without first consulting Mr. Elbert.

All three were delighted that company policies were finally going to be specified. Mr. Powers urged the president "to define policies prohibiting smoking and eating in the plant" because current practices were hurting production. Mr. Seeger wanted the president to set down "clear-cut policies regarding salesmen's compensation, prompt deliveries, and scheduling of incoming orders," for they would help him in his sales efforts. Mr. Fingert wanted policies "covering problems such as the number of voucher copies to be submitted for cash disbursements and the allocation of expenses for repairs and maintenance," which had been the source of misunderstanding.

Questions

1. Should Mr. Elbert follow his men's suggestions?
2. Are policies needed to solve these problems?
3. What would you do if you were Mr. Elbert's consultant?

II | 3

The Call to the Reserves

The Montclair Manufacturing Company has a policy that employees who are called to military service may return to their previous jobs if they report back to the company within three months after an honorable discharge. Since policy also states that military service does not interrupt their seniority in the firm, returnees can claim a better paying job than the one they left. Although these policies are stated in the personnel handbook as a company decision, it is interesting to note that Montclair is merely stating provisions required by law.

Charles is a punch press operator who had joined the reserves a number of years ago and still faces the possibility that he will be called to active duty should his unit be activated. A few days ago he gave his supervisor notice that he was quitting his job, having found a better paying position elsewhere. He gave the company one week notice. Two days thereafter he came to his foreman and told him that he had changed his mind, was not quitting, and wanted to stay on. Since no new employee had been hired to take his place and since his supervisor had not as yet requested the personnel department to record his termination, his boss agreed and promised to forget the whole thing. A week later Charles informed his supervisor that he had received a call from his reserve unit requesting him to report for military duty for an undetermined length of time. The foreman was somewhat surprised at the coincidence and upon further investigation learned that Charles had heard about his call to duty one day after he had expressed his decision to quit his job. Obviously his change of mind was caused by this notice and by his desire to benefit from the military leave policy of the company.

Questions

1. What should the foreman do under the circumstances?
2. Do the company policy and procedures regarding military service apply in this case?

II | 4

The Need for New Plans

The Gardner Manufacturing Company produces potentiometers and other electronic devices and employs about 150 people. Mr. Hal Whitaker, the president of the firm, had just attended a series of lectures on new and better ways of managing a business and motivating employees. The lecturer had convinced Mr. Whitaker of new approaches, and he was ready to put them into effect in the plant. Therefore, he called a meeting for all managers of the production department, namely the factory superintendent and his ten foremen.

Among other things, he told his managers that he intended to discard all time cards and put all production workers on a weekly salary instead of paying them on the usual hourly rate. He also intended to introduce a plan called Flexi-time, which would enable the worker to set his own hours as long as he put in 40 hours weekly. Mr. Whitaker had heard that this was being done abroad and lately in this country and believed it to be successful. He also wanted to eliminate the usual assembly line and introduce in its place production unit centers made up of ten employees. These centers would assemble an entire part. The employees could choose in which center they would like to work. This, he contended, would put informal groups and their beneficial aspects to their best use. He pointed out that each assembly center would be overseen by a supervisor and that such supervisory positions would carry at least as much prestige, authority, responsibility, and remuneration as the present supervisory jobs.

Mr. Whitaker, of course, realized that all of this would take some time, but he wanted to proceed with the changeover without undue delay. The president felt sure that the changes would raise morale, increase productivity, reduce absence and turnover, and even reduce the amount of scrap, returns, and defective parts. All these plans, he was certain, would lead to a highly motivated work force and, ultimately, to higher profits for the company. After presenting his plans, Mr. Whitaker did not ask for comment or further questions but said that another meeting would be held in a week or so.

The superintendent and the foremen were stunned to hear of these far-reaching changes. However, they realized that if this was what the president wished, it eventually would become reality, for he originated all major directives. Nevertheless, the assembled second- and third-line managers had many objections about the workability, advisability, and desirability of the president's plans. Their most prevailing concern, however, was what the effect of this would be on the plans they had made for their areas of activity.

Questions

1. Place yourself in the position of a foreman and discuss effects of the changes on your plans.

2. What would you think if you were the superintendent of the plant?

3. Which of these changes should be made first?

4. What would you urge the president to do if you were the superintendent of the plant?

II | 5

The Closing of Middletown

The Waggoner Electronics Company, with annual sales over $30 million, has four manufacturing plants. Headquarters and one operating unit are located in Chicago, another plant in California, one in the New England area, and a fourth plant in Middletown, Indiana. The last plant was bought at a low price right after the Korean War. At that time it seemed more expedient and economical to buy than to build a new modern plant in a more suitable location.

However, as the years went by, the rapid growth of Waggoner Electronics ended, at least temporarily, and the firm found itself with excess capacity. Therefore, at the end of 1971 the question of closing the Middletown plant arose in the meeting of the Board of Directors. Middletown was a small town of about 25,000 people, with two large factories employing a total of about 5,000. The Waggoner plant, a smaller enterprise, was located in an older multi-story building, and cost studies indicated that the plant's efficiency was significantly less than that of the other three Waggoner plants. The Middletown factory employed about 250 people, of which 35 were managers and supervisors. The employees of Waggoner, Middletown, were primarily men. They belonged to a strong union but had established no contract provisions for plant closure or separation pay.

Most members of the board could easily see the advisability of closing this factory, but some voiced serious concern about the impact such a closing would have on the local community, for most of the workers were middle-aged and family wage earners and had little prospect of finding employment in the two large factories still operating. Also, there seemed little likelihood that the building could be sold or leased because no new industry seemed to be moving into Middletown. Some of the directors pointed out that a firm has social responsibilities; others took the opposite view, stating that their decision would be based only on company considerations. After a lengthy discussion, the board appointed a three-man committee to work out proposals to ease the social impact of closing the plant and to submit its plans to the board of directors.

Questions

1. Which side of the board would you have supported?
2. If you were on the committee, what areas would your proposal cover and what plans and provisions would you make?

III ORGANIZING

THE ORGANIZING FUNCTION.
Organizing is based on the goals
and objectives of the organization that
are formulated through the planning
process. It reflects management's
thinking on the structure of and the
relationships among the various parts
of the organization.

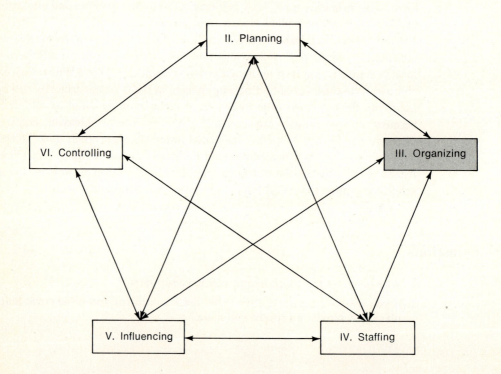

Rarely are systems concepts so well demonstrated as in the organizing functions of management. Organizing by its very nature requires management to think in terms of systems and to design relationships among activities in a way that assures efficient achievement of the organization's goals. The design that evolves reflects management's perception of the relationships among the parts of the organization and the kind of feedback system needed to control it.

The roots of organizing lie in planning. The designs emerging from the planning effort reflect the social, economic, and technological experience of the firm and express its expectations in concrete form. The organizing process then enables an organization to accomplish its designs by helping management to plot the activities needed to attain them. These activities form subsystems that are synchronized and harmonized into a larger system, which is often called the *formal organization*. The organizing function thus provides links among subsystems and coordinates them in a manner that creates the organizational structure.

In other words, organizing flows directly from the objectives and plans of management, establishing relationships among work functions. Obviously the goal of these relationships must be to aid in the implementation and accomplishment of the plans and objectives. Giving structure to work relationships is the fundamental act of organizing. How the structure turns out, what it looks like, and how it works depend upon many factors — organizational objectives, size, technology, culture, and so on. The important thing to realize is that the organizing activity is impersonal; work relationships are established without regard to the people who will function in them. Thus, the tone in which we discuss the organizing process must be impersonal. Later, in the parts of the book dealing with staffing and influencing, we introduce personal elements into formal organizational structure.

Although they are very closely related, the planning and organizing functions are a study in contrasts. Planning is probably the least well developed of the management functions; organizing is the most researched and discussed. Recently, studies in the latter area have accelerated still further. In addition, researchers and writers in the behavioral sciences have found the organizing function congenial to their own concepts and research skills.

The study of complex organizations has grown to include subjects traditionally treated in other functional areas: for example, decision-making (usually treated as part of the planning function), small group motivation and morale (influencing), communication (influencing and controlling), and incentives (staffing and influencing). The incorporation of more and more subject matter leads some to believe that the integration of management theory will occur within the framework of organization theory or systems theory. For our purposes, however, we retain the conventional breakdown and analytic separation of the five management functions and deal here with classical organization concepts. Nevertheless, many new notions in modern organization theory will be introduced in this section, as well as in other parts of the book.

Classic organizational theory rests on several major premises — that *division of work* is essential for efficiency, that *coordination* is the primary responsibility of management in the organization of work, that the *formal structure* is the main vehicle for organizing and administering work activities, and that the *span of management* sets outside limits on the number of people responsible to a given manager.

Classical organization theory continues to have great relevance to basic managerial problems of work relationships, authority, responsibility, coordination, delegation, and so on. Classical theory has a reasoned, rational approach, which managers can use for problem-solving. However, this theory has its limitations; it is not universally applicable. Before one can truly appraise its real worth and shortcomings, one must know its many dimensions.

CHAPTER 9

Coordination

Division of labor creates the need for coordination. Specialization of work is the most elementary of all the social processes in which man engages. It arises from the fact that dividing work into smaller, specialized tasks permits a group of people, performing together, to accomplish more than one individual attempting a whole task alone can do.

EVOLUTION OF THE DIVISION OF LABOR

The practice of dividing labor is as old as history, but in no area of human endeavor is it more evident than in warfare. From earliest times, armies have been divided into service units — archers, infantry, cavalry, and supply — whose effectiveness resulted from their coordinated use in a commander's strategy and tactics. These military divisions remained unchanged for centuries. An appreciation of the benefits of the division of labor also appears in the classics. Cicero, for example, called it the basis for civilization.

Specialization and Efficiency

Centuries later economists viewed the division of labor as the most important factor in commerce. Adam Smith in his famous book *The Wealth of Nations*, published in 1776, discussed the division of labor at length, using as his example the manufacture of a pin. The production of such a seemingly insignificant item required several operations. Smith observed that several persons, each doing the entire pin-making tasks, produced far fewer pins in a day than did several specialists working together. That is, production increased when each activity in pin-making became the responsibility of a person specialized in that task. Thus, the drawing of the wire, the cutting and sharpening of the point, the fitting of the head to the shaft, and the placing of the completed pin in a card were separated. The coordinated use of workers doing each of these tasks created high pin productivity.

The clear connection between specialization and efficiency has led manufacturers to attempt to increase the division of labor. In addition to greater efficiency, division of labor permits the use of relatively unskilled people in simple routine tasks. This, of course, reduces labor and training costs. Division of labor was made possible in part by the availability of massive numbers of unskilled workers. These workers, many of them immigrants, have provided the backbone to industrial development in the United States since the late eighteenth century. This situation is changing, however.

Perhaps the greatest monument to specialization and the division of labor is this country's automobile industry, pioneered by Henry Ford in the 1920's. Today the mass production of cars using semiskilled workers in large numbers is commonplace. The same is true of the radio and television, home appliance, and garment trades. There is little doubt that the division of labor and specialization gave impetus to mass production, which in turn provided the basis of industrialization and the increasing levels of affluence in our society.

The division of labor also resulted in social evils with which we have contended for nearly a century. In the early stages of American industrialization, vast numbers of immigrant workers were concentrated in large urban areas. The human misery associated with slums in New York, Pittsburgh, and Chicago is well known. The attendant evils of crime, suicide, and exploitation are also recorded. We need not review all this, but our discussion would not be complete without the recognition that industrialization in the United States has not been an unmitigated good.

The Need For Coordination

Nevertheless, the division of labor has been intensifying, and paralleling its intensification has been the need for coordination. One can only marvel at the coordination required for a modern automobile assembly line. Thousands of parts must be fed from subsidiary lines into the main line at precisely the right time to make a car according to specifications. This operation, we must be careful to note, requires division of labor and coordination not only in production processes but also in management.

Management provides the systems that divide all labor into specialized tasks. It then coordinates these tasks so that the objectives of the organization may be achieved. Division of labor and coordination are the natural imperatives of organization management; they exist in the smallest informal groups and in the largest corporations. Both are central to the understanding of the organizing process, for the division of labor is the reason for organization.

Steps in the Division of Labor

Through the division of labor, tasks are broken down as naturally as possible to allow both mental and physical specialization. Perhaps the most primitive basis for dividing labor is sex. The various activities associated with having and caring for a family are most efficiently performed if the work required is divided among the males and females of a species. But organizations grow beyond the size of the family unit; tasks multiply, technology and products become more sophisticated. In this complex industrial and technological age, man constantly seeks the one best way to

Figure 9-1. Division of Work in a Growing Company

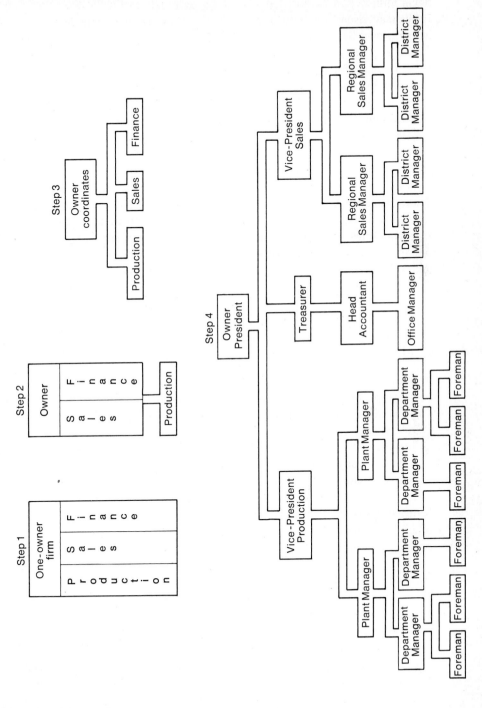

achieve efficiency. His quest is reflected in the increasing specialization of organizational forms.

We may visualize the division of labor by starting with a set of tasks that need to be performed by any business organization: say production, sales, and finance (see Figure 9-1). In a one-man business, the owner performs all these functions (Step 1). If he is successful and the business grows, he hires people and delegates to them responsibility for making the product (Step 2). Here we see the first phase in the division of labor.

During the next phase of growth, the original owner employs specialists to perform all the functions, while he coordinates their efforts (Step 3). When the company reaches a moderate size, the division of labor is still greater. The organization's profile now appears in the conventional form of a pyramid (Step 4).

It should be noted that what Figure 9-1 actually shows is the division of labor among managers in a company. It is really a diagram of management specialization. Of course, division of labor is present also among those who do not have managerial responsibilities. Thus, we find jobs broken down into specialized positions throughout an organization, as we saw in the automobile plant, where job content is small and requires very low levels of worker skill. The development of management specialization, of course, requires relatively high levels of skills, training, and education.

THE MEANING OF COORDINATION

Definitions and Interpretations

Regardless of where and on what level in the organization the division of labor takes place, there arises simultaneously the need for management coordination. Because the division of labor is universal in organizations, coordination is a universal process too. Coordination is the conscious process of assembling and synchronizing differentiated activities so that they function harmoniously in the attainment of organization objectives.

As Fayol saw it, coordination pulls together all the activities of an enterprise to make possible both its working and its success. The well-coordinated enterprise, he believed, bears the following marks: Each department works in harmony with the other departments; each department, division, and subdivision knows the share it must assume of the common task; and each department and subdivision adjusts its working schedules to circumstances. However, Fayol found that these requirements are not always fulfilled and postulated three reasons for this. First, each department knows and wants to know nothing of the others; second, watertight compartments exist between divisions and offices of the same department exactly comparable to those between different departments; and third, no one thinks of the general interest. He wrote: "This attitude on the part of the personnel, so disastrous for a concern, is not the result of preconcerted intention but the culmination of non-existent or inadequate coordination."[1] To remedy this situation, Fayol suggested a weekly con-

[1] Henri Fayol, *General and Industrial Management*, trans. Constance Storrs (London: Pitman, 1949), p. 104.

ference of department heads to facilitate a coordinated and current plan of action. If such weekly meetings could not be held at all or if they could only be held at longer intervals, Fayol urged the use of liaison officers to link departments.

Other writers view coordination differently. For example, Ralph C. Davis looks at coordination primarily as a vital phase of control.[2] L. A. Allen cites coordinating as a managerial function alongside planning, organizing, motivating, and controlling.[3] However, he goes on to say that most coordination will be accomplished automatically if sound objectives, policies, procedures, and organization are established.[4] James D. Mooney defines coordination as "the orderly arrangement of group effort, to provide unity of action in the pursuit of a common purpose."[5] He calls coordination the first principle of organization. By this he means that coordination embraces all the principles of organization in toto — nothing less. Mooney's statement best expresses the universality of the coordination process; coordination means unity of action in the accomplishment of objectives.

Ordway Tead provides another definition of coordination: "Coordination is the effort to assure a smooth interplay of the functions and forces of all the different component parts of an organization to the end that its purposes will be realized with a minimum of friction and a maximum of collaborative effectiveness."[6] Coordination, in effect, synchronizes the actions of people within an organization, and one of the important goals of every management is to achieve this synchronization. Chester I. Barnard even goes so far as to say that under most circumstances "the quality of coordination is the crucial factor in the survival of organization."[7] Coordination is not a separate and distinct activity of management; it is a part of all the managerial functions, transversing the entire management process.

Coordination and Cooperation

The term "coordination" should not be confused with "cooperation"; there is considerable difference between them. Cooperation indicates an attitude of a group of people: their willingness to help each other. Coordination is more inclusive, requiring more than desire and willingness. For instance, consider a group of men attempting to move a heavy object. Even if they are sufficient in number, willing and eager to cooperate, are trying to do their best to move the object, and are also fully aware of their common purpose, in all likelihood they will fail. Only when one of them, the manager, gives the proper orders to apply the right amount of effort at the right place and the right time will their efforts succeed. It is conceivable that,

[2] Ralph C. Davis, *The Fundamentals of Top Management* (New York: Harper and Row, 1951), p. 19.

[3] Louis A. Allen, *Management and Organization* (New York: McGraw-Hill, 1958), p. 24.

[4] *Ibid.*, p. 43.

[5] James D. Mooney, *The Principles of Organization*, rev. ed. (New York: Harper and Row, 1947), p. 5.

[6] Ordway Tead, *Administration: Its Purpose and Performance* (New York: Harper and Row, 1959), p. 36.

[7] Chester I. Barnard, *The Functions of the Executive* (Cambridge, Mass.: Harvard University Press, 1938), p. 256.

by coincidence, mere cooperation could have brought about the desired result. But management cannot rely upon coincidence. Thus, although cooperation is always helpful, and its absence could prevent all possibility of coordination, its presence will not assure coordination. Coordination must be a conscious managerial effort exercised through the functions of planning, organizing, staffing, influencing, and controlling.

Self-Coordination

Although coordination is management's job, the subordinate is not exempt from doing all he can to help the effort. Alvin Brown calls the subordinate's effort "self-coordination," which he defines as "the effort of independent responsibilities to achieve the harmonious or reciprocal performance of their own responsibilities."[8] In other words, each person in a group must recognize the effects of his own performance upon others and coordinate his activities with those of others.[9] Herbert Simon speaks of self-coordination in a similar way.[10] However, neither self-coordination nor self-adjustment is a substitute for the over-all coordination introduced by management, which is necessary to the success of the enterprise.

COORDINATION IN ACTION

The Difficulties of Coordinating

Coordination is not easily attained. Each interest group stresses its own view of how organizational purposes should be accomplished and tends to favor the policy that will further its interests. These differences in viewpoint are a problem to all levels in a managerial hierarchy. It takes thoughtfulness, listening power, and good will to see and understand the relationships involved in working with higher and lower groups.

In spite of cooperative attitudes and self-coordination by each member of a group, duplication of action and conflict of effort will occur unless management synchronization exists. Through coordination, management can bring about a level of accomplishment far greater than the sum of the individual parts.

The task of securing coordination belongs solely to management and cannot be delegated to a specialist. Management is in a better position than any special "coordinating department" to view the organization's various functions and to determine how they should be coordinated to bring about desired results. Although it is absurd to think that the task of securing coordination can be shifted and assigned to a department created expressly for this purpose, liaison men can sometimes aid in the coordination effort, as we shall see later in this chapter.

---

[8] Alvin Brown, *Organization of Industry* (Englewood Cliffs, N.J.: Prentice-Hall, 1947), p. 354.
[9] *Ibid.*, pp. 108–28.
[10] Herbert A. Simon, *Administrative Behavior* (New York: Macmillan, 1958), p. 104.

The difficulties of achieving coordination arise for various reasons, one of which is the growth of the enterprise. With growth the task of synchronizing the increasing number of jobs and multiplying daily activities becomes more complicated and more important. A complex organizational structure involving more subordinates also adds problems of communication. Moreover, advanced products and methods bring about new man-machine relationships, which create coordination needs unheard of before. Now man, machine, and function all have to be coordinated within the framework of sophisticated space-age technology. Organization theory has just begun to feel the effects of these developments.

Human nature itself can also lead to coordination problems. Often a manager, preoccupied with the work in his own unit, hesitates to become involved in other areas even though his activities might have significant bearing on them. He, likewise, tends to think primarily of the welfare of his own department and does not consider the over-all welfare of the enterprise. Such tendencies may lead to suboptimization — the maximizing of the returns of one division or department at the expense of the firm as a whole. This is particularly likely to happen if the manager's total compensation is based on his department's financial performance.

Types of Coordination

Vertical

One must distinguish among three different types of coordination — vertical, horizontal, and diagonal. Vertical coordination exists between different levels of an organization — between the vice-president in charge of production and the plant manager and between the plant manager and department manager, for example (see Figure 9-1, Step 4). Vertical coordination is secured by delegating authority together with the means and manner of supervising and controlling. As the preceding sentence implies, delegated authority carries great weight. However, vertical coordination cannot be achieved by threat alone. Instead, it must be the result of a superior's efficient and expert performance of his managerial functions.

Horizontal

Horizontal coordination refers to coordination between men and departments on the same organizational level. For example, planning and implementing a new promotional program might involve the working arrangements among the vice-president in charge of production, the vice-president in charge of sales, and the vice-president in charge of finance. Horizontal coordination is needed so that when the sales department is ready to sell the new item, the production department will be able to fill the orders. Financial arrangements will already have been made to establish the required amount of outstanding credit and to ensure that the necessary funds are available for raw materials, parts, and so on. Each of the executives involved in this coordination manages his own department and has no authority over either of his associates. Horizontal coordination, like vertical, cannot be commanded; it must result from superior managerial skills. If horizontal coordination is insufficient or inconclusive, however, a matter can be carried to a level of the managerial hierarchy high enough to be responsible for all the activities in question.

Diagonal

In a small enterprise, coordination between the various functions and managers of different departments is facilitated by the proximity of working arrangements, close contacts, and short lines of communication. However, in a large organization, the problems become more complicated. In fact, in certain large organizations whose structure is dominated by its projects, diagonal coordination appears. In this situation, both levels and positions on a chain of command are superseded so that all can take advantage of a special service. For example, operating departments and individual projects may all have access to a centralized computer service (see Figure 9-2). The allocation of the computer service resources, in this case, often has to be coordinated by negotiation between the users and the computer personnel. This process involves complex interrelationships that cannot be coordinated by resorting to "the next level in the chain of command." Often, responsibility for coordination must be assumed by the parties themselves.

Figure 9-2. Diagonal Relationships

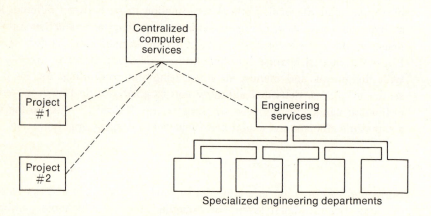

Specialized engineering departments

The Principles of Mary Parker Follett

Mary Parker Follett, in her discussion of coordination, has presented several fundamental principles of organization.[11] She states that coordination — agreement on methods, actions, and ultimate achievement — can be attained most easily by direct horizontal relationships and personal communications. She also points out that

[11] Henry C. Metcalf and Lyndall F. Urwick, eds., *Dynamic Administration: The Collected Papers of Mary Parker Follett* (New York: Harper and Row, 1942), p. 297.

coordination can be achieved more readily in the early stages of planning and policy-making. If the executive of one department meets with the executives of other departments and confronts them with a finished policy, coordination naturally becomes difficult. But "if the head of the production department, *while* he is forming his policy, meets and discusses with the other heads the question involved, a successful coordination is far more likely to be reached. That is, you cannot, with the greatest degree of success for your undertaking, make policy-forming and policy-adjusting two separate processes."[12]

In a third principle of coordination, Follett illuminates the process of communication. She states that all factors in a situation are reciprocally related. That is, when A works with B, who in turn works with C and D, each of the four finds himself influenced by all the persons in the total situation: "This sort of reciprocal relating, this interpenetration of every part by every other part, and again by every other part as it has been permeated by all, should be the goal of all attempts at coordination."[13] As a fourth principle, Mary Parker Follett states that coordination is a continuing process that cannot be left to chance. Managers must constantly work at it so that they will not be suddenly confronted by unforeseen developments.

Coordination and the Five Managerial Functions

Committees are often formed to ensure voluntary coordination among individuals and departments. Some writers strongly recommend this practice because it gives unit heads a reason to hold formal and informal meetings.[14] Often management sets up committees expressly to bring together the people whose activities must be coordinated, and by doing so provides a setting that will foster voluntary horizontal coordination.

When management plans, it must immediately coordinate. Top executives should discuss various plans and alternatives, while they are still flexible, with the managers of all departments so that everyone will have the opportunity to express doubts and objections at once. If these managers are involved in planning at the initial stages, the chances for coordination are good. For instance, the thoughtful manager will plan an advertising campaign in conjunction with the production manager, the sales manager, the vice-president in charge of finance, the publicity manager, and so on, thereby synchronizing the efforts of all individuals involved.

Concern for coordination should also permeate organizing activities. It should be foremost in management's mind as it groups and assigns various activities to subordinates and creates departments themselves. In the process of organizing, management should establish departments and define their relationships in such a way that coordination will result. For instance, placing related activities that must be closely synchronized in the same administrative unit will facilitate coordination.

---

[12] *Ibid.*, p. 298.

[13] *Ibid.*, p. 299.

[14] For example, see Ernest Dale, *Planning and Developing the Company Organization Structure*, Research Report No. 20 (New York: American Management Association, 1952), p. 116.

Often poor coordination is caused by a lack of understanding of who is to perform what or by the failure of management to delegate authority and responsibility clearly. Such fuzziness can easily cause duplication of effort instead of synchronization. This is most likely to happen when two executives both feel responsible for the same activity. The heads of the purchasing department and the maintenance division, for example, might both consider it their function to buy repair and spare parts.

Management should also bear coordination in mind when considering staffing decisions. It should make certain that it has the right number of executives in the various positions to assure the proper performance of company objectives.

In influencing, management is again involved with coordination. The purpose of giving orders, instructing, coaching, teaching, and generally supervising subordinates is to coordinate their various activities in such a manner that the over-all company objectives will be reached in the most efficient way. In assessing the relationship of good supervision to coordination, Alvin Brown defines coordination as "that phase of supervision which is devoted to obtaining the harmonious and reciprocal performance of responsibilities of two or more deputies."[15] The supervisor can never completely relieve himself of the duty of watching the progress of the various activities under his direction.

Finally, coordination is directly related to controlling; the very nature of the controlling process brings about coordination. Frequent evaluation of operations helps to synchronize the efforts of subordinates. If management finds that performance is not proceeding as planned or directed, it should immediately take remedial action to correct whatever deviations have occurred. This action should at least assure future coordination.

Good communications are immeasurably helpful in all coordination efforts. Personal contact is probably the most effective means of communication. However, written communications, reports, procedures, bulletins, and the numerous modern mechanical devices that ensure speedy dissemination of necessary information to various subordinates are also helpful. Recent developments in electronic data processing can aid considerably in communication efforts, as can devices like PERT.

Liaison Men

Although coordination will always remain the line manager's responsibility, special employees have sometimes been charged with coordinating tasks. In situations where executives cannot maintain sufficient personal contact to provide all the informal information desired, a liaison man may be utilized. Such a person must be thoroughly familiar with operating conditions in his division so that he can explain them to the other divisions with which he is in close contact. He then must report conditions in other divisions back to his own unit. In large business concerns with widely scattered headquarters, offices, plans, and branches, a liaison man's usefulness and appropriateness can at times be justified.

[15] Brown, *Organization of Industry*, p. 354.

Liaison men, however, do not have the authority to commit their operating divisions, and their use should never be considered a substitute for more direct means of securing coordination. The practice of relying on liaison men became widespread during World War II, when the position of coordinator or expediter or liaison officer was created to assure coordination among departments, suppliers, resources, and subcontractors. No doubt this was appropriate and filled a need in time of war and emergency; such measures might also be advisable as a temporary relief in any management situation. However, if under normal conditions a constant need for coordination exists, the organizational structure and the manner in which management functions are performed should be checked. There should not be any need for specialists who do nothing but coordinate.

External Coordination

In addition to the need for internal coordination, there exists a need for coordination with factors external to the enterprise — changes in the competitive situation, government activities, technological advances, and the interests of the general public, the owners, and the employees. Coordination must also exist between an organization and other related enterprises such as shippers, suppliers, and carriers, as well as between the organization and the economy at large. All these external factors add to the already difficult task of internal coordination.

Much is being written about relationships among independent but integrated firms such as power companies in an electrical distribution network. Obviously coordination among these firms must be highly sophisticated and is of crucial importance. Daniel Wren discusses what he calls the interface relationships between such firms, analyzing behavior among the companies at the point where they are tangent to each other.[16]

It should be pointed out that, through new tools and devices and through a more thorough understanding of managerial functions, knowledge of how to obtain coordination is becoming broader. Management's ever-increasing problems of coordination can thereby be offset by ever-increasing knowledge of how to perform its managerial skills.

New concepts of coordination such as project and matrix organizations are emerging. These forms of management coordination are discussed in subsequent chapters. We move next to span of management, which is a logical extension of the concept of the division of labor and the process of coordination.

Discussion Questions

1. One of the most persistent problems with which management has to deal is trying to reconcile forces that tend to split organizations and forces that tend to

---

[16] Daniel A. Wren, "Interface and Interorganizational Coordination," *Academy of Management Journal* 10, no. 1 (March 1967): 69–83.

integrate organizations. How would you analyze this statement in terms of co-ordination and division of labor?

2. Why does self-coordination take on added significance when we consider organizational situations in which diagonal relationships are important?

Supplementary Readings

Carzo, Rocco, Jr. "Organizational Realities." In *Dimensions in Modern Management,* edited by Patrick E. Connor. Boston: Houghton Mifflin, 1974.

Lawrence, Paul R., and Jay W. Lorsch. "New Management Job: The Integrator." In *Dimensions in Modern Management.*

Litterer, Joseph A. *The Analysis of Organizations.* New York: Wiley, 1965. See chapters 8–11.

Mooney, James D. *The Principles of Organizations.* New York: Harper and Row, 1947. See chapter 2.

Pfiffner, John M., and Frank P. Sherwood. *Administrative Organization.* Englewood Cliffs, N.J.: Prentice-Hall, 1960. See chapter 8.

Raube, S. Avery. "Principles of Organization." In *Dimensions in Modern Management.*

Wren, Daniel A. "Interface and Interorganizational Coordination." *Academy of Management Journal* 10, no. 1 (March 1967): 69–83.

CHAPTER 10

The Span of Management

The establishment of departments and the creation of levels of management are not ends in themselves. They are not intrinsically desirable. They are expensive; they require the employment of department managers and staff. Furthermore, as departments and levels are created, difficulties are encountered in coordination and control. Why then should an organization departmentalize? The answer lies in the concept of span of management, a concept that refers to the number of subordinates who can effectively be supervised.[1]

THE MEANING OF SPAN

It is obvious that no one can manage an infinite number of subordinates. Therefore, management must create departments — distinct areas of activity having a manager in charge. The manager receives authority from top management and delegates it to as many subordinates as his management can effectively span. Thus, span of management defines the limits of departmentalization and delegation of authority. These in turn are related to the division of labor and coordination.

An Ageless Concept

Management's inability to supervise unlimited numbers of subordinates is not a new problem. Moses ran into it, and the manner in which he handled the problem is described in Exodus 18:17–26. Moses' father-in-law gave him this advice: "For this thing is too heavy for thee. Thou art not able to perform it thyself alone. . . . I will give thee counsel. . . . Thou shalt provide out of the people able men and place such over them, to be rulers of thousands, and rulers of fifties, and rulers of tens. And let them judge the people at all seasons; and it shall be that every great matter they shall bring unto thee, but every small matter they shall judge; so shall it be easier for thyself and they shall bear the burden with thee." Moses took this advice and he chose "able men out of all Israel and made them heads over the people, rulers of thousands, rulers of hundreds, rulers of fifties, and rulers of tens. And they judged the people at all seasons; the hard causes they brought unto Moses, but every small matter they judged themselves."

[1] The term "span of management" is often called span of control, span of responsibility, or span of supervision.

The same problem, of course, prevails today: How many subordinates can a manager effectively supervise? Much has been written on this subject since biblical times, and some empirical research has been done. Nevertheless, it is not possible to pinpoint the number of subordinates a manager can supervise. Some surveys say that, at the upper level, the span of management can embrace four, five, or even eight subordinates. General Eisenhower, as supreme commander of the Allied Forces, had only three line subordinates reporting to him. In contrast, General Ian Hamilton says in a book published in the early 1920's that from three to six is the optimum number of upper-level subordinates:

The average human brain finds its effective scope in handling from three to six other brains. If a man divides the whole of his work into two branches and delegates his responsibility, freely and properly, to two experienced heads of branches he will not have enough to do. The occasions when they would have to refer to him would be too few to keep him fully occupied. If he delegates to three heads he will be kept fairly busy whilst six heads of branches will give most bosses a ten hour day. Those data are the results of centuries of the experiences of soldiers, which are greater, where organisation is in question, than those of politicians, business men or any other class of men.[2]

At intermediate levels, however, the span of management can be larger, and at the lowest or supervisor's level it can include twenty-five, depending, as we shall see later, upon the many factors of which span is a function.

Relationship to Organizational Levels

Let us look more carefully at the relationship between the span of management and organizational level. As an example, imagine a situation where there are 256 subordinates on one organizational level reporting to one executive. Then assume that the executive decides that 256 subordinates are too many and that only 4 should report to him. There would now be 64 employees reporting to each of four subexecutives. By creating subexecutives, however, we have established two levels of organization and a total of five executives. Now, assuming that 64 subordinates are still too many and this figure is cut to 16, the organization will require three executive levels totaling twenty-one executives. Each of the five executives on the upper levels will have four subordinates reporting to him and each of the sixteen executives on the lowest level will have sixteen subordinates. The span of management has thus been reduced considerably from the original 256.

This admittedly extreme example, shown graphically in Figure 10-1, illustrates what occurs when one begins to narrow the span of management. It is obvious that the narrower the span, the more levels are needed. Since each level must be managed by executives, the more levels there are, the more executives will be introduced into the organization. Depending upon the number of levels, the organization will end

[2] Sir Ian Hamilton, *The Soul and Body of an Army* (London: Arnold, 1921), p. 229.

Figure 10-1. Organization Levels and Spans of Management

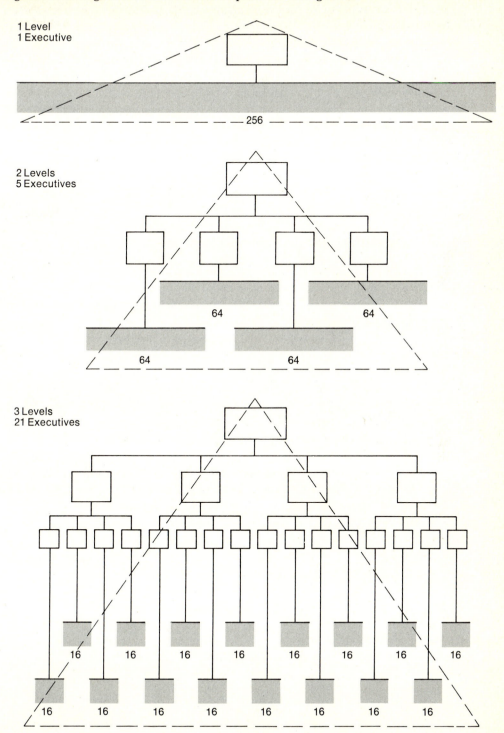

up either as a shallow, flat, broad pyramid having a span of 256 subordinates like the first diagram in Figure 10-1, or as a tall pyramid like the last example showing only 4 subordinates in each of the upper spans of management. This is what is meant by the terms "shallow organization pyramid" and "tall organization pyramid."

Consider another example: an enterprise of moderate size with five employment levels — the chief executive, senior managers, junior managers, foremen, and clerks or workmen. In this organization 10 people report to each foreman, and on each higher level 6 managers report to each superior manager. Thus, the chief executive with the help of 6 senior managers, 36 junior managers, and 216 foremen can supervise 2,160 clerks and workmen or a total of 2,418 employees. This illustrates the fact that with a small number of supervisory levels and a reasonably small span, a fairly large enterprise can be effectively managed (see Table 10-1).

DETERMINING THE PROPER SPAN

Organizational Relationships and the Theory of Graicunas

In 1933 V. A. Graicunas published an article entitled "Relationship in Organization."[3] Graicunas analyzed the problem of subordinate-superior relationships and developed a mathematical formula that showed that the number of such relationships increases exponentially with an increase in the number of subordinates. Graicunas did not derive his formula from empirical observation but based it on a mathematical projection of what would happen to an organization if the span of management were changed at the top.

When calculating the total number of relationships, Graicunas considered not only the direct relationship between a superior and his immediate subordinates but also the superior's relationships with different groupings of subordinates and, furthermore, the cross relationships among the subordinates. For example, in a particular organization a superior has direct single relationships with his three immediate subordinates, B, C, and D. He also has direct group relationships with each possible combination of subordinates. In this case there will be a total of nine

Table 10-1. Levels of Supervision

Level	Typical position	Number of persons on this level	Total supervised directly by this level
1	Chief executive	1	6
2	Senior managers	6	36
3	Junior managers	36	216
4	Foremen	216	2,160
5	Clerks and workmen	2,160	—

[3] Reprinted in Luther Gulick and Lyndall F. Urwick, eds., *Papers on the Science of Administration* (New York: Institute of Public Administration, 1937), pp. 183–87.

Table 10-2. Total Possible Relationships with Variable Number of Subordinates

Number of subordinates	Total number of possible relationships
1	1
2	6
3	18
4	44
5	100
6	222
7	490
8	1,080
9	2,376
10	5,210

direct group relationships. In addition, cross relationships will arise from the need of the supervisor's subordinates to consult with one another. Whereas the supervisor's own direct relationships with individuals increase in proportion to the addition of subordinates, the group and cross relationships increase much more than proportionately.

Graicunas' formula is expressed by this equation:

$$R = n\left(\frac{2^n}{2} + n - 1\right)$$

where R equals all types of relationships that might concern management and n is the number of subordinates. By substituting various values for n, we can determine their effect on R. The results of substituting values of one to ten are shown in Table 10-2.

From this table, we can see that four subordinates and their superior can engage in forty-four relationships. If, however, one more subordinate is added, one hundred relationships result. This illustrates the exponential increase that results from adding even one subordinate. A 25 per cent increase in the number of subordinates will result in a 127 per cent increase in relationships.

Graicunas' formula, however, gives us only the total number of potential relationships. It does not deal with the actual performance, the frequency, or the importance of each of the various types of relationships that make up the total. Yet it does dramatically emphasize how complex a situation can become if a manager has too many subordinates reporting to him. In reality, the magnitude of relationships which a given manager must handle will probably not be so great as the total indicated by the formula. Newman points out that as an enterprise grows in size, the employees seldom engage in all the relationships with each other that are theoretically possible, any more than a new telephone subscriber makes calls to all the people theoretically within his reach.[4]

---

[4] William H. Newman, *Administrative Action* (Englewood Cliffs, N.J.: Prentice-Hall, 1951), p. 261.

Graicunas also qualified his observations by stating that cross relationships or contacts among subordinates of a common superior render the task of supervision more difficult. This difficulty will not be as prevalent where the work requires few such cross contacts among the subordinates concerned. This qualification is based on the same premise stated by Hamilton: "The smaller the responsibility of the group member, the larger may be the group."[5]

Factors Influencing the Magnitude of the Span

A considerable number of factors determine not only the actual number of relationships within a management span but also their frequency and intensity. These factors will greatly alter the figures a mathematical formula produces, so they must be observed and investigated. That is, instead of merely juggling alternative numbers of subordinates, theorists must consider the factors that determine the frequency and relevance of the various human relationships encompassed within the span of management. We shall cite the most important of these.

Organization Policy

The type of management and organization policy practiced by a particular enterprise markedly influences the span of management. What a manager does with his time is of utmost importance. Problem-solving takes more total time if a manager decides every problem individually than it does if he makes policy decisions that anticipate problems. Clear and complete policy statements simplify a manager's personal decision-making. The same rationale applies to other administrative processes that routinize decisions — defining responsibility and authority, and developing performance standards, procedures, and budgets. If an enterprise's policy encourages these programmed practices, then its span of management can probably be broader.

Availability of Staff

Because management depends on having a certain amount of work of a particular nature done, the availability of staff will have a bearing on the management span. If specialized staff makes a full range of expert advice and service in specific areas available to management, a manager's time will be freer and his span can be wider. However, the presence of personal staff does not necessarily broaden management's span. Since a manager must supervise even an effective assistant fairly closely, he might find it more economical to upgrade the responsibility of a lower-level manager than to designate a new personal staff assistant.

[5] Hamilton, *The Soul and Body of an Army*, p. 229.

Qualifications of Manager and Subordinates

The qualifications of the manager and his subordinates are another important factor influencing the span of management. Obviously, the training and personal qualities of some managers enable them to handle more subordinates than others, thus facilitating a broader span. Similarly, the greater the training, capacities, and self-direction of subordinates, the fewer contacts they will need with their superiors.

Type of Activities Performed by Subordinates

The nature and importance of the activities assigned to subordinates are also significant. If such activities are uncomplicated, a larger number of subordinates can be supervised effectively. Part of the reason for this is that supervision is often built into work processes. For example, the pace of work on an assembly line is controlled by the speed of the conveyors. If, on the other hand, the activities to be supervised are highly important and complicated, management's span must be small or management must delegate a great deal of authority. In general, the simpler and more uniform the work, the greater is the number of persons who can be supervised by one superior.

This point is emphasized time and again by Lyndall Urwick. He states, for example, that if the work of subordinates does not interlock, there is less need for extensive subdivisions or levels of control, and a broader span is possible. He cites Sears, Roebuck, to illustrate that there is no reason why twenty stores situated in different towns and operating on a more or less standardized pattern should not be controlled effectively by a single executive.[6] In contrast, the district manager of a company that runs a chain of small discount or outlet stores in several cities will probably be fully taxed by supervising just five or six store managers. Competitive factors are more intense: "The stores are harried by the unfriendly attitude of local merchants and the outright opposition of some manufacturers. There is little policy or procedure to guide him, so the store manager is forced constantly to refer to headquarters or to try to gather facts and decide himself on most operating and management problems."[7]

Applicability of Objective Standards

Another factor that influences relationships and thereby determines the span of management is the degree to which objective standards are applied. If there are enough objective control standards available so that managers can check whether they are on the right track, they will not need to report to their superior as frequently.

[6] Lyndall F. Urwick, "The Manager's Span of Control," *Harvard Business Review* 34, no. 3 (May–June 1956): 45.

[7] Louis A. Allen, *Management and Organization* (New York: McGraw-Hill, 1958), p. 76.

Also, objective standards enable a manager to concentrate on exceptions, areas where performance is deviating from expected results. In general, we may say that where work is routine and carefully detailed and where supervision is engineered into a work system, the machinery does some of the supervision. Therefore, a manager's duties are lessened and he can have many employees under his supervision.

The Conflict of Span Versus Level

The span of management, as we have seen, is limited by many factors. It has been established that the narrower the span, the larger the number of managerial levels that will be needed. This poses a problem: Should an organization have a broader span or more levels? There are advantages and disadvantages to both. Let us first consider the disadvantages of additional levels.

Disadvantages of Levels

The presence of many organizational levels necessitates a larger number of executives. They, in turn, incur a larger expense in executive salaries. R. C. Davis showed that changing the executive management span from six to four and the first-line supervisory span from twenty to ten in an enterprise with 12,000 operative employees necessitated a 120 per cent increase in executives.[8] In addition to extra salaries, the firm will have to pay the costs connected with extra staff and clerical personnel. Therefore, levels cost money.

The addition of levels has another disadvantage: Increasing the number of executives makes communication more cumbersome. Communications often become distorted as they go up and down the channels of command. This tendency is particularly acute when the communications must pass through several layers or levels of supervision in order to get from one part of an organization to another. The more layers through which they must pass, the greater is the danger of distortion, omission, and misinterpretation.

In order to avoid the inefficiencies caused by *layering,* some executives have decided that contacts between units should be carried out in the most direct way — laterally. However, at the same time, each member of the organization is to keep his superior fully informed, thereby ensuring one level of vertical communication. If this is not done, an executive might find that his colleagues have received information from one of his subordinates before he has and that they might even have taken action on the basis of such information. One way to remedy this difficulty is to encourage lower-level managers to develop cross relationships. If such a practice is advocated and accepted by management, many matters can be solved quickly and

---

[8] R. C. Davis, *The Influence of the Unit of Supervision and the Span of Executive Control on the Economy of Line Organization Structure* (Columbus: Ohio State University, Bureau of Business Research, 1941).

satisfactorily at lower levels. Fayol suggested such a solution and proposed a "gang plank" or a bridge to overcome the effects of layering.[9]

Another disadvantage of an excessive number of levels is the loss to morale which they can cause. The subordinate who finds himself far down on one of the last levels of the executive hierarchy might feel sensitive about never hearing directly from the "boss." Considering himself far removed from the chief executive, he might allow the quality of his work to decline. However, this particular situation is hard to remedy; in large organizations communication throughout all levels is virtually impossible. Consequently, efforts to improve human relations have been aimed mainly at the point of direct contact between an immediate superior and his subordinate.

Criticism of Span

Interestingly enough, the problem of morale has been the basis for criticism not only of the excessive use of levels but also of the excessive widening of the management span. Some writers have objected to the idea of a limited span on the grounds that it prohibits democratic participation. Those advocating a flat organization pyramid with a wide span of control and few levels of management maintain that this allows a minimum of social and administrative distance. In reply, writers such as Urwick point out that nothing rots morale more quickly and more completely than poor communication and indecisiveness — the feeling that those in authority do not know their own minds: "And there is no condition which more quickly produces a sense of indecision among subordinates or more effectively hampers communication than being responsible to a superior who has too wide a span of control."[10]

Another criticism of a wide management span comes from Herbert Simon, who questions its theoretical validity. He maintains that "a contradictory proverb of administration can be stated which, though it is not so familiar as the principle of span control, can be supported by arguments of equal plausibility. The proverb in question is the following: Administrative efficiency is enhanced by keeping at a minimum the number of organizational levels through which a matter must pass before it is acted upon. . . . In many situations the results to which this principle leads are in direct contradiction to the requirements of the principle of span of control."[11] He goes on to say that a restricted span of control inevitably produces excessive red tape, "for each contact between organization members must be carried upward until a common superior is found."[12]

[9] Henri Fayol, *General and Industrial Management,* trans. Constance Storrs (London: Pitman, 1949), pp. 34–36.

[10] Urwick, "The Manager's Span of Control," p. 43.

[11] Herbert A. Simon, *Administrative Behavior,* 2d ed. (New York: Macmillan, 1958), p. 26.

[12] *Ibid.,* p. 28.

There is no doubt that a careful balancing of the inefficiencies of levels against those of span is necessary. Nevertheless, extending the executive's span of management beyond what he can reasonably handle in order to reduce the number of levels is not necessarily the cure for administrative distance. Of course, it is desirable to restrict the number of levels as much as possible and to eliminate any level which is not vital. "But in determining the number of levels which are necessary, prime regard should be paid to the span of control, not vice versa."[13]

Tendencies Toward a Broader Span

In spite of the criticisms of Urwick and others, the concept of a narrow span of management is often disregarded. In many instances the span has been increased in an attempt to encourage democratic participation and discourage feelings of distance. In addition, executives desiring to demonstrate advancement and status by their position as high up as possible in the executive hierarchy have forced increases in span. In other cases, management's desire to keep the chain of command as short as possible has resulted in the same response. Then again, managers may wish to take a personal interest in as many aspects of their position as possible. They may distrust the ability of subordinates, fear possible rivals, or desire power. Other managers might feel that overly close supervision discourages initiative and self-reliance among subordinates and realize that such supervision would be physically impossible if the span of management were large.

Taking these considerations into account, between 1940 and 1947, International Business Machines Corporation eliminated one of its levels of management entirely. By doing this, it enlarged the job content of foremen and plant managers and reduced that of middle management.

Another classic example of a flat organizational structure or shallow managerial pyramid is that of Sears, Roebuck. This company organized one group of stores within its chain along conventional lines with the usual steep organizational pyramid, and another comparable group with a wide span of management. In this second group, approximately thirty merchandise managers reported to one superior. Sears then studied sales volume, profit, and morale and found that the stores with the flat type of organization were superior in all respects to those organized along more conventional lines. Their studies indicated that the flat organization had been successful because managers who had a large number of subordinates reporting to them had no choice but to delegate authority. This improved not only the subordinates' morale but also the quality of their performance. Also, a store manager, knowing that he must delegate a considerable amount of authority, took greater care in choosing, guiding, and training his subordinates. Moreover, because many stores were assigned

[13] Urwick, "The Manager's Span of Control," p. 45. Also see Urwick, "The Span of Control — Some Facts About the Fables," *Advanced Management* 21, no. 11 (November 1956): 5–15; and Herbert A. Simon, "The Span of Control: A Reply," *Advanced Management* 22, no. 4 (April 1957): 14.

to relatively few area supervisory offices, district managers were kept from exercising too detailed a control of any one store. James C. Worthy summarizes the Sears experience:

The company has gone directly counter to one of the favorite tenets of modern management theory, the so-called "span of control," which holds that the number of subordinate executives or supervisors reporting to a single individual should be severely limited to enable that individual to exercise the detailed direction and control which are generally considered necessary. In an organization with as few supervisory levels as Sears, it is obvious that most key executives have so many subordinates reporting to them that they simply cannot exercise too close supervision over their activities. By this means, substantial decentralization of administrative processes is practically guaranteed.[14]

The Bank of America, likewise, has a flat organizational structure. Its nine hundred branches in the state of California and in various foreign countries, offering more than sixty kinds of banking services, report directly to corporate headquarters at San Francisco without any intervening layer of district offices. Top management feels that this enables branch managers to be self-reliant local businessmen with a maximum opportunity to make judgments and decisions in many highly specialized and divergent areas on their own. At headquarters, specialists are available if needed to provide functional guidance in each of the many categories of activities. But this does not alter the fact that the nine hundred branch managers are directly accountable to the president.

IBM, Sears, and Bank of America are just a few examples of the recent trend toward a broader management span. Clearly, less weight is being given today to theories of early writers such as Urwick, who stated that "No superior can supervise directly the work of more than five or, at the most, six subordinates whose work interlocks."[15]

Nevertheless, there is no doubt that many situations do demand close supervision. This is especially true when jobs are simple, repetitive, and require low skill levels; it is much less true when jobs are complex, creative, and require greater skill. Therefore, a manager may be able to effectively supervise as many as fifteen scientists doing complex jobs. Although his supervision is not direct or close, results may be far better and morale higher because he has delegated sufficient authority to achieve a wide span.

[14] James C. Worthy, "Factors Influencing Employee Morale," *Harvard Business Review* 27, no. 1 (January 1950): 61–73. Also by the same author, see "Organization Structure and Employee Morale," *American Sociological Review* 15, no. 2 (April 1950): 169–79; *Discovering and Evaluating Employee Attitudes*, Personnel Series, no. 113 (New York: American Management Association, 1947); and "Democratic Principles in Business Management," *Advanced Management* 14, no. 1 (March 1949): 16–21.

[15] Lyndall F. Urwick, *Scientific Principles and Organization*, series no. 19 (New York: American Management Association, 1938), p. 8.

The Trade-Off Problem

In the last analysis, the problem of spans versus levels is resolved by compromise. Basically the compromise requires a trade-off of spans for levels or vice versa. If a company wishes to reduce layering it must increase the span of management. Often this requires granting greater discretion to subordinates so that they may work effectively without continual direct supervision. Granting greater discretion may in turn mean that the quality of subordinates has to rise. Thus, management is actually substituting the cost of numerous managers for the cost of subordinates of higher quality.

Discussion Questions

1. In what ways do span of management ideas apply to family life? Think of a family with one child and compare it with a family having four children.

2. The trade-off in costs between span and levels, between more managers and higher-quality employees, has been discussed in this chapter. Do you think a one-to-one exchange exists? Can you mention any other factors that enter into this trade-off?

Supplementary Readings

Koontz, Harold. "Making Theory Operational: The Span of Management." In *Dimensions in Modern Management,* edited by Patrick E. Connor. Boston: Houghton Mifflin, 1974.

Litterer, Joseph A. *The Analysis of Organizations.* New York: Wiley, 1965. See chapters 8, 9, 10, and 11.

Scott, William G., and Terence R. Mitchell. *Organization Theory.* Homewood, Ill.: Irwin, 1972. See pp. 40–41, 49–50.

Stieglitz, Harold. "Optimizing Span of Control." In *Management in Perspective,* edited by W. E. Schlender, W. G. Scott, and A. C. Filley. Boston: Houghton Mifflin, 1965. See pp. 333–41.

CHAPTER 11

Departmentalization

Departmentalization results from the division of work, the span of management, and the need for coordination. It is the process of grouping activities into natural units. A department is such a unit; it is a distinct area of activities over which a manager has been given authority and for which he has accepted responsibility. Management has a great number of alternatives for grouping activities and thus for creating departments.

Departments are commonly organized by function, product, territory, customer, process and equipment, time, or project. In addition, departments are sometimes organized by simple numbers. This kind of departmentalization occurs where sheer numbers are crucial, for example, in filling a request for one hundred farm hands. However, simple number departmentalization has declined as the advent of specialization has made it more convenient to group according to skills.

DEPARTMENTALIZATION BY FUNCTION

Grouping activities by the functions of an enterprise is one of the most widely used patterns of departmentalization. All organizations create some product or service. In addition, they often must market their product or service and finance their ventures. Thus, firms frequently have production, sales, and finance departments because these three major functions are found in nearly every business and non-business organization.

The terminology describing basic functions varies considerably. In a distributorship the production function will be called "buying." In an airline or railroad, production is called "operations" and sales "traffic." One hardly finds a distinct selling function in a hospital, but the "delivery" of health services is common.

Often sales, finance, and production departments are combined with product, territorial, or customer departmentalization. That nearly every enterprise has some functional departmentalization is especially evident in young enterprises, which almost always begin with this type of organizational structure. A functional structure seems to be well suited to businesses created by one or a few people and closely supervised by the proprietor(s). Here, the immediate problem is to get things done and therefore the emphasis is on operations. At a later time, after the enterprise has grown, the problem of changing to a different type of departmentalization may arise.

147

Examples

Departmentalization by function groups work to be done into major functional areas. All work of the same or a related kind is placed under a single chain of command. Therefore, the manager of manufacturing is in charge of all manufacturing activities throughout the enterprise, regardless of where the plants might be located and regardless of how many product lines are being manufactured. For example, in a company that has been organized to manufacture wooden and metal furniture, both types of furniture are produced in the same plant and both types are sold by the same sales people (see Figure 11-1). As the enterprise grows, additions are made to the already existing functions. Such growth, however, necessitates separating the production and sales of wood furniture from those of metal furniture. Separate departments now handle these functions, as is shown in Figure 11-2. This departmental increase adds levels to the areas that the managers of functional departments must supervise.

Figure 11-1. Functional Departmentalization in a Small Company

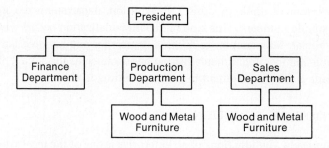

In most companies the managers of the production, sales, and accounting departments report directly to the chief executive, usually the president. These departments usually have large budgets and employ many people. However, a major department may occasionally become a minor one. For instance, wartime shortages may transform the duties of a sales force into the mere allocation of the available finished products to many orders. This situation changes when hostilities end and, with the return of a buyer's market, selling again becomes a major function. Such a change could also work in reverse. Many firms have found that owing to the acceleration of technological competition in the industry, the once minor function of research and development has become their lifeblood.

Advantages

Functional departmentalization has many advantages. As we have demonstrated, it provides a logical way of arranging activities. Also, by facilitating specialization, it leads to economic operations. It groups functions that belong together and are performed by the same specialists with the same kind of equipment and facilities. With functional departmentalization each department and its manager are concerned with one type of work. If production is concentrated in a single department, for example, peaks and valleys in the demand for one product can very likely be minimized by the peaks and valleys of a second product. Thus, both equipment and facilities are used optimally. Additional economies result from pooling and combining a number of administrative activities such as receiving, shipping, maintenance, and the like. Functional departmentalization can also improve coordination within a single function because one executive will take the responsibility for all related activity. Coordination is more easily achieved if a single function is not diffused into several different divisions. Finally, functional departmentalization gives the whole enterprise the benefits of the outstanding abilities of one or a few individuals. Louis Allen explains:

The reason for this is that, in the functional organizational structure, only the president is so placed, organizationally, as to be able to coordinate problems and make decisions having to do with one or more of the major functions. As a result, the structure itself forces all such decisions to the top and ensures that the special abilities of the chief executive can be transmitted to the point of action in most of the important affairs of the company.[1]

Disadvantages

The advantages of functional departmentalization may eventually turn into disadvantages as an enterprise grows in size and diversity. With growth, centralization may become excessive and delays in decision-making may result. Exercising control

Figure 11-2. Functional Departmentalization in a Larger Company

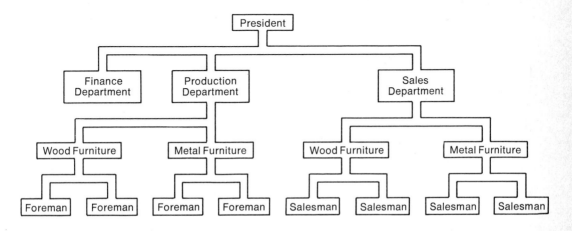

[1] Louis A. Allen, *Management and Organization* (New York: McGraw-Hill, 1958), p. 84.

and measuring performance also become increasingly difficult. As a company grows, moreover, additional organizational levels must be created and a larger total number of people must report to supervisors. This slows down communications because, as we already noted, in a functional organizational structure coordinating decisions that affect two or more functions can be accomplished only by the chief executive.

Effective control is also difficult in an organization that is functionally departmentalized. For instance, if the manufacturing department produces all products, it is difficult, if not impossible, to single out the cost of any one product. For a long time such departmentalization prevented the Chrysler Corporation from determining accurately the cost of producing a Plymouth or any of its other cars, whereas other automobile manufacturers who operated on a product division basis could readily establish the cost of one of their particular makes.

Finally, an organization that is functionally departmentalized does not possess a good training ground for all-around managers. Its managers have little opportunity to learn to manage the entire range of the different functions. Instead, they become expert only in their particular function and tend to de-emphasize the importance of other functions. Once transferred from a functional position to an executive job, a manager may emphasize the function from which he originally came. A former sales executive who becomes the president of a company often remains concerned with sales and neglects his over-all management functions. This, of course, is not really a shortcoming of departmentalization; it is the fault of the executive. However, departmentalization can easily lead to this particular kind of managerial preoccupation.

MODIFICATION OF FUNCTIONAL DEPARTMENTALIZATION

If an organization continues to grow, sooner or later it must modify its functional departmentalization and adopt another system. When should this change be made? A thorough analysis of the organization must occur before such a decision can be made. The amount of sales in itself is an insufficient basis for the decision. A firm doing less than $10 million business a year, for example, might efficiently departmentalize by products or territories rather than by functions. On the other hand, it is interesting to note that in 1920, when General Motors switched from a functional structure to product divisions, its annual sales were in excess of $500 million.

Departmentalization by Product

When functional departments become obsolete, management may turn to departmentalization by products. In this scheme each product or group of closely related products in a product line is established as a relatively autonomous, integrated unit within the company. Emphasis shifts from the function to the product to be manufactured and sold.

Under product departmentalization an executive is in charge of and responsible for *all* activities relating to a particular product — manufacture, sales, service, and engineering. It is of no importance where the division is located, whether it is close to the home office or geographically far removed; the division is organized around a product and not a territory.

Product departmentalization divides a large company into smaller and more flexible administrative units. Such units recapture some of the advantages of a smaller functional organization that disappear when the functional organization grows to a large size. An emphasis on products encourages expansion, improvement, and diversification. There is no doubt that in a functional organization certain products receive more emphasis than others. Although such emphasis is perfectly normal and understandable, it may harm some of the products, particularly those which require more promotion and more sales effort in order to achieve their place in the market. Problems of this sort are more easily resolved in a product division.

Examples

Let us assume that our hypothetical firm now manufactures plastic as well as metal and wood furniture. Having decided to departmentalize on a product basis, the organization takes the form indicated by Figure 11-3, with each product grouping now coordinated at the divisional level. The president retains his own centralized advisory groups, which help him in the over-all management of the enterprise. Product departmentalization has proved successful in all functional areas except labor relations, finance, and the like. Since the labor relations department may deal with large national unions, it is essential that it remain centralized. For obvious reasons, it is also desirable that the president and top management should control financial management. Similarly, market research and research and development should be located on the corporate level. Operating as staff groups, men involved in

Figure 11-3. Product Departmentalization

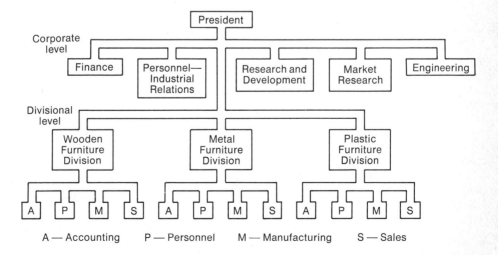

A — Accounting   P — Personnel   M — Manufacturing   S — Sales

these activities can lend valuable assistance to all divisions as well as perform needed research functions for the corporation as a whole.

An organization should consider departmentalizing by products if the characteristics of the manufacturing, engineering, and selling of the particular products lend themselves to it. Each product should be suitable for separation from other products and should be optimized by its own production facilities and sales organization. The various divisions of General Motors — Buick, Cadillac, Chevrolet, and the others — remain among the best-known examples of product departmentalization. The Du Pont Company is another excellent example of an enterprise that, around 1921, decided that product expansion and diversification could best be facilitated by grouping its departments or divisions along principal product lines. Within each division, production, sales, and research are established as line functions. The managers of these three functions are on the same level and report directly to the general manager of the individual product division.

Other leading companies also are organized by product division. All department stores, for example, organize each department along merchandise lines. One finds the same product departmentalization, so to speak, in commercial banks. Their loan activities, for example, are broken down into separate departments for commercial, personal, and industrial uses.

This departmental grouping can at times lead to coordination difficulties within the organization structure. Perhaps a successful manager of a product division will try to enlarge his empire by acquiring more and more power. Dangers of this sort can be prevented by the existence of a general staff, by centralization of finances, and by major policy determination by the top management of the enterprise. This, broadly speaking, is the arrangement at General Motors Corporation, Du Pont, and other large enterprises: decentralized product divisions with centralized control — particularly of financial matters — at headquarters.

Geographic Departmentalization

Another way to departmentalize is by territories. This type of organization is frequently used by physically dispersed enterprises where the various branches produce the same good or perform similar services at each location. For example, the United States Postal Service and the Federal Reserve System are departmentalized by territories. In all twelve Federal Reserve districts and in all post offices, basically the same functions are performed.

Advantages

Private businesses use geographic departmentalization for several reasons. Often the needs of the customers or the characteristics of the product demand it. There is little doubt that territorial departmentalization serves the local markets with greatest efficiency. It permits managers to consider particular local circumstances that might be overlooked if activities were functionally departmentalized at headquarters. It also permits the utilization of local salespeople who are familiar with local conditions. Furthermore, territorial departmentalization produces certain economies. It reduces the cost of transporting raw materials to the plant and finished products to the customer. It cuts delivery time. In addition, geographical groups supply a good training ground for versatile managerial talent. Because territorially departmentalized enterprises perform almost all functions in all territories, a manager's experience will be well rounded. Figure 11-4 shows an organization departmentalized on a geographical basis.

It is top management's responsibility to balance the advantages derived from geographic departmentalization against the additional expenses involved. This kind of departmentalization has obvious advantages for companies engaged in the insurance, telephone, railroad, and oil industries. Geographic decentralization is also important where perishability is a problem, as in the processed food industry. The advantages of geographic departmentalization are particularly important in production and sales, and therefore they are often handled in this manner. In contrast, there seems to be little reason to departmentalize finances on a territorial basis. As a matter of fact, financial management succeeds best if it remains centralized at

Figure 11-4. Geographic Departmentalization

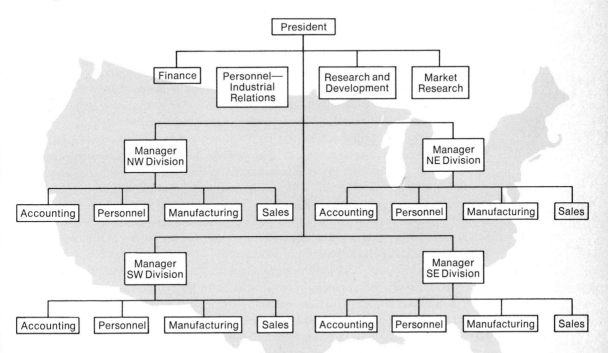

headquarters. The same reasoning holds for the over-all personnel function and, generally, for industrial relations. Of course, each region has its own local personnel and finance staff in addition to the centralized staff at headquarters.

Although top management at the home office often decides that each region within the country should be a self-contained unit with its own facilities for production, sales, and all other auxiliary functions, management may decide to departmentalize only one of the functions on a territorial basis. Sales, for instance, are almost universally organized along geographical lines. Most firms divide the country into sales territories, and all selling activities are regulated accordingly. In such cases, other functions, such as production, personnel, and finance, remain centralized.

Departmentalization by Customer

Management can also base its groups on customer consideration, thereby showing its paramount interest in the welfare of its customers and in the attention given to them. There are many examples of organizations departmentalized along customer lines, such as a university whose night programs and day programs comply with the requests and special needs of its various "customers." Department stores are often partially departmentalized by customer as well as by product. Many stores maintain budget departments that carry a full line of merchandise, but of a different quality and at a lower price. Then, again, customers may be classified by age, as are the clientele of the teen shop in a department store. Manufacturers of motors, likewise, may distinguish among industrial users, distributors, and institutional customers.

Sales activity is often the function best suited to departmentalization on a customer basis. A salesman who calls on industrial users is better qualified to deal with them than if he were also to call on distributors and institutional customers. The various groups of customers have different needs to which the enterprise must cater. However, the production function of an enterprise should not necessarily be departmentalized in a similar manner. It is unlikely that a manufacturer of electric motors would differentiate in his line between motors bought by industrial users, distributors, or other customers, although he might manufacture different types of motors to suit each set of customers. There is also little likelihood that the over-all finance function would be broken down along customer lines. However, derivative finance functions such as consumer credit are separated as distinct activities. The General Electric Credit Corporation is an example.

The advantages of customer departmentalization also bring with them disadvantages. Additional problems of coordination arise, for instance. Frequently there will be pressure for special treatment and special consideration for certain customers. Also, customer departmentalization may result in the underutilization of some company facilities. In some instances the disadvantages of customer departmentalization are overshadowed by the advantages; an enterprise has much to gain by catering to the special and individual needs of its customers.

Departmentalization by Process and Equipment

Activities can also be grouped according to the process involved or the equipment used. This form of departmentalization, often employed in manufacturing enterprises, can often bring great economic advantage. For instance, in order to achieve maximum economy, it might be necessary to run a particular piece of equipment around the clock. Blast furnaces in steel mills must be kept in constant operation. The decision to departmentalize by process or equipment is usually made on the basis of cost, that is, on the basis of economic considerations.

Departmentalization by Time

Another common practice is to departmentalize according to time. Enterprises such as hospitals and public utilities, which function around the clock, often organize activities on this basis. Everyone is familiar with the second or night shift. Undoubtedly, functions performed at these hours are similar to or the same as those performed during the regular day shift. Nevertheless, such groupings create serious organizational questions. How self-contained should each shift be? What relationships should exist between regular and special shift executives?

A COMPOSITE ORGANIZATION STRUCTURE

Departmentalization is not an end in itself; it must lead to the realization of enterprise objectives and permit coordination. To achieve this, management often uses more than one method of departmentalization, thereby ending up with a mixed structure. Because each method of departmentalization has its advantages and disadvantages, management must balance the gains derived from one kind against the disadvantages of another.

It is possible, for instance, that an organization may organize its selling function first by territories and then, farther down the line, by customers. A large enterprise producing office machinery could conceivably break up its Manhattan sales activities in the following manner: The downtown office calls on banks and brokers; another office handles insurance companies; a midtown office is for the textile and retail trade; and an uptown office serves the petroleum, manufacturing, and transportation industries. Or a divisional sales department may be organized along customer lines and at lower levels along territorial lines. Any mixture is perfectly acceptable as long as it fulfills the purpose of the enterprise.

Figure 11-5 shows a company that has been departmentalized by functions at the primary level. On the intermediate level, production has been departmentalized by products and sales by territory. On the next level, the production function has been departmentalized by the process and equipment used. The territorially grouped sales districts have been further regrouped along narrower territorial lines and, at the lowest level, have been departmentalized by customer — industrial users,

Figure 11-5. Composite Departmentalization

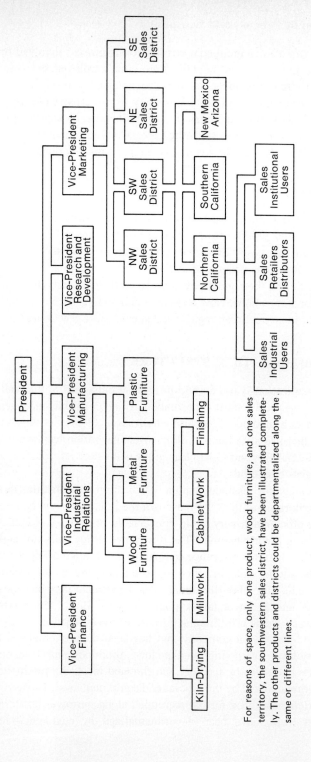

For reasons of space, only one product, wood furniture, and one sales territory, the southwestern sales district, have been illustrated completely. The other products and districts could be departmentalized along the same or different lines.

retailers and distributors, and institutional users. Figure 11-5, then, shows a hybrid structure with departmentalization along function, product, process and equipment, territorial, and customer lines.

Discussion Questions

1. Departmentalization is the practical manifestation of the span of management. If spans were purposefully made wide, few departments would exist in a particular organization. This being the case, how would coordination be achieved?

2. One authority observed, "Departments establish artificial boundaries in organizations. The best we can expect from them is the encouragement of empire building." Do you agree or disagree? Why?

Supplementary Readings

Barnard, Chester I. "The Theory of Authority." In *Dimensions in Modern Management,* edited by Patrick E. Connor. Boston: Houghton Mifflin, 1974.

Davis, Ralph Currier. *The Fundamentals of Top Management.* New York: Harper and Row, 1951. See pp. 263–66.

Price, James L. *Organizational Effectiveness.* Homewood, Ill.: Irwin, 1968. See pp. 24–30.

Weber, Max. "The Three Types of Legitimate Rule." In *Dimensions in Modern Management.*

Woodward, Joan. *Industrial Organization: Theory and Practice.* London: Oxford University Press, 1965. See pp. 109–11.

CHAPTER 12

Organizational Authority: The Classical View

Authority is a difficult concept and one which we should lead into gently. It has many interpretations, including the one adopted in this chapter: Authority is an attribute of a managerial position in an organization. Authority in this case is an impersonal feature of the organizing activity, indispensable as a means of achieving coordination. This is a traditional view, but one that is useful because it promotes an understanding of processes such as delegation and notions such as the unity of command.

Authority is also a method of achieving influence. Legitimacy, power, and leadership are important dimensions of the authority concept. We shall consider them when we present the influencing function in Part V.

Every successful manager knows that coercion provides a poor means of inducing subordinates to perform their duties. In practice many managers speak now about their "responsibility" or "tasks" and "duties," not about their authority to punish. In a loose sense, semantics thereby allows management to avoid the big stick.

Our attention in this chapter focuses on the authority that is associated with position, role, or function in the organization — authority that can be delegated. Expertness in a given field and personal qualities or attractiveness of an individual yield other forms of authority that cannot be delegated.

THE SOURCE AND NATURE OF AUTHORITY

Early students of management took authority for granted and had little doubt about its nature, purpose, and origin. To them it was a necessary building stone in the formation of an organization. Henri Fayol spoke of authority as "the right to give orders and the power to exact obedience."[1] He went on to say that authority was not to be conceived of apart from the sanctions, rewards, or penalties which go with the exercise of power. However, since Fayol's time, two different views of the nature and source of authority have arisen. One is called the formal authority theory and the other is known as the acceptance theory of authority.

---

[1] Henri Fayol, *General and Industrial Management*, trans. Constance Storrs (London: Pitman, 1949), p. 21.

Formal Authority Theory

The formal authority theory is a top-down theory since it traces the delegation of authority downward from basic social institutions to top management to subordinates (see Figure 12-1). Even the president of a company receives his authority from the board of directors who, in turn, receive their authority from the owners or the stockholders. In formal theory, the ultimate source of managerial authority in America is the Constitutional guarantee of the institution of private property: "Under our democratic form of government the right upon which managerial authority is based has its source in the Constitution of the United States through the guaranty of private property. Since the Constitution is the creature of the people, subject to amendment and modification by the will of the people, it follows that society, through government, is the source from which authority flows to ownership and then to management."[2]

Figure 12-1. Flow of Delegated Authority

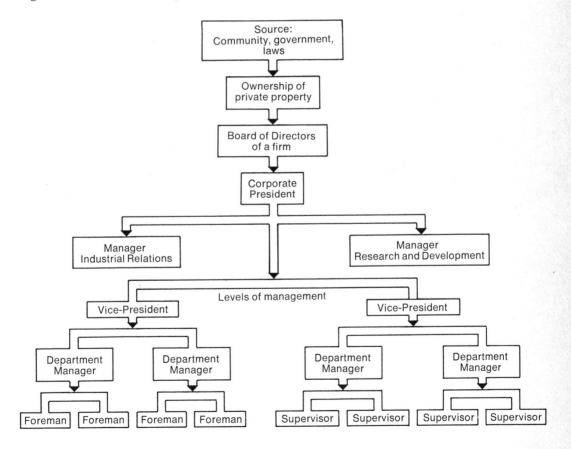

[2] Elmore Peterson and E. Grosvenor Plowman, *Business Organization and Management,* 4th ed. (Homewood, Ill.: Irwin, 1958), pp. 84–85.

Acceptance Theory

A large group of writers do not agree with the formal authority theory. Their position, summarized in the following definition, stresses the acceptance theory of authority:

Authority is the relationship that exists between individuals when one accepts the directive of another as authoritative, that is, when the individual receiving the directive weighs the consequences of accepting it against the consequences of rejecting it, and decides in favor of acceptance. The authoritative nature of the directive is confirmed when the person accepting the directive acts in accordance with it, within the confines of his understanding and ability.[3]

This definition, reflecting a bottom-up approach, is based on the points of view of Chester Barnard, Mary Parker Follett, Herbert Simon, Robert Tannenbaum, and others. They all agree that management's authority is bestowed on it by subordinates. Barnard expresses his "approximate definition of authority" as follows:

Authority is the character of a communication (order) in a formal organization by virtue of which it is accepted by a contributor to or "member" of the organization as governing the action he contributes; that is, as governing or determining what he does or is not to do so far as the organization is concerned. According to this defini-tion, authority involves two aspects: first, the subjective, the personal, the accepting of the communication as authoritative . . . ; and, second, the objective aspect — the character in the communication by virtue of which it is accepted. . . .

If a directive communication is accepted by one to whom it is addressed, its authority for him is confirmed or established. It is admitted as the basis of action. Disobedience of such a communication is a denial of its authority for him. There-fore, under this definition the decision as to whether an order has authority or not lies with the persons to whom it is addressed, and does not reside in "persons of authority" or those who issue these orders.[4]

The key aspect of acceptance theory is that a manager has no effective authority unless and until subordinates confer it upon him. This is essentially Barnard's position. He equates the acceptance of a communication (order) with acceptance of authority. Even though management may have formal authority, this authority is effective only if subordinates accept it. Barnard also states that a subordinate can and will accept a communication as authoritative only when four conditions are met simultaneously: (1) when he can and does understand the communication, (2) when he believes that it is not inconsistent with the purpose of the organization, (3) when he believes it to be compatible with his personal interests as a whole, and (4) when he is able mentally and physically to comply with it.

---

[3] Daniel J. Duffy, "Authority Considered from an Operational Point of View," *Journal of the Academy of Management* 2, no. 3 (December 1959): 167.

[4] Chester I. Barnard, *The Functions of the Executive* (Cambridge, Mass.: Harvard University Press, 1938), p. 163.

Barnard maintains that each individual possesses "a zone of indifference," which is extremely important to acceptance theory. An order in this zone will be accepted without conscious question. Such orders fall within the range of requests and duties that were generally anticipated by the subordinate when he accepted employment. As long as this is the case, the subordinate will see the orders as acceptable and will comply with the authority which initiated them (see Figure 12-2).

Figure 12-2. Expectations, Communications, and Acceptance of Authority

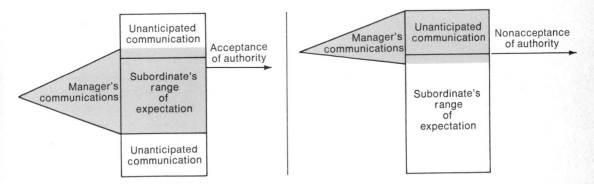

Proponents of the acceptance theory look at authority without considering its sanctions, thereby dismissing the concept of power. This is logically correct but is not the whole story. Authority and power are distinct but related management concepts. Whereas authority may be based on acceptance by subordinates, power is derived from control of resources. It is impossible to conceive of any management situation in which either authority or power is totally absent in superior-subordinate relationships. All theorists agree that authority is one of the foundation stones of organization and probably its key:

The concepts started with authority being placed in one person who then delegated it downward to other persons who acted for him in various capacities. The influence of the military command can be seen here. The next step was the idea that authority was connected with the work to be done and appeared throughout the organization as a necessity for the accomplishment of tasks. Finally, we arrive at the notion that authority does not exist unless it is effectively executed and that it is therefore something which is granted by a subordinate to his superior or to someone else. Thus the meaning of the word has come full circle. While all these concepts are valuable to our understanding of the subject of administration or management, they have certainly stretched the meaning of one word to its limits.[5]

[5] Merten J. Mandeville, "The Nature of Authority," *Journal of the Academy of Management* 3, no. 2 (August 1960): 117.

Several decades ago, Henri Fayol called attention to the fact that a "distinction must be made between a manager's official authority deriving from office and personal authority, compounded of intelligence, experience, moral worth, ability to lead, past services, etc. In the makeup of a good head personal authority is the indispensable complement of official authority."[6] Merten Mandeville suggests taking the slight liberty of substituting the word "leadership" for the term "personal authority."[7] This does not alter the meaning of Fayol's writing but indicates that Fayol recognized the difference between leadership and authority.

Mandeville concludes that the arguments and confusion concerning the nature of authority arise from different ways of looking at organization. Should an organization be considered a structure built to achieve some objective or "a dynamic aggregation of social beings"?

We share with Mandeville the opinion that when behaviorists discuss authority, they probably mean not authority but leadership or influence: "The nature of authority seems to be the right to see that tasks are accomplished. There is something more fundamental in the concept of 'authority' than the inclination of someone to work or not to work for an organization."[8] The "something else" is probably a mixture including the acceptance by subordinates of their superior, the power of the superior to give rewards and impose sanctions, and the responsibility of the superior to do an effective job. A realistic appraisal of any managerial roles must include these elements of authority.

Limits of Authority

There are limitations to the authority a manager can derive from his position, some stemming from internal and others from external sources. Among external limits are codes, mores and folkways, and laws. Over time, many legal, political, ethical, social, and economic considerations also have limited the concept of authority. The laws referring to collective bargaining and the establishment of labor unions, for instance, clearly limit managerial authority. Contractual obligations such as statements of management's role in handling workers' complaints and grievances impose further limitations.

Articles of incorporation and by-laws set internal limits on the authority of officers. An executive's authority is also restricted by the enterprise's objectives, policies, procedures, and programs. Furthermore, most managers are subject to the specific internal limitations of their positions, spelled out in the assignment of duties and delegation of authority. For example, a branch manager of a manufacturing plant may have been given the authority to make capital expenditures up to five thousand dollars, whereas a local warehouse manager is limited to one hundred dollars. Generally, the scope of authority becomes more limited as one

---

[6] Fayol, *General and Industrial Management*, p. 21.
[7] Mandeville, "The Nature of Authority," p. 111.
[8] *Ibid.*, p. 118.

descends the management hierarchy, as shown in Figure 12-3. This pattern reinforces the tapering concept of authority.

DELEGATION OF AUTHORITY

No subordinates and hence no organization can exist without the delegation of authority. By delegating, management vests subordinates with portions of its own authority, thereby creating levels and degrees of authority. However, delegation does not mean surrender. Management always retains its over-all authority to perform its functions. Instead, delegation grants the authority to subordinates to operate within prescribed limits.

The Scalar Chain

Through the dynamics of delegation, authority is distributed throughout an organization. In a corporation the president, although subject to the higher authority of the board of directors and the stockholders, is, for all practical purposes, the single source from which authority is transmitted to the rest of the organization. The line

Figure 12-3. Tapering Authority

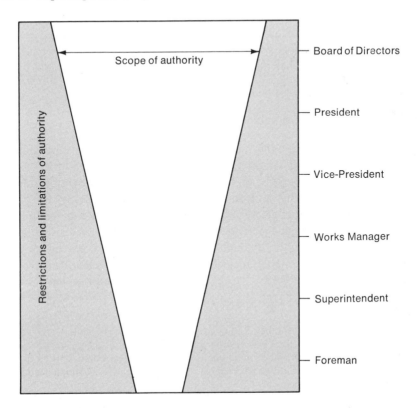

of vertical authority relationships from superior to subordinate throughout the organization is commonly called the scalar chain.

"The scalar chain is the chain of superiors ranging from the ultimate authority to the lowest ranks. The line of authority is the route followed — via every link in the chain — by all communications which start from or go to the ultimate authority. This path is dictated both by the need for some transmission and by the principle of unity of command, but it is not always the swiftest."[9] However, the chain of command must be understood and followed or else authority might be undermined, thereby ultimately jeopardizing organizational effectiveness.

Unity of Command

Except in instances of shared authority and applications of functional authority to be discussed later, the delegation of authority flows on a one-to-one basis. That is, a subordinate is accountable only to the superior from whom he receives his authority and to no one else. This is known as unity of command.[10]

The unity of command principle is highly regarded by classical theorists because it provides one of the major avenues to coordination. Through unity of command, responsibility for coordination can be pinpointed; people are not confused by having two bosses; lines of accountability are clear. Figure 12-4 contrasts two situations, one with unity of command and the other without it.

Ever since biblical times, people have observed that it is difficult to serve two masters. Such a situation often leads to confusion of authority and results in unsatisfactory performance by the subordinate. The subordinate does not know which of his two superiors has the authority to delegate duties to him and which duties take precedence.

The Effect of Delegation on Organizational Growth

Delegation is the force underlying the vertical growth of an organization. The extent to which management delegates authority — how much or how little — is important. A manager who delegates authority freely tends to create an organization with decentralized authority, and one who delegates little authority tends to create a centralized organization. Notice that the delegation of authority tends to produce a certain result but is not a guarantee. Nonetheless, a management that is not willing to delegate enough authority tends to limit the number of executives and the size of the enterprise, for in order for an organization to grow, management must delegate increasingly more authority. We shall discuss the decentralization of organizations in greater detail in Chapter 14.

[9] Fayol, *General and Industrial Management*, p. 34. Also see James D. Mooney, *The Principles of Organization* (New York: Harper and Row, 1939), pp. 14–15.

[10] The unity of command principle is discussed in several other contexts in this book, in connection with line authority relationships. The frequent mention of this principle emphasizes its importance to management.

Figure 12-4. The Unity of Command Principle

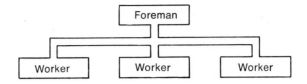

Unity of command: Each subordinate has only one superior, the foreman.

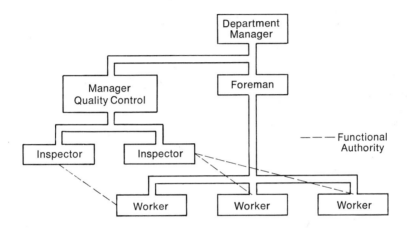

Violation of unity of command: Each worker is respon-sible for an aspect of his work to the Quality Control Department, provided this department has functional authority over the line. Workers are also responsible to their foreman.

THE PROCESS OF DELEGATION

William H. Newman notes three chief and inseparably interrelated aspects of the delegation of authority: (1) the assignment of duties by an executive to his immediate subordinates; (2) the granting of permission (authority) to make commitments, use resources, and take all actions which are necessary to perform the duties; and (3) the creation of an obligation (responsibility) on the part of each subordinate to the delegating executive to perform the duties satisfactorily.[11]

Assignment of Duties

When assigning duties, a manager must decide how to allocate work among sub-ordinates in order to achieve a balance between an effective span of management and

[11] William H. Newman, *Administrative Action*, 2d ed. (Englewood Cliffs, N.J.: Prentice-Hall, 1963), pp. 185–86.

a reasonable number of managerial levels. In checking his own functions and duties, the manager will see which ones he can delegate to others and which he cannot. Some duties are so routine that they could be done best by another. Other functions can be delegated only to subordinates who possess the skill to perform them effectively. Still other functions cannot be delegated at all and must be done by the manager himself. Some decisions will not be so clear cut; a number of management duties could fall into any of the three groups. In these cases, the decision to allocate a specific duty to a subordinate will often depend on management's general attitude and the number and quality of the subordinates available.

Granting Authority

Newman postulates that the second aspect in the process of delegation is the granting of authority to make commitments, use resources, and take actions necessary to perform allocated duties. In this stage, management confers upon the subordinate the right to act and to make decisions within a limited area. Naturally, it is necessary for management to determine the scope of authority to be delegated to a subordinate. This scope depends on the area of authority that top management itself possesses and is intrinsically related to the duties assigned to the subordinate. Any change in those duties will necessitate a change in the scope of authority. The scope of authority delegated to a subordinate should be adequate for the successful performance of the assigned duties.

When management grants authority, it must remember that such authority needs to be intrinsically and directly related to the duties assigned to a subordinate and the results expected from him. Management must make sure that it has delegated enough authority so that the subordinate is able to obtain the results expected from him. The subordinate, on the other hand, can be expected to accept responsibility only for the functions encompassed by his authority. If he is given more authority than he needs, loose management will result.

It is obvious that the scope of authority of each subordinate must be clear in order to have clear lines of organizational authority. It is not enough that clarity exists in the mind of the delegating executive; the scope must be just as clear to all managers involved. Ambiguous authority often leads to reduced performance. Charts, manuals, and job descriptions aid considerably in management's clarifying endeavors.

Preferably, a delegating executive sets down in writing the scope of delegated authority, for this will provide a clear guide at all times. However, having done so, the executive's duties are not finished. He still is obliged to check from time to time to see whether the subordinate is keeping within his delegated limits. As conditions and circumstances change and as duties are reassigned, additional clarification and interpretations of the scope of authority might become necessary.

It must be remembered that duties are assigned and authority is delegated not to people but to positions within the enterprise. Unless these positions are manned by people, however, the assignments and the delegation of authority are meaningless. That is why one commonly speaks of the delegation of authority to subordinates instead of the delegation of authority to subordinate positions.

Specific or General Delegation

Management must recognize the nature of a particular organizational situation before determining whether to delegate authority specifically or generally. Very often the nature of the task that must be performed is a decisive factor in the decision. For example, management can delegate authority specifically if a task is routine and requires little skill like digging in a gravel pit or working on an automotive assembly line. However, if the task is that of a research physicist, management may wish to delegate authority generally, thereby giving scope to the full range of that physicist's talents.

There are times when the scope of authority cannot be made very specific even though specificity may be desirable. This is particularly true in a new enterprise or in a new venture within an existing organization. In such cases, management itself might not fully realize the scope of a new activity and it therefore would not know how much authority to delegate. However, once the task has begun to take shape, conferences clarifying the nature of authority can be encouraged.

The Exception Principle

The scope of delegated authority defines the area within which a manager has decision-making responsibility. If situations arise outside his scope, he must refer these exceptional problems upward, thereby conforming to what is commonly known as the exception principle.

This principle is often overused. Incompetent and insecure managers often attempt to refer too many exceptions upward. By doing so, they weaken the delegation of authority. Sometimes top management is tempted to make a decision in an area where it has delegated the decision-making authority. Even though it may have formerly made decisions in this area, management must now refrain from making such decisions unless dealing with an exceptional problem.

Shared and Splintered Authority

Management may at times delegate joint authority to two or three subordinates, because it may want the decisions in a given situation to be shared by them. For example, the president of a corporation might want the vice-president in charge of production, the sales manager, and the chief engineer to decide jointly which products will be carried in the product line for the coming year. In many respects, shared authority is the wave of the future, particularly in space-age industries.

In addition to shared authority, the concept of splintered authority is frequently found in organizations. This concept reflects a situation in which an individual manager possesses all the authority he needs to make decisions within his own department but faces a problem that bridges more than one department. In order to solve this particular problem, several managers pool their decision-making authority.

Revoking of Delegated Authority

Management always has the right to revoke whatever it has delegated. As activities change, authority relationships often need realignment and reorganization. This often means that management must revoke authority and either exercise the revoked authority itself or redelegate it. Management may even delegate more authority if circumstances demand it. Naturally, such realigning and reshuffling of authority should not take place too often. Most people in an organization can understand the necessity for reassigning authority from time to time, but if this happens too frequently they will become demoralized.

Delegation by Results Expected

When management states exactly what it expects, when it expects it done, and by whom, it is said to delegate authority by the results expected. Naturally, it is management's responsibility to make certain that a subordinate knows the results expected of him. Edward Schleh points out the significant advantages that delegation by results will produce:[12] (1) It produces real accomplishment by a subordinate instead of "spinning wheels." (2) Through it, management can set up job standards to provide a basis for judging performance and can establish a system of controls. (3) It helps to minimize politics in an enterprise. If expected results have been clearly laid out and standards to measure them defined, some tangible record of performance is available to judge an individual's contribution to the organization.

Responsibility

The third major aspect of delegating authority mentioned by Newman is the creation of an obligation to perform assigned duties satisfactorily. The acceptance of such an obligation by an individual creates responsibility. Without responsibility, the process of delegating authority is not complete. Therefore, the concepts of responsibility and authority are closely related, as the substitution of such expressions as delegating responsibility or carrying out a responsibility for duty, task, activity, or authority indicates.

Responsibility is the obligation to perform a duty or carry out granted authority. The essence of responsibility is obligation. By accepting employment, by accepting the obligation to perform assigned duties, an individual implies the acceptance of his responsibility. In other words, responsibility results from a contractual agreement in which a person agrees to perform certain duties in return for certain rewards.

[12] Edward C. Schleh, *Successful Executive Action* (Englewood Cliffs, N.J.: Prentice-Hall, 1956), pp. 19–33.

Responsibility may be a continuing process, or it may be terminated by the accomplishment of a single action. The relation between the president of a corporation and the works manager is an example of continuing responsibility. On the other hand, the responsibilities existing between the president and someone from outside the firm hired to spend some time evaluating the salary structure of the company will be terminated when the study is finished and recommendations are made.

Accountability

In addition to the concept of responsibility, some writers have employed the concept of *accountability*. Although this term is largely used by the military, where to be accountable means to keep accurate and adequate records and to safeguard public property, the term is also used by a few writers in the area of management who distinguish between it and responsibility. Only the term responsibility will be used in this text, although "being accountable" is at times relevant and therefore used in the discussion of control.

Authority and Responsibility

As we have already noted, authority and responsibility should be commensurate. Inequality between delegated authority and responsibility produces undesirable results. If authority exceeds responsibility, a misuse of authority can easily occur. On the other hand, embarrassment and frustration can only be the result if one accepts responsibility without adequate authority to take the necessary actions to perform required duties and fulfill obligations.

In some situations, however, authority and responsibility cannot be equalized. For instance, in emergencies executives often exceed the bounds of their authority without criticism. Sometimes managers are delegated authority for a task for which they cannot be entirely responsible. Consider the case of a sales manager. He is often given the authority to sell the entire output of a factory and is required to accept the responsibility for obtaining the planned sales volume. He has accepted responsibility for something for which he cannot be held responsible. He cannot compel customers to buy. He cannot foresee changes in economic conditions or unexpected maneuvers by competitors that may greatly affect sales. The sales manager has accepted responsibility to use all material and human resources available to him to obtain the best results possible. He can be held responsible only for making his best effort, not for more.

The need for balance between authority and responsibility is widely recognized. However, it must be applied with discretion, and from time to time it has been questioned. Urwick, although generally advocating the principle of parity between authority and responsibility, agrees with Barnard that at times individuals are placed in a position where they have responsibility but cannot have authority.[13] Often

[13] Lyndall F. Urwick, *Notes on the Theory of Organization* (New York: American Management Association, 1952), pp. 51–52.

executives wish for subordinates who are more willing to assume responsibility. Dalton McFarland believes these executives are actually inviting their subordinates to bid for authority that they have not yet seen fit to grant them and to accept responsibility that they have not yet been asked to assume.[14]

FUNCTIONAL AUTHORITY

We will conclude this chapter with a final important concept, that of functional authority. Although functional authority is a classical idea, it is often misunderstood and misapplied. It is one of the more difficult ideas to group in the analysis of authority relationships. Functional authority can be defined as the authority delegated to an activity (or its staff) that gives members of the activity the right to command. This right is based on the members' expertise in a narrow area of specialization such as quality control. The delegation of functional authority enables managers to exercise control over those who are not their subordinates. However, authority granted in this manner is confined to the specialized area for which it was delegated.

A simple chart, Figure 12-5, reflects the relationships brought about by the delegation of functional authority in a production department. The chart shows that the quality control manager through his inspectors has functional authority over the work of foremen in other departments. This means that if the quality inspectors find an operation "out of control" they can require that operation's foreman to suspend production until the problem is corrected.

Functional Authority Versus Unity of Command

There is no doubt that functional authority violates the principle of unity of command by introducing a second superior for one particular element of work (see Figure 12-5). Although functional authority is often called "limited authority," this is a misnomer; a person either has authority or he does not. Functional authority gives its holder full right and power to command — but in a restricted and specialized area.

Either line or staff personnel can assume functional authority. However, such authority is usually conferred upon a staff man because of his knowledge of specialized subjects such as engineering, law, accounting, packaging, and design. Functional authority given to a line officer is known as functional line authority; that given to a staff man is known as functional staff authority.

Functional Staff Authority

Personnel

One of the duties of an organization's personnel staff is to oversee union contracts, interpreting clauses and implementing grievance procedures. This staff guides,

---

[14] Dalton E. McFarland, *Management Principles and Practices* (New York: Macmillan, 1958), p. 217.

Figure 12-5. Functional Authority

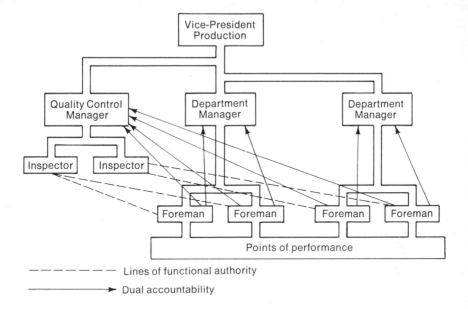

Vice-President
Production

Quality Control
Manager

Department
Manager

Department
Manager

Inspector   Inspector

Foreman   Foreman   Foreman   Foreman

Points of performance

— — — — — — Lines of functional authority

————————▶ Dual accountability

counsels, and advises management on the handling of grievances brought before it. However, it generally does not have the authority to decide and settle grievances. Its recommendations are usually incorporated into management decisions issued under the authority of the appropriate line personnel.

However, the president of the organization may decide that, since a particular staff man is an expert in handling grievances, he should decide and settle those grievances and thus ensure uniform interpretation throughout the company. In this case, functional staff authority having been conferred upon the staff personnel expert, he finds that he has full authority to determine whatever settlement he considers appropriate. He is now able to issue a settlement order and sign it in his own name. In other words, in this situation the authority for settling grievances has been conferred by line management upon a member of the staff. Within the limits of the specialized functional area for which authority has been delegated, the staff man's characteristics have been changed completely. He has now been clothed with functional staff authority — authority that formerly belonged to line and line alone.

Although the orders issued by staff managers with functional authority are not really orders but merely representations of management's final decisions, the effect of these orders is the same as if they had come down through the direct channels of command. The line supervisor is responsible for seeing that they are carried out. If he feels that a particular order is wrong or unwise, he may appeal to his senior line executive for a change. Following a more expedient route, he might first see the staff members who issued the order. However, until and unless the order is changed, the line manager is expected to see that it is carried out.

Accounting

Let us consider another example of functional staff authority, this time in a manufacturing enterprise with headquarters in New York and manufacturing plants in St. Louis and Los Angeles. Each of these plants is run by a manager who has been given sufficient authority to take full charge of local operations. He also has full authority over all employees in the plant regardless of the functions they perform. Each plant maintains some separate accounting records and, naturally, the local manager is given full line authority over the accounts in his plant. However, it is the task of the chief accountant at the central office in New York to maintain accounting records for the entire enterprise. In order for him to be able to fulfill his responsibility, he needs the necessary authority. Therefore, the chief executive of the enterprise has conferred upon him the functional staff authority to determine the methods and manner in which the individual plant accountants are to perform their work. Without this authority, he would be unable to ensure consistency in the records of the entire company and might become involved in serious conflicts with local plant managers. For instance, it is conceivable that the accountant in the St. Louis branch might charge depreciation on machinery at a much higher rate than that applied at the Los Angeles plant but at a much lower rate than the one used at headquarters.

In other words, the chief accountant has functional staff authority over the accounting activities in the St. Louis and Los Angeles plants, and the local plant manager has the authority and responsibility to see that the local plant accountants perform their work exactly as prescribed by the chief accountant. This, of course, violates the unity of command principle because the local plant accountants now have two superiors, the chief accountant and the plant manager. However, this disadvantage is offset by the advantages of company-wide standard accounting procedures.

Flow

Generally speaking, functional authority is most effective and expeditious when exercised over the operating line manager most directly concerned, bypassing several intermediate operating layers (see Figure 12-6). However, the senior line executives in these intermediate positions should be kept informed of the delegation decision.

Although this type of delegation is expedient, it can create problems. For instance, a man in a functional unit might need to issue directives to a manager who is actually his superior; thus, recalling our previous example, a vice-president could receive instructions from someone below him in rank who is in charge of accounting procedures. In this situation, a subordinate exercising functional authority is actually using a small portion of his superior's authority. If the individual exercising functional authority is technically competent and if his use of the authority is clearly understood and accepted, the arrangement will succeed. Functional authority can thus provide an effective short cut in accomplishing objectives.

Functional Line Authority

The following example illustrates the concept of functional line authority: In most manufacturing operations product packaging is overseen by the department of production, managed by the manufacturing superintendent and, above him, the vice-president in charge of production. In the phonograph record industry, however, packaging is very important. Since packaging has such an exceptionally strong influence on sales, if the sales manager of a certain record manufacturing company were an expert on modern packaging and design of the covers, he might be assigned packaging authority. The authority so assigned is functional line authority; it enables the sales manager to issue orders to a man not normally his subordinate — the manufacturing superintendent.

Figure 12-6. Flow of Functional Authority

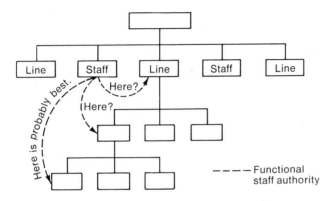

In our example, authority for packaging is ultimately vested in the president of the company. He, in turn, delegates it not to the vice-president in charge of production but to the vice-president in charge of sales. By doing so, he violates the principle of unity of command. However, there are very good reasons why the vice-president in charge of production cannot perform this function as well as the sales manager. His lack of detailed knowledge in this specialized area forced the president to assign the functional authority to the sales manager. It is worth repeating, however, that the sales manager can give orders to the superintendent only within the narrow confines of packaging.

Advantages and Drawbacks

The main advantage of the delegation of functional authority is that it permits maximum effective use of staff specialization. A staff member given functional authority can intervene in line operations at any point that management designates. The price of this advantage is, of course, violation of unity of command. This drawback may indeed cause real frictions in some organizations. However, many feel that giving staff direct authority in restricted areas of line performance contributes more to efficiency and coordination than it detracts.

The problem that functional authority poses — conflict between the principles of unity of command and of specialization — has no general solution. Often the way this problem is solved depends on a particular company's technology. Woodward[15] indicates that large, relatively labor-intensive firms are likely to emphasize unity of command over functional authority, whereas firms requiring a high degree of automation are likely to stress the reverse.

This completes our discussion of the classical concepts of authority. The next chapter shows how these concepts are translated into organizational structures.

Discussion Questions

1. A foreman in a manufacturing company was heard to say: "These guys from the production control department come down here, restudy jobs, and change job standards. Then they walk away and leave us to sell our men on the idea they should work harder to make the same money." What problem in organizational authority is bothering this foreman?

2. If you have ever had to delegate authority, what rules did you use in determining what you would delegate and what you would retain?

Supplementary Readings

Avots, Ivars. "Why Does Project Management Fail?" In *Dimensions in Modern Management,* edited by Patrick E. Connor. Boston: Houghton Mifflin, 1974.

Carlisle, Howard M. "Are Functional Organizations Becoming Obsolete?" In *Dimensions in Modern Management.*

Nisbet, Robert A. *The Sociological Tradition.* New York: Basic Books, 1966. See chapter 4.

Pfiffner, John M., and Frank P. Sherwood. *Administrative Organization.* Englewood Cliffs, N.J.: Prentice-Hall, 1965. See pp. 74–80.

Scott, William G., and Terence R. Mitchell. *Organization Theory.* Homewood, Ill.: Irwin, 1972. See chapter 12.

[15] Joan Woodward, *Industrial Organization: Theory and Practice* (London: Oxford University Press, 1965), ch. 7. This chapter deals with the general problems of line-staff relationships and gives considerable attention to functional authority as it is related to technology.

CHAPTER 13

Organizational Structure

In this chapter and the next we explore common organizational structures. These structures are, of course, the practical result of the organizing process by which management attempts to achieve useful relationships among functions and levels of authority. This chapter deals with the two structures encountered most frequently in business — the line organization and the line and staff organization.

THE LINE ORGANIZATION

The simplest of all organizational relationships assumes the line form. In this form, a primary chain of command exists, extending from chief executive to subordinate. Inseparable from this chain of command is the authority carried along the same chain. Thus, the path of line authority refers to the line of command extending from a superior to his subordinate. The scalar principle states that within an organization the line of superior-subordinate relationships runs from the top of the organization to the bottom. Figure 13-1 shows a direct line of authority from the board of directors to the president of a corporation, to the vice-president in charge of production, to the plant manager, and from him to the superintendent, to the foreman, and finally to the workers.

Figure 13-1. Chain of Command

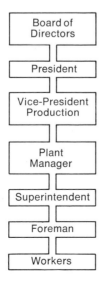

This uninterrupted line of authority from the president to the foreman permits any superior to exercise direct command over his subordinate. Likewise each subordinate obeys only one superior. Line authority, therefore, is the authority to give orders, to command. It is the authority to direct others to implement decisions, plans, policies, and goals. The primary purpose of line authority is to make the organization work by evoking action from subordinates.

This structure is found in all military organizations and is sometimes called military line authority. It has the advantage of clarity: Each subordinate knows whose orders he has to obey and to whom he can, in turn, give orders. It also has the advantage of directness and unity; results can be achieved precisely and quickly. There is no doubt about who has authority over whom and who is responsible for what.

The Primary Lines

Thus far we have been using the phrase "*the* line organization." More precisely, however, we should say "line organizations" because three primary lines exist: There is a line for the creation (of goods or services) function, one for distribution, and one for finance. Each represents a basic function and has its own chain of command.

The division of line authority into three parts served well when organizations were less complex than they are today. Now, however, activities have become so specialized and complicated that the simple line structure is no longer adequate.

Growth of the Line Organization

Organizational line structure can grow in two directions, vertically and horizontally. Vertical growth occurs through the delegation of authority; horizontal growth occurs through the division of labor. Take, for example, the business of furniture refinishing. It requires removing the old finish, sanding the bare surface, applying coats of oil or varnish, and finally waxing and polishing. One person can do this job, but if many pieces are to be done on a continuing basis, several specialists would be more

Figure 13-2. Horizontal Growth

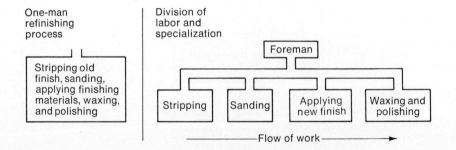

Figure 13-3. Levels of Authority and Specialization

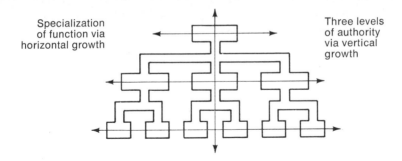

Specialization of function via horizontal growth

Three levels of authority via vertical growth

efficient. Thus, if specialization were to be introduced we would have a process of horizontal growth whose nature resembles the diagram in Figure 13-2. The degree of horizontal growth or specialization can proceed until further work division becomes uneconomical.

However, a line organization is the product of the division of labor and the delegation of authority acting concurrently. Therefore, the typical organization is a combination of levels of authority and functional specialization on each level (see Figure 13-3).

THE LINE AND STAFF ORGANIZATION

A staff organization assists the line in performing its functions. The addition of staff specialists to a line organization represents a further horizontal extension of the organization through the division of work.[1]

Ultimately, every line organization reaches a point where specialized staff contributions are required. Because the typical executive — even a chief executive — cannot be a master of all the information necessary for successful decision-making, he hires staff groups to supply technical data and advice. Staff work revolves around the performance of specialized activities, the utilization of technical knowledge, and the creation and distribution of technical information concerning the functions which are important to line management.

Historical Evolution of Staff

Staffs can be found in the history of many organizations. Most followed a similar pattern of development: As the organizations became larger and larger, top management could not possibly fulfill all the demands of its position. It needed the help of others in carrying out its job. A convenient way for management to enlarge its scope

[1] A staff department may have a line or chain of command of its own. Often we speak of primary and secondary lines to distinguish between the chains of command associated with the basic business functions and those associated with staffs, respectively.

was to make use of various kinds of aides. One finds applications of the staff concept in ancient Athens and Rome, in the College of Cardinals, and in the different divisions of the Curia who serve as advisers to the Pope. Today, the President of the United States can call on many staffs. For instance, the Council of Economic Advisers gives staff advice on economic conditions.

The staff concept has also been developed for centuries within European armies. Traces of staff are found as far back as the days of Julius Caesar. The Prussian general staff, conceived in the early nineteenth century by General von Scharnhorst, was created to help commanders in the field handle the many auxiliary functions related to running an army. Many of the ideas developed for this staff are still in use. One of them, the concept of rotating officers between staff and line duties, can be seen in business today. This practice enables staff personnel to have first-hand experience with operating problems and line personnel to learn the advantages of staff assistance. International Business Machines is a prime example of the many companies which follow this idea in the training of their executives.

Evolution of Staff in Business

As a business grows, the chief executive, like his counterparts in other institutions, expands his responsibilities. Because he is the only coordinating officer who can handle certain duties properly and because there probably is no one to whom he can delegate some of his responsibilities, he must do more and more himself. At some point, he will attempt to remedy the situation by introducing subordinate managers into the organization. As time goes on, however, he finds that he has so many people reporting to him that he cannot add any more and give them all adequate attention. He may also discover that he is not able to coordinate available information or plan properly.

Under these conditions the executive may appoint one or more assistants, thus creating a personal staff that will help him to perform duties he cannot delegate. As the enterprise continues to grow, the executive may increase the number of his personal staff assistants. Although these assistants can provide general aid, in all likelihood none of them is well enough qualified to advise and guide the executive in the more difficult aspects of such areas as labor relations and law.

Eventually, the personal staff becomes inadequate. Not only the chief executive but also other managers now seem to need expert advice and guidance on problems of scheduling, operations research, input-output theory, taxes, new concepts of engineering, marketing, and so forth. The foremen need help in recruiting workers, assistance in training them, and advice in handling their complaints and grievances. They need the expertise of skilled technicians to set up quality standards, to schedule production, and to perform many other associated activities.

At this point, specialized staffs are developed within the organization. The chief executive creates staff positions, each in a special field, to provide advice and counsel to any division or member of the organization in need of a particular type of aid. This development is traced in Figure 13-4.

Figure 13-4. The Evolution of Staff

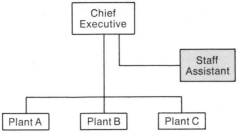

First stage: Personal staff created

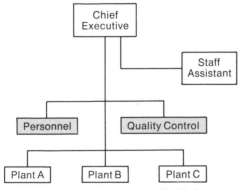

Second stage: Specialized staff added

Role and Authority of Staff

As we have stated, the staff guides, advises, counsels, and serves the line personnel. In reality, the staff does what the chief executive might do himself if he possessed all the necessary special knowledge.

Much of the information and advice that the staff provides flows to the line personnel, and it is their privilege to accept, alter, or reject this advice. Since in most instances staff has been established to provide good counsel and advice, it is usually in the interest of the line manager to follow staff suggestions. However, he is under no obligation to do so. When he does follow the staff suggestions, he transforms them into line commands which are issued under his name as line orders.

Basically, we can see that line and staff possess different authority. Staff authority is not inherently inferior to line authority. Line authority is derived from the chain of command or the organizational hierarchy based on superior-subordinate relationships. Staff authority is based on expertise in specialized activities.

It is conventional, and correct in most instances, to say that "staff authority" provides expert advice and counsel to the managers who have "line authority" but lacks the right to command them. There are two exceptions to this concept of staff authority. First, a manager of a staff department exercises line authority over the subordinates in his department. This relationship provides no real organizational problem since a line within a staff is merely a secondary chain of command attached to a primary line organization. Second, a staff may have functional authority. If this is the case, staff may exercise special, but restricted, command over the line. We discussed this type of functional authority in the last chapter.

Figure 13-5. Company-wide Staff Service

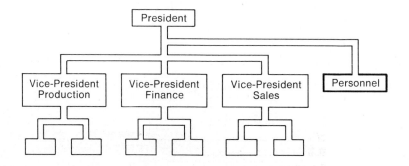

The Functions of Staff

If an organization is large enough, staff work itself becomes differentiated into five functions: service, advice, control, initiation, and innovation.[2]

Service staff groups usually render some specialized function such as maintenance. Their activities are indispensable to the organization, yet they are passive because they must be called into action by others.

Many staff groups, like market research, supply information and may suggest strategies. Such groups are responsible for generating appropriate data on request and on their own. As indicated before, the line has the option to use the data and recommendations or reject them.

Staff also helps to implement the control function. For example, the quality control staff group checks to insure that actual performance meets standards. However, staff performing in this capacity must act after the fact, after action has been initiated by the line.

Some staff groups, like production control or scheduling, set actions into motion rather than monitor results. These staffs aid in synchronizing many activities which contribute to the output of a complex operation such as the assembly of a car.

Finally, some staffs create new ideas. While all staffs may innovate to some extent, certain staffs like those in research and development have innovation as their primary responsibility.

[2] These categories were suggested in Leonard Sayles, *Managerial Behavior* (New York: McGraw-Hill, 1964), ch. 6.

Since staff work is dynamic, the responsibilities of a particular staff may not always remain the same. Indeed, several of the staff groups can extend their influence so that they are not merely passive reactors to the line, but rather active agents of organizational change.

THE RELATION OF STAFF TO LINE

Staff-line relationships involve both structural and human aspects. They are reflected in the three basic problems discussed here: the levels of staff participation in organization, the relationship between line growth and staff growth, and the human relations problem of line and staff.

Figure 13-6. Staff Service to the Basic Business Functions

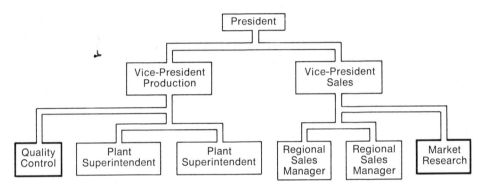

Levels of Staff Participation in the Organization

Company-wide Service

In general, staff groups either perform company-wide service or are in one of the three specialized basic business functions. The personnel department is company-wide in scope. Figure 13-5 shows the personnel staff attached to the line organization between the president and the vice-presidents.

This does not mean that the personnel manager is higher in company rank than the vice-presidents. All it tells us is that the personnel department is available to give service and advice to the manager of each of the line departments. Each such department has problems with which personnel can help. These problems range from the recruitment, selection, and placement of personnel to training, employee service, and wage administration.

Service Within a Function

The other common form of staff participation, service within one of the basic functions of the company, is shown in Figure 13-6. Notice the positions of the staff departments under consideration. The quality control staff is concerned with the maintenance of standards at the point of production. The market research staff gathers data to assist in the development of marketing strategies and programs. The authority of these staff groups does not cut across the entire organization. Rather, their work is limited to the functional area where their specialized knowledge is best utilized.

Corporate and Divisional Service

As organizations grow and relationships become more complex, staff groups can be established both on the corporate and on the divisional level. Figure 13-7 shows three ways in which these groups interrelate. First, it shows that personnel activities at the division level are coordinated by the industrial relations chief at the corporate level. This allows uniform administration of a labor contract, for instance, across the three divisions.

Second, the marketing department on the corporate level can supply consumer research data or coordinate sales efforts in the three divisions or both. This department may assume the pure staff functions of supplying information and advice to the divisions' sales managers. Or in another organization it might have both line and staff roles, coordinating and supervising activities as well as giving information.

Third, although research and development does not have continuous direct relationships with the divisions, its work in areas such as new product development and the improvement of internal operating methods and techniques eventually affects all of them.

Staff Growth Patterns

According to the law of functional growth, as the amount of work in an organization increases, the functional relationships increase at a faster rate. Since staff exists to facilitate line activities, it is reasonable to suppose that after a certain point has been reached in organizational size, the staff will increase at a faster rate than the line.

Research on this matter has not been conclusive. Older studies seem to show that such a tendency holds true. However, more recent research does not support this conclusion. For example, Alan Filley[3] finds that there is no simple relationship between the growth of line and the natural increase of staff. Instead, he sees staff emerging at any point in a company's life span as a result of executive decision-making. Therefore, the addition of staff does not follow some natural law. Instead, it is a product of management decisions that are unique and suited to an organization at a particular time.

[3] Alan C. Filley, "Decisions and Research in Staff Utilization," *Academy of Management Journal* 6 (September 1963): 220–31.

Figure 13-7. Corporate and Divisional Staff Organizations

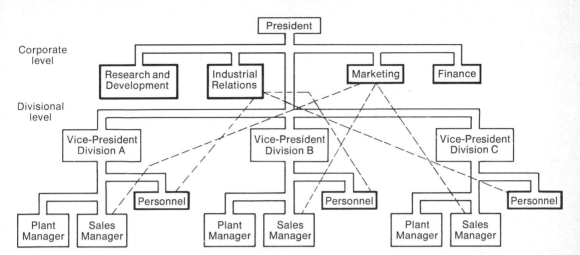

Human Problems of Line-Staff Relations

Although relationships between line and staff have been clearly specified, conflict often arises. In many enterprises, in fact, there is continuous warfare between line managers and staff, sometimes open and sometimes concealed. At times, this antagonism exists in both the higher and the lower echelons of the organization. In all fairness it should be stated that there are also many cases where line and staff work together as a team and solve problems with the greatest amount of cooperation and coordination.

Line Complaints

However, where staff-line conflict does exist, it may diminish the functioning and productivity of the enterprise. How does such conflict arise? One of a line manager's most common complaints is that staff wants to usurp line authority. Another common complaint is that the advice of staff is academic, theoretical, and unrealistic. Line management contends, moreover, that since staff personnel are not responsible for ultimate results, they tend to propose untried and untested ideas. However, line would sometimes willingly put these ideas into effect if the staff would discuss and explain them properly. But such explanations are often expressed so technically that they are difficult for line to understand.

Another complaint is that staff thinks in a vacuum. Line management feels the staff specialist is so involved with his own specialty that he does not think in terms of the objectives of the enterprise as a whole. This complaint is common and at times quite valid. Equally justified are those who point out that line management will be blamed for project failures but staff will try to take the credit for project successes.

Staff Complaints

However, staff people have their case, too. One of the most frequently heard staff complaints is that line management resists new ideas and is not willing to accept the rapid progress of a particular specialty. Another common complaint is that line does not make the proper use of available staff; those line managers who need specialized advice the most often hesitate to ask for it. Such line people seem to think that asking for staff advice is admitting ignorance or defeat. Then, again, staff often complains that some line managers, after going through the motions of asking for advice, reject the suggestions either because they really did not want them in the first place or because they distrust the staff adviser. Another complaint frequently made by staff is that it does not have enough authority. Staff people often feel that if they have arrived at the best solution they should be able to put it into action.

These line-staff problems result in large part from the confrontation of two kinds of authority — the authority based on position (line authority) and the authority based on expertise (staff authority). Since each requires special personnel qualifications, it is no wonder that line managers possessing different training, aspirations, and expectations disagree with staff over organizational and operational problems.

OTHER SPECIALIZED ORGANIZATIONAL FUNCTIONS

Several other organizational positions cannot strictly be called either line or staff. The preponderance of these are held by "assistant-to" and liaison personnel.

"Assistant-to"

As discussed earlier in this chapter, the assistant-to belongs to a single executive's personal staff. Usually assistant-to functions are performed by one person who does a wide variety of jobs for the executive. He does not have line authority. Rather, the assistant-to acts as an "extension of the arms and the mind" of the executive, gathering information, doing special research projects, and generally acting to relieve the executive of details which cannot be delegated to a staff group or left to his secretary. From time to time this role of assistant-to is used in management training to show young executives how top officers function.

Liaison

The liaison function is quite a different kind of activity. Liaison people act as representatives for their firm in dealings with other firms. For example, a large aircraft manufacturer often has liaison representatives in the plants of some of its suppliers to insure that components are produced according to standards and to help the supplier overcome whatever technical problems he might encounter. Very often liaison people are used to coordinate public utility firms operating in the same power network system (see Chapter 9). Liaison work is also used between government agencies and private contractors.

THE TRADITIONAL ORGANIZATION STRUCTURE

Our discussion has treated what is frequently called the traditional structure of formal organizations. The label "traditional" is used for several reasons: First, the structures that it represents are those most often encountered in the real world. Second, its forms are those that have received the most attention in the past from scholars of management and sociology. Indeed, the German sociologist Max Weber's work on the nature of bureaucracy established the foundations of formal organization theory. And, third, such systems are those found in historical studies of the military, government, or church. In other words, the traditional model of organization is not restricted historically to business.

The traditional model has been much criticized, however. A number of scholars say that it has internal inconsistencies and therefore does not work well, that it is not responsive to the needs of the people in the organization, and that it does not adapt easily to change. These criticisms are valid under certain circumstances. Nevertheless, traditional theory is still most appropriate for organizations that

1. exist in a relatively stable environment
2. employ a high proportion of semi-skilled and unskilled workers
3. use a fairly unadvanced technology in achieving a relatively uncomplicated product
4. are not gigantic in size, judged by the number of people employed

These four points more or less define the limits of the traditional model. Most business firms fit within these limits and therefore find this form of organization quite useful.

Discussion Questions

1. If you were the manager of a staff department, which function would you like your department to perform for the rest of the organization? Service? Advice? Control? Initiation? Innovation? Why?

2. We say that most organizations have three organic functions — creation, distribution, and finance. What do hospitals create and distribute? How about a university?

Supplementary Readings

Allen, Louis A. *Management and Organization.* New York: McGraw-Hill, 1958. See chapter 10.

Hall, James L., and Joel K. Leidecker. "Lateral Relations in Organization: Theory and Practice." In *Dimensions in Modern Management,* edited by Patrick E. Connor. Boston: Houghton Mifflin, 1974.

Litterer, Joseph A. *The Analysis of Organizations.* New York: Wiley, 1965. See chapters 16, 17, 18.

Logan, Hall H. "Line and Staff: An Obsolete Concept?" In *Dimensions in Modern Management.*

Sampson, Robert C. *The Staff Role in Management.* New York: Harper and Row, 1955. See chapters 4, 8, 15.

Sinclair, Upton. "The Hierarchy." In *Dimensions in Modern Management.*

Preparing Formal Organization Charts and Manuals

This discussion is concerned with the details associated with depicting and explaining management organization charts and manuals. Although many firms utilize these tools, a surprising number have never formally adopted any of them.

ORGANIZATION CHARTS

Organization charts graphically portray an organization's structure and are relatively easy to construct. They show the skeleton of the organization's structure and depict only basic relationships and groupings of positions and functions. Most of the time, charts begin with the function under consideration shown as a rectangular box. Each box represents one function. The various boxes are then interconnected to show the groupings of activities that make up departments, divisions, or other parts of the organization. By studying the position of the boxes in their scalar relationships, one may readily determine who reports to whom.

Organization charts can be of considerable assistance to management because they not only portray the existing organization, but also can be used to improve communications and personnel relations and to analyze the organization for future planning purposes. Some organizations, in fact, have two charts, one depicting the existing organization and another — a so-called master plan that the company has designed as a long-term objective — showing the ideal organization.

Often management does not recognize the numerous uses and purposes of charts. Managers who do not chart their organization give several reasons for neglecting this valuable tool: concern that the chart is likely to emphasize an individual's superiority or inferiority, or to give a person occupying a rectangular box an exaggerated feeling of security and a lifetime claim to his position. Other managers feel that it is easier for them to change the organization if there is no chart, or they believe that if one has been drawn up, it should be kept secret. These objections indicate that management does not fully understand a chart's purpose, advantages, and limitations.

Advantages

As its graphical portrait is drawn, an organization is being analyzed. Through this analysis, structural faults, duplications of effort, and other inconsistencies leading to lowered performance are revealed. Situations of this nature occur most frequently in enterprises where rapid expansion has occurred and where management, because of the speed of expansion, did not pay much attention to the organization per se.

Organizational charting can also be a great help in personnel administration. An organization chart will often indicate a possible progression line for managers in firms concerned with management development programs.

Charts provide a simple guide to organizational make-up. Most people within an organization have a keen interest in knowing where they stand, where their superior stands in relation to the higher echelons, and so forth. When organizational adjustments are made, publication of "before and after" versions of the organization chart can provide one of the most effective means of informing the members of the enterprise of the various changes.

Limitations

In most instances an organization chart is merely a snapshot of the existing structure, and it holds true only as long as the organizational status quo is maintained. As soon as changes occur, the chart is as outdated as yesterday's newspaper. It is therefore imperative to chart changes within the organization at once.

As we have implied, the information transmitted by a chart is limited. It shows only what is on the surface. It does not show informal relationships, which may be numerous and important. The chart also fails to show precise functions, amounts of authority, and responsibility. Although these shortcomings are substantial, they do not negate the value of the chart.

Responsibility for Charting

When securing data for organizational charts, some companies are concerned only with current structure and do not make any attempt to inject organizational analysis. Other companies, however, combine data procurement with a systematic approach to organization planning.

Responsibility and authority for the preparation, review, and final approval of the organization chart lies with line management, generally with the chief executive. In individual departments this responsibility would probably rest with the head of the department. However, especially in large corporations, a specialized staff department at the corporate level often is charged with the duty of advising line management on the preparation of its organization charts. In some companies, this is done by the organization planning department or the department on organization. In either case, the individual who is charged with the preparation of the organization chart usually gets most of his data from the incumbents in various positions. In addition, he speaks to the heads of units to get an over-all idea of how each unit is organized. After all the data is collected, a temporary draft is prepared and reviewed by those concerned with the chart. Once the draft has been verified, the final organization chart is drawn up and distributed as a portrayal of the organization structure. Regardless of the amount of help and advice such a department will give in preparing, reviewing, and drawing the organization chart, approval and endorsement of the final document are the responsibility of line management. Final approval for the publication and distribution usually comes from the chief executive.

Figure 13A-1. Conventional Forms of Organizational Charting

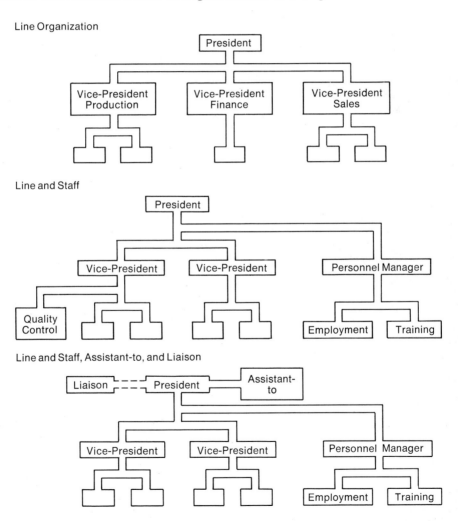

Types of Chart

Vertical

Although different types of organization chart are available, a company should plan to use consistently whatever type it has selected. About 95 per cent of all companies choose the vertical organization chart, which presents the different levels of organization in a step arrangement, with the senior executive placed at the top of the chart and the successive levels of management depicted vertically in pyramid form. This type of chart shows functional relationships, chains of command, and interconnecting lines of subordinates, and gives enough captions to clarify the structure.

Special relationships can be indicated, as they are in Figure 13A-1, by the positioning of functions and lines on the chart. The straight-line organization chart should show the lines of authority clearly, the functional relationship of activities (i.e., sales, production, etc.), and, to the greatest extent possible, the activities that are on the same level (i.e., vice-president, production; treasurer; and vice-president, sales).

Often it is impossible to tell from an organization chart whom management considers to be staff. This situation can be corrected easily by drawing a horizontal line from one of the vertical trunk lines of the primary organization to the staff function (quality control, personnel, etc.) and its secondary chain of command, as in Figure 13A-1, second part. Other special organizational personnel can also be designated on the vertical chart and related to the basic organization. In the third part of Figure 13A-1 we see how this is done in the cases of a liaison person and an assistant-to.

One of the chief advantages of vertical organization charts is that they can be easily read and understood; the downward flow of delegation, for instance, is clearly shown by connecting lines. One of their limitations is that, like all organization charts, the information they convey is only partial. Another limitation is that unless a special device is adopted, either line or staff, even if on the same level, will appear subordinate to the other, depending upon which appears higher on the chart. The same impression results if one division of an organization has more levels than another. For instance, an organizational unit of three levels may show the foreman on the lowest level, whereas he may be on the third level in an organization having five levels.

Horizontal

Although vertical organization charts are the most conventional type, horizontal charts which read from left to right are occasionally used (Figure 13A-2). One of the advantages of this type of chart is that it minimizes the importance of levels. There is no clear ascendancy in this chart and therefore people using it "may not be so likely to make erroneous inferences about differences in status or importance."[1]

[1] *Charting the Company Organization Structure*, Studies in Personnel Policy No. 168 (New York: National Industrial Conference Board, 1959), p. 17.

Figure 13A-2. Horizontal Organization Chart

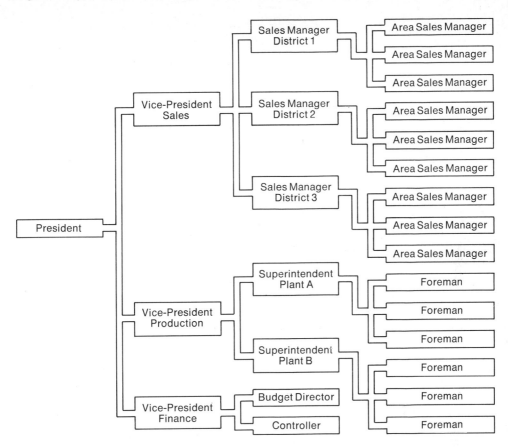

Circular

A third type of organization chart, commonly known as the circular chart, is illustrated in Figure 13A-3. In this chart the position of the chief executive is located in the center of concentric circles. Positions of equal importance lie on the same concentric circle. This arrangement eliminates any position at the bottom of the chart and shows the flow of formal authority from the chief executive in many directions. Unfortunately, at first glance a circular organization chart may seem somewhat confusing.

Additional Charting Considerations

Many other considerations should be kept in mind when charting an organization. Charts may have differing purposes: Organizations can be charted according to functions, products, or geographical location. Chart makers may choose to ignore

Figure 13A-3. Circular Organization Chart

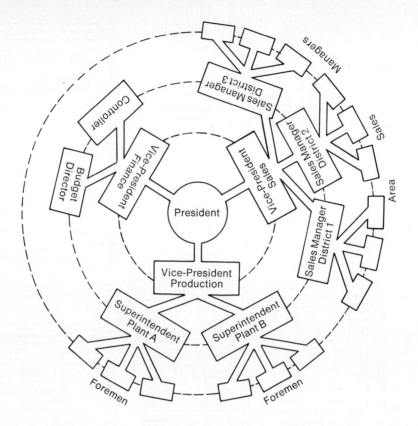

certain factors: In some charts no attempt is made to distinguish between line and staff functions, and they are shown on the same reporting level. Other charts differentiate line and staff by means of light and heavy lines or by the position of the lines, as we have done. Managers must also remember charting difficulties: They must consider the difficulty of drawing up a chart so that it reveals the true relative status of the positions and the various departments shown. In addition, mechanical considerations may appear important: Executives may be concerned by the placement and orientation of a chart on the page, the balancing of the chart, simplicity, amount of white space, identification of contents, dating of the chart, conserving space, and so forth.

ORGANIZATION MANUALS

The organization manual is another helpful tool for effective organization. Although compiling a manual involves a considerable amount of work and expense, larger enterprises have found the effort worthwhile. A manual provides in comprehensive written form decisions regarding the company organizational structure; it defines the scope of authorities and responsibilities of management positions and the channels to be used in obtaining decisions or approvals of proposals; it is also helpful in selection, orientation, development, and appraisal of management personnel. A manual specifies the scope of each manager's job and its relationship to the other positions within the organization. A manual also serves to reiterate for the individual executive the long-term objectives of the enterprise.

Naturally, some drawbacks to organization manuals exist. As we have indicated, compiling them and keeping them up to date are time-consuming. Also, manuals sometimes have a confining effect. Likewise, they may reveal sensitive relationships.

Content

An organization manual normally pictures an entire organization with its various departments and functions. In it can be found a statement of the objectives of the company, its policies, a definition of terms, a definition of organization principles, a discussion of organization problems, job descriptions, a guide to the use of names and titles, organization charts, and so on. An organization manual often contains a brief statement of the firm's underlying philosophy. Such a statement might cover the quality of company products, pricing, teamwork, service, good citizenship, and the like.

Job Descriptions

All manuals contain job descriptions, although some contain more than others, depending on the size of the group for which the manual is intended. Job descriptions generally indicate the principal duties and functions of the position, the scope of authority, and its channels.

In compiling job descriptions, as in drawing organization charts, information is usually obtained from the incumbent. Again, such work can expose organizational discrepancies — dual responsibilities, fuzziness of lines, overlapping of efforts. Checking and verifying position descriptions with the incumbent can often lead to clarifications and to necessary reorganization. Other advantages, revealed in the discussion of charting, also apply here.

Before we leave this topic, we should note that there is some confusion in the use of the terms "job description" and "job specification." Generally speaking, the former objectively describes the elements of a position, whereas the latter specifies the qualities a person must possess in order to perform the job adequately. In certain companies, job descriptions are extended to include some personal qualities. Where this is not done, such specifications must be drawn up separately.

Titles

There is little agreement on the use and meaning of titles. For instance, the chief executive officer of one of the divisions of the Du Pont Company is called the general manager. In this capacity, he presides over a division empire whose capital investments and sales probably each run into the hundreds of millions of dollars. On the other hand, the chief executive officer in another enterprise with the same or, more likely, a considerably lower volume of investment and sales would probably be called the president.

Although the use of titles may vary considerably among different organizations, within a single organization titles must have a definite meaning and must be used consistently. Therefore, the organization manual should clearly specify the allocation of titles to executives in both staff and line operations. Doing so permits prompt identification of comparable status within organizational levels. Such comparability is often facilitated by using a basic title, such as manager, to which an adjective is added connoting the rank, for example, assistant manager. Possibly another or several more adjectives will be included to describe the activities of the particular executive, for instance Assistant Sales Manager, Fuel Oil, West Coast.[2]

Preparation and Revision

Although ultimate responsibility for the organization manual rests with the chief executive, he is usually aided in its compilation by an assistant or by the staff department primarily concerned with organization planning. Because making an organization manual is costly, its scope should be confined to the important targets of top management activities. Also, unless a manual is revised regularly, it can quickly become outdated. Therefore, annual, semi-annual, or even quarterly revisions are necessary.

[2] For a "Roster of Executive Titles" see William H. Newman, *Administrative Action* (Englewood Cliffs, N.J.: Prentice-Hall, 1951), p. 306.

CHAPTER 14

Decentralization of Authority

Decentralization is closely related to the subjects covered in Chapters 12 and 13 — organizational authority and structure. Although the terms centralization and decentralization are usually used as if their meanings were clearly understood, they often have completely different meanings to different people. To one individual the statement that an organization is decentralized may mean that its management delegates a great deal of authority to the lower echelons in the managerial hierarchy. To a second it might signify the existence of several plants at different locations. Even if decentralization did connote delegation of authority to the second person, he might view the areas and extent of delegated authority in an entirely different manner. It is necessary in each instance, therefore, to state the exact sense in which the term decentralization is used.

We have already discussed the centralization of activities and occasionally referred to the centralization and decentralization of physical facilities. Here we turn our attention to the centralization or decentralization of authority, to the problem of where in the administrative hierarchy operating and policy decisions are made.

"Centralization is not a system of management good or bad of itself, capable of being adopted or discarded at the whim of managers or of circumstances; it is always present to a greater or less extent."[1] Hence, from the organizational standpoint, the extent of centralization or decentralization (depending upon which way one looks at it) is a matter of how much authority has been or will be delegated to different organizational levels. As Fayol put it, "everything which goes to increase the importance of the subordinate's role is decentralization, everything which goes to reduce it is centralization."[2]

Before proceeding, it is necessary to clarify the relationship between decentralization and delegation. Decentralization is an extension of delegation. Delegation refers mainly to the granting of authority and the creation of responsibility; decentralization is the result of that systematic delegation throughout the organization. Delegation can occur without decentralization, but decentralization cannot occur without delegation.

[1] Henri Fayol, *General and Industrial Management*, trans. Constance Storrs (London: Pitman, 1949), p. 33.
[2] *Ibid.*, p. 34.

Centralization represents upper management's systematic and consistent reservation of major policy-making authority. Neither centralization nor decentralization is absolute. Their extent depends on the amount of independent judgment and discretion executives can exercise, the degree of authority delegated, and the qualitative nature of the decisions made on each level of the organization. Ernest Dale illustrates this point well in his statement that the decentralization of authority in an organization increases with four factors:

1. the number of decisions made lower down in the management hierarchy
2. the importance of decisions made lower down in the management hierarchy (The greater the sum of capital expenditure that can be approved by the plant manager without consulting anyone else, the greater will be the decentralization in this field.)
3. the increase in functions affected by decisions made at lower levels (Companies permitting only operational decisions to be made at separate branch plants are less decentralized than those also permitting financial and personnel decisions at branch plants.)
4. the less checking required on the decision (Decentralization is greatest when no check must be made; less when superiors have to be informed of the decision after it has been made; least if superiors have to be consulted before the decision is made. The fewer people to be consulted, and the lower they are in the management hierarchy, the greater will be the decentralization.[3])

CENTRALIZATION

Centralized authority is common in small enterprises and is often necessary if the enterprise is to survive in a competitive environment. Here the chief executive is in close touch with all operations, makes all decisions, and gives all instructions. In certain organizations small enough to have this type of centralized administration, the chief executive does not care to or is in no position to delegate any authority. On the other hand, many small firms in the electronics and space industries are loosely organized. In them, the management has delegated a great deal of authority to highly trained and educated scientists and engineers. Here, such decentralization provides the best way to make effective use of valuable human resources.

DECENTRALIZATION

Limited Decentralization

Variations on the degree of decentralization of authority are innumerable. In some situations, authority is decentralized to a limited degree. Top management initiates policies and programs but delegates their applications in day-to-day operations and

[3] Ernest Dale, *Planning and Developing the Company Organization Structure*, Research Report No. 20 (New York: American Management Association, 1952), pp. 149–50.

planning. In many medium-sized manufacturing firms employing from 100 to 200 persons, such authority is usually delegated to the production manager, but this delegation has its limitations. The production manager is responsible for getting the work out. He schedules the production, requisitions the various materials and supplies, hires employees, and handles personnel matters within the union agreement. He may have, however, a number of questions which require final approval by top management: questions referring to inventory policy, purchasing machinery, hiring supervisors, and changing pay rates. Authority to decide these questions is not delegated to the production manager.

This kind of arrangement is advantageous because it limits the number of executives which a firm needs to employ. In addition, it relieves top management of numerous details, leaving them free for matters of greater importance. There are probably thousands of enterprises in the United States which are organized on the basis of limited decentralization of authority.

Bottom-Up Management: Extreme Decentralization

Extreme decentralization can be seen in what William B. Given, Jr., has called "bottom-up" management.[4] At the time his book was written, Given was the president of the American Brake Shoe Company, an enterprise made up of ten divisions operating sixty widely scattered plants. Utilizing bottom-up management, he tried to release the thinking and encourage the initiative of all subordinates down the line so that the impetus and the ideas would flow from the bottom up.

Given was not merely dealing with the usual concept of decentralization; instead, he was dealing with decentralization carried a step further, with a radically different effect. Call it progressive decentralization, if you wish, assuming progressive to mean spreading from one part to others. Such decentralization not only takes the lead strings off subsidiary presidents and department heads, but also gives superintendents, foremen, chief clerks — people all along the management line — a stimulating sense of personal freedom, freedom to think and plan boldly.[5] Each manager, each division, each unit, feels a proprietary responsibility for its own activities. The manager must plan how to do the job best; he must also do the job. Under such an arrangement, top executives cannot exercise detailed controls. Their principal duties are to help subordinates to do a better job.

The concept of bottom-up management has been employed successfully in the American Brake Shoe Company since the middle 1920's. Apparently this type of thinking is particularly adaptable to companies composed of relatively small, self-contained, independent operating units; the failure of one such unit would not be fatal to the entire company. Assistance from central staffs is available to the various divisions and managers, but if managers feel that they can get better results following their own ideas, no one will object. Bottom-up management no doubt provides a great stimulus for managers to use their ingenuity and initiative creatively to do

[4] William B. Given, Jr., *Bottom-Up Management* (New York: Harper and Row, 1949).

[5] *Ibid.*, pp. 5–6.

the best possible job. It is a dynamic way to raise morale. It also provides excellent training ground for future top executives.

THE DECISION TO DECENTRALIZE

When to Decentralize

Although centralization or limited decentralization of authority is most logical in the early stages of company development, most managements must sooner or later face the problem of when to make a systematic effort to decentralize authority to the lowest possible level. Such a decision will involve major changes in the structure of the organization and in the general managerial philosophy. It also will necessitate changes in the habits and attitudes of individual managers. In Chapter 11, we examined that period in the growth and development of the enterprise when it became necessary for management to switch from a functional departmentalization to product division. The same factors which indicate a need for the establishment of product divisions also indicate that it is time to decentralize authority. As a matter of fact, product division only becomes effective when accompanied by such decentralization. As soon as the enterprise diversifies into product lines, authority must be delegated to the various divisions for maximum results and accountability.

However, factors other than the need for product division can also help to determine the proper time to decentralize. For example, decentralization becomes necessary when management finds itself so burdened with decision-making that the top executives do not have time to perform their planning function adequately or maintain a long-range point of view. In such a situation they will probably want to make a concerted effort to delegate authority to lower echelons.

Occasionally an enterprise must delegate authority in order to keep its position within the market. Decision-making might have become so cumbersome that other companies can adjust to prevailing market conditions more readily and quickly and thus gain a major advantage. Top management might also find that it has few junior managers available to fill higher managerial positions as they occur. Factors such as these will also indicate the need for decentralization of authority.

Pros and Cons

The advantages of decentralization are obvious. By delegating authority, executives are relieved from time-consuming detail work and freed for more important problems. Subordinates can make decisions without waiting for approval from a superior. This increases their flexibility and permits prompter action when speed may be essential. In addition, decentralization of decision-making authority may produce better decisions since the manager on the spot usually knows more about pertinent factors than the manager at headquarters. Likewise, decentralization tends to increase the morale of a lower-level executive, his interest, and his enthusiasm for his work. It also provides a good training ground for junior executives.

The advantages of decentralization become even more important as an enterprise grows. The need for delegation of authority is recognized and appreciated by the managements of all large concerns. To some managements it has even become a fad, and extensive decentralization has been applied where size and complexity do not warrant it.

The disadvantages of decentralization are equally clear. As authority is decentralized, executives increasingly resemble operators of small independent businesses. As a consequence, duplications of service might develop. Also, executives in the field may come to feel that they no longer need the advice of specialists assembled at headquarters. Under these conditions the specialists would not be utilized fully and the division or department managers would not receive technical advice or services that they really could use. Before such a situation arises, top management should make clear to the subordinate managers the extent to which they should utilize central staff.

Another disadvantage of increased decentralization of authority is potential loss of control and the related problem of suboptimization. In this situation, the relatively autonomous units of a company optimize their own profitability, but in so doing decrease the net profit of the corporation. Many large companies devise controls to minimize such a possibility.

FACTORS INFLUENCING DECENTRALIZATION

Management is faced time and time again with the problem of how much decentralization to permit, and naturally it must choose a pattern of delegation that is sound for the organization. Although many executive-subordinate delegations follow a traditional pattern, new problems do arise. Thus, decentralization and delegation of authority are continuous functions requiring constant checks to ensure that they are still appropriate and adequate for the particular organization.

Because no simple formulas exist for determining the appropriate amount of decentralization of authority, management needs to examine the various factors that will influence its decentralization decision and the delegation decisions that must accompany it. These matters must be settled by top management; authority to dispose of them cannot be delegated.

History of the Organization

The historical growth of an organization is frequently a factor in gauging the decentralization of authority. Organizations that expand from within and show little delegation of authority often have grown under the vigorous centralized direction of the founder-owner.

Companies that result from business combinations, amalgamations, and mergers, usually contain a great amount of decentralization. In such cases, recentralization of authority would be foolish. The firm being merged has probably operated for years in a satisfactory fashion, and the acquiring firm hopes to continue this trend.

In time, the acquiring company must provide for proper coordination and controls, but it may still maintain the decentralized structure.

The reverse can also be true, however. Sometimes the existing management of a firm being merged cannot be entrusted with the future of the enterprise; sometimes the controlling group has prior plans to install its own management as soon as the acquisition is completed. In either case, the acquiring company imposes centralization and revokes much of the authority previously delegated to the managers of the merged company.

Boise Cascade is a firm that has grown through mergers and acquisitions, yet has retained centralized control over the strategic financial decisions of its various divisions. These divisions, however, have considerable autonomy in making nonfinancial decisions. Hence the history of an enterprise can show a trend toward centralization of authority, toward decentralization, or toward some combination of the two.

Availability of Managers to Implement Decentralization

Decentralization and delegation of authority cannot occur unless enough managers of sufficient ability are available to discharge the responsibilities involved. It is often taken for granted that enough managers exist to handle the authority delegated to them, but this assumption may be unwarranted. If managers do not have the necessary ability, authority cannot be granted. Thus, management may find itself in a vicious circle of complaining that, without trained executives, it cannot delegate authority, but without receiving authority, its executives cannot obtain the necessary training. In other words, management often deplores this lack of trained people but at the same time uses it as an excuse for not decentralizing.

In order to avoid this impasse, many large firms develop and train managerial manpower by pushing decision-making down into the lower ranks of the organization. In the early stages of a manager's career, his scope of authority will be small, but as he acquires experience, he will be given more authority.

Dispersion of Operations

Geographic dispersion of operations has some bearing on decentralization. Such dispersion increases the problems of communication and coordination. Therefore, one is likely to find more delegation of authority in dispersed operations. Usually, the local manager can manage better than an absentee manager. Yet geographical dispersion does not necessarily result in decentralization. For example, the local managers of chain stores usually have no authority over pricing, advertising, inventory, purchasing; instead, all these decisions are controlled from a central office. In this situation, performance may be decentralized, but authority is centralized. It is evident, however, that dispersion or centralization of activities in and of itself does not provide a clear gauge for delegating authority.

Costliness and Significance of Decisions

The costliness and significance of typical management decisions will greatly affect the degree of delegation and thus the amount of decentralization that is feasible in that company. Generally speaking, costly and significant decisions must be made at the upper level of the managerial hierarchy and cannot be delegated. Costliness can be expressed in dollars and cents, in man hours, or in units of output. Costliness can also be of an intangible nature such as the effect of a certain decision on the reputation of an enterprise. Consider a shoe manufacturing firm where decisions regarding the quality of finished shoes can be made at the operational level. A wrong decision might not affect the company's reputation sufficiently to warrant relocating such decision-making. However, in the quality control of a new antibiotic, an error could devastate the reputation of the company (to say nothing of the health of the population). Therefore, authority for those decisions should be located at a relatively high managerial level, making decentralization in this matter rather unfeasible.

There is no assurance, of course, that top management will not make a mistake in its decision, and possibly a costly one. It is also conceivable that a person closer to it might possibly have made a better decision. However, higher executives usually make fewer mistakes, for they have more experience, more occasions to make decisions, and more training.

Control over Capital Funds

In most enterprises decisions regarding the expenditure of capital funds are not broadly delegated. They are often considered so vital to the life of the enterprise that top management reserves authority for them. Some enterprises, however, have given their managers considerable authority over capital expenditures. In the General Electric Company, the operating department general managers may make commitments up to $500,000. Ralph J. Cordiner, former president of General Electric, has said, "I believe that too much of a fetish has been made in the past of capital expenditures. A manager can lose a lot more money on inventory, foolish pricing policy, careless personnel staffing, or poor production scheduling."[6] Often, a branch manager does more harm by making bad decisions about materials, purchases, or personnel than he would have done if the corporation let him make decisions about capital expenditures.

Size of the Enterprise

The larger the firm, the greater is the number of decisions generated and the more levels at which they can be made, and the more numerous will be the problems of effective coordination. One of the major difficulties in a large enterprise is to achieve efficient and effective teamwork. Realization of the dis-economies of size often leads

---

[6] Ralph J. Cordiner, *New Frontiers For Professional Managers* (New York: McGraw-Hill, 1956), p. 61.

to decentralization or breaking up the enterprise into a number of autonomous or nearly autonomous units. In these units, decisions can be made with more speed and at a point closer to the place of action; time can be saved, paper work reduced, misunderstandings in communication diminished, and frictions held to a minimum. However, it is impossible to define the size of such ideal units. Estimates range from 250 employees to 1,000 or even 2,500.

Of greater significance than the numbers involved is the amount of economic and managerial self-sufficiency that management must grant to the various units in order to make decentralization effective. Usually, managment establishes units along product lines, each product unit embodying all functions of the enterprise. Obviously, a functional department such as sales could not by itself be as independent as a product unit. The existence of such decentralized product units raises the possibility of a lack of policy uniformity and desired coordination. Division managers can easily become so preoccupied with their units that they lose sight of the enterprise as a whole. Therefore, the corporation must, as mentioned earlier, take precautions to ensure policy coordination and the necessary amount of central control. The best example of a large corporation with decentralized operating units and overall controls is General Motors.

Dynamics and Type of Enterprise

The decentralization of authority may also be greatly influenced by the dynamics of the particular business enterprise. If the enterprise is part of an industry expanding much more rapidly than expected — for instance, electronics — top management will be overburdened with numerous decisions that it probably would not have had to make in the normal course of events. This dynamic condition will force top management to decentralize as quickly as possible, even though some managers to whom authority is delegated might make mistakes. In other words, the dynamic growth and rate of change in the industry might make it impossible to completely train enough capable managers in the lower echelons. Delegating authority will give these managers the opportunity to become more experienced.

Even under dynamic conditions, recentralization and reallocation of authority might take place from time to time. In static industries the tendency toward centralization of authority is continuous rather than occasional. One does not find much delegation of authority, for example, in banking enterprises, insurance companies, or railroads. The dynamics or, to be more specific, the slow rates of growth in these industries do not necessitate decentralization.

Firms with highly diversified activities — especially those that cut across several industries — do, however, require a large degree of decentralization. To a conglomerate corporation with divisions in divergent fields such as electronics, lumber, shipping, steel, plastics, and chemicals, considerable delegation of authority is natural and economical. The diversification, however, could easily lead to devastating results if top management has not devised effective centralized controls to go along with the delegation.

Control and Decentralization

In a sense, control and decentralization are opposites. Decentralization, by widening the span of management, implies a loosening of direct control over day-to-day performance. Nevertheless, the presence of some effective control system such as a profit center is essential to ensure that the decentralized units of a firm function consistently with the general objectives of the enterprise.

For example, General Motors has two criteria for appraising and controlling the performance of its decentralized divisions: (1) market penetration and (2) unit costs. The first criterion gives corporate management a reading on the effectiveness of the marketing program. The second gives data on the level of manufacturing efficiency. These criteria are broad and cover a relatively long time span — usually the model year.

Other large corporations tackle the control problem by using a special corporate-level audit staff group. This group monitors activities in the decentralized units and sends performance reports to top management. By acquiring data on a wide variety of activities, the group gives top management a basis for carrying out its control function, and by going directly to the unit itself, the monitoring group by-passes the lengthy chain of command.

Improved Morale

The morale in an organization can also affect decentralization. If morale is low, management may decide to increase decentralization. Generally speaking, the more authority a lower- or middle-echelon manager has, and the higher his status, the more satisfied will he be.

Concomitant with the trend toward upgrading the education and skills of the work force is the trend toward higher expectations among new, young employees. They expect more authority and responsibility and an opportunity to use their independent judgment. Management should be prepared to institute a certain amount of decentralization in order to fulfill these expectations.

Environmental Factors

In our discussion of factors influencing decentralization and the delegation of authority, we have concentrated mainly on those internal to the enterprise. There are also a number of external factors over which the business has little or no control — labor unions, government control over business, and tax policies, to name a few. All these factors have a centralizing effect on business. For example, many firms deal with large unions and negotiate labor contracts on a company-wide basis at corporate headquarters. Therefore, within the area of labor relations, authority for decision-making cannot be decentralized to a large degree. The same effect is produced by various government controls on business such as price regulation.

DECENTRALIZATION IN THE VARIOUS FUNCTIONS

Another way to look at decentralization is through the various functions an enterprise performs. The nature of a function will, to an extent, dictate the degree of delegation of authority and the amount of decentralization that is feasible. As mentioned previously, the main functions in an enterprise are creation, distribution, and finance, and the usual auxiliary activities are personnel, accounting, and purchasing. The importance of these functions and their relationships to one another vary from enterprise to enterprise. Also, unique circumstances sometimes necessitate centralization or decentralization in a particular case. However, some broad conclusions on how these functions lend themselves to decentralization can be drawn. A study by Ernest Dale is pertinent.[7]

In the Major Functions

Creation

Those observing the growth of an enterprise commonly find that management first delegates authority over the creation of goods and services. This is especially true of the production function in manufacturing firms. Moreover, management is likely to delegate the greatest amount of authority in this area, for as the size and complexity of production activities increase, the need for delegation increases.

This generalization seems to hold true whether production facilities are located close to the home office or not. If such facilities are physically dispersed, however, the need for delegation and decentralization becomes even more urgent. Nevertheless, over-all controls must remain with top administration — through planning and examining production and operating budgets, through quality inspections, possibly through a vice-president in charge of all manufacturing, and sometimes through the help of functional staff departments based at the home office.

Finance

As we have noted, the finance function tends to be relatively centralized even in enterprises where authority is broadly delegated. The reason for this is obvious: Only through centralized authority can the proper application of scarce capital resources be guaranteed. In most companies, a particular manager is given a relatively small fund that can be spent without special permission from headquarters.

Operating expenditures are not as strictly controlled. The manager of a manufacturing division is usually granted wide authority over those expenditures. However, they are subject to the usual budgetary controls. Budgets are made up at regular intervals by the operating division and are submitted to top management for review and approval. Once a divisional manager gains budget approval, he has full authority in this field. However, management is becoming increasingly aware that centralized

---

[7] Dale, *Planning and Developing the Company Organization Structure*, pp. 271–82.

authority over operating expenses might be advisable too. Uncontrolled expenditure in this area could also dissipate corporate capital.

Distribution

At first glance, much decentralization and delegation of authority appears to exist within the marketing function. In a growing enterprise, authority over sales activities will be delegated soon after authority over the production function has been delegated. This occurs because sales activities must usually be brought to customers scattered across the country. A sales executive must have authority to adjust to these customers and to rapidly changing circumstances and conditions. Branch managers also need a wide area of discretion so that they can give customers the individual attention that many of them require. Therefore, the nature of distribution seems to make decentralization necessary.

A closer examination, however, shows that much of this decentralization exists in name only. In most instances, no variations in prices and discounts are permitted without the express permission of the home office. Clear limits to the extension of credit usually exist. Travel and entertainment expense ceilings are often specified in detail. George Smith cites the case of a large manufacturing company where, he was told by the general sales manager, the marketing function had been completely decentralized. Certainly, all selling was done by people in the regional divisions. However, executives at headquarters decided upon the product line, set up the prices, conducted sales training programs, hired the salesmen, kept track of sales, carried on the company's advertising campaign, and gave advice to regional sales managers. When the regional managers were asked whether they considered the marketing function to be centralized or decentralized, they described it as exceedingly centralized.[8]

Supporting functions are likewise handled from headquarters, thereby further decreasing the apparent decentralization of the marketing function. In order to achieve economy and full staff utilization, promotions, market research, advertising, and publicity usually come under centralized authority.

In the Auxiliary Functions

Accounting

Very little delegation of authority is usually associated with the accounting function, for accounting is most economically performed by a central department and the information obtained by that department is necessary for effective over-all organizational control. However, if too much centralization occurs, a manager may be unable to obtain fast and accurate answers to his accounting questions. Therefore, some accounting activities are often performed in the lower echelons, thereby enabling the manager at a particular location to be correctly and promptly informed.

[8] George Albert Smith, Jr., *Managing Geographically Decentralized Companies* (Boston: Division of Research, Graduate School of Business Administration, Harvard University, 1958), p. 16.

Personnel

Since managing means getting people to do things, and since people vary widely in their capabilities, attitudes, and responses, managers must have the authority to deal with them as individuals and to modify broad personnel policies to accommodate particular cases. Therefore, within the area of personnel activities there should be as much delegation of authority as possible.

In some personnel areas, however, a high degree of centralization is desirable and, in practice, exists. Union dealings require centralization of authority. Wage and salary administration, appraisal procedure, job evaluation, bonus and fringe benefit arrangements, and executive development programs also tend to be highly centralized.

Purchasing

The amount of decentralization and delegation of authority within the purchasing function depends largely on the types of purchases involved. Capital goods are usually purchased centrally because they represent a substantial capital investment. Although the degree to which authority is delegated for other purchases varies greatly, we may venture to say that in an enterprise with widely scattered plants, authority to purchase basic materials and supplies is probably centralized, whereas authority to purchase other things might be delegated. The central purchasing department will often place a general contract for specific materials and the individual plants will then order directly from central purchasing. Such an arrangement enables the plants to take advantage of special price agreements, yet leaves them free to purchase as the need arises.

In enterprises where the divisions produce different product lines, the tendency toward decentralized purchasing is greater. An enterprise that uses products of a perishable nature probably also delegates purchasing authority. Furthermore, semi-independent and competing divisions usually practice decentralized purchasing. If a division's performance is judged by its income statement, it is only fair to give it a free hand in its purchasing. Even if purchases are widely decentralized, however, a centralized staff usually formulates general purchasing policies and procedures. In some enterprises — those involved in merchandising, for example — almost all purchasing activities are highly centralized. Store managers, however, might have the authority to cater to special local needs and to purchase the appropriate items.

DECENTRALIZATION IN PRACTICE

The Difficulty of Achieving Effective Decentralization

Thus far we may have implied that it is easy for management to achieve the desired degree of decentralization once this degree has been determined. In reality, this is not always the case. Although a given amount of decentralization may be desirable, often obstacles must be overcome before it can be accomplished. For instance, management may find that authority has not been delegated to its full extent. Some managers may retain authority because they feel its delegation may bring a loss of status, a loss of power and control. Others believe that centralized power brings them closer to the president's ear. Still others are concerned by the expenses involved in delegating authority — expenses incurred by duplicating functions, expenses caused by the costly mistakes of junior executives, and the like.

Top management can try in several ways to overcome these obstacles and achieve the degree of decentralization they deem desirable. As stated before, they must indoctrinate the entire management group with the philosophy of decentralization. Management must understand that by carefully delegating authority it neither loses status nor absolves itself of its responsibilities. The willingness and sincere desire to delegate authority must permeate the entire organization. Top management must practice as well as preach delegation of authority. When management extends its span, it has no choice but to delegate. It must remember, however, that it is still responsible for over-all performance and therefore must make certain that managers at all levels are well trained. It must also establish clear policies and guides backed by a good system of controls. Delegating authority in this manner has been strongly advocated by Sears, Roebuck, for instance.

Other firms will not promote a manager until he has developed a subordinate who can take over his position. Thus, they force the manager to delegate authority. Where this is the policy, managers are generally most eager to delegate as much authority as they can as soon as possible.

Cases of Effective Decentralization

The Profit-Center Concept

In spite of the inherent difficulties, many large firms have successfully decentralized certain areas. Such companies as General Motors, Ford, Du Pont, General Electric, and General Foods show that the most effective means of decentralization is through the profit-center concept. Under this concept, each divisionalized unit is established as a self-contained, individual enterprise within the framework of the corporation. In other words, each division is set up as a separate business enterprise with its own management and own staff, and each competes with the other divisions. Likewise, each division manager operates his division as an independent businessman, completely responsible for the profit the division earns or for the loss it sustains.

This profit-center concept assures an aggressive management constantly looking for improvements, additional markets, additional opportunities, and cost savings, all of which lead to a better income statement. The profit-center concept also gives real meaning to decentralization, placing the burden of profit-making on a number of divisional managers rather than on just one or two top executives at headquarters. It puts responsibility for profit close to the point where profits are made, and makes it possible and in fact imperative for the divisional manager to take action. It is likely that he will do so vigorously since his personal security and reputation are at stake.

The General Motors Corporation

One of the most successful examples of profit-center decentralization is the General Motors Corporation. Their operating philosophy, formulated in the early 1920's, is stated in few words: "Decentralized operations and responsibilities with co-ordinated control." A simpler way of expressing it is: "give a man a clearcut job and let him do it."[9] Peter Drucker calls this philosophy "an essay in federalism."[10]

Such federalism was not always the practice in General Motors, however. Originally, under the leadership of W. C. Durant, the company was structured along highly centralized lines. In the early 1920's the corporation found itself in a difficult position. It was experiencing substantial deficits, suffering from inadequate research and engineering activities, from an unbalanced capital situation, and from inadequate budgetary controls. To quote Harlow Curtice, a former president of General Motors:

Operations were neither integrated nor coordinated. There was no consistent policy with respect to production programs. Frequently poor judgment was exercised in making capital expenditures and establishing production schedules. The Corporation did not have a properly developed research and engineering staff nor any sound concept of budgetary control. The central administration did not exercise adequate control over the operations of the individual divisions. There were wide variations in the competence of divisional managements. In short, the Corporation was unorganized and the individual units largely out of control.[11]

In 1921, under the leadership of Alfred P. Sloan, Jr., General Motors centralized and integrated policy-making and administration, yet at the same time made provisions for highly decentralized responsibility and operations. Sloan's concept of the management of a great industrial organization was

to divide it into as many parts as consistently as can be done, place in charge of each part the most capable executive that can be found, develop a system of co-ordination so that each part may strengthen and support each other part; thus not only welding all parts together in the common interests of a joint enterprise, but importantly developing ability and initiative through the instrumentalities of responsibility and ambition — developing men and giving them an opportunity to exercise their talents, both in their own interests as well as in that of the business.[12]

This philosophy carried General Motors from imminent failure to its position as one of the largest and most profitable enterprises in the United States.

[9] *The Organization of General Motors Corporation*, prepared by William M. Collins, assistant secretary, General Motors Corporation (March 1968), p. 2.

[10] Peter F. Drucker, *Concept of the Corporation* (New York: Day, 1946), p. 46.

[11] "The Development and Growth of General Motors," Statement before the Subcommittee on Anti-Trust and Monopoly of the United States Senate Committee on the Judiciary by Harlow Curtice, former president of the General Motors Corporation (December 2, 1955), p. 6.

[12] Quoted *ibid.*, p. 8.

At present General Motors is composed of thirty manufacturing, assembly, and warehousing divisions within the United States and operations in thirty foreign countries. Its worldwide employment in 1972 averaged about 760,000 men and women and about 810,000 in the first six months of 1973. The corporation is owned by approximately 1.3 million stockholders and has sales of over $30 billion. General Motors has decentralized on a profit-center basis in order to benefit from large-scale production while retaining the advantages of a well-managed small business. Decentralization provides GM with the flexibility to change operations and improve its products. It enables GM's managers to make effective use of their talents by giving them maximum scope to exercise their freedom of action. It also gives many individuals additional opportunity to develop executive ability and initiative.[13]

More specifically, profit-center decentralization permits the general manager of each division to manage and operate his own domain. He is responsible for planning, for building his organization, for staffing it, and for controlling his own results. He designs, develops, produces, and sells his own products. He purchases his own materials and parts, either from outside suppliers or from other divisions of the company, his choice depending solely on where he can get the best product at the lowest price. He competes with every other division of General Motors and with every other company which makes a similar product. The division manager is fully responsible for the success or failure of his division and he is rewarded accordingly.

The division manager, however, is not completely autonomous. Recall that General Motors' philosophy envisions decentralized operations and responsibilities with coordinated control. Thus, the manager's efforts are guided by a comprehensive framework of centralized planning, coordination, and control.

All decentralized operations function under the jurisdiction of the board of directors and committees of the board operating within a sphere of authority granted to them by the board. The chairman of the board is the chief executive officer of the corporation. He is directly responsible to the board as a whole. The president of the corporation is the chief operating officer. Within this centralized part of General Motors, it is recognized that policy formulation is separate from administration. Policy-making is the responsibility of two governing committees in the corporation, namely, the finance committee and the executive committee. These two committees both deal with policy at the top level and both report to the board of directors. However, they do not deliberate or establish policy in isolation, for the organizational pattern provides a channel through which policy ideas and suggestions filter up from the line and staff organizations (see Figure 14-1).[14]

In fact, several policy groups meet regularly to consider and recommend policy formulation on such problems as distribution, personnel relations, public relations, engineering, and research. "The balance between decentralized operations, on the one hand, and coordinated control, on the other, varies according to areas. It also varies according to the temperaments and talents of executives, and the way in which they work."[15]

[13] *The Organization of General Motors Corporation*, p. 5.
[14] *Ibid.*, p. 15.
[15] "The Development and Growth of General Motors," p. 6.

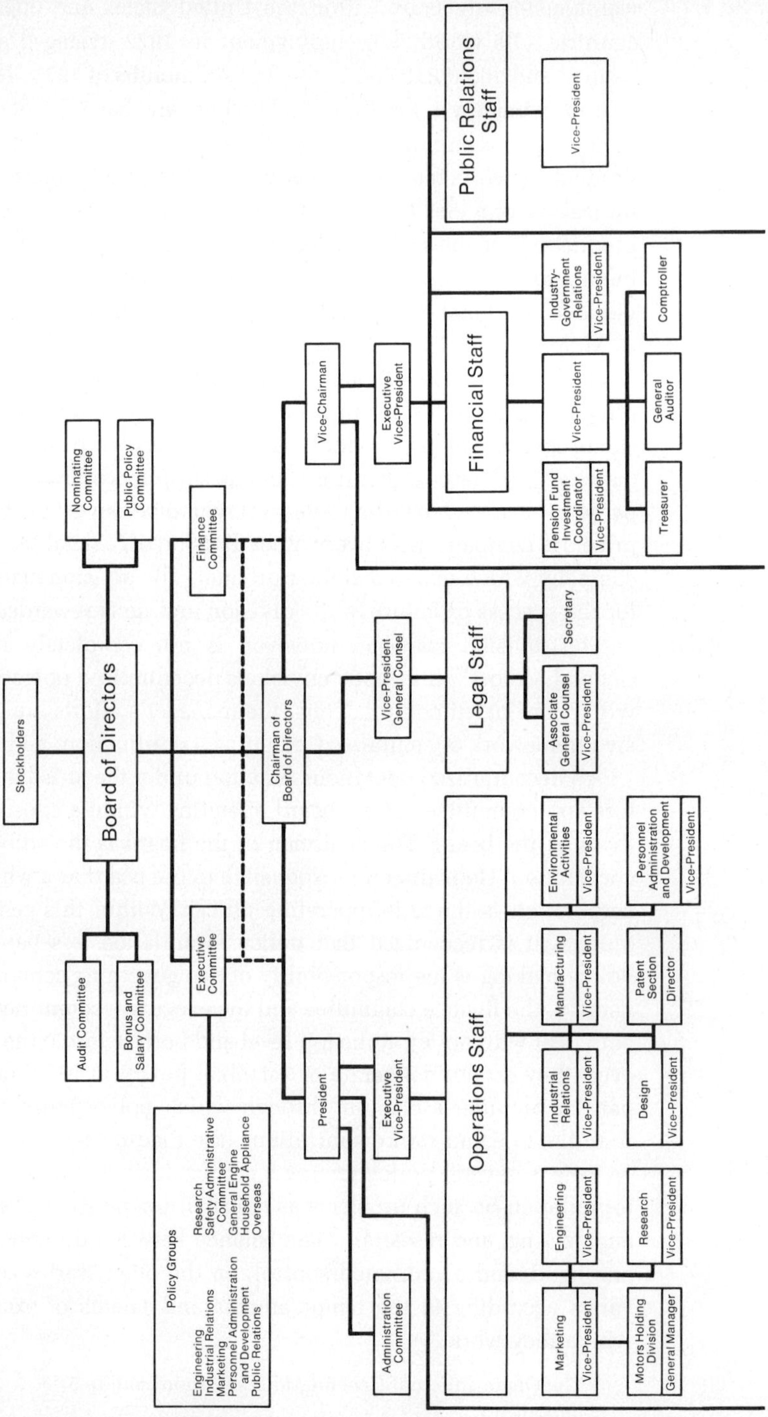

Figure 14-1. General Motors Corporation, January 1973

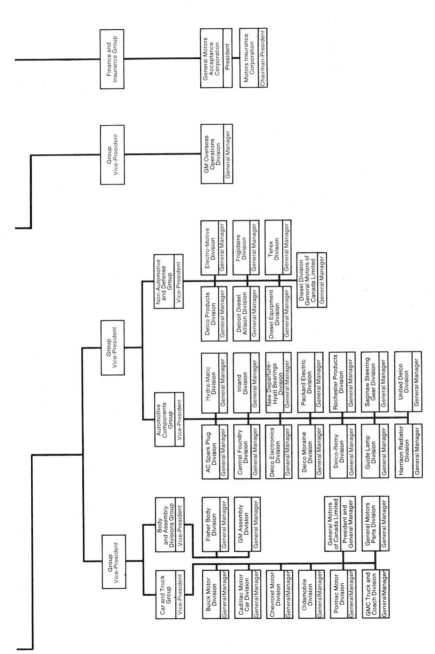

Source: General Motors Corporation. Used with permission.

RECENT TRENDS

The Tendency Toward Decentralization

In recent years decentralization has been a growing trend. In fact, having a decentralization program has become one of the most discussed issues in the world of management. The cost of such a program should be considered as a long-term investment in managerial training and in improved morale among all ranks of the managerial hierarchy. However, each organization must devise its own structure. No two organizations are alike; each has its own history, problems, opportunities, and personnel.

Any organizational structure will change from time to time. Therefore, a program of decentralization cannot be devised, put into force, and then forgotten. Periodic adjustments must be made in the delegations and flow of authority between various units and levels in the company. Smith suggests that management approach this problem with the following thoughts:

> Let us look, perhaps more intently than usual for a while, at the way we have allocated authorities and powers between the headquarters organization on the one hand and the local divisions on the other hand. Let us see if we are having decisions made and actions taken at the levels where they can best be made. Let us ask the divisions what things they would like to decide which they now can't decide. What do they have to decide which they wish the headquarters would decide for them? Let us ask similar questions of the headquarters people.[16]

Such an approach will permit a continuous scrutiny of the decentralization process and will permit some give and take on the part of local executives and the executives at headquarters. Of even more importance, such an approach will stress cooperation and coordination and minimize the idea of a struggle for power.

The Need to Recentralize

From time to time management finds that it needs to recentralize authority. Top management may feel that it has lost control over certain activities, probably because its original controls were not effective. It is also possible that poor business conditions may force top management to recentralize authority over expenditures, sales efforts, or other activities. Moreover, in periods of business decline, top executives might feel that their personal influence and experience are needed to obtain cost reductions, improved operations, uniform standards, checks on expenditures, and so forth. It is also probable that executives will curtail decentralized staff services to the local managers and will require the managers to depend to a greater extent on centralized staff facilities. In general, many companies tend to centralize authority during a market decline and decentralize during the upward movement of the business cycle.

[16] Smith, *Managing Geographically Decentralized Companies*, p. 20.

Assume, for example, that in a manufacturing enterprise with several plants each plant manager has authority to negotiate union contracts. Then suddenly the national union's chief officers present top management with hard bargaining demands. This forces a recentralization of negotiating authority. Similar recentralization may also occur in times of emergency. In wartime, for example, much delegated authority must be recalled in order to adjust activities to a wartime basis. Usually, however, this recentralizing process does not reverse the basic idea of decentralization. Instead, authority over a certain type of activity is centralized wherever that activity is found. In the first example, the local plant manager still has over-all authority. Only his authority to negotiate union contracts has been recentralized.

The Recentralizing Effect of Computer Systems

What effect will computer technology have on the centralization-decentralization issue? It seems probable that computerized decision-making and information systems will slow down or even reverse the trend toward decentralization. Both of these technological innovations encourage recentralization. They do so by eliminating one of the compelling reasons for decentralization — management's inability to keep up with the increasing size and complexity of the enterprise. Aided by computers, management can relocate most decision-making at a central point. There the computers will efficiently process information and rapidly make it available. Computers will enable top management to extend its thinking and decision-making range, thus making delegation of authority less necessary.

No doubt many psychological reasons for decentralization have always existed and are likely to remain. However, they will be counterbalanced by the possibilities which the new information and decision-making systems provide for top management. Through them, management can exercise immediate control over work done at the divisional level.

The effects of computerization may be further amplified by two examples. The first is a large decentralized firm that, after acquiring electronic data processing equipment, attempted to recentralize certain finance decisions that had previously been made in relatively autonomous units. The managers of the decentralized units strongly resisted the change. They viewed headquarters' move as a severe threat to their position. The morale problem became so acute that top management finally decided not to go through with the recentralization program even though it had the technical capacity to do so. Precisely the opposite results occurred in a large insurance company. The firm decided to recentralize a variety of routine activities, such as sending out customer premium notices, making out payrolls, and keeping track of sales records, which had previously been handled in district offices. Most district managers were happy to relinquish these duties to the central computer system because they would have more time to concentrate on selling insurance.

In summary, the influence of the computer on centralization will vary from firm to firm. It is impossible to gauge its impact on important variables such as morale, organizational structure, and the independent judgment of individuals in the organization. The computer does seem to be a force toward centralization; the degree to which management decides to exploit it is another matter entirely. However, at least for the foreseeable future, only the largest enterprises will be able to make economic use of expensive computer installations.

With the discussion of decentralization, we complete the core of ideas surrounding the organizing function. However, two other structural elements in business organizations require close attention — committees and the board of directors.

Discussion Questions

1. The top management of a large company argued at one time, "We are a centralized-decentralized corporation." How will this affect corporate policy on the delegation of decision-making prerogatives?

2. Review your understanding of profit centers. How effective are they as a means of corporate control? What pitfalls do you visualize in the application of profit-center policy?

Supplementary Readings

Dale, Ernest. "Centralization Versus Decentralization." In *Dimensions in Modern Management,* edited by Patrick E. Connor. Boston: Houghton Mifflin, 1974.

Golembiewski, Robert T. *Men, Management, and Morality.* New York: McGraw-Hill, 1965. See chapters 7 and 8.

Kline, Bennett E., and Norman H. Martin. "Freedom, Authority, and Decentralization." In *Management in Perspective,* edited by W. F. Schlender, W. G. Scott, and A. C. Filley. Boston: Houghton Mifflin, 1965. See pp. 345–56.

Learned, E. P., and A. T. Sproat. *Organization Theory and Policy.* Homewood, Ill.: Irwin, 1966. See pp. 38–59.

Newsweek. "The Assembly Team." In *Dimensions in Modern Management.*

Organization Structures of International Companies. Studies in Personnel Policy, Research Report No. 198. New York: National Industrial Conference Board, 1965.

Stieglitz, Harold, and Allan R. Janger. "Degree of Decentralization." In *Dimensions in Modern Management.*

CHAPTER 15

Committees

We have seen that, as an organization grows larger, an executive has increasing difficulty administering its affairs and handling its problems. One way that management copes with this difficulty is by establishing committees and turning over specific problems and issues to them. A committee is a group of people who function collectively. It differs from other units of management in that its members normally have additional duties and devote only part of their time to committee activities.

Mention of the word "committee" evokes various reactions. When properly used and wisely selected, committees can be a great asset to any organization. However, the committee device has often been abused. Badly organized committees often delay action, and many perceive them as useless debating societies — "a collection of the unfit appointed by the unwilling to perform the unnecessary."

In spite of their bureaucratic image, committees — sometimes referred to as boards, commissions, or task forces — are widely used. Government activities generally involve a great deal of committee work. In some instances, government committees are created to investigate certain problems and in others they are created to manage government agencies, such as the Atomic Energy Commission. Educational institutions make extensive use of committees and boards. Religious organizations often depend on them to achieve greater lay participation in church affairs.

Committees are also widespread in business. According to A. C. Filley, in a survey of 1,200 respondent firms, 94 per cent of the firms with over 10,000 employees and 64 per cent of firms with fewer than 250 employees said they had formal committees.[1] A board of directors is a committee established by law for all corporations.

TYPES OF COMMITTEES

Function and Level

Committees can be classified by function and by the level in the organizational hierarchy to which they are attached. In the upper echelons we commonly find policy, executive, finance, audit, bonus and salary, product, and nominating committees, and many others named after the functions they perform. Corporate commit-

---

[1] A. C. Filley, "Committee Management: Guidelines from Social Science Research," *California Management Review* 13 (Fall 1970): 13.

tees, divisional committees, and departmental committees also exist. At the lower levels we find grievance committees, suggestion committees, safety committees, and others. Clearly, the committee device has been used for almost every task. However, management should only use the committee form when group action will be advantageous.

Line and Staff

A committee investigates, debates, and discusses a problem, and concludes its deliberations with some recommendation. If this procedure results merely in guidance, counsel, and advice, the committee is acting in a staff capacity. However, in many instances a subject is presented to a committee for decision. In such a case, the committee is acting in a line capacity, is called a *plural executive,* and is managerial in nature. The Du Pont Company has used this type of line committee management for top policy decisions since 1921.

Although most committees are either line or staff, at times they are neither. Such is the case when a committee is appointed merely to receive and pass information. Whatever its type, the committee is one of several kinds of devices that facilitate lateral relationships in organizations.

Temporary or Standing

Committees can also be classified by longevity. A temporary committee is appointed for a particular purpose and will be disbanded as soon as it has accomplished its task. A standing committee has a permanent place in the organization and deals with recurring problems. Finance and budget functions are handled by standing committees.

Often meetings and conferences arise on the spur of the moment when an executive feels the need to discuss certain matters with several department managers. The executive in this instance is not creating a committee. Large lectures and meetings likewise are not committees, even though the speaker may have to field questions. In both instances, group action — the typical characteristic of committees — is lacking.

ADVANTAGES OF GROUP DELIBERATION AND JUDGMENT

Combined Opinion

If a committee is properly selected and motivated, its group deliberation and judgment can be an outstanding asset to an organization. Committee members can bring to their meetings a range of experience, background, and ability, which one manager could not possess. This is especially important when decisions must be made on questions to which there is no clear answer. Then expert advice in different fields must often be obtained. The interests of various departments must also be properly represented. A committee member from one department or field may be able to direct the attention of other committee members to aspects of the problem that they might not have seen. Because the free oral interchange of ideas stimulates and clarifies thinking, committee members must be able to present their ideas clearly and must be willing to submit them to the critical appraisal of the other members of the committee. In this way, problems can be collectively analyzed. Frequently, staff uses committees to solicit a wide range of opinion and thereby improves the quality of advice given to management.

Coordination and Cooperation in Execution

The committee device can also promote coordination. Each committee member, by listening to other members' suggestions and thinking, becomes aware of the purposes and problems of other departments. He will understand how his activities affect their functions and hopefully will become more considerate of the other departments and more aware of the necessity for synchronizing his efforts with theirs. If a manager has participated in committee problem-solving, he is likely to cooperate more fully in the execution of the solution. Thus, committees promote planning coordination.

Development of Executives

Committee meetings provide an excellent proving ground for executives. Committees afford such men an opportunity to observe other departmental situations and to think about problems from an over-all company point of view. Top management can also observe executives in action in such meetings. These men must be able to present thoughts clearly, defend them, and think through their implications. Committee debates and discussions can certainly broaden an executive's decision-making qualities.

The committee is also an excellent training ground for junior executives. The appointment of such men to committees will enable them to become acquainted with the attitudes of other executives, with the company point of view, and with the way decisions are made. Because the junior executive is not always required to participate actively in committee deliberations, he will benefit most from merely listening and observing.

Associated with training benefits is the continuity of thinking fostered by committee membership. Few committees replace all members simultaneously; instead, they make full members out of junior executives who have previously sat in on committee meetings or they provide continuity by retaining several older members who know the reasons for previous decisions and actions. A desire for continuity also provides a rationale for the election of only one-third of the members of the United States Senate at any one time.

An outgrowth of the idea of using committees as a special training device for young executives is the "multiple management" plan originated in 1932 by McCormick and Company and adopted with modifications by several hundred other companies. McCormick has established four junior boards for younger executives —

the factory board, the sales board, the institutional sales board, and the board of directors. Although none of these junior boards is an official part of the corporate structure, they all examine company policies and operations and can make recommendations to the senior board of directors whenever they unanimously decide to do so. According to Charles P. McCormick, "The purpose of the junior board then, as it is now, would be not to bypass the judgment of the more mature men, but to supplement that judgment with new ideas."[2]

Fear of Delegating Too Much Authority

Often, management does not wish to delegate authority to individuals and will instead form a committee. Although in some cases this practice merely reflects management's inability to delegate any authority, it often reflects management's valid appraisal of a particular situation. This type of situation will be discussed here.

The legitimate fear of delegating authority to an individual is particularly strong in all levels and activities of government, in educational institutions, and in religious organizations. These institutions, therefore, abound in boards, commissions, and committees. We also find examples of this fear in business. The existence of a corporate board of directors may have been brought about in part by the reluctance of property owners to delegate too much authority to a single executive officer. Top policy, salary, and bonus committees are formed for similar reasons. We mentioned previously that the authority to determine company products is often lodged in a product committee. In all these situations, authority is shared by four, five, or six managers from various areas of the enterprise.

Representation of Interest Groups

Committees also give representatives of different interest groups a chance to discuss a subject that affects them all. Thus, the executives and specialists of various departments and activities can work as a team. Each interested party is assured proper representation, morale is improved, and participation and involvement is fostered. As mentioned earlier, committees also help to produce balanced group integration and judgment.

At times, however, concern with proper representation can be carried too far. It is essential to appoint capable rather than just representative members to the committee. A "representative" member may not be able to contribute to the committee or integrate his ideas with those of the rest of its members.

LIMITATIONS OF COMMITTEES

Committees have several disadvantages that an executive should consider before committing a problem to group action. Only after weighing the disadvantages with

[2] Charles P. McCormick, *The Power of People: Multiple Management Up to Date* (New York: Harper and Row, 1952), p. 12.

the advantages can management determine if a particular question should be referred to a committee.

High Costs

Committees consume time. Their pace is slow because each member is entitled to speak and to try to convince other members of his point of view. This process, of course, leads to even further discussion. Meetings are further slowed by a committee member's unnecessary verbiage.

Meetings cost money as well as time. Time spent in committee meetings is not spent elsewhere. Hence, every hour consumed by a committee meeting costs the corporation in dollars and cents. In addition, committees often require travel and its associated expense. Moreover, preparing for meetings and providing a committee staff and often a secretary costs money. Obviously, a single executive could reach a decision in a much shorter time and at less expense. The problem, however, is whether his decision would be as good as the one reached by group deliberation. If it were not, then the benefits of committee action would probably be substantial enough to make up for the additional cost involved.

Effectiveness Limited to Certain Situations

When will a group make a better decision than an individual? This question has received considerable attention, and answers to it vary. Generally speaking, a group makes routine decisions effectively but does not perform as well as the individual in creative problem-solving. This conclusion has profound implications today, when committees are used to make company policy, perform research on new products, build morale, increase worker participation, and train junior executives.

For example, business firms are discovering that they can make effective use of scarce scientific talent by combining engineers and scientists on teams that develop fairly routine products. In other words, the abilities of a growing breed of "organization man" scientists can be multiplied by a large factor when utilized in project teams. Teaming has several additional benefits. Through it, a firm can secure technological progress in a highly competitive research environment and can provide its scientists with professional associations and support from a group of technically qualified people like themselves.

A survey by the American Management Association indicates other types of problems that executives feel are suitable for committee decisions. Table 15-1 presents the survey's analysis of the relative merits of individual versus group action in various management activities. From this we can see that most managers prefer to settle jurisdictional disputes within the company by committee. Many managers prefer that committees formulate company objectives. Although not shown specifically in the survey, the distribution of bonuses and the establishment of salaries for executives are also often determined by committee. In most other functional areas, however, the survey shows that individual action is considered essential. In

Table 15-1. Percentage of Cases in Which Management Functions Can Be Effectively Exercised by a Committee

Management function	A. Can be exercised by committee effectively	B. Same as A, but can be exercised more effectively by individual	C. Individual initiative essential; may be supplemented by committee action	D. Individual action essential; committee ineffective
Planning	20	20	25	35
Control	25	20	25	30
Formulating objectives	35	35	10	20
Organization	5	25	20	50
Jurisdictional questions	90	10	—	—
Leadership	—	—	10	90
Administration	20	25	25	30
Execution	10	15	10	65
Innovation	30	20	20	30
Communication	20	15	35	30
Advice	15	25	35	25
Decision-making	10	30	10	50

Source: Adapted from Ernest Dale, *Planning and Developing the Company Organization Structure*, Research Report No. 20 (New York: American Management Association, 1952), p. 128.

at least 50 per cent of the cases involving organization, leadership, execution, or decision-making, management feels that the use of a committee would be undesirable and, in fact, ineffective.

Divided Responsibility

In addition to the limitations on the types of situations in which committee action is effective, there are limitations on the sense of responsibility it evokes. When a problem is submitted to a committee, it is submitted to a group and not to individuals. Therefore, it becomes everybody's — and nobody's — responsibility. Theoretically, each member of the committee should shoulder the responsibility, but in reality this does not occur.

Many individuals who gladly accept individual responsibility do not seem to feel the same sense of responsibility when serving on a committee. Therefore, committees often are willing to settle for reasonably satisfactory solutions. If such solutions are wrong, "the committee," not the individuals comprising it, is blamed. There is no way to overcome the thinning out of responsibility; it is one of the serious disadvantages of the committee.

Splintered Authority

The phenomenon of splintered authority is closely related to the problem of divided responsibility and is perhaps partially responsible for it. In an earlier chapter, we saw that from time to time managers of different departments pool their authority to make decisions spanning several areas because none of the managers has enough authority in each area to make the decision himself. Such pooling of splintered authority enables department managers to avoid calling on a higher executive to solve many problems. From time to time the use of committees to facilitate such pooling is unavoidable. If, however, committees are used continuously to concentrate authority in one place, then the structure of the organization should be reexamined.

Danger of Weak Compromise Decisions

Committee decisions are often unanimous, even if only majority agreement is required. This tradition is based on politeness, mutual respect, cooperative spirit, and other considerations of this sort. However, a unanimous agreement often signals watered-down action and weak compromise. Very often, in fact, the compromise decision will reflect the lowest common denominator of agreement. Therefore, this type of decision probably will not be as strong, as positive, or as good as it would be if an individual had considered the various aspects and made the decision by himself.

Political considerations are frequently important in lowest common denominator decisions. One member of a committee may lend his support to another with the hope of eventual reciprocation. However, such support usually does not appear in a formal vote. Those experienced in committee work usually oppose formal voting because it tends to split the group instead of promoting cooperation and coordination. A vote on a controversial matter, therefore, is not as beneficial as a consensus of the majority. The few members who disagree will at least not feel formally outvoted and therefore may be willing to cooperate in the execution of the decision.

A committee, however, often reports not only the majority recommendation but also the minority one. Having both opinions will probably be helpful to the executive making the final decision. Also, the danger of a weak compromise is lessened when both majority and minority opinions are submitted.

Strain on Interpersonal Relations

One further limitation of committees in modern organizations exists. They tend to place considerable strain on interpersonal relationships. Some organizations, therefore, establish programs to develop interpersonal competence. Firms like TRW Systems have used sensitivity training to help employees settle problems among themselves. We will have more to say about this training technique in Part V.

EFFECTIVE OPERATION OF THE COMMITTEE

After management has weighed all advantages and disadvantages and has decided to establish a committee, it must make plans that will ensure effective committee operation.

Clear Definitions of Functions, Scope, and Degree of Authority

Management must clearly define the functions and scope of its committees. Committee members must know the range of the subject referred to them and the functions they are expected to fulfill in relation to it. The basic functions of a marketing committee, for example, could be described in this way:

To review and coordinate marketing activities of the various operating and selling units of the company and coordinate them with other management functions, especially manufacturing. To develop plans for more effective analysis and control of distribution costs, pricing, inventory control, market analysis and forecasts, product service, basic advertising, trade mark policies, and market forecasting in so far as they affect the company as a whole.[3]

The scope of the marketing committee could also be delineated:

The duties and responsibilities of this Committee cover all matters concerned with the sale of products by any operating division. The committee shall not concern itself with the normal marketing activities of any individual operating or selling unit of the company unless such activities appear to require consideration from an overall company policy viewpoint.[4]

If a committee has a stated scope and duties, it is not likely to flounder. This statement will also provide committee members and higher executives with a scale on which to judge committee performance. Furthermore, it helps to clarify the committee's relationship to other organizational units and its connections — if any — with a particular executive's job.

Management must also specify the degree of authority it confers on a committee. It must clearly state whether the committee is to serve in an advisory, informational, or decision-making capacity. It must also specify whether it is to function as staff or to perform the job of a plural executive. The degree of authority conferred upon the marketing committee, for example, could be designated in this way: "This committee will serve as a counseling and advisory group to the president. Recommendations resulting from committee action will be presented to the president for his consent when they are of company-wide or major application or involve budget action or changes."[5]

---

[3] Ernest Dale, *Planning and Developing the Company Organization Structure*, Research Report No. 20 (New York: American Management Association, 1952), p. 259.

[4] *Ibid.*, p. 259.

[5] *Ibid.*, p. 261.

Selection of Appropriate Members

The quality of a committee's work is only as good as its members. Members should be capable of working together. They should be willing to see each other's viewpoint, be able to integrate their thinking with that of other members, and be careful to avoid compromise at the least common denominator. They must also respect each other even if they disagree.

Members of a committee are usually of the same organizational rank and independent of each other. This ensures that their deliberations will not have any superior-subordinate connotations. It is difficult and uncomfortable, for instance, for a vice-president to oppose the chairman of the board. If committee members are chosen from different departments, these difficulties of rank are more easily overcome. Selecting members from different departments also helps to assure proper representation of the various interests which will be affected by the committee's actions. The importance of wide representation cannot be minimized. However, as we pointed out previously, representativeness is not as important as ability.

When selecting able committee members, a manager should choose individuals who are familiar with the objectives of the enterprise, who know how the company operates, and who have the imagination and the ability to present their ideas effectively. They also should have the courage of their convictions and the strength to maintain their point of view until proved wrong. Although each member will not possess all these attributes, each should at least be capable of expressing and defending himself in the presence of a group.

Management analysts have found that committee members work together more productively and gain satisfaction from their committee experience if they share goals. However, not all committees should be homogeneous in composition. Some tasks are accomplished more effectively than others in a competitive group atmosphere.[6]

Reasonable Number of Members

A committee should be large enough to provide thorough group deliberation, a wide range of opinion, and broad sources of information. However, it should not be unwieldy. Many believe that a committee should be limited to three or four members, whereas others feel that from six to ten is a reasonable number. Sometimes the purpose for which a committee is established will, by necessity, dictate its size. If a committee has been appointed to coordinate activities, for example, it must include representatives of all the divisions to be coordinated. If a large committee must be formed to consider a particular subject, the group can sometimes be broken into various subcommittees that will consider smaller aspects of the general problem. In order to reduce size, management might also designate certain individuals to be part-time committee members. Such members will attend meetings whenever their special knowledge is pertinent or whenever they can benefit from the day's discussions. Generally, smaller committees, of approximately five members, will per-

[6] Filley, "Committee Management," pp. 18–19.

form tasks most effectively and will supply maximum satisfaction to participating members.

Thorough Preparation for Meetings

In order to make committee meetings more effective, an agenda should be prepared and circulated in advance. Too often members must go into a meeting inadequately prepared because they do not know the committee's agenda. Under these conditions, their contributions cannot be as effective as they otherwise would be.

Staff support is also necessary to effective committee work. Often, a committee is provided with its own staff, which prepares certain information, gathers data, and so forth. If it does not have its own staff, the committee must be able to call on advisory staffs available throughout the organization to supply background information and other detailed material. Such factual material provides a basis for committee evaluation of questions under consideration and gives a broader perspective to committee matters.

Committee Procedures

Committee meetings are more effective if certain procedures are followed — if minutes are composed and distributed to committee members before subsequent meetings, and if such subsequent meetings are planned well in advance and members are appropriately informed. Often, executives who are active on a number of committees find that meeting dates conflict. Although an executive can send an administrative assistant to a meeting as his representative, that assistant usually cannot speak for him and can fulfill only a reporter's role. Such schedule conflicts can often be avoided, however, by proper planning. Some companies have resorted to a scheduling board to keep track of an executive's commitments and actually pin him down for executive meetings.

The Right Chairman

The most important man in every committee operation is, of course, the chairman. His skills will often determine the success or failure of committee activities. He plans the meetings, prepares the agenda, and sees to it that the proper background information is available before the meetings. During meetings he provides leadership, guides the proceedings, calls on speakers, and generally sets the tone of the discussion. A good chairman can minimize many committee shortcomings. He can conduct sessions in a formal or relaxed manner, depending upon the circumstances. He can also integrate committee deliberations. Naturally, the chairman cannot dominate the discussion, for this would annihilate the value of group deliberations. However, he can summarize various discussions and try to integrate them into an effective solution or recommendation.

When, as sometimes happens, a person without much leadership ability is selected as chairman, one of the other members of the committee will very likely become a de facto chairman. In such a case, management would do well to remove the originally appointed chairman from his position and probably from the committee.

Group Interaction

Even without the guidance of a chairman, most committees would eventually arrive at some conclusions through the dynamics of group interaction. However, experience has shown that when several committees deliberate concurrently, some arrive at conclusions — and better conclusions — before others do. This occurs because some chairmen can structure group interaction more successfully than can others. This structuring involves such things as keeping the discussion on the relevant subject, assessing the quality and ability of committee members, and choosing appropriate procedures and methods for the type of individuals and the subject involved. The various members of a committee all have individual patterns of behavior and points of view. The chairman must know how to handle the membership so that the viewpoints and attitudes fuse and an effective team results.

Naturally, each committee member thinks first of how a new proposition will affect him and his working environment. This tendency can easily lead to unnecessary frictions. Therefore, the chairman must develop some common basis for evaluating propositions. He must first establish agreement on the nature of the problem under discussion. Then he must see that everybody understands the issues. Only after these steps have been achieved can the members of the group effectively interact and achieve a successful solution.

Of course, it takes time and patience to form a smoothly interacting social group. Indeed, managers often say that the problems on the conference table are really not as difficult to deal with as the people around the table are. Individuals often react to each other rather than to ideas. For a meeting to be successful, members must forget about personalities and outside allegiances and work together.

Although the chairman plays a pivotal role in all committee interactions, he may appear successively as an autocrat and as a democrat. At times, however, even the most permissive, democratic chairman must exercise tight control over a meeting. The decision to do so will, of course, reflect the chairman's ability to understand and to structure group interaction.

In summary, an effective chairman must master two leadership roles: a role that emphasizes leader control over task activities, and a role that emphasizes group-building and the maintenance of committee social relations. Although it is desirable that the chairman play both roles, they are frequently shared by at least two people.[7]

Follow-Up of Committee Action

If a committee has been acting in a staff capacity, its findings need relatively little follow-up. The chairman will merely report the committee's recommendations to

[7] *Ibid.*, p. 17.

the initiating line executive. Of course, since committee members will be interested in the executive's reaction to their recommendations, he should provide appropriate feedback. If recommendations are not accepted, an explanation would be politic but not absolutely necessary.

If a committee has been acting in a managerial capacity and has been charged with authority to make decisions, a different situation arises. Then a member of the committee itself usually executes its decisions, and that member must be chosen. Usually, the chairman or secretary of the committee will be asked to act in an executive capacity for the committee as a whole. However, sometimes a divisional representative would be more appropriate. If the committee has been dealing with matters that normally belong within the realm of one operating division, it is better to have that particular operating executive execute the decision. In such an instance, functional authority is conferred upon the committee, but executive authority is left to the regular operating executive.

Evaluation of Committee Work

Committees, like other parts of an organization, need periodic evaluation. A line executive must check to see whether the purpose for which the committee was established is still valid and whether the committee is operating efficiently within the terms of its purpose and scope. Without such review, comittees may remain unnecessarily self-perpetuating.

Discussion Questions

1. Under what circumstances (organizational, task) should members of a committee compete with each other? When should they cooperate?

2. In your experience of working with other people in groups, what size of group seemed most effective? In what size of group did you gain most satisfaction from your participation?

Supplementary Readings

Davis, Ralph Currier. *The Fundamentals of Top Management.* New York: Harper and Row, 1951. See pp. 468–84.

Filley, A. C. "Committee Management: Guidelines from Social Science Research." In *Dimensions in Modern Management,* edited by Patrick E. Connor. Boston: Houghton Mifflin, 1974.

Galbraith, John Kenneth. *The New Industrial State.* Boston: Houghton Mifflin, 1967. See chapter 6.

Rubenstein, Albert H., and Chadwick J. Haberstroh. *Some Theories of Organization.* Homewood, Ill.: Irwin, 1966. See pp. 263–78.

CHAPTER 16

Boards of Directors

The classic definition of a corporation was given by Chief Justice Marshall in the well-known Dartmouth College case decided in 1819:

A corporation is an artificial being, invisible, intangible, and existing only in the contemplation of the law. Being a mere creature of the law, it possesses only those properties which the charter of its creation confers upon it, either expressly or as incidental to its very existence. . . . Among the most important are immortality, and if the expression may be allowed, individuality; properties by which a perpetual succession of many persons are considered the same, and may act as a single individual.[1]

The corporation was considered from the start to be an artificial creation. Who would be responsible for its management? Who would decide the questions that in a sole proprietorship or partnership were decided by the owners? The formulators of state laws of incorporation found it expedient to create a board of directors for this purpose — a permanent, formal committee established to function as a plural executive.

The state laws under which businesses are incorporated do not clearly specify the duties of directors; they merely state that directors should "manage" the affairs of the company. Naturally, the board does not handle daily operating details and does not make all the decisions necessary to keep the enterprise running effectively. Instead, day-to-day business is entrusted to the chief executive and his lieutenants. The directors, however, must make certain that this executive is competent and that he and his associates efficiently and properly conduct the corporation's operations. Freedom from involvement in day-to-day operating details enables the board to maintain a broad perspective and far-seeing point of view. Stockholders, employees, and others are thus assured that their long-run interests will not be sacrificed to the expediencies of the moment. However, although the directors are responsible for the welfare of the corporation, they are not legal agents of the stockholders; they are their elected representatives.

Variety among boards of directors is endless. In small family-owned businesses boards are often composed of relatives and serve little purpose but to comply with

[1] The Trustees of Dartmouth College v. Woodward, 4 Wheaton 636 (1819).

the law. On the other hand, vast corporations, with hundreds of thousands of shares of stock listed on the stock exchanges, have boards whose directors are complete strangers to most shareholders. Some of these boards are composed of insiders — directors who are full-time employees or officers of the company. Others consist entirely of outsiders — people who hold leading positions in other companies, professions, or public affairs and who are not active in the day-to-day management of corporate affairs. The frequency of board meetings may also vary. Some meet only once a year; others meet often and regularly. Also, the extent to which boards fulfill their functions and exercise their potential powers differs greatly.

FUNCTIONS

The board of directors has the authority to exercise the powers of the corporation subject to the limitations stated in the corporate charter and the by-laws. Necessarily, the functions, powers, and responsibilities of the directors extend into numerous areas.

Trusteeship

The relationship between the directors and the stockholders of the corporation is a fiduciary one. It is a relationship of trust and confidence in which the stockholders entrust the welfare of the corporation to the directors. It is similar to the relationship between trustees and guardians. Thus, the term "trusteeship" is used in this text in a popular sense to describe the attitude of directors toward their position; no reference is intended to title, to property, or to any other legal implications. In addition to the fiduciary relationship of the directors to the shareholders, the board has a similar relationship to the company's employees, to its customers, and to the general public. This is especially true in large, publicly owned corporations. In practical terms, a fiduciary is not allowed to take advantage of the relationship for personal gain. If he should do so, he would be legally liable.

Establishment of Basic Objectives and Broad Policies

One of the functions of the board of directors is to develop and determine the basic objectives and broad policies of the corporation. The board of directors, while staying within the general provisions of the charter, must provide long-range planning and establish the over-all goals of the company. One of the chief means by which the board guides its operating executives is by its major policy formulations. Sound, consistent policies bind the various parts of the organization together, creating unity of purpose and lessening the dependence of the corporation on any one executive. However, the directors alone do not determine policy. Instead, effective policy is the joint product of the board of directors and the operating executives. The operating staff plays an important role in the preparation of policy by gathering the information that the board needs to act intelligently. Furthermore, in many corporations, and especially in small ones, the spark and initiative for goals and objectives come from the operating people. In such instances, the president or other high executive officers explore new possibilities and submit plans to the directors for their consideration. The directors then accept or alter the plans and policies as they desire. Likewise, the pronouncement of a policy by the board does not make it effective. Unless the policy is workable and understood, and unless it is "accepted in spirit as well as in letter by the operating organization, it will be nullified."[2]

The policy-making function of the board of directors is continuous. Policies must be made when a new enterprise is launched, when the board feels that a major change of course is necessary, and when new problems arise. Frequently, what appears on the surface to be an operating problem may actually be a policy-making one that should be handled only by the directors. For example, when the directors of a downtown department store approve the appropriation for the opening of their first suburban shopping branch, the fact that the directors are inaugurating a change in the character of the company's business is of primary importance.

Election of Corporate Officers

The selection and election of a corporate president is a vital function of every board of directors. Their choice is in the nature of a long-range decision because it will have significant bearing on the future of the corporation. Therefore, electing a president and policy-making are closely related. If the board chooses a candidate who will accept his position without demanding major policy changes, his acceptance constitutes a confirmation and probably a continuation of existing policies; if the board chooses a candidate who will accept only if major policies will be changed, the board in electing him is making a long-run policy decision.

The choice of the chief executive is also likely to have a long-range effect on the board itself. New presidents gain progressively more influence with the directors. A president's advice regarding potential board members will be sought; eventually he may even suggest names of men to be nominated for election to the board. The president will also influence the board's activities, for he decides which operating problems should be referred to it. His decisions will determine to a great extent whether the board has the opportunity to perform the service for which it is intended.

Generally the board of directors has the authority to elect all other officers of the corporation as well as the president. However, for all practical purposes this authority is usually delegated to the president himself. Since corporate officers will work as his subordinates, it is only proper for the president to choose them. As a matter of form, the president submits his choices to the board, which in turn formally appoints them as corporate officers. Although it does not actually select these other officers, the board subsequently often advises them and approves their actions.

---

[2] Melvin T. Copeland and Andrew R. Towl, *The Board of Directors and Business Management* (Boston: Division of Research, Graduate School of Business Administration, Harvard University, 1947), p. 66.

Approval of Important Financial Matters

The board of directors controls corporate purse strings by approving all final budgets. However, the board's purse control involves far more than strictly financial considerations; it involves a great deal of policy. If additional capital appropriations are needed, for example, the directors must decide whether these funds should be borrowed or whether they should be obtained from the sale of stock. If they decide to borrow, they must decide whether the loan should come from commercial banks or insurance companies or from the public in the form of notes or bonds. Board decisions such as those relating to the compensation paid to the various officers also have policy implications.

Distribution of Earnings

Determining how to distribute earnings is one of the most essential functions of the board of directors. The various interests inherent in this type of decision greatly challenge the fiduciary character of a director's position. Generally speaking, a director may distribute earnings in three ways: They may be distributed to the stockholders in the form of dividends; they may be retained in the business for expansion purposes; or they may be used to repay outstanding loans. However, the various regulations of the Internal Revenue Code penalize a corporation with additional taxes if it fails to distribute a certain percentage of its earnings to its shareholders. Aside from such specific legislation, the board must be guided by its position of trusteeship. The distribution of earnings will affect the stockholder, no matter what is done. If the directors decide to retain earnings for expansion purposes, they are forcing the stockholders to reinvest in the corporation. Likewise, if they decide to retain earnings to retire outstanding indebtedness, they withhold dividends from the stockholders.

Over the years many companies have established a policy whereby a portion of the earnings is distributed in the form of dividends and the remainder is retained for further expansion and for the retirement of indebtedness. There are, however, years during which the profits of the company might not be large enough to permit distribution in all three directions. In such cases, the board uses its judgment in determining where the earnings are most needed.

Maintenance and Revision of the Corporate Charter

If, for some reason, the content of the corporate charter or the by-laws has become outdated and a revision is needed, the board of directors must institute such action. Although the statement of purpose in the original charter is usually made as broad as possible, the directors may wish to pursue some new activity not covered by it. In such a case, they must amend the charter. Similarly, if there is to be a change in the number of shares or composition of the outstanding capital stock, the board of directors must approve it and instigate the appropriate action.

Perpetuation of the Corporation

The board of directors must assure the continued life of the corporation. It must also perpetuate itself by holding regular elections and filling vacancies. It is the board's responsibility to recommend to the owners of the corporation desirable future board personnel. In making such recommendations, the present directors must consider both inside and outside members. They must also bear in mind the factor of age. If a board grows too old, it may overlook the advantages of appointing younger members. All boards should also make some provisions for the continuation of management in an emergency.

Delegation of Special Powers

Because board members are not concerned with the day-to-day management of the affairs of the corporation, they must delegate the authority for certain special tasks to the executive officers. For example, the board must determine who may sign checks, sign contracts, open bank accounts, and make loans. However, the board's powers of delegation may be restricted by the corporate statutes of the state or the corporate charter.

Checking on Results

The fiduciary relationship of the directors to the shareowners clearly implies that the directors must check on the results and control the activities of the executive officers. This is more than a policing operation. It includes not only an analysis of the financial outcome at the end of the fiscal year, but also a constant review of operating results throughout the year. A check made only at year's end might be too late. Moreover, a thorough review should extend beyond figures to policies and practices. Although the board delegates authority for executing policies to the operating executives, it remains responsible for ensuring that policies are effectively carried out and that the actual results are those that were anticipated. Such checks do not imply a lack of confidence in the operating executives or friction between them and the board. In fact, the board is actually checking up on itself as much as on the executives, because it naturally had much to do with making the various plans and policies.

Raising Discerning Questions

Another important function of the board of directors is to ask discerning questions. They are a director's principal tool and constitute one of his major contributions to managing the enterprise. "A really discerning question typically opens up a situation where action or at least a thorough review of policy is called for. Discernment, furthermore, is evidenced not only in the opening question but also in the persistence shown in following through beyond the initial reply to the underlying reality."[3] When a director inquires about the sales outlook he is posing a routine question, but when he asks why less than 10 per cent of the products account for 90 per cent of total sales volume, he is posing a discerning question which goes to the heart of the problem. The ability to ask discerning questions comes with experience.

A director should be able to ask pertinent questions without knowing all the details of a situation. He senses when and where and how to initiate searching inquiries. In one case the starting point for such an inquiry may come from some item on the balance sheet; in other cases, it may come from remarks made during a discussion, from a casual comment of an executive, from an item in a special report, or from contrast with the practices and policies of another company. Directors, who in their years of experience have been exposed to a variety of situations, usually acquire an almost intuitive ability to ask pertinent questions.

Executive officers who submit propositions to the board of directors are generally aware that they will be questioned closely. Hence, they will prepare their subject matter thoroughly, studying the problem from all angles in order to have appropriate answers ready. The directors, in turn, will quickly sense the amount of preparation that has gone into a proposal. In asking discerning questions about it, the director is not playing the role of a prosecuting attorney, nor is he interfering in the executive's field of action. Instead, he is attempting to fully understand and evaluate the matter under consideration so that he can constructively participate in the board's deliberations.

Maintaining Close Contact with Owners

An additional function of the board of directors is to maintain close contact with the owners, that is, the stockholders of the corporation. Because the directors are the elected representatives of the stockholders, they must see that those stockholders are acquainted with the company's progress, that they are provided with annual and interim reports. Good stockholder relations are becoming increasingly important, especially to large, publicly held corporations with a great many investors. Yet even in small corporations, it is common for the board of directors to keep in touch with shareholders and to send out annual and quarterly interim reports.

Mediating Between the Organization and the Environment

Recently another dimension has been added to the many functions of the board. Because of the efforts of minorities and special interest groups to make corporations realize and live up to their social responsibilities, boards have accepted the authority to act as a mediating link between them and the organization. It has been proposed[4] that board composition be altered to reflect the needs of the various important interest groups. Even now, in some large corporations, women and members of

---

[3] *Ibid.*, p. 95. Also see John Calhoun Baker, *Directors and Their Functions* (Boston: Division of Research, Graduate School of Business Administration, Harvard University, 1945), p. 19.

[4] Jeffrey Pfeffer, "Size and Composition of Corporate Boards of Directors: The Organization and Its Environment," *Administrative Science Quarterly* 17, no. 2 (June 1972): 218–28.

minority groups have occasionally been elected to corporate boards. How well the board responds to these new external social pressures will affect over-all corporate success.

LEGAL RESPONSIBILITIES OF DIRECTORS

All boards of directors do not fulfill all the functions just discussed; some merely fulfill their legal requirements. The corporation laws of most states do not recognize these differences, however. As a general rule, the same basic principles govern the directors of all corporations. Legal responsibilities remain the same whether a board member is truly a director or merely a front, whether the corporation is a multi-million-dollar operation or a small family business, and whether the director is an outsider or an employee.

Charter Provisions

The corporate charter or the corporate by-laws, of course, set some limits on the directors' authority. Amending the corporate charter, merging with other corporations, and dissolving the corporation are shareholder decisions. Furthermore, some activities are not included in the original statement of purpose of the corporation and are therefore prohibited. If the board of directors engages the corporation in activities that have not been specified in the charter, it is performing extra-charter activities, *ultra vires*. Such activities are illegal. However, for all practical purposes, the charter can usually be amended so that these activities will fall within the scope of the corporation and hence within the competence of the board.

Reasonable Business Judgment

A director managing the affairs of a corporation should exercise his authority with the same degree of energy, diligence, care, and skill that ordinarily prudent men would exercise under similar circumstances. Legally, when a director or board fails to act with proper care and as a result the corporation is harmed, the careless directors can be held personally liable. Taking proper care means, among other things, that the director must attend board meetings and keep himself informed. Within reason, the director can rely on the integrity of the other directors, on the competence of the executive officers, and on the information given to him. However, he cannot passively acquiesce when as an ordinary businessman he would inquire and possibly object.

The director is not liable, of course, for honest mistakes in judgment if he has used ordinary business prudence and has acted in good faith. He can take the same chances that he would take in his own business. However, he cannot be careless or negligent without being legally liable. In the eyes of the law, as long as directors use reasonable business judgment, they have nothing to fear even if their decisions turn out to be wrong.

Loyalty

Loyalty is the other factor determining a director's legal liability. By making the directors responsible for the welfare of the corporation, a relationship of trust and confidence is created between them and the stockholders. The directors are naturally expected to faithfully serve the interests of any corporation on whose board they sit, but they may have loyalties to other people or institutions as well. In today's business world, the extent and limits of a director's various loyalties are often tested. For example, two corporations that have occasional transactions with each other may have the same director. This situation, known as an interlocking directorate, will be discussed later. A director may also hear of opportunities that he could exploit on his own but that also could be exploited by the corporation. There have been many occasions when the courts were forced to define proper behavior in such a situation and to determine whether a conflict of interests existed.

A director should at all times be guided by ethical standards. For instance, it is unethical for a director to learn of a location that the corporation intends to buy, purchase the land himself, and then resell it to the corporation at a higher price. In this case the director's disloyalty to the corporation is clear. In other cases, however, his decision to pursue an opportunity might be more ethically troublesome.

Liabilities Under Federal Laws

A number of federal laws set standards for directors of corporations whose stock is registered on a stock exchange. Under the Securities Act of 1933, directors must, to a reasonable degree, determine the truthfulness and completeness of the factual representations made in securities registration statements. If a director does not do so, he may be criminally penalized and may be held personally liable to any security buyer who suffers losses because of the misrepresentation for which he is responsible.[5]

In addition to this, the Securities Exchange Act of 1934, together with its 1964 amendment, requires that directors of corporations whose stocks are listed on a stock exchange promptly report significant events affecting the corporation. They also must submit to the stock exchanges and to the Securities and Exchange Commission an initial report of all their holdings of the corporations' equity securities and, within a stated time, must submit additional reports of any changes in those holdings.[6] Moreover, the law restricts the directors from engaging in certain stock transactions commonly known as short-swing profits of insider trading. This measure is obviously intended to prevent directors from taking advantage of inside information. More specifically, Section 16b of the Securities Exchange Act of 1934 states that directors must turn over to the corporation any profit realized from the purchase and sale or sale and purchase of the corporation's stock completed within a span of less than six months. Any stockholder or the corporation itself can sue the

---

[5] Securities Act of 1933, Sec. 11, 15 U.S.C.A. 59, P.P. 77k and Sec. 24, 15 U.S.C.A. 59, P.P. 77x.

[6] Securities Exchange Act of 1934, Section 16 (a), 15 U.S.C.A. 78(p) (a).

director to recover this possible profit. Section 16c of the Act similarly restricts short sales by directors.

These statutory limitations on the speculations of insiders have, no doubt, had a salutary effect. However, laws cannot completely eliminate the use of inside information. Nevertheless, recent and pending court and administrative decisions concerned with new and broader restrictions on stock dealings based on inside information may close some of the gaps.[7]

On the other hand, a pattern of by-laws, charter provisions, state corporate statutes, and insurance coverage is emerging to protect directors against excessive legal liability. Their objective is to broaden legal protection to the fullest extent possible so that competent men will remain willing to serve as directors.

Nevertheless, the number of lawsuits against directors instigated by irate stockholders, environmentalists, and special interest groups has been increasing. Thus, the liability hazard is becoming an obstacle to recruiting directors. In order to overcome this risk, corporations have been requested by their board members to carry director liability insurance — expensive insurance coverage whose validity has not been sufficiently tested in court. However, it provides the director with some psychological comfort and assures management that it will have assistance in case a suit should be brought.

Interlocking Directorships and Conflict of Interest

Interlocking directorships between large companies have long been prohibited by Section 8 of the Clayton Anti-Trust Act. This provision was initially aimed at large companies in direct competition, but it has been extended to those companies in partial competition. In 1968, under the threat of anti-trust action, many of the nation's largest companies — especially those in the auto, petroleum, and rubber industries — agreed to break up interlocking directorates. Auto makers and oil companies, for instance, could not share directors because each sold items such as batteries and spark plugs in the auto market.

In recent years, the Federal Trade Commission has established that a conflict of interest exists when a director serves on the boards of two companies that make different but competitive products. For instance, the Federal Trade Commission contends that the steel and aluminum industries compete in the auto bumper market and in the industrial building siding field.

Obviously, the broadening interpretation of interlocks and conflicts of interest is going to make the recruiting of sufficiently qualified outside directors more and more difficult. Since regulatory agencies and the courts, reasoning that stockholders and the public must be protected and free competition ensured, have begun forcing sterner interpretations, conflicts of interest have become an increasingly sticky problem for top corporate executives who serve on boards of directors.

[7] The Cady, Roberts and Company Case, Securities Exchange Act Release No. 6668, November 8, 1961, and S.E.C. v. Texas Gulf Sulphur Company et al., C.C.H. Fed. Sec. L. Rep. No. 91805 (S.D.N.Y. 1966).

COMPOSITION OF THE BOARD

The most desirable board of directors is balanced with proper representation of company management and outsiders including large ownership interests and with members who have varied skills and experience. Much of the most recent information concerning the composition of boards of directors is found in a research study conducted by the National Industrial Conference Board in cooperation with the American Society of Corporate Secretaries.[8] In this study 753 industrial and commercial companies reported on their latest directorship practices. Of these, 456 were engaged in manufacturing and 297 in nonmanufacturing. Much of the factual data presented below is based on this survey.

Inside and Outside Directors

Although a balanced board is usually considered desirable, some companies do not believe that typical balance is necessary or desirable. Such companies might have boards entirely composed of inside directors or they might, with the exception of a single person (the chief executive officer), have boards selected entirely from outside. There has been a continuous trend toward placing a majority of outsiders on corporate boards.

The Inside Director

The term "inside director," or "employee director," is applied to two different groups. First, there is the inside director who devotes his entire time to sitting on the board of a particular corporation. He has no other executive duties, is fully employed by the corporation as a director, and is compensated accordingly.

Second, there is the inside director who, in addition to being a board member, is also an officer of the corporation — vice-president in charge of production, of sales, etc. This type of director should be known as an officer director. Such an executive wears two hats. At times he is an upper-level operating manager, at times an inside director. Some difficulties are created by such a dual function.

Both types of inside directors know the internal problems of the corporation thoroughly and generally are also familiar with the problems of the industry. In addition, they are vitally interested in the successful operation of the company, for their income and livelihood depend on it. They cannot have any conflicts of interest. An employee director is readily available. However, there are a number of disadvantages to this kind of director. He is so closely connected with the operations of the company that he may be unable to view a situation objectively and independently. This criticism is primarily leveled against the officer director, as is the charge that this type of inside director often has difficulty reconciling his own short-run goals with over-all company operations. Furthermore, insiders selected by the chief

[8] Jeremy Bacon, *Corporate Directorship Practices,* Studies in Business Policy No. 125 (New York: National Industrial Conference Board, 1967).

executive are less likely to question their superior's proposals seriously and fear-
lessly.

The Outside Director

Outside directors are frequently officers of banks, insurance companies, or other
financial institutions that regularly serve the company to whose board they belong.
Outside directors may also be attorneys, members of other professions, presidents of
other corporations, retired executives, prominent businessmen in the community
or the country at large, or educators.

Outside directors can view a corporation with objectivity. They bring to the board
a variety of backgrounds and experience helpful in dealing with different problems.
Because of their diversified outside activities, they may also have contacts valuable
to the corporation. Although outside directors depend heavily on operating executives for facts and recommendations, their final judgment can be completely independent of inside — and sometimes in-grown management — thinking.

However, a few serious disadvantages to having outside members on the board
exist. Normally, they cannot devote as much time and thought to the problems of the
corporation. This being the case, they are often unable to gain a thorough understanding of the problems of the company on whose board they sit. An outside director may have some special and possibly conflicting interests arising from the fact
that his own organization does business with the corporation of which he is a board
member. Experience seems to indicate that the presence of bankers and especially
investment bankers on a board restricts the options open to that board. However,
bankers can always give advice and counsel, for this is part of their business. A
recent survey indicates that lawyers and their legal questions inhibit boards. However, the lawyers who conduct themselves first as businessmen and second as lawyers make effective outside directors.[9]

Professional directors, clearly outside directors, devote all their time to serving
simultaneously on the boards of several noncompeting corporations. They are common in Great Britain but are not widely used in the United States. However, the companies that use them have found them to be effective.

Recent Use Trends

The National Industrial Conference Board has periodically studied trends in the
use of inside and outside directors by both manufacturing and nonmanufacturing
companies. Their studies of manufacturing companies show that in 1938 there was
an even split between boards having a majority of outsiders and those having a
majority of insiders. By 1953, outside directors constituted a majority on about 54
per cent of the boards of manufacturing firms surveyed. Five years later, in 1958,
57 per cent of the manufacturing company boards had more outside than inside

[9] Based on a report published by H. R. Land, *Building a More Effective Board of Directors*
(Los Angeles, October 1972).

directors and by 1961 outside directors were in the majority in 61 per cent of the manufacturing companies surveyed. This trend has continued. The 1966 NICB survey showed that the number of manufacturing company boards with more outsiders than insiders had jumped to 63 per cent.[10] The survey also indicated that in all cases the president of the corporation served on his own board. About half of the surveyed companies reported that the chairman of the board was a fully employed inside director.[11]

The composition of the boards of nonmanufacturing companies differs noticeably. Outside directors are in the majority in 85 per cent of the cases included in the 1966 NICB study. Owing to the nature of their activities, banks and insurance companies usually have fewer employee directors and more outside directors on their boards. However, in most of the nonmanufacturing companies, the president of the corporation also serves on the board, and in half of them the chairman of the board is, like his counterpart in manufacturing firms, a fully paid employee of the company.[12]

During the last few years, as conglomerates have evolved and flourished, the use of inside directors has experienced a slight comeback. This has occurred primarily when officers of the acquired companies were placed on the board of the conglomerate parent company and outside members were dropped. Conflict of interest problems have also led to an insider increase. Because of their multi-faceted activities, conglomerates in particular have found it increasingly difficult to find outside directors free from interlocking directorships or potential conflicts of interest. The broader the interpretation of conflict of interest becomes, the harder finding suitable outside directors will be.

Women and Members of Minority Groups

Very few women serve on boards either as inside or as outside directors.[13] The few who do have usually been placed there because they hold substantial blocks of the company's stock. However, as feminist pressure has increased, more women have gotten such positions. Members of minority and special interest groups are also slowly achieving acceptance. Their election to a board, like that of women, should be based primarily on the contributions they can make to the board's deliberations, not on outside pressure.

Legal Eligibility and Membership Qualifications

State statutes govern the eligibility and qualifications of directors. Most states have relatively few restrictions. Some allow statements of eligibility and qualifications to be placed in the certificate of incorporation or even in the by-laws. In certain types of businesses, federal statutes place additional restrictions on who may serve

[10] *Ibid.*, p. 6.
[11] *Ibid.*, p. 10.
[12] *Ibid.*, p. 18.
[13] *Ibid.*, p. 23.

as a director, but it is beyond the scope of this book to explore these restrictions in detail.

There is a widespread belief that in order to be a director one must also be a stockholder. This is not so. When such a provision does exist, it usually calls for only token holdings. For all practical purposes, then, a director need not be a company stockholder.

Critics of this situation feel that if a director possessed an investment in the company he might work harder, show more interest in the corporation, and have a greater sense of responsibility for it. In response to this criticism, one might reply that directors are appointed for their judgment and ability rather than for their financial interest in the company. If one were to insist upon directors being major shareholders, the insistence would increase the difficulty of finding good directors. However, although stock ownership is no prerequisite to directorship, large shareholders or their representatives do form key groups on many boards.

Age of Directors and Retirement Policies

The 1967 Conference Board Report states that the average (median) age of members of boards of directors is fifty-eight years. In most companies the age of the directors ranges between fifty-five and sixty-four years. Rarely does the average age on a particular board fall below fifty years. The age of the directors on the boards of nonmanufacturing companies seems to be slightly higher.[14]

Should the retirement of directors be enforced? About half of the companies participating in the 1967 survey have established age limits or other conditions that make retirement from the board mandatory. Generally speaking, about the same number of companies have retirement provisions for both outside as well as inside directors. Of course, the stipulations of the retirement provisions vary widely and depend to some extent on the industry. Retirement ages for directors in manufacturing industries are lower than in nonmanufacturing industries. These two groups also differ in the age limits set for inside and employee directors. Over half of the manufacturing companies retire employee directors at sixty-five, whereas only two-thirds of the nonmanufacturing enterprises set retirement at this early age. Seventy years is the most frequently reported retirement age for outside directors of manufacturing firms, whereas seventy-two is considered appropriate by most nonmanufacturing companies. The reasons for establishing these age limits are similar to the reasons underlying the establishment of retirement policies for all employees; the company is best served by alert, active, and interested directors who in due time must automatically make room for younger men.[15]

Recently it has become increasingly common to nominate a retiring board member as an honorary or emeritus director. About one-fifth of all participating companies indicated that they follow this practice. This practice recognizes the retiring director's contribution, retains access to his counsel, and makes retirement more acceptable to him. The honorary directorship is conferred either by board resolution

[14] *Ibid.*, p. 92.
[15] *Ibid.*, pp. 82–86.

or by a provision in the by-laws. An honorary director emeritus may attend board meetings and participate in discussions, but he has no voting rights. He acts in an advisory capacity and is free of the responsibility of a director.[16]

Length of Service

In most corporations the directors are elected for a one-year term, and the entire board is re-elected annually. A small number of corporations elect their directors for a three-year period and stagger their terms of office.[17] This practice ensures a certain degree of continuity. Even when corporations have annual elections, however, the over-all time which the directors spend on the board is usually considerable. Approximately half of all directors serve ten years or more and 20 per cent serve as many as twenty years or more on the board.

These figures are significant for several reasons. First, it takes a director many years to absorb the traditions of a corporation and thus to see a long-range point of view. Second, years of service are an important factor in enabling a board to serve as a live repository for broad, accumulated experience. Third, the continuity of board policy is more easily maintained if at least a few directors have served lengthy terms.

Size of the Board

Generally speaking, boards, like committees, should be kept as small as circumstances permit. They should not be so large that they are unwieldy and unworkable, nor so small that a broad viewpoint is unobtainable. The size of the board usually varies with the size of the company.

OPERATION OF THE BOARD

Boards of directors usually operate through regular meetings conducted by the chairman of the board and through smaller meetings of special board committees. Frequently, boards also operate in conjunction with general stockholders' meetings. This occurs if the board members have approved a proposition at their own meeting but seek wider sanction.

Board Meetings

Most corporation boards meet once a month. However, some boards and particularly those of smaller corporations meet only quarterly or once a year. Increasingly, corporations attempt to keep their directors well informed and to prepare them for their board meetings by providing pertinent prior information. An agenda is usually sent to each director at least a week before a meeting. Along with it, the directors will frequently receive financial statements, operating statements, budgets, forecasts,

---

[16] *Ibid.*, pp. 88–91.
[17] *Ibid.*, p. 24.

minutes of the preceding meeting, and other information. Even in companies where the board meets only quarterly, monthly financial statements are often sent to the directors. Information of this nature is particularly important for the outside directors. Employee directors are deeply involved in the daily activities of the corporation and are therefore more familiar with operating details. Nevertheless, thorough preparation of all directors for the board meetings is bound to increase their effectiveness.

The Chairman

The functions of the chairman of the board are often not clearly defined. This is especially true when the chairman is also the chief executive officer of the corporation and must function in the day-to-day management of company affairs as well as in long-range planning and over-all corporate policy-making. If the chairman is not the chief executive officer of the company, his position is more that of an advisor or an elder statesman. In either case, however, the chairman must convene and preside at the meetings of the board, plan the agenda, keep the directors advised, and sign, together with the president, reports to the stockholders.

In his position as presiding officer, the chairman of the board must draw out directors' contributions skillfully. He must direct the attention of the board to policy matters needing consideration and he must make sure that adequate information is available so that the board comprehends the policies on which it is asked to take action. He must also see that the board is constantly aware of its trusteeship role. He must maintain proper relations between the board and the executive management group on one side, and between the board and the shareholders on the other side. The chairman of the board frequently presides at stockholder meetings as well as board meetings.

Committees

State corporation laws confer power on the board of directors as one body; the individual director has no legal power as such. However, especially in large corporations, the board often appoints one or more committees to function between full board meetings and to be readily available whenever needed. Examples are the executive committee, the finance committee, and the audit committee.

Such board committees can be created by a resolution of the directors in accordance with the corporation's by-laws. These by-laws frequently permit committees to hold such powers and duties as are deemed necessary to conduct the affairs of the corporation. Board committees can also be approved by the stockholders or can be sanctioned by the state statute that governs incorporation. Usually, all members of the committees must be directors of the corporation. These committees must either advise the board or actually exercise board authority. If any committee has non-directors as members or if it advises the president rather than the board, it is not a board committee.

The executive committee is the most frequently established board committee. The by-laws of larger corporations usually specifically provide that the executive committee shall have full authority whenever the board is not in session. However, this committee can assume only those powers not reserved to the full board by the statutes of the state or by the by-laws of the corporation. In addition, the full board might at times reserve certain powers for itself, thereby also limiting the type of authority which can be delegated to its executive committee.

The functions of executive committees vary widely. In most instances they report on their activities to the full board of directors in order to provide adequate information, obtain approval, or both. In some companies all action taken by the executive committee must be submitted to the full board for approval. In others, the committee is a de facto board of directors, and in still others, it merely serves as a screening committee for the board. Whatever its role, the executive committee usually meets regularly. In a few companies it meets daily; in others it meets once or twice a week or perhaps only once or twice a month.

In addition to the executive committee, the board of directors of most of the large corporations also establishes a finance committee, an audit committee, a salary and bonus committee, possibly also a stock option committee, a contributions committee, an investment committee, a policy committee, a nominating committee, and any other committees which serve the particular needs of the company.

Seeking Stockholders' Approval

It has become increasingly common for a board of directors to seek stockholders' approval for corporate plans that the board or one of its committees possesses the authority to formulate. Among the matters most frequently referred to the stockholders are propositions involving the inauguration or modification of pension and retirement plans, stock option plans, incentive and profit-sharing plans, and plans for deferred compensation. In addition to these matters, the board of directors often submits propositions relating to changes in capitalization, additional financing, mergers, consolidations and acquisitions of businesses, other recapitalization plans, selection of independent auditors, and the like.

There are several reasons for seeking the shareholders' approval of matters of this kind. First, state corporation laws may not clearly delegate authority to handle a particular problem to the board. To avoid any errors such problems are submitted to the stockholders for their approval. At times the board of directors also feels a moral obligation to secure the stockholders' approval. This is especially true if self-interest might be involved, as in consideration of pension and retirement plans and stock option plans. At other occasions, the board might feel it wise to seek stockholders' approval in order to obtain the weight of their backing for the proposition in question.

The securing of stockholders' approval promotes good stockholder-board relations and avoids unpleasant discussions later on. In some cases, it may even preclude stockholder suits against the directors. On the other hand, there are a number of disadvantages to seeking stockholder approval on propositions which the board clearly has the authority to handle. One of these drawbacks is that the average stockholder is usually not acquainted with management problems and very often is not interested in solving them. Also, if too many matters are referred to them, some stockholders might begin to question the qualifications and the capability of the board. It is after all the board's duty to make decisions; seeking stockholders' approval where none is necessary might lead the stockholders to believe that the board is shirking its responsibility or that there is a lack of harmony among board members. However, soliciting stockholders' approval is becoming more and more the practice.

Compensation

Although the compensation for directors has moved steadily upward, it is still not commensurate with the services expected of them. Fees of outside directors of manufacturing firms range from nothing to $1,000 or more per meeting. The median payment in these firms is $400 per meeting. Larger corporations (in terms of assets) tend to pay higher fees than smaller corporations do. The fees paid by manufacturing companies also seem to be somewhat higher than those paid by nonmanufacturing firms. Many directors are now paid an annual retainer. This trend away from per diem payment began in the 1940's and is still growing. The median retainer paid to directors of manufacturing companies is $3,000 to $5,000. Directors receive their fees and retainers even if they do not attend all meetings.[18]

Should compensation also be paid to inside directors? Some firms pay all directors. However, most companies do not pay employee-directors extra compensation for their board service.[19] They feel that these people are already paid to give their full time to the corporation and therefore need no additional compensation. However, the functions of a high-level administrative manager can be quite different from those of a director. As a director, an individual assumes a responsibility and a contingent personal liability that he does not assume as an executive, and he should be compensated for that assumption in the same way as all the other directors.

The majority of corporations pay additional fees to outside directors who also serve on committees of the board,[20] because committee work is often not shared equally among all board members. Again, employee directors are usually not additionally paid. It is customary, however, to reimburse all directors for expenses incurred while attending directors' meetings or committee meetings. Inside directors participate in all employee benefit plans; outside directors are rarely included in these programs.

A great number of nonmonetary but complex incentives induce leading businessmen to serve on the boards of corporations. Members of a Columbia University symposium on boards of directors held some years ago decided that aside from compensation, there were four chief inducements to accept board membership: the prestige of serving on certain boards, the high value of personal associations with men and

[18] *Ibid.*, pp. 30–31, 40.
[19] *Ibid.*, p. 29.
[20] *Ibid.*

women of outstanding ability, personal interest in the work of the company, and the broadening of individual experience gained by insight into the workings of another company.[21]

BOARDS IN SMALL CORPORATIONS

A small corporation usually has limited management resources. Its board of directors is mainly a token and docile institution designed to fulfill the requirements of state corporation laws. Generally, such a board does not participate in the actual management of the business.[22] In many small enterprises the members of the board are also the officers of the corporation or are members of the families of the owners. In reality, the small corporation board exists in name only and in some cases never meets.

It is regrettable that most small corporations do not use the board of directors as an organizational device, for such corporations could probably benefit most from it. Many problems of small corporations are similar to those of a large corporation, but the small enterprise is not as well equipped to contend with them. Usually specialized line and staff officers are unavailable and expert outside advice unaffordable. Nevertheless, the complexities of small corporation management demand high personal qualifications, education, or experience — qualities that only a few small corporate managers have.

The owner-managers of small corporations are often so involved with the daily affairs of the corporation that they cannot take the time necessary to make balanced policy judgments and long-range plans. Outside board members are better able to provide suggestions and solve policy problems in areas such as the determination of enterprise objectives, the small company's place in the industry, and the future of the business. They are also helpful in protecting the interests of minority stockholders and providing management successors. Succession is often more important in a small corporation than in a medium-sized or large one. The premature death of the owner-manager could easily end the company. Numerous small corporations can operate successfully without the benefit of an effective board while the owner-manager is alive, but no manager can perpetuate himself indefinitely. Some assistance from active and capable outside directors is essential.

Although in most instances distrust of outsiders prevents a small corporation from having an effective board of directors, an owner-manager's feelings of inferiority may be equally at fault. He may fear that bankers, lawyers, other professionals, or businessmen from other corporations would have no interest in being on the corporation's board. Financial remuneration cannot be much of an inducement. However, some business and professional men may seek the education and experience such service would afford. Other public-spirited citizens might consider it an honor and a contribution to the welfare of the community to serve on the board of one or more small local corporations.

[21] Courtney C. Brown and E. Everett Smith, *The Director Looks at His Job* (New York: Columbia University Press, 1957).

[22] M. L. Mace, *The Board of Directors in Small Corporations* (Boston: Division of Research, Graduate School of Business Administration, Harvard University, 1948), p. 87.

In fact, leading businessmen often find it a challenge to offer advice and counsel to small enterprises. Often they consider the enterprise to be a pet project. These outside board members readily see the need for a continuing rather than a sporadic participation in policy formulation and implementation. The manager, therefore, should feel free to call upon them whenever the need arises, without having to wait for the next board meeting.

THE CHANGING ROLE OF THE BOARD OF DIRECTORS

The basic concept of the board of directors is changing. Originally boards were created so that the stockholders could choose representatives who would manage the company for them. At that time, the number of corporate stockholders was very small, and all of them probably had enough knowledge of each other to select directors from among themselves. Today, however, we are confronted with corporations that have hundreds of thousands of stockholders who desire company growth and wish a fair return on their investment but, in reality, are uninterested in corporate affairs. As a matter of fact, the average American stockholder is an impotent force in corporate business. In the early days of the corporation, the stockholder needed the protection of the board of directors because he had no ready market for his stock, if he became dissatisfied and wished to sell. Today the stockholder can easily dispose of his shares, and this is what he is likely to do if he becomes dissatisfied or finds a better investment opportunity.

Much of the criticism leveled against the changing role of the board of directors can be attributed to changing times. Many say that the directors have lost their contact with small stockholders. Boards are also criticized for permitting management, not owners, to select the directors. Employee directorships are particularly criticized here. However, there is no proof that greater stockholder participation in the election of directors would improve the functioning or the composition of the board. Some observers, in fact, feel that ineffective boards and disinterested stockholders are unrelated. Instead, they place the blame squarely on the chief executive, maintaining that numerous chief executives actually do not want a strong and independent group of directors.

However, today's corporations are not and cannot be callous to criticism. As a matter of fact, corporations often lean over backwards to sample shareholders' opinions, to listen to criticism, and in general to maintain a good public image. The larger corporations are recognizing increasingly that an effective board of directors can be of great value in these efforts. They are becoming aware that, in the long run, the success and in fact the existence of the corporate system depends upon public confidence. Hence, today boards of directors are chosen with greater care, are better informed, and generally receive more help from management. The directors, in turn, are discharging their functions more ably and are becoming more active and more effective. This trend should be increasingly evident in the future, as the nature of major stockholders changes. An ever-larger percentage of stock seems to be held by investment funds, trusts, pension funds, mutual funds, and other aggregations of capital. Because of their large holdings, these new collective shareholders could conceivably take a more direct interest in particular corporations and in the composition of boards of directors.

In a world where priorities are changing and where special interest groups, minorities, and dissatisfied stockholders are increasingly vocal, it is becoming increasingly difficult for a board to define a stockholder's interest. Directors must recognize their corporate social responsibilities. They must represent different viewpoints and must challenge practices that once were tolerated or ignored. But in so doing, directors must always bear in mind that they represent all stockholders and not merely a special constituency.

This concludes our study of the organizing function. In Part IV we shall consider the life-giving force of any organization — the people in it.

Discussion Questions

1. Can you think of groups in nonbusiness organizations that function in a manner similar to that of corporate boards of directors? How do the functions of such groups compare to the functions of corporate boards?

2. "Members of corporate boards lack the technical knowledge necessary to be of any real service to modern business organizations. Therefore, they perform primarily ritualistic functions." Discuss.

Supplementary Readings

Bacon, Jeremy. *Corporate Directorship Practices,* Studies in Business Policy No. 125. New York: National Industrial Conference Board and the American Society of Corporate Secretaries, 1967.

Conference Board. *The Board of Directors: New Challenges, New Directions.* New York: Conference Board, 1972.

Drucker, Peter F. *The Practice of Management.* New York: Harper and Row, 1954. See pp. 178–81.

Juran, J. M., and J. Keith Louden. *The Corporate Director.* New York: American Management Association, 1966.

Koontz, Harold. *The Board of Directors and Effective Management.* New York: McGraw-Hill, 1967.

Mace, Myles L. *Directors: Myth and Reality.* Boston: Division of Research, Graduate School of Business Administration, Harvard University, 1971.

Manne, Henry G. "In Defense of Insider Trading." *Harvard Business Review* 44, no. 6 (November–December 1966): 113–22.

Pfeffer, Jeffrey. "Size and Composition of Corporate Boards of Directors: The Organization and Its Environment." In *Dimensions in Modern Management,* edited by Patrick E. Connor. Boston: Houghton Mifflin, 1974.

Vance, Stanley C. *Boards of Directors: Structure and Performance.* Eugene: University of Oregon Press, 1964.

CASES

III | 1

You Cannot Shift Responsibility

A few days ago, Mr. O'Malley, the administrator of St. Jude's Hospital in St. Louis, a 500-bed general hospital, received a written complaint from a patient who was discharged after having undergone surgery. The incident to which the patient referred allegedly took place while he was awaiting surgery, lying on a stretcher in the surgical suite. Because all operating room activities are a part of the nursing function, the administrator contacted Mrs. Krieger, the Director of Nursing Service, and asked for an investigation and a report. She, in turn, immediately contacted Mrs. Rogers, the Operating Room Supervisor.

After waiting a week, Mr. O'Malley phoned Mrs. Krieger and asked for her report. She replied that she had assigned the matter to Mrs. Rogers and had told her that the inquiry was urgent. That was the last she had heard of the matter. The administrator himself phoned Mrs. Rogers and strongly reprimanded her for the delay. Mrs. Rogers replied that because she had no secretarial help she had sent her report to Mrs. Krieger's secretary for typing. Upon investigation, Mr. O'Malley learned that the pertinent secretary in the nursing director's office had been ill for a few days. Mrs. Rogers' untyped report was found on her desk.

Questions

1. Comment on Mrs. Krieger's role.
2. Should Mr. O'Malley have contacted Mrs. Rogers?
3. How can similar situations be avoided?

III | 2

The Manager's Dilemma

The manager of the transportation department, Mr. Wagner, recently received a new directive stating that the plant manager must give permission for all overtime and Saturday work before such work is scheduled. Previously, the department manager had authorized overtime whenever the need for it arose. However, the company was experiencing a severe profit squeeze and was looking for ways to reduce costs and other expenditures. In the past, Mr. Wagner had little occasion to schedule overtime, and therefore he did not think that the new directive would hamper the performance of his duties.

However, a new situation arose. Because of unforeseen delays in production, orders began to pile up. This bottleneck, soon alleviated in the factory, then shifted to the transportation department. Here, the increased work load and unexpected absences combined to slow the shipment of orders. Mr. Wagner feared that some orders would be canceled if they were not shipped before the week was over but felt his men could not complete their task during normal work time. He was convinced that overtime would help the situation. He tried to contact the plant manager and learned that he was out of town at a convention and could not be reached. Mr. Wagner had heard that some time ago the plant maintenance manager had faced a similar problem and, realizing that delay in making the needed repair would have made the job more difficult and costly, had authorized overtime without the necessary permission. When the plant manager had returned, he had seriously criticized his subordinate and instituted disciplinary action.

The transportation manager did not know what to do. If he authorized overtime, he would exceed his authority; if he did not have his employees work overtime, shipping would be delayed and orders canceled. He thought of contacting the president of the company, who was the plant manager's line superior. However, he too was out of town and unreachable. Mr. Wagner decided to be safe and did not ask his people for overtime. Thus some of the shipments did not go out on time and some orders were canceled.

Questions

1. If you had been in charge of the transportation department, what would you have done?

2. What would you do if you were the president of the company?

3. How might a similar situation be prevented?

III | 3

The Good Samaritan Hospital

Sister Estelle Marie is the administrator of the Good Samaritan Hospital in Bedlam, Ohio. She was elected to this position in 1965 by the governing board of her religious community after obtaining a masters degree in hospital administration. Good Samaritan is a general short-term community hospital with beds for 200 patients. Because it is the only hospital within 100 miles, its occupancy rate has been hovering around 90 and 95 per cent, far above the average rate for hospitals of its type. At this time, a new wing containing 100 additional beds is being constructed.

The administrator heads up to the governing board, which is made up primarily of members of her religious order. When Sister Estelle took office in 1965, she decided to appoint a lay advisory board to bring the hospital into closer contact with the needs of the business community and the area in general, to interest the area in

Exhibit III-1. The Good Samaritan Hospital

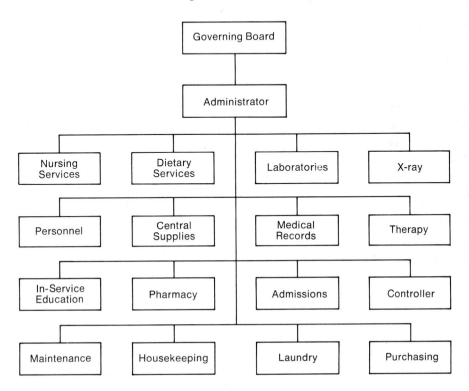

the workings of the hospital, and to serve as a source of sound advice. The board, composed of local lawyers and executives in manufacturing, construction, banking, and retailing, has been meeting monthly for over three years.

The discussion in last month's meeting was prompted by the construction and expansion program underway, and it centered around the hospital's organization. When the administrator distributed a chart showing the current organization (see Exhibit III-1), two or three board members noticed the large number of department heads who reported directly to the administrator. They wondered if the wide span of management were straining the smooth functioning of the hospital, and they suggested narrowing the span, because they expected a 50 per cent increase in facilities and activities in the near future.

The administrator assured them that she had been able to handle the department heads because of their competence. She did not think that the increase in beds would change the picture; the various functions would remain the same, although their magnitude would increase. Therefore, she intended to carry on with the same organizational structure. As further justification she remarked that the manager of the local Sears, Roebuck, store has twenty-three managers directly under him and is apparently able to function efficiently.

Questions

1. Do you agree with the administrator?
2. What changes would you suggest and why?
3. Suggest a revised organization chart.
4. What are the advantages and shortcomings of the lay advisory board?

III | 4

The Office of the President

Irving Bacon is the fifty-five-year-old president of Electro Products Company, a firm manufacturing a broad line of small electrical appliances sold primarily for household use. During fiscal 1971, the company's sales volume amounted to approximately $75 million. Sales have increased each year, and the net earnings have been most satisfactory to management and the board of directors. The following officers report to Mr. Bacon: Mr. Powers, vice-president for production; Mr. Schiller, vice-president for marketing; Mr. Findley, vice-president for finance; the director of personnel relations; and the director of research and development.

Mr. Bacon, who has been president of the company for ten years, recently read in some business magazines that several large companies have abolished the president's position and have instituted an "office of the president" shared by several — perhaps three — officers. Under this plan, each co-president has the authority to make any decision that is brought to the presidential office; each must support every decision made by his co-presidents; and each must keep the others informed.

Mr. Bacon called a meeting with the five officers previously mentioned to discuss the feasibility of implementing this idea at Electro Products. He emphasized that his presidential task was becoming increasingly burdensome, especially since the company had entered international markets and was being pressured by new environmental factors and social responsibilities. He stated that he, of course, intended to remain as one of the three members of the president's office.

Question

1. How would you respond to such a proposal?

III | 5

Blumfield Paper Products

Fred McNulty is the chief executive officer and president of the Blumfield Corporation, a firm manufacturing a broad line of consumer and commercial paper products, ranging from towels and bags to the disposable drapes used in the surgical suites of hospitals. Total company sales during fiscal 1971 amounted to over $200 million.

The Blumfield Corporation has headquarters in Chicago and four manufacturing plants in different parts of the country. The company is departmentalized along functional lines, each function being headed by a vice-president. In other words, all production is the responsibility of the vice-president of production, all sales are under the vice-president of sales, etc. However, the president has the ultimate responsibility for showing over-all profits. Recently, Mr. McNulty has been trying to find ways to decentralize the responsibility for producing profits and to design an organizational system that would highlight each vice-president's contribution to corporate profits. At one time he contemplated arranging Blumfield's activities by product departmentalization, separating the major products into individual product divisions and putting a division manager in charge of each. This scheme would create separate profit centers and would enable each product division's contribution to profits to be readily measured.

However, this plan would not be economical. Many company products are produced by the same equipment from basically the same raw materials in the same manufacturing process. Channels of distribution also often overlap.

Questions

1. Does the president have cogent reasons for changing the organizational structure?
2. What kind of departmentalization would you suggest?

III | 6

The Tasty Food Products Corporation

The Tasty Food Products Corporation manufactures a broad line of frozen TV dinners, frozen vegetables, pizzas, and fruit pies. The company is organized along functional lines: All selling is concentrated under the authority of the sales manager, and all production is under the production manager. The production manager has full authority to purchase raw materials and supplies. In addition, he oversees food preparation and handles all packaging, storing, and shipping.

Company sales figures are leveling off, although total industry sales are up. Marketing believes that the company's sales trend can be attributed to unattractive packaging and has substantiated that belief by observing and questioning consumers. Thus the marketing staff hired a commercial artist to design new wrappers. They would be colorful and up-to-date, and each would cost two cents more than the present wrapper.

The production manager does not believe marketing's story. He feels that the department is merely trying to shift the blame from its meager sales efforts. The production manager also thinks that packaging is his business and that a two-cent increase in the cost of each wrapper would wipe out all profits.

The marketing manager reported this conflict to the president of the company and urged him to let marketing design and develop the outside wrapper. Although the president realized the validity of the marketing manager's argument, he also realized that giving marketing the authority they wished would mean a realignment of production's authority and responsibility.

Questions

1. What would you advise the president to do?
2. What is involved in giving marketing the authority?
3. How else could the dilemma be resolved?

IV

STAFFING

THE STAFFING FUNCTION. *Staffing is the life-giving force of any system. It supplies the human resources that will fulfill corporate plans and vitalize the organizational structure.*

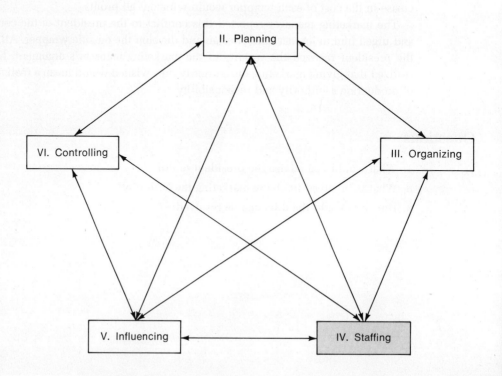

Staffing supplies people to run a planned and organized system. It, like influencing, is a human resource function indispensable to systems of organized behavior.

Traditional organization theory requires that staffing occur only after tasks and task relationships have been established. Work is first defined, then divided, and finally people are found to do it. Staffing includes recruitment, selection, placement, training, appraisal, and compensation of personnel. Traditional theorists make two assumptions about the staffing process — that each executive has the responsibility for staffing his own department and that the executive will staff in such a way that the capability of his people matches their authority. The second assumption is particularly important. If an employee's capability is beneath his authority, he probably will not perform his job satisfactorily. If, however, his capability exceeds his authority, he will not be employed to his full capacity and may become unhappy, thereby wasting the resources of the organization.

To achieve optimal use of human resources, an organization clearly needs a rational staffing program — one that balances job authority with employees' capability. However, such balance is not easily achieved; most executives do not have direct access to the labor market for recruitment, nor do they have the specialized skills needed for the selection of employees. This situation has prompted the development of a specialized staff function — personnel — to aid and advise executives in meeting their staffing needs. As a matter of fact, personnel was the first specialized staff function to achieve widespread departmentalized status in business. Its scope of responsibility and authority varies with the type of organization. In some enterprises, the personnel department mainly recruits low-level employees and maintains the paper work associated with such employment. In other cases, personnel has broad jurisdiction including training, management development, counseling, compensation, fringe benefit programs, and the recruitment of high-level executives. A personnel management department with broad authority, then, is closely associated with staffing. To prevent any misunderstanding, however, we must note that ultimate staffing responsibility rests with the executives who have direct authority over the performance of their subordinates.

Although fundamentally staffing matches capabilities with authority, we should not interpret this function too narrowly. Staffing also has its motivational aspects. Certainly training and development as well as compensation and other staffing activities are sources of motivation and influence. To this extent staffing shades into the influencing function, which we will discuss in the Part V.

In Part IV we stress the theme of education, particularly its role in the development of both young and mature executives. Education is basic to the treatment of appraisal; it also offsets executive obsolescence.

CHAPTER 17

The Staffing Process: An Overview

Staffing, like other functions, is a task that management must perform continuously. In a new organization, the top positions are usually filled first so that key employees can choose their own subordinates. This occurs in the federal government when a new President is elected. One of his first acts is to appoint his Cabinet officers. They, in turn, select the people who will work under them. Staffing an established enterprise is a more common undertaking. The magnitude of such staffing depends on the success of the enterprise, its rate of growth, the type of management and particularly the personnel management practiced, and remuneration policy. Whether staffing a new or a going concern, management must provide well-trained subordinates to satisfy the various managerial needs.

EXTENT OF THE STAFFING FUNCTION

The staffing function involves the placement, growth, and development[1] of the members of the organization with managerial potential. This definition includes "all levels of management because those who will occupy positions in the top two or three levels of management fifteen or twenty years from now are likely to be found in the lower levels today."[2]

It has long been obvious that a successful enterprise needs a constant supply of capable executives. Many say that having good managers is more important than having efficient production methods and more important even than having money in the bank: "The future of any business depends more on the people in it than on any other single element."[3] If management does not ensure that a constant stream of

---

[1] Although the word "training" is frequently used in relation to executive development, it is a poor choice. Training refers to efforts to improve physical skills connected with the operation of equipment. In executive development, it is more advisable to use the terms "growth" and "development."

[2] Myles L. Mace, *The Growth and Development of Executives* (Boston: Division of Research, Graduate School of Business Administration, Harvard University, 1950), p. 19.

[3] William B. Given, Jr., "Experience in the Development of Management People," in *The Development of Executive Leadership*, ed. Marvin Bowar (Cambridge, Mass.: Harvard University Press, 1949), p. 75.

subordinates is recruited, selected, trained, developed, and promoted, it is not ful-filling one of its most crucial duties.[4]

Increased Demand for Capable Managers

The demand for capable managers is increasing. The growing size of business, the complexity of administration, and the intensity of competition all contribute to this trend. The impact of government and unions also intensifies the need for more and better managers. Well-trained, capable, professional executives must make decisions in many areas that vitally affect the owners, the employees, and the public in general.

The situation during World War II revealed the importance of the staffing func-tion's role in the development of managers. At this time, large numbers of capable middle management personnel went into the armed forces, thus reducing the flow of competent young men who normally would have moved up to higher positions and creating substantial gaps in management successions and promotions. Because of this, key executives remained in their positions long beyond retirement dates, until competent successors were found. As a result, many companies in the postwar period discovered that they had competent high-level management, but only a few men in the junior and middle executive ranks. This condition stimulated strong interest in executive development programs; in fact, many such programs were first introduced in the postwar period.

The problem, however, still exists. Presently executive job openings exceed exec-utive supply. This problem threatens to grow worse. If current population trends continue, by 1980 the size of the prime top management age group will actually decrease.

The Needs of Large and Small Enterprises

A variety of factors determines the number of managers needed in any enterprise. Large enterprises, of course, have more managerial positions to fill than small ones do. This does not mean, however, that staffing is unimportant in small enterprises or in family businesses, where son succeeds father. Sons or subordinates in small businesses need training too. Succession in management, which is just as important in small enterprises, can be achieved only if top management fulfills its staffing function.

Factors in addition to size help to determine managerial needs. The structure of the organization, degree of decentralization of authority, span of management, and future expansion plans all influence executive needs. The rate of turnover among

---

[4] Of course an enterprise must also have its share of rank and file employees who must also be recruited, selected, and developed. This, however, is a duty of the first-line supervisor. Discussions of rank and file employment are usually an essential part of personnel manage-ment textbooks and do not belong here.

managerial personnel will also have some bearing on the number of executives who must be kept available.

SPECIAL PROBLEMS OF STAFFING

Certain staffing problems do not occur in other managerial functions. They result from the personal nature of staffing.

The Problem of Measurement

The rewards of adequate staffing are often intangible. What is the value of a large number of junior executives who have received many years of expensive training and who have acquired sufficient capabilities to undertake middle level and top positions? The high quality of executive talent will eventually influence the financial performance of the enterprise. But in the short run, good business conditions may obscure the low quality of executive talent. The reverse, of course, is also possible.

Although no item on the balance sheet reveals the cost of neglecting executive development, poor spirit and low morale are sure indicators of such neglect. "The lack, however, of tangible and concrete cost data does not lessen the desirability of fully developing the skills and capacities of a company's employees."[5] In the long run, management's concern with a systematic executive personnel program will pay off.

The Small Number of Staffers

Few people are involved in the staffing process. Usually, ten to fifty people carry on staffing activities. Even in companies with hundreds or possibly thousands of executives in various ranks, only a small number of people decide whom to hire, whom to fire, whom to promote. However, although the number of staffers is small in relation to the total number of employees, the magnitude of the consequences of their activities can be formidable; obviously, the quality of the executives they select will greatly influence the ultimate success of the enterprise.

Nonstandardized Positions

Another challenge to staffers is the lack of standardization in managerial positions. Even similar positions in different organizations may require differing technical knowledge and skills. As pointed out previously, people who hold the same title in different enterprises do not always hold the same job. Although a sales manager will perform some functions common to sales managers in any enterprise, it is probable that his position in one will include functions not included in another. The

[5] Mace, *The Growth and Development of Executives*, p. 6.

only way to understand a job is to study it. Only by this means can one become familiar with the duties that have been assigned to a certain position in a certain enterprise.

THE GENERAL NATURE OF STAFFING

A Line Function

The responsibility for an executive personnel program starts with top-line management and permeates the entire organization. Each line manager, although he may not be active in original recruitment and selection, must make certain that his subordinates are properly developed, trained, and, in due time, promoted. This line function is as important as planning, organizing, influencing, and controlling. Needless to say, the subordinate cannot be passive in this staffing process; he must promote his own career progress.

Chief Executive's Ultimate Responsibility

Naturally, the ultimate responsibility for an executive personnel program lies with the chief executive, for he and his immediate subordinates are charged with the future of the enterprise. Specifically, the chief executive must monitor and support the staffing program. He must make certain that all executives meet their staffing obligation, sometimes a difficult task. For instance, another high executive may be unwilling to part with a junior executive whom he has trained, even though his promotion would benefit the enterprise as a whole. The executive who resists such a change does not understand the nature of his own staffing function.

Of course, we must recall that the chief executive's staffing responsibility is passed to him by the board of directors. The board, in turn, bears a responsibility to the stockholders to perpetuate the corporation. The directors' duty can be interpreted to mean that they should know what is being done to prepare candidates to replace the top executive and fill other top management positions.[6] It is a duty of the board to formulate a company policy of managerial development throughout the organization. Only by so doing can the board make sure that an orderly succession can occur in the company.

Sometimes the authority and responsibility for staffing are delegated to a committee composed of top executive officers representing the entire range of company operations. This committee is likely to include the chairman of the board, the president, and the vice-presidents in charge of the chief operating units. A staff member from the personnel department may serve as the executive secretary of the committee and may even hold the title of director or coordinator of executive development.

[6] Melvin T. Copeland and Andrew R. Towl, *The Board of Directors and Business Management* (Boston: Division of Research, Graduate School of Business Administration, Harvard University, 1947), p. 4; also see Mace, *The Growth and Development of Executives*, p. 15.

Staff Assistance

Although line management cannot dispose of its staffing responsibility by assigning it to a staff unit, line officers may often call on staff members for help with this program. Staff specialists can be useful in almost every phase of executive development. For instance, they can assist department heads in appraising their subordinates; they can aid them in determining their training needs; and they can help in devising suitable programs for individual cases. They also might guide executives in the coaching and counseling of their subordinates and may keep records of the various training activities.

Staffing Policies

Promotion from Within

One of the most frequently encountered staffing policies is filling responsible positions by internal promotion rather than by importing executives from outside the company. Generally, this policy leads to improved morale and a favorable corporate reputation. In addition, it is often less costly for the enterprise to promote from within. For these reasons, many firms publicly announce in their recruitment programs that they adhere strictly to this promotional policy, and they ensure it by specific administrative measures. The success of such a policy, of course, depends on whether the incumbents are qualified for their new responsibilities and whether they are at least as good as executives in comparable positions in competitors' enterprises.

A policy of promoting from within has limitations. At times employees will question a promotion, feeling that the right person has not been selected. Although an outsider can engender similar complaints, company morale does not seem as much impaired as when the policy of promotion from within seems inequitable. Therefore, if one of three inside executives of equal status must be chosen to fill a position, management might be wise to bring in a new executive from the outside and keep all three where they were. This situation is often encountered in nonbusiness settings, for example, in universities. Instead of selecting a dean from a group of qualified professors, it is sometimes more expedient to bring in someone new from the outside.

A strict policy of inside promotion depends on the constant availability of a sufficient number of qualified executives. However, this may not occur. Sometimes the most promotable junior executives are in training when an opening develops and none is far enough advanced to take over. Promoting only from within also can easily lead to inbreeding. From time to time most organizations can profit from the injection of new blood. This is particularly necessary in an enterprise that depends on fresh approaches for its existence, such as firms in advertising and public relations.

If a company pursues a policy of promotion from within in the strictest sense, current employees are in a more or less monopolistic position. They have only to compete with each other and not with anyone from the outside. Management, however, should be free to select the best possible candidate regardless of his origin. Therefore, a promotion from within policy should be modified by the words "whenever feasible."

Top management may also specify the opposite policy, stating that certain key positions — a minority — should be filled by outsiders. Such a policy is often pursued by companies that depend on a rapidly growing and changing technology. Because inside talent cannot be developed fast enough, these firms must hire outside specialists and experts.

Other Staffing Policies

In addition to formulating hiring and promotion policies, management must also issue staffing rules, procedures, methods, and directives. For example, it may rule that when a vacancy occurs in an important position it must be filled promptly. Procedures and methods for announcing noteworthy promotions must also be detailed. Perhaps such promotions will appear in a special column of an organization's official house publication.

Sequence of Steps in Staffing

The first step in the staffing process is to determine the type of managerial skills needed by an organization. A current organization chart will indicate existing managerial positions and will not forecast future needs. Staffing requires projections of organizational changes. In addition, management also needs written job descriptions enumerating the various duties and responsibilities connected with each of the present managerial positions. This will enable staffers to draw up a list of specifications setting forth the education, experience, ability, and minimum personal qualities required of the people who are to fill each job. With the help of this information, management will know what to look for in a potential candidate.

The second step in staffing is to determine the number of executives management will need and when they will be needed. In order to do this an inventory of available executives must be taken. By looking at those who are currently employed, management can to some degree ascertain who will be available three or five years hence and how many vacancies will occur. By comparing the current picture with the ideal organization structure, management might also find that it wants to create certain new positions. Both the new positions and the vacancies in the old ones will have to be filled. Thus, management's next step is to determine which of the available incumbent managers will be capable of filling them. This necessitates an appraisal of the effectiveness of incumbent personnel in their present jobs and an analysis of their development and promotional potential. Management should provide opportunities for personnel growth. In fact, the fourth step in the staffing process is to set up development programs for just this purpose. Such development programs will, in time, enable executives to move into positions of higher responsibility.

Naturally, the positions at the bottom of the executive ladder must be filled by outside people. Therefore, as a fifth step in the staffing process, the enterprise must initiate a basic executive training program. As a last consideration within the staffing function — but not of least importance — management should devise an executive compensation plan.

Discussion Questions

1. How would you distinguish between staffing activities which may be legitimately performed by the personnel staff and those that must be performed by the line organization?

2. How would you react to a policy that makes your promotion in an organization depend upon the availability of a trained person to take over your job?

Supplementary Readings

Greenwood, William F. *Management and Organizational Behavior Theories.* Cincinnati: South-Western, 1965. See pp. 601–02.

Wortman, Max S. "Manpower: The Management of Human Resources." *Academy of Management Journal* (June 1970): 198–206.

CHAPTER 18

Forecasting Executive Needs

Because every enterprise requires a certain amount of executive manpower, it must attempt to anticipate this quantity by forecasting executive needs. Such forecasting constitutes the first phase of the staffing process and consists of three separate calculations: (1) What types of executive skills are needed? (2) In what amount? (3) When?

Management uses numerous techniques to make these calculations. Position descriptions and skill evaluations are very valuable in determining the types of executives needed. Inventories of current executives and replacement tables are useful in determining the number of existing executives and the time at which they will be needed. These methods help management visualize the total needs of the organization and the broad executive skills and talents required. They also make it easier for management to understand the groupings and relationships of positions.

A broad perspective can provide many advantages to executive forecasters. If railroads, for example, regarded themselves as links in the over-all transportation network rather than as cogs in the rail industry, their plan for meeting future executive needs might be very different. They might imitate the practice of many petroleum companies that view their activities as encompassing the whole field of energy. Sound executive forecasts grow out of such broad vision and expansive goals and policies. That is, they grow out of expectations of the future both within the enterprise and within the surrounding environment. Specifically, an analysis of expectations within the enterprise should include the following factors:

1. expansion plans
2. diversification programs
3. organizational changes
4. goal reorientation[1]

Within the larger external environment, future expectations must encompass:

1. changing consumer demands for products and services
2. economic forecasts, especially those estimating the costs of acquiring effective managerial talent

[1] Adapted from Willys H. Monroe, "Strategy in the Management of Executives," *Business Horizons* 6 (Spring 1963): 35–44.

3. social legislation that requires the employment of women and minority group members
4. technological competition with other firms

These eight elements are basic factors in planning staff requirements. When executive appraisals are added to them, management can accurately forecast its executive needs. Thus staffing rests upon forecasting, and forecasting rests upon planning and executive appraisal. Line executives must assume forecasting and planning functions, although they may call on staff to work out technical details.

DETERMINING THE TYPES OF EXECUTIVES NEEDED

Position Descriptions

Many techniques are available to help management determine executive needs; position descriptions provide one. However, there is no single list of specifications for the "executive position" because each position is unique. However, the duties, objectives, and results expected of each job in each organization should be described in as much detail as possible. Likewise, the experience and specific knowledge required for successful performance of each job should be defined.[2] This is a time-consuming process but a valuable one. An enforced analysis of the content and requirements of positions provides an objective guide for selecting candidates for promotion. It enables management to choose the candidate who best fulfills the specifications of a particular position and hence is likely to succeed in it. A clear catalogue of position descriptions is necessary in order to plan for the growth and development of members of the organization.

Position descriptions also play an important role in the selection of new personnel. A statement of the position's requirements will minimize biases and prejudices among those in charge of the selection process and will provide a definite standard to guide executives who interview prospective employees.

The Need for Continuous Review

Any program runs the danger of becoming calcified. This is clearly the case with a program of position description. Positions must be audited frequently by the personnel staff to determine the extent to which the job content has changed. Any organization will be considerably changed by new technology and the creative efforts of executives occupying top positions. The extent and character of such change must be determined so that accurate information can be provided for forecasting executive needs. This feedback will, in turn, lead to the creation of better plans for executive recruitment and development programs. Figure 18-1 describes this process.

[2] For a full discussion of managerial position descriptions, including many examples, see C. L. Bennet, *Defining the Manager's Job: The AMA Manual of Position Descriptions,* Research Study No. 33 (New York: American Management Association, 1958).

Figure 18-1. Position Description Program

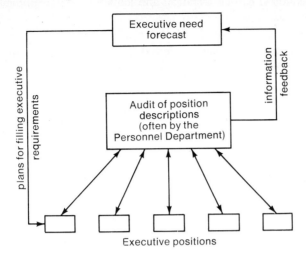

Executive positions

Man Specifications

Because position descriptions merely state the duties, objectives, relationships, and results expected and do not tell specifically what to look for in appraising a candidate, it is therefore necessary to translate duties into man specifications. These specifications outline the experience, age, and personal characteristics thought necessary for each position. It is relatively simple to determine experience specifications by analyzing the duties involved in the present job and the type of previous knowledge and practice required for its successful performance. It is more difficult, however, to quantify personal characteristics. Most of the following discussion, therefore, deals with this problem.

A check list would simplify the job of specifying desirable personal characteristics. Therefore, much effort has been spent in trying to devise such lists. Although the efforts generally result in descriptions that could serve as broad executive standards, they are useless "for the practical purposes of development of particular persons for particular positions in particular companies in particular situations."[3]

Two primary factors invalidate any standard list of executive personal traits. First, there is no generally accepted set of objective criteria for judging a good executive. The success of a worker can be determined by measuring output, but the success of a supervisor must be measured by subjective factors not easily quantified. As one goes higher in the managerial hierarchy, it becomes increasingly difficult to

[3] Myles L. Mace, *The Growth and Development of Executives* (Boston: Division of Research, Graduate School of Business Administration, Harvard University, 1950), p. 20; C. Wilson Randle, "How to Identify Promotable Executives," *Harvard Business Review* 34, no. 3 (May–June 1956): 123.

measure performance objectively. Also, no standardized executive position descriptions exist. As mentioned earlier, technical and job knowledge requirements vary even if job titles are the same.

Since lists of characteristics for the ideal executive cannot be formulated, managerial abilities and capacities must be viewed in their relationship to a specific organizational environment. Management must determine desired personal traits by the content of each job. Among the personal characteristics often mentioned in drawing up job specifications, in appraising candidates, and in planning further executive development are intelligence, analytical ability, initiative, skill in communication, willingness to be a leader and to accept responsibility, a sense of moral values, and soundness of judgment.

The measurement of these executive traits is also extraordinarily difficult. Some organizations, like International Business Machines, have developed elaborate psychological techniques to identify executive talent. However, the evaluation of the character attributes of people in relation to organizational needs remains an intuitive process.

Skills

Robert L. Katz has suggested what he considers a more useful approach to identifying qualified executives. His approach is based not on "what good executives *are* (their innate traits and characteristics), but rather on what they *do* (the kinds of skills which they exhibit in carrying out their jobs effectively).[4] He suggests that effective management rests on three basic skills — technical, human, and conceptual. Technical skill includes the performance and understanding of technical activities. Human skill encompasses understanding and motivating individuals and groups. Conceptual skill implies the ability to coordinate and integrate the activities and interests of the organization and channel them toward a common objective. Katz suggests that this three-skill approach can provide guidelines for the promotion of executives, the development of members of the organization, and the testing and selecting of prospective personnel.

For example, the principal need at lower levels of the administrative hierarchy is for technical and human skills, whereas at the higher levels technical skill becomes less important and the need for conceptual skill increases. At the top level of the hierarchy, conceptual skill is of paramount importance.[5] No doubt it would be helpful to know how much of each skill a man must possess each time he is promoted or progresses in his career development. However, this process still requires job analysis and position description.

[4] Robert L. Katz, "Skills of an Effective Administrator," *Harvard Business Review* 33, no. 1 (January–February 1955): 33.
[5] David W. Ewing, "The Knowledge of an Executive," *Harvard Business Review* 42, no. 2 (March–April 1964): 91–100.

DETERMINING THE NUMBER OF MANAGERS NEEDED

Top administrators often say that their organization "always has room for good men." Frequently, management brings competent executives into an organization without a clear-cut idea of what they are to do. In most cases, the results are devastating. These men either create disturbances and frictions by interfering with the functions of other executives or they become tired of waiting for an appropriate assignment and leave the organization, disillusioned.

Executive Inventories

To avoid situations of this sort, management must carefully determine the kinds of executives needed, how many will be needed, and when. To accomplish this a complete review of current executive inventory is necessary. Even in companies where no fixed retirement age exists, this inventory should include the ages of present executives. Although mortality tables can be of some help, it is impossible to forecast the life span of individual incumbents. Past experience, however, can be a good guide in estimating the number of vacancies likely to be caused by serious illness, resignation, or other separations.[6] Many companies find that reviewing the total number of separations over several years yields a more reliable estimate than would a monthly or quarterly review. In this connection, the level of management where losses occurred should be considered.

An over-all forecast of executive needs will have to be modified if the enterprise anticipates expansion or contraction in the foreseeable future. Obviously, however, such a forecast is highly speculative since numerous changes can take place before it is fulfilled: Expansion plans can accelerate or collapse; personal situations can make projected transfers or promotions impossible; and a variety of external factors can intervene. Yet in spite of such uncertainties, yearly, three-year, five-year, or even ten-year forecasts of vacancies in the executive ranks must be made. These forecasts should be reviewed at least annually.

Replacement Tables

Top management also needs to know the timing of executive vacancies. To obtain this knowledge, replacement tables spanning one, three, five, or ten years are frequently compiled by the chief executive or by the managers of each division. Such tables list each key position, the incumbent in it, and the approximate date when

---

[6] A survey by Arch Patton on the "Trends in Executive Compensation," *Harvard Business Review* 38, no. 5 (September–October 1960): 147–48, reveals that within a six-year period major shifts have occurred in the top management of 55 per cent of a very large sample of major companies listed on the New York Stock Exchange. That this trend has continued is shown in the 1969 survey by the same author, "Executive Compensation in 1969," *Harvard Business Review* 39, no. 5 (September–October 1969): 152–57.

this position may be vacated (see Table 18-1). Of course, these tables are subject to change and should not be regarded as rigid or automatic schedules.

Should first-line supervisory positions be included in replacement tables? No doubt the first-line supervisor is a manager; he directs the work of the people on his lines. However, his particular position requires a considerable amount of technical skill. He must be familiar with the operation of the machinery and equipment, he must be able to make minor adjustments, and must be able to show workers how the work is done. Normally, persons with high managerial potential are not assigned to these partially nonmanagerial supervisory jobs. Instead, management hopes that enough first-line supervisors can be found in the ranks of the workers. Thus, first-line supervisory positions are not included in the replacement tables of most companies.

As a general rule, replacement tables list not only the dates when managerial positions may be vacated but also the reason for vacancies. Some reasons, such as those involving retirement age and ill health, can be deduced from the inventory of current executives. Others, however, may depend upon prior performance appraisals. Such appraisals will indicate who is doing a good job in his present position,

Table 18-1. Executive Need Summary (Department Heads and Above)

Position	Present incumbent	Placement required 1975	1976	1977	1978	1979	Reason
President	J. Brown				X		Retirement
Vice-president, finance	S. Green			X			Possible promotion
Controller	B. Black			X			Possible promotion
Director, management planning	—	X					New position
Vice-president and general manager, "X" division	—		X				New product division to be formed
General sales manager, "X" division	—		X				New division
Manufacturing manager, "X" division	—		X				New division
General sales manager, paint division	S. William	X					Inadequate performance
Manufacturing manager, paint division	G. Gray					X	Retirement
Division controller, paint division	L. Blue		X				Possible early retirement — health

Source: Willys H. Monroe, "Strategy in the Management of Executives," *Business Horizons* 6 (Spring 1963): 38. Used with permission.

who is promotable, who needs additional development before promotion, and who specifically might be capable of filling each position at the time it becomes vacant. An analysis of performance appraisals combined with replacement tables also focuses attention at an early date on those positions for which no replacements or only weak ones are available. This gives management a good idea of the number of positions that can be filled by promotions from within and the number for which outside executives or management trainees will have to be recruited.

Moreover, since premature death, unexpected health problems, and voluntary separations can interfere with even the best planned replacement tables, an enterprise should have available a number of what William Newman calls "runners-up," men who are qualified to "step into an unexpected vacancy in any key post."[7] Large organizations, of course, are in a better position than small ones to have an adequate supply of these men.

For any firm to have a selection of runners-up, however, it must also have made prior performance appraisals of incumbent personnel. Because an appraisal program is so important not only for completing replacement tables but also for planning executive development programs and management trainee programs, we will consider it in detail in the next chapter.

Discussion Questions

1. Consult with a manager and find out the elements of his job that he would include in a job description.

2. C. Northcote Parkinson's famous Parkinson's Law indicates that the forecasting of executive needs is not an entirely rational process, particularly in periods when organizations are contracting. His favorite example is that of the English navy. Read Parkinson's Law, and then see if you can discover any other examples of it. See C. Northcote Parkinson, *Parkinson's Law* (Boston: Houghton Mifflin, 1957), especially ch. 4.

Supplementary Readings

Bassett, Glen A. "The Qualifications of a Manager." In *Dimensions in Modern Management,* edited by Patrick E. Connor. Boston: Houghton Mifflin, 1974.

French, Wendell. *The Personnel Management Process: Human Resources Administration.* 3d ed. Boston: Houghton Mifflin, 1974. See chapter 11.

Monroe, Willys H. "Strategy in the Management of Executives." In *Management in Perspective,* edited by W. E. Schlender, W. G. Scott, and A. C. Filley. Boston: Houghton Mifflin, 1965. See pp. 427–38.

[7] William H. Newman, *Administrative Action* (Englewood Cliffs, N.J.: Prentice-Hall, 1951), p. 332.

CHAPTER 19

Performance Appraisal
of Managers

Performance appraisals hold a key spot in the staffing process. They are essential for planning staff requirements and for trainee selection and development. They also help management identify individuals with promotional potential. Additionally, they provide a source of information about the training and development needs of older managers. However, as their name implies, the main use of performance appraisals is to judge the effectiveness of managers, to judge whether they and the amalgam of units and departments they run are contributing to the achievement of the organization's goals.[1]

APPRAISAL AS A MANAGEMENT TOOL

Usefulness

The appraisal of managers is both a guide for merit rating and a basis for promotions and executive development. When a manager appraises a subordinate to decide if he deserves a salary increase (merit rating), his appraisal is concerned exclusively with the subordinate's performance in his current job. When a manager appraises for purposes of possible promotion, however, he is assessing the incumbent's potential for growth and further advancement in addition to his performance in his present job.

By specifically defining an individual's strengths and weaknesses, an appraisal becomes a basis for improving the quality of current job performance. Only by appraisal is it possible to isolate weaknesses and formulate a development program to overcome them. The early discovery of such weaknesses often prevents them from becoming more serious, resulting in damage to the individual and to the enterprise.

A further aim of appraisal is to let an executive know where he stands with his superior. Most executives are anxious to have this information. Every employee, in

[1] See Stanley Sloan and Alton C. Johnson, "New Context of Personnel Appraisal," *Harvard Business Review* 46, no. 6 (November–December 1968): 14–30.

fact, has the right to know how well he is doing or what he can do to improve his present performance and advance in the company.

In some instances, an employee's desire to know his standing can be interpreted as a request for reassurance about his future in the organization. To carry this idea a bit further, appraisals can be an important incentive to the members of an organization. Often a manager in a large company has the feeling that his individual contributions, which necessarily appear small, are lost and forgotten. Appraisals can serve to dispel such a feeling and to reassure managers that their work is appreciated and that they have development opportunity.

The various uses of appraisals that we have been discussing will be emphasized if we look at Douglas McGregor's summary of their three major purposes.[2]

1. Administrative: Appraisals permit an orderly and rational way of determining promotions, salary increases, transfers, terminations, and so on.

2. Informative: Appraisals supply data to management on performance of subordinates and to the individual on his strengths and weaknesses.

3. Motivational: Appraisals create a learning experience for subordinates that motivates them to improve.

Difficulties in Appraising

Although management appraisal has become routine in most large firms and even in many medium-size firms, there are still numerous executives who do not believe in it. This may be partly because of the difficulties involved in effective appraisal. For one thing, it is very hard to measure the quality of performance of various employees because each of them is an individual with different capacities. In addition, measurement is complicated by the dynamic changes which take place within an individual as he grows in years and experience. Although great efforts have been made to learn more about people, there still is no way of measuring human qualities exactly.

A further difficulty in effective appraisal is that standards for executive performance often do not exist. There is no question that formulating such standards is a line manager's job, but there are many questions as to how precisely these standards can be established. Obviously, a position description alone is not enough; it lists only what a person does. What is needed is a statement of the conditions that exist when a job is done well. Although some larger enterprises have made progress in setting standards of this type, much remains to be accomplished.

Another appraisal problem stems from the fact that appraisals of effectiveness are often based on recent incidents that are not representative of the subordinate's performance. To counteract this, a superior must force himself to draw his conclusions as objectively as possible from over-all performance. He must also try to prevent his own personality from entering and unduly coloring the picture. Even though he attempts to remain as objective as possible, however, the appraiser probably cannot

[2] Douglas McGregor, *The Human Side of Enterprise* (New York: McGraw-Hill, 1960), pp. 82–88.

help but inject some conscious or subconscious bias and prejudice into the appraisal of his subordinates.

THE APPRAISAL PROCESS

Appraisal Forms

Most enterprises use an appraisal form to overcome some of the difficulties mentioned above. These forms reduce the elements to be measured to the most objective terms possible. Although there are innumerable types of forms, most of them include a number of different criteria for measuring job performance, intelligence, and personality. In deciding which criteria are appropriate to its forms, each enterprise should study the specific requirements of its different jobs. These requirements differ, of course, according to the function and level of the position. The number of criteria should be kept to a minimum in order to make the form reasonably manageable. Likewise, the number of categories of evaluation — does this well, needs more instruction, does poorly — should be kept to a minimum, yet should give the appraiser sufficient choice.

Among the specific criteria most frequently mentioned in appraisal forms are quality of work, character, knowledge, ambition, leadership, communication facility, and promotion potential. Since these words often mean different things to different people, further definition is usually included. Explanatory words and phrases are also added to the rating categories in order to assist the appraiser.

Since an evaluation is based on a subordinate's performance of his job, it is essential that the appraiser keep job content in mind. Also, forms often require that an appraiser support his conclusions with evidence. This assures that the appraisal is made with thoughtfulness and diligence and helps to avoid superficial approval or disapproval. A request for evidence can, for example, discourage what has been termed the "halo effect," in which a high rating on one factor leads to unmerited high ratings on other factors.

Who Should Appraise?

In most firms a man's immediate superior fills out the appraisal forms, but in some enterprises, the appraisal is made by the superior together with two others from the superior's level who know the man being appraised. Other companies prefer to have the appraisal made by a group consisting of the immediate superior and two members at the superior's level, one of whom does not know the man to be appraised. Of course, the immediate superior can generally make the most effective appraisal of how a man has actually performed on his job. He is in the best position to observe him and to judge how well he handles his work, how he gets along with others, how he delegates authority, how much initiative he displays, and how well he normally carries through on his assignments. Although there is no substitute for the firsthand knowledge and experience of the immediate superior, it is possible that his appraisal would have certain shortcomings. It is understandable though not pardonable for some executives to underrate a good subordinate so they will not lose him. For instance, a division manager might hesitate to recommend a man for promotion to a position outside the division.

To avoid such injustices many companies have instituted group appraisals. Sometimes one rater can add to the knowledge of another. Also, such committee deliberations help to assure the use of uniform standards in judging an individual's performance. Of course, it is advisable that an individual's job description and any standards of performance be clearly understood before the members begin the appraisal.

Some companies believe that appraisals are more accurate if made independently by the appropriate executives rather than in conference. Such companies attach considerable significance to the contrasts between these ratings. They feel that they have removed the danger of single-member dominance of rating committees. No matter how rating groups are organized, however, they should include the immediate superior of the appraisee and the superior above him. In addition, they should include two or more managers who have had some contact though not necessarily a close working relationship with the appraised candidate.

During the evaluation, the appraisers should not see copies of prior appraisals. This restriction will ensure that the employee is judged on the basis of present performance alone. If appraisals are made independently by several different appraisers, a staff person might be called upon to summarize the various conclusions or the appraisers might meet in subsequent discussion to transcribe the results.

Regularity of Appraisal

Appraisals of management personnel should be made routinely once a year. This period is normally considered long enough for growth and change to manifest themselves. If a person has just started a new and more responsible position, however, he should be appraised after six months. Periodic appraisal reminds an individual that he has not been forgotten. He knows that whatever improvement he has made will be noted and will very likely carry him to higher positions.

How Far Down?

Most companies appraise all managers from first-line supervisor to top executive. They do not, however, appraise hourly workers and try to locate, develop, and utilize potential executive manpower from their ranks. The reason often given for this is that union rules and the slowness of promotions make it impractical to conduct such appraisals.

However, a number of companies periodically appraise all employees and conduct individual superior-subordinate appraisal discussions. Such firms are often considered to be good places to work and to get ahead. Managements that do not follow this practice might re-examine their policy, as some members within the hourly wage earners group undoubtedly have administrative potential.

Review of the Appraisal

By a Higher Executive

If an appraisal is made only by an individual and not a committee, it should be reviewed by the appraiser's superior. Such a policy insures that the appraiser will make the evaluation as thoroughly and objectively as possible because he knows that he will be called upon to justify it to his own superior. Discussing the appraisal will keep the higher superior informed of the promotability, potential, and need for improvement of executives in his department and, at the same time, will enable him to check the effectiveness of the rater's own appraising, coaching, teaching, and directing ability.

With a Subordinate

Of greatest importance is the appraisal conference between superior and subordinate. Some managers feel that such a review is unnecessary, because they are in daily contact with their subordinates. This, however, is not enough. The subordinate knows that he has been appraised formally and is understandably eager to have a first-hand report. He may also have things on his mind which he does not want to discuss in everyday contacts. It is not an easy task, however, for a superior to discuss an appraisal with a subordinate. Positive judgments can usually be communicated effectively, but it is difficult to communicate criticism without generating resentment and defensiveness. Day-to-day criticism is much easier to accept than the formal criticism of an appraisal. Day-to-day criticism is not threatening, whereas formal criticism is. However, the effective manager can channel such criticism into positive suggestions for self-development and growth. Counseling an executive about preparation for new responsibilities and ways to improve his performance is an art, and each interview must be adapted to the individual case.

At times the relationship between a superior and his subordinate in this appraisal process has been compared to the relationship of a farmer to his crop. The farmer does not grow the crop. The crop grows itself, but its success or failure depends to a large degree upon what the farmer does or does not do to help it grow.[3] Likewise, in the process of "growing" managerial talent, the appraiser can do much to fertilize the development of managerial potential through his interviews with budding subordinates. Not only will the interview have critical significance for the career of the subordinate, but it will provide the subordinate with a pattern for subsequent counseling of his own subordinates. Much of the art of counseling depends upon being a good listener and getting the appraisee to think and express himself in terms of his further growth and development, his needs and goals.

[3] Myles L. Mace, *The Growth and Development of Executives* (Boston: Division of Research, Graduate School of Business Administration, Harvard University, 1950), p. 113

Conducting the Interview   Although an appraisal interview should be held shortly after the appraisal has been performed, the appraiser should still refresh his memory regarding the reasons for the opinions expressed. At the outset, the appraiser should emphasize that the appraisal is a training device designed to benefit the individual and the enterprise. If the subordinate, though not an outstanding person, performs satisfactorily in his present position, the superior should minimize criticism and suggest one or two moderate improvements as his goal. If the appraisal indicates that the subordinate is highly proficient in his present position, much of the interview will center around the types of experiences which can further his growth and development and help him attain promotion. An interview succeeds best when a manager plays the role of a coach helping an individual to determine his targets and the steps necessary to reach them.

Negative Judgments   In the discussion thus far, we have not mentioned the possibility that an executive might have to be removed. Top management must be sure that all managerial positions are properly filled. Changes may be necessary if an employee has not lived up to the potential predicted for him. Conceivably, periodic appraisals will reveal that a promotion has been a mistake or that a manager's performance has fallen below expectations. When this becomes evident, performance appraisals form the basis for possible demotion or discharge. The supervising executive is often reluctant to face this situation because, in all probability, he was instrumental in placing the person in his present position. However, it is his duty to correct the situation. In most instances, the correction will amount to no more than reassignment to a position of lesser importance. But, if an individual has had several opportunities to show his ability and has been unable to perform the functions assigned to him, discharge is the only solution left. Regardless of how unpleasant such action is, an executive is not fulfilling his responsibilities properly if he shirks it.

CRITICISMS AND RECOMMENDATIONS FOR PERFORMANCE APPRAISAL

Many have criticized the ways in which performance appraisals are conducted by businesses. Their criticisms fall into two categories.

"Playing God"

Some say that performance appraisal allows the superior to "play God" with the subordinate. The appraisal is an extremely powerful instrument in the superior's hand, as the career progress of the subordinate often depends upon it. A bad appraisal, which is, of course, recorded and made a part of the individual's permanent personnel file, stays with him throughout his employment at the company.

   As a consequence, some employees feel that they must conform to the wishes of their superiors even though the employee might believe that his boss's decisions are not in the best interests of the company. It may even develop, as Harold Leavitt explains, that "the young executive finds it hard to separate good from his boss's approval of it."[4] Thus, performance appraisal of the conventional type places the employee in a highly dependent position, which could stifle initiative and creativity.

To overcome this problem, William Evan suggests a system of appeal.[5] This would give the individual the right to take his case to a higher management board, if he feels he has been unjustly appraised. Such a right would free the individual from the pressing need to conform. However, programs of this type are by no means prevalent in industry, partly because the feeling against bypassing one's immediate superior is deeply ingrained.

Performance Not Really Measured

Other critics have pointed out that a performance appraisal is misleading since it does not really measure performance. This is a valid criticism because the conventional paper and pencil kind of evaluation cannot measure results in any significant way. It simply reflects a manager's subjective judgment of a subordinate, which is based on rather vague personal qualities.[6] It does not give a meaningful indication of how the subordinate is really doing.

Management by Objectives

To deal with the inadequacies of routine appraisal programs, George Odiorne suggests a technique known as management by objectives.[7] The technique suggests that:

1. the organization's common goals be specified along with measures of organizational performance
2. revisions in the organizational structure be made if necessary
3. a superior confer with each of his subordinates on that subordinate's goals
4. the superior and his subordinate agree about the subordinate's goals
5. feedback on interim results, measured against predetermined milestones, be given to subordinates
6. review of the subordinate's results be made
7. review of the total organization's performance be made before the cycle is begun again

The dynamics of this process involve close consultation between superior and subordinates. For instance, in steps (3) and (4) both the manager and the person under him jointly agree on what areas of performance will be subject to appraisal

---

[4] Harold J. Leavitt, *Management* (Chicago: University of Chicago Press, 1964), p. 127.

[5] William M. Evan, "The Organization Man and Due Process of Law," *American Sociological Review* 26 (August 1961): 540–47.

[6] See Patrick E. Connor, "Interpersonal Effectiveness and Performance Effectiveness: Some Thoughts for Management," in *Dimensions in Modern Management*, ed. Patrick E. Connor (Boston: Houghton Mifflin, 1974).

[7] George S. Odiorne, *Management by Objectives* (New York: Pitman, 1965).

and what the appraisal criteria will be. Suppose a regional sales manager and a district manager are concerned about setting sales quotas for the next six months. The regional manager feels that a 5 per cent increase over last year is a reasonable expectation. The district manager believes that only 2 per cent is possible. The regional manager and district manager meet and discuss the reasons for their figures. As a consequence, a 4 per cent increase is agreed upon, and it becomes one of the standards on which the performance of the district manager is judged. The same sort of process can be pursued to define and measure other results and standards of performance.

To repeat, the significant feature of the management by objectives technique is the *joint* determination of performance objectives and criteria of measurement. The technique involves a high degree of appraisee participation in all aspects of the appraisal process. The appraisee participates in the review and analysis of results at the end of the appraisal period; he helps to decide the kind of management development or training program he thinks is necessary to improve his own effectiveness; and he helps set the standards for the next appraisal period.

In addition to its participatory aspects, this type of program requires a continuous reassessment of organizational goals and standards. Feedback is useful not only to the person being appraised but also to management in its role as policy-maker and organizational designer.

Conventional programs of appraisal are also criticized because they fail to consider the needs of those appraised. This is another shortcoming that management by objectives attempts to overcome. Such a program opens a two-way channel of communication between superiors and subordinates. However, more is required than merely formalizing the subordinate's role in the appraisal process. An environment has to be developed in which a person believes that he can legitimately express his feelings without fear of reprisal from his superior. More is said of this in Part V.

Discussion Questions

1. Design a system of management by objectives which could be applied in the present management course that you are taking.

2. What would you imagine to be the advantages and pitfalls of an appeal system that would allow a subordinate to appeal an appraisal given to him by his superior using convenfional performance appraisal techniques?

Supplementary Readings

Connor, Patrick E. "Interpersonal Effectiveness and Performance Effectiveness: Some Thoughts for Management." In *Dimensions in Modern Management*, edited by Patrick E. Connor. Boston: Houghton Mifflin, 1974.

Labovitz, George H. "In Defense of Subjective Executive Appraisal." In *Dimensions in Modern Management.*

McConkey, Dale D. "Measuring Managers by Results." In *Dimensions in Modern Management.*

McGregor, Douglas. *The Human Side of Enterprise.* New York: McGraw-Hill, 1960. See chapter 6.

Odiorne, George S. *Management by Objectives.* New York: Pitman, 1965.

Whisler, Thomas L., and Shirley F. Harper. *Performance Appraisal: Research and Practice.* New York: Holt, Rinehart and Winston, 1962.

CHAPTER 20

Executive Growth and Development

In most cases, an effective appraisal program will highlight the areas in which many middle-level executives need additional development, either to improve their present performance or to ready themselves for higher positions. Top management is obligated to provide opportunities for such development. The opportunities usually take two forms — those obtained through in-company career line development and those obtained in programs outside the company environment.

EXECUTIVE OBSOLESCENCE

Both types of executive development programs help to provide managers with the skills they need for successful job performance and career progress. They also help to overcome executive obsolescence. Although the first view of executive development is positive and the second view negative, it is not clear precisely where the first ends and the second begins.

Although executive obsolescence is hard to define for research purposes,[1] it is a fact of business life brought on not only by changing technology but also by an organizational environment that does not help its executives cope with change. In today's atmosphere of rapid change, such obsolescence has become a key issue. Unless an executive keeps himself up to date and is encouraged to do so by his firm, he may quickly find his skills outmoded and may feel apathetic about learning anything new.

The problem of obsolescence is particularly evident among engineers in the aerospace industry. Assume, for example, that an optical engineer is assigned to work for two years on an exotic project such as a missile guidance system whose design specifications are frozen. At the end of two years, when the project is completed, the engineer may know more about optical guidance systems for missile X than anyone in the world. But who will need these skills? More than likely, new families of missiles have been developed and missile technology has advanced. Unless the engineer has maintained his technical knowledge, he is in trouble. Lockheed Aircraft Corporation, recognizing this problem, has set up a development program requiring continuous education for project engineers.

[1] Frederick C. Haas, *Executive Obsolescence*, Research Study No. 90 (New York: American Management Association, 1968), pp. 11–12.

Admittedly, the problem of obsolescence is more acute among engineers than among managers in less technical work. Nevertheless, the analysis of the difficulties is quite similar: The dimensions of the problem can be reduced to industrial specialization, individual inertia toward change, transitions in the industry and in the individual firm, and lack of company initiative in helping executives adjust.

Executive obsolescence will probably become a more important issue, for the factors causing it are not likely to abate. In fact, the matrix form of company organization, which we discuss in Chapter 24, encourages higher levels of specialization and thus more rapid obsolescence of managerial and engineering talent. Consequently, those concerned with future executive development must address themselves to this problem of maintaining the human resources of a firm in the face of change.

IN-COMPANY DEVELOPMENT PROGRAMS

The most effective way of fighting obsolescence is by performing a job in which a positive relationship exists between boss and subordinates. Under the guidance of their superior, managers learn skills and develop the potential for advancement. No substitute has been found for such on-the-job managerial development. In fact, some companies consider it so important that they provide opportunities for managers to gain experience in a number of appropriately chosen positions of differing nature and increasing degrees of responsibility. These positions, however, are not created for this express purpose. Each time management moves an individual into such a position, it does so because it wants the job filled by a capable candidate and at the same time wants to give that candidate an opportunity for development so that he may become eligible for promotions to higher levels. Each new assignment carries the full responsibility for satisfactory performance.

Planned Progression Systems

Many enterprises have formalized their rotation practices so that they constitute a planned progression system. Their plan provides executives with the knowledge necessary to fulfill higher-level responsibilities. There are differing opinions, of course, on whether executives should be well versed in the technical aspects of their positions. There is little doubt, however, that the manager of the production department, besides being thoroughly familiar with managerial functions, ought to know production processes, techniques, and methods in order to do an effective job of managing the plant. Equally, there is little doubt that the sales manager ought to know what is involved in performing various sales functions, and it is preferable that he gain this knowledge through experience.

The path of progression from the lower to the upper levels of the organization can often be traced by studying the company's organization chart and job requirements. Planned progression is not a rigid path, however; it can be changed or modified to meet prevailing conditions or to allow capable individuals to be promoted into certain jobs more quickly. Most companies, in fact, have several progression paths rather than a single one, since substantially similar business experience can be secured from several different positions.

Even those companies that consider planned progression to be the main avenue to further executive growth and development should realize that deviations are sometimes necessary. It is unwise to plan an executive's path of progression in detail. One of the difficulties is that individuals do not progress at the same rate. Some perform very well up to a certain level, but do not seem capable of going further. Innumerable causes, both personal and business, can upset even the best planned schedule.

Lateral Transfers

Planned progression can limit an entire progression path to a specific function, so that a person who starts in production, for example, is expected to progress only through production department positions. Such a pattern can lead to complaints by the sales department that production people do not recognize their problems and complaints by the production department that the sales people have no understanding of the production and procurement processes. In order to resolve these misunderstandings, some companies have found it advisable to transfer men across functional lines. Such lateral shifts are often used for lower- and middle-level management but less frequently for top management.

The values derived from lateral transfers are numerous. They broaden a manager's technical knowledge and understanding of many of the functions of the enterprise. They enable him to coordinate and supervise an increasing number of units concerned with different functions. They afford him an opportunity to acquire new managerial skills. Also, they give the manager an opportunity to work under several different executives whose coaching can be of great benefit to him. If an enterprise has a program of lateral transfers, it will have an increased number of channels for advancement to higher positions. Such a program will also increase the number of competitors for promotions.

There are some drawbacks to lateral transfers. Naturally, a manager dislikes seeing a subordinate leave his department after he has developed him into a capable understudy. It is also conceivable that the ambitious members of a department will become disturbed whenever a young executive moves in from another department. This drawback can be overcome, however, if management shows that there are just as many promotions out of as well as into a division.

Lateral transfers can, of course, be effectively incorporated into a planned progression program. As an example, consider a company whose head of engineering seems to be the best man for the president's job — a position that, because of retirement, will be open in a few years. The head engineer has demonstrated outstanding managerial capabilities in the designing and engineering sections of the enterprise. However, the board of directors, responsible for grooming a presidential replacement, is not certain how effective he would be as the head of the production department where he previously held a subordinate line position. They also wonder whether he would treat the various functions of the enterprise in the proper balance. As a test, they place the chief engineer in charge of production for several years.

After that he is made general manager of an entire product division encompassing all kinds of activities ranging from production to sales and finance. Since his performance remains good in both instances, when the president retires the directors of the company elect this candidate to that high position with full confidence.

Special Projects

If exposure to a series of jobs cannot be arranged, there are other means for giving managers opportunities to acquire experience. They can, for example, be assigned to a special project or to some new activity in which the enterprise plans to engage. They may be put in charge of an electronics committee created to assess the feasibility and advisability of automation for the enterprise. They may be asked to introduce a new product. On such a special project, managers usually have a great amount of freedom because the newness of the project makes it difficult for top management to confine and prescribe their area of authority precisely. This gives developing executives a chance to show their initiative, perspicacity, and the many other qualities that top management is trying to appraise.

Temporary Assignments

Temporary assignments are also often used to provide on-the-job development. When a manager is away from his position because of illness, vacation, or an extended leave of absence, another executive typically takes over temporarily on an acting basis. This gives him a fine opportunity to gain experience in the higher level job. The immediate superior of the absentee manager is available to counsel and instruct the substitute, hence minimizing the risk that such substitution might otherwise entail.

Although the knowledge gained through this experience is of great value to the substitute, his performance in such a temporary assignment cannot be gauged effectively for selection and promotion purposes. First, the department or activity will probably carry through on its own momentum, and no one will expect the temporary manager to undertake radical changes. Furthermore, no responsible acting manager would deviate greatly from the established pattern, knowing that he will not be around when the results — or the failures — of such changes manifest themselves. Since temporary assignments are likely to cause a certain degree of disturbance within the regular operations, it is advisable that their number at any given time be kept to a minimum.

Assistant-to Positions

It was noted earlier in this section that shifting of men across functional lines at the upper levels of management is not usually feasible. Often, however, an executive destined for a top-level position lacks knowledge in some particular function. Occasionally, firms have tried to overcome this gap by creating upper-level assistant-to positions.

Although, as we will see in Chapter 21, the assistant-to position is frequently successful as a developmental tool for junior and lower-level executives, it is not as successful when used for upper-level people. First, upper-level employees are higher salaried, and whatever contribution they can make as an assistant-to would not be commensurate with the expenses that the host department would have to pay. Also, an assistant-to can seldom demonstrate how well he has learned his functional duties because he does not have any responsibility. The amount of knowledge he gains largely depends on the efforts which the departmental specialists make to teach him. Each of these limitations is serious; thus the assistant-to position is rarely used as a device for further development of upper-level managers.

Coaching and Counseling

Whether a company has a planned progression system and a program of lateral transfers or whether it has more informal executive practices, it will need to stress the diligent coaching of executives by their immediate superiors because the benefits the subordinate derives from any type of on-the-job development effort depend largely on this practice. Day-to-day relationships provide a superior with innumerable opportunities to strengthen and develop his people's capabilities.

Coaching is clearly a line duty. The executive does not fulfill his staffing function unless he realizes that on-the-job development of his managers is his responsibility alone. Although the staff of the personnel department or of the executive development group within that department can help, it is in no position to perform the coaching job for the line manager. Executives resent being trained by personnel staff and often wonder whether personnel people, many of whom have never administered anything, can tell them how to become better managers. Likewise, the coaching duty cannot be shifted to outside consultants, although they too can supply help and assistance, especially at the beginning of a development program.

Since the theory supporting any on-the-job development program is to learn by doing, the superior must provide ample opportunity for the subordinate to perform on the job. There can be no development without delegation. Only by having real authority and responsibility can a person's managerial qualities be tested and strengthened, and only by giving such authority and following through can superiors fulfill their coaching function.

One of the most important aspects of coaching is counseling — teaching the subordinate the art of management. In counseling, the counselor discusses with the subordinate his performance of specific activities. Such discussions usually include critical analysis of administrative skills, personal adjustments, problems of personalities, job knowledge, leadership, and so on. Relating this counseling to the job done in a particular situation will contribute effectively to the development of the subordinate. As Miles Mace puts it:

Counseling by the superior constitutes an effort to augment and strengthen the learning process which starts with doing tasks on the job. Given opportunities to perform, the subordinates will learn from these experiences, but they will learn more quickly and develop faster and further if their mistakes are the basis for suggested corrective measures afforded by the superior. The distinction here is probably that between unguided learning and guided learning.[2]

There is no single method of counseling. Specific techniques and styles used by one executive might be of little value to another. The important thing is to make the counseling procedures fit the specific case; each working situation might require a different method of counseling.

A Climate of Confidence

A climate of confidence between superior and subordinate must exist if coaching and counseling are to be effective. Confidence cannot be achieved merely by using gimmicks or techniques like the well-known "open door policy." The manager must be available not only physically but also psychologically. To tell people to come in at any time will not create confidence if the ensuing discussions are handled in a discouraging, curt, or discourteous manner. The reduction of threat in the counseling atmosphere is essential to establishing confidence. An inappropriate remark or a thoughtless comment may shatter the rapport which has taken so long to establish. However, the climate should be such that both the strengths and shortcomings of employees may be discussed frankly.

Getting Superiors to Coach

Since the extent and rate of managerial development depends greatly on coaching, it is important to impress upon executives the magnitude and significance of this duty. The degree of coaching practiced within a company is usually determined by the example set by the chief executive. If he practices coaching and believes firmly in it, his attitude will probably permeate the organization. In many cases, management should continuously stress coaching responsibility, pointing out that one of the factors on which each executive is appraised is his ability to develop subordinates.

In order to impress managers with their responsibility, some companies state that no one will be promoted unless he has prepared a successor. Although such a rule can be helpful, it is not applicable in all instances. Some individuals cannot be promoted no matter how many subordinates they may coach. Others have no further administrative ambitions.

OUT-COMPANY DEVELOPMENT PROGRAMS

Modern business organizations have undertaken many development activities which are conducted off company premises. These activities offer broadening experiences to executives, but are less directly tied to specific job functions than are in-company

---

[2] Miles L. Mace, *The Growth and Development of Executives* (Boston: Division of Research, Graduate School of Business Administration, Harvard University, 1950), p. 123.

programs. One is immediately impressed by the variety of activities available: They range from studies of classic literature to sensitivity training.

Most of these activities are conducted by universities and colleges, consulting firms, trade associations, management associations, and specialized organizations like the NTL Institute. Many companies recommend graduate programs to their executives. Sometimes they urge pursuit of a definite goal — an advanced degree. Other times they merely suggest that an executive take a particular course or two. Occasionally, formal educational activities take place at schools and staff colleges sponsored and maintained by the enterprise itself. Of course, only the very large enterprises can afford such an arrangement. General Electric, for instance, has established a Management Research and Development Institute at Crotonville, New York. If an enterprise does not have its own company school, it might call in instructors from nearby universities. All in all, diversity characterizes out-company executive development programs.

College and University Programs

Generally, major college and university training programs are based on one of two models. In the first, the executive leaves the business scene for a specified period of time, from three weeks to six months. He will meet with executives drawn from a number of firms around the country. They will live together, usually in a campus environment, and will study different subjects including policy formulation, business conditions, economics, and finance. These have been the most popular kinds of programs by far. They allow the executive to get away from daily business pressures and to interact with other businessmen from different industries. In the process, these men are exposed to the many points of view of their fellow "students" and of the faculty responsible for running the courses.

The second college model is built around a more formal academic curriculum and often leads to a master's degree in business administration. Executives who participate in this type of program pursue a course of study similar to that offered to regular students.

Special Institutes

The popularity of special institutes that train executives in a more restricted subject area is growing. A good example of such an institute is the NTL Institute. Executives who attend NTL programs receive training to improve their interpersonal skills so that they can become more effective leaders. In addition to NTL, there is a huge number of special institutes run by professional groups. The American Management Association is particularly active in this area.

Use of Consultants

Frequently, firms use a consultant in conjunction with their own training director to create and present a development program that will satisfy the firm's special needs.

This approach has been quite popular in developing programs for first-line supervision and has been used extensively for higher levels of management as well.

The subject matter in these specially-designed programs is diversified, but it focuses mainly on leadership skills and management processes. Usually the programs are condensed versions of introductory management courses that cover planning, organizing, staffing, influencing, and controlling. The degree of emphasis on each of these topics will vary from program to program depending on the needs of the firm's executives. More often than not, consultants conduct these programs in a live-in environment away from the company. A hotel, a resort, or a college campus frequently provides the facilities.

TECHNIQUES AND TRENDS IN DEVELOPMENT

With few exceptions, modern executive development programs tend to use methods which directly involve the participants in the subject matter. Certainly the case approach, pioneered by Harvard University, effectively achieves participation. In almost all development programs some variation of the case approach, simulating actual or supposed business conditions, is used.

However, other methods are evolving. Group dynamics are thought to be an extremely effective means of improving the leadership qualities of managers. The technique is also used to improve the work climate of an organization. Generally, development programs are focusing more and more on the individual executive as an agent of organizational change. At present, this philosophy is not universal. However, the modern business environment does seem to be forcing executives to give more consideration to their role in facilitating organizational adaptation. Certainly training activities aimed at improving executive abilities in this area should be much favored in the future.

How can the effectiveness of executive development programs, especially those conducted outside the company, be measured? How can management know whether these programs do what they claim to do — improve leadership, increase interpersonal skills, make managers better agents of change? Lack of follow-up and evaluation is a serious deficiency in most executive development activities. However, management seems to be increasingly concerned with the need to check the effects of its training and development methods.

Discussion Questions

1. Suppose you are the chief executive of a small company in a rapidly changing, highly technical industry. What kind of a development plan would you consider appropriate to offset executive obsolescence?

2. Check around your school or area and see what sorts of "out-company" management development programs are offered. Report on the content and structure of a program to your class.

Supplementary Readings

Argyris, Chris. *Interpersonal Competence and Organizational Effectiveness.* Homewood, Ill.: Irwin, 1962. See chapters 6, 7, 8, and 9.

Bennis, Warren G. *Changing Organizations.* New York: McGraw-Hill, 1967.

Schein, Edgar H. "Management Development as a Process of Influence." In *Dimensions in Modern Management,* edited by Patrick E. Connor. Boston: Houghton Mifflin, 1974.

Scott, William G. "Executive Development as an Instrument of Higher Control." In *Dimensions in Modern Management.*

Scott, William G., and Terence C. Mitchell, *Organization Theory.* Homewood, Ill.: Irwin, 1972. See chapter 16.

CHAPTER 21

Selecting and Developing Management Trainees

A crucial part of the staffing process is ensuring the continuity of management by providing an adequate flow of potential young managers into the company. The quality and quantity of this flow are determined by the forecast of executive requirements and also by the evaluation of managerial talent, which is part of the appraisal process.

In earlier decades, the natural flow of young men into the business sector seemed to be sufficient to supply almost all corporate needs. As enterprises began to grow in size, however, and as other appealing avenues of employment opened up in society, business firms began to find their existing sources of potential executives inadequate. Thus, they found it necessary to undertake an active search for new sources of talent. Across the country their recruiters combed the campuses of colleges and universities for suitable personnel. The now annual parade of "body snatchers" on the campus each spring is a sure sign that the academic year is nearing its close. Some companies prefer graduates from the liberal arts colleges, whereas others lean toward the graduates of schools of business administration. Although campus recruitment has become common in recent years, a number of companies followed this practice as long ago as World War I.[1]

For all practical purposes, then, junior executive training means the preparation of college graduates for managerial jobs. No doubt some schools provide their graduates with a better background on which to base such training than others do. Each company will sooner or later find its best source. A college education, however, is not an absolute prerequisite for entry to a management training program. Every employee of an organization, regardless of his formal education, should have the opportunity for promotion. Foremen should be asked to nominate candidates from the worker ranks for preparatory training, and those who pass the usual tests and executive interviews should be selected as management trainees. In most instances, though, this source provides only a fraction of the total number of executive trainees needed. Hence, colleges have increasingly become *the* source of candidates for management training programs.

---

[1] Henning W. Prentis, Jr., "The Task of Managing," in *Top Management Handbook*, ed. H. B. Maynard (New York: McGraw-Hill, 1960), p. 119. Mr. Prentis, the former chairman of the board of Armstrong Cork Company, describes his firm's experience with campus recruiting.

As a rule, college graduates are given general introductory preparation for a number of years, after which time they are appointed to junior executive positions. After additional development and experience, they are usually then promoted to higher positions. By entering a college graduate in such a program, the enterprise runs virtually no risk. The candidate has already been academically trained in the scientific approach to problem-solving, he thinks logically, he is intelligent, and he can communicate well. American higher education has eliminated the need for corporate executive "farm clubs," much as it has eliminated this need for professional football and basketball teams.

THE DECISION TO ESTABLISH A TRAINING PROGRAM

Each firm must decide if it should establish a formal training program. Past experience will help indicate to top management if such a program is necessary. In reaching a decision, management must also consider plans for expansion and diversification. Surveys have shown that larger firms tend to engage in training programs more frequently than smaller ones do. Although only a small percentage of all firms presently have such programs, almost all larger firms have adopted them.

Determining the Number of Trainees Needed

Once top management has decided that it needs a junior executive development program, the next question, a most crucial one, is how many trainees should be brought into the enterprise each year. The obvious purpose of the program is, of course, to develop a sufficient number of executives. If it fails to do so, the enterprise will have to go to the outside to attract qualified managers. However, having too many trainees is equally undesirable and costly. Young people may become impatient while waiting for the proper opening and may possibly leave the enterprise after they have been trained. Stockpiling young managers is unfair to the individual and inefficient for the company.

As we mentioned in Chapter 18, a record of past executive replacements will give top management an approximate idea of the annual rate of attrition. In deciding the number of trainees, some firms follow a ratio of one to one between selectees and the number of probable openings. Other companies feel that out of any initial group of trainees, fewer than 50 per cent will be available for appointments five years thereafter. Naturally some good people will be lost, but the only way to prevent this would be to have an organization made up of mediocre talent that no competitor would want. This is too high a price to pay for stability. As time goes on and the enterprise gains experience in its selection process and training program, it will probably be able to improve and narrow the ratio between the number of selectees and the number of probable openings.[2]

---

[2] The Armstrong Cork Company, an enterprise that has had an effective college trainee program ever since World War I, has trained approximately fifteen hundred young men during the twenty-year period from 1938 to 1958. Of these, almost 60 per cent were still employed by the company at the end of 1958. Prentis, "The Task of Managing," p. 121.

Management of the Training Program

Organizing the training program is a function of the line executive. Often a director is appointed to head the program, and he should be a line man who is part of the upper managerial ranks. However, in companies where the program is of considerable size, top management should assign a staff member or a staff agency to provide line management with the necessary expert advice and administrative help.

RECRUITMENT AND SELECTION

It is interesting to observe the recruitment activity on university campuses from year to year. Larger firms recruit consistently, regardless of business conditions. They realize that the aging process of executives continues through good years and bad ones. Other companies, those that have not yet solidified their junior executive training program, may allow hiring to fluctuate with general business conditions. This is a shortsighted view and one that indicates that some managements are not yet fully convinced of the benefits of a regular recruiting effort. Sporadic hiring of outstanding young people will sooner or later be reflected in a poorly balanced or unbalanced age distribution among upper level executives.

Initial Screening

The first step in the recruiting process is *screening*. This takes place when the firm's recruitment officer — a member of the personnel staff or a line executive — visits university campuses and speaks to potential candidates. It is especially important that a corporation send as recruiters individuals who are well informed about their company and who know what kind of trainees to seek. Large corporations like General Motors hire as many as one thousand graduates each year and, in order to get them, they may have to interview twenty-five thousand.[3] A well-qualified recruiter can develop valuable relationships between his company and college placement counselors, thus facilitating the process of getting the right students into the right spots.

Each firm has certain minimum hiring requirements, and in the first interview a good recruitment officer should be able to eliminate candidates who do not fulfill them. Although there is a great diversity in these requirements, almost all firms stipulate that an applicant be young, for it will be years before he is ready for a senior executive job. If the applicant is approximately twenty-five to twenty-eight years old, at the age of forty-five or forty-eight he could, theoretically, step into a top executive position and still serve the firm for approximately twenty years before retirement at age sixty-five. Therefore, the upper age limit that most enterprises usually set for management trainees is about twenty-five to twenty-eight.

[3] "What Makes College Recruiting Go Wrong?" *Business Week* (January 14, 1961), pp. 70–71. Also see George S. Odiorne and Arthur S. Hann, *Effective College Recruiting* (Ann Arbor, Mich.: Bureau of Industrial Relations, University of Michigan, 1961).

The recruiter must also try to learn many other things about the candidate in this preliminary interview. Although it is difficult to judge maturity, the recruiter will get an impression of some of its facets — the candidate's interests, the views he holds, the common sense he expresses, and the drive and initiative he demonstrates. It is always easier to eliminate candidates who are obviously unfit in these respects than to determine degrees of fitness for those who do seem to qualify.

The recruiter's next task is to encourage applicants who have not been eliminated to become active candidates for the training program of his particular enterprise. He will, of course, discuss compensation with the potential trainee. Starting salaries have become a problem. They must be comparable to what other firms offer, but they must also be consistent with the company's over-all compensation system, thereby assuring that reasonable increases can be given to the trainee after he is on the job. In order to woo a candidate, the recruiter will often roll out the red carpet, a practice that obviously cannot be continued after he is hired.

Interviewing and Final Selection

The next step in the recruitment process is the initiation of a series of thorough interviews, which are normally conducted at the headquarters of the firm. Although the interviews are usually supervised by the officer in charge of the training program, a number of other corporate executives also participate. It is necessary that line officers interview the candidates so that the final selection decision reflects a consensus of several different types of experienced executives.

In assessing a candidate, the interviewer will look for intelligence, analytical capabilities, facility in communicating, personality, interests, and motivation. The intelligence of the candidate can be determined by checking his scholastic record and various aptitude tests which he has probably taken before and during his college career. In order to assess the candidate's analytical ability, the interviewer may present him with a certain problem and observe how he solves it. Because the same problem is given to all candidates, the interviewer can rate the quality of particular solutions. The candidate's interests and his ability to communicate are easily appraised during an interview. His personality and motivation are more difficult to assess; however, some help is provided by McClelland's work on n(achievement), discussed in Chapter 1.[4]

In all its trainee interviews, management must beware of the tendency to pick candidates who are too much alike. Since great stress is often placed on the need to secure adaptable young people schooled in managerial skills, greatly concerned with human relations, and displaying characteristics that will make them good members of a smooth working team, organizations often neglect individuals with new and even unorthodox views who will question existing practices and generate ideas for constructive change. To do so disregards the dynamics of business and neglects the need for innovators.

[4] David C. McClelland, "Business Drive and National Achievement," *Harvard Business Review* 40 (July–August 1962): 99–112.

MANAGEMENT RECRUITMENT AND PUBLIC POLICY

The Fair Employment Practices Act has been enforced as an anti-discrimination code by the federal level of government for a number of years. This act, administered by the Department of Labor, is aimed at eliminating discrimination in employment because of race, religion, sex, or national origin. Although the law is directed at all organizational levels, its enforcement has been most vigorous at the level of hourly rated employees.

Most recently, legislation at both state and national levels has been passed to encourage the recruitment of minorities into managerial and professional positions. Currently pending nationally is a constitutional amendment prohibiting discrimination against women. Some states have already passed constitutional amendments relating to sex discrimination.

Given these developments in public policy, recruiters will have to extend their range to women and minorities when seeking out qualified applicants for managerial training programs. That such efforts are underway is evident; however, equal opportunity for employment in executive positions of corporations and nonprofit organizations is still a distant goal.

TRAINING

The candidates who survive the selection process and join an organization usually find that a rugged training schedule awaits them. The steps outlined in the following discussion merely suggest a possible sequence of training activities; they ought not to be considered definitive.

Induction

Shortly after the individual has been selected for a training program, he will need to learn the history and tradition of the enterprise, its position within the industry, its market standing, its objectives and policies, its general structure and organization. This information is often available in books, booklets, manuals, or brochures; if not, lectures are given.

Presupervisory Work

After becoming acquainted with the enterprise, the trainee will enter a period of presupervisory work. The length of this period varies greatly from a brief six months to one or two years and sometimes even longer. The presupervisory period is intended to give the trainee experience in all kinds of nonmanagerial jobs. For instance, in a manufacturing concern the trainees may go first into the stock room, from there into the shipping room, and then spend several months on the production floor. They may also spend some time in the production control department, scheduling department, purchasing department, accounting department, and in the general offices. Later, they may be placed for several months in the sales department at headquarters, probably selling to the customers in the field. The exact order and selection of the nonmanagerial jobs will differ depending on the needs and character of the enterprise. All trainees will not do the same job at the same time. After a given amount of time is spent at a certain job, the trainees are reshuffled. Thus, by the end of several years, all will have had approximately the same amount of diversified work experience.

Advantages and Shortcomings

The advantage of varied presupervisory work experience is obvious: It affords the trainee an opportunity to perform differing jobs. It also has, however, certain disadvantages. Some trainees learn the details of a job in a shorter time than others and therefore waste much of the time they spend on the job. Many regular employees resent trainees because they are the chosen few who will eventually be promoted into higher positions. A further disadvantage is that those in charge of the particular departments used for training will have to bear the costs of training the junior executives, knowing that they will probably not remain long enough to make a productive contribution. Nevertheless, these and numerous other disadvantages are far outweighed by the great advantage of having trainees who have done many jobs. Furthermore, if all the trainees follow an established presupervisory route, supervisors eventually will accept this procedure as a matter of course, and with time, much of the friction will disappear.

Appraisal of Trainee

At the end of each presupervisory assignment the management trainee will be rated and appraised by the executive under whose supervision he has worked. This executive, in turn, will usually send his appraisal to a staff man from the personnel department, or more specifically from the executive development program, who serves as trainee administrator and counselor. From time to time this counselor will review the record of each individual trainee in order to decide whether he actually has the capacity for further advancement, whether he should be kept within the organization, or whether he should be encouraged to leave. This decision should be made in the first years of employment, for in the long run frankness can only be beneficial to the young man or woman.

Additional Presupervisory Training

In addition to presupervisory experience in actual work situations, many firms use other devices to broaden the exposure of trainees before assigning them to supervisory levels. Two of the more commonly used are work in an assistant-to position and rotation in observation posts. Through these devices the trainee is exposed to certain aspects of company operations without actually doing the work himself.

Assistant-to Positions

The assistant-to position connected with an executive training program differs from the assistant-to position associated with line and staff. In the latter instance, the assistant is assigned to an overburdened executive to relieve him of some of his duties. In executive training, the position is created primarily to help the trainee by exposing him to the manager's daily activities. Most companies feel that it is more effective to put a trainee into such a position after he has had some kind of work experience within the enterprise rather than when he is fresh out of school.

Assistant-to positions for trainees are usually not permanent, and only a few executives are assigned a trainee. The trainee is there to learn and only adds to the burdens of the executive. The executive, of course, is generally responsible for the success or failure of the assistant-to position as a training device. If the executive makes a real effort to be a good teacher and coach, the trainee will certainly benefit. For this reason, only executives who have proved that they have these capacities participate. In the beginning, no duties are given to the assistant-to other than doing some of the leg work for the executive. However, if the executive is a good teacher, he will as time goes on be able to make more and more use of the trainee, and the trainee will be exposed to a multitude of managerial activities. This, of course, presupposes not only the superior's ability to teach but also the trainee's desire to learn. Hence, the assistant-to position is often created especially for a particular trainee, and after it has served its purpose it is abolished.

Observation Assignments

The observation assignment also permits trainees to gain exposure to various managerial functions. When it is used, trainees are assigned on a rotating basis to different managers whom they observe as they perform their functions. The obvious disadvantage of this training device is that the trainee might not know what to look for. He might not be far enough advanced in his training to distinguish between the activities that are worthwhile observing and those that are not. In addition, some managers feel that the trainee should not be allowed to observe certain confidential activities and decisions. Also some managers resent observation assignments because the trainee actually performs no work, although his salary is charged to the department.

Nevertheless, under proper auspices, observation assignments are beneficial, for they give the trainee a chance to examine and discuss thoroughly the work being done. It is questionable, however, whether an observation assignment will improve managerial skills because it does not involve any practice or impose any responsibility for action. The special value, therefore, lies in the information gained.

Assignment to Managerial Positions

After a sufficient exposure to presupervisory experiences, the trainee is appointed to a supervisory job. From then on, he must show what he has learned, and he will continue to learn by managing. He will have to direct the efforts of subordinates toward achieving the enterprise goal. He will change from doing things himself to getting things done by others; he will plan, organize, staff, influence, and control.

For his first supervisory job a trainee will be assigned to one of several line or staff positions. Sometimes the trainees who prefer staff positions are assigned to line jobs to qualify them for operating functions later on. At other times trainees will be placed in fields completely different from those in which they specialized in college, thus improving their adaptability and versatility. Initial supervisory assignments are by no means permanent. Generally, the trainee is rotated just as he was in his nonmanagerial, presupervisory period. The type and extent of rotation depends, among other things, on the needs of the enterprise, its plans for expansion, and the dynamics of the industry. In addition, it depends on the needs of the person himself.

A junior executive who has progressed to the supervisory level usually spends several years at a certain job. During this time he must prove his value before he can progress to another job. If top management has decided on such a system of rotation as a training device, then certain managerial jobs must be set aside and manned only by executive trainees. These are regular managerial positions within the organization, but positions that will offer the trainee-manager a suitable opportunity for development and experience. Because there will be a rather rapid turnover rate in departments staffed by trainees, top management should minimize the loss in efficiency by making certain that the positions above and below the one being filled by a trainee-manager are held by experienced individuals.

One of the greatest advantages of this kind of rotation is that the trainee-manager gains an understanding of interdepartmental relationships and the importance of coordination and cooperation. One of the major disadvantages, in addition to the difficulty of selecting suitable positions and the initial loss of efficiency, is the lowering of morale among subordinates who work in the departments that trainee-managers supervise. These subordinates resent the fact that, although they may be qualified, they will never achieve a managerial position within their department because such positions always go to a trainee. Those who are ambitious and feel that they are at a dead end will probably leave the enterprise, whereas older subordinates, unable to leave, will remain and be resentful. This is a disadvantage that usually cannot be overcome, and top management must make certain that it is outweighed by the advantages derived from the rotation procedures.

ADDITIONAL TRAINING DEVICES

Some supplementary devices can be worked into the junior executive training program. These include use of committees, junior boards, conferences, courses, university programs, trade association programs, and many other arrangements that contribute to a well-rounded training experience.

Committees

There is little doubt that service on committees is of considerable educational value to executive trainees. It is useful to place a young manager on a committee composed mostly of experienced executives so that he will become acquainted with various company problems and points of view. He will have the opportunity to observe how department managers defend their attitudes and opinions in front of a committee and how they adjust themselves to the over-all needs of the enterprise. This will broaden the trainee's knowledge, for the problems under consideration usually have causes and consequences far exceeding any one member's area of competence. Committee experience will also warn the young executive against believing that his point of view is always right; it will show him the importance of having an open mind on all complex issues.

Junior Boards

The junior board is a committee created for training purposes and is composed only of junior executives. In this arrangement, junior executives at various levels meet as a quasi–board of directors, deliberating over problems they have encountered and suggesting changes and ideas that they consider proper and good for the enterprise. Their suggestions are passed on to regular managerial boards and, if they warrant, to the real board of directors. Participation in this kind of deliberation no doubt broadens the outlook of the trainee.

The problems selected by junior boards are usually fairly general. This affords the trainee an opportunity to acquire considerable knowledge in almost all aspects of the enterprise. It is a sign of recognition for a young man to be elected and re-elected by his fellow trainees for membership on a junior board. In fulfilling his assignments as a board member, the young executive has a chance to develop important skills such as leading a discussion, leading the investigation of a problem, preparing and presenting a report. Junior boards are a good additional training device for potential executives; the suggestions they generate are also of substantial benefit to the enterprise.

Training Outside the Firm

Management often sends trainees to conferences held by trade or management associations. Much can be learned if these conferences are properly conducted and if they come at the right time in the trainee's development. In addition to conferences, top management often decides to enroll trainees in formal university courses or university programs. These and innumerable other external training devices are desirable if they stem from well-qualified sources.

When a young person completes his training and probationary period, he becomes a member of the executive cadre. He is appraised constantly through his early employment with a firm, and appraisal by his superior continues after his "graduation." In large part, appraisal for him as for the more established executives determines compensation, the subject of Chapter 22.

Discussion Questions

1. What expectations do you have for company managerial training in your first job?

2. Discuss the recruiting process engaged in by organizations on your campus. Has there been any change in patterns over, say, the last five years?

Supplementary Readings

Dill, W. R., T. L. Hilton, and W. R. Reitman. *The New Managers.* Englewood Cliffs, N.J.: Prentice-Hall, 1962.

French, Wendell. *The Personnel Management Process: Human Resources Administration.* 3d ed. Boston: Houghton Mifflin, 1974. See chapter 13.

Given, William B. *Bottom-Up Management: People Working Together.* New York: Harper and Row, 1949.

Odiorne, George S. *Training by Objectives.* New York: Macmillan, 1970.

Schein, Edgar H. "Management Development as a Process of Influence." In *Readings in Human Relations,* edited by Keith Davis and William G. Scott. New York: McGraw-Hill, 1964. See pp. 340–59.

CHAPTER 22

Executive Compensation

Usually when we think of executive compensation we think of the money and the various other kinds of financial incentives offered to management. Although monetary matters occupy a good deal of our attention in the present chapter, we should be aware that business also contains nonfinancial rewards that provide powerful incentives. These less tangible incentives will be explored later in this chapter.

SALARY DETERMINANTS

A company needs an equitable system of executive compensation that will satisfy executives as well as stockholders. It is management's responsibility to build such an executive salary structure even if a few executives do not fit into it properly. In the long run, having a logical basis for managerial compensation is just as important as having a sound pay structure for the rest of the organization.

Compensation Factors

Compensation surveys show that the rate of executive pay is affected by company size, type of industry, and the importance of the decision-making role. Generally, for comparable positions, a large company pays higher salaries than a smaller one, for larger firms have greater financial resources at their command. Also, although the nature of managerial activities may be similar, the magnitude of responsibility for the manager of a large company will be greater. He will probably need to handle larger budgets, more subordinates, and the like.

Surveys show that executive salaries vary greatly from industry to industry. For example, in 1969, retail trade firms with $400 million in annual sales paid their chief executives between $90,000 and $168,000 annually, whereas the petroleum industry paid between $151,000 and $323,000.[1]

Earlier figures, compiled in Table 22-1, show the salary relationships between the four highest paid positions in about 600 companies. The table indicates that this relationship remained stable in the seven-year period studied. In 1961, the number two

---

[1] See The Conference Board, *Top Executive Compensation*, Report 501 (1970), pp. 47–49, 50–53.

Table 22-1. Salary Relationships Among Top Executives (Per Cent of Chief Executive's Salary Received)

Position	1954	1955	1956	1957	1958	1959	1960	1961
Chief executive	100	100	100	100	100	100	100	100
Number 2 executive	70	71	70	69	73	72	73	71
Number 3 executive	58	58	57	57	60	60	61	59
Number 4 executive	51	51	51	52	55	55	54	54

Source: Arch Patton, "Trends in Executive Compensation," *Harvard Business Review* 38, no. 5 (September–October 1960): 144–54; "Executive Compensation in 1960," *Harvard Business Review* 39, no. 5 (September–October 1961): 152–57.

executive received an average of 71 per cent of the compensation of the chief executive; the number three executive received 59 per cent; and the number four executive received 54 per cent. More recent figures show a narrowing of the gap between the pay levels of the top executive and his immediate subordinates.[2]

We have stated that the magnitude of an executive's decision-making role is crucial in determining his salary level. This statement, however, raises an interesting question. Is an executive really paid on the basis of the size of his responsibility, or is he paid on the profitability of his unit's operation?[3]

Classic economic theorists state that, ultimately, the revenue produced by the executive determines his salary. However, there is substantial evidence to indicate that the magnitude of responsibility, not profitability of the activity, is becoming the crucial factor underlying salary. Arch Patton, for example, talks about the "disassociation of pay and profits" and states that this is a relatively recent development. To substantiate this he points out that in 1965, "only a few industries were detected which showed a positive correlation . . . between the level of top management pay and return on sales or invested capital."[4] He makes the interesting observation that if salary were a function of sales volume (which in turn is a function of company size) rather than of profits, we would raise the spectre of profitless prosperity.

Internal Consistency and External Competitiveness

The three factors we have just discussed are not the only determinants of executive compensation. They are supplemented by two closely related and somewhat overlapping considerations: internal consistency and external competitiveness. *Internal consistency* requires that the salary system reward jobs according to their impor-

[2] Arch Patton, "Top Executive Pay: New Facts and Figures," *Harvard Business Review* 44, no. 5 (September–October 1966): 94–98.
[3] Malcolm S. Salter, "What Is 'Fair Pay' for the Executive?" *Harvard Business Review* 50 (May–June 1972): 6–13, 144–46.
[4] Patton, "Top Executive Pay," p. 96. Also see "For the Chief, Sales Set the Pay," *Business Week* (September 30, 1967), p. 174.

tance in the organization. It attempts to minimize the pay inequities which arise when one job has fewer responsibilities than another, but carries a higher salary. *External competitiveness* demands that executive compensation meet that of other firms. The reconciliation of these two factors is often difficult. Frequently, the market demand for certain specialists like computer technologists and systems analysts does not respect the internal salary structure of any particular firm.

Internal Evaluation of Management Positions

In order to achieve an equitable internal alignment of management positions, it is necessary to determine the proper relationships among the salaries of the positions; and in order to do this it is necessary to evaluate each position systematically. This procedure, called *job evaluation,* is a standardized method of appraising the worth and value of each job in relation to other jobs. Although job evaluation methods can be used for any position, the present discussion is concerned only with the evaluation of management positions. Such evaluations should be performed by a committee of representative top-level managers to assure that all types of managers receive equal attention and concern. Once a number of such positions are appraised and their worth and value determined, it is a simple matter to figure out the relative compensation for each management job. The compensation of the chief executive and of a limited number of other very high corporate officers is determined by the board of directors.

The evaluation of executive jobs for compensation purposes has been criticized because such evaluation is concerned with the job itself and not with performance. Some say that carrying this factory-oriented concept of job evaluation to executive positions brings an unrealistic rigidity into the compensation structure, particularly at upper levels. As Patton puts it: "The closer to the top of the company pyramid an executive climbs, the more he makes his own job."[5] In other words, Patton believes that it is pointless to speak about job evaluation of top positions, in reality, because evaluation can only relate to what an individual manager has made of his job in comparison with what others have made of theirs. In his opinion the critical element in evaluating the upper-level positions is the contribution managers in such positions make to the decision-making process. Although it is relatively easy to distinguish major decisions from the less important ones, it is much more difficult to determine who makes or influences which decisions and whose decision-making contributions go beyond his functional responsibilities.

External Compensation Alignment

An executive compensation structure must also align equitably with those of other firms. Otherwise, the enterprise will not be able to retain its capable managers or, when necessary, to attract executives from the outside. Because of the differing size,

[5] Arch Patton, "What Is an Executive Worth?" *Harvard Business Review* 39, no. 2 (March–April 1961): 71.

nature, and specific job characteristics of enterprises, it is much more difficult to obtain proper external alignment than to achieve internal balance. Clearly, many executive duties performed in one enterprise may not exist in another.

In addition to direct compensation, many companies provide supplementary benefits which are not readily quantifiable and comparable. The report on trends in executive compensation published by the Conference Board is a good source of information on such supplementary benefits as well as on other aspects of compensation. These reports analyze the compensation data of about 1,200 companies listed on the major stock exchanges. Management can use such data to see whether its own executive compensation structure is sound internally and externally.

OTHER FORMS OF FINANCIAL COMPENSATION

As we have just stated, other forms of financial remuneration round out a company's executive compensation program. These range from offering managers financial incentives designed to increase their short-term profits to providing deferred income for retirement, a policy that provides distinct tax advantages. Table 22-2 lists both the objectives and techniques of the major compensation practices.[6]

Let us look at each of these practices in more detail.

Incentive or Bonus Systems

Many firms have bonus systems to satisfy their managers' desires for increased income. Bonuses should be looked upon as an extra payment beyond base salary. Not

Table 22-2. Compensation Practices

Technique	Objective
Incentive compensation	1. Dollar profit improvement 2. Increased return on investment 3. Improved individual performance
Stock option	1. Proprietary attitude towards costs and profits 2. Dollar profit improvement
Qualified profit-sharing plan	1. Increased individual attention to company profits 2. Dollar profit improvement
Qualified retirement pension plan	1. Greater loyalty to the company 2. Lower turnover

Source: *The Use and Effectiveness of Management Compensation Programs* (New York: Cresap, McCormick and Paget, Management Consultants, 1963), pp. 1–4.

[6] For a more detailed account, see George W. Hettenhouse, "Cost/Benefit Analysis of Executive Compensation," *Harvard Business Review* 48 (July–August 1970): 120–21.

only do they provide additional income and incentive for the executives, they also provide great advantages for the enterprise. Because improved returns to the company mean additional income to them, executives are truly motivated. Also, an enterprise might be able to gain the services of a particularly well-qualified executive without interfering with its established basic salary structure by offering appropriate bonuses. Instead of paying an executive a high annual salary, management might pay him an incentive bonus. In this way, the incentive paid for outstanding performance in one year will not become a permanent ingredient in the salary structure.

One of the problems with this type of system, however, is that it is often difficult to measure the degree to which the efforts of a particular executive have contributed to the results of a particular year. The business may have done very well during a year because economic conditions were unusually good; success may have had little to do with the efforts of particular executives. As a matter of fact, it has been found that executives often exert more effort when economic conditions are poor; yet, company profits will necessarily remain low.

Clearly, the basis of incentive compensation presents a problem. Theoretically, it would be a good idea to relate the standard of measurement to the work of the individual. A sales manager, for example, would receive incentives based on the amount of sales; for other managers, the bases might be production output, reduction of costs, and so on. But none of these bases necessarily provides an accurate reflection of true managerial performance. Increased sales might result from good general business conditions or the poor performance of competitors; they might also be a by-product of inflation. Increased production could be caused by overwork, speed up, and other devices which will look good in the short run but will eventually harm the enterprise. The same applies to incentives based on savings in costs and expenses. A manager might postpone needed replacements, repairs, and maintenance in order to earn himself a bonus. Adequate controls can, however, minimize these problems.

Generally, incentives should be related to over-all performance of the enterprise; they should, therefore, be based on profits. This usually occurs among firms where only one or a few executives are involved. In large companies, a bonus fund is frequently established whereby a fixed percentage of the net profits, reflecting not so much the contribution of an individual as the teamwork of all executives, is set aside. In some cases, this percentage is set aside regardless of the return on invested capital; in others, it is not set aside until a certain percentage return is earned on such capital. The division of the bonus fund among participating executives is determined by the board of directors or by a special bonus committee. Naturally, the larger the enterprise, the larger the fund will be and the larger the number of executives who will participate in it.

One extreme case can be found at General Motors, where the bonus fund for 1972 operations (distributed in 1973) amounted to over $101 million, distributed among approximately 7,100 employees of the corporation. The amount of money available for employee bonuses is determined by a complicated formula based on the corporation's net income. In the same year, the bonus fund for the Ford Motor Company amounted to over $64 million, disbursed among approximately 6,800 managers of the company. The amount was based on 6 per cent of the profits after 10 per cent of the capital used in the business had been deducted.

Incentive payments are frequently made in the form of cash. This has the advantage of satisfying the immediate financial needs of executives, whose needs are usually at a peak during the early and middle stages of their careers. However, as the executive progresses into higher income tax brackets, a growing portion of the cash payment will be consumed by taxes. Therefore, deferred payment plans with their tax saving features have become increasingly popular. There is, however, the danger that preoccupation with tax saving and emphasis on retirement will cause some of the incentive value of the bonus to be lost.

Stock Options

Stock option plans have, during the past years, become a major device for attracting and retaining capable executives. These plans give company executives the right to purchase a certain amount of the company's stock at a stated fixed price. From 1950 until 1964, options could be granted at as much as 15 per cent below the market price of the stock on the day they were granted. Under changes introduced by the Internal Revenue Service in 1964, the options cannot now be granted at less than current market price on the day they are declared. There is no obligation on the part of the executive ever to exercise his option, and naturally he will not do so unless the market price of the stock advances far enough so that it pays for him to take action. In other words, if an option is declared when the market price of the stock is $50 per share, the executive might want to wait until its price goes up to $55 before exercising his option to buy at $50. This waiting period, however, cannot extend beyond five years from the date the option is declared, whereas prior to 1964 the option expired in ten years. Profits derived from stock options are considered long-term capital gains and are taxable as such, provided the buyer holds the stock for at least three years. Before 1964, a six-month holding period was sufficient to qualify for the lower capital gains tax rate.

Such arrangements are attractive to executives who are in the high income tax brackets. For them, stock options are preferable to a substantial salary increase, which would be taxed away as normal income. By this means, an enterprise can attract and keep executives whose income is in the high tax brackets. However, the effects of the 1964 and, subsequently, the 1969 revisions of the tax law do "virtually eliminate the possibility of capital gains profits from options."[7] The law plus severe slumps in the stock market have hampered the incentive value of stock option plans.

Although it probably would be within the prerogatives of most boards of directors to grant stock options to executives, they usually first submit the option plans to the stockholders for approval at the annual meeting. This practice probably devel-

[7] Arch Patton, "Are Stock Options Dead?" *Harvard Business Review* 48 (September–October 1970): 26.

oped because of the severe criticism made of stock option plans. Recently, the frequency with which such plans are established has raised the fear that they are getting out of hand.

Profit-sharing

Profit-sharing is a popular form of executive compensation. Much like bonus-type incentive plans, profit-sharing generally provides an annual distribution of funds to executives based upon over-all company performance. Unlike regular incentive plans, however, cash distributions are not made in the year earned. Rather, they are credited to the executive's account and allowed to accumulate over the years. Frequently, these funds are invested in the common stock of the firm with the anticipation of future appreciation. Such anticipations were certainly fulfilled in the case of the celebrated Sears, Roebuck plan in which modest dollar investments grew to sizable proportions for the participants.

Because of their deferred character, profit-sharing plans are being integrated with retirement programs. Typically, an executive must be with a company some years, usually five to ten, before he gets any vesting privileges in the firm's contributions. This means that he cannot take any of the company's contributions to the program with him if he changes jobs before the vesting period expires. Such a feature is a strong incentive for an executive to stay with the company. Indeed, in some companies, funds do not vest until retirement age is reached.

Deferred Compensation

As pointed out on previous occasions, high income tax rates have led top management to devise forms of deferred executive compensation. Prior to retirement, such compensation is not subject to income taxes. Executives are often much more interested in an assured income after they retire than in an increase in income at a time when they are already receiving high salaries. This is one reason why the popularity of pension and retirement plans has greatly increased. A pension plan provides the executive with a reduced though still sizable income after he has retired from his company activities. It has been estimated that the average chief executive's pension amounts to 26 per cent of his compensation in his highest earning years.[8] He will still have to pay income taxes on the pension in those years when he receives it, but his tax bracket will by then be considerably lower.

Aside from these tax considerations, it is only fair that an executive, after having spent many years with an enterprise, be entitled to receive a retirement income from it. So that this will not be too great a burden on the firm, however, a multitude of

[8] The full picture is obscured because seemingly modest pension programs are often supplemented by substantial consulting agreements between a retired high-level executive and his former firm.

regulations permit the amounts paid out for pension purposes to be considered a deductible business expense. It is advisable, therefore, that management consult the services of an expert before devising any pension plans.

In addition to pension plans, there are other types of deferred executive compensation. For example, some enterprises enter into contractual agreements with executives stating that when they retire they will be available on a consultant basis to the enterprise at a fixed income. Other arrangements establish compensation levels for executives if they are elected to the board of directors. Still another form of deferred compensation involves a contract made between the enterprise and the retired executive, paying him a sum of money for not working for any other firm, particularly for a competitor. In all these arrangements, care must be taken that there is no doubt about the deferred nature of the income and that the device is not merely intended to evade current taxes. Expert advice about legality and tax considerations should always be obtained.

NONFINANCIAL COMPENSATION

Business offers its executives many rewards not directly related to income. Among the most important are power, social acceptance, and an opportunity to demonstrate ability. The larger the firm, the greater is the degree to which an executive is likely to realize these rewards. Thus, it can be said that the motivation underlying organizational growth is linked to nonfinancial as well as to financial incentives.

The first of these less tangible incentives — power — means, in one sense, control over organizational resources. A manager achieves greater power by expanding his responsibilities. He is able to make a larger claim on the resources of the firm if he controls a sizable unit in it. This becomes, then, an avenue of influence for him, an avenue by which he is able to have considerable impact on company policy.

Business firms provide an outlet for the talents, skills, and education that thousands of persons acquire in order to earn a living. A business firm is really not just a place to work, it is also a place to be creative and to contribute to society. In fact, for many executives work is not a burdensome chore. Instead, it carries intrinsic personal satisfactions. Business organizations provide the opportunity for many to use work as a form of self-expression. Hence, if the proper work environment exists, the chance to do a good job is another nonfinancial incentive for a manager. This incentive is closely related to the process of influencing in which, as we shall see in Part V, motivating factors beyond money also exist.

Discussion Questions

1. What are the implications of the trend toward paying executives for the magnitude of their responsibility instead of for their profit-making ability or efficiency?

2. Is anybody really worth a salary of $500,000 a year?

Supplementary Readings

Business Week. "There's Big Money in the Fringes." In *Dimensions in Modern Management,* edited by Patrick E. Connor. Boston: Houghton Mifflin, 1974.

Hettenhouse, George W. "Cost/Benefit Analysis of Executive Compensation." *Harvard Business Review* 48 (July–August 1970): 114–24.

Lewellen, Wilbur G., and Howard P. Lanser. "Executive Pay Preferences." *Harvard Business Review* 51 (September–October 1973): 115–22.

Patton, Arch. "What Is an Executive Worth?" In *Dimensions in Modern Management.*

Salter, Malcolm S. "What Is 'Fair Pay' for the Executive?" *Harvard Business Review* 50 (May–June 1972): 6–13.

CASES

IV | 1

The Conrad Manufacturing Company

Carl Miller started working for the Conrad Manufacturing Company at the age of twenty and has been there for the last twenty years. During this time, he worked his way up through various jobs and now holds the position of superintendent. He is in charge of all production and works directly under Mr. Earl Lang, the works manager, who is sixty-four years old. For the past five years, Mr. Lang has not provided the leadership and management that his position requires. Carl has submitted to him plans for a number of important changes and improvements that he considers necessary to keep the productive facilities up to date and to make the company a more desirable and challenging place for the employees. However, his suggestions have not brought results. Mr. Lang listens to them but does nothing more, even when inaction is clearly inappropriate.

Mr. Miller is seriously considering leaving the Conrad Manufacturing Company to accept a superintendent's position in another firm in the city. He is completely frustrated and believes that as time goes on his reputation in the eyes of top management might suffer. Of course, he understands that as soon as Mr. Lang leaves he would become the works manager. He thinks that he has been most patient and understanding. However, he is now forty years old and thinks this is the right time to make a change. On the other hand, he is reluctant to forgo the possibility of advancement in his present firm.

The president of the company, Mr. Probst, is aware that Mr. Lang has not been performing well for several years, and this is also known to the personnel director, Mr. Boland. Carl has expressed his feelings and thinking informally on several occasions to the personnel director, who realizes that the company may lose Carl. The company has no fixed retirement policy; otherwise Carl would know when he could expect things to change.

Questions

1. What should Carl Miller do?
2. Should the personnel director become involved in this situation?
3. What actions, if any, should the president take?

IV | 2

Pickens Versus McDougal Aerospace Company

Charles Pickens worked for the McDougal Aerospace Company for twelve years, having started there in August 1960 after graduating from State University as a mechanical engineer. During this time, he was employed as an engineer in one of the electromechanical sections of the engineering department. He had advanced to the rank of a senior engineer in his department, having been there five years longer than any of the six engineers in his section. During all these years, the company was highly satisfied with his work and attitude.

In recent years, the workload of the electromechanical section, of which Mr. Pickens is a part, has been decreasing steadily because company projects have required less and less technical support of this nature. On October 20, 1972, Charles Pickens was laid off. The other engineers in his section with less seniority were not laid off. Mr. Pickens' letter of dismissal stated that the action was taken in accordance with company policy after long and serious consideration and that the company had no other choice. The workload of the company had shifted and would continue to shift from electromechanical work to electronics work and his qualifications in electronics were far below those of the others of his section.

Naturally Mr. Pickens was very disturbed and intends to try to have his dismissal decision reversed. At this time, he is deliberating the steps he should take and the reasons he should cite in support of his position.

Questions

1. What would you advise him to do?
2. What arguments should he put forth in order to show the fallacy of the company's point of view?

IV|3

Simmons Retail Chain Store — Selection of an Auditor

Harry Jamison, the employment manager of the Simmons Retail Chain Store Company, returned to his office from a luncheon engagement with two assistant controllers where several important matters had been discussed. Among them was the company's expansion program, which included the establishment and acquisition of new stores throughout the southwestern part of the country. These changes, plus the normal amount of turnover, had greatly increased the need for additions to the company's accounting and internal auditing staffs.

Several of the traveling auditors had been promoted to more responsible positions, some were made regional controllers, and others were brought into the Chicago office as department heads. Two experienced men had retired during the past year, and four had left the company to take positions with other companies. As a result of these changes and difficulties in hiring new auditors as replacements, eight requisitions for either experienced accountants or auditors were in the employment office. It was desirable but not necessary that the auditors be certified public accountants.

The assistant controllers were convinced that ten years of accounting or auditing experience was necessary for an individual to qualify as a retail chain store auditor. Harry Jamison believed that it might be possible to employ college graduates with specialized training in accounting, place them on a planned job rotation program, and develop them into auditors in five or six years. Simmons' policy, however, was to hire only experienced personnel, so Mr. Jamison usually sought auditors through newspaper advertisements and private employment agencies.

The pressing problem of the moment was to fill the immediate vacancies with qualified men. In recent years, Jamison had experienced extreme difficulty in hiring new auditors. Part of the problem was that the starting salary paid to a new auditor was somewhat lower than the prevailing rate in the Chicago area (about $500 a year lower). Jamison believed, however, that most of the problem lay in the nature of the job itself. Simmons' auditors were required to travel extensively and to be away from their homes for long periods of time, sometimes several months. Qualified accountants with family responsibilities objected to the long absences from home, and often turned down positions at Simmons because of this problem. Several auditors had resigned in the past specifically because they disliked being away from their homes on extended assignments.

Reprinted from Joseph W. Towle, Sterling H. Schoen, and Raymond L. Hilgert, *Problems and Policies in Personnel Management*, 2d ed., by permission of Houghton Mifflin Company.

Harry reached into his pocket and pulled out a newspaper clipping which the chief controller, Mr. Griffin, had given to him. It was a section from the want ads and was heavily marked with pencil. It read:

Wanted

Position in accounting or auditing work by well qualified man with 25 years of financial experience with two corporations and one bank. Long service in responsible positions marred by one human error, an embezzlement. Interested in discussing employment with corporations executive needing the services of good accountant, controller or auditor. Single. Will travel. Box M-103.

The penciled notation indicated that Mr. Griffin was willing to talk to this man. However, Harry knew that Mr. Griffin was aware of the company's unwritten policy against hiring people with prison records. In addition, this applicant was probably in his late forties or early fifties, and the company seldom hired men over 40 years of age.

Just then the telephone rang. It was Mr. Griffin.

"Harry," said Mr. Griffin, "how about my requisitions for accountants and auditors? Look, boy, this thing is getting serious. We need men and fast."

Jamison answered, "Griff, I've been saying for years that we need to establish some type of policies or training program in regards to where, when, and how we're to get and keep qualified auditors. It's going to be a tough proposition to find eight experienced men right away."

"Maybe so," replied Mr. Griffin, "but the problem is that we need auditors today. I say, let's get whatever men we can get today and worry about the policies some other day when we can afford to think about them. Do you think we should talk to the guy in the want ad who has the prison record?"

For a moment, Jamison pondered what his reply should be.

Questions

1. Should Mr. Jamison reply to the ad and set up an interview?

2. What do you think of the company's unwritten policy against hiring people with prison records?

3. What should the Simmons Company do to avoid such a dilemma? Would hiring accounting majors after graduation be the answer?

IV|4

The Informal Promotion

Betty Nichols, R.N., graduated from the local university with a bachelor's degree in nursing and, after a few years as a regular staff nurse, was persuaded to take a head nurse's position in the medical-surgical division of St. John's Hospital. This job involves the supervision of many beds and a good number of R.N.'s, L.P.N.'s, nurses aides, and orderlies.

Time was always a problem to Miss Nichols. Although she believed in and practiced delegation, she could not resist remaining involved in direct patient care more than she should. This demanded time that she needed to oversee the daily round of administrative problems that came to her.

When Miss Nichols found that one of her employees, an experienced L.P.N. named Miss Rose Simpson, was eager to take on additional responsibilities, she began to assign some administrative work to her. Rose Simpson did an excellent job and began to handle more and more administrative details for Miss Nichols. After some time, she in effect filled the job of an assistant head nurse, although such a position did not exist on the hospital's organization chart.

After many months had passed, during which this informal arrangement worked smoothly, Miss Nichols requested a promotion for Miss Simpson to the position of assistant head nurse. The Director of Nursing Services was willing and able to create such a position. However, she felt that Miss Simpson lacked adequate formal education for the job and was certain that the hospital accrediting agency would insist that an R.N. hold such a position.

This situation left Miss Nichols with a difficult problem. She could not get a change in status for Miss Simpson or even a salary increase for her because she was already receiving top wages as an L.P.N.

Questions

1. What should Miss Nichols do?
2. Should Miss Nichols have allowed Miss Simpson to perform the administrative work?
3. What should Miss Simpson do?

IV | 5

The Gamma Electronics Company

Early in 1971 the board of directors and president of the Gamma Electronics Company, realizing that the vice-president of the engineering division was approaching retirement age, started discussions concerning the selecting of his replacement. The company had a written policy of promotion from within whenever feasible and had been practicing it to the fullest extent.

While searching for likely candidates for the position, the board naturally considered the four department heads in the engineering division: Arthur Clayton, the head of Customer Service Engineering; Ben Simpson, the head of Research and Development; Jack Stillwell, the head of Product Engineering; and Otto Fitch, the head of Equipment Engineering. All four executives had been with the company for many years and were well known and respected. When the board asked the retiring vice-president to state his preference, he commented that any of the four men would be capable of dealing with the technical aspects of the position.

After deliberating for some time, the board decided to offer the position to Mr. Clayton. The board and the president thought that he showed more managerial ability than the other three and that his past divisional experience was broader than that of the others.

The other three men apparently accepted the decision with good grace and pledged their continued support to the newly appointed vice-president. However, within a year and a half, two of them had resigned, stating that more challenging positions were offered to them elsewhere.

Questions

1. How can the resignations be explained?
2. Should the company change its policy of promotion from within?
3. Could the resignations have been avoided?

IV | 6

The Appraisal Interview with Mr. Lorenz

Jack Baker, the director of marketing for the Ace Distributing Company, has just finished the annual evaluations of his immediate line subordinates. Among them was an evaluation of Henry Lorenz, his sales manager. Mr. Lorenz has been with the company several years. Although he is doing a good job in the field, in a number of areas he has serious shortcomings. Mr. Baker has tried to discuss these areas with him many times but to no avail. Mr. Lorenz simply will not accept criticism and has done nothing to correct his shortcomings.

While thinking of the forthcoming evaluation interview, Mr. Baker decided to contact his former professor at the university to see whether he could suggest how to approach Henry Lorenz. The professor suggested that Mr. Lorenz be asked to evaluate himself. Mr. Baker sent Mr. Lorenz an evaluation form and requested that he return it in a week. Mr. Lorenz returned it promptly, and Mr. Baker found that Henry Lorenz had given himself a superior rating on each point and had concluded that he was ready for a more challenging position in the company.

Mr. Baker was studying the evaluation again as the door opened and Mr. Lorenz came into his office for his evaluation interview.

Questions

1. How desirable are self-evaluations?

2. Did Mr. Baker's former professor give him poor advice?

3. Should Mr. Lorenz accept and correct his shortcomings?

4. How would you handle the evaluation interview with Henry Lorenz? Role-play the interview.

V INFLUENCING

THE INFLUENCING FUNCTION. Influencing enables management to evoke goal-directed action from others in the organizational system. Like staffing, it is a human resource function, one particularly concerned with behavioral responses and interpersonal relations.

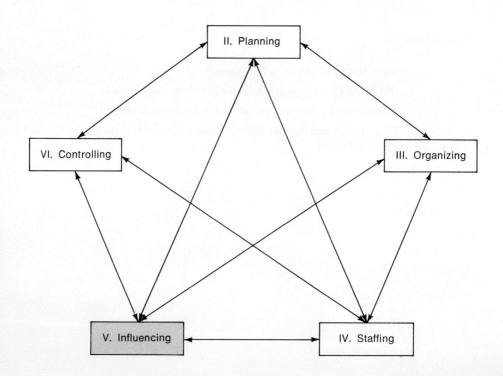

In order to perform effectively, every manager has to be aware of the human activities of which he is a part and must understand how he affects other people and how they affect him. Sensitivity to interpersonal relationships is essential if a manager expects to influence any of the people who surround him. And, clearly, management must influence in order to fulfill its roll of getting things done through others.

A statement such as "an administrator needs human as well as technical skills" highlights the fact that influencing others in a planned, purposeful way is indeed a skill. In the past, however, influencing was done on a hit or miss basis. Little purposeful or scientific planning was involved, except that provided by the early management pioneers in the form of work incentive programs. Moreover, negative persuasion or coercion through disciplinary action seemed to be more common than were positive incentives. This state of affairs was largely a result of the fact that traditional organizational theory was dominated by the notion of hierarchy. Generally speaking, the vertical chain of *command* was considered to be the only relevant system for evoking action in an organization.

As we saw earlier, not until the 1930's were the behavioral sciences introduced into management theory and practice, offering new dimensions to management's understanding of human motivation and group behavior. No longer did management have to rely on the limited ability of economic incentive systems or the use of power to secure action. The behavioral sciences pointed to new, more effective methods of influence.

Today, the influencing process is mainly concerned with the interpersonal and intergroup relationships that each executive must manage in order to obtain collaboration and cooperation in achieving organization goals. Older fields like human relations and newer ones like organizational behavior and organizational development contribute directly to the influencing process. Their contributions are felt in two ways, through research and conceptual development and through the training methods they have devised to help executives become more effective influencers.

In management circles the influencing function is known by many names. Sometimes it is called motivating; at other times, actuating; and often, directing. Regardless of the name, the behavioral view of the influencing process focuses on the question, "How does a superior get the most and best out of his subordinates and at the same time create a climate in which they find personal satisfaction?" In other words, "What constitutes effective superior-subordinate relationships?"

Recently, behavioral analysis of the influencing process has been applied to other kinds of organizational relationships, notably to the interaction among managers of roughly the same rank. The complex organizations of today contain numerous managerial specialists, whose presence compound the number of existing lateral or horizontal relationships. New technologies, complicated structures, well-educated employees with high levels of expectations, all make management's influencing function more challenging. The modern organization is clearly an intricate network of influence patterns. It cannot be easily categorized into a series of superior-subordinate relations.

Thus, the theoretical climate has changed and with it our thinking. We now speak of interdependencies among elements and functions of organizations; we discuss horizontal, vertical, and diagonal flows of information and resources. The behavioral sciences help us to find meaning in these new concepts; they provide the knowledge that enables management to perform its influencing function more effectively.

CHAPTER 23

Communication

At its basic level, communication is the process of passing information from one person to another. It entails imparting ideas and making oneself understood by others. At a more complex level, however, communication provides a way of motivating and influencing people. Further, people have a need not only to perform their jobs effectively but also to achieve psychological and social satisfaction. Therefore, it is appropriate to begin Part V with a consideration of communication. Communication spans all the managerial functions and is a major means of securing integration and coordination in organizations.

THE NATURE OF COMMUNICATION

A verbal exchange is successful only when mutual understanding results. Because managing includes getting things done by various people, clearly management has to communicate with many members of the organization. It has been estimated that a manager spends 90 per cent of his time sending or receiving information. However, to assume that in all this activity communication is taking place would be erroneous. Just because a manager sends and receives messages does not mean that he is an expert in getting ideas across. The appearance of frequent misunderstandings, confusion, and disagreement is evidence that true communication often does not take place.

Communication always involves at least two people, a sender and a receiver. A man who is stranded on a deserted island and who is shouting at the top of his voice does not communicate. This fact is not so obvious to a manager who is sending out a memorandum. He is inclined to believe that once he has sent it, he has communicated. However, this is not so until and unless information and understanding have passed between him and the receiver.

Understanding is a personal matter. If the idea received is the one intended, communication has taken place. However, people may interpret messages differently. If the idea received is not the one intended, communication has not taken place; the sender has not communicated, he has merely spoken or written. This does not mean that the receiver must agree with the statement of the sender; he must merely understand it.

Each person is endowed with some capacities for communication. However, some persons are much more effective communicators than others. The personal effectiveness of a manager is determined in part by his ability to communicate. If he cannot transfer information and knowledge so that he is understood, he will not achieve his desired results. Also, he must know how to receive knowledge and understanding from the messages sent to him by others. Only through such effective interchanges can company policies and practices be formulated and administered, misunderstandings ironed out, long-term plans achieved, and activities coordinated and controlled.

CHANNELS OF COMMUNICATION

An organization's communication network has two distinct, important channels — the official or formal and the informal. Each carries messages from one person or group to another downward, upward, across, and diagonally.

Formal Channels

Formal channels are established primarily by the organization structure through the establishment of formal systems of authority and responsibility and by explicit delegation of duties.

Downward Communication

The chain of formal command suggests that someone at the top issues an order that the next person in the hierarchy passes along to those who report to him, and so on down the line. Management relies on this downward movement for the communication of directives. Through this channel, policies are transmitted to lower levels of the organization for implementation. Downward communication helps to link the levels of the hierarchy and to coordinate activities on many different levels. Generally speaking, it initiates subordinates' actions and is primarily directive.

Upward Communication

Upward communication informs and reports. It carries control information about what has happened at various points of performance, as well as the opinions and attitudes of subordinates to their superiors; it must carry reports on work-related activities and actions. Management should encourage such communication, for this is the only means by which it can determine whether messages have been transmitted and properly received and whether the enterprise is operating efficiently. Upward communication shows whether proper action has taken or is taking place to accomplish company objectives. The chain of command not only establishes the downward line of communication, which enables a manager to transmit directives and information to subordinates, but, working in reverse, it also creates a path for the upward line of communication, which the subordinate can use to convey information to superiors.

Lateral Communication

Lateral communication is also essential for efficient organizational action. Such communication occurs across departments or between people on the same level in the managerial hierarchy. For example, the manager of the production department will certainly have to communicate with the managers of the sales and accounting departments. Without such lateral communication the coordination of various functions cannot occur.

Diagonal Communication

Diagonal communication occurs when messages flow between decision centers which are not on the same lateral plane of the organization's structure. Communication between line and staff groups occurs diagonally. We also frequently find this form of communication in project-type organizations, which we discuss at length in Chapter 24. Figure 23-1 illustrates diagonal communication as well as the other formal types that we have been discussing.

Informal Channels — The Grapevine

Although it is important to develop sound formal channels of communication, students of organization have repeatedly pointed out that groups often tend to create additional channels of communication as well. Every organization has its grapevine [1] — a network of constantly recurring casual personal contacts forming spontaneous channels through which facts, half-truths, and rumors pass.

The grapevine is a natural and normal outgrowth of informal organization, of people's social interaction, and their natural desire to communicate with each other. The grapevine fulfills a person's need and desire to be kept posted on the latest information. It gives the members of the organization an outlet for their imagination and an opportunity to relieve their apprehensions in the form of rumors. At the same time it offers management insight into what others think and feel.

Operation

At times, the grapevine carries factual information and news, but as we noted above it also carries inaccurate information, private interpretations, suspicions, and all kinds of distorted information. Like the formal communication channels, it carries such information in four directions — up, down, across, and diagonally. In addition, it carries information in an unpredictable, flexible, meandering pattern not fixed by an organization chart. The path followed yesterday is not necessarily the same as that of today or tomorrow.

Being spontaneous and having no definite pattern, the grapevine also has no stable membership. Normally, only a small number of people are active participants

[1] Keith Davis, *Human Behavior at Work* (New York: McGraw-Hill, 1972), pp. 261–70.

Figure 23-1. The Flow of Information Along Formal Communication Channels

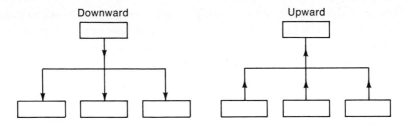

Downward

Upward

From a higher to a lower level: Carries policies, orders, directives, and performance standards. Is used to evoke action from subordinates and coordinate activities.

From a lower level to a higher level: Carries control information pertaining to performance. Is used as a feedback device.

Lateral

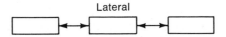

Between functions on the same organizational level: Carries information vital to the effective performance of work between functions that are interdependent. Is used to coordinate activities by the exchange of data. Also used by staff for transmitting technical information necessary to facilitate the work of other functions.

Diagonal

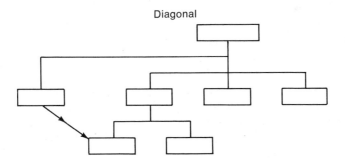

Between special staff groups and line functions: Used by staff to transmit information and advice to line. Sometimes used by staff to exercise functional staff authority.

in it. Although the vast majority of people in an organization listen to the grapevine, few actually pass information along it. Although any person within the organization is likely to become active in the grapevine on one occasion or another, some individuals tend to be more active than others. They feel that their prestige is enhanced by providing the latest news, and in doing so they do not hesitate to give the news new "completeness" and "accuracy."

In periods of excitement and sudden change, the grapevine becomes more active than at other occasions. During these periods of insecurity and great anxiety, the grapevine gives members of the organization an outlet for their fears and apprehensions. It serves as an emotional safety valve.

Uses

The grapevine often carries important information which, if properly utilized, can help to clarify and to disseminate formal communication. In fact, it frequently spreads information which could not be sent through the official channels of communication. For example, occasionally an executive suddenly "resigns." Although management cannot state publicly what actually took place, it may not want to give the impression that the executive was the victim of some unfair top management action. In such a case, a top manager may reveal to a member of the grapevine — under the seal of secrecy — what really occurred.

A manager can no more eliminate the grapevine than he can abolish informal organization. Managers sometimes feel that the grapevine should be stamped out since it often carries false, malicious, and uncontrollable rumors. However, it does perform useful functions and is an important part of organizational life. It transmits information with amazing speed. "With the rapidity of a burning powder train, information flows like magic out of the woodwork past the water fountain, past the manager's door and the janitor's mop closet."[2] It is unrealistic to expect that such a spontaneous phenomenon can be stamped out.

Since the grapevine represents an enduring portion of the channels of communication, a manager should learn how to live with it and make good use of it. In order to do so, he must tune it in and learn what it is saying. He must listen and look for the meaning of the grapevine's communication, not merely for the words. He must find out who its leaders are and who is likely to spread information. He must learn that by feeding the grapevine facts he can counter rumors and half-truths. By doing this, the manager can effectively utilize the grapevine's energy, and serve his own interests. Although the best way to minimize rumors is to improve the official channels of communication, the grapevine channels should not be ignored. An organization without a grapevine is unthinkable.

THE COMMUNICATION MEDIA

Words, pictures, and actions are the media for communication.[3] Because words are the most important symbols used, a manager must be able to employ them effec-

---

[2] Joseph K. Shepard, "I Heard It on . . . the Grapevine," *The Indianapolis Star Magazine* (October 2, 1955), p. 4.

[3] Machines communicate by means of electrical impulses. Analysis of the communication network in a system must account for machine-machine, man-machine, and man-to-man communication.

tively. Words can be transmitted orally and received by listening, or they can be transmitted in written form and received by reading.

Pictures, the visual aids that a manager may resort to from time to time, are powerful too and are particularly effective in association with well-chosen words. Business has made extensive use of pictures — blueprints, charts, drafts, models, posters, and the like. The popularity of motion pictures and comic strips also clearly proves the ability of pictures to communicate and especially to contribute to understanding.

Action is also an important factor in communication. A manager must not forget that what he does is interpreted as a symbol by his subordinates and may be more powerful than his words. Because of a manager's status, all observable acts communicate something to the subordinate whether he intends them to or not. Purposeful silence, gestures, a handshake, a shrug of the shoulder, a smile, all have meaning.

By the same token, inaction communicates. Unexplained action, however, often communicates a meaning which is not intended: For example, if a manager orders the removal of machinery from the production floor without telling the workers why, it may upset them considerably, especially if the workers fear a shutdown or think that the plant will be moved to another city.

Written Communication

Because words are the most important means of communication, we should look at their uses more carefully. Words are used in both oral and written communication. Although oral communication is more frequent, a well-balanced communication system must utilize both media. Serious inefficiency can result if, for example, a manager tries to communicate with his subordinates and colleagues entirely by writing. An executive who rarely calls anyone for a face-to-face conference and who only rarely uses the telephone must spend all his time dictating memos, leaving little time for other more important business. His subordinates would have to spend an equal time reading and preparing replies to his communications as he did in dictating, reading, and signing them.

Written messages are indispensable at times, however. They provide a permanent record to which the receiver can refer as often as necessary in order to make sure that he understands what has been said, whereas the spoken word generally exists only for an instant. Moreover, detailed instructions may be so lengthy that they must be put in writing so that they can be studied at leisure. Also, the written medium is frequently best for widespread dissemination of information that may concern many people. Finally, written communications have a degree of formality that orally delivered messages usually do not carry.

Oral Communication

Nevertheless, in most instances a manager can achieve better understanding and save time by communicating orally — by telephone or face-to-face conversations. Face-to-face conversations, particularly those conducted between supervisor and subordinate or line and staff managers on a day-to-day, man-to-man basis, are the heart of an effective communication system. They provide the most frequently used opportunity for the exchange of information, points of view, and instructions. No form of printed communication — nor even the telephone, the public-address system, or other artificial oral media — can equal oral contact between the various levels of management, the supervisor and the worker, and among the entire work group. ✷The greatest single advantage of oral communication is that it provides immediate feedback. Although the response may be only a facial expression, the sender can judge how his message has been received. Oral communication enables the sender to find out immediately what the receiver hears and what he does not hear. It enables the recipient to clarify meanings and resolve unexpected problems instantly. The human voice can give a message a meaning and shading that even long pages of written words simply cannot convey.[4]

Because oral communication is the most effective and frequently used tool of the manager, he must be skilled in it. He must know how to speak well and be aware of his listener. He must be concerned with the total impact of his presentation. More than words are involved in face-to-face communication; meaning is conveyed by tone of voice, manner, facial expression, gestures. These modes of expression do make oral communication more meaningful, but at the same time they may lead to misunderstanding.

BARRIERS TO COMMUNICATION

The speaker and the listener are two separate individuals who live in different worlds. Many fundamental factors can interfere with and distort the message that passes between them. Every manager is familiar with the misunderstandings, frictions, and inconveniences that arise when the communication network breaks down. Most managerial problems (and human problems in general) result from poor or nonexistent communication. Breakdowns not only cost money but also injure teamwork and morale and therefore are significant obstacles to effective influence.

Although the variety of communication barriers is large, the most important ones can be placed into four general groupings. Some are caused by the nature of the organization's structure, some by status and position, some by language, and many by people's inclination to resist change.

Organizational Structure

The intricate structure of most enterprises today involves several layers of supervision, long communication lines, complex relations among staff and line assignments, and considerable distance between workers and the top levels of management. Communication may break down because of faulty transmission in any level

---

[4] That oral communication is in fact more effective than written (and face-to-face communication more effective than telephone) has been shown by Jake Huber, "An Efficacy Comparison of Vocational Instructional/Curriculum Material Survey Techniques" (Ph.D. diss., Oregon State University, 1973).

of supervision. To forestall potential breakdowns, management must consider the nature and complexity of the organization's structure and determine the best channels and the most effective ways to overcome communication barriers. For instance, management might decide to reduce the number of supervisory levels, shorten the lines of authority, provide for more participative practices, or increase delegation and decentralization.

Status and Position

Obviously, the president of a company and the vice-president in charge of production are on different levels in the corporate hierarchy. Differences in status and position become apparent as one level communicates with another. In addition to the barriers to communication that usually exist between human beings on the same social level are barriers of social distance caused by the different echelons in an organization.

When a subordinate listens to a message from his superior, several factors become operative. The receiver evaluates what he hears in terms of his own position, background, and experience, and he also unconsciously evaluates the sender. It is difficult for the receiver to separate what he hears from the feelings he has about the person who sends the message. Often he attributes nonexistent motives to the sender. Union members often interpret management statements adversely because they are convinced that management is trying to weaken and undermine the union. Often a company's newspaper is considered to be a propaganda organ and mouthpiece of management, and regardless of the truth and interest of its information, the workers read it with suspicion. Such attitudes, however justified, do not promote understanding.

A good communicator will realize that negative feelings, prejudice, and barriers created by differences in status and position often result from the divergence between the listener's and sender's interests. The superior can help to overcome this by putting himself in the subordinate's position and analyzing and anticipating his reaction before he sends the message. Often, the reactions of several subordinates must be considered. The president's announcement that the enterprise is buying a concern in a different part of the country might be interpreted by the sales manager to mean a larger sales potential for him and his sales force, whereas the production worker in the old plant may feel the action will threaten his position.

The same status and position barrier also appears in the upward flow of communication because a subordinate wants to impress his boss. Consequently, he screens the information he passes up the line, emphasizing what the superior likes to hear and omitting or softening what is unpleasant. At times, a subordinate tries to cover up his own weaknesses when talking to a person in a higher position. Often a supervisor fails to pass on important subordinate attitudes or grievances because he believes that such information would reflect unfavorably on his supervisory ability. After two or three selective screenings of this sort, a message is likely to become extensively distorted.

Language

Normally words serve well as a basis for communication, but frequently the same word may suggest quite different meanings to different people,[5] and the particular orientation of different groups will give different meanings to the same words. In such a case, the words themselves constitute a barrier to communication. For example, when a manager speaks of "profits," he considers them essential for an enterprise to continue as a growing business, to buy new equipment, to expand, and to provide more jobs. However, many employees may think that "profits" suggest unearned or unfair excess earnings derived from paying inadequate salaries. Some union members do not understand — or else understand too well — the competitive position of their employer and therefore cannot accept the employer's explanation of his position. Their orientation and interests are different, developed from another way of life.

The problem of word meanings is aggravated by the status barrier. People on different levels often "speak different languages." There are many instances in which a frustrating conversation ends with this admission. In order to avoid a breakdown in communication, the communicator should attempt to use the language of the listener. He should realize that some words carry a symbolic meaning for some people and that when he uses such words he may find himself communicating something he did not intend to say. Expressions such as "management prerogatives" have acquired different symbolic meanings for management and for union representatives. The word "efficiency" has different meanings to a union leader, a worker, a manager, and an engineer.

People also speak languages geared to the specialized work they do. The existence of staff and technical experts in a large number of fields makes organizations sound like modern towers of Babel. Each expert uses his own jargon, making understanding difficult for those uninitiated in the field. Often technical reports must undergo "translation" so top management can use them as a basis for policy-making. Of course, the forces that have led to this situation, such as advancing technology and growing organizational complexity, cannot be reversed. Nonetheless, their existence emphasizes the importance of communication in the influencing process. If technical experts cannot be understood, they cannot effectively influence opinion and action.

Resistance to Change

Resistance to change builds yet another communication barrier. All too frequently, listeners do not properly receive messages conveying new ideas. Although the tendency to resist change is unhealthy, it is natural. The listener's receiving apparatus works like a filter, rejecting new ideas if they conflict with what he already believes.

---

[5] An entire field of study called semantics is devoted to the analysis of the meaning of words. According to one semantic principle, the structure of a person's language influences the manner in which he understands reality and behaves with respect to it.

Sometimes this filter works so efficiently that he doesn't hear at all. Ultimately, the listener hears what he expects to hear. If he is insecure, worried, or fearful, this barrier becomes even more powerful. Sometimes a listener, determined to refute what he expects to hear, pays only marginal attention to a communication instead of trying to understand it.

Others

Many other barriers arise from specific situations — emotional reaction; deeply rooted feelings and prejudice; physical conditions such as heat, noise, and cold. All these obstacles can cause serious barriers to communication and unless the sender knows of their existence he is in no position to overcome them. For this reason, every manager must acquaint himself with all potential and actual barriers to communication. No manager should blithely assume that his message will be received as it was intended. Instead, since managerial effectiveness depends largely on the accurate transmission of information and orders, the manager must do all within his power to overcome communication barriers.

MEANS FOR OVERCOMING BARRIERS TO COMMUNICATION

Although perfect understanding may be impossible, there are many techniques available for improving communication. The executive ought to be familiar with several of them in order to maximize his success in communicating.

Feedback

Feedback is probably the most important method of improving communication. Most people are automatically aware of feedback. When sending messages, they are alert to the reactions of their receiver; they constantly seek clues from him that show that they are being understood.

The following experiment testing the importance of feedback was conducted by Alex Bavelas at M.I.T.[6] Two students were placed in different rooms, with identical grids in front of them and a set of dominoes. One student was asked to communicate to the other by telephone the position of an interconnected series of dominoes, explaining their relative positions in any way he felt advisable and necessary. The receiver was then to arrange his dominoes like those of the sender. The receiver could listen to the sender's instructions but could not respond or ask questions. Although the sender explained the pattern carefully and minutely, the receiver was unable to successfully complete the task. This and similar experiments indicate that some kind of feedback is essential if complex information is to be communicated success-

[6] See Elmer L. Lindseth, "Management Communication," in *The Management Team*, ed. Edward C. Bursk (Cambridge, Mass.: Harvard University Press, 1954), pp. 24–25; George Strauss and Leonard R. Sayles, *Personnel: The Human Problems of Management* (Englewood Cliffs, N.J.: Prentice-Hall, 1960), pp. 203–04.

fully. At best a yes or no response to the sender's question of whether the message is understood would be helpful. However, as subsequent portions of Bavelas' experiment indicate, the speed and efficiency of communications increase as feedback increases.

The simplest way to obtain feedback is to observe the receiver and analyze his nonverbal responses. Observation of expressions of comprehension or bewilderment, the raising of an eyebrow or a frown, is possible only in face-to-face communications. Therefore, one of the outstanding advantages of any oral communication is that it provides immediate feedback.

If a sender wishes to test comprehension verbally, he may ask the receiver to repeat complex information. This is much more effective than merely asking whether the statement is understood or the instruction clear.[7] If the receiver can state the gist of a message, the sender will really know what the receiver has heard, whether he has understood, and what he has not understood. This process might also reveal that the receiver ascribed special meaning to a particular message that the sender did not intend. Also, during a face-to-face conversation the receiver may ask additional questions and make comments, thereby making immediate feedback even more meaningful. Additional feedback can be obtained simply by observing whether a person behaves in accordance with the communication. If direct observation is not feasible, the sender must watch for reports and results.

Sensitivity to the World of the Receiver

As we have stated previously, in order to communicate successfully, a sender must be sensitive to the world of the person who will receive his message. Once a manager determines the message he wants to convey, he should try to predict its impact on the feelings and attitudes of the receiver. A common ground for understanding must be established, especially if the backgrounds and experiences of receiver and sender differ considerably. If the relationship between the two is close, the superior will know much about the world of the subordinate and can more easily anticipate how he will interpret a message.

Managers often ignore the need for sensitivity to the world of the employee. They attempt to communicate with employees in management terms through company newspapers filled with analyses of economic conditions, the prospects for the company, competitive problems, and so forth. However, employees often are not interested in problems of this sort. Management is merely projecting its own interests and in doing so does not succeed in communicating its messages.

Effective Listening

A sender can often overcome barriers to communication by spending more time listening. In order to get a receiver to hear what he wants to tell him, the speaker should first listen to the receiver. In many instances, this will give the speaker some

[7] See Huber, "An Efficacy Comparison of Vocational Instructional/Curriculum Material Survey Techniques."

clues about the receiver's values and his relationships to his world. However, listening cannot be accomplished by a mere expression of attention. One who hears with the intent of finding fault and correcting is likewise not listening. Better communications are achieved if biases and prejudices are put aside. There is no need to agree with a speaker, but there is every necessity to try to understand him.

It is the listener's job to listen to the meaning of an idea rather than to the individual words of the speaker. The listener must be careful to discover any hidden content — the *latent content,* as distinct from the *manifest content.* Although the listener should keep his imagination in check, he must ask himself what is really meant. From time to time the listener might ask, "Is this what you mean?" The listener must also often listen patiently even though he may believe what he hears to be irrelevant.

Listening greatly improves communication by reducing misunderstandings. By listening while talking, a speaker can adjust his message to fit the responses of the receiver. The adjustment opportunity provided in oral communication is, as we pointed out earlier, one of its chief advantages.

Actions Speak Louder Than Words

The manager communicates as much by his actions as by his words. One of the best ways to give meaning to a message is to act in accordance with it. Because of his status, the manager is often the center of his subordinates' attention, and he communicates by all observable actions regardless of his intention. Naturally, barriers to communication will be overcome if verbal announcements are reinforced by action. But if a manager says one thing and does another, sooner or later his subordinates will "listen" mostly to what he does. For example, a manager's statement that he is available at any time to see an employee who has a problem has no meaning if he keeps his door closed.

Slight Redundancy

A certain amount of redundancy often helps to overcome communication barriers. This is especially true if each word is important and directions are complicated. In such cases repetition in various forms may be necessary. The sender, however, must remember that if too much redundancy occurs the message may be ignored as too familiar and too simple. It would defeat communication if the listener no longer paid attention to a message because he knew exactly what was going to be said. How much redundancy is permissible will depend largely on the content of the message and the experience and background of the receiver.

The Importance of Being an Expert

One other aspect of effectiveness in communication should not be neglected. Because of the growing technical complexity of organizations, more and more people having professional and scientific skills are being employed. It has been found that they will more readily accept their manager's communications if they perceive the manager to be scientifically well qualified. They tend to reject messages from those they think to be technically less competent or incapable of meeting the requirements of their specialized jobs. This tendency seems to hold true regardless of how the scientific and technically trained subordinates feel about their manager personally, as an individual, apart from his technical skills. We will elaborate on this point more fully in the next chapter when we discuss the authority-influence relationship in greater depth.

Discussion Questions

1. Contrast the possible content of messages carried through formal channels of communication with that of messages carried on the grapevine.

2. Don't you imagine that it is a little sneaky for a manager to listen to the grapevine and then to try to manipulate behavior by utilizing what he has heard or by pumping in new information?

3. How many forms can feedback take in organizational communication?

Supplementary Readings

American Management Association. "Ten Commandments of Good Communication." In *Dimensions in Modern Management*, edited by Patrick E. Connor. Boston: Houghton Mifflin, 1974.

Beer, S. *Cybernetics and Management*. New York: Wiley, 1959. See chapters 4 and 5.

Chase, Stuart. "Executive Communications: Breaking the Semantic Barrier." In *Dimensions in Modern Management*.

McGregor, Douglas. "Difficulties in Communication." In *Dimensions in Modern Management*.

March, James G., and Herbert A. Simon. *Organizations*. New York: Wiley, 1958. See pp. 161–69.

Pfiffner, John M., and Frank P. Sherwood. *Administrative Organization*. Englewood Cliffs, N.J.: Prentice-Hall, 1960.

Planty, Earl G., and William Machaver. "Stimulating Upward Communication." In *Dimensions in Modern Management*.

Scott, William G., and Terence R. Mitchell. *Organization Theory*. Homewood, Ill.: Irwin, 1972. See chapter 8.

CHAPTER 24

Organizational Authority:
Emerging Views

Few subjects have commanded as prolonged attention from behavioral scientists as have authority and power. First discussed by political theorists such as Machiavelli, then by sociologists such as Max Weber, they are now being dissected by numerous psychologists and social psychologists. These two matters have received such continuous attention because they provide major sources for influencing human behavior; they are means by which people have been motivated through the ages to comply with commands and accomplish objectives.

In an organizational setting, the structure of authority is an important source of influence. Robert Bierstedt maintains that "authority is always a property of social organization. Where there is no organization there is no authority."[1] Authority, in other words, is vested in organizational roles. In no way does it belong to the individual who occupies a particular role. Although individuals have the privilege of exercising the authority inherent in their position in an organization, they do not retain this privilege when they leave.

Influence, however, stems not only from the authority vested in organizational roles, but also from an individual's capacity to affect the actions of others. Behavioral scientists have given considerable attention to this form of influence and have frequently related it to the concept of power as distinct from authority. Power, however, receives mixed treatment in the literature. Some scholars believe that it is almost entirely a matter of personal capacity; others feel that it embodies both organizational and personal elements.

At any rate, it is around authority and power that this chapter is organized. Of course, we are also concerned with other forms of influence. But such concepts as coercion, acceptance, incentives, sanctions, and so on relate either to power or authority, or to both. The nature of their relationships will become clear as our discussion unfolds.

[1] Robert Bierstedt, "The Problem of Authority," in *Freedom and Control in Modern Society,* ed. M. Berger, T. Abel, and C. Page (New York: Van Nostrand, 1954), p. 72.

THE CHARACTER AND OPERATION OF AUTHORITY

Authority is a form of influence through which a manager obtains his subordinates' compliance to orders, communications, policies, and objectives. This compliance occurs because the subordinate is willing to accept the manager's legitimacy as the person in command. As we emphasized in Chapter 12, authority is accepted by subordinates because they believe that the person issuing orders and setting goals has the *right* to do so. Such acceptance begins the moment an employee takes a job and goes to work. By his actions at this time, he implicitly agrees to comply with the directives of a legitimate source of authority.

An organization cannot exist without being permeated by such authority. Each manager has a certain amount of it. Top management utilizes its authority when it sets broad objectives and integrates the various functions of the business; lower levels of management utilize it in the operation of their departments or divisions.

When making these statements, however, we must be sure that our terms are clearly defined. We mentioned in Chapter 12 that a distinction exists between authority and power. We reinforce this point here in order to avoid any confusion between these two types of influence. Power rests upon *domination*. Persons with power have the ability to distribute or withhold resources as rewards or punishment. Authority is based on willing *acceptance* by others of a person's organizational *right* to distribute or withhold resources. As Weber put it, authority is legitimate power. Anyone doubting the importance of the distinction between legitimate authority and domination by power need only reflect on the invasion of Czechoslovakia by the Soviet Union in 1968.

Sources

Scholars in the behavioral sciences identify three types of legitimate authority: traditional authority, functional authority, and personal authority. A manager might possess all three, but need not. We shall discuss them separately and then see how they interact.

Traditional Authority

Traditional authority is based on acceptance of the position that a manager holds in an organization. Although we have already discussed this source of authority extensively, there are several more ideas connected with it.

Traditional authority is, in a sense, institutional. Subordinates accept the legitimacy of a manager because they recognize him as an agent of an organization which they believe has social validity. Therefore, traditional authority is impersonal; it resides in the position and in the organization in which it is found.

Ultimately, traditional authority is bestowed by society. We have already seen that the right of management to manage is inherent in the institution of property which, in turn, is supported by law flowing from the people themselves. This concept applies not only to private property, but also to property that is state owned as in socialist countries. In the first case, the delegated right to manage comes from individuals who personally own property; in the second instance, it comes from the state which administers property in the collective interest of the masses.

We find traditional authority in other than business organizations, of course. Religious, military, educational, fraternal, and service organizations also have it and their structures likewise rest upon social acceptance of those who occupy their positions of authority. Employees, church members, or soldiers may not like a particular manager, clergyman, or officer, but they accept him because of the legitimacy of the position he holds. How many times do soldiers hear, "You do not salute the man but the uniform"?

Conventional organization theory has concentrated almost exclusively on this traditional authority vested in social organizations. As a consequence, vertical superior-subordinate relationships have been the focal point for discussions of authority as a form of influence. There are, however, other dimensions to authority which are not based upon the legitimacy of command.

Functional Authority

People will accept, follow, or be influenced by any expert. Authority based on such expertness is called functional authority.

However, the influence that an expert exercises is quite different from command authority. We accept the expert because we recognize that he knows more about a subject than we do. However, an expert's knowledge must be needed by others in order for him to influence them. The needs of students of management, for example, draw them to professors of management and businessmen, not to engineers and technicians.

Functional authority exists in all the traditional branches of learning and crafts as well as in business and arises from the division of labor and specialization of work. In business, functional experts emerge in organizational planning, sales, finance, accounting, production, research and development, personnel, and so on. The expertness enjoyed by men in a particular functional area often creates a firm bond of allegiance between superior and subordinates.

Whereas traditional authority is impersonal, functional authority is mixed. In one sense, it is highly personal; an *individual* possesses knowledge, skill, and information. On the other hand, society in general and organizations in particular require that specialized roles be filled. Rewards are offered to encourage people to gain the skills needed to perform the functions of these roles. If the functions become obsolete, those having skills in them are displaced. We frequently label this technological displacement, but the notion can be applied more broadly. For example, there is less demand today for scholars of classical Greek than for scientists.

In conclusion, functional authority, like traditional authority, rests on acceptance. However, functional authority stems from a legitimate base of knowledge rather than from a legitimate social institution.

Personal Authority

We will not devote much time to personal authority here since we analyze a parallel subject in the next chapter — leadership. However, several points need to be set forth at this time. First, personal authority — sometimes called charismatic authority — is closely associated with an individual. Unlike traditional or functional authority, it is not based in social institutions. As its name conveys, it is a personal attribute of an individual: a kind of personal magnetism by which a leader is able to attract a following.

In fact we can say that leadership and personal authority are practically synonymous. People accept personal authority because they see that the stated aims of the leader are consistent with their own individual needs. The appeals of the great national and religious leaders of the past have attracted those who felt similarly and therefore were quite willing to accept the legitimacy of the spokesman.

However, personal authority is not restricted to well-known historical figures. It is found among managers in business organizations, administrators in education, and so on. Although the scope of the leader's appeal is restricted in these cases to people in immediate contact with him, the influence of his personal authority on behavior is real nonetheless. It is capable of motivating people to spontaneous cooperation in pursuit of individual as well as collective goals.

The Interaction of the Sources of Authority

We have now seen in broad outline the three types of legitimate authority in organizations. A manager relies on them to secure willing collaboration from his subordinates. If he does not possess at least one of these types, his effectiveness as a manager will be reduced considerably or blocked completely.

In most modern organizations, in fact, management cannot rely exclusively on a single source of authority to ensure acceptance. In the past, most people believed that it was sufficient to base one's right to manage on the legitimacy of the social institution. This attitude was related to the idea that managers would automatically get compliance and acceptance from subordinates because they represented the property rights of owners.

Such views, however, have changed tremendously. Now authority is seen as something that must be earned, by expertness in a given area, by personal leadership ability, or by both. Business itself, as we saw in Chapter 1, is experiencing major technological changes that are forcing modifications in the occupational character of employees. More and more experts in specialized areas are being employed. They in turn place greater weight on the role of functional authority.

Much the same can be said regarding personal authority. People entering the work force today expect more than economic satisfaction to flow from their jobs. Therefore, management must develop a climate of satisfaction designed to fulfill a wide range of human needs.

However, these newer developments do not entirely undermine the practical significance of traditional authority as a form of influence. Traditional authority is still important, but modern business and contemporary managers view it as one of several ways in which they can gain acceptance.

Compliance

As we have seen, people comply with the authority they perceive to be legitimate. They accept it because they feel that the goals and communications established by such authority are consistent with their personal needs and values. This is the only way that spontaneous and willing collaboration can be produced. Much of authority's legitimacy used to be based upon an employee's automatic acceptance of vertical chain-of-command-type relationships. However, with the growing complexity of firms and the increasing need for technical experts in business, other kinds of organizational relationships are becoming important. These include the lateral (horizontal) relations among managers, which we discuss later in this chapter.

Such relations, rather than being based on the chain of command, are founded in the interdependency of functions. These relationships foster an entirely different form of managerial behavior, one in which compliance, cooperation, and coordination of tasks are achieved through activities such as

1. creative problem-solving — where effective managerial teams produce inventive decisions which are satisfying to the organization and to the individuals on the team
2. bargaining and negotiation — where managers mutually exchange resources in order to improve the performance of their departments
3. win-lose conflict — where two managers or groups of managers compete, the outcome resulting in a defeat for one and a victory for the other

Thus, compliance and coordination are much more challenging to achieve when functional and personal authority supplement conventional reliance on traditional authority. Employees cannot be "ordered" to act on the assumption that they accept the chain of command.

POWER

Superficially, power is a straightforward concept. It is a form of domination giving its possessor the ability to direct the actions of others toward predetermined goals. As applied to organizations, this definition of power is based on two important ideas.

First, an organization's management is able to influence the behavior of others because it controls some of the organization's resources. These resources, which management can distribute to subordinates or withhold from them, consist of the values that people seek from employment. They include money, opportunity for advancement, security, and satisfying work assignments. Although these values are stated in positive terms, they also have a negative side if any or all are withheld.

Second, the reason that power is necessary is also implicit in our definition. People do not always willingly and spontaneously accept authority. Power is latent in every organization; it is an ever-present potential available to secure action when authority fails. It is natural that people bring to organizations diverse motives and needs. Frequently, these motives and needs will correspond to organizational objectives, but occasionally they will not. When this incongruence between organizational goals and individual goals occurs, power must be used to influence.

Sources

Power rests upon management's right to administer incentive and sanction systems. These systems are in turn based on the resources controlled by management. Therefore, power, like traditional authority, is institutional and impersonal.

However, we have also said that power is latent. It appears only when legitimate authority is not perceived by subordinates. Thus, whether power is needed or not, the extent of its application is highly personal and depends greatly on the kind of interpersonal relationship existing between superior and subordinates. If subordinates willingly accept their superior, he will seldom need power to achieve his goals. Of course, the reverse is also true. Clearly, the application of power relates directly to an individual's leadership ability and situation within a particular department or other organizational unit.

Moreover, it is a matter of personal administrative skill to know when to use power and also to know what kind of power to use. Management has at its disposal several types of positive incentives and negative sanctions. Their appropriate use and timing is crucial for the effective operation of an organization.

Outcomes

It is interesting to examine the views of Herbert Simon on the use of power because they are shared by many contemporary management scholars. Simon believes that dominating employees by power is not an effective way to manage an enterprise; he therefore speaks of the "poverty of power."[2] He sets forth several reasons for this belief.

First, power is not a one-way street. Although management can derive seemingly overwhelming power from the resources at its disposal, employees can retaliate in a number of ways — through absenteeism, waste, minimum compliance, slowdown, malicious obedience.[3] Overreliance on power to secure objectives is dysfunctional from an influencing standpoint. In other words, power meets resistance, which tends to require more power to overcome, generating more resistance, and so on.

[2] Herbert A. Simon, "Authority," in *Research in Industrial Human Relations,* ed. Conrad M. Arensberg et al. (New York: Harper and Row, 1957), pp. 108–10.

[3] A maliciously obedient employee actually complies to the letter of a command and eliminates all flexibility from the execution of the task. Often this results in the failure of a project and the embarrassment of the superior, without blame to the subordinate, "who was only following orders." See Peter C. Reid, "A Case of Malicious Obedience," *Supervisory Management* 8, no. 7 (July 1963): 4–8.

Second, although management's control of positive motivators such as financial rewards may seem to provide them with a strong source of influence, this source is not as strong as it appears to be. Behavioral scientists have shown that employees work for more than money. Therefore, influence based on financial incentives alone is likely to produce insufficient results.

Third, in a very practical sense, using power costs more than securing compliance through acceptance.

THE DYNAMICS OF THE AUTHORITY-POWER RELATIONSHIP

A mixture of authority and power exists in any concrete administrative situation. Of course, it is desirable that managerial authority be accepted in any such situation; to the extent that it is not, power fills the *influence gap*. Figure 24-1 visually portrays the nature of this idea.

Figure 24-1. Power, Authority, and the Influence Gap

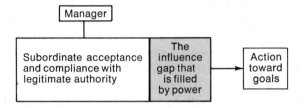

This figure shows a situation in which the manager has much, but not total, subordinate acceptance. To compensate for the deficiency, he uses some of his potential power to move the group toward departmental objectives. This influence gap may merely represent one employee who has not wholly accepted the manager's authority, or it may be that the whole work group has backed off slightly from full acceptance. Whatever the case, power is necessary for the achievement of the aims of the department.

The sociologist Robert Nisbet presents a somewhat different conception of the relationship between authority and power.[4] He feels that these two concepts are different sides of a single coin — and that the coin itself is influence.

Still another view of the authority-power relationship is provided by the influence continuum shown in Figure 24-2. It is hard to conceive of any management situation where both elements are not present to some extent. However, one element tends to predominate. Nevertheless, because there are an infinite number of points on any continuum, there can be an infinite number of power-authority mixes. The crucial factor from a management standpoint is to pick the optimal mix for the situation. At Point 1 in Figure 24-2, the use of power predominates. This might occur

[4] Robert A. Nisbet, *The Sociological Tradition* (New York: Basic Books, 1967), pp. 3–7.

when a manager supervises a number of low-skilled manual workers who have little, if any, identification with the values of the organization.

At Point 2, we might assume that the manager is supervising a number of highly trained scientists who possess considerable professional commitment and a greater identification with the goals of their department, if not the whole firm. To influence his men successfully in this situation, the manager must build on the acceptance of legitimate authority rather than power. For a variety of reasons, most of which we have already discussed, today's management submerges power as far as possible beneath the surface of superior-subordinate relations.

Figure 24-2. The Influence Continuum

In summary, a manager must mix authority and power in a manner suitable to the human and organizational variables that he confronts. Part of the art of management lies in selecting the mode of influence that will most effectively lead to the accomplishment of the business's objectives and concurrently provide satisfaction for the people in the firm. Another part of the art lies in creating a mix of power and authority that will optimize flexibility and adaptation to change. Critics say that reliance on power to obtain compliance unduly rigidifies the organization. Acceptance of authority, on the other hand, facilitates change.

Emerging Forms of Organizational Relationships

As the emphasis in superior-subordinate authority relationships shifts from traditional to functional forms, we may expect to find the emphasis on vertical organizational forms to be modified as well. In fact, organizational structures are changing, and the lateral and diagonal interrelationships among managers are becoming increasingly significant. The new lateral and diagonal forms are incorporated in contemporary systems such as the project or matrix organization.

Lateral Relations

As we know, traditional formal organization structure is centered on vertical, superior-subordinate relationships. Some modern organizations are shifting their emphasis to existing lateral (horizontal) relationships. They are stressing the behavior of managers who have different functions yet depend on each other, although they do not have scalar command authority built into their relationships.

Organizations are becoming more interested in these horizontal relationships for several reasons. First, the enormous structural and technical complexity of some modern organizations causes the neat distinctions between line and staff within the chain of command to blur. Second, the needed coordination in these kinds of organizations cannot be achieved entirely by the application of classical principles. Third, functional interrelations are critical to effective performance. If such interrelations are to be effective, if cooperation among differentiated activities participating in a common task is to occur, a high degree of lateral communication must take place. According to Leonard Sayles, the lateral interdependency of managers arises from three different types of relationships[5] — trading relationships, work flow relationships, and service relationships.

Trading Relationships

Trading among lateral managers necessitates establishing future relationships, involving one manager as "seller" and another as "buyer" of departmental goods or services. Such relationships ensure both managers that after the terms of a trade have been set, resources like computer data will be readily available in exchange for some other commodity like storage space. Trades of this kind among managers in the same company are more similar to barter than to actual sales for a fixed dollar price. However, the process of bargaining and negotiating terms is akin to that occurring in typical market-place transactions.

Work-Flow Relationships

Lateral work-flow relationships are easier to comprehend. They encompass the inevitable interactions that occur when different departments all contribute to the same final product, and the output of one department becomes the input for the next, as in Figure 24-3.

Figure 24-3. Work-Flow Relationships

In this situation it is important for each manager to secure stability of operations in his department. Naturally, inputs and outputs have to be balanced in order to avoid shortages and surpluses. Since this is not a typical assembly line situation, the usual methods of obtaining balance cannot be applied. Using the engineering department as the example, let us see what can be done, however. Obviously, the managers of the engineering department will have to engage in intensive lateral communication with the managers of the other concerned departments. This will ensure proper coordination and the availability of the final output at the time specified.

---

[5] Leonard R. Sayles, *Managerial Behavior* (New York: McGraw-Hill, 1964), ch. 5.

Balancing the inputs and outputs of each department is extremely important if available engineering talent is to be used effectively.

Service Relationships

The third type of lateral transaction discussed by Sayles is the service relationship. In a particular organization, auxiliary activities are often grouped into service departments that support the organization's major operations. These service departments facilitate economies of scale and take advantage of specialization.

Service departments have many functions. Some are concerned with warehousing, some with traffic, maintenance, legal matters, or systems and procedures. A service department has two noteworthy characteristics: It is centralized, and it offers a scarce resource. The economy of centralized warehousing, for example, is obvious. What is less obvious is that some operating executives see the value of warehouse space in more personal terms. Therefore, they will compete among themselves for available warehouse space. Trade-offs may occur between competing executives and between those executives and the warehouse managers. Behavior thus becomes similar to that described under trading relationships.

Summary

Many of the operating affairs of a firm are conducted by managers at roughly the same level on a traditional vertical organization chart. However, their lateral interface behavior is quite different from that found in conventional superior-subordinate relationships. The differences are shown in Table 24-1.

Table 24-1. Interface Behavior of Managers

Content of superior-subordinate relationships	Content of lateral relationships

Authority
  Position
  Command
  Acceptance
	Bargaining
	
	Trading

Power
  Reward
  Punishment
	Negotiating
	Compromise

THE PROJECT ORGANIZATION

The project organization (at times called the matrix organization) is the direct outcome of the vastly complex demands that advanced military and space technology has placed upon American industry and is one of the most important developments in contemporary management theory and practice. Although project organization can be applied effectively to nonmilitary work, it was established to handle contracts for weapon systems.

The purpose of the project organization is to secure a higher degree of coordination than could be obtained in a conventional line structure. Work is organized around a project rather than around specialized departments as in the typical line organization. The project organization is in a sense an overlay on conventional organization structure. Although it draws upon traditional structure for various skills, as we see in Figure 24-4, projects themselves are clearly identified and directed independently from their inception to the manufacturing stages. The need for this type of structure is evident especially when a firm has several projects under way.

Two basic organizational segments can be seen in Figure 24-4: the conventionally organized engineering departments and the three project activities. Each project has its own manager who sees the project through to completion. He draws the people he needs from the engineering departments and coordinates their work from the design phase to testing and manufacturing. When a project is ended, personnel may return to their engineering departments to be reassigned to new projects.

The project organization has a number of advantages. It eases coordination and allows for rapid assessment of the status of any given project. It makes the job of maintaining effective contact between the contractor and contractee simpler. In addition, it provides an orderly way of phasing projects in and out of an organization.

The project organization introduces whole new sets of relationships.[6] Whereas conventional structure and classical management theory stress vertical chain-of-command relationships, the project structure emphasizes horizontal and diagonal relationships. Clearly, the lateral relationships are necessary if the required exchanges among project management and conventional department management are to occur. The material in the preceeding section on lateral relationships is then applicable here.

Advanced technology, new products, work specialization, and higher skills have forced organizations to modify their structures. Although a number of these modifications have been discussed in this chapter, they merely suggest some of the events that are taking place. How are management leadership and employee motivation affected by these changes? These subjects are considered in the next two chapters.

Discussion Questions

1. The matrix organization and the process of project authority violate the unity of command principle. What are the theoretical *and* practical reasons for such a violation?

2. If possible, give examples of organizations based entirely on consent and entirely on coercion. Why is it so difficult to find cases falling purely in one of these categories or the other.

[6] See David I. Clelland, "Understanding Project Authority," *Business Horizons* (Spring 1967): 63–70.

Figure 24-4. Project Organization

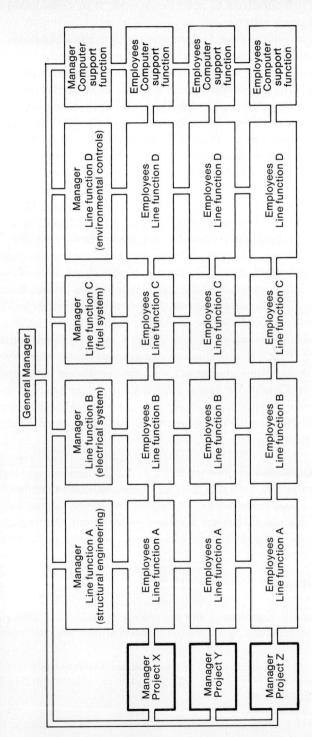

Supplementary Readings

Bennis, W. G., E. H. Schein, and D. E. Berlew. *Interpersonal Dynamics.* Homewood, Ill.: Dorsey Press, 1964. See part 3.

French, John R. P., Jr., and Bertram Raven. "The Bases of Social Power." In *Dimensions in Modern Management,* edited by Patrick E. Connor. Boston: Houghton Mifflin, 1974.

Nisbet, Robert A. *The Sociological Tradition.* New York: Basic Books, 1966. See pp. 141–50, 292–300.

Peabody, Robert L. "Perceptions of Organizational Authority." In *Dimensions in Modern Management.*

Sayles, Leonard R. *Managerial Behavior.* New York: McGraw-Hill, 1964. See chapters 5–7.

Scott, William G., and Terence R. Mitchell. *Organization Theory.* Homewood, Ill.: Irwin, 1972. See chapter 12.

CHAPTER 25

The Climate for Motivation

Behavioral scientists have demonstrated that human satisfaction, productivity, turnover, waste, and a host of other variables important to a cooperative system depend to a large extent on motivation, organizational climate, and leadership. In this chapter, we will consider these three interrelated factors, so vital to the success of an organization.

THE NATURE OF HUMAN MOTIVATION

Man's unsatisfied needs motivate his actions. A person needs food; therefore he eats. He needs a sense of achievement; therefore he strives to advance in business. He needs a sense of creative fulfillment; therefore he writes poetry. Each action springs from sources within the person — sources molded by the individual's upbringing, training, environment, that combine to form his personality.

Some motivations are stronger and more urgent than others. Strong motivations are most likely to lead to successful action. Likewise, greater rewards tend to engender more forceful action. John Atkinson summarizes these propositions when he states that the strength of an individual's motivation is a function of the strength of a particular motive, the probability of success, and the nature of the reward.[1]

Attitudes

Underlying motives are an individual's attitudes — his feelings or predispositions — about something. Several people may, for example, have strong achievement needs. However, one individual might seek fulfillment of these needs in business, another in government, another in education. The individual's attitudes, feelings, and prejudices will determine his choice. Therefore, attitudes in this case have determined the route but not the basic goal.

To summarize, attitudes underlie motives, which underlie action. Actions — or goals — are determined by unmet needs. Successful action or accomplishment of a goal provides feedback to the individual, whose needs are satisfied and attitudes reinforced. Unsuccessful action leads to dissatisfaction and frustration.

[1] John W. Atkinson, "Motivational Determinants of Risk Taking Behavior," *Psychological Review* 30 (November 1957): 359–72.

The Hierarchy of Needs

Man never seems satisfied. He is forever restlessly fulfilling needs. One success seems to be merely a springboard for another round of pursuit. These commonplace behavioral observations have been expressed by the well-known psychologist Abraham Maslow in the form of theory that has gained considerable acceptance. Maslow postulates a hierarchy containing five levels of needs. We may visualize it as a pyramid (see Figure 25-1).[2]

The lowest order of needs are physiological. These needs encompass all man's biological demands — hunger, thirst, sex, elimination, and so on. Safety needs follow. These involve relief from certain physical threats in the environment — for example, safety from attack. The need for love appears on the next higher level. It is usually expressed as a person's need for warm supportive relations with others, such as family and friends. The need for esteem is dual in nature and quite complex. Man needs self-esteem, which often comes from mastery over part of his environment — for example, being the best hunter in the tribe or being an outstanding accountant. He also needs others to esteem and recognize his accomplishments. The linkage between these two aspects is evident. However, it seems likely that esteem of self often takes precedence over esteem from others.

Self-actualization, the highest level of need, is the most difficult to describe. It has been said that this is the need "to become what one is capable of becoming." It is here that we find the key to the meaning of fulfillment. Unlike the other four needs, which may be satisfied, self-actualization is never fully realized. This failure may result from the potential of man's spirit. Once activated, it seems capable of limitless expansion and variation.

Figure 25-1. Hierarchy of Needs

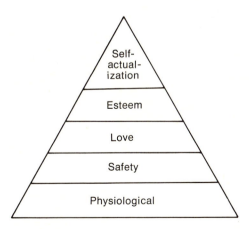

[2] Abraham H. Maslow, *Motivation and Personality,* 2d ed. (New York: Harper and Row, 1970), ch. 4.

The hierarchy of needs seems to relate to age. That is, each level appears to be associated with certain periods in an individual's life span. Physiological and safety needs are paramount in an infant's life. As the child grows older, affiliative (love) needs become important to him. When he reaches young adulthood, esteem needs dominate his energies. If he is successful in satisfying these needs, then he *may* move on to self-actualization later in life. This last step does not necessarily follow, however, since social or organizational demands may arrest his progress at the esteem level or lower. This problem is the basis of the conflict between organizational and individual goals.

The Level of Aspiration

Closely related to the need hierarchy is a person's level of aspiration. Aspirations are dynamic. They represent the ever-changing shift of goals which occurs as need satisfaction is achieved. That is, when needs are satisfied at one level, the individual usually readjusts his sights to higher levels. Suppose an individual is highly motivated by a need for achievement in business. He then will not be satisfied by a low-level executive position. Once he obtains such a position, he will strive for the next higher position and so on. After achieving a top position in his firm, he may shift his objectives to, say, social or governmental activities where other possibilities exist that will satisfy his achievement needs.

This endless personal search for alternatives to satisfy increasing aspirations is an important source of individual motivation. It is also a powerful factor in the concept of influence, because the wider the range of need satisfaction that an organization is able to supply, the greater will be the individual's commitment to that organization.

Achievement Motivation

One of the more interesting behavioral studies is David McClelland's research in patterns of achievement motivation — n(achievement) as he calls it.[3] McClelland relates levels of aspiration directly to achievement motivation and says that such motivation is learned. In some societies, the culture, the up-bringing of children, and various traditions produce a low level of achievement motivation among the people. In the United States, there is a high level of achievement motivation. However, n(achievement) is not equally distributed throughout the population. Business leaders tend to score highly on n(achievement) tests. Since achievement motivation is learned, McClelland reasons, it may be possible to teach young people and lower levels of management to raise their motivation. If such is the case, then executive development programs may truly affect these groups.[4]

[3] David C. McClelland, *The Achieving Society* (Princeton: Van Nostrand, 1961).
[4] David C. McClelland and David G. Winter, *Motivating Economic Achievement* (New York: Free Press, 1969).

ORGANIZATION CLIMATE

The Conflict Between Individual and Organizational Goals

A major cause of personal dissatisfaction in business firms arises from the conflict between organizational and individual goals. The first systematic analysis of this problem was made by Chris Argyris.[5] Argyris saw a conflict between the individual who seeks activity and independence through psychological development and the bureaucratic, formalized organization which keeps the individual in an infantile state of passive dependence. The organization's work climate, as Argyris described it, stifles an individual's natural desire for freedom and self-determination. Because of this condition, many conflict symptoms manifest themselves in turnover losses, waste, slowdowns, lower productivity, lack of innovative and creative behavior, nonacceptance of leadership and authority, and so forth. However, probably the most serious consequence of bureaucratic organization is that it blocks the individual's psychological maturation. This represents a lamentable squandering of human resources.

Generally the blame for this situation must be placed upon the organization itself. It is often so inflexible, so dedicated to rigid bureaucratic norms, so divided into specializations of labor, that it is incapable of providing the opportunity for individuals to achieve a wider range of work satisfactions. These conditions, combined with centralization of authority and autocratic managerial behavior, submerge the individual in the system and cut off much hope that he will ever find in his work an opportunity for self-realization.

The Ability to Cope with Change

Although the foregoing thoughts have been stated in an extreme manner, they do reflect a major thrust in current management theory. Clearly organizations must create an improved climate if they are to fill the legitimate needs of the people in them. In fact, numerous forces are present in modern society which make such an improvement in organizational climate imperative.

Among these forces, as we noted in the last chapter, are advancing technology, highly skilled labor, professionalization of management, and the rising expectations of employees that they will have a more satisfying work experience than their fathers. But of all the new and dynamic forces which have confronted the modern organization since the close of World War II, perhaps the most important of all is the phenomenon of change itself.

That we live in a rapidly changing world is a commonplace observation. This change has forced on organizations a need for flexibility and adaptability never before experienced. Many writers, notably Warren G. Bennis,[6] have stated that the

---

[5] Chris Argyris, *Personality and Organization* (New York: Harper and Row, 1957), ch. 2.

[6] Warren G. Bennis, *Changing Organizations* (New York: McGraw-Hill, 1966).

key criterion for judging organizational health is its ability to cope with change. Moreover, they go on to say that the typical bureaucratic, highly formalized organization is poorly suited to the demands for change.

A crucial factor affecting an organization's ability to cope with change is its "climate." Work in the behavioral sciences has shown that certain leadership styles, decision structures, communication patterns, and participation levels are more conducive to facilitating and gaining acceptance of change than others are. We look now at two pioneering approaches to the issue of how management can develop an organizational climate flexible enough to adapt to change and able to produce effective motivation, thereby helping to resolve the conflict between individual and organizational needs and goals.

Theories Relevant to Organizational Climates

Theory X and Theory Y

Douglas McGregor has postulated that men placed in an organizational climate will behave in a particular manner based either on the assumptions of Theory X or those of Theory Y.[7] A manager who fits into the Theory X group leans toward an organizational climate of close control, centralized authority, autocratic leadership, and minimum participation in decision-making. This manager is willing to accept this combination of characteristics because he makes certain assumptions about behavior. Theory X assumptions, according to McGregor, are:

1. The average man dislikes work and will avoid it to the extent he can.
2. Most people have to be threatened or forced to make the effort necessary to accomplish organizational goals.
3. The average individual is basically passive and prefers to be directed rather than to assume any risk or responsibility. Above all else he prefers security.[8]

A "Theory Y" manager operates with vastly different assumptions. He feels that an effective organizational climate has looser, more general supervision, greater decentralization of authority, less reliance on coercion and control, a democratic style of leadership, and more participation in decision-making. The assumptions upon which this type of organizational climate is based are:

1. Work is as natural to man as play or rest and, therefore, is not avoided.
2. Self-motivation and inherent satisfaction in work will be forthcoming in situations where the individual is committed to organizational goals. Hence, coercion is not the only form of influence that can be used to motivate.
3. Commitment is a crucial factor in motivation and is a function of the rewards coming from it.

[7] Douglas McGregor, *The Human Side of Enterprise* (New York: McGraw-Hill, 1960), ch. 4.
[8] *Ibid.*, pp. 33–34.

4. The average individual learns to accept and even seek responsibility, given the proper environment.

5. Contrary to popular stereotypes, the ability to be creative and innovative in the solution of organization problems is widely, not narrowly, distributed in the population.

6. In modern organizations human intellectual potentialities are just partially realized.[9]

In a later book, McGregor observes that these assumptions are not simply ends of a continuum.[10] He believes that they represent distinctly different views of man. Theory X views man mechanistically; he is simply a depersonalized factor of production. Theory Y sees man as an interacting organic system, affecting and being affected by other systems surrounding him. As such, he simply cannot be depersonalized or taken for granted. McGregor underscores the notion that Theories X and Y represent beliefs held by management about the nature of man. Thus, they constitute the foundations upon which organizational philosophy and climate will be built.

Which management philosophy and organizational climate will produce the best results? One is inclined to say that fostered by Theory Y because on the surface it is humanistic and less harsh than that of Theory X. It is also more optimistic about human motives at work. However, sentiments alone are not sufficient for judging the effectiveness of an organizational climate or leadership style. Thus, we must evaluate organizational climate separately in each situation. For now, let us say that under some conditions Theory X works best and under other conditions Theory Y works best. Although this is not a complete answer, we shall discuss the matter further after we look at another theory of organizational climate.

Likert's Theory

Rensis Likert's concept of organizational climate in many ways resembles McGregor's, yet contains several differences. Likert proposes four systems of organizational climate: System 1, Exploitive; System 2, Benevolent Authoritative; System 3, Consultative; and System 4, Participative Group. Each of these systems is composed of six elements, which Likert feels are key ingredients of organizational climate. The six are leadership, motivation, communication, decision, goals, and control. Their dimensions can be measured on a continuous scale so that a manager may rate his organization's climate.[11]

Obviously, Systems 1 and 4 define organizational extremes. They embody autocratic and democratic leadership climates, respectively (in McGregor's terms, a Theory X climate and a Theory Y climate). Likert observes that the climate found in most American industry lies in the center — somewhere between System 2 and

[9] *Ibid.*, pp. 47–48.
[10] Douglas McGregor, *The Professional Manager* (New York: McGraw-Hill, 1967), pp. 79–80.
[11] For a full discussion see Rensis Likert, *The Human Organization* (New York: McGraw-Hill, 1967), pp. 14–24, 120–21.

System 3. Interestingly, however, when asked, "What is the most effective climate?" the majority of managers tend to select the democratic end of the scale. This leads Likert to conclude that managers do not execute what they, in essence, believe to be successful leadership styles and organizational practices.

The chief difference between McGregor's and Likert's theories is that McGregor does not view organizational climate as a product of managerial strategy, whereas Likert does. Superficially, this may appear to be a small distinction, but in reality it has wide implications. Likert feels that an effective management is one that operates in a climate on the participative (democratic) end of the scale. He thinks that managers should consciously strive to mold their organizational climate in this manner because people working within it will experience higher levels of need satisfaction and, hence, will become better employees.

McGregor, while endorsing the positive human values flowing from democratic management, says implicitly that Theory X, or an autocratic climate, may be more effective in certain situations. Management should not be locked into a strategy which may prove inappropriate to its particular situation.

The Current Consensus

An article in *Fortune* magazine gives us some insight into the consensus on the question of what is the best organizational climate.[12] Most writers appear to underscore the situation as the leading determinant of organizational climate. Thus, in organizations having a stable environment and using employees of low-level skill, a more nonparticipative, autocratic kind of climate appears to be effective. However, in rapidly changing firms with highly educated and skilled employees, more democratic forms of management get the best results.

However, writers who admit the value of autocracy in some cases will say in the same paragraph that organizations which find this type of climate conducive to effective influence are dying out. In twenty to thirty years, autocratic bureaucracy will be nothing more than a curiosity. The forces bringing about this change and requiring a more democratic climate are again those that we have mentioned so many times — technology, education, and professionalization of management.

Organizational Design

As we have by now often observed, the changes produced by new technology, new consumer and employee demands, and new ecological awareness are placing extraordinary demands upon management.[13] Study after study has indicated that the type of organizational design best suited to cope with such change is the organic system[14]

---

[12] Robert C. Albrook, "Participative Management: Time for a Second Look," *Fortune* (May 1967), pp. 166–70, 198–200.

[13] See Alvin Toffler, *Future Shock* (New York: Random House, 1970), for a discussion of present-day environmental turbulence.

[14] For an early study that pointed the way, see Tom Burns and G. M. Stalker, *The Management of Innovation* (London: Tavistock, 1961).

— a type of design that emphasizes openness, flexibility, and maximum employee participation in the implementation of organizational goals.

Closely associated with organizational adaptation to change are the processes of integration and differentiation.[15] As organizational change occurs, the degree of differentiation or specialization in organizations increases. Likewise, as specialization increases, integration must increase. In other words, greater specialization requires greater coordination. Consequently, management must increase the degree of collaboration that exists among various segments of its organizational structure. Various techniques help in this process. They include analyzing the design of structural relationships, training and developing managers' interpersonal skills, and improving the climate for task accomplishment and individual satisfaction.[16]

A very important variable in the success of any integration scheme, which we have merely noted in passing, is leadership. Ultimately, management leadership is responsible for establishing the kind of climate which facilitates motivation and influence. Naturally the climate must be tailored to each firm by its leadership. Thus, management has a great responsibility to read each situation correctly, to remain sensitive to changes over time, and to develop an appropriate type of organizational climate and corresponding leadership style.

THE LEADERSHIP PROCESS

Leadership is a process by which people are directed, guided, and influenced in choosing and achieving goals. In any undertaking, a leader mediates between the organization and the individual so that the degree of satisfaction to both is maximized. Viewing leadership as a process directs our attention to functionality. What does a leader do? Why does he do it? A first step in answering these questions lies in understanding something about leadership roles.

The Diversity of Leadership Roles

Most of us have seen the various individual roles usually enacted in a group situation. One person organizes the group to achieve a goal, another raises a stream of objections, another provides comic relief, still another synthesizes the ideas of all, and a final historian evaluates all present action in the light of what was done in the past. These roles and many others are essential for group life. They fulfill needs of individual members of the group and are vital to group accomplishment.

Some of these roles involve leadership, whereas others do not. Researchers in the behavioral sciences have devoted considerable attention to this distinction. They have found that, generally, leadership roles fall into two broad classifications — task and emotive.

[15] Gene W. Dalton, Paul R. Lawrence, and Jay W. Lorsch, *Organizational Structure and Design* (Homewood, Ill.: Irwin, 1970).
[16] Wendell L. French and Cecil H. Bell, Jr., *Organization Development* (Englewood Cliffs, N.J.: Prentice-Hall, 1973).

Task Roles

When a leader organizes and influences a group to achieve some specified set of objectives, he is playing a task role. Whether such objectives are imposed on a group from above, whether they are imposed laterally, as in a work flow, or whether they arise spontaneously from within the group itself, the leader must still play his task role in order to remain a leader and to facilitate the accomplishment of the goals of the group.

Emotive Roles

Emotive roles are equally important, for they allow the individual needs of the group's members to be satisfied. Sometimes these needs are related to goal accomplishment; at other times they are unrelated to goals. In either case, the emotional needs of people are social and psychological in nature. The leader playing the emotive role plays a dual part: He helps the members of the group to experience need satisfaction, and at the same time he smoothes the way for task performance.

Frequently we say that the ideal leader is one who plays both task and emotive roles effectively. However, the leadership of a group can be shared without diminishing group performance or morale.[17] In such a situation, one person takes the task role and another the emotive role. These are not unusual circumstances. The nature of the formal organization often forces a manager to be most concerned with getting a job done. If he can be accepted by his subordinates on this basis, he has gone a long way toward being a true leader and not merely the head of his group. However, he must anticipate that normal group processes might also select another informal leader who will function in the emotive role.

Leadership Theories

In our concern for the functional aspects of the leadership process, we must not overlook research done on the characteristics and behavior of the leader himself. This subject has long received considerable attention from observers of society.

Early Genetic Theory

For hundreds of years, a continuous stream of observers recognized leadership as the ability to influence people in such a manner that they willingly strove toward an objective. It was believed that this ability was not a part of official position. Certain people were born to be leaders, it was said, having inherited a set of unique traits or characteristics that could not be acquired in any other way. Leadership was thought

[17] Amitai Etzioni, "Dual Leadership in Complex Organizations," *American Sociological Review* 31 (October 1965): 688–98.

to be inherited, simply because it emerged frequently within the same prominent families. In reality, however, strong class barriers made it impossible for most people outside these families to acquire the skill and knowledge needed to become a leader.[18]

Trait Theory

As the social and economic barriers were broken down and as leaders began to emerge from the so-called lower classes of society, the early genetic theory underwent some modification. The change was partly a result of the fact that in the middle 1930's behavioral scientists began to contribute to the literature on leadership. The first work was by writers who maintained that leadership traits could be acquired through experience, education, and training.[19] These writers tried to focus upon all the traits, whether inherited or acquired, that were found in men regarded as leaders.[20] The traits frequently included physical and nervous energy, a sense of purpose and direction, enthusiasm, friendliness and affection, integrity, technical mastery, decisiveness, intelligence, teaching skill, and faith.

The inadequacy of the trait approach soon became apparent. Seldom, if ever, did any two lists enumerate the same essential leadership characteristics. Moreover, the lists were confusing; they used different terminologies and contained different numbers of characteristics. Nonetheless, the trait approach was widely accepted for a long time. Its hypotheses seemed highly plausible because studies of various successful leaders almost always indicated numerous similar personality and character traits. However, the intensity and degree of the traits often varied. Likewise, theorists could reach no satisfactory consensus about the number of traits necessary for leadership, or whether a person could be a leader if he lacked some but possessed others. Neither could theorists determine how to isolate and identify all the specific traits common to leaders. Moreover, writers used different terminology and did not indicate which traits were the most important and which the least important. A further weakness of the trait approach was that it did not distinguish between the characteristics needed for acquiring leadership and those necessary for maintaining it.

Although the trait approach is partially discredited today, research does show that leaders do have in common certain very general characteristics — intelligence, communication ability, and sensitivity to group needs. Such traits found interwoven in the personality of the leader must always be viewed in the context of the group, however. In other words, the most intelligent person in a group will not necessarily emerge as the leader. Instead, the person with the combination of traits best suited to the situation in which the group finds itself will assume leadership.

[18] Thomas Gordon, *Group-centered Leadership* (Boston: Houghton Mifflin, 1955), p. 47.
[19] *Ibid.*
[20] Prominent among exponents of the trait theory were Ordway Tead, *The Art of Leadership* (New York: McGraw-Hill, 1935); and Erwin H. Schell, *The Technique of Executive Control*, 8th ed. (New York: McGraw-Hill, 1957).

Situational Response

In their search for universal leadership traits, behavioral scientists discovered the importance of situational factors which predispose certain persons to leadership. The proponents of the situation approach do not deny that the characteristics of individuals also play an important part in leadership. However, they point out that leadership is also the product of situations in particular groups. They argue that leadership will differ in each group situation. Who becomes a leader of a group engaging in a particular activity and what leadership characteristics he will need constitute a function of the specific situation in which the group finds itself.[21]

In their desire to de-emphasize the trait approach, some behavioral scientists may have gone overboard in emphasizing the situation. In doing so they may have overlooked the possibility that some people possess certain characteristics that predispose them to attain leadership positions or at least increase their chances of becoming leaders.[22] Indeed, both characteristics and situation are involved in the concept of leadership.

Follower Compromise

A more sophisticated concept of leadership acknowledges the follower's personality and needs. Those holding this composite approach maintain that the follower must also be studied, because the type of individual who will carry out leadership functions depends upon the characteristics of the followers as well as the specific needs of the group at a given period of time.[23] "It is the follower as an individual who perceives the leader, who perceives the situation and who, in the last analysis, accepts or rejects leadership. The follower's persistent motives, points of view, frames of reference or attitudes will have a hand in determining what he perceives and how he reacts to it."[24]

The follower approach does not neglect the importance of the situation, nor does it fail to consider that certain characteristics will help one person to emerge as a leader and others to emerge as followers. It stresses the idea that the leadership function must be analyzed and understood in terms of the dynamic relationship existing between the leader and his followers. Group members will follow a leader because they see in him a means for personal need fulfillment. Yet they see that leadership is essential if the group is to act as a unit. Therefore, group members choose a leader not only because he possesses characteristics such as intelligence, skill, drive, and ambition, but also because of his functional relationships to them.

Although a leader may emerge as a result of agreement among group members that he, more than anyone else, serves as the best means for achieving their need

---

[21] William O. Jenkins, "A Review of Leadership Studies with Particular Reference to Military Problems," *Psychological Bulletin* 44, no. 1 (January 1947): 54–79.

[22] Gordon, *Group-centered Leadership*, p. 49.

[23] *Ibid.*

[24] Fillmore H. Sanford, "Leadership Identification and Acceptance," in *Groups, Leadership and Men*, ed. Harold Guetzkow (Pittsburgh: Carnegie Press, 1951), p. 159.

satisfaction, he may also arise in the reverse fashion. His own need satisfaction may cause him to seek out the leadership of a group. He may want to accomplish an objective which can only be attained if he can direct the activities of other people. A manager formally appointed to a leadership position within an organization usually is in this situation.

Leadership Style

A leader is an individual who is perceived by other group members to be in harmony with the needs of their group and responsive to the group situation. Leaders must always be recognized as such by group consensus. Appointed managers, who do not necessarily reflect subordinate group choice, are not usually regarded as leaders at the outset, though they may become leaders. Obviously, if the influencing function is to be efficiently performed, it is desirable that subordinates quickly accept their manager as a leader and not merely as the head of their department. This is where leadership style enters, in three categories — autocratic, democratic, and free rein.

Autocratic

Autocratic leadership reflects a narrow span of management, tight supervision, and a high degree of centralization. Those who utilize the autocratic style tend to be repressive and to withhold communication other than that which is absolutely necessary for doing the job. Autocratic management unilaterally makes decisions, vesting little if any participative rights in the group. Thus, this style tends to minimize the degree of involvement of groups and individuals in the organization.

Democratic

Democratic leadership emphasizes a nonpressure orientation that maximizes group and individual participation in the decision-making process. A free flow of communication is encouraged among all members of a department so that a climate of understanding can be built upon a foundation of honesty and trust. The democratic style is fully consistent with a decentralized organization and a wide span of management.

Free Rein

Under the free rein or laissez faire style of leadership, the organizational climate is such that people, assumed to be self-motivated, do their jobs virtually without supervision. The individual with authority leaves the group to its devices and provides little specific direction. However, he is available in a consultative capacity to help out if requested.

Leadership Style and Organizational Climate

Obviously, each of these styles has its place in management practice, and a good leader knows when and when not to use them. As a rule, it has been shown that free rein is most useful for establishing an organizational climate for professional people — university professors, research scientists, and others — who desire independent work and have shown the capacity for it. Free rein situations are relatively rare in industry.

A democratic style is appropriate to an organization in which rapid change is evident. Because such a style creates a fairly free environment, skilled and educated people — engineers, technicians, and craftsmen — seem to thrive under it. Some writers believe that a democratic leadership style is beneficial to all organizations. However, this position is not overwhelmingly accepted, mainly because some scholars believe that the autocratic style is necessary to produce results among unskilled workers who are poorly prepared to participate in decision-making and might be uncomfortable if urged to do so.

The preceding discussion reinforces our statement that leadership style must be adapted to a specific situation. However, in general a more democratic, more open, and less pressure-laden style leads to greater leader acceptance than does an autocratic one. This factor is important because the democratic climate, as we have said before, is capable of greater flexibility in the face of change.

Figure 25-2. Influence Triangles

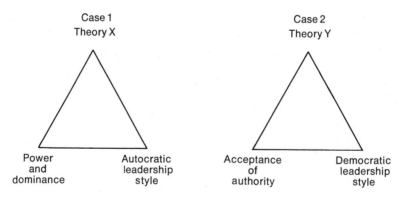

Case 1	Case 2
Theory X	Theory Y

Power and dominance — Autocratic leadership style

Acceptance of authority — Democratic leadership style

INTERRELATIONSHIPS AND INFLUENCE

We are now ready to tie together several of the ideas that we have developed in this and in the preceding chapter. To do so, let us speak of the *influence triangle*, which relates the ideas of organizational climate, authority, power, and leadership style.

In Case 1 of Figure 25-2 we have pictured a Theory X climate based generally on power and dominance. Its prevailing leadership style is autocratic. Case 2 exhibits a Theory Y climate where acceptance of authority is high and the need to rely on power and dominance is low. We have seen that the democratic style is appropriate for reinforcing this climate.

We have stressed throughout this chapter the situational character of management practice. Frequently, cases occur where the Case 1 triangle applies and should be used by management. However, the thrust of organizational change is carrying industry and management further and further within the boundaries of the Case 2 triangle. Its methods are viewed by more and more management scholars and practitioners as the approved and most effective way to run an organization.

In a sense, we have now made a complete circle. We started this chapter by saying that man is motivated to action by his unsatisfied needs. Then we went on to show how organizational climate and leadership style must be designed to fulfill employees' needs. What determines these needs in a particular individual on a particular job? We shall soon see that needs are a function of an employee's expectation. Each person has certain ideas about what he wants from his work situation. In the next chapter we shall discuss some of them.

Discussion Questions

1. How would you relate an individual's level of aspiration to his achievement motivation? Give some examples.

2. What relationships exist between Theory X and Theory Y and the organic and mechanistic organizational designs?

3. "It's easier to change the nature of jobs than it is to change the nature of individuals." What implications does this statement have for leadership theory and management development?

Supplementary Readings

Dalton, Gene W., Paul R. Lawrence, and Jay W. Lorsch. *Organizational Structure and Design*. Homewood, Ill.: Irwin, 1970.

Fiedler, Fred E. "Engineer the Job to Fit the Manager." In *Dimensions in Modern Management*, edited by Patrick E. Connor. Boston: Houghton Mifflin, 1974.

Hersey, Paul, and Kenneth H. Blanchard. *Management of Organizational Behavior*, 2d ed. Englewood Cliffs, N.J.: Prentice-Hall, 1972. See chapter 4.

Likert, Rensis A. *The Human Organization: Its Management and Value*. New York: McGraw-Hill, 1967. See pp. 13–47.

McClelland, David C. "That Urge to Achieve." In *Dimensions in Modern Management*.

Tannenbaum, Robert, Irving R. Weschler, and Fred Massarik. "How to Choose a Leadership Pattern." In *Dimensions in Modern Management*.

CHAPTER 26

Employees' Expectations

Each employee, whether manager, engineer, clerk, or assembly-line worker, hopes in his work to satisfy his needs and reinforce his attitudes. Needs and attitudes together give rise to expectations, and the extent to which these are met in large measure determines not only personal satisfaction but also group morale.

The fulfillment of employees' expectations depends upón organizational climate, leadership style, perception of legitimate authority, use of positive incentives, and the like. Because these factors also determine the effectiveness of management's influence, the function of influencing appears in sharper focus against the background of employees' expectations.

SATISFIERS AND DISSATISFIERS

Frederick Herzberg, a psychologist who has done a great deal of research on job satisfaction, has defined a number of conditions upon which satisfaction is based.[1] By analyzing the responses employees have made to a survey, he has measured how often satisfiers and dissatisfiers appeared in work-related events described by his survey respondents and how long they produced either a marked improvement or a marked reduction in job satisfaction. Herzberg found that the most frequently mentioned determinants of improved job satisfaction (satisfiers) are achievement, recognition, work itself, responsibility, and advancement. The factors most frequently involved in events causing job dissatisfaction (dissatisfiers) are company policy and administration, supervision, interpersonal relations, and working conditions. Figure 26-1 summarizes Herzberg's findings about satisfiers and dissatisfiers along both the frequency and duration dimensions. The length of each box in the figure indicates frequency and the width indicates duration.

Herzberg's Conclusions

In Figure 26-1, the first five factors are satisfiers. If these factors are unfulfilled they can produce dissatisfaction, as shown by the extension of the bars to the left of point 0. If they are fulfilled, they can be strong motivators. Achievement, for example, is

---

[1] Our discussion is based on Frederick Herzberg, "New Approaches in Management Organization and Job Design," *Industrial Medicine and Surgery* 31 (November 1962): 477–81.

mentioned most frequently as a source of satisfaction, but the length of time a person derives satisfaction from any particular achievement is short. Conversely, responsibility is a long-term satisfier. Dissatisfiers tend to be relatively short-term. It is interesting to note that the factors that bring about job satisfaction are not the same as those that cause job dissatisfaction. The satisfiers pertain to the content of the job, whereas the dissatisfiers reflect the job environment. Both are one-dimensional in their effects. That is, the factors that appeared frequently on the right side of the scale showed up infrequently on the left side and vice versa. To emphasize these differences, Herzberg calls the dissatisfiers "hygiene factors" because they are environmental and prevent improved job satisfaction. He calls the satisfiers "motivators" because his study seems to indicate that they promote higher performance and achievement levels.

Figure 26-1. Factors Affecting Job Satisfaction

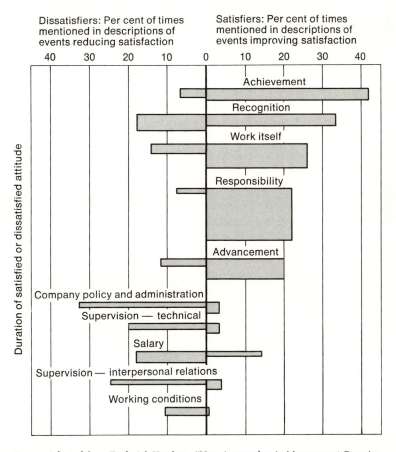

Source: Adapted from Frederick Herzberg, "New Approaches in Management Organization and Job Design," *Industrial Medicine and Surgery* 31, no. 11 (November 1962): 480.

Implications

Herzberg's findings have important managerial implications. First, even though management strives for good organizational "hygiene" by promoting equitable wage administration programs, enlightened supervision, good working conditions, and so forth, it may not achieve a strong motivational climate. The effect of its efforts minimizes the dissatisfiers rather than maximizes the satisfiers. Furthermore, because satisfiers and dissatisfiers relate to different aspects of the employment situation, minimizing dissatisfiers does not stimulate motivation.

Second, it seems that management must develop a two-pronged strategy, directed at hygiene and at the development of motivation. This strategy must be based upon two sets of human needs: the need to avoid unpleasantness, which comes largely from dissatisfying conditions; and the need for personal growth, which comes largely from the fulfillment of satisfying conditions. The second need is closely related to Maslow's concept of the need for self-actualization.

In addition to Herzberg's findings, other evidence also shows a direct relationship between satisfaction and a work climate that facilitates the realization of employees' needs. The opposite is equally true, of course. The greater the inconsistency between employees' goals and the goals of the organization, the lower is the level of satisfaction.

These straightforward statements may obscure what is essentially a complex problem. If everyone entered an organization with the same expectations, it would be fairly easy to create an environment that would satisfy all. However, expectations and needs vary from person to person, group to group, and occupation to occupation. Even a moderate-size organization contains a great amount of human diversity. Engineers have different expectations than salesmen, line executives than staff specialists, management decision-makers than rank-and-file workers.

The environment of an organization should be responsive to this diversity. To be responsive, the organization's subunits must be sufficiently free to be able to adapt their climates to the particular kinds of people found within them. It is virtually impossible to impose a uniform style of management upon an entire organization. This becomes especially apparent as the size and complexity of an organization increase.

Bearing this discussion in mind, we can now make several recommendations that will enable the performance of the influencing function to be more successful:

1. Management should foster decentralization to allow lower managerial levels the freedom to work out the climate best adapted to the satisfactions sought by the people supervised.

2. Managers should increase their awareness of the needs of their subordinates and the kinds of satisfactions they require.

3. Responsiveness to human satisfactions should in no way be interpreted as "soft management." Instead, it reflects a philosophy designed to facilitate organizational adaptability and to accommodate a wide variety of changing human requirements.

MORALE AND SATISFACTION

Many writers distinguish morale from satisfaction. They say that satisfaction is associated with an individual's experience whereas morale pertains to the spirit of a group. It is correct for a manager to say, "The morale of the people in my department is high," when he is referring to his subordinates as a group. When speaking of individuals, the manager might say, "Charlie is satisfied with his job." This seems to be a natural usage, so we will preserve it. However, a difficulty exists: In behavioral research the factors used to measure group morale are often also used to measure individual satisfaction. Thus terminology can become confusing. However, this is partly a methodological problem, and we will try not to let it distract us as we discuss morale.

The Components of Morale

Morale is widely studied and, as one might expect, it is defined in many ways. Yet most scholars agree about some aspects of it. The consensus is that morale is a group feeling that results in intense goal-directed effort. This feeling is caused by group members' perception that they share similar values about the accomplishment of a worthwhile objective. When working together is essential for achieving a goal, morale often makes the difference between success and failure. This is true in any collective undertaking — business, educational, military. We may elaborate upon our definition of morale by looking at its four components more closely:

1. *Group feeling:* This may be thought of as a type of togetherness, a belonging with others who are dedicated to accomplishing similar ends. The stronger this feeling is, the more intense will be the effort expended in goal-directed behavior.
2. *Goal-directed behavior:* Since group action is not directionless, this component is indispensable to morale. Goal-directed behavior must always aim at something; it may be task-oriented, recreational, social, protective to the group, etc.
3. *Shared values:* A group's behavior becomes welded around a perception of shared values, acknowledged by group consensus. If the group shares values, by implication it shares mutual and compatible expectations. This allows them to act as one in achieving their objective.
4. *Worthwhile objective:* The last factor actually expresses the norms that determine acceptable group behavior and rewards which come from group effort. In general, the higher the rewards, the greater will be the group effort.

The Determinants of Morale

Many determinants affect the way these four factors will function in a specific group situation. That is, the level of morale in any group results from conditions both inside and outside the group. Separating the internal from the external determinants is not easy because they interact closely. However, for purposes of simplification, we will try to make such a separation.

Internal Determinants

Values and Objectives   The higher the rate of agreement among members of the group on values and objectives, the higher will be the morale. It is only natural that such agreement will reduce potential conflict and allow group members to concentrate their energies on goal accomplishment.

Probability of Success   The higher the probability that joint action will accomplish goals, the higher will be the morale, because group members perceive a strong likelihood of success from their collaboration. If the reverse is true, morale tends to be lower.

Actual Success   This is also an important determinant of morale, because if the group achieves its goals, morale tends to be high, but if the group constantly fails, morale tends to be low.

Individual Satisfaction   The higher the degree of individual satisfaction of group members, the higher the morale of the group as a whole. However, morale is not merely a sum of individual satisfactions; a circular relationship exists between these two factors. High personal satisfaction leads to high morale, which in turn tends to raise the level of satisfaction even higher, and so on. In other words, individuals get personal satisfaction from being in a high-morale group.

External Determinants

Job or Task   Work itself is intrinsically satisfying if it is geared to the needs, skills, experience, and education of group members. Because managers to a large extent determine the content of jobs, they must have a good program of personnel administration to assure satisfactory selection, placement, appraisal, promotion, and transfer of people according to their interests and desires. The personnel program must also meet the staffing needs of the firm. At one time, it was felt that the nature of a job was fixed by technology and nothing could be done to alter it. However, we now know that work can be changed within a given technological framework to make it more stimulating.

Type of Supervision   We have already seen that a good deal of research supports a policy of looser, more general supervision that allows a higher degree of individual and group determination of work activities. A direct relationship seems to exist between the amount of worker participation and the level of morale. The interpersonal skills of a manager also have much to do with morale levels.

Nature of the Control Systems and Amount of Pressure at Work   These related factors also have considerable influence on morale levels. Morale tends to be lower when control systems are tight and output pressure is high. In the process of automobile assembly, workers are paced (controlled) by an assembly line and experience great pressure to get work done.

Group Identification with the Goals and Values of the Organization   When people feel that they work for an organization that has worthwhile objectives, their morale is favorably affected. Of course, the organization's objectives and the way they are implemented are a function of management's philosophy and the administrative skill of the executives.

The Outcomes of Morale and Job Satisfaction

Even though high morale and job satisfaction are values that management must endorse and attempt to achieve, they do not exist apart from other important variables. We must ask, therefore, what relationship they have to turnover, absenteeism, accident rates, and productivity. This question is of considerable importance to management because it relates directly to cost and to the efficient use of human resources.

A tremendous amount of research in the behavioral sciences has been formulated to shed light on these relationships. Victor Vroom, who has reviewed this literature extensively, has pointed out some emerging patterns:

1. Higher morale and job satisfaction result in lower turnover. This pattern is consistent throughout the research.

2. Although high morale and job satisfaction also result in lower absenteeism, this pattern does not appear quite as strongly.

3. The same kind of statement seems to apply to the relationship of morale and satisfaction to accidents. However, because of the small number of research studies in this area, the evidence is inconclusive.

4. Finally, and most interestingly, research findings do not give a clear picture of the relationship between morale and productivity.[2]

For years it was assumed that a positive relationship existed between morale and productivity, that high productivity would result from good morale. Indeed, many respectable early research findings did show that this relationship prevailed in some enterprises. The human relations movement was inspired by such findings. One of the chief aims of this movement was to devise means to improve morale so that management would experience lower unit labor costs from satisfied high-producing employees.

Researchers in the early 1950's, however, created doubts that the results of earlier studies could be generalized. One study conducted in an insurance company showed no convincing evidence of a connection between positive employee attitudes and productivity. As more findings were published, it became clear that the morale-productivity relationship could appear in many forms — low morale and high productivity, high morale and low productivity, high morale and high productivity,

[2] Victor H. Vroom, *Work and Motivation* (New York: Wiley, 1964), ch. 6.

low morale and low productivity. Such findings suggest that morale and productivity may be independent, rather than interdependent, variables. In arguing for this interpretation, Vroom holds that the conditions providing job satisfaction are not necessarily identical to those that lead to higher employee performance.[3]

The present state of affairs is not satisfying to people looking for straight answers. Management could easily justify the cost of installing morale-building human relations devices in firms if it could be proved that they work better than traditional incentive systems do. However, management must now think twice. This is only part of a complex story that we must consider in greater detail.

JUSTIFICATION OF MOTIVATIONAL PROGRAMS

The need to justify motivational programs that depart from traditional incentive plans is often a real road block to progressive managers. Even though it may be demonstrated in a given company that application of more enlightened forms of Theory Y or System 4 management will probably increase productivity, reduce turnover, and cut absenteeism, unit costs may not be reduced commensurately. Management's reaction to this is often, "Why bother experimenting if we cannot achieve a more favorable profit, or cost, or market position?"

Human Asset Accounting

Rensis Likert introduces the notion of human asset accounting[4] as a partial answer to this question. He warns that conventional accounting systems do not adequately reflect the use of human resources in a business. He argues that human assets, like accounting assets, can be depleted or increased and that a company can likewise be better or worse off as a result of their increase or depletion. Table 26-1 compares the accounting concept of assets with Likert's human concept of assets.

There is no doubt that the quality and quantity of an organization's human assets will determine its performance in achieving both long- and short-range goals. Human assets directly affect the levels of sales, profitability, waste, and efficiency, which are short-range targets. In the longer run, human assets will also determine an organization's ability to adapt to change, its rate of innovation, and ultimately its capacity to survive. Thus, it is evident that accounting measures do not fully reflect the health of an organization. This fact is particularly important when management attempts to project long-range prospects. Such projections must not only account for the present value of human assets but they must also consider the future expansion of these assets.

For such reasons, Likert feels that motivational programs designed to satisfy diverse and changing employee expectations are justified and necessary. This, of course, is not the only justification. Other authors have different opinions. Let us continue to look at them.

[3] *Ibid.*, p. 187.
[4] Rensis Likert, *The Human Organization* (New York: McGraw-Hill, 1967), ch. 9.

Table 26-1. Accounting Assets Compared with Human Assets

Accounting assets	Human assets
Current	
Cash	Level of intelligence and aptitude
Inventory (completed and in process)	Level of training
	Level of performance goals and motivation to achieve organizational success
	Quality of leadership
Fixed	Capacity to use differences for purposes of innovation and improvement, rather than allowing differences to develop into bitter, irreconcilable interpersonal conflict
Equipment	
Buildings	
	Quality of communication upward, downward, and laterally
Intangible	Quality of decision-making
Patents	Capacity to achieve cooperative teamwork versus competitive striving for personal success at the expense of the organization
Goodwill	
	Quality of the control processes of the organization and the levels of felt responsibility which exist
	Capacity to achieve effective coordination
	Capacity to use experience and measurement to guide decisions, improve operations, and introduce innovations

Source: Adapted from Rensis Likert, *The Human Organization* (New York: McGraw-Hill, 1967), p. 148. Copyright © 1967 by McGraw-Hill, Inc. Used with permission of McGraw-Hill Book Company.

Participative Management

If employees have a say in affairs and are able to influence those that directly affect them on the job, their satisfaction is higher and sometimes so is their productivity. A number of years ago, Lester Coch and John French, in a study of a garment manufacturing firm, showed that by allowing employees to participate in decisions that affected their work assignments and job content, turnover was reduced, learning new jobs was accelerated, and change was accepted, not resisted.[5]

Increased employee participation and an expanded definition of such participation have increasingly become the theme of management philosophy. Whereas earlier studies stressed the need for factory workers to have greater say in their jobs, today the meaning of participation has broadened to become almost synonymous with democratic management. However, the basic idea remains: When people —

[5] Lester Coch and John R. P. French, Jr., "Overcoming Resistance to Change," *Human Relations* 29 (1948): 512–32.

and this includes rank-and-file workers, technical specialists, and managers — receive the opportunity to exercise more responsibility, judgment, and discretion in their jobs, they derive more satisfaction from work.

All this makes good sense if we relate it to what we previously said about technology and the changing character of the work force. People are entering the labor market today with more education and greater skills than ever before. Furthermore, they are conditioned to expect more from work than economic satisfactions. Because of such widening expectations, a repressive work climate will stifle an employee's innovative capacities. As Likert would say, such a climate is likely to produce a decline in human assets. Such a decline will occur if an employee quits and goes to a company where there is a better climate and more satisfaction. If employees do not make such a move, human resources will still be wasted in a hostile environment.

Whether called participation, decentralization, democratic leadership, System 4, or Theory Y, modern management philosophy and practices are changing to accommodate the expectations and stimulate the motivations of present-day employees. Warren Bennis observes that this change is indeed inevitable — that is, it is necessary if an organization is to stay healthy and survive.[6]

Just Treatment

Without a doubt, employees expect justice at work. Arbitrary treatment by superiors and unjust management policies will reduce employee satisfaction. Research indicates that if employees perceive that they are being treated unjustly or arbitrarily, their turnover will be higher than that of employees who do not have this perception.[7]

Distributive Justice

Two aspects of justice are important to management, distributive and corrective. According to Wendell French, distributive justice is a process whereby management deals out rewards or punishments in proportion to the contributions made by individuals to the company.[8] An individual's perception of distributive justice is always based on how that individual feels his treatment compares with that received by others, usually his working peers. Thus, two managers having equal responsibility and the same experience, education, and length of service with a company would expect to receive equal salaries. If a substantial salary difference existed, we could predict that the manager getting less money would feel unjustly treated.

[6] Warren Bennis, *Changing Organization* (New York: McGraw-Hill, 1966).

[7] Charles S. Telly, Wendell L. French, and William G. Scott, "The Relationship of Inequality to Turnover Among Hourly Workers," *Administrative Science Quarterly* (June 1971): 164–72.

[8] Wendell French, *The Personnel Process: Human Resources Administration*, 3d ed. (Boston: Houghton Mifflin, 1974), ch. 8.

Many management practices are used to create a system for just distribution of rewards and punishments. Job evaluation is one example. Its major aims are to pay people uniformly for the work they do and to scale pay according to the amount of responsibility involved in the job.

Corrective Justice

The possibility of unjust treatment exists in any human organization. The purpose of corrective justice is to right such treatment. Many systems exist to give people an opportunity to express grievances and obtain satisfaction. Most familiar is the *grievance procedure,* which is part of most labor-management contracts. It gives the individual a chance to obtain satisfaction if he feels his contractual rights have been violated. Suppose a foreman disciplines an employee for refusing to do a job assignment by imposing a three-day layoff, and the employee claims that the job was hazardous and not within the area of his responsibility. This situation may be submitted to the grievance procedure.

Corrective justice procedures not negotiated between labor and management also exist. For instance, management may unilaterally grant the right of appeal to all employees.[9] Such systems of appeal generally provide a channel of communication, by-passing the formal chain of command, through which an individual can get a hearing if he feels he is being treated unjustly. These appeals cover a range of complaints and grievances, from the trivial to the major. They may be used by employees on all organization levels, including management.

In summary, we may say that just treatment is an important employee expectation. Along with participative management and human resource accounting, just treatment represents a way of fulfilling employee needs, promoting satisfaction, and raising morale.

The Current Trend

Employees are expecting more from an organization's climate today than they did a generation ago, and there is little doubt that the next generation will make even greater demands than the present one. Organizations must respond to these demands not only for the good of the employees, but also for their own sake. The viability of a business depends on how well it can cope with change. The repressiveness of traditional organization is no longer justifiable. The truly responsive organization maximizes individual freedom and responsibility and thus fulfills rising employee expectations.

We need to discuss one more important ingredient of satisfaction, morale, and behavior at work — the small group. This is such an essential aspect of the influencing process that we devote the next chapter to it.

[9] William G. Scott, *The Management of Conflict* (Homewood, Ill.: Irwin, 1965).

Discussion Questions

1. What do you view from your position as a student to be the motivation and hygiene factors in your situation?

2. If morale is not related to productivity in any systematic way, how can it have any significance for management?

Supplementary Readings

Campbell, John P., et al. *Managerial Behavior, Performance, and Effectiveness.* New York: McGraw-Hill, 1970.

Herzberg, Frederick. "The Motivation-Hygiene Concept and Problems of Manpower." In *Dimensions in Modern Management,* edited by Patrick E. Connor. Boston: Houghton Mifflin, 1974.

Herzberg, Frederick. "New Approaches in Management Organization and Job Design." In *Management in Perspective,* edited by William E. Schlender, William G. Scott, and Alan C. Filley. Boston: Houghton Mifflin, 1965. See pp. 357–66.

Herzberg, Frederick. *Work and the Nature of Man.* Cleveland: World, 1966. See chapters 5–8.

Scott, William G. *Management of Conflict.* Homewood, Ill.: Irwin, 1965. See chapters 2–3.

CHAPTER 27

The Informal Organization

The individual and the formal task structure constitute two main elements of a complex organizational system. A third and equally significant element is the informal organization. The informal organization — powerful as a source of influence — interacts with and modifies the other two elements. Most of what is known about the informal organization comes from sociology and social psychology. Studies conducted within these two disciplines center on small group behavior and provide what is perhaps the most convenient approach to the subject. Adopting this approach, we will begin by asking why people join small groups. This will involve us in a more specific inquiry: What benefits are derived from small group participation? Next we will broaden our discussion and delve into the nature of the informal organization and its relationship to formal organization. Finally we shall briefly observe informal working relationships that seem to incorporate other patterns.

Before beginning, however, we must recognize that there is a basic difference between the small group and the informal organization. The small group is a component of the informal organization and constitutes its nucleus. In the first sections of this chapter we will discuss the small group. Then, we shall expand our discussion to the informal organization.

WHY PEOPLE FORM GROUPS

Why do people form groups?[1] What advantages do they gain from these associations? Why do smaller subgroups emerge within large aggregations of people? People have a basic need to associate with their fellow men in groups small enough to permit intimate, direct, and personal contact among individuals. The satisfactions which are derived from these kinds of associations cannot be obtained from working in a big organization, living in a large city, or learning in a sizable high school or college. Thus, the group provides the individual with satisfactions different from those that he can get from any other source.

---

[1] The basic reference in group behavior is George C. Homans, *The Human Group* (New York: Harcourt Brace Jovanovich, 1950).

Attraction to Specific Groups

Individuals, however, do not gravitate randomly to just any small group. They follow a pattern that has certain general characteristics. First, the group must arise spontaneously within larger aggregations of people. It usually has no more than ten and at times as few as two members.

Second, small groups attract individuals who share similar values. These people interact, mainly by communicating, to produce a consensus on values and standards of behavior, which is essential to the group's effective accomplishment of its objectives.

Third, all groups have certain goals that they seek to fulfill. The goals are important to the group and to each individual member. These goals usually involve task achievement and emotive satisfactions. The task often involves some specific outcome that can be achieved only by group collaboration — such as neighbors getting together for a cook-out. Emotive satisfactions are the rewards each individual experiences from participating in the group endeavor. Task and emotive satisfactions are often closely related. Important exceptions are discussed later in the chapter.

Figure 27-1 sums up these three characteristics. Small groups process inputs to create outputs. The inputs are individuals with various interests, values, and goals. The group processes of interaction, communication, and collaboration allow the members to reach a consensus, without which the outputs of goal accomplishment would be difficult to achieve.

Now that we know something about small groups, we can turn to more direct answers to the question of why people join groups.

Figure 27-1. General Characteristics of Small Groups

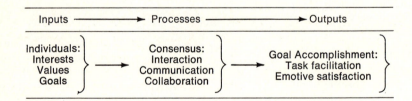

Benefits from Group Participation

Satisfaction

Because an individual in a group is surrounded by others who share similar values, the group reinforces the individual's own value system. This is a formal way of saying that it is usually more comfortable to be around people who think the same way we do. Such an explanation illuminates the basic kind of satisfaction a person gains from group participation. Formation of groups to supply this satisfaction is as natural to man as eating or sleeping.

However, additional factors are present. Groups help men to accomplish tasks that they cannot accomplish alone. As we have already noted, task facilitation provides personal satisfaction through cooperative effort. The tasks may be essentially economic, like work, or they may be social and recreational. Barn raising, common among pioneer farmers, was both a work and a social event.

As we know, group output includes both task and emotive content. On the emotive side, the group is a source of psychological satisfactions. For example, the group provides a person with status by enabling him to belong to a distinct and more or less exclusive little organization. It also allows an individual an opportunity for self-expression — it provides a kind of forum and generally sympathetic listeners. The individual participating in a group thus gets satisfaction for his recognition, participation, and communication needs. In some instances, a person can even find in the group an outlet for his leadership drives.

A good deal of evidence shows that in a business setting such satisfactions are often not available from work itself. However, jobs that are boring, fatiguing, and monotonous are offset to some extent by social relationships among workers. The value of small groups of managers, on the other hand, presents a more complex problem, and unfortunately little research has been done in this area.

One study by Tom Burns, however, focuses on the formation of such a group among managers who had reached the end of their career progress in a company.[2] These managers used the group as a way of reassuring each other that they were not actually personal failures in business — that other forces outside themselves were responsible for ending their advancement. Thus, they derived emotive satisfaction from their group and also mutual support — another of the major benefits of group participation.

Support

Group reinforcement of individual values is, of course, a form of support. However, the concept of support goes beyond this; the group in a very real way insulates the individual from the complexity and hostility of a vast, impersonal society. Often when people enter an organization for the first time they feel considerable anxiety. Their surroundings are unfamiliar, their future uncertain. The first inclination of these people is to seek out others in a similar situation and to form a friendship with them. Where several people are in the same circumstances, a small group may arise on this basis alone. However, usually it does not last very long after the initial fear of the new environment wears off.

More lasting are groups that arise from the members' perception that collective action is necessary to prevent the encroachment of outsiders. People who perceive that they will be involved in an organization for a long time may form such groups in an attempt to maintain the status quo. We find examples of this in prisoner of war camps, in teen-age gangs, and to a degree in business organizations.

[2] Tom Burns, "The Reference of Conduct in Small Groups," *Human Relations* 32 (November 1955): 467–86.

In business, groups may restrict worker output. Such restrictions have been interpreted as a protest or a protective form of behavior. Protests usually occur against high standards of output or other aspects of working conditions. Protective behavior may attempt to ensure that output standards will not be increased even though higher productivity may easily be possible.

To generalize, whenever people mutually perceive that their environment creates a need for protection or protest, they may form small groups. They do so because they realize that action is most effective when engaged in collectively. Often such groups form the embryo of a larger, more formalized organization. Certainly, the labor movement had its beginnings in a few informal groups of workers.

Information

A third reason why people form groups is to secure information. As we have seen, the grapevine is an important means of satisfying the communication needs of individuals. Of course, a person does not have to be in a small group to receive information from the grapevine, but it does help.

Figure 27-2. Communication Patterns of Small Groups

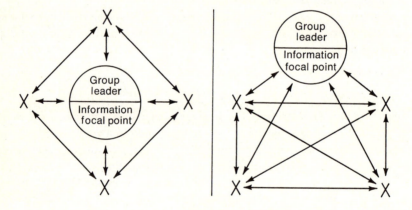

In fact, research into communication patterns shows that people tend to form groups in an effort to cluster around the individual who is the focal point in a communication network (see Figure 27-2). Thus, possession of information may be considered to be a prerequisite of group leadership. This is true whether we are talking about formal or informal organization. An individual who has information is able to satisfy the communication needs of others and can reduce a great deal of uncertainty in others' minds. The small group facilitates this process, even though the information transmitted may be false or misleading.

NATURE OF INFORMAL ORGANIZATIONS

We turn now to a larger entity, the informal organization, of which small groups are a part. Before analyzing its structure and behavior, it is necessary to reaffirm one important point. Both the informal organization and its main component small groups exist in a still larger social system. The nature of social systems vary from that of a neighborhood in a city, to a unit in the military service, to the formal structure of a business firm. Often such a system is so large that the individual feels lost in it. Therefore, he forms small groups. Now that we are aware of this pattern, we can turn to the characteristics of the middle-level organizational structure — the informal organization.

Structure

The structure of the informal organization is determined by the different status positions people have in relationship to the organization. There are four status positions: (1) group leader, (2) member of the primary group, (3) fringe status, and (4) out status. By using sociometric techniques to measure the type, duration, and frequency of contact among people located in a close geographic area, we are able to determine who holds which status position and thus draw a picture of the informal organizational structure. Suppose, for example, that we wanted to determine the structure of a group of nine girls working in an office. These girls are located in a close general area and there are no artificial barriers, like walls, to prevent them from frequently associating with one another if they wish. Common sense tells us, however, that each girl will not associate with each other girl with equal frequency. Rather, they will be selective in their associations, regularly including some and excluding others.

This is the phenomenon that we want to measure, and sociometry is the device that measures it. Through a simple questionnaire and some rough observations, an outsider can get in a rather short time an accurate picture of the informal organization of the girls. On paper the picture looks something like the model of the atom often described in elementary science books (see Figure 27-3).

The solid square in the nucleus represents the leader of the small group. Clustered around her are four other members. Their association is close, and their interaction and communication is intense. In a practical sense, the girls enjoy each other's company, go to coffee and lunch together frequently, and often meet for dinner and maybe a show after work. The girl who is the leader is the dynamic force in the group, crystallizing opinions, setting objectives, and the like.

The three people in the fringe shell of the informal organization are newcomers. They are being evaluated by the smaller group for acceptance or rejection. Eventually they will move either into the nucleus or into the out shell.

The person in the out shell has been rejected. Although part of the informal organization, she is not accepted by the members in the core group. Such rejection can

Figure 27-3. A Model of Informal Organization

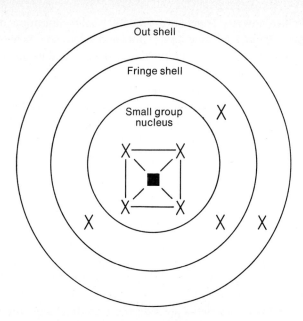

affect that girl's behavior profoundly, especially if she wants badly to belong to the nucleus group. Of course, if the rejection is mutual, the person in the out shell can survive easily.

We must stress that the entire informal organization is a system of interaction. The structural diagram that depicts it cannot capture much of its behavioral content. Most certainly, the interactions of the nuclear group members modify each member's individual behavior. This group's behavior also has a marked impact on the individuals in the two surrounding status shells. Conversely, the people outside the nuclear group could have a marked impact on those inside. They could, for example, be perceived as threats. If so, the nuclear group will modify its behavior toward them. Finally, the informal organization as a whole interacts with other organizations about it, particularly with the formal organization.

Behavior

We have just indicated that the informal organization influences its members' behavior regardless of their status within it. This is an obvious but exceedingly important observation. A manager cannot hope to understand individual behavior without knowing the forces that shape it, and the informal organization is a significant force.

In order to understand why the informal organization has influence over individual behavior, we can refer to our earlier discussion of the reasons for joining groups. There we stated that groups are capable of granting or withholding the advantages of group membership. Thus, if the individual wants acceptance by a nucleus group in an informal organization, he must modify his behavior so that it corresponds to the standards and values of the group. However, indifference to group acceptance does not eliminate him from the informal organization. He is still in the system, and his behavior will be influenced to a greater or lesser degree by the values and behaviors that predominate there.

Another characteristic of behavior in the informal organization is that it resists change. It does not resist all changes, however; only those that are interpreted as a threat. Let us assume, for example, that a group of staff engineers has been working together for some time in a close area of a department and has evolved a satisfying social relationship. Management may decide, however, that it would be more efficient to reorganize the office. This decision could involve shifting the engineers to several different locations in the department. The move would probably break up the pattern of social relations among the engineers, destroying the group. Often threats of this type of change are countered by resistance — complaining, slowing work, reducing quality, being absent, and so on. Without understanding the dynamics of group behavior, management could not possibly hope to influence the group's acceptance of change.

Leadership

Many of the concepts of leadership previously discussed apply to leadership in the informal organization. For example, leadership in such organizations is situational, and the selected leader tends to have the optimum combination of intelligence, sensitivity, and communication skills appropriate to the situation. However, several additional points on group leadership need particular emphasis.

First, the group leader is democratically chosen. He acquires the leadership role by consensus of the group he leads.

Second, the leader is the dominant personality in the group. He functions to help satisfy both task and emotive needs of group members. However, from time to time we observe groups where these aspects of the leadership role may be shared. The sharing may be brief, depending on the needs of the group. For example, one person may assume leadership of the group because he has some skill the group requires to accomplish a particular task. The regular leader, sensitive to the group's need, will take a back seat temporarily.

Third, we often observe a division of labor in a group. In addition to bringing specific task skills to the group, we find members playing other roles both in the task and the emotive categories. The leader integrates these diverse activities so that the processes of the group work well.

RELATIONSHIPS BETWEEN FORMAL AND INFORMAL ORGANIZATIONS

The informal organization is clearly a product of natural human social processes. This kind of organization will appear wherever people gather together to gain benefits that the larger, containing organization cannot provide. Thus, the informal organization can aid the formal organization distinctly; it supplies satisfaction for individuals and high morale for work teams.

Some early theorists tended to picture the informal organization as antagonistic to the formal organization's goals. They viewed management's role as one of trying to manipulate the group into accepting formal goals. However, management should be aware of the positive nature of the informal organization and cease to dwell upon it as a source of conflict.

Currently, theorists realize that a clear distinction between formal and informal organizations does not exist at all. Instead, they consider both formal and informal organizations to be parts of a complex system. These organizations are seen as interacting within the system, each modifying the other in the process of achieving goals. This does not mean that the goals of these subsystems are necessarily the same; they may be mutually reinforcing, conflicting, or may bear little or no relationship to one another. Regardless of the nature of the goals, however, there is no question that behavior will interact. Thus, the expectations and satisfactions of the people in both formal groups and informal subsystems will be influenced in several directions.

Of course, management must constantly strive to create an organizational climate in which the legitimate satisfaction and expectations of individuals and their informal groups can be fulfilled. It is folly for management to suppose that the functioning of the formal system alone can provide the entire range of satisfaction necessary for high spirit among employees. The informal organization has a positive contribution to make in this respect. As such, it should be nurtured by management.

Figure 27-4. By-passing the Chain of Command

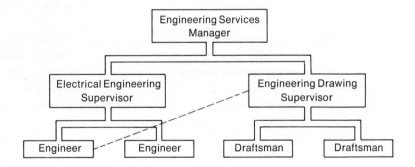

INFORMAL WORKING RELATIONSHIPS

Just as the informal organization is a departure from the specific structure that exists in formal charts and manuals, so are informal working relationships. They are less dramatic but nonetheless profoundly influential in organizational behavior. Informal working relationships encompass all the job-related activities that are carried out in ways not specified in formal organizational documents or in ways different from those specified. Behavior pertains to work, but it deviates from formally pre-scribed patterns. The most obvious example of this is the informal by-pass of the chain of command that many use to communicate on some aspect of work (see Figure 27-4).

In Figure 27-4, electrical engineers working on circuit design cut directly across the chain of command to consult with and take work to the supervisor of draftsmen. The dotted line shows the informal relationships between them. This bypass speeds up requisitioning drawings and working out technical details. Following the pre-scribed channels of communication would be burdensome and time consuming.

It is impossible to describe all the informal working relationships that can exist within formal organizations. The point to remember was made by a management scholar who observed that if everyone adhered to the formal organization in the day-to-day operation of a company, nothing would get done. Informal working re-lationships introduce a considerable degree of flexibility into any organization.

Discussion Questions

1. When you first arrived at college, what kinds of group associations did you make? What goals did you have in making these group connections?

2. What relationships exist among the individual, the small group, the informal organization, and complex systems?

Supplementary Readings

Homans, George C. *The Human Group.* New York: Harcourt Brace Jovanovich, 1950.

Pfiffner, John H., and Frank P. Sherwood. "Non-Formal Aspects of the Organization." In *Dimensions in Modern Management,* edited by Patrick E. Connor. Boston: Houghton Mifflin, 1974.

Sayles, Leonard R. *Managerial Behavior.* New York: McGraw-Hill, 1964. See chap-ters 5–8.

Scott, William G., and Terence R. Mitchell. *Organization Theory.* Homewood, Ill.: Irwin, 1972. See chapter 7.

Tannenbaum, A. S. *Social Psychology of the Work Organization.* Belmont, Calif.: Wadsworth, 1966. See chapters 2–5.

CASES

V | 1

The New Directive

For the past fifteen years the Claymont Manufacturing Company has produced valves and other small parts to be used in aerosol spray cans. Most of its employees have worked for the company for a long time and are not unionized. For many years Mr. Williams, the president of the company, has wanted to change working hours during the summer months to help his employees avoid some of the rush-hour traffic and to enable them to enjoy more daylight hours after work. The regular working hours for all factory and office personnel are from 8 A.M. until 5 P.M., with one hour off for lunch. Mr. Williams intends to change these hours to span the period from 7:30 A.M. until 4 P.M., with only half an hour off for lunch.

He knows that many of his employees would prefer the new hours. However, he also knows that this new arrangement will cause hardships for a number of employees. Some of the women drive to work with their husbands; others are in car pools; and some depend on babysitters to take care of their children. Some employees like to sleep late in the morning. Mr. Williams also expects some objections from those whose work depends on the work of outsiders whose day begins later and ends later.

Recently, Mr. Williams has entertained the idea of "flexi-time," a plan that would permit an employee to set his own time schedule as long as he put in eight hours a day and as long as those eight hours fell between 7 A.M. and 5 P.M. However, Mr. Williams can foresee that such a plan would cause many new problems on the production line and in the office.

Therefore, Mr. Williams has decided to go ahead with his first plan. Although he fully realizes that he could submit this change to his employees for group deliberations and group decision-making and although he is aware both of the problems of introducing the change and of the benefits of employee contributions, he nevertheless intends simply to announce the new working hours four weeks before they will take effect, so that his employees can make all the arrangements that will be necessary.

Questions

1. Is Mr. Williams doing the right thing?

2. What would you prefer if you were (1) the president of the company, (2) one of the employees?

3. What are the advantages and disadvantages of group decision-making?

4. What problems are usually encountered when changes need to be introduced?

V | 2

Jack and His Department

Jack Armstrong, age thirty, is a supervisor of the stores room for the Dunhill Manufacturing Company. He has been working for the company for five years and for the last three years has been an assistant to one of the buyers in the purchasing department. This assignment familiarized him with many of the materials, parts, and supplies needed by the company. When the job of supervisor of the stores room became vacant, he asked for the position; after further discussions, he was given the job. Because it was a promotion, he was eager to succeed in his new position. However, the job was a challenge, for the operation of the stores room had always been a source of many complaints in the company.

Jack installed many new procedures for record-keeping, issuance of materials, and controls, and after one year or so his department seemed to be functioning smoothly. Jack had six employees working for him when he started. Within two years, four of the six had left the company and had to be replaced. All four had been with the company for a number of years. The two who remained were older employees who would be unable to find comparable jobs in other companies.

When the personnel director called this situation to the attention of the plant superintendent, under whose authority the stores room operates, the superintendent suggested that someone ought to determine the reasons for the turnover. The plant superintendent asked his assistant to do this, and after speaking with the former employees and with other employees of the company, the assistant submitted his report. He had found that Jack was a hard worker, was eager to succeed in his job, and was very knowledgeable. Many of the new methods and procedures he originated were very good, and the department generally functioned well. However, Jack's major weaknesses seemed to occur in the area of directing, motivating, communicating and leading. Jack seemed to be a rigid and formal young man who, in his desire to succeed, ran the department with a firm hand, thereby creating considerable resentment among his employees. At times he had embarrassed his subordinates by taking disciplinary action in public.

The plant superintendent would like to know what to do. Jack certainly is doing a good job with the material aspects of his job, but seems deficient in the personnel area.

Questions

1. What are the major problems in this situation?
2. Should Jack be replaced? If not, what action would you recommend?

V|3

The Right of Appeal

The employees' handbook of St. Mary's Hospital states that an employee has the right to appeal to the next highest line superior if that employee thinks he has been wronged. The administration of the hospital realizes that, in order to have good organizational hygiene, it is necessary to make provisions for a wrong to be righted. By and large, their grievance procedure worked satisfactorily until a case came up that had some ramifications never encountered before.

John, an orderly in the nursing services, had repeatedly violated the no-smoking rule. After initiating preliminary steps — a friendly informal talk, a formal oral reprimand, and a written warning — but to no avail, his supervisor imposed a three-day disciplinary layoff upon him. John appealed to the director of Nursing Services because he felt that his punishment had been too severe. When he went to this director, John brought along his colleague Bill, another nursing orderly, who was to plead the case for John. John was afraid that he could not make a good case for himself, for he easily becomes tongue-tied when nervous and excited. The director refused to listen to Bill. She insisted that John must plead his own grievance and dissatisfaction and also maintained that no provisions existed allowing a person to be represented by another at such a meeting. Both John and Bill left the nursing director's office without discussing the case; instead of returning to work, they both quit their jobs at the hospital.

Questions

1. Does the hospital invite problems when it offers such an appeal procedure?

2. Was the director of Nursing Services right in her contention?

3. If you had been in her place, how would you have handled the situation?

V|4

The Administrative Assistant

Dr. Wesselman is the chief of medicine at the Methodist Hospital in St. Louis. As such, he is a full-time employee of the hospital in charge of all aspects of the department of medicine. He is paid a substantial annual salary and, whenever he sees private patients, his fees are paid to the hospital. He has a staff of about seventy-five people, comprised of physicians, scientists, technologists, and clerical employees. In order to ease his many administrative duties, he has hired Charles Gorham as his administrative assistant. Mr. Gorham, who holds the degree of bachelor of science in business administration, has helped Dr. Wesselman greatly by ensuring that the department functions smoothly, thereby enabling the chief to concentrate on the medical and scientific aspects of his job.

The department contains specialized groups, one of which is composed of endocrinologists headed by Dr. Miller. A number of physicians, scientists, and technologists work in this specialty; all of them are full-time employees of the hospital. One of the bright young men in this area is Dr. Conway, a resident who came to the hospital with an outstanding record of achievements in other hospitals. He had come to Methodist Hospital with high expectations and great hopes for pursuing his research.

Mr. Gorham, who is well liked by most people in the department, has learned that Dr. Conway seems highly discouraged and dissatisfied and is on the verge of turning in his resignation. His chief complaints center around the fact that Dr. Miller burdens him with routine work and does not allow him any time to pursue his own area of research. He was hired with the understanding that he could and should pursue the promising work he had started in other hospitals.

Mr. Gorham does not know what to do. He definitely considers it his duty to do all in his power to keep Dr. Conway on the staff of the hospital. He does not know if Dr. Miller is aware of Dr. Conway's intentions. However, he does know that Dr. Miller would resent it if Mr. Gorham were to discuss the matter with him. On the other hand, Mr. Gorham is reluctant to discuss Dr. Conway's case with Dr. Wesselman because it is not an administrative matter. Also, if he approached Dr. Wesselman and Dr. Wesselman, in turn, discussed the case with Dr. Miller, Dr. Miller would either resent Gorham's interference or would think that Dr. Conway had gone directly to Dr. Wesselman to express his dissatisfaction.

Question

1. If you were in Mr. Gorham's position what would you do?

V|5

The Chemical Laboratory

The Alpha Laboratories develops chemicals, oils, coloring, and other ingredients for use in the cosmetics industry. The firm employs a number of chemists, engineers, technologists, and clerical workers. All the chemists and engineers hold at least a bachelor's degree; the technologists have one or two years of junior college or a high school education and a great deal of on-the-job training.

The president of the firm assigned each project to be worked on to a chemist, who then carried it through to its completion. During this period the chemist could request the help of other chemists, engineers, or technologists. No particular technologist or number of technologists was assigned to a chemist. This informal arrangement always worked well; there were always technologists available to tackle new tests; and no significant delays were caused by the overuse of equipment or apparatus.

As time went on, however, the number of projects increased. The president enlarged the laboratory by adding chemists and technologists. At the same time he rearranged the organizational setup, creating a pool of technologists with a chief technologist in charge. By creating a pool, the president hoped to conserve resources, avoid waste, and make technologist support available to all on an equal basis. Under the new scheme, whenever a chemist needed certain tests, he was to channel his request through the chief technologist, who would then assign someone from the pool to do the job.

After some time, great dissatisfaction and many delays began to occur, and it seemed that the new system was not working. Chemists complained that they could not get their test results back quickly enough. The technologists became dissatisfied and complained that the chief technologist placed too much pressure upon them. Often, they said, the unavailability of testing equipment caused the delays. More technologists were put to work and more equipment was bought. Still, the complaints persisted to such a degree that, after one year, the president was tempted to go back to the informal working arrangement that he had previously used.

Questions

1. Could these problems have been avoided?
2. Why didn't the pool produce the desired results, even though its organization was rationally based?
3. The number of projects is continuously increasing. What should the president do?

VI

CONTROLLING

THE CONTROLLING FUNCTION. Controlling is the process that measures performance against standards and ensures that organizational goals and objectives are being met. Controlling is closely related to planning because through it the effectiveness of the organization can be gauged.

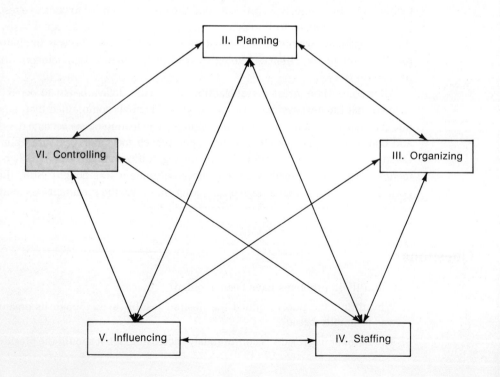

Many misconceptions about the controlling function exist. One of the most serious is that controlling is concerned only with events after their occurrence. This misconception probably stems from two causes. The first is that in most management textbooks, as in this one, the controlling function is discussed last, giving the impression that it occurs after the other functions have been performed. Second, in certain practical applications of control such as quality control in a factory, deviations from standards are not picked up until after a mistake has been made or faulty workmanship has been discovered.

This after-the-fact interpretation of controlling only gives half of the picture, however. We must remember that control goes on simultaneously with the other functions in a system. Control decisions affect plans, for example, just as planning decisions affect controls. In the process of planning, management sets goals, objectives, and policies, and these become the standards against which performance is checked and appraised. If any deviations occur between achievements and goals, management has to take corrective action, and this action itself may entail new plans and new goals.

Although the relationship between planning and controlling is particularly close, control is interwoven with all management functions. Indeed, their relationship is circular. The better management plans, organizes, staffs, and influences, the more effectively it can perform its function of control, and vice versa. Clearly, the interrelatedness of the functions in the management system does not allow any one function to remain first or last in a sequence.

The after-the-fact view of controlling can be further modified when we consider that control, like planning, should be at least partially forward-looking. Higher levels of management should adopt controls that anticipate potential sources of deviation from objectives and standards. As we have said, control and planning are linked. Planning sets objectives, and high-level control seeks ways to offset situations that may interfere with their accomplishment. Past experience can be of considerable help in anticipatory controlling. Management may study the past in order to learn what has taken place and where and possibly why certain standards were not met. It can then take the necessary steps to assure that action in the future does not follow the mistakes of the past. It is in this sense that control is forward-looking, utilizing the past to anticipate the proper measures for the future.

In practice, however, the anticipatory aspect of control is seldom emphasized or realized. Instead, control is usually backward-looking. Deviations *are* corrected after the fact, rather than anticipated. Thus, the part of the control process that receives the most attention is reaction. The reactive aspect enables men to detect deviations from standards or objectives, to receive feedback information, and to correct deviations at the point of performance. We must always keep in mind, however, that proper use of the control function requires understanding not only of its corrective aspect but also of its anticipatory potential.

We would be remiss if we did not take note of another important aspect of control: the response of people. This factor pervaded our discussions of the organizing, staffing, and influencing functions. For this reason, we do not have a chapter specifically devoted to it in Part VI. However, we would like to make several points concerning it here. Control means nothing more or less than placing constraints on behavior so that what people do in organizations will be predictable. Important techniques of control that facilitate this purpose arise from specialization and specification of function, from organizational structure, and from the reward and punishment systems through which managers exercise power. Group norms — nonplanned or consciously introduced into the system by management — also exert powerful controls over behavior.

The amount of control or constraint exercised in a particular situation is obviously subject to management's discretion. Management literature mentions two extremes — tight control and loose control or close supervision and general supervision. What these extremes define is the degree of freedom an individual has and how much discretion he is permitted to use in performing his job. This is an important matter because the nature and degree of control over people's discretion relates directly to the climate of motivation discussed at length in Part V.

We saw that management is increasingly widening this area of discretion in an effort to obtain greater organizational flexibility. They realize that, if control is loosened and human satisfactions on the job are enhanced, the facility of the organization to adapt to change will be increased. Looser control is, of course, accomplished by less functional specification, greater decentralization, and more participation in the decision-making process, among other things.

The degree of control can also be related to the organic or mechanistic character of an organization. An organic organization has free-flowing communication and an open structure that depends less on lines of authority. A mechanistic organization functions in the opposite manner. It has a rigid chain of command that forms a path for the movement of information along official channels of communication. Obviously the mechanistic organization has a more closely controlled and formal, bureaucratic system. As we

have said, management is tending to move away from this type of organization toward more open, organic systems. This point is discussed further in Chapter 31.

This movement, however, should in no way suggest the complete disappearance of control in organizations. Such a situation is an impossibility. What we see is in part a reaction to the tight, often inhuman character of traditional control systems. However, we must keep in mind, as we have observed previously, that organizations are not universally susceptible to the reduction of human controls. Technology and the educational levels of the work force make the difference. Those organizations most open to loose control structure are the ones that utilize advanced technologies, are subject to rapid change, and employ large numbers of professionally educated people.

CHAPTER 28

The Control Process

Control is the function in the managerial system that ensures that performance carries out the prescriptions of plans. In Henri Fayol's words: "Control consists in verifying whether everything occurs in conformity with the plan adopted, the instructions issued and principles established. It has for its object to point out weaknesses and errors in order to rectify them and prevent recurrence. It operates on everything, things, people, action."[1] Planning, organizing, staffing, and influencing are the preparatory steps for getting work done. Controlling makes certain that it gets done. Without controlling, management could not do a complete job of managing. Indeed, control is necessary whenever management assigns duties and delegates authority to a subordinate. Managers cannot simply delegate and sit back. They must exercise control over the actions taken under the delegated authority. They must set standards, check results against them, and take corrective measures when necessary.

Although planning and setting objectives, goals, policies, and procedures are indispensable to the efficient management of an enterprise, they are not means of control. Objectives, goals, and policies generate the need for control, but they do not fulfill that need. Neither does organization. Management must thus develop separate and distinct techniques for control purposes. Before we turn our attention to them, however, let us review a general model of control.

A GENERAL MODEL OF CONTROL

The concept of feedback lies at the heart of the control process. For any system to operate properly it must have readings on how well it is doing in relation to its environment and its internal activities. Feedback supplies this kind of information. The most commonly cited example of a feedback system is the thermostat. This instrument controls the air temperature in a room by turning on and shutting off a furnace. It constantly compares the actual room temperature with the desired temperature and takes regulating action when the actual temperature rises or drops sufficiently to trip an actuating device.

Control systems in organizations work on the same principle. They compare actual with desired performance. When and if the actual deviates unacceptably from

[1] Henri Fayol, *General and Industrial Management*, trans. Constance Storrs (London: Pitman, 1949), p. 107.

385

Figure 28-1. Control Model

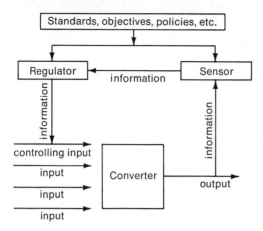

desired levels, corrective action is instituted. These similarities allow us to speak of a feedback principle in organizational control systems. More specifically, we can develop a general model of control which applies to a wide variety of systems. Figure 28-1 illustrates such a model.

The model represents a closed loop system composed of six elements: the inputs, the converter, the output, the sensor, the regulator, and the information which flows through the system. The controlling data — standards, objectives, policies, and the like — are inputs to the system. They originate in a larger system of which the model is a part. Similarly, if an individual sets a thermostat at 72 degrees, that individual represents a larger system providing controlling objectives for the subsystem.

Given the objectives, the closed loop system works in the following manner: The converter processes inputs to produce an output. The output is sampled by the sensor to discover if it conforms to the standards set by a higher system. If it does, the sensor takes no action. If it does not, the sensor activates a regulator, which adjusts a controlling input. Note that the regulator functions on only one input, not on all. This one input is crucial; by varying it, the control desired of the converter can be achieved. In other words, the converter will resume producing outputs in line with standards.

This model can easily be applied to many kinds of organizational situations. The most obvious example is quality control in a manufacturing operation (see Figure 28-2). The closed loop system in this illustration applies to nail manufacturing. The inspector samples the nails being produced. If the rejection rate exceeds the allowance, the foreman is notified. He acts on one of the inputs, in this case labor, to reduce the number of faulty nails. He suspects that the reason for the defective output is a poorly trained new employee. After correcting this input, the convertor or production line should then be able to produce more nails which meet quality standards.

Figure 28-2. Control Model Applied to a Quality Control System

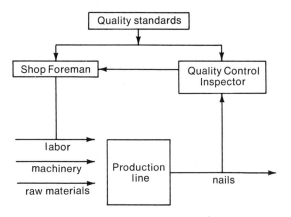

THE HUMAN ASPECTS OF CONTROL SYSTEMS

Response of People to Control

As we stated in our introduction, a crucial aspect of control is the response of people to control systems. This factor pervaded our discussions of the organizing, staffing, and influencing functions. However, we would like to make several additional points in reference to it here.

Freedom and Control

The amount of control that exists in an organization determines how much freedom of action an individual has when performing his job. However, an individual's perception of freedom is not necessarily maximized by an absence of control. Some control is conducive to maximizing human perception of freedom. Control restricts not only one's own behavior, but also the behavior of others. The existence of control assures the individual that he will be able to predict, within limits, the behavior of others toward him. If, for example, an individual could not predict the reaction of his boss, he might feel quite constrained in his behavior.

A certain amount of formalization and control, therefore, appears essential to regulate behavior in all situations. Because controls limit arbitrary, capricious, and erratic behavior, they make a positive contribution to the individual's perception of freedom. Theorists now think that perception of freedom is optimized when a balance is achieved between the degree of discretion and the degree of formalization in an organization. In other words, neither the extreme of tight control nor that of complete freedom is optimal for achieving organizational effectiveness. Somewhere between these extremes are mixes of control and freedom which maximize organizational effectiveness and individual satisfaction.

The Ideal Mix

However, the ideal mix differs for each organization and even for each department within an organization. For example, psychiatrists in mental hospitals usually feel more satisfied with their positions and perform more effectively if they are free of detailed supervision by nonprofessionals. However, in less professional positions and in those requiring minimum skills, greater organizational effectiveness appears to result from tighter controls and closer supervision of work details.

The optimal mixture of control and freedom is closely related to organizational centralization and management style, which we treated in previous chapters. Its basis is entirely situational. The greater the professional competence of people in the organization, the greater should be the decentralization of decision-making and the use of democratic leadership style. When the degree of professionalization drops, the reverse is true.

However, all this involves a major difficulty. We seek two outcomes from a given control mix: organizational effectiveness measured by standards of efficiency and productivity, and individual satisfaction measured by standards of morale. According to James Price's review of the literature on this subject, theorists seem to agree that loosening control over professional employees creates both organizational effectiveness and individual satisfaction.[2] For nonprofessionals, the picture is not quite as clear. Tight controls do produce organizational effectiveness, but may reduce individual satisfaction and group morale.

Thus, the effect of controls on people is still an open question. Researchers in the behavioral sciences are giving some answers, but they are situational ones that are not very satisfying for those seeking absolute laws. All we can say at this point is that managerial discretion continues to be pre-eminent in deciding upon appropriate mixes of freedom and control. With this in mind, we turn to the specific aspects of the control function.

REQUIREMENTS OF AN EFFECTIVE CONTROL SYSTEM

Understandability

The first requirement of an effective control system is that the controls be understandable. Managers throughout the system must understand how the controls work and must recognize the standards that are to be achieved. People seem to find it easier to live with a problem they cannot solve than with a solution they cannot understand. In practical terms, this means that the system of control should be designed so that it will become less complicated as it extends farther down into the managerial hierarchy. Certainly, it must be understood by the level of management that is to apply it. This factor frequently leads to conflict between the specialists who devise systems of controls and the managers who must apply them. The incompre-

---

[2] James L. Price, *Organizational Effectiveness* (Homewood, Ill.: Irwin, 1968), ch. 3.

hensible technical language of specialists often provides a communication barrier to understanding by lower levels of management.

Adherence to Organizational Design

In the process of organizing, activities are grouped, duties are assigned, and authority relations are established. Once this has been done, it is easy to identify the manager of a particular activity that is to be controlled. For a control system to be workable, it must follow the organizational design. Organizational design and control are therefore inseparable. Problems of who controls what, who provides the information, who inspects whom, and so forth can be solved only if the planning and control model is designed to meet the specific needs of the organization.

Rapid Reporting of Deviations

An effective control system requires the reporting of deviations without delay. The sooner management is aware of such deviations, the sooner it can take corrective action. Indeed, it is more desirable to have deviations reported quickly even if substantiated only by approximate figures than to wait two or three weeks for exact figures. Management cannot afford such a time lag; it must find means to learn of deviations expeditiously. The organizations that use electronic data processing equipment have the great advantage of receiving data almost immediately.

Another reason for rapid reporting is that managers are prone to exert less and less pressure as time passes. They tend to concentrate on events that took place during the last few days and report them to their superiors, ignoring those that are past history. Often the reviewing manager ends up focusing on this last bit of information instead of on the more enduring problems that should be under review. The timeliness of control information is therefore essential.

Inevitably, however, in higher levels of the organization, the control period lengthens. A parallel to this exists in the planning function. We noted that the typical planning period of first-line supervision is much shorter than that of middle managers, and the middle-managerial period is shorter than that of top management. Similarly, in the control process the first-level supervisor may get rapid feedback on performance, but top management may have to wait a longer period of time to receive meaningful control data. However, top management generally gets integrated feedback on broad segments of the system, whereas the supervisor gets data pertaining only to his small slice of the organization.

Situational Appropriateness and Adequacy

Controls must always be appropriate to the activity they monitor. The tools of control that are suitable to a sales department are different from those used in manufacturing. Even within manufacturing, the control tools used by the vice-president in charge of production are different from those used by the supervisor on the floor.

Likewise, the controls found in a small organization are not as elaborate as those employed by a large enterprise.

Some control techniques, however, are used in one form or another by almost all enterprises. These include standard hours, standard costs, budgets, break-even points, and financial ratios. Management adapts these and other techniques in order to devise a control system which adequately reflects the activities and needs of the particular enterprise. The size and type of enterprise will, of course, help to determine the criterion of adequacy. Any system of control should require no more reports, data, figures, and statistics than are absolutely necessary.

Flexibility

Since the environment of every organization constantly changes, controls must be flexible. Unforeseen circumstances play havoc with the best plans. Even if management prepares planning premises thoroughly, they are still estimates of the future and are by their very nature uncertain. As Billy Goetz puts it, it is always possible that some particulars within a managerial plan will fail: "The control system should report such failures and should contain sufficient elements of flexibility to maintain managerial control of operations in spite of such failures."[3] A good control system, in other words, must be designed to keep pace with the continuously changing pattern of the organization's environment. Unless control devices are flexibile enough to permit change just as soon as it is required, the control system is bound to deteriorate.

The practical importance of this can be illustrated by considering the budgetary control device. Typically, the amount of expense allowed in a department is based on expected sales for the coming period. If, however, the sales during that period double, the manager cannot be expected to stay within his allotted budget. There must be enough flexibility built into the system so that he can cover the added expenses resulting from this substantially increased amount of business. Similarly, in their desire to stay within budgets, executives themselves should not refuse to recognize early indications of change in the internal or external environment. If they overlook such indications, they will not be able to keep pace with altered conditions as rapidly as they should.

Economic Criteria

In a workable control system, the controls must be economical and must be worth the expenses involved. At times it is difficult — although always worthwhile — for management to ascertain how much a particular control system is worth and how much it really costs. They must bear in mind certain economic criteria: the relative contribution the control system makes in relation to the size of the enterprise, the expenses involved, and the consequences that might follow if the controls did not exist.

---

[3] Billy E. Goetz, *Management Planning and Control* (New York: McGraw-Hill, 1949), p. 229.

Indicative of Corrective Action

Effective controls must show the way to corrective action. It is not enough for a control system to reveal deviations; it must also show who is responsible for them and where they have occurred. At times, however, this information is not readily available. Often a report submitted to top management has been oversimplified, and too many items have been consolidated under a single heading. Such a summary report does not clearly indicate below-the-surface facts. Perhaps a favorable showing in one area prevents a poor showing in another from appearing. Management can discover such occurrences by insight, accident, or by a thorough study of the detailed financial control information on which their incomplete summary is based.

BASIC STEPS IN THE CONTROL PROCESS

To set up an effective control process, management must plan three basic activities. First, in order to ascertain whether performance is in accordance with plans, they must set standards. Then they must ensure that performance is checked and appraised. Finally, if a deviation occurs, they must have set up an apparatus for corrective action. To control effectively, these activities should be followed in the sequence indicated.

Setting Standards

Standards are criteria against which to judge results. In planning, managment sets the objectives and goals that the enterprise hopes to achieve. They then divide these over-all objectives into narrower objectives for individual departments. From these narrower objectives specific goals are established. Specific goals may relate to quality, production cost, time standards, sales quotas, schedules, budgets, and many other areas of detailed operations. These goals become the standards for exercising control.

Types of Standards

Because the variety of specific goals is so large, the average enterprise will have a multitude of standards. Most of these will be of a tangible nature, although some will be intangible and therefore much more difficult to work with.

Tangible Standards The most common tangible standards are physical, cost, revenue, and capital. Normally, physical standards form the basis of all planning. They encompass the actual operation of the enterprise: where goods are produced, services rendered, and workers employed. These standards are both quantitative and qualitative. Quantitatively, they define the number of units to be produced per hour, the number to be obtained out of a certain quantity of raw material, and so forth. Qualitatively, they refer to the durability of the product, the content of the mixture, the dimensions, closeness, and precision of machining operations, the finish, smoothness, hardness, toughness, strength, and the like. Both types of physical standards are what Goetz calls "the building blocks of managerial planning."[4] At the same time they are the physical criteria of control.

Cost standards are established by attaching monetary value to the expenses necessary to reach planned goals. Cost standards include direct and indirect labor costs per unit, standards per hour, standard cost for the material per unit, selling costs, overhead costs, and other direct and indirect costs.

Revenue standards are obtained by attaching monetary value to sales. Management can easily set these standards by multiplying the number of units which are forecast to be sold by the price of each unit. The revenue standard thus calculated is the expected sales volume of the enterprise for a particular period. In planning the annual sales of a department store, for example, the revenue standard might be set at a figure 10 per cent above the previous year's sales. This, then, will be the expected volume for that year. The revenue standard for a hospital might be based on expected room occupancy and revenue per bed. Inflationary trends need to be considered, of course, when setting revenue standards.

Capital standards are related to the amount of capital invested in an enterprise. The return on capital invested forms a frequently used standard. Other capital standards often used in analyzing the balance sheet of a firm include the ratio of current assets to current liabilities, of fixed investment to total investment, of equity capital expressed by capital stock to debt financing by debentures, notes, or bonds, and the ratio of debt to net worth.

Intangible Standards   Although it is relatively easy to measure performance against tangible standards, intangibles such as relationships, attitudes, beliefs, morale, and the success of certain programs such as advertising, public relations, and executive development are much more difficult to assess. Whereas it is simple to measure the units produced per hour against the standard, it is exceedingly difficult to measure whether the enterprise has reached the standards of good community relations, high employee morale, or complete customer satisfaction, which it set for itself.

Tools that will aid executives in appraising intangible standards and drawing appropriate conclusions are being developed. Psychologists and other behavioral scientists are constantly evaluating new tests and attitude surveys. Although some of these tools will be helpful to management, they are far from exact. Indeed, the further away a characteristic is from the production line or the accounting department, the more difficulty management has in setting up specific standards and measuring performance by them. Nevertheless, management must not overlook the importance of intangible standards in achieving a balanced system of controls.

Strategic Control Points and Standards

The staggering variety of tangible and intangible control standards available makes it necessary for organizations to be selective in their use. One author suggests that at least two important steps should be taken by management before attempts to com-

---

[4] *Ibid.*, p. 93.

pare actual operations with standards. First, "if control is to have effective influence on performance, the administrator should make sure that the goals are properly identified with individual responsibility."[5] Second, since the administrator will find it impossible to review all aspects of performance, he must select certain points that will give him adequate information about what is going on.

It is impractical, in other words, to check the performance of each activity against all the standards that might be applied to it. As operations become more complex or as the area of management authority increases, such minute control becomes increasingly infeasible. Management must concentrate, therefore, on certain strategic control points. In taking this approach, management selects for use only the standards that best reflect its goals and best show whether those goals are being met.

Guides for Selecting Strategic Standards   It would be helpful indeed if management could be given specific suggestions for selecting strategic standards. Although this is not possible, it can adopt certain general guidelines. It should choose standards that are timely, economical, and that permit comprehensive and balanced control.

The need for timeliness is illustrated by manufacturing standards. In many factories, early quality control points have been established to check partially finished output before additional processing costs are incurred. Many department stores set up an "open to buy" limit designed to regulate buying activities before firm commitments to purchase the merchandise are made. Another example of timely controls should be found in the company personnel and hiring policy. In the words of William Newman, "the time to check the hiring of wrong people or the placing of them in the wrong positions is when the initial selection is made, rather than after they have been put on the job."[6]

The second consideration in selecting strategic standards is whether they can be observed economically. This factor has already been discussed under the requirements of an effective control system and does not need further elaboration here.

Third, we have said that the selection of strategic standards should provide comprehensive coverage and promote balanced performance. When selecting strategic control points on which to base strategic standards, management must take into consideration the fact that one point might adversely affect another. Overemphasis on quantity of production, for example, will affect quality. Likewise, if expenses are selected as a strategic control point, the quality of the service or the product may suffer. When looking for a control point which permits comprehensive coverage, management should examine the point where several operations are summarized and consolidated. For example, many heads of small and medium-sized businesses insist on signing all checks themselves. They feel that this act gives them comprehensive control of all activities. Similarly, it is not uncommon for heads of small and medium-sized enterprises to open and read the morning's mail because it enables them to oversee what is happening in all departments. For the same reasons, executives might insist that carbon copies of all outgoing mail be sent to them.

---

[5] William H. Newman, *Administrative Action*, 2d ed. (Englewood Cliffs, N.J.: Prentice-Hall, 1963), p. 421.

[6] *Ibid.*, p. 427.

It is obvious that, out of the great number of strategic control points, executives must select those that are most effective for their particular undertaking. By such selection management can limit the number of standards necessary to achieve a comprehensive and balanced control system which accurately reflects the goals of its specific activities. It should always be remembered that what serves well in one enterprise will not necessarily serve in another.

Checking on Performance

The second of the three activities in the process of control is to check performance. This can only occur after standards have been set. Then work can be observed, output measured, and figures and reports compiled. Checking against standards is a continuous process, which, depending on circumstances, must be performed daily, weekly, or perhaps monthly.

Subsequent Checking or Prior Confirmation

Checking performance is usually carried out by the superior after his subordinate has performed his functions. When the superior delegates authority for these functions to his subordinate, he should make certain that enough controls exist to enable him to take corrective action in case the subordinate's performance does not meet the standard. In the final analysis, the superior never shifts his responsibility for the function. He merely exercises control after the fact.

Occasionally, however, superiors insist on checking work before a subordinate can proceed. Prior confirmation may be required for numerous reasons: The superior may be reluctant to delegate authority because he is unable to state control standards clearly. The superior may not as yet have completed all his planning functions and thus may not be able to set the standards which he expects the subordinate to achieve. This lack of complete planning with its consequent lack of standards might be caused by the development of a new area or by a superior's ignorance of the functions involved in a particular area. In cases of this nature, the superior should have the subordinate check with him before he proceeds, thus requiring prior confirmation instead of subsequent controlling.

In certain other cases, however, prior confirmation is less justified. Some executives, unwilling to delegate authority and clarify standards, also require prior confirmation instead of a subsequent check. This practice delays action, is cumbersome, and denies the subordinate an opportunity for personal development. Such prior checks seem to indicate that the manager lacks confidence in his subordinates; in actuality they may indicate that the manager cannot plan properly.

The Exception Principle

A superior checking the activities of a subordinate will find most of his performance to be adequate. He can pass over satisfactory areas and concentrate on the exceptions, namely, on matters where performance deviates significantly from the standard. This technique, named the exception principle, was first expressed by Frederick Taylor.[7] When applying his principle to the control process, Taylor felt that a manager should give detailed attention to unusual or exceptional items because only they warrant executive attention. A manager might even request a subordinate not to send any reports on activities that are wihin pre-established standards.

In order for the checking process to be successful, a sense of mutual trust and confidence must exist between subordinate and superior. The superior must know that the subordinate will not hesitate to report functional exceptions or deviations, and the subordinate must know that his superior maintains confidence in his over-all performance.

Before ending our discussion of the exception principle, we must make sure that its concepts have not become confused with those of strategic control points. Strategic control points indicate only the points to be watched, whereas the exception principle refers to significant deviations that must be watched regardless of where they occur.

Means of Checking

There are numerous ways for management to check performance. It may require written reports and summaries with or without oral presentation. The reports serve a good purpose and are necessary. However, they cannot substitute for direct observation and personal contact. Although an executive will find that checking on performance by personal observation is time consuming, and although he will find that inspecting operations personally at all the strategic control points is almost impossible, he will find the techniques to be valuable. If the president of a company, for example, wishes information regarding his company's products, its reputation, the effectiveness of its publicity campaigns, there is no better way to obtain such information than to travel with area salesmen even for short periods. Through this process the president will gain a firsthand picture of whether the enterprise is reaching its tangible physical standards — a quality product, for instance — and its intangible standards of reputation, customer goodwill, salesmen's effectiveness.

To cite another example, the chief executive of a large department store makes it his practice to walk through the store at least once every day to observe the myriad activities that would never appear in written reports. By doing this he probably fails to perform other functions in his office, but he feels that only in this way can he know what is going on.

Corrective Action

The third activity in the process of control is taking corrective action. Management does not truly control unless it performs this step whenever it is needed. If no devi-

[7] Frederick W. Taylor, *Shop Management* (New York: Harper and Row, 1919), pp. 126–27.

ations from established standards occur, then of course controlling is fulfilled by the first two control activities. However, if there is a discrepancy or a variation, the controlling function is not completed unless corrective action is taken.

Reasons for Deviations

Management should check into the reasons for variations from standards before prescribing specific corrective measures. For example, a deviation could result from ill-chosen planning premises. It could result from the dependence of production quotas on some other department. For instance, the production quota of a machine shop could be based on the fact that it would receive a certain number of units from the casting department. A check on performance might point out that the deviation in production was caused by an insufficient foundry supply. The corrective action in this instance would be directed toward the casting department.

Deviations might also occur if a subordinate is unqualified or has not been given proper directions and instructions. If the latter is the case, additional training might solve the problem. If this is not sufficient, a replacement must be sought. Before taking such a step, however, the superior should be sure that the subordinate understands what is expected of him.

Taking Appropriate Action

After reviewing the different reasons for deviation, management must decide upon and carry out necessary corrective action. This action might consist of a revision of standards, of replacing certain subordinates, or of a revision of plans.

To visualize the entire control process let us assume that an economic upswing has been forecast and that standards have been set accordingly. If the upswing does not materialize as anticipated, then the standards must be lowered. In this instance, corrective action will also include a revision of plans. At the moment management revises its plans it starts a completely new cycle of all managerial functions. The new plans might necessitate changes in organization, changes in staffing, changes in influencing, and, of necessity, creation of new standards for the control process. These will require checking and reappraisal, that is, a comparison of results with the new standards. If new deviations occur, additional correction will have to be taken. This example clearly shows the continuing circular movement of the controlling function and the management process in general.

Discussion Questions

1. It is becoming popular in management to talk about "planning" and "control" in almost one breath, such as in the phrase "planning and control models." Why is this the case?

2. In the text the statement is made that it is easier for a manager to live with a problem he cannot solve than with a solution he cannot understand. Do you find

this to be the situation with problems you encounter in your college course work? What accounts for the similarities or differences between the problem-solving experiences of a student and those of a manager?

Supplementary Readings

Anthony, Robert N., John Dearden, and Richard F. Vancil. *Management Control Systems.* Homewood, Ill.: Irwin, 1965. See chapter 1 and pp. 645–47.

Emery, James C. *Organizational Planning and Control Systems.* New York: Macmillan, 1969.

Litterer, Joseph A. *Organizations.* New York: Wiley, 1969. See volume 2, part 4.

Livingstone, John Leslie. "Management Controls and Organizational Performance." In *Dimensions in Modern Management,* edited by Patrick E. Connor. Boston: Houghton Mifflin, 1974.

Price, James L. *Organizational Effectiveness.* Homewood, Ill.: Irwin, 1968. See chapter 5.

CHAPTER 29

The Budget: Control Aspects

The budget is probably the most widely used of all available control devices. Indeed, when properly applied, budgetary control is one of management's most effective tools. Budgets express the plans, objectives, and programs of an organization in numerical terms. Therefore, the preparation of the budget is a planning and decision-making function. However, its administration is a controlling function. In this sense, then, budgets are pre-established standards to which operations can be compared and adjusted. Like other control techniques, budgetary standards measure the progress of actual performance against the plan and, in doing so, provide information that enables management to take necessary action to make results conform with the plan.

BUDGETING AND BUDGETARY CONTROL

Budgetary plans generally regulate all phases of an organization's operations for a definite period of future time. Management usually plans an over-all budget for the organization and a number of sub-budgets detailing departmental and divisional plans. For instance, the sales budget states revenue goals, and the expense budget states the expense limitations that cannot be exceeded if a business firm, for example, wants to realize planned income. Other budgets specify the plans for inventory levels, cash requirements, financing, production, purchasing, labor requirements, capital additions, and so forth.

The term "budgetary control" refers to the use of budgets to control day-to-day operations so that they will conform to organizational goals. Budgetary control involves not only constant evaluation of actual results in relation to the established goals but also corrective action when necessary.

Comprehensive and Partial Budgeting

If all phases of the operations of an organization are budgeted and if departmental budgets are consolidated into the over-all budgetary program, then comprehensive budgeting is in use. Although many managers prefer comprehensive budgeting, a number prepare only partial budgets. For example, some prepare only a sales budget to serve as a basis for setting sales quotas and a production budget to cover activities in the production department. Others use budgets extensively for planning but not for control. Unquestionably, such partial budgeting is of greater value than no budgeting at all, but the full benefits of budgeting and budgetary control can only be realized if a comprehensive program covers all organizational aspects and is utilized for both planning and control purposes.

Numerical Expression

Although the numerical terms specified in budgets are frequently monetary, not all budgets are expressed in dollars and cents. Many are expressed in nonfinancial numerical terms. A raw materials budget is expressed in pounds, tons, gallons, or yards of specific materials. Personnel budgets are expressed in terms of the number of workers needed for each type of skill or the number of man-hours necessary to perform a certain activity. Likewise, finished goods budgets are expressed mostly in units of products. If nonfinancial budgets were expressed in monetary terms, they might be too general. A company might appear to have an adequate total inventory if its budget shows only the dollar value of all raw materials together. However, if one or two particularly important items are not in inventory, production will stop. Likewise, a monetary budget would not be detailed enough to show price changes in raw materials, although such changes might greatly influence the outcome of the production plan. Nevertheless, over-all budgeting needs some common denominator, and generally this is dollars and cents. Ultimately, even nonfinancial budgets must be translated into this system so that they can be incorporated and condensed into companywide estimates and over-all budgets.

MAJOR COMPONENTS OF A BUDGETARY PROGRAM

If an organization budgets its entire operations, numerous subsidiary budgets must be prepared before a master budget can be formulated. Although budgeting could begin in almost any area, the management of business firms usually starts by requesting the development of a sales forecast or sales budget by the sales division. Since advertising and the extent and expense of distribution also affect total sales potential, these budgets are prepared in conjunction with the sales budget.

Once the sales budget is prepared and tentatively approved, a large number of other sub-budgets can be generated almost simultaneously. For example, when the sales budget and the policy regarding the finished goods inventory are determined, managers can prepare a production budget enumerating the timing and materials required. Then having established production requirements, managers can develop budgets for direct material requirements, direct labor requirements, and the various manufacturing expenses. At the same time, other departmental managers will be engaged in preparing budgets for administrative expenses, research outlays, capital expenditures, financial expenses, and cash. After all these budgets have been established, they are summarized in the income statement, sometimes called the profit and loss statement or the balance sheet.

Sales Budget

As we noted previously, formulation of the sales budget is usually the initial step in budgeting. To do this, management must predict sales for the coming year by relying on past experience, anticipated market conditions, and all other planning considerations. Let us assume that only one product is manufactured. If no seasonal fluctuations occur, the annual sales budget can be broken down into quarters or monthly periods by simple arithmetic. If, however, a seasonal fluctuation exists and other departments such as production, advertising, and finance must coordinate their efforts with the sales department in order to meet the fluctuating demand, management must calculate separate sales estimates for each of the twelve monthly sales periods. The resulting budget will then show the number of units to be shipped each month. If we assume that each unit is sold at a constant price, then multiplying the number of units by the price will give us the monetary value of shipments for each month.

Finished Goods Budget

Most firms will use their sales budget as a basis for a production budget. The sales budget does not necessarily reflect the production schedule, however, because in most instances an enterprise must carry at least some inventory so that it can fill orders promptly. Thus, a finished goods budget is usually a prerequisite of a production budget. The finished goods budget will indicate the monthly opening inventory and the monthly closing inventory. At certain times of the year, the closing inventory level will be higher than at other times.

Production Budget

The production budget determines the number of units that must be manufactured in order to meet monthly sales requirements and maintain desired inventory levels. Suppose, for example, that a sales budget was based on anticipated shipments of fifty thousand units for the month of January. On January 1, the finished goods budget indicated an opening inventory of ten thousand units and a desired closing inventory of twenty thousand. The production budget for the month would have to be sixty thousand units. By using the finished goods and sales budgets in this fashion, the manufacturing division is able to prepare a production budget that specifies individual monthly figures.

Materials and Materials Purchases Budgets

The materials budget is concerned with the number of units of raw material that a company must have in order to produce the units of goods specified in the production budget. The exact quantity of each raw material required is known to the production department, and this information provides the basis for the materials purchases budget that is transmitted to the purchasing department.

Although the materials budget is stated in terms of physical units, the purchasing department will reduce it to monetary units. This materials budget can then form an element in the computations that must be made for all materials and supplies before a summary purchase budget can be formulated. When formulating its summary budget, the purchasing department must also consider the company policy on excess raw material inventories. In addition, the purchasing department should make certain that the timing of purchases is budgeted to coincide with inventory policy and production schedules.

Personnel Budgets

To achieve complete budgeting, management must also estimate personnel and labor requirements. As an ingredient of this, the manufacturing division must prepare a direct labor budget based on the production budget. This labor budget, normally expressed in terms of standard labor hours, specifies the types of personnel needed — unskilled workers, skilled workers, salesmen. The seasonal fluctuations that appear in the production budget must appear in the personnel budget. If such a budget is given to the personnel department at the beginning of the year, that department will be able to prepare accordingly. Curtailment of production will necessarily be reflected in a curtailed personnel budget, and if the personnel department knows of these happenings in advance, it can carefully prepare layoffs and discharges.

Additional Expense Budgets

An organization incurs many expenses other than those for materials and wages. Included are advertising expenses, distribution expenses, administrative expenses, insurances, taxes, interest, depreciation, utilities, and so forth. There are also selling expenses and supervisory expenses, losses caused by bad debts, and many other items of this nature. Because these expenses are often substantial, they too must be budgeted at least tentatively for the ensuing period.

Capital Expenditure Budget

In contrast to the additional expense budgets, the capital expenditure budget is often projected over a long range such as five or ten years. This budget outlines in specific terms expenditures for things such as plant expansion, machinery, equipment acquisitions, and other permanent capital additions. Only the portion of the long-range capital expenditure budget that will materialize during the current year is taken into consideration in the summary budget. Since capital expenditure budgets result in monetary investments that can be recovered from operations only after a long period has elapsed, they must be planned with the greatest care. Plant and equipment expenditures have far-reaching significance not only for the future of the particular enterprise but also for the national economy. Indeed, the over-all figures of capital expenditure budgets are used as one of the indicators of national economic activity.

Cash Budget

Another important budget is the cash budget, usually prepared by the organization's treasurer. This budget indicates estimated cash receipts, disbursements, and resulting cash fluctuations throughout the year. In preparing the cash budget, the treasurer includes only those items that actually involve cash. He must bear in mind that cash disbursements do not always coincide with expense totals since items such as depreciation and bad debts are recorded as expenses but are not considered to be cash outlays. Conversely, a number of items which are not normally treated as expenses do require cash outlays. When the enterprise invests cash in new machinery, for example, the machinery is not charged directly to expenses but is recorded as an asset. Still, such machinery requires cash outlays. The treasurer also knows that the sale of merchandise on credit increases company assets but cannot increase cash receipts until the merchandise is paid for by the customer.

A properly prepared cash budget will indicate whether there will be enough cash available to meet the company's obligations whenever they become due. In other words, it will show management at the beginning of the year when the enterprise will probably run short of cash. This knowledge enables management to choose in advance whether to secure additional capital or change the various budgets. If the cash budget shows that the need for additional funds is only temporary, the treasurer will probably meet the current deficit by making arrangements to borrow from a bank. The cash budget will indicate in advance how much will be needed and for how long a period. At the same time, the treasurer will make plans for repayment and will determine the size of installments. Arrangements of this nature are particularly important in industries that have strong cyclical fluctuations in sales and consequently in cash receipts. Many companies in such industries depend heavily on seasonal borrowing. These transactions are clearly indicated and projected in their cash budgets.

A cash budget is particularly necessary for a firm that operates on a narrow cash margin. A cash budget is also important to enterprises that have large funds available in excess of the cash needed for current operations. In such situations, the cash budget will show the amount of excess cash and the period during which it will be available. Knowing that such a situation will exist, the treasurer then can invest in short-term bonds or treasury notes, if he wishes, instead of keeping idle cash in the bank.

Budgeted Income Statements

Data from the budgets just discussed can be consolidated into what is called a budgeted income statement. This statement provides management with an estimate of the profit and loss from operations for the budgeted year. Many companies prepare such a statement on a monthly as well as a yearly basis. This, of course, entails additional work, but if the monthly income budget is used as a control device, it can be of great help. Like the annual budgeted income statement, it will show management approximately what can be expected under prevailing conditions during the budgeted period. If the indicated results seem to be satisfactory, management will not need to revise the budgets. If, however, the consolidated income statements indicate poor results, management will probably review all supporting estimates in an effort to change plans and achieve a better outcome.

The Budgeted Balance Sheet

A comprehensive budgetary program usually has a budgeted balance sheet that indicates the effect of the budgeted plans on the assets, liabilities, and net worth of the enterprise. The chief finance officer compiles this balance sheet, basing his figures on the various budgets just discussed. This balance sheet will indicate to management and, if need be, to creditors, the probable financial picture of the company at the end of the budget period. In evaluating a budgeted balance sheet, management should compare it with the final balance sheet that appeared at the beginning of the year. By making such a comparison, management will be able to observe if and how the various items making up the assets and liabilities of the enterprise will shift by the end of the budgeted period.[1]

PREPARATION OF THE BUDGET

Because budgets serve to effectuate all plans, budget preparation engages management in one of its most basic decision-making activities. For budgetary purposes management cannot merely say that production is likely to increase during the second half of the year or that selling expenses should be lower. These planning premises must be quantified and dated. There is considerable difference between making general forecasts and attaching numerical values to plans. The figures that are put into the budget represent actual operating plans; they are no longer merely predictions. They will be generally regarded as the basis for daily operations and as the standards for control. This kind of rigorous budgeting is bound to improve the quality of planning.

A Line Function

Broad Participation in Determination of Budget Estimates

Not only top management but also line managers who will administer and function under the budgets must have a part in their preparation in order to assure the advantage of improved planning that comes from budget-making. People resent arbitrary orders; therefore, management must include all those responsible for executing budgets when determining budget allowances and objectives. In order to bring about such participation, management must direct each manager to submit his own budget. This is known as grass-roots budgeting.

[1] For a thorough discussion of the subject, see Glenn A. Welsch, *Budgeting: Profit-Planning and Control* (Englewood Cliffs, N.J.: Prentice-Hall, 1957); J. Brooks Heckert and James D. Willson, *Business Budgeting and Control*, 2d ed. (New York: Ronald Press, 1955).

Participation does not mean, however, that the entire responsibility for budgeting rests with subordinate managers. Before executives request managers to submit their budget estimates, they must ensure that the managers are supplied with all available information concerning past performance, new developments, and any other facts that would assist them in preparing an intelligent and attainable estimate. Once budget proposals are submitted, sponsoring managers must substantiate them in a free and spontaneous discussion with their superiors. Later, in cooperation with top management, they will set and adjust the final figures.

This is what is meant by broad participation in budget-making. A successful budget program cannot be handed down by a budget director or "budget administrator." Active support and cooperation on the various levels of line management is necessary to achieve a good budget.

Of course, the budget suggestions of subordinates do not always prevail. A superior may feel that they are inadequate or incorrect. Indeed, top management — the group with final budgeting authority — should accept no budget plans without carefully studying and analyzing them. Top management should also resolve any differences regarding budget estimates and should be sure that a definite decision is reached.

Often budgets that have been formulated through the broad participation of all managerial levels tend to be loose. This occurs because some individuals deliberately set their budget estimates at a level that presents no challenge. Obviously their motive is self-protection. Usually a manager who exceeds his sales budget or stays under his allotted expense budget is at least temporarily praised, whereas a manager who has set a stiff budget for himself and does not live up to it is rarely complimented for what he tried to accomplish. Management can check the tendency toward budgetary looseness by making it clear that although it scrutinizes unfavorable variations between actual performance and the budget estimate, it will also scrutinize favorable performance.

Submitting realistic and attainable budget estimates provides one of the criteria on which a manager will be appraised whenever his over-all rating as supervisor and executive takes place. An effective budgetary program indicates the inefficiency as well as the efficiency of individual managers. For this reason, when managers develop such a budgetary program, they may encounter many problems and may run into active or passive opposition. These problems must be solved, and full managerial support must be gained. If all levels of management are drawn into budget preparations, and all are encouraged to give the budget serious thought not only from a narrow departmental view but also from a company-wide vantage point, support will probably be forthcoming.

Ultimate Responsibility

In the final analysis, of course, the ultimate responsibility for the budget program lies with the chief executive. Although he may be assisted by other line officers and by staff specialists, he cannot turn over the authority for budget-making to a staff unit. Although it is reasonable and often necessary to enlist staff help in constructing the budget, budget-making is always a line function. Nonetheless, let us look more carefully at the type of staff help the chief executive may enlist.

Staff or Committee Assistance

Budget Director

In many organizations much of the work connected with the preparation of a budgetary program is performed by the budget director or the controller. Often this individual is associated with the top echelon of management, but he holds a staff position and performs an essential but supporting function. The budget director provides technical assistance and advice to line personnel. He also supervises the process of bringing the budget estimates together in final form after they have been prepared by the operating executives.

Budget Committee

Many enterprises have found it expedient to establish a budget committee. This standing committee is often composed of the president, the vice-presidents, and the budget director. In a manufacturing firm, it may consist of the president, the sales manager, the production manager, the controller, and the treasurer. In some organizations, the budget committee merely advises and in this capacity contributes greatly to top-level coordination. In other organizations, the budget committee adopts a line function and assumes responsibility for the complete budgetary program. Under these conditions, the budget committee considers all departmental estimates and makes any required revisions. No estimate becomes effective without committee approval. Moreover, the budget committee receives reports comparing performance with budgeted figures and, if necessary, makes changes in the budget.

Approval by the Board

Top management, in most cases the president, gives final approval to the budgetary program. However, after his approval and before distribution, the complete budgetary program is usually placed in broad outline before the board of directors. A budget submitted to the board will be accompanied by a statement saying that this is what management intends to accomplish, this is why they wish to do so, and this is the probable outcome. The president points out that the budgetary program is based on certain forecasts regarding the foreseeable future, and that if unforeseen conditions should develop the budget would be resubmitted. The presentation of the budgetary program to the board is somewhat of a formality, but it is desirable that board members understand its major aspects.

FLEXIBILITY OF THE BUDGETARY PROGRAM

It is extremely important for an organization to build flexibility and adaptability into its budgetary program. This will enable it to cope with rapidly changing conditions. It will also permit the organization to revise those parts of the budget that may prove to be incorrect.

There are many devices for building flexibility into a budget. Among those that we shall discuss are the length of the budget period, alternative budgets, variable expense budgets, supplemental monthly budgets, and budget reviews.

Length of the Budget Period

Although the length of the budget period will vary among organizations, most will choose a yearly period. Many firms break down the planned yearly budget into quarters. Some specify months only for the first quarter. Others divide the entire planning period into months at the time of the original budget preparation. The selection of a definite yearly budget period and its constituent sub-periods is commonly referred to as periodic budgeting.

If reasonably accurate budgetary estimates cannot be made for a whole year at a time, an enterprise will use what is called continuous budgeting. In this case, monthly, quarterly, or semi-annual budgets will be prepared. These, then, will be revised each month by dropping the month just ended and adding the following month. This technique ensures a highly accurate budgetary picture, capable of reflecting short-term conditions and events.

It is quite common for organizations that use either periodic or continuous budgeting also to use budgets that extend over long terms such as three, five, ten, or even more years. Long-term budgets of this nature are formulated by top management and the board of directors. They are not direct operating budgets.

Alternative Budgets

Another device for securing flexibility in budgeting is to follow the system of alternative budgets. This system requires that separate budgetary programs be set up for different operating conditions. At the beginning of the budget period, managers prepare three different kinds of budgets: one geared for a high level of operations, another for a medium level, and a third for a low level. All three must be approved. At the beginning of each month or each quarter, managers are told which budget will be in effect. Since such an arrangement is cumbersome and time-consuming, three alternative budgets are not frequently made. Instead, managers commonly prepare only two budgets: one for a high level and another for a low level of activity. From these, management can estimate mathematically or graphically what the various budget items should be under each alternative. Of course, management must wait until operations for the particular budgeted period are completed in order to know the level of activity. Only then can it see how the various items compare to the amounts budgeted. Although it is relatively easy to determine budgetary standards for different levels of activity, it is impossible to obtain an estimate of how well the organization is doing until the budget period is over. Moreover, this system of alternative budgets is suited only to an enterprise that produces a single product or performs a single service. This device also assumes that costs will vary directly with volume at a constant rate, which is not always the case.

Variable Expense Budgets

Similar to the system of alternative budget is that of the variable expense or flexible budget. Whatever its name, this budget is concerned only with expenses. "It is completely separate and apart from the planning budget but can be used to complement the planning budget."[2] Under a variable budget, expenses are also estimated and allowances computed for different levels of activity. After the budget period is over and the level of actual activity known, management can determine what the proper amount of expenses should have been. For example, the variable budget may indicate an allowance of a thousand dollars per month for supplies plus ten dollars per one hundred direct labor hours worked. Budget allowances for supplies can easily be computed for the various volumes of activity by adding to the one thousand dollar base the multiple of ten dollars per hundred direct labor hours. This provides an expense standard adjusted to the rate of activity, a particularly useful device for the control of expenses.

Variable expense budgets, however, do not set a level of operations until after the activity has been performed. They are therefore of little value to the over-all budgetary program. It is not possible for the purchasing agent, for instance, to wait to determine his materials purchase budget until after the month is over. Variable expense budgets do, however, help to explain overexpenditures and unfavorable variances. Nonetheless, they are a supplement to, not a substitute for, a comprehensive budgetary program.

Supplemental Monthly Budget Plan

Flexibility can also be achieved through the use of a supplemental monthly budget plan. Under it, a basic minimum budget for the company's operations is set up. Then, a supplementary budget is prepared each month, "designed primarily for management use in pushing sales volume and controlling costs and expenses."[3] This additional budget, prepared about ten days before the beginning of the month covered, gives management funds above those already specified in the basic budget, in accordance with expectations.

[2] Welsch, *Budgeting: Profit-Planning and Control*, p. 38.
[3] J. Brooks Heckert, *Business Budgeting and Control* (New York: Ronald Press, 1946), p. 77. The second edition of this book, co-authored by James D. Willson, does not make special mention of the supplemental monthly budget plan.

Budget Review or Budget Revision

Since management usually realizes that flexibility in budget application increases the chances of achieving or even bettering goals, they often assure flexibility by regular budget revisions. At periodic intervals of one, two, or perhaps three months, they review the established budget and change it if necessary. At these times, they compare actual performance with the budget. If operating conditions have been appreciably altered or if the comparison indicates that the budget cannot be followed in the future, they will have to revise the budgetary program.

In comparing actual results to budgeted data, however, management must look for the cause of variation in order to be able to make the appropriate corrections and adjustments in future plans. According to J. H. Hennessy, Jr., "Variance analysis, whether it be for budgetary purposes or for day-to-day operating control, is the procedure employed in deciding when and where a predetermined level of performance is not being met and, to varying degrees, in exposing fundamental causes."[4]

An unfavorable variance by itself is not sufficient reason for changing the budget. It is a symptom and indicates the need for further investigation and explanation. A failure to reach standards, for example, could result from the supervisor's inability to keep products moving through his department. In such circumstances, budget revision would probably be unnecessary. On the other hand, a thorough analysis may indicate that sales revenue has declined because of the reduction in selling prices brought about by an industry price war. This external condition may necessitate internal budgetary changes. Similarly, management may find that an inventory loss has resulted from a drop in raw material prices. A budget revision may also be in order to accommodate changes caused by the competitive situation. The proper action, however, cannot be taken unless management makes a thorough analysis to discover the causes for the variations from the budgeted amounts.

When this analysis indicates a definite need for revision, management must decide whether significant or only minor changes are required for the remainder of the period. A significant revision may involve considerable work, but it is a worthwhile effort. In contrast, management may allow minor effects to "show up on the budget reports as *explainable* variations rather than to go to the trouble of revising the budget."[5]

Regular budgetary review and revision seem to provide the best means for assuring the necessary flexibility within a budgetary program. They enable the budget to be a living, growing document rather than a strait jacket. At the time of revision, management can usually make quite accurate predictions of the new operating conditions. Therefore, the adjusted budget will remain a good standard of performance for management's control purposes.

[4] J. H. Hennessy, Jr., "Looking Around," *Harvard Business Review* 38, no. 3 (May–June 1960): 40–42.

[5] Welsch, *Budgeting: Profit-Planning and Control*, p. 256.

THE RELATIONSHIP OF BUDGETING TO OTHER MANAGERIAL ACTIVITIES

Budgets and Control

Budgets, as we just noted, permit comprehensive control — the continuous effort that enables management to know if their pre-established objectives are being met. Control, in other words, means measurement, and the yardstick for measurement is provided by the budgetary program. Budgeting does not in itself control; management controls using the budget as an effective device. Knowledge of the budget enables a manager to compare and measure actual performance against plans.

In setting up budgets for control purposes, management should follow the existing organizational structure and accounting systems. As we shall soon see, this organization structure will indicate budget responsibility. The accounting system, on the other hand, will provide the categories that must be included somewhere in the over-all budgetary program. Let us consider the relationship between budgeting and accounting first.

Budgets and Accounting

In order to ensure the success of the budgetary program, management must arrange for good, common-sense accounting. Because reliable historical data form the basis of many budgetary estimates, accounting records are heavily depended upon. These records, however, cannot substitute for actual budgeting. Traditionally, by analyzing accounting data, executives can compare current results with those of some past period. However, such a comparison is often defective. Conditions or prices may have changed, new products may have been added, productivity may have increased, or possibly the previous period's performance may have been unsatisfactory. Thus, a meaningful analysis of present performance can only be provided by the goals set out in the budget. However, since accountants' reports of actual operations, costs, revenues, and other financial amounts must be compared with budgeted amounts, budget and accounting categories must be identical. Comparisons would be meaningless if the classifications did not coincide.

The accounts must also accurately reflect the areas of managerial responsibility. Extreme care should be taken to make certain that no supervisor has any item in his budget over which he has no control. Moreover, close budgetary supervision requires that if several department heads are responsible for semifinished inventory, separate inventory accounts must be kept for each department.

Budgets and Organization

Logically, the quality of the budget will be influenced by the precision of the organization structure. In other words, if budgets are to be effective, they must be prepared for each unit of the administrative organization and the managers of each unit must have clear authority to execute them. Thus the person responsible for each department and for any performance that does not meet the budget must be clearly designated. As we implied in the previous section, confusion over authority and responsibility will also make it difficult for managers to secure the data necessary for constructing the budget in the first place.

Budgets as an Aid for Coordination

Budgets also aid in achieving coordination. The existence and availability of the various budgets promote balanced activities among the departments. For example, sales and production departments must coordinate closely so that sales does not plan to sell more than production can produce. Since the production budget tells precisely how much can be expected and when, the sales manager can adjust the activities in his department accordingly. This kind of specific information is more meaningful to sales management than a general prediction that production will be increased.

Moreover, the utilization of a budgetary program is bound to improve coordination and maintain a proper balance not only between production and sales, but also among many other areas. Because work is usually interdependent, department managers, for example, will often seek information from one another while in the process of preparing the budget. This open communication and interchange of information will greatly aid in the coordination of the various plans and budgets, and will often reveal imbalance. Budgeting, therefore, can illuminate possible inconsistencies at an early stage, while they can still be easily adjusted. Moreover, because budgetary plans must take into consideration the objectives and problems of each department and of the enterprise as a whole, they facilitate over-all planning coordination as well.

The relationship of the budget to the task of coordination and, by implication, to the organizing function cannot be emphasized too strongly. This is one of the reasons why the Department of Defense undertook its celebrated "Planning-Programming-Budgeting System" (PPBS). PPBS was instituted in recognition of the fact that "integrated combinations of men, equipment, and installations whose effectiveness could be related to our national security objectives" must be treated as program elements and regrouped in meaningful units of activity.[6]

The problem with conventional budgeting is that it tends to segment the organization into labor budgets, material budgets, and so on. Such budgets are inappropriate to matrix-type organizations. These organizations are forcing management to think in terms of coordinated program budgets. This is an important contemporary development that has wide impact on many functions, especially planning, organizing, and controlling.

---

[6] Charles J. Hitch, *Decision-making for Defense* (Berkeley and Los Angeles: University of California Press, 1965), p. 32.

Budgets and Human Problems

Budgets necessarily represent restrictions, and for that reason people often dislike them. In fact, people often approach budgets defensively, an approach they have acquired through painful experience. Many times budgets appear only as barriers to spending or as an excuse for not granting raises. In the minds of many employees, therefore, the term "budget" is often associated with penurious behavior rather than with planning and direction.

This one-sided impression must be corrected. Managers need to point out that budgeting is a trained, disciplined approach to all problems, necessary for maintaining a standard of performance. The budget should be presented as *both* a planning and a control device. A budget "may be symbolized by two wooden sticks — one neatly divided into thirty-six one-inch spaces, and the other sharply pointed at one end."[7] The planning concept of budgets is expressed by the yardstick, the control concept by the pointed stick. Every manager should know that the yardstick concept often will bring forth the voluntary effort, whereas the pointed stick concept will bring about reluctance and minimum performance. A study conducted by Chris Argyris concerning human relations problems and budgets led to the tentative conclusion that when budgets are used as a pressure device "they tend to generate forces which in the long run decrease efficiency." This study concluded that budget pressure seems to unite the employees against management, to place the supervisor under tension and cause him to see only the needs of his own department. Ultimately the budget, in and of itself a neutral thing, often gets blamed for many problems.[8]

Most of these problems naturally arise at the point of budgetary control. It is there that deviations are discovered and that employees are censored for exceeding budgets. Deviations from the budget necessitate explanation, instruction, and decisions. Such discussions presuppose that a satisfactory working relationship exists between the subordinate and his immediate superior. Of course, managers should be certain that enough flexibility is built into the budget system to permit the common-sense deviations which serve the best interests of the enterprise.

In the final analysis, the effective utilization of budgetary procedures will depend on management's attitudes toward the budget system. On the one hand, management can consider the budget as a part of over-all planning, ensuring that action will be by design rather than expediency and that a guide for spending will be available. On the other hand, management may view the budget as a control device to secure greater efforts. Management must carefully scrutinze its own motives and attempt to balance its position between these two factors.

[7] James L. Peirce, "The Budget Comes of Age," *Harvard Business Review* 32, no. 3 (May–June 1954): 59.

[8] Chris Argyris, "Human Problems with Budgets," *Harvard Business Review* 31, no. 1 (January–February 1953): 97.

Discussion Questions

1. What similarities and differences do you see in your personal budgeting and in the managerial control technique of budgeting?

2. Do you think budgeting would be easier during periods of forecast organization growth, stability, or contraction?

Supplementary Readings

Argyris, Chris. "Human Problems with Budgets." *Harvard Business Review* 31, no. 1 (January–February 1953).

Business Week. "Direct Costing to the Rescue." In *Dimensions in Modern Management,* edited by Patrick E. Connor. Boston: Houghton Mifflin, 1974.

Dudick, Thomas S. *Profile for Profitability.* New York: Wiley, 1972.

Hanson, Ernest I. "The Budgetary Control Function." In *Dimensions in Modern Management.*

Lewis, Robert W. "An Industry View of Budgeting." In *Management Control Systems,* edited by Robert N. Anthony, John Dearden, and Richard F. Vancil. Homewood, Ill.: Irwin, 1965. See pp. 71–81.

CHAPTER 30

Techniques to Control
Over-all Performance

$\mathbf{I}$n addition to the budget, management has a number of other control devices at its disposal. Some of these are used along with the budget; others are completely separate. In the first category are the statistical data available for control purposes. These data can be presented either in tabular form or in the form of charts. Whereas certain managers are adept at interpreting and understanding tables of figures, most seem to find it easier to work with data presented in chart form. Thus, a number of organizations use a chart system as a control tool.

Other control tools management may use are the internal audit, the control unit, and break-even point analysis. Also, both PERT and CPM are control techniques as well as planning devices. Finally management has control techniques to monitor the over-all financial performance of the organization.

THE CHART SYSTEM

The Du Pont Company is probably the most frequently cited enterprise that has relied heavily on a chart system to supply management with control information about each of its diverse operations. The company recently modified its procedures somewhat. Instead of standard chart formats, members of the industrial departments may use whatever charts they think will be most helpful. In spite of this change, the general principles discussed here remain applicable.

The charts in the original system did not replace the financial statements usually used by management; they supplemented them. They permitted each department to periodically measure actual performance against past and forecasted performance. They also facilitated company-wide comparisons. Managers prepared more than four hundred charts, each showing the results of departmental operations for the current and previous year against a background of comparable data for the ten preceding years and against a forecast for the next twelve months.

Advantages

The corporation chose this chart system because it had special merits. First, charts can be presented without narrative. This prevents the individual who reviews the figures from bogging down "under the weight of particular words or phrases that might be chosen to explain a given development."[1] However, the chart supervisor is present to answer questions. This type of quantitative presentation makes it "comparatively easy to hold the attention of an entire group to one item at the same moment."[2] Another advantage of the chart system is that all figures can be presented on a uniform basis thereby offering a common measurement of performance for all investment lines. If, because of changing conditions, a new approach is needed, then all the data for the current year and the ten preceding years can be reset on the new basis. In this way, the charts can be kept comparable.

Each month an executive committee met to go over charts, reviewing the performance of two or three departments at each monthly meeting. By doing this, they could examine each of the twelve industrial departments of Du Pont every third month. The general manager whose department was being discussed was on hand to explain the performance and answer any questions the committee raised.

The physical arrangement in the chart room where the executive committee met enabled a graphic presentation and a related tabulation of data to be presented side by side. The charts and tables, therefore, spoke for themselves and required little explanation when reviewed. They focused attention on the underlying factors that cause satisfactory or unsatisfactory performance and spotlighted the areas requiring further analysis and action. This arrangement permitted the members of the executive committee to fix their discussion with each general manager directly on the trouble spots. In addition to the departmental charts, a "Summary Du Pont" set of charts summarized the operations of all twelve industrial departments. This was reviewed each month. Taken as a whole, the system provided an effective control tool to members of the executive committee. Let us look at its control implications briefly.

Control Implications

The Du Pont Company bases its control of over-all performance on the ratio of earnings to the investment of capital. The return on gross investment is the ultimate measure of success for each department's operations. The factors affecting return on investment are broken down through a succession of detailed charts in order to pinpoint the cause and effect relationships between working capital, permanent investment, sales, and costs. All these charts are powerful control tools; management can trace any indication of poor performance to its source and can focus its attention on that point where the operation is out of line with expectations. The charts also indicate those operations which provide a less than satisfactory return on investment in comparison with other operations. Later in this chapter, the substance of the chart system and its connection with control of return on investment will be discussed in more detail.

---

[1] *Executive Committee Control Charts,* AMA Management Bulletin No. 6 (New York: American Management Association, 1960), p. 15.

[2] *Ibid.*

INTERNAL AUDITING CONTROL

Another control tool available to management is internal auditing. Modern internal auditing performed by a staff of specialists began to flourish as organizations, rapidly expanding during World War II, found an increased need for close accounting supervision. Since then, modern internal auditing has become one of the most important ways to establish and maintain management control. However, since it was born of accounting, many executives limit internal auditing activities to verification of accounting transactions. Nevertheless, authorities in the field of accounting view internal auditing as a management control function.[3]

Meaning and Scope

The Institute of Internal Auditors defines the internal audit as an independent appraisal within an organization that can serve as a basis for protective and constructive help and service to management. This type of control functions by measuring and evaluating the effectiveness of other types of control. Internal auditing is concerned primarily with accounting and financial matters but it may also deal with matters of an operating nature. Lamperti and Thurston in their thorough analysis of internal auditing conclude that it is associated closely but objectively with every activity and transaction which contributes to the profit of enterprise operations. "It issues no orders, originates no transactions, but is everywhere as a searching, appraising, and open evaluating function, with the object of helping those who do issue orders or originate transactions."[4]

In more specific terms, internal auditing is concerned with finding out whether management's policies are as effective as management intends them to be and whether the members of the organization are carrying out such policies with thoroughness. In this way, internal auditing ascertains the adequacy of the procedures in force and if necessary facilitates finding improved procedures. It also checks whether records are properly prepared and maintained. In brief, "internal auditing is the inspection unit of the system, constantly on the alert for any weakness or breakdown of controls."[5]

Position Within the Organization

Obviously, it is difficult to discuss the functions of internal auditing control in specific terms since they vary considerably with the size and type of each organization. However, in most established auditing systems a basic pattern of continuous measuring and evaluating of all other controls exists. Most auditing systems also require an internal auditor who must be independent of all departments in which

---

[3] Frank A. Lamperti and John B. Thurston, *Internal Auditing for Management* (Englewood Cliffs, N.J.: Prentice-Hall, 1953), p. 86.

[4] *Ibid.*

[5] *Ibid.*, p. 90.

he performs audits. In other words, he should not be attached to the controller's or the treasurer's office, but should report either to the chief finance officer or even to the head of the control unit. (The control unit concept is discussed immediately below.) It is also conceivable that, in some cases, the internal auditor may report directly to the president. Internal auditing is usually considered to be a staff function. Therefore, internal auditors cannot take line personnel to task for some of the shortcomings which they might discover. Instead, the internal auditing staff must report the situation to the responsible operating management, generally to top management. They then decide whether to pursue the auditor's suggestions.

THE CONTROL UNIT

A recent development that has aided in effective control of over-all performance is the centralized control unit, sometimes called the management control department, the management service department, the control department, or the control section. This unit is a significant top management tool and represents an important step in the evolution of managerial control. Generally, a control unit is a fact-finding and recommendations section with no administrative or operating responsibility. Normally, the over-all control unit reports to the president, but such units can be utilized in lower levels of organization if the department they supervise is large enough to require internal control activity. In defining the control unit, Lamperti and Thurston state that

it is simply the gathering of all these [control] activities into one coordinated unit under the supervision of a top executive. This places new emphasis on these functions, acknowledges their importance, and usually results in substantial economies in the cost of effecting proper control of the business. Duplication of effort, work at cross purposes, overemphasis on the importance of one function at the expense of another are eliminated. Erroneous interpretations or lack of unity of purpose, which can happen unintentionally when two people examine the same situation independently, are eliminated. The whole flow and channeling of control data from source to directive action is coordinated under uniform guidance and without extraneous motion.[6]

Need

It is difficult to define the circumstances that make a centralized control unit worthwhile. Obviously, it is not needed in a small, compact enterprise where most of the control functions can easily be performed by the chief executive and his staff. The need for a centralized control unit is more apparent in a large organization. However, what is large? Some people regard an organization with a thousand employees as

[6] *Ibid.*, p. 95.

large, whereas others might not consider any firm that employs less than ten thousand as large.

In addition to size, the dispersion of operations may indicate the need for a centralized control unit. The more dispersed the operations of the company are, the greater is the need. Complexity also bears significantly on the decision to establish such a unit. The Koppers Company, referred to later in this chapter, is an excellent example of a highly diversified company producing a wide variety of products and services for the use of other industries. The complexity of its operations makes a centralized control unit mandatory.

Purpose

Clearly no hard and fast formula determines whether a control unit is applicable to a particular organization. By the same token, if such a unit is established, its functions and duties must be tailor-made for the enterprise in which it will function. Nonetheless, we can say that the purpose of a control unit in almost all enterprises is to facilitate orderly, efficient administration and planning by supplying a continuous flow of facts to top management.

More specifically, the purpose of the control unit is to assist the president in discharging certain phases of his duties by providing the centralized information necessary to control. It is conceivable that similar control units will exist in each major division to assist the divisional managers in discharging their control responsibilities. In a large organization where top management is distant from the supervisory level and problems of coordination are more involved and time consuming, the central control unit can help top management to be well informed about operations at all levels.

Position Within the Organization Structure

The centralized control unit is a staff department usually associated with the top echelon reporting to the president. This situation conforms with sound organizational principles. Wherever a staff department must serve two or more divisions impartially and equally, it should report to a level of management above these divisions. Although management may be tempted to merge the functions of the control unit with those of the controller, to do so would be unwise. The head of the control unit should be a different executive from the controller. Even if the title "controller" is not already used in the enterprise, it is inadvisable to give this title to the head of the control unit. Traditionally, the controller is the chief accounting executive of most enterprises, and it is not generally appropriate to expand his function to include the areas of planning, policy control, and so forth. The centralized control unit is concerned with much broader functions than those of the traditional accounting activities.

range. Outside this range, the pattern could change. The relevant range may be thought of as the variation in volume which is reasonably anticipated for the company. "What the analysis purports to show is what fixed costs should be and how variable costs should act within the relevant volume range as determined by existing managerial policies."[10] As long as performance remains within this range, operations can be assumed to be relatively stable and therefore predictable on a straight-line basis.

As we have seen, the general terminology used in break-even analysis is that some costs are "fixed" while others are "variable." Fixed costs or stand-by costs are so named because they do not vary as volume changes. They are those costs that "because of organization structure, style of operation, capital availability, methods of selling, size of productive capacity, and stored-up knowledge of key individuals, cannot be added or dropped at will through wide ranges of activity rate fluctuation."[11] Normally, fixed costs include depreciation, property insurance costs, property taxes, minimum fee service contracts, costs of administrative officers, costs of keeping sales offices, and so forth.

Those costs which do vary with volume changes are, of course, the variable costs. Direct labor costs, direct material costs, and commission rates on sales are examples of variable costs. Many consider variable costs to be the costs of *doing* business; stand-by costs to be the costs of being *in* business.

These two broad groupings often shade into each other. As evidence, management often attempts to classify some costs as semi-variable. In other words, within each account classification the costs are neither always completely variable nor always completely fixed. For instance, it could normally be assumed that inspection costs would vary closely with the rate of productivity. However, regardless of productivity the enterprise must maintain a reservoir of supervisory inspection ability. The reservoir is necessary even if production should be at a complete standstill. To this extent, then, inspection costs would be a fixed cost. Similarly, because of differences in organizations, corporate structure, or industry type, certain other costs that are considered fixed in some enterprises are variable in others.

Control Implications

In general, the break-even chart and the break-even point reflect the efficiency and quality of the management of an enterprise. If operations are under close control, the chances are that the actual break-even point will not fall very far from the planned break-even point. If, however, no effective control exists, the break-even point could shift extensively. This may be caused by a lag in control action, the law of diminishing returns, shifts from high to low margin lines, growth of the company,

[10] Glenn A. Welsch, *Budgeting: Profit-Planning and Control* (Englewood Cliffs, N.J.: Prentice-Hall, 1957), p. 265.

[11] Fred V. Gardner, *Profit Management and Control* (New York: McGraw-Hill, 1955), pp. 28–29.

loose management thinking, and many other reasons. "In itself, a break-even point moves only with changing conditions and, in moving, flashes a warning. To ensure follow-through from this warning requires a detailed control."[12]

Of course, an almost unlimited number of areas within an organization are subject to managerial controls. Each of these areas is concerned with one of the many functions or activities of the company. Controls are needed, as we have seen, in the broad areas of production, sales, personnel, costs, and so on. Control over policies, organization, and procedures is also necessary. More specifically, management must control operations, the product line, pricing, rate of output, quality of the product, research and development, wages, salaries, quality of personnel, and industrial relations. Likewise, it is imperative that management control capital expenditures. Many of these areas are included in the control of general financial performance.

GENERAL CONTROLS OF A FINANCIAL NATURE

By and large, most general controls are of a financial nature. Unless the enterprise shows a profit or a good return on investment it cannot stay in business. For this reason, financial control of over-all performance seems to be the most effective control type.

Profit and Loss Control

The profit and loss statement is probably the most widely used means of controlling general performance. This statement shows all the revenue, expenses, and income for a given period and, as such, is an excellent control tool for the operations of the enterprise. It serves to hold each operating department, plant, or unit rigidly accountable on a profit and loss basis.

In some organizations "both budgetary control and profit-and-loss control are used. These systems actually complement each other and, taken together, make a very effective plan of control. The budgetary control then becomes the forecast or objective, and the profit-and-loss statements are compared with the estimates to determine actual accomplishments."[13] In other words, using the budgeted income statement as a standard, management can make a valid comparison between it and the profit and loss statement. Profit and loss control will also become more meaningful if management has comparative income statements showing financial results for a number of consecutive years. By highlighting the increases or decreases occurring from year to year, these statements help management to do a better job of controlling.

Profit and loss control is effective not only in appraising the performance of the entire enterprise but also in appraising fully integrated parts of it such as regional

---

[12] *Ibid.,* p. 124.

[13] For a detailed analysis see Paul E. Holden, Lounsbury S. Fish, and Hubert L. Smith, *Top-Management Organization and Control* (New York: McGraw-Hill, 1951), p. 209.

divisions, subsidiaries, or product divisions. This type of control, of course, calls for a profit and loss statement for each such division or subsidiary. Obviously, these statements necessitate considerable accounting work which in itself is expensive and cumbersome. However, this is the only way that the contribution of each division to the income of the entire enterprise can be ascertained. Divisional profit and loss control requires that the manager of each division have ample opportunity to run his division as he deems best. Naturally, he does not have authority to determine over-all corporate expenses such as those for research and administrative overhead. These will be prorated for each division.

The accuracy of a divisional profit and loss statement increases with the integration of the particular division. If the enterprise is departmentalized by products or if its organization follows territorial divisions, control through divisional profit and loss becomes more meaningful because each of these organizational units is responsible for its own production and marketing operations. In such a situation, the profit and loss statement will truly represent management's effectiveness.

Enterprises with purely functional organizational structures cannot easily use divisional or departmental profit and loss control because they cannot determine the "income" of the various departments. For instance, the cutting department will "sell" its product and service to the assembly department which, in turn, "sells" its product to the sales department. One of the obvious shortcominges of such a functional arrangement is the number of accounting records which have to be kept and duplicated. Problems of allocation of burden and general overhead costs will also cause many misunderstandings, as will the price at which transfers should be made. If a transfer to the sales department is recorded at the cost price, the assembly department will show no profit. However, if the assembly department charges a profit, the department manager would be behaving monopolistically, since he knows that the sales department is compelled to buy his product. Furthermore, although staff and service departments could conceivably "sell" their services, profit and loss control is not really appropriate to their intangible output. Therefore, staff and service departments are usually controlled through a straight expense budget.

Although numerous problems would occur if profit and loss control were applied to certain departments and divisions, it is still one of the most effective tools for controlling the general performance of an enterprise. It requires little effort to compare the profit and loss statements for a number of consecutive years to gauge over-all past performance, and it is likewise easy to compare the current profit and loss statement to a tentative, budgeted statement to see how operations are progressing in comparison to the established future goal.

Control Through Return on Investment

When management controls performance through return on investment, it must consider profit not as an absolute figure but as a return on the capital invested in the business. Management's goal is still to maximize profits, but only if they will maximize the return on investment.

Figure 30-2. Relationship of Factors Affecting Return on Investment

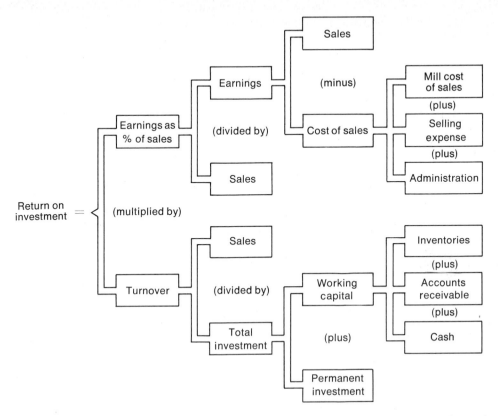

Source: *Executive Committee Control Charts,* AMA Management Bulletin No. 6 (New York: American Management Association, 1960), p. 4.

The Du Pont Example

Although a number of companies have been employing this yardstick since the end of World War II, the Du Pont Company has used it since 1919.[14] Figure 30-2 illustrates what Du Pont considers to be the relationships among the various factors that affect return on investment. By multiplying the turnover by the earnings as a percentage of sales, the return on investment figure is reached. Tying turnover to earnings as a percentage of sales in this way means that management clearly acknowledges that one division with a high profit rate but a low capital turnover may not be as profitable as another division which shows a high capital turnover but a low ratio of earnings to sales. Earnings as a percentage of sales reflect management's success or failure in maintaining satisfactory control of costs. Turnover shows how

---

[14] The discussion of Du Pont's return on investment control is based on information in *Executive Committee Control Charts,* AMA Management Bulletin No. 6 (New York: American Management Association, 1960).

rapidly the capital committed to the operation is being utilized. Turnover itself is computed by dividing sales by total investment. In this case, total investment is considered to be working capital and permanent investment. Working capital, in turn, consists of inventories, accounts receivable, and cash.

In total, then, Figure 30-2 shows that executives, by properly managing an operating investment, can potentially improve the return by reducing costs or working existing investment harder. Return on investment and earnings as a percentage of sales are calculated both before and after income taxes. The purpose of this is to analyze the kind of job being done by the industrial departments and to keep operating management aware of the impact of income taxes on profits.

Figure 30-2 also indicates the return on investment technique used by Du Pont. As mentioned previously, their executive committee was supplied with a series of charts that illustrated each item appearing in Figure 30-2. It is interesting to see how much information the figure provides. For instance, it indicates that decreased turnover might result from increased inventory as well as from lower sales. Tracing the root causes of this development, managers would find that if the permanent investment remained constant, an increase of total investment must be the result of additional working capital in the system. Then, checking the working capital charts, they might spot the trouble in inventories. Finished product inventories might be out of control, for example. The reason for these higher inventories could in turn be traced to greater production, which was planned to take care of sales which had been forecast but did not materialize. Hence, the cycle of events can be summarized: Excess production built up the finished product inventories, which increased working capital and investment. Together with lower sales, rising investment resulted in an appreciably lower turnover of capital. At the same time, however, the higher production led to lower mill cost for goods sold as a percentage of sales. This can be traced through lower costs of sales, higher earnings, and better earnings per sales dollar, showing an improving net return on investment.

Now the real value of the chart system comes into focus. It indicates that although net return is up, all is not right; probably an inventory problem exists. Through use of various charts, management may discover this problem before it throws operating results into a tailspin and while corrective steps can still be taken. To correct the problem, management will have to curtail production in order to work off the finished product inventory. This will, in turn, lead to an increase in unit mill cost and a drop in earnings as a percentage of sales. Simultaneously, sales will drain off the excess inventory thereby increasing turnover. Thus, operations will return to a more normal level.

In calculating return on investment Du Pont does not take into consideration any reductions for current or other liabilities or any reserves for depreciation. The company is aware that many different views of how return on investment should be computed exist. For its purposes, Du Pont holds that the "capital, liability and reserve positions of an enterprise are largely a reflection of the philosophy of top management as to how the business should be financed."[15] Its reasons for basing its

[15] Ibid., p. 22.

calculations of return on investment upon *gross* operating investment and earnings net of depreciation are stated as follows:

Since plant facilities are maintained in virtually top productive order during their working life, the depreciation reserve being considered primarily to provide for obsolescence, it would be inappropriate to consider that operating management was responsible for earning a return on only the net operating investment. Furthermore, if depreciable assets were stated at net depreciated values, earnings in each succeeding period would be related to an ever-decreasing investment; even with stable earnings, Return on Investment would continually rise, so that comparative Return on Investment ratios would fail to reveal the extent or trend of management performance. Relating earnings to investment that is stable and uniformly compiled provides a sound basis for comparing the "profitability of assets employed" as between years and between investments.[16]

This return on investment device for controlling over-all performance is applied to the managers of the various Du Pont divisions. Top management has found it to provide a fair yardstick for measuring the effectiveness of individual operations. Many other firms have since adopted a similar concept.

Other Examples

The Monsanto Chemical Company's return on investments technique, for example, also uses the gross value of fixed assets without deducting the reserve for depreciation. "Actually, the fixed assets are used to produce net income during their entire life, and therefore the full cost value is considered a part of investment until they are retired from use."[17] The company, however, deducts current liabilities from assets in order to arrive at the investment figures.

The H. J. Heinz Company, in its computations for return on invested capital control, shows fixed assets at net depreciated values. The company states that the depreciation reserve represents that part of the initial investment which has been recovered through write-offs and has been reinvested in other fixed assets or has been used as working capital. "Eliminating depreciation from the base gives a realistic investment figure which our operating people can accept without raising the question of duplication of asset values. At the same time, this treatment places a relatively greater demand for earnings on the new, modern installations than on the old, worn, and partially obsolete ones."[18] This enterprise carries control even further; it has established a return on investment control by product lines.

[16] *Ibid.*

[17] Earl J. Wipfler, *Return on Investment: A Program of Financial Planning and Controls, The Monsanto Chemical Company,* Financial Management Series No. 103 (New York: American Management Association, 1953), p. 7.

[18] T. G. Mackensen, *Return on Invested Capital: How H. J. Heinz Manages Its Financial Planning and Controls,* Financial Management Series No. 106 (New York: American Management Association, 1953), p. 42.

Appraisal of Return on Investment Control

There are many advantages to using return on investment as a control device. It is particularly effective in large companies since it gives management a basis for measuring if invested capital is being efficiently employed. Such a yardstick focuses management's attention on the central objective of the enterprise: the best utilization of the investment. It provides top management with a fair measure for comparing the activities of the division managers. Through this device these managers, in turn, develop a broad corporate outlook. Before requesting additional large capital investments for his division, a manager will stop to consider the impact of this on the enterprise as a whole and on the showing of his division. The system also permits the manager to detect speedily the source of any difficulty that is unfavorably affecting the return on his investment. The Du Pont Company example illustrates how management can trace the source of weaknesses which are harmful to over-all performance.

Although these advantages are of great importance, particularly for larger firms, return on investment control also has certain disadvantages. How are certain general overhead expenses to be allocated? How should expenses be apportioned among divisions and departments? If some assets are used jointly how should they be allocated to the different divisions? Also, should assets be charged at original cost, depreciated value, or replacement value? This problem is especially important in periods of inflation.

We should also note that management's emphasis on return on investment often produces too much consideration of financial factors. As a result, the divisional manager might conveniently overlook technical development, the development of junior executives, the morale of the employees, public relations, and many other factors which do not contribute directly or financially (at least for the time being) to return on investment. In addition, management must determine what constitutes a reasonable return on investment. It is difficult to establish an optimum return for a particular enterprise. As a matter of fact, comparisons within the industry might not even be valid, because each firm has its own idiosyncrasies and policies. Nevertheless, many large enterprises are using return on investment to control performance and are achieving good results.

External Auditing Control

In almost all enterprises, outside accountants are engaged to perform an audit of the financial transactions and accounts of the business at least once each year. This audit is an examination, performed either by public, certified public, or chartered accountants, that serves as a basis for "an expression of opinion regarding the fairness, consistency and conformity with accepted accounting principles, of statements prepared by a corporation."[19] It is important to stress that the external audit does not

---

[19] Lamperti and Thurston, *Internal Auditing for Management*, p. 129.

establish the factual accuracy of the statements audited; it is merely "an expression of opinion." Although all members of a corporation are supposed to prepare their statements in anticipation of the audit, this is generally thought of as the accountant's job and he does most of the work involved.

The usual form of audit used by outside accountants is a balance-sheet audit, which includes detailed verification of all important balance-sheet accounts and test checks of profit and loss accounts with particular emphasis on those that are closely related to balance-sheet items, such as fixed assets and depreciation. In a balance-sheet audit, all major asset, liability, capital, and reserve accounts are verified. The certified public accountant has the responsibility to determine the extent of verification. He makes no appraisal of the value of physical property contained in the balance sheet, but merely certifies that such items are valued in accordance with accepted accounting principles.

It is incorrect to think that because a public accountant certifies a statement, he assumes primary responsibility for the accuracy and reliability of its financial data. Management and management alone has this responsibility. The certified public accountant, of course, is responsible for exercising reasonable care and diligence in conformance with established standards while performing his audit. He also, as we said, is responsible for expressing an opinion as to whether generally accepted accounting principles have been followed. However, this is usually all he does. Most outside accounting firms limit their audit to the verification of the accounts and do not extend it into additional functions which the internal auditing staff might perform such as the checking up on plans, policies, and procedures.

External auditing obviously does not directly control over-all performance of the enterprise. However, by assuring that generally accepted accounting principles are met, it does exercise an indirect control, or a degree of control, over the operations of the enterprise. Although a certain amount of flexibility of viewpoint is to be expected in determining whether this is the case, no certified public accountant would certify an account where a major item had been charged off as an expense rather than being capitalized.

This concludes our discussion of control of a financial nature. We have been principally concerned with the budget, internal auditing, break-even point analysis, profit and loss analysis, return on investment, and external auditing. We have also seen that techniques such as the chart system and the control unit can provide control over various physical aspects of the organization such as sales, rate of output, and so on. These various measures of organizational performance go a long way in helping management to assess effectiveness. However, other dimensions to organizational effectiveness exist. They will be discussed in the next chapter.

Discussion Questions

1. Why can the chemical industry in general, and Du Pont in particular, easily adopt chart control techniques?

2. How does one resolve the apparent paradox between the need for a control unit and the need for decentralization in large organizations?

3. Business organizations usually measure their general performance in financial terms. How do you suppose nonprofit organizations would measure such performance?

Supplementary Readings

Anderson, Clayton W. "Disclosure of Assumptions — Key to Better Break-Even Analysis." In *Administrative Control and Executive Action,* edited by Bernhard C. Lemke and James D. Edwards. Columbus, Ohio: Merrill, 1961. See pp. 628–33.

Heiser, Herman C. *Budgeting.* New York: Ronald Press, 1959. See part 3.

Lamperti, Frank A., and John B. Thurston. *Internal Auditing for Management.* Englewood Cliffs, N.J.: Prentice-Hall, 1953.

Lemke, Bernhard C., and James D. Edwards. *Administrative Control and Executive Action.* Columbus, Ohio: Merrill, 1961. See part 2.

Lewis, R. W. "Measuring, Reporting and Appraising Results of Operations with Reference to Goals, Plans and Budgets." In *Management in Perspective,* edited by William E. Schlender, William G. Scott, and Alan C. Filley. Boston: Houghton Mifflin, 1965. See pp. 619–30.

Newman, William H., Charles E. Summer, and Warren E. Kirby. *The Process of Management.* Englewood Cliffs, N.J.: Prentice-Hall, 1967. See chapter 30.

Patrick, A. W. "Some Observations on the Break-Even Analysis." In *Administrative Control and Executive Action,* edited by Bernhard C. Lemke and James D. Edwards, Columbus, Ohio: Merrill, 1961. See pp. 634–43.

Strong, Earl P., and Robert D. Smith. "Break-Even Charts." In *Dimensions in Modern Management,* edited by Patrick E. Connor. Boston: Houghton Mifflin, 1974.

Wallace, Michael E. "Behavioral Considerations in Budgeting." In *Dimensions in Modern Management.*

CHAPTER 31

Organizational Effectiveness

The degree to which an organization achieves its goal is called its effectiveness.[1] Effectiveness compares performance with criteria composed of past achievements and future expectations. Therefore, effectiveness is always a dependent variable; it can be assessed only in relation to other standards. In business those standards are relevant to the relationship between the performance of an organization and its specified goals. Hospitals, for example, have goals encompassing health care services. They include the successful treatment and release of people admitted to in-patient care, the use of out-patient clinical facilities, and the rate of bed occupancy and turnover. If a hospital can successfully achieve its goals in these areas, it is probably achieving a high degree of effectiveness.

MAJOR VARIABLES IN MEASURING ORGANIZATIONAL EFFECTIVENESS

Because organizational goals vary, so also will the standards used to measure their effectiveness. Therefore, every organization must develop its own performance criteria. These criteria appear to fall into three general categories:

1. Output is the quality and quantity of a good or service created, and the efficiency with which it is produced.
2. Adaptability is the long-term ability to cope with change in technology, culture, and behavior.
3. Flexibility is the short-term ability to shift resources to cope with unexpected contingencies.[2]

A library system serves as an example of how these three variables apply to a given organization. Libraries have a service goal; their output in large part is measured by circulation (quantity). However, they must also possess the kinds of books most demanded by their clientele (quality). Furthermore, they must be able to process books for loan efficiently, maintain accurate records, and minimize loss and damage (efficiency). A library system also has to plan for long-range change in

[1] James L. Price, *Organizational Effectiveness* (Homewood, Ill.: Irwin, 1968), pp. 2–3.
[2] Paul E. Mott, *The Characteristics of Effective Organizations* (New York: Harper and Row, 1972), pp. 17–20.

its clients' needs and tastes. A library district faced with the long-term aging of its borrowers will plan to order different books than one anticipating that it will serve a large number of young, school-aged children. It must consider adopting new technologies — duplicating techniques, microfilm, and so on. These long-range changes are related to the criteria of adaptability. Finally, a library system needs to have sufficient flexibility so that it can make its holdings available to subunits. Some systems have mobile libraries that give rural users and shut-ins the opportunity to borrow books.

Different organizations will give different meaning and value to the three effectiveness criteria. Their definitions of the variables will depend on their organizational goals ánd the types of performance that they select for measurement. Business organizations have typically stressed quantitative yardsticks to measure performance. However, as we discuss later, qualitative standards are now being seriously studied.

THE RELATIONSHIP OF ORGANIZATIONAL EFFECTIVENESS TO OTHER MANAGERIAL FUNCTIONS

Control

The budget and other financial controls that we mentioned in Chapters 29 and 30 clearly are designed to measure performance. These are traditional forms of measurement that are essential in appraising organizational effectiveness. However, they are concerned mostly with the output criteria previously mentioned. Although flexibility is an important factor in certain budget considerations, conventional techniques of management financial control do not focus primarily on measuring such organizational flexibility and adaptation.

The increasing complexity of organizations, the expanding relationships between organizations and their environment, and the growing turbulence created by technological change require that organizations introduce new methods of evaluating performance. Effectiveness criteria must be developed that cover a broader range than those covered by the economic and efficiency controls. These new organizational factors — including social and behavioral ones — need control criteria so that management can compare actual organizational performance against stated objectives. More often than not these criteria will be qualitative.

Regardless of whether the criteria are qualitative or quantitative, they still must be implemented within the control function. If deviations exist beyond allowable variances, management still has to institute corrective action. However, since control does not exist apart from other management activities, organizational effectiveness is related closely to decision-making and planning.

Other Management Processes

Organizational effectiveness has its origins in decision-making. Utilizing the decision-making process, management will set basic directions for the organization and will allocate resources for programs and activities. For example, corporate management may decide to fund an employee college tuition program. This will require the diversion of some stockholder earnings. Management's decision, of necessity, will involve all decision-making steps from the evaluation of alternatives to the appraisal of outcomes. In short, it will encompass all those mental calculations required by the decision-making process. Thus, decision-making initiates the consideration of organizational effectiveness.

Next, management must plan its program since, through planning, basic goals, objectives, and standards are formulated. If a hospital starts an educational program dealing with preventive medicine, basic objectives have to be established. Is the program going to be community-wide? Is it going to involve only certain age groups? Is the program going to focus on certain subjects like drug abuse or prenatal care? On the basis of goals formulated by answering such questions, standards of performance can be formed. How many people should become involved? By what level should drug usage be reduced? How many expectant mothers can one hospital expect to counsel? The projections derived from these further questions provide guidelines to measure future effectiveness.

Organizational design is also part of the planning function. Management must explicitly assign responsibility to people for implementing plans. To facilitate this process, management may need to establish special departments, delegate authority, or hire new people with required skills. Organizational design, in this respect, is crucial to control since effectiveness is very difficult to measure unless those responsible for specific activities are clearly identified.

Thus, although organizational effectiveness is associated in an immediate sense with control, it also incorporates decision-making, planning, and organizational design. Naturally, organizational effectiveness can be applied to many kinds of organizations. However, we will only examine how it is developing in business.

ECONOMIC MEASURES OF ORGANIZATIONAL EFFECTIVENESS

Typically organizational performance has been appraised in economic terms expressed in the form of profit, efficiency, or cost. Business organizations use these measurements extensively. Indeed, the quantitative expressions of monetary gains or losses are interpreted as the final statement of the worth of management. However, business is not alone in the use of quantitative standards of performance. Other organizations, which do not have dollar profit as a goal, use quantitative measures of efficiency as indicators of managerial effectiveness.

The preoccupation of modern organizations with quantitative measures of effectiveness is shown by the central role they give financial control. Their preoccupation is a result, of course, of the basic expectations people have of the organizations that serve them. Business owners expect profit and appreciation in value; the government expects dollar accounting for tax purposes; the customer expects a quality product at a low unit cost; and employees expect to maximize their income and fringe benefits. Thus management's devotion to the economic measures of effectiveness is in large part a response to the expectation of the people it serves. Since our society is basically materialistic in its values, it should not be surprising that we expect the performance of organizations to be accounted for in quantitative terms.

Although it is an oversimplification, the criteria of economic effectiveness can be expressed by the equation, $E = O/I$. This equation is the statement of efficiency, and it implies general economic guidelines for managerial decision-making and organizational behavior. The equation says merely that efficiency equals outputs divided by inputs. The idea behind this statement is deceptively simple, but its rules for application are profound.

The first rule is that efficiency should be increased. By doing this productivity is increased, costs are reduced, volume is expanded, and the organizational payoffs to owners, managers, employees, customers, and society are improved. Given these targets, then the next rule is that management should make adjustments in O or I so that the value of E is increased. For example, management can allow output to remain constant and inputs to decrease; it can allow output to increase and inputs to remain constant; or it can allow outputs and inputs to vary so long as the value of E goes up.

Ultimately, the various engineering, economic, and accounting measures of effectiveness embody the values expressed by the efficiency equation. The life or death of business organizations depends on management's ability to work the output-input relationship. The executives' worth is decided by the way they manage the rules of efficiency. The well-being of the clients of the organization as well as the health of the organization itself depends on earnings. Earnings, in turn, depend upon how well the resources of the organization are used to produce goods or services.

Some Applications of the Rules

There are dozens of examples of how the rules of efficiency are applied to organizational practice. Just a few will have to serve the purposes of this chapter. As a first example we should recall previous discussions of the budget and other financial controls. These provide financial examples of the workings of the efficiency principle because they are aimed at getting maximum benefits for the organization at minimum costs. As we emphasized, the calculations behind budget considerations permeate the cost benefit analysis involved in all managerial functions.

Management uses production control standards to determine various levels of resource utilization and thereby to reduce cost. One specific application of these controls is management's establishment of output standards for labor engaged in various jobs. Similar calculations are made for expected expenditures for capital investment in plant and equipment.

In summary, the efficiency calculus is based on the assumption that the more intensive is the use of resources, the more effective is the organization. Most of the time this aspect of the calculus is reduced to quantitative terms. For example, if sales volume can be doubled without increasing the sales force, management has a positive, concrete indicator of increased marketing effectiveness. The efficiency equation is most apt to be reduced to quantitative terms in organizations with a high degree of departmentalization, specialization of labor, and mechanization of production. These conditions occur primarily in conventional manufacturing organizations, although they could also occur in organizations that process large quantities of paper work on a routine basis.

As we stated, the efficiency equation is an oversimplification. Many management decisions cannot be reduced to quantitative terms. Because of this, the measurement of effectiveness by strict efficiency standards is impossible.

Other Effectiveness Considerations

The difficulty of measuring organizational effectiveness becomes compounded when organizational complexity increases, when decision-making time horizons get longer, and when a number of conflicting factors in organizational performance have to be balanced.

Management faces a number of internal organizational problems when complexity grows. Top management, obviously, wants to optimize the performance of the entire organization. However, in concerns with semiautonomous subdivisions, such a goal could mean that certain segments of the organization would be forced to operate at less than the degree of efficiency that might otherwise be attained. For example, a firm could require that its manufacturing departments "purchase" the components they use internally, even though comparable products are available on the open market at a lower price. This policy, while increasing the unit cost of the product of a manufacturing division, contributes favorably to the over-all performance of the organization.

Implicit in the simplified version of the efficiency equation is the assumption that the time span of effectiveness is measured in the short run. However, organizations dealing with advanced technologies, with research and development programs, and with extensive capital investments must take a long-range view of organizational effectiveness. Immediate appraisal of research and development activities, for example, might show their adverse effect on earnings, or the installation and use of new capital equipment could result in a short-term decline in efficiency. Nevertheless, if an organization is to stay healthy in the long run, such short-term sacrifices have to be made.

Finally, management's attempts to balance the interests of organizational clients are bound to affect the efficiency equation adversely. As illustration, one executive in the electronics industry said that customers expect every television set produced to work perfectly. However, he pointed out, given the technology of mass production, there are going to be duds. In these cases, the best a company can do is to offer warranties or to replace defective sets. To make every unit perfect would involve such vast costs that the final price would be outside the reach of the mass market. Many examples like this one show that effectiveness often is a compromise between what is possible in an engineering sense and what is necessary in order to make a product or service available to a wide market.

The quantitative and qualitative economic aspects of organizational effectiveness have concerned management for quite some time. Although the answers to the questions raised by economic considerations are imperfect, managers have evolved an approach to settling issues of economic effectiveness. However, organizational effectiveness is beginning to lap over into areas of social welfare and social responsibility. Here few answers exist; in fact, not many people know the appropriate questions.

MEASURES OF EXTERNAL SOCIAL EFFECTIVENESS

Americans today expect more from their organizations than the efficient production and distribution of goods and services. They feel that business and other organizations have social obligations and responsibilities. External social responsibility includes the obligations that an organization has to the general public and to specific interest groups. They arise from organizational activities that affect society to a greater degree than do the organization's ordinary affairs. A company's obligation to maintain renewable resources involves the welfare of society as a whole. For example, a forest products firm has a strong economic and social responsibility to replant trees in areas where it has cut lumber. Likewise, an organization located in the ghetto may feel a strong social obligation to develop programs to train and employ hard-core unemployed minorities.

Management's decision to become involved in areas of social responsibility can be either voluntary or legally imposed. For instance, local communities, states, and the federal government have pollution control standards. In order to comply with such laws, an organization might install a pollution control system sufficient only to meet minimum legal local standards for water quality. Another organization, however, could voluntarily decide to exceed legal standards. As a further example, no legal requirements for support exist in such areas as business aid to higher education. Therefore, the decision to engage in such support activities is in the realm of private managerial discretion.

Thus, certain social responsibilities are imposed on management. In these cases, a national consensus exists, expressed in the form of public policy. Federal standards on nondiscriminatory hiring practices comprise such a policy. However, no national consensus or public policy exists for many social issues. The nation is still debating the appropriateness of a firm's doing business with South Africa. Some believe that a company should not judge the national policies of sovereign countries. Others feel that it is immoral for a firm to trade with countries that enforce racial exclusion.

The nature of an organization's social activities and programs stems initially from management's choice of areas of participation. Its basic decisions are translated into social goals and social policies. George Steiner gives a number of examples of such policies. They include statements like these: "Research and development will be oriented, to the extent possible, to produce products which are nonpollutants." "Advertising will avoid statements which take advantage of unsophisticated buyers, such as children and the less educated, shall avoid exploiting emotions, and shall be honest."[3] Policies such as these, in turn, become the social criteria against which organizational performance is measured. Clearly, unless management formulates policies based upon imposed or voluntary obligations, criteria for organizational effectiveness cannot be stated.

Even if management has established social policies, the problem of judging organizational effectiveness is only partially solved. What measures of effectiveness shall management use? Obviously, the usual economic and accounting measures of performance are hard to apply to qualitative social actions. If obligations are imposed, as fair hiring practices and pollution control have been, legal requirements may provide adequate control standards. For instance, they might include a measure of the pollutants emitted in a time period or might establish the ratio of minority employees to the total number of employees in an organization.

Table 31-1. Abt Associates, Inc., Social Balance Sheet (Year Ended December 31, 1971, with Comparative Figures for 1970)

	1971	*1970*
Social Assets Available		
Staff		
Available within one year	$ 2,594,390	$ 2,312,000
Available after one year	6,368,511	5,821,608
Training investment	507,405	305,889
	9,470,306	8,439,497
Less accumulated training obsolescence	136,995	60,523
Total staff assets	9,333,311	8,378,974
Organization		
Social capital investment	1,398,230	1,272,201
Retained earnings	219,136	—
Land	285,376	293,358
Buildings at cost	334,321	350,188
Equipment at cost	43,018	17,102
Total organization assets	2,280,081	1,932,849
Research		
Proposals	26,878	15,090
Child care research	6,629	—
Social audit	12,979	—
Total research	46,486	15,090
Public services consumed net of tax payments	152,847	243,399
Total social assets available	$11,812,725	$10,570,312

Source: "First Attempts at a 'Social Audit,'" *Business Week* (September 23, 1972), p. 89. Used with permission.

[3] George A. Steiner, *"Social Policies for Business"* (Paper prepared for Center for Research and Dialogue on Business in Society, Graduate School of Management, University of California, Los Angeles, 1972), pp. 16–17.

Table 31-1 (Continued)

	1971	1970
Social Commitments, Obligations, and Equity		
Staff		
Committed to contracts within one year	$ 43,263	$ 81,296
Committed to contracts after one year	114,660	215,459
Committed to administration within one year	62,598	56,915
Committed to administration after one year	165,903	150,842
Total staff commitments	386,424	504,512
Organization		
Working capital requirements	60,000	58,500
Financial deficit	—	26,814
Facilities and equipment committed to contracts		
and administration	37,734	36,729
Total organization commitments	97,734	122,043
Environmental		
Government outlays for public services consumed,		
net of tax payment	152,847	243,399
Pollution from paper production	1,770	770
Pollution from electric power production	2,200	1,080
Pollution from automobile commuting	10,493	4,333
Total environmental obligations	167,310	249,582
Total commitments and obligations	651,468	876,137
Society's equity		
Contributed by staff	8,946,887	7,874,462
Contributed by stockholders	2,182,347	1,810,806
Generated by operations	32,023	8,907
Total equity	11,161,257	9,694,175
Total commitments, obligations, and equity	$11,812,725	$10,570,312

For the most part, however, such explicit standards do not exist, nor are there guidelines to help management judge the larger problem of the relative desirability of various types of social action. The discovery of criteria and standards for measuring organizational performance is the chief problem in social effectiveness.

The social audit represents one attempt to overcome this problem. There is little agreement about what the social audit is, but there are many opinions. For example, two authors[4] suggest that in order to do a social audit management should: (1) list all its activities that have a social impact, (2) explain what circumstances led to these activities, (3) informally evaluate the programs that seem most important, and (4) judge how well these programs tie into the objectives of the organization and society.

[4] See the discussion of Bauer and Fenn in "The First Attempts at a Corporate 'Social Audit,' " *Business Week* (September 23, 1972), pp. 88–92. See also George A. Steiner, "Should Business Adopt the Social Audit?" *The Conference Board Record* (May 1972), pp. 7–10.

These points provide general guidelines for social audit procedures. However, the concept of an audit implies that more tangible criteria must exist to appraise effectiveness. To meet this difficulty, some organizations have attempted to quantify their social efforts. Table 31-1 is a "social ledger," in which a company assigns dollar values to its own internal and external social commitments, obligations, and equity.

Accounting for social programs in financial terms may be useful for illustrative and comparative purposes. However, it is misleading to suppose that precision is enhanced by assigning numbers to qualitative activities. Social accounting may be a start in developing measures to judge effectiveness in this sphere, but we emphasize it is just that — a start.

MEASURES OF INTERNAL SOCIAL EFFECTIVENESS

The measurement of internal social performance in organizations has to include at least two types of data — that obtained from measuring the value of human resources and the company's investment in them and that obtained from measuring the over-all capacity and capability of management. The first measurement constitutes an experimental "accounting" approach. The second has been conducted for a number of years in the form of the management audit.

Human Asset Accounting

Convinced that people in organizations are assets that can be enhanced or depleted, Rensis Likert, a management consultant, has proposed a plan of "human resource accounting."[5] He places a dollar value on the human assets of an organization; it shows up as a "bottom line" figure on annual statements. Likert argues that organizational performance, or lack of it, can be traced to the quality of the people employed. Thus, expenditures to improve the quality of human resources can be looked upon as an investment rather than as a cost. For example, training programs or executive development programs are typically written off as expenses. However, under Likert's scheme, such expenditures could be treated as an investment that increases the assets of the concern.

One company, the R. G. Barry Corporation, figures human resources as an investment in its annual reports. However, such figures are unaudited and are not obtained by conventional accounting practices.[6] Although its techniques are experimental, nevertheless executives in this company claim that the data obtained are useful in appraising the true cost of employee turnover and helpful in making financial decisions.

[5] For a description of Likert's technique, see "A New Twist to People Accounting," *Business Week* (October 21, 1972), pp. 67–68.

[6] See "Firm's Accounting Covers 'Human Resources' Data," *Wall Street Journal* (March 21, 1972).

Although it possesses interesting potential for determining organizational effectiveness, human asset accounting is just a quantitative estimate of qualitative changes in an organization. As such, it is a primitive technique, not likely to be accepted in conventional practice very quickly.

Management Audits

Management audits are becoming increasingly significant. They are substantially different from those performed by public accountants because they are not concerned with verification of financial data. They are performed for top management, the stockholders, or other owners, in order to survey from the broadest possible point of view management resources and, by implication, the over-all position of the enterprise. Management audits start where balance-sheet audits leave off. At times, such an audit is undertaken by management itself, but more frequently outside help is called in.

Periodic Management Self-Audit

In the 1930's, James O. McKinsey advocated that a periodic self-audit be held in order to discover and correct management errors. The self-audit amounts to an appraisal of all aspects of the enterprise. In order to do such an audit, management must determine not only the company's present position but also where it is heading and where it will be in five, ten, or fifteen years. Moreover, management must look beyond the present and future position of the company in the industry to appraise the outlook for the entire industry. The self-appraisal must cover policies, organizational structure, personnel practices, personnel inventory, physical facilities, financial resources, and all other aspects bearing on the outcome of the company's operations.

Management should perform a self-audit once a year or, at the very least, once every two or three years. The obvious difficulty with a self-audit, however, is that in most instances management does not find the time to perform it. There also is a danger that because of its proximity to the situation and because of company politics and personal considerations, management is not as well equipped to perform an audit as an outsider would be.

Audit by the American Institute of Management

The American Institute of Management, a private nonprofit organization, has conducted management audits for many years. This organization has devised a list of several hundred questions to determine the quality of the management of a particular enterprise. The questions cover ten areas encompassing economic functions, corporate structure, health of earnings growth, fairness to stockholders, research and development, composition of the board of directors, fiscal policies, production efficiency, sales, and executive evaluation. A maximum number of points is assigned to each area.[7]

The individual questions, grouped by areas, are submitted to corporate officers and to outside sources. Members of the institute then analyze the resulting answers in order to determine how many points out of the maximum attainable rating are to be given for each answer. The points are added to achieve a total for each of the ten areas. The relationship between the total number of points achieved and the maximum attainable will determine management's rating.

External Management Audit by Outside Consultants

Management audits conducted on an annual basis by outside management consultants are also increasing. They examine a company's performance, its position within the industry, its organizational structure, and the operations of its divisions and departments. If such audits are conducted regularly, management can compare current findings with prior conditions in order to discover what has been achieved and what is still required. External management audits performed by management consultants are similar to external financial audits performed by outside accountants.

Because the quality of an enterprise's management is of utmost importance to the long-run performance of the company, it may be that, as time goes on, management audits by outside firms will become just as routine as the annual audit by independent certified accountants. This trend could even lead to the establishment of a certified management audit performed by an outside firm whose staff is thoroughly trained and qualified to objectively appraise the effectiveness of an organization's management. At present, however, the prospects for such certification are remote.

ORGANIZATIONAL CHANGE

Warren Bennis believes that the only true criterion of organizational health is its ability to adapt to change.[8] However, most measures of organizational performance are not designed to give readings on organizational adaptation. The effectiveness criteria that we have reviewed give snapshots of organization performance at points in time. However, we need a moving picture to measure effectiveness as an organization adapts to change over time. Many theorists, including Bennis, think that the chief test of managerial effectiveness will also measure how well an organization copes with change. Change is one of the basic facts in organizational life; successful adaptation or little adaptation to changing environmental conditions can make the difference in organizational survival.

---

[7] Jackson Martindell, *The Scientific Appraisal of Management* (New York: Harper and Row, 1950), p. 280. Also see Jackson Martindell, "Management Audit Simplified," *The Corporate Director*, Special issue no. 15 (December 1951), pp. 1–6; and Jackson Martindell, *The Appraisal of Management* (New York: Harper and Row, 1962).

[8] Warren G. Bennis, *Changing Organizations* (New York: McGraw-Hill, 1966), p. 44.

While techniques do not presently exist to give a dynamic "moving picture" of adaptive effectiveness, three areas — the social, the technological, and the administrative — will have to be included when such techniques are established.

Social Adaptation

The measurement of social adaptation must include external and internal criteria. However, emphasis would have to be shifted from the quality of past performance to the effectiveness of planning and decision models in anticipating changes in the social climate and adjusting to them. For example, manufacturers that today exceed existing air quality standards by using advanced pollution control techniques, are probably forecasting that social and legislative pressure for cleaner and cleaner air will occur.

Technological Adaptation

Management is more likely to adapt to technological change than to any other type. Advancing technology has produced the need for vastly different organizational designs encompassing highly educated and skilled people. How well organizations have adapted to this need must be determined. However, how can we judge how well an organization is able to foresee technological change and make the adjustments necessary in order to accommodate it?

Administrative Adaptation

Measuring administrative adaptation is the most difficult process of all because in a sense it means measuring just about everything that goes on in the organization. Nevertheless, certain aspects of management adaptation can be singled out. For example, the relationship of leadership style to organizational needs is important. If an organization exists in a turbulent environment where change is rapid and response has to be innovative, management might wish to give the maximum amount of discretion possible to those at subordinate levels. Clearly, a restrictive form of leadership would be inappropriate in this situation because it would not facilitate adaptation. The organizational climate that management fosters is also crucial to adaptation.

Adaptive Behavioral and Organizational Designs

As the result of research,[9] the organic model of organizational design is now thought to be the most adaptable to a rapidly changing environment. In order to understand the organic model, we can contrast it to the mechanistic model. The mechanistic model is similar in structure to classical formal organization or bureaucracy. Such

[9] See Tom Burns and G. M. Stalker, *The Management of Innovation* (London: Tavistock, 1961).

a design is believed to be closed, repressive, rigid, and insensitive to change. The organic model is supposed to be open, relatively free, flexible, and highly sensitive to change. Therefore, an organic organizational design is recommended for firms involved with innovation, a skilled and educated work force, and the necessity to react quickly to change.

However, how can an organization change from older organizational forms to newer forms more suitable to current conditions? The need to create new organizational designs and leadership styles has led some writers to examine the problem of organizational renewal. Robert Golembiewski points out that renewal requires a shift in emphasis from stability, predictability, loyalty to an organization, strict hierarchy, coercion, and stable work relationships, to change, creativity, and commitment to the effective completion of task, freedom brought about through self-direction and self-control, and satisfying work relations that can be dissolved when no longer relevant.[10] Some of the techniques used to implement this transition are sensitivity training and organizational development, which we have discussed in previous chapters. The chief difficulty with these techniques is similar to that we have found with others — finding criteria to measure their effect.

Management is just beginning to probe the value of measuring organizational effectiveness by means other than conventional economic criteria. Techniques like the social audit are only now being applied to decision-making, planning, and control. However, as a recent Harris Poll shows, Americans' confidence that business is discharging its social obligations is at the lowest point ever. If such is the case, then pressure may mount on organizations to account for their activities in the social realm. This accounting will require measures and criteria of the sort discussed here, measures that will extend far beyond those of economic effectiveness.

Discussion Questions

1. What do you suppose would be the motivation of management to go beyond imposed legal requirements to meet social obligations? Pick a specific area of social concern where legal standards of conduct prevail and discuss steps management could take to exceed these standards.

2. Adaptation seems to relate closely to organizational effectiveness. Discuss the usefulness of this relationship in different types of organizational environments. In what situation is it most appropriate; in what, least appropriate?

Supplementary Readings

Bennis, Warren G. *Changing Organizations.* New York: McGraw-Hill, 1966.

Bennis, Warren G. "The Coming Death of Bureaucracy." In *Dimensions in Modern Management,* edited by Patrick E. Connor. Boston: Houghton Mifflin, 1974.

[10] Robert T. Golembiewski, *Renewing Organizations* (Itasca, Ill.: Peacock, 1972), p. 8.

Buchele, Robert B. "How to Evaluate a Firm." In *Dimensions in Modern Management.*

Mott, Paul E. *The Characteristics of Effective Organizations.* New York: Harper and Row, 1972.

Peterson, Richard B., and James S. Garrison. "Culture as an Intervening Variable in the Technology Organization Structure Relationship." In *Dimensions in Modern Management.*

Seashore, Stanley. "Criteria of Organizational Effectiveness." In *Dimensions in Modern Management.*

Steiner, George A. "Should Business Adopt the Social Audit?" *The Conference Board Record* (May 1972), pp. 7–10.

Ways, Max. "Tomorrow's Management." In *Dimensions in Modern Management.*

CASES

VI | 1

The Elysée Manufacturing Company

M_r. Wagner is the president of the Elysée Manufacturing Company, a small, Chicago-based manufacturer of womens' belts. The company's total annual sales have been approximately $1 million for the past few years. The annual after-tax profit is small. Because of the size of the company, the amount of accounting work is not enough to warrant mechanized facilities, and records are kept manually. Therefore, the accounting department requires quite some time to prepare the monthly closing figures. Mr. Wagner usually has to wait until the fifteenth of the following month to learn the past month's financial results. Since the company is small and has meager financial resources, he is monitoring operations and affairs closely. He has repeatedly told the accounting department that he would prefer to have approximate figures of each month's performance available within two or three days after the close of the month than to wait for the exact figures until the fifteenth or even later.

The chief accountant has tried to convince Mr. Wagner that all closing figures must be gathered first and that it would waste effort and incur needless double work to submit the preliminary figures to him right after the month closed. He maintains that such figures would not be correct or meaningful until all figures — returns, allowances, discounts, salesmen's commissions, inventory fluctuations — were correctly assembled. He has even said that the president would be taking real risks if he were to base plans or act on any figures other than the final ones. Because the president does not have much knowledge of accounting and the company's financial resources are small, he has submitted to the accountant's point of view. However, he still wishes he could receive some relevant information sooner.

Questions

1. Do you think the president's point of view has any merit?
2. What are the disadvantages and advantages of acting on the basis of approximate data and information?
3. Why should the accountant's contention be supported?

VI│2

The New Budget

The Belmont Community Hospital has doubled its facilities during the last ten years and at present has 250 beds. Total revenues amounted to $7.5 million during the last year. Recently, a completely new board of trustees has been elected. In one of their first meetings, the question of budgets was brought up. The executive director of the hospital told the board that at the beginning of each fiscal year he and the controller would plan an over-all budget for the hospital but that only a few major departments such as nursing services would have a departmental budget. When one of the trustees asked why each department would not have its own budget, the director replied that most departmental supervisors were not familiar with budgeting and would not know how to function within a budget. He pointed out that the mere mention of the word "budget" aroused disturbing and even hostile feelings in many supervisors. He stated that the controller would be keeping an eye on all departmental operations, so complete budgeting would not be necessary.

After a lengthy discussion, the trustees passed a resolution asking the finance committee to take immediate steps to devise a complete budgetary system for each department. They also asked the finance committee to be responsible for budget reviews and revisions. The trustees felt that in this manner they could assure the success of the budgeting process.

Questions

1. What steps should be taken and who should begin the budgeting project?
2. When budgets have been set, how can meaningful reviews and revisions be made?

VI | 3

The Nytron Division

In December 1970, Mr. Leo Simmons was hired as president and general manager of the Nytron division, a wholly owned subsidiary of Citronics, Inc. He was given full authority to manage the division, and it was agreed that the parent company would in no way interfere with him. His performance was to be judged at year's end against two criteria: the rate of profit after taxes in relation to sales and the rate of profit after taxes related to the assets invested in the division. Headquarters made it clear that sales should be increased 10 per cent above those of the previous year, that the present rate of 8 per cent profit on sales should rise to 10 per cent, and that the return on assets was to be 15 per cent. Mr. Simmons agreed to these goals, and they became the mutually agreed upon objectives. Mr. Simmons understood that he would be subject to severe criticism and possibly discharge if he failed to achieve them. He was well compensated in his job, and throughout the year he was left free to run the division to the best of his abilities.

Table 1. Headquarters Figures

	1970	1971
Sales	20,000,000	22,000,000
Assets	16,000,000	16,000,000
Profits after taxes	1,600,000	2,000,000
Return as per cent of sales	8%	9%
Return as per cent of assets	10%	$12\frac{1}{2}$%

When the year was over, the president of Citronics, Mr. Ashburn, and the corporate controller confronted Mr. Simmons with figures that indicated that the Nytron division had not reached its goals (see Table 1). When Mr. Simmons checked the figures and compared them with those prepared by the division controller, he found that headquarters considered his research and development expenditures of $500,000 to be an expense, whereas the Nytron division had capitalized this amount. Mr. Simmons contends that the amount spent in research and development will lead to substantially increased profits over the next five or ten years and should not be considered an expense at this time. Either it should be expended as soon as the new developments in the form of new products produce revenues, or it should be amortized ratably. The division's figures were based on this rationale (see Table 2).

Headquarters did not agree with Mr. Simmons' figures and stated that his divisional practices did not conform to those accepted by corporate headquarters.

Table 2. Divisional Figures

	1970	1971
Sales	20,000,000	22,000,000
Assets	16,000,000	16,500,000
Profits after taxes	1,600,000	2,500,000
Return as per cent of sales	8%	11%
Return as per cent of assets	10%	15%

Questions

1. Which position would you support?
2. Are issues other than those of controlling involved in this disagreement?
3. How could this misunderstanding have been avoided?

VI | 4

The Fledgling Company

For fifteen years, Mr. Rubin had been a traveling salesman for the Star Manufacturing Company of New York. The company sold an assortment of women's scarves, which were either produced by the firm or imported from abroad. Mr. Rubin sold these scarves to department and specialty stores in the East. He had established a good following and a fine reputation during the many years he worked for this company. His income was substantial, and he was able to save enough money to realize his ambition: to go into a similar business for himself.

About two years ago he was able to secure sufficient bank loans and additional credit to open his own manufacturing company. Ever since, his business has grown and prospered. After two years, his annual sales amount to about $250,000, and last year's operations showed an after-tax net gain of $20,000. Of course, Mr. Rubin worked, so to speak, day and night, personally supervising all phases of the small, growing company. He designed the scarves, watched the production, made trips abroad to select the imports, sold his products, took care of the correspondence, watched the flow of finances, and did everything else involved in building a new business. As time went on, he realized that there was a limit to how much he could do. Therefore, he placed a superintendent in charge of production and the workers, and he hired a salesman. He already had two good office employees who had joined the company when it was founded.

Mr. Rubin knows that in order for his company to grow, he must assign activities to others and delegate to each the authority necessary to manage his own department. He is perfectly willing to do so, but he is greatly concerned that when he does he will no longer be familiar with and involved in every detail. This worries him considerably. He has invested all his savings in the company and has even pledged his personal belongings to the bank as collateral for the various loans. He does not wish to lose his investment. Although he has a great deal of confidence in his subordinates, he knows that he should still watch all aspects of the business. He has read somewhere that "to delegate authority does not mean to lose control," and he is wondering how to set up a control system that would enable him to let others take charge of some of the aspects of the fledgling company while he remains fully aware of what is taking place.

Questions

1. How would you set up controls so that Mr. Rubin will be aware of what takes place in his small company?
2. Design a system that would provide Mr. Rubin with strategic control points to examine and at the same time would leave him with time and opportunity to expand his business.

VI|5

The Administrator's Problem

Mr. Jones is the administrator of St. Mary's Hospital, a general short-term community hospital in Cincinnati. It has 500 beds and operates most of the time at maximum occupancy. Its total revenues amounted to $18 million for the last year. While reviewing last year's operating statement, the board of directors found that the operating surplus had dwindled to a negligible amount compared with that of other years. The board is searching for the reasons for this change and for ways to cut expenses and eliminate unnecessary expenditures.

An outlay that received much of the board's attention was $75,000 for continuing education for the employees. It covered such items as travel to meetings, membership fees for professional organizations, tuition reimbursements, educational material, books, subscriptions to journals. It did not cover the expenses for interns and residents. The account represented all expenditures made in connection with the hospital's efforts to give its employees the chance for additional development, education, and training.

When the board asked the administrator about this account, he replied that such provisions are necessary in today's labor market. Unless they are available, good employees eager to advance in their professions will not stay with the hospital. Also, only by exposing employees to meetings, seminars, and talks can the hospital achieve and maintain its goal of providing the best quality of patient care. After the administrator had cited these and other reasons, the board could see the need for the expenditure.

The board then asked Mr. Jones, the administrator, what tangible results he could show for his program and how he ascertains the effects of these development costs. The administrator admitted that he did not have a solid answer to that. He said he would try to set up a control system that would enable the hospital to check and appraise the validity and benefits of the expenses.

After the board meeting, Mr. Jones called Mr. Tibauld into his office. Mr. Tibauld is an administrative resident fulfilling the residency requirement for his master of hospital administration degree. Mr. Jones told Mr. Tibauld what the board wanted to know and asked him to devise a system to measure the effectiveness of spending $75,000 a year for continuing education.

Question

1. How should Mr. Tibauld go about this task? What approaches to the problem might the administrator give him?

COMPREHENSIVE CASES

1/ Lennert Company Limited

Harry Fielding spent the evening of June 24, 1963, confiding to a close friend who he hoped would give him a different perspective on a major decision he would have to make within the next two days. At the time he was the vice-president of sales of the Lennert Company of Oshawa, Ontario, a nationally known manufacturer and merchandiser of powered lawn mowers and garden equipment. The essence of his conversation was:

"In July 1962, I left a promising job as sales manager for Kelly Foods to work with Glen Hayes when he bought Lennert. I came with him mostly because I was anxious to see how a guy who buys and sells companies works . . . The past 11 months, since we took over, have really been rough. Although I've worked like a dog, the company is not going particularly well. It will take at least four more years to turn it around, diversify the product line and get some long-run stability. I've done well with the company so far; the sale of common stock Hayes gave me when I joined him has netted me a capital gain of close to $25,000. But why should I stick with it when there are so many other opportunities that look so much better. Hayes has already checked out a couple of possibilities, and I've got a couple in mind that he doesn't know about. Also I left my old company with a standing offer, that would soon get me to the top rank of the New York head office."

"I'm sure Hayes will slowly drop out of active participation in Lennert now that the stock price has dropped. Besides he's not the kind of guy who sticks with any company for very long unless there is a capital gain potential. When he goes there is no one but myself that is presently capable of taking over. If I stayed with Lennert, the whole operation would probably be mine, with a big salary, in four or five years . . . And it could be argued that I have some responsibility to the shareholders to keep the thing going."

COMPANY HISTORY

The Lennert Company was founded in 1933 by Carl Lennert of Oshawa. The original assets of the company were a new idea for producing hand lawn-mowers and $4,700 that Carl Lennert raised by mortgaging his farm. Although sales were confined to the Oshawa–Toronto area, the company was able to survive and grow in the depressed market of the 1930's. However, due to material restrictions Carl Lennert suspended operations in 1940 and enlisted in the army.

This case was prepared by George S. Day, lecturer, under the direction of Professor Donald H. Thain, as the basis for class discussion rather than to illustrate either effective or ineffective handling of an administrative situation. Copyright 1963 by the University of Western Ontario, School of Business Administration. Reprinted by permission.

In 1946 Carl Lennert was joined by two other ex-servicemen, who were able to supply some of the skills the company previously lacked. Their first major success came in 1947 when a large department store ordered 500 mowers. Money was borrowed to finance the sale and operations were expanded. For the next 10 years the three owners were fully engrossed in the company. They worked seven-day weeks, there were few vacations for anyone, salaries were limited and all expenses were carefully controlled. All problems were faced by the three men as a team. Both individually and together they had a strong determination to grow and succeed.

By 1958 the company was apparently financially sound (see Exhibit 1-1) with an established position in the field. The early diversification into power mowers and cultivators had proven very successful in capitalizing on the suburbanite's desire to work on his own lawn and garden.

The attainment of a measure of success and security was followed by a change and a broadening of the owners' motivations and interests. One believed that the company should diversify into less seasonal products, the second became active on the local town council, and Carl Lennert, then 55, became concerned about having all his funds tied up in the company. In addition he lost his previous enthusiasm for new product development and was less interested in working long hours.

The changes in the owners' attitudes took place at the same time that the company's once bright future prospects were noticeably dimming. Despite the warning signs the owners found it increasingly difficult to reach any agreement among themselves as to the company's future operations.

By 1962 the company was still able to generate satisfactory profits, but faced the following adverse trends:

1. In 1958 two large U.S. manufacturers entered the Canadian power lawnmower and power garden equipment market. The impact of their consumer advertising and aggressive merchandising was beginning to be felt.

2. Private brand business had grown from 41% of sales in 1958 to 69% in 1962. The two largest private brand customers, a department store and an automotive supply chain accounting for 35% and 22% of the company sales respectively, were pressing for price reductions.

3. At the same time, consumers were switching their preference to cheaper private brands, from the premium-priced brand names.

4. The May 1962 dollar devaluation and import surcharge had abruptly stopped all imports of a popular gasoline-powered garden tiller that Lennert merchandised

Exhibit 1-1. Summary of Financial Results ($000's), December 31

	1954	1955	1955	1956	1957	1958	1959	1960	1961
Sales	$1,019	$995	$1,265	$1,478	$1,550	$1,920	$2,380	$2,451	$2,550
Earnings (after tax)	22	(3)	10	40	67	75	110	125	120
Working capital	201	230	225	303	340	328	465	505	490
Net worth	280	300	297	307	331	406	464	545	595

under its own name. The garden tiller was an integral part of the product line although sales volume was too low to warrant manufacture and assembly by Lennert.

5. Industry annual sales of power lawn-mowers were expected to decline slightly in the next five years as the market in existing homes became saturated and the rate of new home formations declined.

On June 27, 1962, the three owners completed negotiations for the sale of the company to Glen Hayes. Hayes had spent the previous two months inquiring into the problems of the company, after being introduced to one of the co-owners. The reasons for his growing interest in the situation, as he studied the company, became clearer with a better understanding of his background and motivations.

Glen Hayes was born in 1931, into a middle-class Hamilton, Ontario, family. He showed great promise and intelligence by ranking at or near the head of most of his classes in public school, private preparatory school, and engineering at McGill University. Following graduation from McGill and two years working for a large oil company, he enrolled in the MBA program of a well-known western U.S. business school. His pattern of behavior at the business school was noticeably different from McGill, where he participated in extracurricular activities. Although an excellent athlete, and previously active in student affairs, he was just "too busy" to spend time on these extracurricular activities. To his classmates he appeared aloof and reserved. In class he was regarded as a skeptic, one who constantly challenged many of the basic ideas and concepts that most others readily accepted.

During the time in the MBA program, his ambitions, while complex, crystallized to the point where one stood out to his intimate friends "to make a million dollars before I'm 30." To help achieve this objective he spent the two years following his graduation working for a well-known corporation lawyer in New York City. The lawyer, who was mainly involved in "setting up companies," had a widely known reputation as a sharp financial manipulator. Hayes had an opportunity to learn the lawyer's methods from close personal observations as he appraised various investment opportunities, planned company reorganizations, and worked on the broad problems of defining corporate strategies and structures under the supervision of the lawyer.

Hayes left the lawyer's firm following a fundamental disagreement about the prospects of a proposed speculative electronic apparatus manufacturer. To back up his conviction about the bright future of this company he borrowed heavily and bought enough common shares to gain a controlling interest in this company. He was 28 at this time. Three months after his 30th birthday his controlling interest in the company was acquired for a $1,500,000 cash payment by a large electronics company.

Following this success, he and his Canadian wife decided to return to Canada, primarily because he saw Canada as an interesting geographical area for "creative strategic opportunities." A big advantage, in his view, was the much debated lack of initiative or entrepreneurial drive of Canadians, and the consequent lack of domestic risk capital. The four months following his return to Canada were spent intensively studying a number of "potential investment" opportunities. On June 27, 1962, he purchased the Lennert Company Limited.

TAKE-OVER BY GLEN HAYES

Hayes found all three owners very receptive to his offer to purchase their interest in the company. Since both parties were well aware of the company's clouded and difficult future, the price of $500,000, based on a compromise between the capitalized earnings and adjusted net worth was reached after a short, uninvolved period of negotiations. Before the negotiations were started the owners had separately expressed their concern over the lack of adequate estate provisions for their families and the problems that the death of one of the top management trio would create.

The agreement called for an immediate cash down payment of $20,000 which amounted to an option-to-purchase, and a lump sum payment of $480,000, before the end of October 1962. Hayes's intent was to pay the balance owing with the proceeds from a large stock placement. The placement was to be made in the name of a newly-formed holding company, Lennert (1962) Limited, with an authorized share structure of 100,000 common. The first asset of the company was the option-to-purchase, which Hayes assigned to the company in exchange for 15,000 shares of Lennert (1962) Ltd.

After the holding company was established, Hayes worked out an arrangement with an investment broker who had a reputation for specializing in "risk situations," and who would arrange an over-the-counter placement for about 10% of the proceeds. It was agreed that 56,000 shares, priced at $10.00 per share would find a ready market among the investment broker's "lists and customers." The necessary legal and accounting arrangements were handled by a lawyer, who settled for 2% of the proceeds, and a chartered accountant, who agreed to a fee of $9,000, which was about 2% of the proceeds.

To pave the way for the stock issue, planned for September 1962, Hayes retained a well-known firm of public relations consultants. Their job was to publicize the change in management, the proposed product changes and innovations, and the impetus that the transfusion of capital would provide. A series of brochures and bulletins were planned to constantly publicize the company's "enlarged prospects and bright future." For further help in creating "a dynamic and successful image" he approached a good friend, Harry Fielding, a graduate of the University of Western Ontario MBA program, with a reputation as a shrewd and resourceful marketing man. His work with Kelley Foods Co. had been publicized on a number of occasions.

HAYES'S OFFER TO FIELDING

The substance of Hayes's comments during his dinner meeting with Fielding was: "This operation is going to be too big for me. Only one of the previous management group is remaining with the company, and I don't have too much confidence in him. I want someone in here with me who thinks as I do. Besides the big problems are all in the marketing area where you can really exercise your skills . . . If you come aboard you'll have your present salary plus 2,500 common shares of Lennert (1962) Limited that I will give you in exchange for a contract to stay with the company for two years.

"As I see it, we'll either make or break it within the next two years. But, regardless of what happens you'll be able to sell your common for a big gain. This offer doesn't mean that you have a long-term commitment to me — you can be on your own in two years if you wish."

Harry Fielding spent most of his time during the next week pondering the offer. He realized that the offer was an unparalleled opportunity, which might not present itself again, to learn the pattern on which many business fortunes were made. He recalled that many times in bull sessions back at school he and his classmates had agreed, "You'll never make money on a salary. You've got to get into a small company, own a piece of the action and go for capital gains." He couldn't help but consider, at the same time, a situation with which he was personally familiar. A friend, and the owner of a successful medium-sized company, was 64 years old and seriously concerned about the condition of his estate. In Fielding's estimation, the situation would be "ripe for a change" in about three years time, and if properly handled could be highly profitable.

The offer meant facing up to some basic personal questions that he had never before considered. The attraction of the stimulating kind of life that Hayes led, and the assurance of large financial gains, overcame his uncertainty about substituting a secure job in a large corporation for what was admittedly a risky situation.

ACTIVITIES — SEPTEMBER 1962 TO JULY 1963

The broker encountered some resistance to the issue of Lennert (1962) Ltd. common, despite the favorable publicity received during the summer. The poor response was blamed on the continuing lack of confidence of the small investor in common stocks of any kind, following the sharp price decline in the spring. Nevertheless, by October 12, 1962, the 57,000 common shares were sold at a price very close to $10.00 per share and the purchase was completed.

During October and November the stock market rose strongly from the summer's low point. The general price rise, combined with the continuing stream of publicity pushed the price of Lennert (1962) Ltd. Stock to $14.00 per share in December. Both Hayes and Fielding instructed their broker to feed as many of their own shares into the market as could be absorbed without causing a price break. By May 1963 each man had disposed of over 70% of his personal holdings at a net capital gain (after brokerage fees) of $14.00 per share.

During this time, both men devoted the majority of their time to the problems of the business. Despite their efforts the adverse market and competitive influences were only partially countered. The December 31 statement for 1962, made public on June 20, 1963, after a deliberate two months delay, showed that the past sales levels were maintained only at the cost of a reduction in after-tax earnings to $47,000. Two days after the news was released, the common stock price dropped to $8.50 per share, despite carefully planned publicity that explained the temporary nature of the reverse. Hayes asked Fielding to sit down with him later in the week, to appraise their current position and prospects.

2/J. R. Sanford Corporation (A)

In August, 1958, Richard Trent, a member of the small business consulting firm of Baker and Trent, Inc., was wondering whether to make an offer to purchase the J. R. Sanford Corporation. The Sanford company was a leading producer of certain kinds of automatic paper-handling equipment for use in offices and printing shops; net sales were about $400,000 in 1957. However, the company was near bankruptcy, and Mr. Trent had been asked if he wished to make a purchase offer.

MR. TRENT'S BACKGROUND

After graduation from high school in 1936, Mr. Trent spent the next six years with a Boston utility company, working his way up from office boy to assistant to the vice-president. From 1942 to 1945, he served in the army. He then completed the undergraduate course at Harvard in three years and followed that by attending the Harvard Business School. From 1950 to 1952, he was in the planning department of a large West Coast aircraft manufacturer, and from 1952 to 1955 he served on special assignments with National Metals, Inc., a small manufacturing firm. He left the company in 1955 to establish a business consulting firm with Arthur Baker, who had formerly held administrative positions in several small firms. During the next three years, Baker and Trent provided business consulting services for many small businesses and also acted as brokers in finding buyers for certain firms.

Although Mr. Trent had earned a living from consulting, he had found the experience to be frustrating. One problem was the difficulty in getting businessmen to recognize problems and to take corrective action. He said, "Many men acquire or found a business for noneconomic reasons, related more to a way of life than making a profit. They do not think in terms of improving their return on investment, but rather in terms of maintaining a comfortable existence. If the consultant makes a suggestion, such as the development of specific accounting data bearing on one of the firm's problems, the manager may reject the advice, more because he dislikes working with figures than because he has thought through the suggestion.

"Another problem is that many managers of small businesses think a consulting firm is a nonprofit institution. Consulting is like medicine in that the patient may decide in retrospect that his recovery was so easy the doctor or consultant couldn't have done much and wasn't worth the fee. They have an emotional resistance to paying fees of $100 per day, which are needed to ensure the consultant a reasonable

This case was prepared by A. C. Cooper and R. B. Wood under the direction of Professor W. A. Hosmer, Harvard University, Graduate School of Business Administration, as the basis for class discussion rather than to illustrate either effective or ineffective administration. Copyright © 1960 by the President and Fellows of Harvard College. Reprinted by permission.

return after providing for business expenses. A consultant cannot afford to get a reputation as a man who has to sue to collect, so he is foredoomed to failure." Because of these difficulties, Mr. Trent was considering leaving the consulting field when, in November, 1957, Baker and Trent was asked to advise the J. R. Sanford company, located in Middletown, Massachusetts.

HISTORY OF THE SANFORD COMPANY

The company was founded by J. R. Sanford, in Middletown, Massachusetts, in 1949. Mr. Sanford, an engineer, designed the paper-handling equipment which the company had been selling since that time.

The company's products included collating machines and machines making carbon snap-out forms. Collating machines arranged sheets of paper in a designated order as part of the process of making booklets or of assembling office papers. With a folding device attached, the collator could assemble flat sheets of paper into complete booklets of up to 64 pages. The Sanford machines were automatic and, depending on the size, could collate from 18,000 to 72,000 sheets per hour. The price of these machines ranged from $4,000 to $16,000 apiece. Forms-making machines were used to glue sheets of paper together along one edge with little spots of glue. Carbon interleaved business forms were a typical product of this process. The price of these machines ranged from $1,100 to $2,800.

There were two principal competitors in the collating machine market. One was the Thompson Equipment Company, a manufacturer of printing equipment and supplies. Thompson Equipment sales totaled $35 million in 1956, which was the last year for which data were available at the time Mr. Trent came to consult with Sanford in 1957. The other principal competitor, American Office Equipment, Inc., specialized in office supplies and equipment, and had sales of $70 million in 1956. For both companies, sales of collating machines were only a small percentage of total company sales. Competition in the forms-making machine market came from several very small companies, each of which accounted for only a small fraction of industry sales.

Exhibit 2-1. Comparative Performance Data for Collators[a] as Determined by Sanford Management

Company	Price[b]	Speed (sheets per hour)	Size (floor space in sq. ft.)
American Office Equipment	$5,700	5,000	12.4
Thompson Equipment[a]	$4,700 to $6,900	16,000	25.0
Sanford[a]	$3,800 to $4,500	18,000	4.9

Source: Dealer bulletin prepared by the Sanford company in 1957.

[a] Four-station machine without folding attachment.

[b] Depends upon the sheet sizes.

Exhibit 2-2. Income Statements for Years Ending December 31, 1949–1956

	1949	1950	1951	1952	1953	1954	1955	1956
Gross sales	$220,760		$608,111		$515,438	n.a.	n.a.	$453,418
Less: dealer and cash discounts	15,774		73,023		55,128	n.a.	n.a.	49,565
Net sales	$204,986		$535,088		$460,310	$365,667	$415,993	$403,853
Beginning inventory[a]	$ 33,672		n.a.		$ 69,626	n.a.	n.a.	$ 87,170
Purchases	66,982		n.a.		139,397	n.a.	n.a.	123,502
Direct labor	n.a.		n.a.		33,983	n.a.	n.a.	43,118
Manufacturing overhead	n.a.		n.a.		77,361	n.a.	n.a.	131,301
Total	$100,654	M	n.a.	M	$320,367	n.a.	n.a.	$385,089
Less: ending inventory[a]	10,989	I	n.a.	I	72,089	n.a.	n.a.	97,737
Cost of goods sold	$ 89,665	S	$247,086	S	$248,278	$240,837	$312,562	$287,352
Gross margin	$115,321	S	$288,002	S	$212,032	$124,850	$103,431	$116,501
General and administrative expenses	n.a.		n.a.		n.a.	n.a.	n.a.	$102,641
Selling and shipping expenses	n.a.	I	n.a.	I	n.a.	n.a.	n.a.	38,103
Total	$ 70,775	N	$255,706	N	$159,649	$160,102	$131,023	$140,744
Net operating profit	$ 44,546	G	$ 32,296	G	$ 52,383	$ (35,253)	$ (27,593)	$ (24,243)
Other income	—		7,685		—	495	—	314
	$ 44,546		$ 39,981		$ 52,383	$ (34,758)	$ (27,593)	$ (23,929)
Less: interest	n.a.		n.a.		n.a.	n.a.	n.a.	2,299
Net profit (loss) before taxes	$ 44,546		$ 39,981		$ 52,383	$ (34,758)	$ (27,593)	$ (26,228)
Less: taxes	14,116		12,755		20,597	(9,255)	(9,627)	n.a.
Net profit (loss) after taxes	$ 30,430		$ 27,226		$ 31,786	$ (25,503)	$ (17,965)	$ (26,228)

Note: These income statements were available to Mr. Trent at the time he was asked to advise the Sanford company in November 1957.

n.a. = not available.

[a] Inventories include only material and direct labor.

Industry sales of automatic forms-making machines were estimated at $300,000 for 1956, of which Sanford accounted for about 80 percent. Sanford sales of collating machines totaled about $160,000 in 1956, which was about 20 percent of the industry total. Both markets were expected to grow with the increased tendency toward automated office procedures; it was expected that the collating market would grow more rapidly.

Net sales of the Sanford company climbed from $205,000 in 1949 to $535,000 by 1951. The Sanford management believed its machines to be more economical, more compact, and faster than competitive machines. Comparative performance data for collators as prepared by the Sanford management in 1957 are given in Exhibit 2-1. However, sales dropped after 1951, and were $403,000 in 1956. Losses occurred in all years after 1953. Available financial data for the years 1949 through 1956 are given in Exhibits 2-2 and 2-3.

THE SITUATION

In attempting to assist the Sanford company, Mr. Trent investigated various company activities. He found that all products were marketed through a network of 140 United States dealers and through two company-owned sales offices in Chicago and New York. The dealers received a 25 percent discount from list price, and were expected to install and service the machines as well as train the operators. All dealers also handled other items of printing and office equipment. Dealerships were not exclusive; for example, in Los Angeles there were seven dealers.

Mr. Sanford also personally arranged direct sales to any customers who answered the company's advertisements in trade magazines; dealers were not given a commission on these sales. In 1957, about 50 percent of total sales were made in this way. This created a problem in that dealers were reluctant to service machines they had not sold. In Mr. Trent's opinion, this practice was disrupting the morale of the dealers and converting them into mere order takers.

The company was housed in a modern building containing 20,000 square feet of floor space, which was being used at about 50 percent of capacity in 1957. The building was owned by a separate corporation which was wholly owned by Mr. Sanford; rent was $1,100 per month and did not include heat, taxes, or insurance. In November, 1957, there were 25 employees in the Middletown plant, two of whom, in addition to Mr. Sanford, served in an executive capacity. However, it appeared to Mr. Trent that most decisions in all areas of company activity were being made by Mr. Sanford.

There were also eight engineers in a research and development laboratory located in Chicago; the cost of maintaining this laboratory was approximately $50,000 per year. In the income statement, this was charged in part to manufacturing overhead. Few improvements or developments had come out of this laboratory, apparently due in part to a rapid turnover in technical personnel. Mr. Trent thought this turnover was due to personal differences between Mr. Sanford and the technical men involved.

Exhibit 2-3. Balance Sheets as of December 31, 1949–1956

	1949	1950	1951	1952	1953	1954	1955	1956
Assets								
Cash		$ 16,204	$ 1,353		$ 8,103	$ 2,719	$ 1,128	$ 2,390
Accounts receivable		102,698	43,193		79,384	42,205	55,574	38,667
Inventory[a]		17,538	54,629		72,089	76,937	87,170	97,737
Total		$136,450	$ 99,175		$159,576	$121,861	$143,872	$138,794
Machinery and equipment (net)		n.a.	n.a.		n.a.	n.a.	n.a.	n.a.
Furniture and fixtures (net)		n.a.	n.a.		n.a.	n.a.	n.a.	n.a.
Total		$ 14,765	$ 46,500	M	$ 53,516	$ 64,194	$ 65,134	$ 61,292
Reserve (finance company)				I	$ 4,860	—	$ 1,795	$ 4,328
Deposits		$ 9,656	$ 9,918	S	2,719		4,346	—
Other				S		34,423	24,715	5,303
Total		$ 9,656	$ 9,918	I	$ 7,579	$ 34,423	$ 30,856	$ 9,631
Total assets		$160,861	$155,593		$220,671	$220,478	$239,861	$209,717
Liabilities and capital				N				
Accounts payable		$ 22,523	$ 21,164	G	$ 37,714	$ 52,923	$ 85,159	$ 85,380
Notes payable		—	—		—	6,144	18,706	8,184
Accrued payroll and expense		—	—		1,200	6,221	4,887	6,678
Withholding taxes payable		736	1,012		3,526	b	b	b
Customers' deposits		—	—		—	4,466	13,293	10,815
Taxes accrued		47,792	16,380		25,508	23,504	6,075	15,228
Total		$ 71,051	$ 38,556		$ 67,948	$ 93,258	$128,120	$126,285
Long-term note		—	—		—	—	$ 2,486	$ 408
Capital stock outstanding		$ 46,390	$ 46,390		$ 46,390	$ 46,390	$ 46,390	$ 46,390
Retained earnings		43,419	70,646		106,333	80,829	62,864	36,635
Total		$ 89,809	$117,036		$152,723	$127,219	$109,255	$ 83,025
Total liabilities and capital		$160,861	$155,592		$220,671	$220,478	$239,861	$209,717

Note: These balance sheets were available to Mr. Trent in November 1957.
n.a. = not available.
a Inventories include only materials and direct labor.
b Included in taxes accrued.

Production involved machining of certain parts, assembling, painting, and buffing. The operations performed were typical of many machine shops and, in Mr. Trent's opinion, did not require any special skills. The equipment included lathes, drill presses, and assembly benches — all in excellent condition. Mr. Trent thought there was enough equipment to produce for annual sales of about $1 million.

Mr. Sanford owned 90 percent of the stock. The remaining 10 percent of the stock was owned by Ralph Beller, who did general administrative work. Although records were incomplete, it appeared that Mr. Sanford was drawing a salary of about $50,000 per year and was also charging about $50,000 per year in personal expenses to the company. Loans on accounts receivable and equipment totaling about $13,000 had been obtained from a local finance company at interest rates of 18 percent per year.

Apparently, records were not kept in a consistent manner, and some transactions were not even recorded. There was no knowledge of product costs, and it appeared that the financial statements had not been prepared with sufficient care to be reliable. Such records as had been prepared had not been preserved systematically, so that,

Exhibit 2-4. Income Statements for Year Ending December 31, 1957, and for Six Months Ending July 30, 1958

	1957	1958 (unaudited)
Gross sales	$453,041	$199,076
Less: dealer and cash discounts	49,468	29,338
Net sales	$403,573	$169,738
Beginning inventory[a]	$ 97,737	$ 81,586
Purchases	127,954	38,088
Direct labor	32,356	12,752
Manufacturing overhead	122,752	44,784
Total	$380,799	$177,210
Less: ending inventory[a]	81,586	59,124
Costs of goods sold	$299,213	$118,086
Gross margin	$104,360	$ 51,652
General and administrative expense	$113,092	$ 67,710
Selling and shipping expense	29,770	9,440
Research and development	—	2,082
Total	$142,862	$ 79,232
Net operating profit	$ (38,502)	$ (27,580)
Other income	1,469	—
Total	$ (37,033)	$ (27,580)
Less: interest	1,847	2,647
Net profit (loss) before taxes	$ (38,880)	$ (30,227)
Less: taxes	—	—
Net profit (loss) after taxes	$ (38,880)	$ (30,227)

Note: In addition to earlier financial statements, these were available to Mr. Trent in July 1958.
[a] Inventories include only material and direct labor.

Exhibit 2-5. Balance Sheets as of December 31, 1957, and July 30, 1958

	1957	1958 (unaudited)
Assets		
Cash	$ 576	$ 2,094
Accounts receivable	38,628	38,523
Inventory[a]	81,586	59,124
Total	$120,790	$ 99,741
Machinery and equipment (net)	n.a.	n.a.
Furniture and fixtures (net)	n.a.	n.a.
Total	$ 58,143	$ 48,321
Reserve (finance company)	$ 6,425	$ 5,923
Deposits	—	825
Other	6,557	13,932
Total	$ 12,982	$ 20,680
Total assets	$191,915	$168,742
Liabilities and capital		
Accounts payable	$ 89,471	$ 72,821
Notes payable	11,981	23,093
Accrued payroll and expenses	4,080	3,749
Customers' deposits	10,192	4,664
Taxes accrued	20,772	9,867
Total	$136,496	$114,194
Long-term note	$ 1,275	$ 7,297
Capital stock outstanding	$ 46,390	$ 46,390
Donated surplus	10,000	33,333
Retained earnings	(2,246)	(32,472)
Total	$ 55,419	$ 54,548
Total liabilities and capital	$191,915	$168,742

Note: In addition to earlier financial statements, these were available to Mr. Trent in July 1958.
n.a. = not available.
[a] Inventories include only material and direct labor.

as can be seen in Exhibits 2-2 to 2-5, some of the balance sheets and income statements were missing entirely.

After his investigation, Mr. Trent made a number of suggestions designed to improve the management of the company. However, Mr. Sanford did not follow the suggestions; Baker and Trent therefore broke off the association. Eight months later, in late July, 1958, Mr. Trent received a distress telephone call from Mr. Sanford.

Mr. Trent arrived to discover that the company's position had deteriorated considerably. Records indicated there had been a net loss of $38,000 for 1957. Financial data for 1957 and the first six months of 1958 are given in Exhibits 2-4 and 2-5. From a consideration of liabilities and assets, Mr. Trent estimated that the company would have a negative net worth of $30,000 if liquidated at that time. Two signatures were already on a bankruptcy petition. Back payroll taxes had not been paid for two years.

It appeared that Mr. Sanford might be liable personally for certain of the company's debts, in which case he might lose his home, his car, and the building.

Mr. Trent told him that he could have aided him eight months or even six months before, but that it was now too late. Mr. Sanford replied by offering to sell his share of the company to Mr. Trent. He pointed out that since the financial situation was so urgent, a decision would have to be made within 24 hours.

THE DECISION

Mr. Trent did not have time to secure an audit of the company's records. He was aware that errors or misrepresentations might exist in the records. He made a personal examination of the inventory and decided that it was undervalued and was probably worth at least twice the $59,000 listed on the balance sheet. Although his previous association with the company as a consultant had been brief, he was aware that a number of improvements could be made in the management of the company. It also appeared to him that the company's products were well designed and superior to competitive products.

Although Mr. Trent had no personal funds that he could invest, he knew of a friend from whom he could secure a long-term loan for $10,000. He had about decided that consulting with small businesses was a dead-end street. He had seen the poor management practices of many managers of small enterprises, including a lack of knowledge of costs and an inability to think in economic terms. It might be easier, he thought, to compete against small businessmen than to advise them.

Mr. Trent realized that, except for his judgment based upon inspection of the inventory, he had little evidence of assets. He was not at all sure the financial statements showed all the liabilities. He was not so familiar as he would wish to be with customer relations and with attitudes of customers and dealers toward the company. Nevertheless, he realized that he would have to give Mr. Sanford an answer the next day.

3/ Self-Serve Shoe Stores

DESCRIPTION AND HISTORY OF SELF-SERVE SHOE STORES

The Self-Serve Shoe Stores of Portland, Oregon, were opened during 1961 and operated as an outlet for both "distress" and popular priced shoes for the entire family. Store No. 1, which was located on a heavily traveled highway just outside the city, was opened in April, 1961. Store No. 2, located on an artery in the city, occupied a part of the same building with a self-service laundry and was situated across the street from an elementary school. It was opened in May, 1961. Store No. 3, also located on an artery, but occupying an entire building adjacent to a self-service laundry, was opened in December, 1961.

Each of the locations displayed shoes in open individual boxes placed upon plain wooden racks. Sizes were plainly penciled on the boxes, and children's, men's, and women's shoes were located in different sections of the store. There was a small amount of warehouse space in each store, but most of the storage room was located in Store No. 1, which also served as the headquarters for the general manager.

The stores were organized as a corporation and owned by six stockholders, but the organization was primarily the brain child of Mr. Wesley Baldwin, who operated two "legitimate" or full-service men's shoe stores in the same city. Mr. Baldwin had opened his first shoe store some five years earlier and three years later opened a second store in a suburban shopping center. The trend toward self-service merchandising of shoes and the possibilities for profits in this type of operation provided the motivation for the organization of the new business. Although the business was that of shoe retailing, the same as Baldwin's previous business, the two ventures were for the most part non-competitive in that their appeals were to different groups of customers.

Although Wesley Baldwin was the instigator of the new self-service shoe stores, he owned less than half of the stock in the corporation. The ownership was divided as follows:

Wesley Baldwin	26.5%
Ronald Brown	22.5
David Ware	22.5
Larry Kliever	13.5
Ned Casey	10.0
Harry Stagg	5.0
	100.0%

Reprinted from Justin G. Longenecker, *Principles of Management and Organizational Behavior*, 2d ed. (Columbus, Ohio: Merrill, 1969), pp. 670–75, by permission of Charles E. Merrill Publishing Co.

THE BOARD OF DIRECTORS

Each of the stockholders also served as a member of its board of directors and participated actively in decisions pertaining to the operation of Self-Serve Shoe Stores. Most of the stockholders also had other business interests. As noted earlier, Wesley Baldwin was the owner and manager of two full-service men's shoe stores. He also served as president of the Self-Serve Shoe Stores but did not serve as its full-time executive in day-to-day administration. The responsibilities or other connections of the remaining members of the board were as follows:

Ronald Brown — employed as a shoe salesman for a major shoe manufacturer, traveling over most of Oregon and part of Washington.

David Ware — employed by a Portland industrial concern as a millwright.

Larry Kliever — employed as a shoe salesman for a manufacturer and also traveling over most of Oregon.

Ned Casey — employed as general manager of Self-Serve Shoe Stores on a full-time basis.

Harry Stagg — employed as store manager of Wesley Baldwin's second full-service shoe store.

The board was no "rubber-stamp" board. Each of the directors took a personal interest in the business, and a number of them made personal contributions of their own services to the new stores. For example, Ronald Brown and Larry Kliever located lots of distress merchandise as they called on different shoe stores and were able to arrange favorable purchases for resale in Self-Serve Shoe Stores. David Ware, having a good background in maintenance, performed all maintenance and minor construction work in adapting and keeping the store buildings in good operating condition.

STORE MANAGEMENT BY NED CASEY

The salary agreement with Ned Casey, the general manager, provided for a base salary of $500 per month with two stores in operation. Starting with Store No. 3 in December, 1961, the contract provided for $90 additional salary per month for each additional store. In addition, he was to receive one-half of one per cent of total gross volume as a bonus, payable every six months. Stores were required to do $50,000 sales volume before this bonus was paid.

The general manager was responsible for directing all store personnel. Each of the three stores had two employees, one of whom was designated as store manager. The store manager received about $80 per week, and the other employee received about $45 per week. The stores stayed open from 9 A.M. to 9 P.M., and the shifts of these two employees were overlapped so that both would be present during rush hours. Shifts were alternated so that one employee did not constantly have the late shift. Ned visited each of the stores as frequently as possible. He was in Store No. 1 daily, but he did not always visit the other two stores each day.

One of Ned's primary functions was buying shoes for sale in all three stores. It was in this particular area that he was recognized as being most skilled. In fact, one of the other stockholders described him as a "walking encyclopedia" of the shoe business. Ned had worked in the sale of shoes for many years and was thoroughly conversant with shoe styles and trends. He was also recognized as being a sharp bargainer in negotiating for the sale of distress merchandise. A jobber might call on Ned to show him some shoes that he had purchased from a bankrupt shoe store. Ned could quickly look at a few of the samples, size them up, and ask concerning the offering price. At once, drawing on his knowledge of shoes, he could reject the purchase, accept it, or make a counter offer that would secure for him the more attractive items in the lot or that would secure a type of shoe that was in short supply in his own stores.

In the use of systematic management and controls, Ned had little experience and seemingly little interest. He kept his greatest supply of information on shoe supplies, requirements, and orders in his own head. He supplemented this knowledge with a rather haphazard record system, involving notes to himself, copies of invoices, and other miscellaneous items of information. These were completely unorganized and unfiled, but, surprisingly enough, Ned could usually come up with necessary figures at the time they were needed. In fact, it was a source of amazement to his colleagues that he could keep the situation under control as well as he could with what appeared to be such a completely inadequate set of records.

Ned was criticized in particular for his lack of ability in personnel relations. He had several incidents in which employees became somewhat unhappy because of his brusque manner of dealing with them. Although he did not use a great amount of tact in dealing with these employees, he was basically big-hearted and never dismissed any of the employees in spite of his rather gruff exterior. Seemingly, some of the employees were able to adjust to Ned and his techniques once they discovered that his "bark was worse than his bite."

RELATIONSHIP OF THE BOARD TO THE GENERAL MANAGER

The close personal interest of the board members in the business and their individual responsibilities in store management meant that they would inevitably be thrown into close contact, and possible conflict, with the general manager. The stockholders and directors did not always consider their services and judgment to be limited to their participation in board meetings; they also liked to discuss store administration and store policies with Ned between board meetings.

Some of the directors felt that Ned was somewhat slow in considering their suggestions and unwilling to give their ideas a full and fair trial. As one expressed it, "Ned is bull-headed and will not consider an idea from one of us fairly. He is brilliant in his knowledge of shoes, but he can't stand to listen to or to discuss a suggestion from one of us. It is a matter of pride with him." Among the types of suggestions, practices, and policies that these directors liked to discuss with Ned were his record and control system, store layout, merchandise purchases, and transfer of certain lots of merchandise from one store to another.

Ned viewed many of the suggestions coming from his associates as an intrusion into an area of management in which they had little knowledge or experience. (The possible exception as far as his own willingness to listen was concerned was the president, Wesley Baldwin, who also was an experienced shoe man.) As Ned expressed it, "I think the fellows sincerely mean to help me, but they simply don't see the entire picture. For example, they want me to buy ahead for a possible, tentative opening of a new store. But I can't build up an inventory for a store that may never materialize. They are free to criticize me when a purchase looks questionable, but they change to smiles and become very quiet when the shoes start selling and bringing in the profits."

The conflicts of ideas and close personal interest of all members in store administration resulted, then, in considerable friction among the members of the organization. In spite of the conflict, each member of the group held considerable respect for the other members and recognized the importance of the contribution that each was making to the success of the business as a whole.

Some of the individual responsibilities of different directors had grown out of this early period of development in which the organization was feeling its way along in its attempt to provide a proper organization that would assume all necessary responsibilities. The advertising function and the maintenance function would normally come under the direction of the general manager, but they had been turned over to the particular directors who had special experience and were expected to work in cooperation with the general manager. He was not in a position, however, to issue orders and instructions to them as he might be able to do in the case of a subordinate. The general manager did manage to obtain final authority over all purchases. Even though the two salesmen-stockholders would locate prospective purchases, they were never given the authority to make purchase commitments. Each of these was referred to Ned, often by telephone, and it was his decision as to whether a particular lot should be purchased or refused.

One of the plans being contemplated by the president of the corporation was an arrangement whereby the purchasing function would be split from the store administration function. As general manager, Ned had the responsibility for both areas. If the functions were split, however, Ned would limit his activities to the purchasing and warehousing of shoes. If an organizational pattern of this type were adopted, the store managers would report to the president, board of directors, or some other chief executive.

There was also a question as to the precise status of the store manager. In particular, a question existed as to whether he might be given responsibility similar to that of a store manager in a full-service shoe store. At the time, he served as a working leader with only minor authority in running his particular store.

4/ Rendell Company

$\mathbf{M}$r. Fred Bevins, controller of the Rendell Company, was concerned about the organizational status of his divisional controllers. In 1959, and for many years previously, the divisional controllers reported to the general manager of their divisions. Although Mr. Bevins knew this to be the practice in many other divisionally organized companies, he was not entirely satisfied with it. His interest in making a change was stimulated by a description of organizational responsibilities which he obtained from conversations with the controller of the Martex Corporation.

The Rendell Company consisted of seven operating divisions. The smallest had $10 million in sales, and the largest over $100 million in sales. Each of the divisions was responsible for both the manufacturing and the marketing of a distinct product line. Some parts and components were transferred between divisions, but the volume of such interdivisional business was not large.

The Rendell Company had been in business and profitable for over 50 years. In the early 1950's, although it continued to make profits, its rate of growth slowed considerably. Mr. Hodgkin, the president, was brought in in 1954 by the directors because of their concern about this situation. His first position was controller. He became executive vice president in 1957 and president in 1958. Mr. Bevins joined the company as assistant controller in 1955. He was then 33 years old. He became controller in 1957.

In 1954, the corporate control organization was primarily responsible for (1) financial accounting, (2) internal auditing, and (3) analysis of capital budgeting requests. A budgetary control system was in existence, but the reports prepared under this system were submitted to the top management group directly by the operating divisions, with little analysis by the corporate control organization.

Mr. Hodgkin thought it essential that the corporate control organization play a more active role in the process of agreeing on budgets and in analyzing performance. He personally took a more active role in reviewing budgets and studying divisional performance reports and brought in several young analysts to assist him. Mr. Bevins continued to move in the same direction after his promotion to controller. By 1959, the corporate organization was beginning to be well enough staffed so it could, and did, give careful attention to the information submitted by the divisions.

Divisional controllers reported directly to the division general managers. The corporate controller was always consulted prior to the appointment of the new division controller, and he was also consulted in connection with salary increases for division controllers. The corporate controller specified the accounting system to which the divisions were expected to conform, and the general procedures to be followed in connection with budgeting and reporting performance. It was clearly understood, however, that budgets and performance reports coming from a division were the responsibility of that division's general manager, with the division controller acting as his staff assistant in the preparation of these documents. For example, the division general manager personally discussed his budget with top management prior to its approval, and although the divisional controller was usually present at these meetings to give information on technical points, his role was strictly that of a staff man.

Mr. Bevins saw increasing difficulties with this relationship as the corporation introduced more modern control techniques. For one thing, he thought the existing relationship between himself and the divisional controllers was not close enough so that he could urge the development and use of the new techniques as rapidly as he wished. More importantly, he thought that he was not getting adequate information about what was actually happening in the divisions. The division controller's primary loyalty was to his division manager, and it was unreasonable to expect that he would give Mr. Bevins a frank, unbiased report of what was happening. For example, Mr. Bevins was quite sure that some "fat" was hidden in the divisional expense budgets, and that the divisional controllers had a pretty good idea as to where it was. In short, he thought he would get a much better idea of what was going on in the divisions if reports on divisional activities came directly from controllers working for him rather than from controllers working for the division manager.

Mr. Bevins was therefore especially interested in the controller organization at the Martex Company as he learned about it from Mr. Ingraham, The Martex controller.

Until his visit to Martex, Mr. Bevins had not discussed the organization problem with anyone. Shortly thereafter he gave Mr. Harrigan, his assistant controller, a memorandum describing his visit (see Appendix) and asked for Mr. Harrigan's reaction. Mr. Harrigan had been with Rendell for 25 years, and had been a division controller before coming to headquarters in 1956. Mr. Bevins respected his knowledge of the company and his opinion on organizational matters. Mr. Harrigan was accustomed to speaking frankly with Mr. Bevins. The gist of his comments follows:

"I don't think the Martex plan would work with us; in fact, I am not even sure it works at Martex in the way suggested by the job descriptions and organization charts.

"Before coming to headquarters, I had five years' experience as a division controller. When I took that job, I was told by the corporate controller and by my general manager that my function was to help the general manager every way I could. This is the way I operated. My people got together a lot of the information that was helpful in preparing the divisional budget, but the final product represented the thinking and decisions of my general manager, and he was the person who sold it to top management. I always went with him to the budget meetings, and he often asked me to explain some of the figures. When the monthly reports were prepared, I usually went over them looking for danger signals, and then took them in to the general manager. He might agree with me, or he might spot other things that needed looking into. In either case, he usually was the one to put the heat on the operating organization, not me.

"We did have some problems. The worst, and this happened several times a year, was when someone from the corporate controller's office would telephone and ask questions such as 'Do you think your division could get along all right if we cut $X out of the advertising budget?' Or, 'Do you really believe that the cost savings estimate on this equipment request is realistic?' Usually, I was in complete agreement with the data in question and defended them as best I could. Once in a while, however, I might privately disagree with the 'official' figures, but I tried not to say so.

"Questions of this sort really should be asked of the general manager, not of me. I realize that the head office people probably didn't think the question was important enough to warrant bothering the general manager, and in many cases they were right. The line is a fine one.

"This business of the division controller being an 'unbiased source of information' sounds fine when you word it that way, but another way to say it is that he is a front office spy, and that doesn't sound so good. It would indeed make our life easier if we could count on the division controllers to give us the real lowdown on what is going on. But if this is to be their position, then we can't expect that the general manager will continue to treat his controller as a trusted assistant. Either the general manager will find somebody else to take over this work unofficially, or it won't get done.

"I think we are better off the way we are. Sure, the budgets will have some fat in them, and not all the bad situations will be highlighted in the operating reports, and this makes our job more difficult. But I'd rather have this, than the alternative. If we used the Martex method (or, rather, what they claim is their method), we can be sure that the division controller will no longer be a member of the management team. They'll isolate him as much as they can, and the control function in the division will suffer."

APPENDIX: NOTES ON MARTEX CONTROLLER ORGANIZATION

Mr. Ingraham, the Corporate Controller, reports directly to the President and has reporting to him all Division Controllers and other accounting, data processing, and analysis groups. Organization charts and descriptions of responsibility are included herein (Exhibits 4-1, 4-2, 4-3, and 4-4) and indicate the structure and function of the organization.

The Controller's organization is charged with the responsibility of establishing cost and profit standards in the corporation and of taking appropriate action to see that these standards are attained. It reviews all research projects and assigns names and numbers to them in order to coordinate research activities in the various Divisions and their Central Research. The organization also handles all matters involving cost and profit estimates.

The present size of Division Controllers' staffs ranges from three to twenty-two. Division Controllers are not involved in preparing Division P and L Statements; these are prepared by a separate group for all Divisions and the Corporation.

Line-Staff Relationships

A Division Manager has no staff of his own, not even a personal assistant. He receives staff assistance from two sources.

First, he has some people assigned to him from the general staff, typically a controller, an engineer, and a purchasing agent.

All division management and all of the corporate staff are located in the corporate headquarters building. However, the "assigned staff" are located physically with their staff colleagues; for example, a Division Controller and his assistant are located in the Controller's section of the building, not near his Division Manager's office.

Second, the Division Manager can call on the central staff to the extent he wishes. The divisions are charged on the basis of service rendered for these services. The central staff units are listed in the "General Staff Services" box of Exhibit 4-2.

Division Manager–Controller Relationship

The success of the Martex Controller organization and its relations with Division Managers appears to be largely the result of Managers and Controllers having grown up with the arrangement and accepting it long before they arrived at their managerial positions.

Some additional factors which appear to contribute to their successful relationship are:

1. a uniform and centralized accounting system
2. predetermined financial objectives for each Division
   a. growth in dollar sales
   b. profit as a per cent of sales
3. profit sharing by Managers and Controllers

Accounting System

The Controller's Division has complete control of the accounting system. It determines how and what accounts will be kept. The Controller's Division has developed an accounting system which is the same for all divisions, Mr. Ingraham pointed out that no division had a system perfectly tailored to its needs, but they felt the disadvantages to the divisions were more than offset by having a system uniform over all divisions and understood by all concerned. Mr. Ingraham indicated it is likely that if Martex Divisions were free to establish their own accounting system, every division would have a different accounting system within two years and interpretation by corporate management would be difficult, if possible at all.

The accounting system appears to provide a common basis for all Division financial reports and analyses, and aids in maintaining the bond of confidence between Division Managers and Controllers.

Division Objectives

The corporation has established two financial objectives for each division. These are:

1. growth in dollar sales
2. profit as a per cent of sales

These objectives are determined in advance by recommendations of the Controller's Division with the advice and counsel of division managers. The objectives are long-range in nature; the target profit has been changed only three times since 1935.

The particular per cent of sales selected as the target profit rate is established by considering several factors, among which are (1) the patentability of products, (2) return on investment, (3) industry margin of profit, and (4) industry rate of return on investment. These factors and others are incorporated in the profit rate finally selected.

Within limits, attainment of these financial objectives represent the primary task required of Division General Managers by Corporate Management.

Profit Sharing

Division Managers receive about 75% of their total compensation from profit sharing and stock options. Division Controllers receive about 25% of their compensation from profit sharing: half from a share in division profits, and the other half from corporate profits.

Division Managers' View

Mr. Ingraham indicated that Division Managers like to have Division Controllers report to the Corporate Controller because (1) it gives them an unbiased partner armed with relevant information, (2) the Controller is in a better position to do the analysis needed for decision-making, and (3) when cost reports are issued there is little or no argument about them among affected parties.

Exhibit 4-1. Position Descriptions from the Martex Management Guide Book

---

Controller

The trend of modern business management is to change the basic concept of the Controller's position from an administrative function concerned largely with accounting detail to that of an important position in management as it relates to the control of costs and the profitable operation of the business as a whole.

The more our business becomes diversified with operations scattered throughout the U.S.A., the greater is the need for an officer to whom the president delegates authority with respect to those factors affecting costs and profits in the same manner as he may delegate authority to others in strong staff positions.

In our vertical type of organization there is great need for an appointed officer whose responsibility it is to establish budgetary standards of operations and objective per cent of profit on sales targets for each of the operating divisions and domestic subsidiaries. He shall also establish budgetary standards of operation for staff functions in line with divisional and over-all company profit objectives. When the standard of operations or profit target is not attained, the Controller has the right and the responsibility within his delegated authority to question the failure and recommend changes to accomplish the desired result.

The Controller shall work with the various divisions of the Company through divisional controllers assigned to each major operating division and staff function. It is not intended that the Controller take the initiative away from the division managers since the responsibility for efficient operations and profits are assumed by the managers. However, the Controller and his staff should have the right and the responsibility to expect certain operating results from the division head and when a difference of opinion occurs as to the reasonableness of the demand for results the matter should then be referred by either party to the President.

Along with the foregoing, the following responsibilities are an essential part of the position and apply to the corporation and its subsidiaries:

1. the installation and supervision of all accounting records
2. the preparation, supervision and interpretation of all Divisional and Commodity Profit and Loss statements, operating statements and cost reports, including reports of costs of production, research, distribution and administration
3. the supervision of taking and costing of all physical inventories
4. the preparation and interpretation of all operating statistics and reports, including interpretation of charts and graphs, for use by Management Committees and Board of Directors
5. the preparation, as budget director, in conjunction with staff officers and heads of divisions and subsidiaries, of an annual budget covering all operations for submission to the President prior to the beginning of the fiscal year
6. the initiation, preparation, and issuance of standard practice regulations and the coordination of systems, including clerical and office methods relating to all operating accounting procedures
7. he or his designated representative shall be a member of all Division and Subsidiary Management Committees

He shall be responsible for the selection, training, development, and promotion of qualified personnel for his organization and their compensation within established company policy. He shall submit to the President an organization plan for accomplishing desired objectives.

The Controller may delegate to members of his organization certain of his responsibilities but in so doing he does not relinquish his over-all responsibility or accountability for results.

Treasurer and Assistant Treasurers

Subject to the rules and regulations of the Finance Committee, the Treasurer is the chief financial officer and generally his functions include control of corporate funds and attending to the financial affairs of the corporation and its domestic and foreign subsidiaries wherever located. More specifically the duties and responsibilities are as follows:

Banking: He shall have custody of and be responsible for all money and securities and shall deposit in the name of the corporation in such depositories as are approved by the President all funds coming into his possession for the company account.

Credits and Collections: He shall have supervision over all cashiers, cash receipts and collection records and accounts receivable ledgers. He shall initiate and approve all credit policies and procedures.

Disbursements: He shall authorize disbursements of any kind by signature on checks. This includes direct supervision over accounts payable and payroll departments and indirect supervision over all receiving departments for the purpose of checking and the accuracy of invoices presented for payment. He shall maintain adequate record of authorized appropriations and also determine that all financial transactions covered by minutes of Management and Executive Committees and the Board of Directors are properly executed and recorded.

General Financial Reports: He shall prepare and supervise all general accounting records. He shall prepare and interpret all general financial statements which includes the preparation of the quarterly and annual reports for mailing to stockholders. This also includes the preparation and approval of the regulations on standard practices required to assure compliance with orders or regulations issued by duly-constituted governmental agencies and stock exchanges.

He shall supervise the continuous audit (including internal controls) of all accounts and records and shall supervise the audit and procedures of Certified Public Accountants.

Taxes: He shall supervise the preparation and filing of all tax returns and shall have supervision of all matters relating to taxes and shall refer to the General Counsel all such matters requiring interpretation of tax laws and regulations.

Insurance Property Records: He shall supervise the purchase and placing of insurance of any kind including the insurance required in connection with employee benefits. He shall be responsible for recommending adequate coverage for all ascertainable risks and shall maintain such records as to avoid any possibility of various hazards not being properly insured. He shall maintain adequate property records and valuations for insurance and other purposes and if necessary, employ appraisal experts to assist in determining such valuations and records.

Loans: He shall approve all loans and advances made to employees within limits prescribed by the Executive Committee.

Investments: As funds are available beyond normal requirements, he shall recommend suitable investments to the Finance Committee. He shall have custody of securities so acquired and shall use the safekeeping facilities of the banks for that purpose. As securities are added or removed from such vaults or facilities, he shall be accompanied by an authorized officer of the Corporation.

Office Management: Will be responsible for the coordination of all office management functions throughout the Company and its domestic subsidiaries.

Financial Planning: He shall initiate and prepare current and long-range cash forecasts particularly as such forecasts are needed for financing programs to meet anticipated cash requirements for future growth and expansion. He shall arrange to meet sinking fund requirements for all outstanding debenture bonds and preferred stock and shall anticipate such requirements whenever possible.

He shall have such other powers and shall perform such other duties as may be assigned to him by the Board of Directors and the President.

The Treasurer shall be responsible for the selection, training, development and promotion of qualified personnel for his organization and their compensation within established company policy. It is expected that since he will have to delegate many of the duties and responsibilities enumerated above, he shall confer with and submit to the President an organization plan and chart.

The Treasurer may delegate to members of his organization certain of his responsibilities together with appropriate authority for fulfillment; however, in so doing he does not relinquish his over-all responsibility or accountability for results.

The Treasurer is a member of the Finance, Retirement, and Inventory Review Committees.

Exhibit 4-2. Martex Corporation, Division A, January 1, 1959

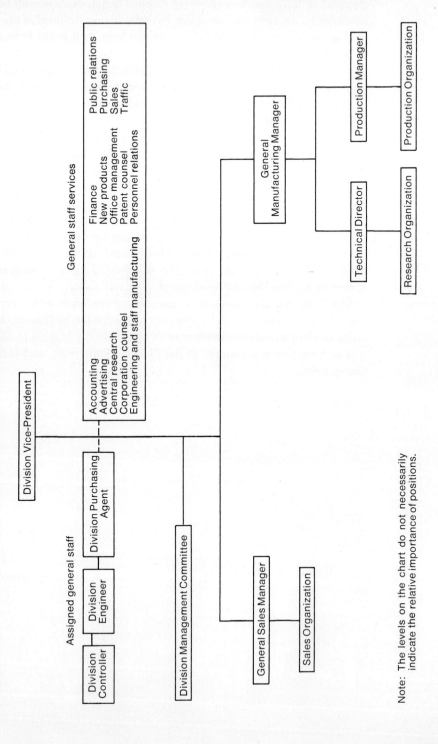

Note: The levels on the chart do not necessarily indicate the relative importance of positions.

Exhibit 4-3. Martex Corporation, Controller's Division, January 1, 1959

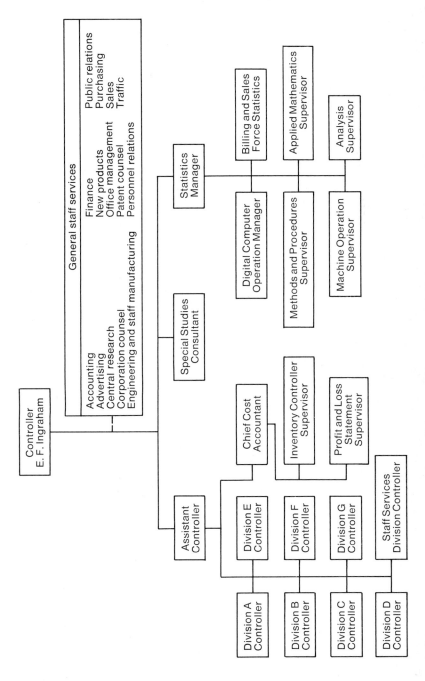

Exhibit 4-4. Martex Corporation, Treasurer's Division, August 1, 1959

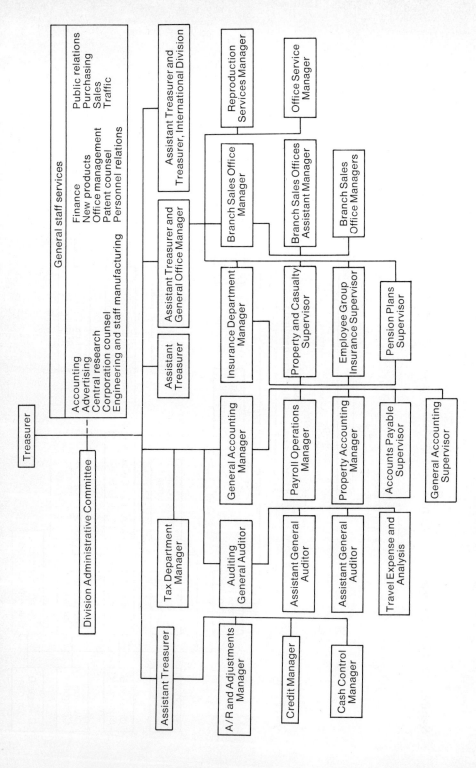

Note: The levels on the chart do not necessarily indicate the relative importance of positions.

5/Fox Press Corporation

In August, 1949, the board of directors of the Fox Press Corporation appointed Mr. Edward Klein, then fifty-one years old, as executive vice-president. Prior to this appointment, Mr. Klein, who had joined the company in 1944 as treasurer, had been serving as treasurer, office manager and chairman of the executive committee.

CORPORATE HISTORY AND PRODUCT DEVELOPMENT

The Fox Press Corporation was known as a manufacturer of custom-made heavy machinery, specializing in industrial presses ranging from 100 to 4,000 tons capacity. Usually prospective customers submitted drawings of the parts they wanted to have stamped or manufactured and the Fox Press Corporation would submit the specifications of the machine it recommended for the task and the price at which it would make and sell the press. Customers consisted primarily of automotive manufacturers and allied companies, stove, refrigerator and airplane manufacturers and die shops. Some of the customers were such large users of presses that they designed their own presses and merely submitted specifications of the desired machines to the Fox Press Corporation, which then quoted a sales price. Presses ranged in price from $12,000 to $200,000.

The company was founded in 1933 by Mr. Richard Jones, who, at that time, had twenty-five years' experience in the industrial press field. Mr. Jones planned to make presses of welded steel, whereas up to that time, they had been made of castings. His innovation offered a stronger press at lower cost and one which was more readily adaptable to custom-made machines. Mr. Jones interested some Chicago investors, who furnished much of the capital and received common stock in return. In the spring of 1950 four of these investors were still on the board of directors and took an active part in all major financial decisions of the company. A machinery dealer and the executive vice-president of the Fox Press Corporation, along with Mr. Jones, made up the seven-man board of directors.

The Fox welded press was gradually accepted by the industry. By 1950 Fox was producing approximately one-fourth of all heavy press machinery. Much of the success of the firm was due to the personal efforts of the president, Mr. Jones. From the start he had made all the important and many of the relatively unimportant decisions. In addition he had been personally responsible for securing many important orders. Although the company had many capable executives, it was clearly recognized that Mr. Jones was the decision maker and chief executive.

Reprinted from Thomas J. McNichols, *Policy Making and Executive Action*, 2d ed. (New York: McGraw-Hill, 1963), by permission of the author and the Graduate School of Management, Northwestern University.

Until 1940 annual sales consisted of only one or two machines. The national defense program and subsequent war needs created a tremendous demand for Fox machines. The establishment of new complete stamping shops created a demand for thirty to forty machines for a single company. Despite the rapid expansion of facilities, the Fox Press Corporation, as late as 1947, had a backlog of orders of about two years' production. Many of these orders were for machines designed previously so that product engineering was relatively unimportant. Production, however, became very important. Sales engineers acted primarily as liaison men between customers, the government and the company in the submittal and approval of specifications, checking of priorities and in maintaining good will.

CORPORATE ORGANIZATION UNDER AN EXECUTIVE VICE-PRESIDENT

Because of the added pressures of wartime conditions, Mr. Jones wanted to hire an executive who could relieve him of his many responsibilities. Early in 1944 Mr. George Cooper, a fifty-five-year-old executive of an automotive concern, was appointed executive vice-president. In December, 1946, he was made a member of the board of directors. Mr. Jones then moved his office to the downtown area and merely visited the plant, located in an outlying district of the city, once or twice a week. He received daily written reports stating the number of machines ordered, the number put into production and the number shipped. In addition he received a weekly balance sheet and profit and loss statement.

Mr. Cooper reorganized the company's fast-growing operations by setting up departments for all important functions. He put great pressure on subordinate executives to carry out the reorganization plan. (See Exhibit 5-1 for organization chart.) When department heads submitted reasons why a particular schedule was impossible to maintain or why other problems interfered with certain other plans, he would go into a rage and say: "I don't care how you do it — just do it, or else I'll get a man who can."

Mr. Frank Michals, who started with the company in 1933 as a lathe hand, was the works manager. He was a big, rough and rugged individual who thought production and only production was the essential part of any business. He purchased the equipment needed in the plant and had one of the best-equipped shops in the Chicago area. He spoke openly and freely, often in derogatory fashion, concerning other phases of the business — primarily sales, purchasing and engineering. From all indications he liked Mr. Cooper, but it was known among his co-workers and subordinates that he wanted to become vice-president and that he was envious of the authority vested in Mr. Cooper.

Mr. John Bartel, the chief engineer, was the originator of the patents which the company possessed on its machines and was widely known as a good press engineer. He, like Mr. Michals, was one of the original employees of Mr. Jones and had held the position of chief engineer since the beginning of the company. He was responsible for the company's original welded design. For several years prior to 1950, Mr.

Exhibit 5-1. Fox Press Corporation, 1944

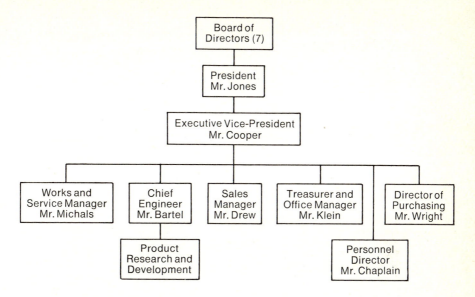

Bartel had put forth little effort in research and new-product ideas. Some of his staff in the engineering department resigned because Mr. Bartel constantly disregarded their ideas. Mr. Cooper had no technical knowledge concerning presses and consulted Mr. Bartel in these matters.

MANAGEMENT CHANGES UNDER MR. COOPER

As sales manager Mr. Cooper retained Mr. Ralph Drew, but the latter actually functioned as an ordinary sales engineer because Mr. Cooper took an active part in sales and assumed all the usual responsibilities of the sales manager. He determined territories, approved all expense accounts, and was on the road extensively. Many times Mr. Cooper would call on customers without informing the company's salesman in the territory about the call. The sales engineers generally seemed to be in disagreement with Mr. Cooper over sales matters. For example, the backlog of orders necessitated deliveries of seventeen to twenty-four months. Salesmen often complained that presses scheduled for delivery on their orders were delivered instead to one of Mr. Cooper's business friends much in advance of scheduled deliveries.

Because of the backlog of orders in the postwar period, and the attitude of Mr. Bartel, product research and experimental work were at a standstill. Most of the presses shipped represented basic designs developed before the war, and only minor modifications, if any, were made for each sale. When contacting customers, Mr. Cooper heard criticisms concerning the machines and related this information to Mr. Bartel, who invariably regarded the information lightly and insisted the presses were well designed.

Exhibit 5-2. Fox Press Corporation, 1948

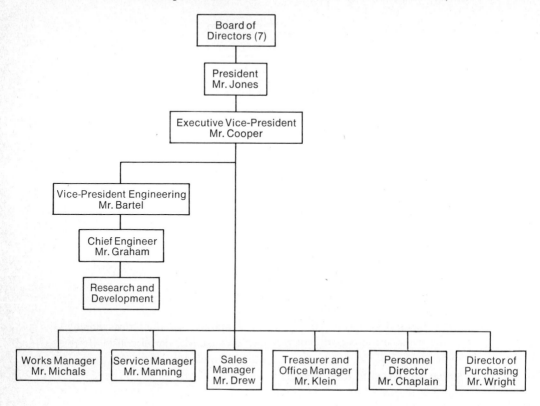

Mr. Cooper, however, became concerned about various customer complaints and was anxious to correct them with a minimum of engineering and still maintain maximum production. Mr. Cooper felt that his lack of technical knowledge was a hindrance in dealing with both Mr. Bartel and Mr. Michals, so he employed Mr. Charles Manning, a press specialist from an automotive concern, as service manager. This action was resented by Mr. Michals, who up to this time had been service manager as well as responsible for production. Mr. Manning spent much time in the plant looking over production procedures, questioning machinists and assemblers. He also visited many customers to discuss problems they might be experiencing in the use of Fox presses. Mr. Manning had no knowledge of the differences among the Messrs. Michals, Bartel and Cooper and thought the whole organization wanted to know about customer desires and complaints, so he wrote extensive reports on his findings and distributed copies to the Messrs. Cooper, Bartel and Michals. Mr. Cooper used the reports in trying to change the attitude of Mr. Bartel. Mr. Jones, the president, read some of the reports and demanded an explanation from Mr. Bartel. The latter blamed his assistant, who was immediately dismissed by Mr. Jones.

Mr. Cooper interpreted the close friendship between Mr. Bartel and Mr. Jones to mean that it would be impossible to dismiss Mr. Bartel, so he did what he thought to be the next best thing. He promoted Mr. Bartel to vice-president in charge of engineering. In this capacity he would act as a consultant to both the company's engineering department and its customers. Mr. Ralph Graham, who had been employed as chief engineer for two large competitors, was hired as the new chief engineer. (See Exhibit 5-2 for organizational changes.)

RESIGNATION OF MR. COOPER

Mr. Bartel and Mr. Michals became increasingly apprehensive about the reports Mr. Manning, the service manager, was submitting. In addition to reports about customer complaints, he was writing reports on the shortcomings of the company's production procedures and engineering standards. They discussed their discontent with Mr. Jones, the president, who promised to look into the matter. Mr. Jones discussed the reports with some other executives of the company and some salesmen, most of whom were of the opinion that the reports in themselves were satisfactory, but that the way Mr. Cooper used them was detrimental to the morale of the employees and caused low efficiency. Their opinion was that Mr. Cooper seemed to be interested in making the Messrs. Bartel and Michals look incompetent so he could justify their eventual dismissal with Mr. Jones. While Mr. Cooper was on a business trip in Europe, Mr. Jones discussed his findings with the board of directors. The board requested and Mr. Cooper gave his resignation in October, 1948. He later accepted an executive position with an automotive concern.

EXECUTIVE COMMITTEE MANAGEMENT

Instead of appointing another executive vice-president, Mr. Jones and the board of directors appointed an executive committee consisting of the following officers — treasurer, director of purchasing, vice-president in charge of engineering, works manager and sales manager. (See Exhibit 5-3 for organizational changes.) Mr. Klein, who was then both treasurer and office manager, was made chairman. His background had been predominantly financial. Before coming to the Fox Press Corporation, Mr. Klein, a C.P.A., had been in public accounting work. He also had been comptroller of a large publishing concern. After joining Fox, he introduced tabulating machinery, new office equipment and procedures and set up a new cost control system.

The committee immediately dismissed the personnel director, Mr. William Chaplain, who had displayed a strong loyalty to Mr. Cooper and had supported him in measures believed to have been detrimental to the company. The assistant personnel director, Mr. James Moon, was appointed personnel director as the initial step in a policy of promoting from within instead of securing men from the outside — a policy which the committee hoped would become standard practice in the future. About four months later, through the influence of both Mr. Michals and Mr. Bartel, Mr. Manning, service manager, was discharged. Mr. Michals again was named service manager in addition to his other duties as works manager.

Exhibit 5-3. Fox Press Corporation, January 1949

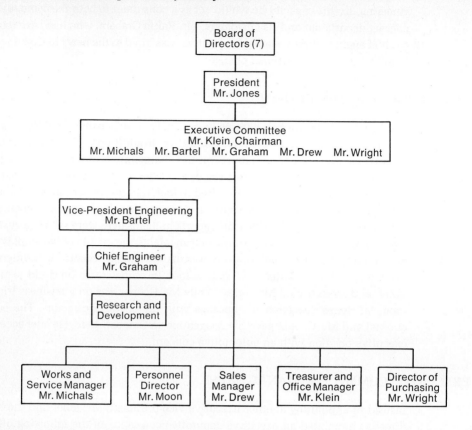

REPLACEMENT OF EXECUTIVE COMMITTEE WITH AN EXECUTIVE VICE-PRESIDENT

After the committee had functioned for six months, Mr. Jones, the president, was convinced that the committee was not operating as he had anticipated. In August, 1949, the board of directors appointed Mr. Klein, the chairman of the executive committee and treasurer, to the position of executive vice-president.

Mr. Klein's first decision was to replace Mr. Drew, the sales manager, with Mr. Chester Bowling, who had been with the company ten years, including four years as a sales engineer. (See Exhibit 5-4 for organizational changes.) Mr. Drew had experienced a heart attack about three months prior to Mr. Klein's appointment as executive vice-president and was not expected back to work for at least another month. Mr. Klein and Mr. Bowling planned to use Mr. Drew as a sales engineer when he returned to work. The other executives considered this a diplomatic way of relegating Mr. Drew to greatly lessened responsibility inasmuch as Mr. Klein had mentioned on various occasions that Mr. Drew was a top salesman but lacked the qualifications of a sales manager.

Mr. Bartel, vice-president in charge of engineering, devoted much of his time to the engineering department discussing engineering problems with the various designers. He travelled little, and his only customer contacts were with such customers as visited the company. All production departments, as well as the service department, planning and scheduling department, shipping and machine hour estimating department reported to Mr. Michals, the works manager, who was quite sensitive about any encroachments in his broad area of responsibility. Problems involving these departments with other departments in the company when reported by Mr. Michals to Mr. Klein invariably were accompanied by statements regarding the shortcomings of engineering, purchasing or sales — seldom manufacturing.

By May, 1950, sales in heavy industrial equipment had been decreasing and the Fox Press Corporation was affected accordingly. The third shift and overtime on the other shifts were eliminated. Mr. Bowling employed additional salesmen and worked vigorously in hopes of capturing a greater percentage of the existing market for presses. Mr. Klein spent considerable time in the field getting acquainted with customers. He continued the weekly meetings of the old executive committee.

Exhibit 5-4. Fox Press Corporation, August 1949

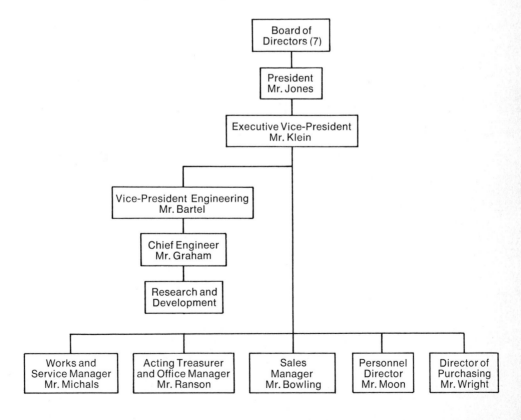

Exhibit 5-5. Balance Sheets, 1937–1948

	1937	1938	1939	1940	1941	1942
Cash	$ 276,766	$ 641,088	$ 436,372	$ 372,189	$ 644,560	$1,102,470
Receivables, net	235,987	91,065	489,730	1,013,944	1,128,581	1,225,328
Inventories, cost or market	124,173	61,656	391,515	438,560	888,915	2,183,850
Total current assets	$ 636,926	$ 793,809	$1,317,617	$1,824,693	$2,662,056	$4,511,648
Land, buildings, machinery, and equipment, net	354,510	663,349	770,573	835,723	1,265,742	1,113,525
Miscellaneous, including investments and patents	237,814	93,624	138,018	184,812	240,866	394,066
Total assets	$1,229,250	$1,550,782	$2,226,208	$2,845,228	$4,168,664	$6,019,239
Provision for taxes	$ 51,429	$ 64,995	$ 76,428	$ 86,341	$ 239,022	$ 709,640
Notes payable	10,675	139,763	320,767	89,040	124,554	196,492
Accounts payable	137,800	101,130	316,495	407,834	1,329,354	2,321,000
Total current liabilities	$ 199,904	$ 305,888	$ 713,690	$ 583,215	$1,692,930	$3,227,132
Preferred stock	450,000					
Common stock	45,000	191,667	200,000	200,000	200,000	200,000
Surplus	534,346	1,053,227	1,312,518	2,062,013	2,275,734	2,592,107
Total liabilities and net worth	$1,229,250	$1,550,782	$2,226,208	$2,845,228	$4,168,664	$6,019,239

Exhibit 5-5 (Continued)

	1943	1944	1945	1946	1947	1948
Cash	$1,252,253	$1,346,776	$ 837,480	$1,584,366	$2,126,160	$2,661,274
Receivables, net	1,047,804	709,786	2,305,772	1,745,928	1,916,580	1,138,363
Inventories, cost or market	1,928,301	1,113,259	1,634,685	2,118,613	2,297,610	1,414,403
Total current assets	$4,228,358	$3,169,821	$4,777,937	$5,448,907	$6,340,350	$5,214,040
Land, buildings, machinery, and equipment, net	1,150,287	906,908	733,266	1,389,338	1,831,052	2,236,294
Miscellaneous, including investments and patents	289,901	343,673	76,635	92,640	3,540	2,022
Total assets	$5,668,546	$4,420,402	$5,587,838	$6,930,885	$8,174,942	$7,452,356
Provision for taxes	$ 219,801	$ 268,846	$ 229,653	$ 220,230	$ 64,274	$ 7,548
Notes payable	1,289,816	174,139	289,280	389,965	450,204	366,591
Accounts payable	1,144,263	793,907	1,617,996	1,775,618	1,486,743	803,449
Total current liabilities	$2,653,880	$1,236,892	$2,136,929	$2,385,813	$2,001,221	$1,177,588
Preferred stock					656,250	776,750
Common stock	212,000	212,000	212,000	424,000	2,650,000	2,650,000
Surplus	2,802,666	2,971,510	3,238,909	4,121,072	2,867,471	2,848,018
Total liabilities and net worth	$5,668,546	$4,420,402	$5,587,838	$6,930,885	$8,174,942	$7,452,356

Exhibit 5-6. Income Statements, 1937–1948

	1937	1938	1939	1940	1941	1942
Gross profit	$ 524,886	$ 566,298	$ 561,380	$ 613,757	$ 871,809	$2,530,019
Selling and administrative expense	186,741	189,363	227,975	276,659	352,236	459,995
Operating profit	$ 338,145	$ 376,935	$ 333,405	$ 337,098	$ 519,573	$2,070,024
Taxes	49,432	66,527	55,706	56,147	199,182	1,559,000
Net profit	$ 288,713	$ 310,408	$ 277,699	$ 280,951	$ 310,391	$ 511,024

	1943	1944	1945	1946	1947	1948
Gross profit	$1,596,894	$1,682,180	$1,427,799	$3,407,858	$4,386,930	$2,295,860
Selling and administrative expense	454,986	553,334	609,687	873,341	931,688	833,246
Operating profit	$1,141,908	$1,128,846	$ 818,112	$2,534,517	$3,455,242	$1,462,614
Taxes	670,196	791,471	555,755	979,652	1,274,977	572,888
Net profit	$ 471,712	$ 337,375	$ 262,357	$1,554,865	$2,180,265	$ 889,726

6/ The Case of the Unplanned Promotion

The following case, based on actual situations, is disguised. While neither the company nor its employees exist in fact, the problems discussed in this case do, and are relevant to managers in all companies, at all levels.

"Well, Dave . . . I just got quite a jolt! Sam Roswell came in and told me he was leaving us to go with the Lighthill Company. And I'm sure it was because he didn't get that assistant's job we gave to Tom O'Hara at the beginning of the month."

Sitting in the office of Dave Marks, personnel director of the Radom Manufacturing Company, was Twill Moore, the company's purchasing agent. The incident which Moore was discussing was the rather sudden loss of Sam Roswell, one of the brighter young men in his purchasing department.

The Radom Manufacturing Company, located in a northern industrial state, manufactured and assembled electromechanical parts for a wide variety of industrial products. The bulk of Radom's production consisted of motor-actuated devices such as timing switches, electric pumps and circulators, blowers, and so on. The company subcontracted the manufacture of a number of special parts, which it in turn incorporated into its assembled products.

Radom employed about 450 people, nearly 325 of whom worked in the manufacturing group. This group, under the direction of the plant superintendent, consisted of about 50 manufacturing staff personnel, as well as a line organization comprising a force of 275. Three general foremen and eight foremen supervised the initial assembly, secondary assembly, and test work. Exhibit 6-1 depicts the manufacturing organization. The company enjoyed harmonious labor relations with its independently unionized employees.

Tom O'Hara had worked for Radom since his return from the service shortly after World War II. He had graduated from high school six years before, and after almost three years of machinist's work in a small machine shop had entered the Army in 1942. O'Hara was a devout churchgoer, had been married for 15 years, and was the father of four. Although his formal education included only a high school diploma, he had completed evening courses in industrial engineering, techniques of supervision, methods and time study, and quality control in his early years at Radom. During that time, he did assembly work and later became a foreman in the assembly department. Radom's growth during the Korean conflict led to a division of the assembly work into initial and secondary segments; in 1953, O'Hara was installed as general foreman of the initial assembly section.

This case was prepared by Stephen A. Greyser and appeared in *Harvard Business Review* 40, no. 6 (November–December 1962): 157–62. Copyright © 1962 by the President and Fellows of Harvard College; all rights reserved. Reprinted by permission.

Exhibit 6-1. Radom Company, Manufacturing

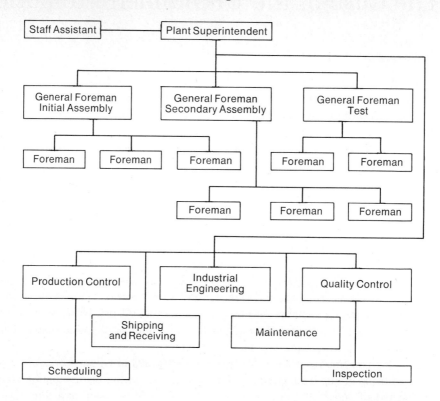

By nature friendly and gregarious, O'Hara was conscientious both in the performance of his work and in his concern for those working in his group. He knew all of the employees in the assembly lines under his own foremen's supervision, and many of the employees in the other lines as well. Convivial, he frequently stopped off with some of the men for a beer after work, and had long been one of the stalwarts of Radom's team in the local industrial bowling league. O'Hara's attendance record was exemplary, except during the three months after he suffered an injured back in an on-the-job accident five years ago.

Sam Roswell had come to Radom three years before, after graduation from a local college where he had received his bachelor's degree in business administration. Roswell was hired to be an expediter in Radom's purchasing department, where his eagerness and interest quickly marked him as a candidate for promotion. Zealous in developing his expertise in the purchasing field, Roswell kept *au courant* with ideas, news, and developments in purchasing via avid reading of trade publications and frequent conversations with older and more experienced members of the purchasing department. He was a member of the local Purchasing Association.

With the approval and encouragement of Radom's purchasing agent, Roswell — drawing both from his college studies of new technical approaches to purchasing problems and from his conversance with activities in the trade — developed several programs which, after experimental use, resulted in department-wide application:

1. Learning-curve pricing, a system whereby prices on purchased special parts are adjusted and reduced gradually as the vendor company acquires greater manufacturing experience, was instituted by Roswell on several contracts. The results proved highly satisfactory both to the vendors and to Radom. Subsequently, this system was adopted on numerous contracts, and its application was credited by Radom's purchasing agent with savings of 5%–10% where applied.

2. Vendor quality ratings, which had existed only as unrecorded impressions in the minds of Radom's purchasing personnel for years, were rigorously maintained by Roswell on vendors with which he dealt. Problems were followed up and corrections made by subcontractors in subsequent deliveries.

Roswell's assiduous and industrious efforts had earned him rapid advancement in the purchasing department. Within six months, he moved from expediter to junior buyer and a year later was promoted to buyer. His salary had been increased from the $4,200 he initially received to $5,400. Shortly after his last promotion, he had married, and recently became the proud father of a baby boy.

When Twill Moore's assistant purchasing agent decided to leave the North because of his wife's illness, Moore knew there would be problems in filling the post.

Radom's purchasing department consisted of about 20 people. Headed by Moore and an assistant purchasing agent, the organization also consisted of six buyers, three junior buyers, three expediters, and several clerks and secretaries. One of the long-service buyers worked on administration of high-dollar subcontracts.

Moore discussed the assistant's position with Dave Marks, Radom's personnel director, who usually was consulted on such matters.

Moore: This is a tough one, Dave. I've thought about who would be the best man for the job, but I'm not sure any of my men are ideal.

Marks: What about your senior man, George Foster?

Moore: Well, George is certainly familiar with all the red tape of the department. He does a steady, capable job and he seems to get along with the other men too. But I don't think he has the creative ability and the talent to do the kinds of things the assistant's job calls for.

Marks: What do you mean?

Moore: Well, right now the assistant purchasing agent's job is really a good step up from the buyer's — and the work is considerably different. Besides having to be able to handle problems or emergencies when they come up, the person in this spot must always be thinking of better ways to do things, and has to coordinate our quality and vendor rating program with the manufacturing department people. He works with all the buyers on the cost-cutting and delivery schedule improvement efforts which we've been making.

Marks: What about young Sam Roswell? I recall your talking about some of the new ideas he helped develop. Of course, he is pretty young, but maybe he's your man.

Moore: Sam's a good man, with a good head, but I don't think he's quite ready. He's been with us for less than three years; and, while he's come a long way, he doesn't have the breadth of experience I think the assistant's job calls for. Besides, I think that Sam's elevation so soon could cause some morale problems in the department.

Marks: What about your other buyers? Are any of them likely candidates for the job?

Moore: Again, I don't think the shoe fits any of them very well — one has just recently been promoted to buyer, another has only a little more experience than Sam, but without Sam's self-application. The other two buyers — both department veterans — say that they are happy doing what they do, and don't act as though they are interested in the job. What I've really got is a contrast. The older men, whom I inherited from my predecessor, seem to be more interested in keeping things calm and steady than in complicating their jobs. The younger men are perhaps basically more capable, and more eager, but just aren't ready to move up. Sam Roswell is good, but, as I said, he still needs experience.

Marks: Did any of them approach you when word of the opening came up?

Moore: Well, after I told the department, I talked about the situation with George Foster, because he *is* the senior man of the group. He seemed to waver a bit on actually coming out and asking to be moved up; and, when I pressed him a bit, he emphasized how happy he was in his present slot. My own view is that he doesn't really want the job, particularly since he's already making almost as much money as the post calls for. But he's not really in favor of anyone else for it, either. In fact, when I asked which of the others he thought most qualified, he finally said he didn't think there was any *one* who stood out.

Marks: And Sam?

Moore: Well, Sam acted a bit funny for a day or two, and then caught me the other afternoon and asked how things were going. I told him that we hadn't made any decision yet. He said that he thought he deserved a chance at the job and had earned it with his efforts in the department. He added that he knew he was young but believed he could handle the job.

Marks: And you said . . . ?

Moore: That I recognized and appreciated the good work he had done, but that I didn't think he was ready for the assistant's post, though he might well be in a year or two. Of course, I'm summarizing — actually we talked for over an hour, and I tried to let Sam know how well he was doing and what a "live wire" he was. He's still got the idea that he's being "used." . . . He mentioned again my department report from last year, and the fact that his contributions were the highlight, although he wasn't singled out personally. I got the feeling he was a little disappointed, but his work since then doesn't seem to have been affected.

Marks: Have you ever thought about Tom O'Hara as a possibility?

Moore: Tom? Gee, no . . . he works fairly closely with us, particularly on quality and delivery, but I always thought he was interested in staying in the plant.

Marks: Well, he and I were talking last week, and he seemed interested in the possibility of making a change if something came up.

Moore: That's interesting . . . let me think about it.

The conversation to which Dave Marks referred had occurred several weeks before. He and O'Hara had first become friendly when Marks was organizing Radom's bowling team and O'Hara helped get things rolling. They had maintained the friendship and from time to time discussed things happening around the plant. It was during one of these chats that Tom O'Hara discussed his reactions to his job.

O'Hara: You know, Dave, I enjoy my job, and especially working with the fellows I've known for years. But I think it's getting to be a bit tiring for me. You know, I've been a general foreman here for eight years, and even though I still like the work, I think I'm kind of in a rut, going stale. Sometimes I wish that Jim (the plant superintendent) would disappear, and I could get a chance to see what I could do there.

Marks: That comes as a bit of a surprise, Tom. You've always given the impression that you really enjoyed your job. I . . . .

O'Hara: Don't misunderstand me — I don't mean that I don't like it. Hell, I'd have said something long ago if I weren't happy. No, it's just that I think I'd enjoy doing something different.

Marks: You've worked with quite a few other people at Radom besides those in the assembly departments, haven't you?

O'Hara: I guess you're right . . . at least I've worked with a lot of different groups. Back when I was an assembly foreman, I did a lot of work with methods engineering, and since becoming a general foreman, I've always tried to keep our department alert to any possible methods improvements. And then when we got involved with more and more subcontracted items, I went with our engineers on visits to suppliers' plants to watch components being made, and to talk with their production people on things like specifications and design changes. And later I worked with the engineering group again in helping our subcontractors set up their production of subassembly parts. In the last year or so, I've been helping out some of the purchasing people on their vendor ratings — you know, like delivery schedules and quality. I know some of the older guys over there pretty well. And I guess I've been around so long I know just about all the parts and materials we use — even know the part numbers on most of them — and I can see pretty easily when things aren't going well.

Marks: Tom, you mentioned that you'd be interested in the plant superintendent job. Why do you think you'd like to try that?

O'Hara: Well, first of all, of course, it's different . . . and I think that would be a good change. And it's a move up — I'd like that. Besides, I pretty much know the other general foremen's jobs and I don't think they'd be that much different from my own.

Marks: Have you ever thought about what the plant superintendent has to do?

O'Hara: I suppose so . . . though I've never quite sat down and figured it out. I guess there's a lot of responsibility in the job.

Marks: You know, Tom, you said that you were interested in something "different." I wonder if you know just how *really* different that job is from yours?

O'Hara: What do you mean, Dave?

Marks: Well, think about these as just a couple of examples:

He has to report to management on costs, quality, and scheduling.

On the accelerated performance program we have, he has to keep after improvement in things like scrap reduction, improved quality, and better production records.

He's on a budget, and must know the cost situation in each department. He must be able to discuss it with all of them, just as he discusses your department's costs with you.

He has to plan personnel requirements for both the plant and his staff departments.

He has to watch everyone's schedule, and while he can see quickly enough when one of the assembly groups, for example, is a bit behind, he himself has the responsibility for the over-all plant not getting behind. And, of course, if things did get out of control, it would be a lot more serious since a whole month goes by between *his* reports to top management.

O'Hara: Gee, I never realized he had to know and do so many things. I don't really know whether those are the kinds of things I'd be able — I'd want — to do.

Marks: Well, Tom, I'll let *you* be the judge of that. Maybe you'd be interested, though, if something came along that was more down your alley. If it does, would you like me to talk to you about it?

O'Hara: Well, Dave . . . yes, I would.

It was only natural, then, for Dave Marks to have brought up Tom O'Hara's name to Twill Moore when the opening in purchasing developed.

In considering O'Hara for the post, the purchasing agent believed that on several major counts O'Hara was a desirable candidate:

Knowledge: While O'Hara had no actual buying experience, his familiarity with the parts and subcontractors and his involvement with the vendor quality and delivery rating system were mitigating factors. Moore recognized that for a while he himself would perhaps have to handle some of the emergencies which might arise.

Capability: Moore looked favorably on O'Hara's willingness to learn, and his ability to pay attention to detail and follow-up. O'Hara's experience in the problems of actual assembly use and his personal relationships with the foremen and others "on the floor" were seen as a plus. With an increasing number of special items being produced, Moore believed that O'Hara's experience would be helpful to the buyers.

Personality: O'Hara was known to be friendly with the older members of the department. Moreover, Moore knew of no instances where O'Hara had had any troubles during the course of his work with purchasing in the past year. An informal "sounding out" of his senior buyer led Moore to believe that little if any resentment among department members would be engendered by the move.

After Moore indicated his basically favorable reaction to the idea, he and Marks discussed the job at length with O'Hara, and a few days afterward the latter accepted it. Moore informed his department members of the move, and two weeks later Tom O'Hara began his new job as Radom's assistant purchasing agent.

Three relatively tranquil weeks had passed when Sam Roswell walked into Twill Moore's office and told him that the Lighthill Company had made him an offer "too good to pass up — they're giving me a 10% boost to $6,000, plus the promise of a chance to move up in the department as soon as I'm established."

Twill expressed surprise, and regret, at Sam's decision, and said that he'd appreciate it if he could talk to Sam again later. At that point, he visited Dave Marks's office and made the comment that opened this case.

7/ The Case of the Punctilious President

The following case, based on an actual situation, is disguised. But the problems it raises are real, and will be meaningful to many managers, especially those in companies with strong differences in the way various departments operate.

"It seems to me that the president of a company should have a lot of things more important to worry about than how much time people spend on coffee breaks, and what time they get back from lunch. You just can't run a marketing organization the way you do a production shop — on an 8:00 to 5:00 schedule. If he tries to force that on us, we'll not only lose efficiency, but we'll probably lose some of our best people too."

Pete Samuels, marketing manager of Boswell Corporation, was talking to Hal Eames, the chief engineer. Also present in Eames's office was Bill Pearl, Boswell's personnel manager. They were all concerned about a meeting of department heads which had been scheduled for that afternoon by Carl Preston, Boswell's recently promoted president, to discuss attendance, tardiness, and housekeeping.

Boswell was a medium sized manufacturer of communications equipment for the military and the commercial market. Its growth in the 20-odd years of its existence was attributable, in the eyes of its former president, largely to its ability to sense the trends of the market and to have innovations and new products ready to meet them. Marketing and engineering had always worked together closely in this regard; in fact, senior engineering people frequently made sales trips and presentations, while marketing personnel attended the product-design meetings in their areas of interest.

The engineering and marketing staffs generally operated in an informal atmosphere. Indeed, production employees occupying an adjacent building often referred to their neighbors as "the country club" because of the flexible working hours and the relatively relaxed atmosphere that prevailed in those departments.

Manufacturing, in contrast, had always been a "taut ship," with very strict conformance to working hours and schedules, and meticulous housekeeping that made the plant the pride of management when there were visitors to show around. (Outsiders rarely saw the inside of the engineering labs.)

Boswell's top management group was considered an experienced and effective one in the industry.

This case was prepared by Joseph J. Hansen and appeared in *Harvard Business Review* 43, no. 6 (November–December 1965): 161–63, 171. Copyright © 1965 by the President and Fellows of Harvard College; all rights reserved. Reprinted by permission.

Sensing that marketing and engineering were the two departments that would come under fire at the afternoon meeting, Pete Samuels and Hal Eames were discussing how best to approach this meeting to combat policies which they thought were not in the company's best interests, yet avoid putting themselves in the role of renegades unwilling to acknowledge the authority of their new superior.

Hal: I agree with Pete. The problems in engineering differ from those in marketing, but we're not basically geared to rigid working hours either. Carl has already made several comments about the number of coffee breaks some of my engineers take in a day. I wonder whether he knows where we finally figured out how to get the last two pounds off that transceiver so we could meet specs — in the cafeteria!

Bill, you've seen several top men come and go around here, each one with his own ideas of how the place should be run. What do you think?

Bill: Well, every successful manager has his own style of operating, and it extends into areas beyond punctuality and housekeeping. Carl is no exception. When he ran manufacturing, he kept a firm hand on everything; he had a highly disciplined organization and always resented the morale problems you fellows gave him by being easier on your people.

I can't agree with Pete that this is too petty a matter for Carl to concern himself with; he has to be his own judge when it comes to that. I'm not out to interfere with the way you run your departments, but from where I sit, it *does* strain our relations with the union when we dock a production employee's pay if he's five minutes late, yet a technician next door seemingly can stroll in when he pleases. These things invariably are brought up at contract negotiations too.

Pete: Then you think Hal and I should crack the whip and fire anybody who won't comply?

Bill: No, I think you should act as responsible members of management by giving Carl your honest assessment of his orders and your recommendations for action, if any. Then you should go along with whatever decision he makes.

Hal: I've been making some notes while you've been talking. *(He holds them out.)* Rather than argue the thing out on an emotional basis, let's look at some pros and cons for the "tight" versus "loose" personnel control policies. Suppose we talk out the merits of these arguments so we can be one step removed from an emotional reaction. We'll show Carl that we've approached the issues in a mature way.

With a few more minutes of work, the three of them added to the chart that Hal Eames had started. They agreed to use it as a basis for their side of the discussion that afternoon.

After lunch, the meeting was held in Carl Preston's office. Present were Carl Preston, Hal Eames, Pete Samuels, Bill Pearl, and Jim Metcalf (Boswell's manufacturing manager).

Carl: I think you all know why we're here. I've talked with each of you individually about bringing the prima donnas in your departments under control. Each one of you is paid primarily to *manage,* and that's just what I expect from you. Of course, every department can't be run the same way, but there *are* limits. I thought if we got together, we could agree on some basic company-wide rules regarding such things as working hours; then it will be up to you to enforce these rules.

Hal: I'm glad to hear you say that different departments have to be run in different ways, Carl, because, to me, this is central to our discussion. Jim has a production line that runs from 7:00 a.m. to 4:00 p.m., five days a week. If he has a vacant spot in the line, the work piles up, and he has downtime until he plugs the hole. In contrast, I could send half of my department to Timbuktu and have them mail in monthly progress reports.

Pete: And half of *my* department *is* out of town at any given time. When a man gets in from a trip at midnight, I don't expect him in the office at 8:00 or even 9:00 the next morning.

Bill: How about the chart, Hal? You're starting out just the way you said you wanted to avoid.

Hal: Right . . . Pete and I got together this morning to discuss these problems between ourselves. Bill was good enough to join us to give us the benefit of his experience and professional outlook. We summarized some of the problem areas on a chart which I have here . . . *(He puts the chart up on an easel.)* You see, we've listed the issues in question and the pros and cons of "cracking down." I think you can see that those favoring tight controls apply more to a manufacturing environment than to engineering or marketing.

Pete: Furthermore, the "tight control" arguments are largely concerned with superficial appearances; those on the opposite side of the ledger pertain to results. If I really tried to run things the way Jim does in his shop, I'd lose some of my best salesmen — men who have been with us for years and know our products and customers inside out. Why, they'd be working for Hunter [Boswell's No. 1 competitor] before you could say, "Sales off 25% from last year."

Jim: Pete, I know you and Hal believe that a lot of your people would quit if you asked them for an honest day's work, but I bet you'd be surprised if you really tried it. Sure, you might lose one or two, but you'd probably be better off without them anyway. Most of the boys would just grumble a little and then accept it. People tend to take as much as they can get away with. Once you suffer through the initial problems and overcome the legacy of looseness, you'll find your section heads and other supervisors will have an easier time of it, and your whole department will run better.

Hal: I agree 100%, Jim — *if* you're talking about manufacturing. What you don't seem to realize is that you just can't treat engineers that way.

Bill: Maybe not, but there probably isn't another company in the area where they get away with as much as they do here. There's been a lot of belt-tightening in the industry in the past year or so.

Jim: That's right, Bill, and it's pretty hard for some of my people to understand that they have to find ways to get pennies off the product cost when they know that the salesmen are flying high on their expense accounts.

Carl: Well, I'm glad to see that you fellows have at least taken a hard look at some of the things your people have been doing. But I can't agree that good control over people only goes in manufacturing. Just yesterday afternoon, I went down to the chem lab with a potential customer, and there wasn't a person in the place! To make matters worse, the whole lab looked just like a bachelor's kitchen that hadn't been cleaned up for a month — glassware all over the place, papers and books stacked on the benches and chairs, and so on. I suppose *I'm* the one who was stupid for bringing him down there in the first place.

Hal: I can appreciate how it must have looked, Carl, but that group worked right through the previous night, trying to find out what suddenly went wrong with the coil-coating resin over in production. They solved the problem, too, and the lines were running the next morning.

Jim: That's true. You really got us out of a hole.

Pete (sarcastically): Maybe we need two sets of labs — one for show, with plate glass windows and a visitors' gallery, and one where the work is done.

Carl (angrily): All right that's enough of that! People don't have to be a bunch of slobs to get a job done. Even though you're getting good results now, I think you'd find they'd be even better if you practiced good housekeeping and kept some control over working hours.

You've been drawing a contrast between your departments and the production line . . . maybe there are some similarities too. Nobody here works in a vacuum. You just can't work efficiently if you never know whether the people you have to consult with are going to be around when you want them. We have a bunch of star players, but not a team.

In another sense, these problems indicate something about *our* attitudes. I'll admit that your people all come through in good style when there's an emergency, but how many months do you think are unnecessarily added to the development time for a new product; how much longer than necessary do we take to wrap up a sale? When you have no discipline, people work on what they're interested in, rather than what's going to make a profit for us. If they can't take direction on something as simple as when to be in at work, how can we expect them to follow instructions in other areas? If nothing happens to them when they come in late and leave early, day after day, why should they think schedules have any meaning? Boswell's making a profit right now, but *in spite of* our poor practices. The challenge that I'm giving you is: *How much better* can we run it?

Exhibit 7-1. Selected Key Personnel, Boswell Corporation

Carl Preston (age 52) had recently become president of the company, after five years as manufacturing manager. Prior to joining Boswell, he had advanced from chief industrial engineer to shop general foreman in the production organization of a large competitor. During his 30-odd years in industry, he had developed a hard-boiled attitude toward people and their problems, and liked to characterize himself as "specializing in doing the impossible."

Although not particularly well liked, he was respected for his accomplishments as manufacturing manager. He was a strong protagonist of realistic schedules and budgets, but in a crisis he invariably met the company requirements that were placed on him. His penchant for setting high goals and then striving with near-fanatical zeal to meet them had often brought him into conflict with other members of the organization. On one occasion, the purchasing agent had threatened to resign when Carl personally called the president of several supplier firms whose late deliveries had put his own schedules in jeopardy.

Bill Pearl (age 58) had been with Boswell for nearly 20 years, over 15 of them as personnel manager. In addition to his official functions as head of industrial relations and chief union negotiator, his long experience at Boswell and his excellent rapport with employees at all levels had led him to become an "informal consultant on just about everything" to management. Everyone naturally turned to him, as unofficial historian at Boswell, when a question regarding events of prior years came up, and hardly a problem could arise on which he was unable to cite a meaningful precedent. To many employees, he represented an element of stability in an otherwise variable management. "He's seen these fads come and go," is how one foreman put it.

Pete Samuels (age 55) was a newcomer to Boswell, having joined the company less than a year ago. Marked at the outset as a "typical salesman" and a "name dropper," he had since earned the respect of Boswell's management and his own staff by bringing in contracts in areas where the company had hitherto been unsuccessful. He had argued successfully for a reduction of manufacturing bid rates, on the grounds that this would result in increased volume which would enable them to be realized. Although this idea was bitterly opposed by Preston ("we'll go broke first") when the latter was manufacturing manager, greater volume did result, and business had never been better.

Pete had been a manufacturer's representative for over 10 years, but had sold his company when two of his major lines decided to establish local direct sales offices in his territory. His acquaintances in the industry were numerous; when an important marketing decision hinged on obtaining a key fact, Pete seemed always to be able to get the information with a telephone call or two.

Hal Eames (age 41) had worked in every engineering department in the company during his 14 years with Boswell. He had always had and still enjoyed the reputation of a "hot-shot" engineer who worked on the company's most difficult and technically challenging problems. Fully one third of Boswell's company-owned patents bore his name as inventor or co-inventor.

He strongly believed that creative engineering was fundamental to the company's growth and that it would continue to be so. He held technical progress meetings in his office weekly on all important programs, and showed an amazing capacity to understand and retain the details of these efforts. In fact, he "made the rounds" of the labs at least once a day, talking with engineers, scientists, and technicians, listening to their problems, and often making suggestions. He liked to say that he judged his people by results and by no other yardstick.

He delivered technical papers at conferences and symposiums several times a year, and encouraged others to do the same and to stay abreast of the "state of the art."

Jim Metcalf (age 40) had been hired by Carl Preston five years ago, specifically to be groomed as his replacement as manufacturing manager. During this period, he had been assigned to supervisory positions in assembly, parts fabricating shops, scheduling, material control, and, finally, as head of the cost estimating and bidding group. He had frequently been given assignments requiring liaison with other departments in the company, and often others had contacted him directly on interdepartmental matters rather than going to Preston.

Exhibit 7-2. Chart Prepared by Eames, Pearl, and Samuels

Issues
   Working hours — late arrivals, early departures
   Coffee breaks
   Long lunch hours
   Housekeeping

Factors favoring tight control
   Effect on morale of other groups (e.g., manufacturing)
   Appearance to visitors, customers
   Efficiency of operation
   Effect on union-management relations

Factors favoring loose control
   Creative work can't be routinized
   Long coffee breaks and lunches promote teamwork
   Too much housekeeping disrupts lab setups
   A salesman is "on call" 24 hours a day
   Engineers and scientists do some of their work at home
   Our results have been good, so why change?
   Valuable people will quit if they lose their freedom

8/ Barrett Trumble

Professor Floyd Hall of Bristol University was visiting his old friend Barrett Trumble, president of Green & Richards, the leading quality department store in Gulf City, one of the fastest-growing metropolitan centers of the South. Hall read at breakfast of Trumble's election as president of the Community Fund.

Trumble said, "You might wonder, Floyd, why I would accept this job. I've already done my stint as general campaign manager for the Fund. I guess most people consider this kind of work an important community responsibility but, at the same time, enough of a headache to expect others to take over after you've done your share. I feel differently about it. Unless business leaders continue to spearhead the private sponsorship of needed community agencies, their functions, which must be performed by someone, will more and more be taken over by the Federal, state, and municipal governments."

Trumble went on to say, "I played hard to get for quite a while. I told the boys I wouldn't take the job till we had firmed up our plans to raise funds for the next three years, including agreement on and acceptance by three executives who will take over successively as general campaign managers. Also, I insisted on the Fund setting up an advisory council of business executives, consisting of company presidents. I find that if we are going to get anything done around Gulf City, the way to do it is through the top brass. Now we have twenty business leaders on this council and I am sure there is nothing we want to have done that we can't swing through this group. Then again, I think it's good for G & R for me to be out front in this type of job. As you can see from the morning's paper, we get pretty good publicity. In addition, I intend to have all meetings of the council and some meetings of the more important committees in our executive dining room in the store. And I am sure it won't turn out to be too much work. A job like this is just a job of getting it organized."

TRUMBLE'S OUTSIDE ACTIVITIES

Professor Hall suggested, "It sounds as though you have it well organized. However, don't you think you will still be harassed by personal appeals and requests from all the other agencies in Gulf City and from others who are interested in community welfare?"

Trumble replied, "Frankly, Floyd, I wouldn't tell this to anyone else, but I must confess that if I didn't have these outside interests, I'd just be twiddling my thumbs down at the store."

Reprinted from Thomas J. McNichols, *Policy Making and Executive Action*, 4th ed. (New York: McGraw-Hill, 1972), by permission of the author and the Graduate School of Management, Northwestern University.

Hall was surprised. He knew that Trumble served on the boards of five other businesses: the First Federal Savings and Loan Association, the Commercial National Bank, the Equitable Casualty Insurance Company, Intercontinental Textile Products Corporation, and National Laboratories. He was also a trustee of the Franklin Museum of Modern Art, the Gulf City Symphony Orchestra, Hambletonian College, and the National Retail Merchants Association. Barrett was also a member of the business advisory committee to the Department of Commerce and the treasurer of the Gulf States' Republican Committee.

Barrett explained, "But these other activities don't really take much of my time. Most of these boards have no more than one meeting per month, and they are not very active during the summer months. Of course, when I am on any board committees, it takes a little more time. Then, down at the store, we have things so well organized that the operation pretty well runs itself. Ever since I brought in Tom Jenkins as executive vice-president, I only find it necessary to get into things at the overall policy level."

TRUMBLE AND HIS VICE-PRESIDENTS

Hall recalled that when Jenkins joined Green & Richards, the vice-presidents in charge of customer relations and store operations had resigned to go with other merchandising firms. Trumble pointed out, "Of course, their resignations made it possible for us to promote two outstanding junior executives who were coming along so fast that we couldn't have kept them in the business if we hadn't been able to move them up the ladder. We now have eight vice-presidents reporting to Jenkins; one each for ready-to-wear merchandising, home-furnishings merchandising, store operations, personnel relations, customer relations, control, advertising, and research. Tom and his eight vice-presidents constitute an executive council which meets twice a week. I sit in on all the meetings and have an opportunity to keep in touch with major policy questions. Once in a while I find it necessary to step in where there is a strong difference of opinion, but I can usually rely on Tom to straighten things out without my intervention."

Hall asked, "Don't you find it necessary, as president, to meet with the heads of other businesses in town on questions which involve all the stores in town? For example, don't you have common problems like retaining the importance of the central business district as a shopping center or instituting charges for customer services which you can no longer render free of charge?"

"Yes, you have a point there. I could spend a lot of my time doing this, but the other boys are really better qualified than I am to make a contribution to joint meetings with other stores. For example, take the question of charging for deliveries, which is a hot subject right now. I think it is something all the stores must consider seriously. But why should I spend the time sitting in on the series of harangues among the other merchants in town when Jack Ogleby (vice-president for store operations) is really up to date on this question and can quote chapter and verse when they get down to brass tacks in their discussions? Anyway, before anybody does anything about this, the question will come before our executive council, and I will get in on it at that point."

HOW TRUMBLE SPENDS HIS TIME

Hall wondered how Trumble used the rest of his time in directing the operations of Green & Richards. "Well, I guess I spend a good 10 per cent of my time with the board of directors — in regular meetings of the board, in preparing for these meetings, and in individual conferences with some of the more interested members of the board. For example, Frederic Pellham (senior partner of the leading law firm in Gulf City) is on my neck now, pressing us to come up with a ten-year plan for our business. He thinks we should be looking to the future growth and development of G & R rather than concentrating on today's profits alone. However, the board as a whole now has enough confidence in me so that the others don't needle me the way Fred does.

"Also, the Green family is concerned with maintaining a good steady return on their investment. They aren't interested in spending the kind of money we would need over the next few years if we were going all out to become the largest department store in the South, which is what Fred would like to see.

"Then, I meet with the executive council twice a week. I have a regular meeting every Monday morning with Tom Jenkins. I am always available to talk with the other vice-presidents about any of their problems. They know that I won't make any decision on the matters they bring to me, but I am always glad to toss ideas around with them for whatever help that may be. But I guess I would have to say that most of my time in the store is spent just going through the business as much as I can. I spend between three and four hours a day walking through the store, particularly in the sales departments, just seeing how things are going, chatting with the people as I go, doing everything I can to help give people a lift. It helps keep me in touch with the way things are moving out on the selling floor, and I am sure that the people down the line feel better to see me around, because they know that I am not trying to run things from an ivory tower."

OPERATING RESULTS OF G & R

"How has the store been doing the last couple of years, Barrett?"

"I certainly can't complain, Floyd. I would say our sales and profits are excellent. Every quarter, for the last three years, we have done better than our budgeted dollar sales, gross profit, and net profit. By the way, I have always found it useful to present to the board of directors a highly conservative sales and profit plan so there won't be any unpleasant surprises when the final reports are in. Our reports are better than the Federal Reserve reports for Gulf City as a whole and better than the National Retail Merchants Association averages. Looking ahead, with defense spending the way it is, creeping inflation, population trends in general, and the growth curve for

Gulf City, I don't see how we can miss. Sometimes I wonder if we might show even better results if I put a little more pressure on the boys or if I spent a little more time myself in some of our major problem areas. But here we are, the major downtown store, with three suburban stores (two of which we did not have six years ago) and with our sales increasing every year somewhere between 4 and 6 per cent. Our operating profits before income taxes have averaged 7.6 per cent of sales for the last five years."[1]

DELEGATION AND MANAGEMENT DEVELOPMENT

"And now I have built a team. As I see my job, it is to help select and develop competent people for our key jobs and then let them go ahead and do the things they are qualified to do and for which they are being well paid. It seems to me you either delegate responsibility and authority or you don't. The trouble with most store heads with whom I am familiar is that they talk a lot about delegation but they spend a lot of their own personal time going around and asking the department heads why they bought this, what they think of that, why don't they do so and so. One of our mutual friends, who runs a store up North, tells me that he thinks his job is one of constantly impressing department heads with the fact that he is thoroughly familiar with the way things are going in each department. He watches each department's figures like a hawk and calls people on the phone or on the carpet to discuss what they have in mind to correct things in the future. I don't see why we spend a lot of time developing people and pay them the money that we do if we don't rely on them to take the kind of action that is good for business and therefore for themselves."

Floyd asked Barrett if he was satisfied with his executive staff. "I would think you would have problems from time to time, humans being what they are."

Trumble replied, "Sure, like any other big happy family, we have our troubles from time to time. For example, Malcolm Donaldson (vice-president for personnel) gets himself steamed up on a special training course for executives and makes the mistake of bringing it up cold at the executive council meeting. The boys kick it around but finally decide that department heads have too many pressing problems confronting them; that it would be unwise to take them away from their operations for extended training sessions. Mal's idea gets voted down. Then, later in the day, he comes to me to see if he can get my backing for the idea, knowing that I am all for more and more executive training.

"What Mal ought to do is talk with some of the other vice-presidents ahead of time and get them interested in the idea and at least briefed to the point where they understand thoroughly what Mal has in mind. Most things get settled in our business outside of council meetings; the interested executives are covered individually or in small groups ahead of time, so that when the issue comes to a vote at the council meeting, it is pretty much a matter of rubber-stamping the proposal.

[1] The National Industrial Conference Board had reported that the previous year's operating profits of large department stores averaged 5.6 per cent of sales.

"Mal really needs a lot of help, anyway. We have just employed a personnel consulting firm, with an annual retainer of $20,000. They keep us in touch with what is going on in other businesses, union trends, etc.; they work with Mal on employee training courses and do a lot of other things for us. For example, I learned the other day that one of their communications specialists is helping Mal write employee bulletins before they come to me for my signature."

BOARD RELATIONS

"You were saying, Barrett, that you don't have much trouble with the board of directors."

"No, except for Fred Pellham, who is a little troublesome from time to time. He has made it a point to dig into our business more deeply than the other directors. He gets his own industry figures direct from the Fed, National Retail Merchants, and Harvard Business School, so that he can compare our operations with what others are doing. As I told you, he is trying to get us to think further ahead and anticipate the changes that are likely to happen ten years from now, so that we will be able to make the necessary moves today in terms of what is going to happen then, instead of struggling year by year to keep abreast as things shift. Of course, most merchants realize that department store business is, at best, a ninety-day business; we have to be quick on our feet to meet day-to-day changes. No one has a good enough crystal ball to be able to forecast several years ahead.

"The other directors now accept almost anything I propose as a sound idea. Over the last five or six years, I have been careful to make sure that the things that I brought before the board were thoroughly explored and based on conservative projections. As a result, I no longer find it necessary to justify most of the things I want to do. Sometimes I wonder if they are a little too easy on me. However, I don't know; it is certainly a lot more comfortable this way. I can't say that I would like to repeat the struggles that I had in selling the board this idea or that idea during the first year or two I was in this job. I guess no president wants a board of directors that is as active in the business as their own stockholders expect them to be. From my own experience in serving as a director on these other boards, I find it pretty easy to put the management on the spot by raising questions which are not self-evident from the figures presented to the board. Before every board meeting in these other concerns, I spend a lot of time going over the material they send us ahead of time, because I think I have the responsibility, both legal and moral, as a director to serve as His Majesty's loyal opposition, so to speak."

OTHER ACTIVITIES

"By and large, it looks to me as though things are in pretty good shape at Green & Richards, but every once in a while I wonder where I am going. Here I am, close to fifty, doing well financially — my directorships alone give me a pretty good income. Of course, income is not important in my tax bracket, and I definitely feel that my

serving on these outside boards is a good thing for the store. Too many of my re-
tailer friends aren't in touch with the methods and viewpoints of other businessmen.
I think I have the advantage over them as a result of these contacts outside our own
trade.

"Apart from these business and community activities, I seem to have plenty of
time for golf; I get in three rounds a week on the average, except when Jane and I are
away on vacation. I guess I told you that we are leaving the middle of next month
for a cruise around the world. In a way, this will combine business and vacation. It
will give me an opportunity to touch base with some of our important resources from
whom we import in the Far East and Europe. Our merchants are over there regularly,
but I think it means something from time to time to have the head of the business
pay them a visit. I get a real kick out of meeting their families, going through their
operations, and talking about the problems they are up against. It seems to me that
they get something out of it, too. In one sense, it does the same thing I try to do when
I walk around the store each day — and maintaining good relations with our key resources, both domestic and foreign, is almost as important as good employee relations, I think. I also try to spend as much time as I can in our domestic markets —
especially in New York and on the West Coast."

Since Trumble was thoroughly wound up, Hall continued to listen without
comment.

SATISFACTION THROUGH CONTRIBUTION

"I get a good deal of satisfaction out of things I am doing. I thoroughly enjoy my
regular job. I feel that Green & Richards is making an important contribution to our
growing community.

"I am convinced we help raise the cultural standards of Gulf City through our
emphasis on quality merchandise and good taste; through constantly making available to our customers exciting new items, many of them exclusive with us; through
concerts, Christmas and Easter festivities, art shows, and many other events throughout the year. I think our reputation for courteous service (and there is nothing more
important), for making good on all commitments, for integrity and fairness in all
dealings with customers, resources, and employees, sets an example for others in
the community. And I believe that my chief contribution to Green & Richards is to
help other people understand, believe in, and apply these principles to their day-
to-day problems. My job is to help our executives grow and develop to the full limit
of their capacities, to the point where they can operate on their own, within our
guiding policies and principles. To the extent I am successful in doing this, I not
only improve the sales and profits of the store but also feel, in some degree, the kind
of satisfaction you derive from your teaching — the satisfaction which one gets
from helping others.

"I would hate to give up any of my outside business interests or directorships.
As for the Community Fund, the Museum, and the other community service activities, I consider them too important to give up — they make it possible for me, in a

small way, to repay the community for my own good fortune. You said you wanted to talk with me, Floyd, about the kind of problems I find most troublesome. I guess my problem is that I don't have any real problems at the present time. Of course, if we had a real recession, I would have my hands full down at the store without any of these outside interests. However, from the looks of things, there isn't going to be too much for me to sink my teeth into in the near future."

EARLIER PROBLEMS AS GENERAL MERCHANDISE MANAGER

"Sometimes I find it hard to look back to nine years ago with G & R. I'm sure you remember how Jane used to complain about the way I worked around the clock and never had any time for her or the youngsters. At that time, we were in really bad shape. During the preceding five years, the store had slipped from first position to a shaky fourth in relation to the other stores in Gulf City. Someone had to get in and work closely with the buyers, one after another. I practically lived with each merchant, helping him get his department back on its feet. In some cases, we found it necessary to replace them with seasoned buyers from other stores. I hated to bring in so many executives from the outside, but we simply didn't have enough good people coming along at the lower levels to do much promoting from within.

"And the store had developed such a poor reputation in some markets that I was forced to work personally with many leading apparel, accessories, and home-furnishings resources before we were in a position to carry their lines again. With conditions as they were and with our competitors doing everything they could to keep us from regaining our No. 1 spot, this was a job I had to tackle myself, as general merchandise manager. The divisional supervisors and buyers just weren't strong enough to deal with the presidents and owners of some of the finest manufacturing establishments in this country and abroad. It was hard work, but it was also a lot of fun."

WHERE DO I GO FROM HERE?

"I can't help wondering what the next stop should be. Young Barrett and Sheila are well along in college and, except for summers, have flown the nest. The only way I can continue to grow is to keep on tackling new, challenging problems. I know that some of my friends think I'm already spreading myself too thin. From the look on your face, Floyd, it may be in your mind, too. I think I am pretty close to the boys down at the store, but it may be that they, too, think I am becoming an absentee president. However, as I have already said, I believe thoroughly in the significance of the causes for which I am working outside of the business, and I also believe each of them, in one way or another, helps contribute to the success of Green & Richards. Besides, I just can't see myself sitting in the office down at the store, reading a newspaper and waiting for someone to come in with a problem.

"Every so often, I have thought about trying a few years of government service. Through my work on the business advisory council of the Department of Commerce, I am in touch with a good many of the key people in the Administration. If they knew that I might be available, I suspect there would be an opportunity for me to move in at a level challenging enough to be more than just another bureaucratic job. Several of my friends have even had the temerity to suggest my name for governor, but in this state, a Republican candidate has lost the race before he starts. I think what I would really like to do is talk with you a little bit about your own experiences as a teacher. Perhaps, at this point in my career, I could get the greatest satisfaction from helping pass on to young people coming along some of the things I think I have learned in business. What do you think, Floyd?"

Hall arose as the two wives entered the room and said, "Why don't we let things soak a bit? You've given me so much to think about I hardly know where to begin."

TRUMBLE'S BACKGROUND

Floyd Hall recalled that Trumble had graduated from Hambletonian College. With business conditions as they were at the time, he had gone on to take his M.B.A. at the Tuck School of Business Administration at Dartmouth. All of his business life had been spent in retailing. Barrett had started as an assistant buyer of women's ready-to-wear at Fisk Brothers in Buffalo, New York. He progressed rapidly to the place where he was merchandising their entire ready-to-wear line. After eight years, he left Fisk to become divisional merchandise manager of a leading Southeast department store. Four years later, he became assistant general merchandise manager of a nationally known high-quality store on the East coast. He joined Green & Richards as vice-president and general merchandise manager and became president two years later. Hall recalled that Trumble had always been active in community affairs, wherever he worked. In the twenty-odd years Hall had known him, Trumble had never shown any evidence of being under pressure. Hall considered this unusual in an industry noted for heavy demands it made on its executives. Trumble had always had time for a full social life and an opportunity to take advantage of his consuming interest in golf. Barrett had been runner-up twice in the national intercollegiate golf championship while in college. He continued to play top-drawer golf after graduation, reaching the quarter finals of the National Amateur in his midforties. Two years earlier, he had been runner-up for the Gulf State Championship and had been club champion of the Jefferson Davis Country Club for six years running.

THE "SERMON"

Floyd Hall remembered that Trumble had sent him a copy of a talk he had given before the Parkville Presbyterian Church shortly after he became president of G & R. When he returned to Bristol, he found it was still in his files.

The Opportunities and Responsibilities of the Christian Layman in the Community

Excerpts from Barrett Trumble's Talk

Parkville Presbyterian Church
Wednesday Evening — November 28

It is very good to be with you, and I am sure that you understand that I am not here to preach. . . . But I thought that perhaps we could all think out loud, in an informal way, about the subject at hand, namely, the layman's opportunity and responsibility in the community.

The first thing we should ask ourselves is: What is a Christian layman? Obviously, a Christian layman is a follower of Jesus Christ and, in essence, stands for and believes, with his heart, in the teachings of Jesus. In this conjunction, it might be interesting to point out that Jesus Himself was a layman. Although he was called Rabbi (that is to say, teacher), there is no record of His attending a theological school. Further, Jesus surrounded Himself with laymen from the common walks of life, and although the message came down out of Heaven through Christ into the church, it was carried out of the church into life by laymen who preached the Gospel. There was really no other way to do this. . . .

. . . We might stress the qualities Jesus stands for and the kind of person He wants the Christian layman to be.

Taking great liberties with Matthew: In Chapter 5, Verse 3, which begins, "Blessed are the poor in spirit for theirs is the kingdom of Heaven" and goes on through the various beatitudes that Jesus mentioned, it seems quite clear that (1) kindness and consideration for others — giving the other fellow a second chance, (2) aggressive courage — going the second mile for good causes, (3) courtesy — coming from the heart, (4) thoughtfulness and understanding, (5) fairness, (6) integrity and vision, and (7) faith are some of the vital qualities that we should strive to possess in our everyday living if we would measure up to Jesus' standards.

. . . These very same qualities that Christ taught us to strive and stand for are the ones that make for true success in everyday life. I think it important to emphasize here that I am talking about inner spiritual, rather than material, success — the sort which would lead a man such as Disraeli to want to be a great man rather than a great lawyer. These qualities make for true success in every walk of life, whether one is engaged in teaching, farming, a profession, business, or household duties. The old idea that to be successful one had to be ruthless, unscrupulous, and tough with people just doesn't stand up today and it is my honest opinion that the inability to handle, work with, and influence people is probably the cause of the greatest number of personal failures in life. Time and time again, I have — and I am sure you have — seen brilliant people who appeared to have just what it takes for success fail utterly because they overlooked the fact that one rarely succeeds alone but rather succeeds because others make one successful. . . .

I have been very fortunate in my life to have met and watched a great number of prominent people at work. I think you will agree with me when I say that a Charles Wilson or a George Marshall or a Dwight Eisenhower exemplifies fully these qualities that I have listed. I have never met a more humble, homespun, or thoughtful man than Charles Wilson; nor a more kind, considerate, and honest one than Marshall; nor a more thoughtful, fair, or courageous man than Eisenhower. As a matter of fact, it seems to me that the greater the man, the fewer the pretenses and the more down-to-Christian-fundamentals he is. . . .

Let me quote, again, from the text: Ephesians 4:32 — "Be ye kind one to another, tender-hearted, forgiving." In Barrie's play, Little White Bird, a young husband is waiting at the hospital for his child to be born. He has never been unkind to his wife, but he wonders if he has been as kind as he might have been. "Let us make a new rule from tonight," he says, "always to be a little kinder than is necessary." . . . "Somehow, I never thought it paid," said Lincoln, when his friends urged him to make a stinging reply to a bitter, untrue word spoken about him. In the end, kindness, even to those who have been unkind to us, is never regretted. "A little kinder than is necessary" is the finest of the little arts of life, if not its final joy. The only things we are never sorry for are the kind things said and done to others. They make a soft pillow at the end.

. . . What are the obligations of the layman to his business or profession? In this regard, we have a great obligation to attempt to do the best possible job that we can in the field we are in, whatever that field might be. I believe it was Plato who said, "The source of the greatest happiness is in a job well done." Furthermore, by doing a good job in our field, whether it be as a mother in a home, a teacher in the school, a doctor in the hospital, or a businessman, we raise the standard of living and happiness of all those around us, and I am sure you will agree this is a most worthwhile goal.

Then there is the obligation of the layman to his fellow worker. To realize the dignity of man, to make his working and living conditions as pleasant as possible, to treat him with inner courtesy — coming from the heart. . . .

More directly and to the point of our subject, there is the obligation of the layman to his community, and I mean this in the large sense — the community being either local, national, or worldwide. Now, this interest in the obligation to the community can take the form of helping to improve the school system, of working with the sick and needy through the hospitals and in other ways helping to take care of the less fortunate. It can take the form of interest in striving for better, more enlightened, and honest government or in working for world peace. And finally, it can take the shape of interest in the church and in what the church stands for. Certainly, in some small way to help improve the lot of one or all of these five community efforts would be a most Christian thing to do — certainly something that Jesus urges us to pursue. Schools need better facilities, and teachers need more pay; the sick need care — the needy, relief from want; the government needs to understand and work for world peace and tolerance. And, certainly, the church, of all these community needs, should always be in our minds as an ever-present source of spiritual guidance, helping us to live every day a better and more Christian life. As I see it, going to church once a week isn't enough. We must also strive in our everyday living to live by the examples and teachings of Jesus. . . . It is not enough to just accept these teachings of Jesus. We must make these teachings work for us in our daily life.

... A Christian church is not a religion of monuments, but a religion of life. Of course, all of us must work for the physical needs of the church. But we must realize that the human race can never be saved by priests and monks and ministers alone, but rather by the Christian layman courageously setting a living example and aggressively selling, if you please, the teachings of Christ in his community. Every great idea must express itself in form. There must be an organization, but organization alone is not enough. Any religion worth having must demonstrate a power that makes changes in the lives of people who profess it. . . .

In conclusion — so many times I have heard people say that working for all these causes is fine, but what can I do about it — I am only one individual. . . . Of course, if everyone lived as Jesus taught us to live, there would probably not be need for helping other people. . . . If we solve our problems from a Christian and spiritual standpoint, we have taken a great step toward helping to solve the world's problems. Secondly, one doesn't have to head up organizations to be helpful. There are all levels of responsibility in community work for . . . anyone who wants to help. Finally, the argument that one is too busy would seem highly unjustified when the old expression, "When you want a job done, give it to a busy man," is so true.

9/ The Case of the Disputing Divisions

The following case, based on an actual situation, is disguised. While the details may not be exactly the same, the problems discussed in the case do exist, and they are relevant to many companies in many industries.

"This is one of the toughest decisions we've ever had to make. . . . There are damn good arguments on both sides, and no matter which way we decide, there'll be howls."

Sitting in the controller's office of the Pollard Appliance Corporation was Austin Frederick, the company's pricing policy manager. The situation which Frederick was discussing with Controller Will Packer involved a pricing dispute between the corporation's Chrome Products Division (manufacturing) and its Electric Stove Division (marketing). The dispute centered on which division should be charged for costs associated with a quality improvement in the tops of the company's electric stoves.

The Pollard Appliance Corporation was a large integrated manufacturer of all types of home appliances. The company had a decentralized divisional organization, consisting of four product (marketing) divisions, four manufacturing divisions, and six staff offices. An organization chart appears in Exhibit 9-1.

Each division and staff office was headed by a vice president. The staff offices had functional authority over their counterparts in the divisions, but they had no direct line authority over the divisional general managers. The company organization manual stated: "All division personnel are responsible to the division manager. Except in functional areas specifically delegated, staff personnel have no line authority in a division." Note, further, that:

The product divisions designed, engineered, assembled, and marketed various home appliances. They manufactured very few component parts; rather, they assembled the appliances from parts purchased either from the manufacturing divisions or from outside vendors.

As for the manufacturing divisions, they made most of their sales (about 75%) to the product divisions. Parts made by a manufacturing division were generally designed by a product division; the manufacturing divisions merely produced the part to specifications provided to them.

Interdivisional pricing was an important element in divisional profitability because of the high proportion of the manufacturing divisions' production that was

This case was prepared by John Dearden and appeared in *Harvard Business Review* 42, no. 3 (May–June 1964): 159–70. Copyright © 1964 by the President and Fellows of Harvard College; all rights reserved. Reprinted by permission.

Exhibit 9-1. Pollard Appliance Corporation

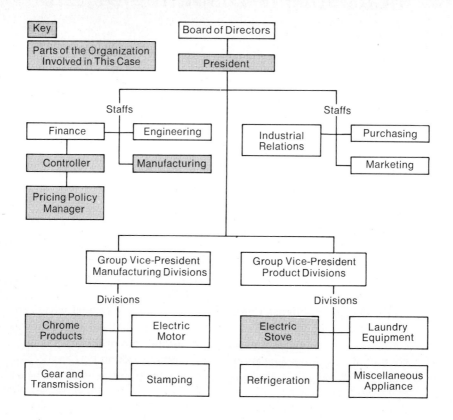

sold to the product divisions. The divisions were expected to deal with one another as though they were independent companies; and parts were to be transferred at competitive prices arrived at by negotiations between the divisions. Competitive price levels were generally determined from actual prices paid to outside suppliers for the same or comparable parts. These outside prices were adjusted to reflect differences in the design of the part bought from a supplier from that of the part made by Pollard. Also, if the outside price was based on purchases made at an earlier date, it was adjusted for changes in the general price level since that date.

In general, the divisions established prices by negotiations among themselves. If the divisions could not agree on a price, they could submit the dispute to the finance staff for arbitration. Responsibility for settling pricing disputes rested with the pricing policy manager, who reported to the company's controller.

Negotiations between divisions were not always conducted as though divisions were independent companies. This was true because the product division doing the buying did not have the power to decide whether to buy from within the company or from an outside supplier. Once a manufacturing division began to produce a part, the only way the buying division could change to an outside supplier was to obtain permission of the manufacturing division, or in case of disagreement, appeal to the purchasing staff. The purchasing staff had the authority to settle disputes of this kind between the product and manufacturing divisions. In nearly every case of dispute the purchasing staff had decided that the part would continue to be manufactured within the company. When the buying divisions were instructed to continue buying a part inside, the manufacturing division had to price the part at the level that the buying division could purchase the part from an outside vendor.

In the case of new parts, the buying division had the authority to decide on the source of supply. However, a manufacturing division could appeal to the purchasing staff to reverse a decision of a product division to purchase a part from an outside vendor.

The dispute between the Chrome Products Division and the Electric Stove Division had been going on for several months, and concerned the chrome-plated unit which fitted on top of the company's stoves. Pricing Policy Manager Frederick explained the situation to Controller Packer.

Frederick: As you know, our Chrome Products Division produces chrome-plated stove tops for the Electric Stove Division. They have been making them since the beginning of last year, when the Electric Stove Division stopped buying it from outside.

Packer: Were there problems that led to our wanting to make the top ourselves?

Frederick: Well, the unit has to be corrosion and stain resistant, and also it must remain bright and new looking. I suspect that having it made inside the company meant better quality control.

Packer: Was the stove-top unit affected by President Pollard's quality improvement program?

Frederick: Actually, that's what gave birth to the problem. After Mr. Pollard got Hind's staff into the quality improvement business, quality control standards on the stove-top unit were changed.

About the middle of 1962, President Pollard became concerned over customer and dealer complaints about the quality of the company's products. A consumer survey indicated that in the previous year the company's reputation as a producer of quality products had deteriorated. Although this deterioration in reputation was caused principally by the poor performance of a new electric motor — a fault which was soon corrected — the president had come to the conclusion that the over-all quality of the company's products had been deteriorating for the past several years; furthermore, he believed it was essential for the company to reestablish itself as a leader in the production of quality products. Accordingly, in early 1963 the pres-

ident called in Lee Hind, the manufacturing staff vice president, and told him that for the next six months his most important job was to bring the quality of all Pollard products up to a satisfactory level.

Packer: What were the changes?

Frederick: As I understand it, when the stove-top unit was first manufactured by the Chrome Products Division, it went through a five-step process — buffing, nickel plating, more buffing, chrome plating, and a final buffing. The quality control standards for rejection or acceptance were a corrosion test and an appearance test. And . . .

Packer: . . . the appearance had to be improved!

Frederick: Exactly. Hind apparently decided that the appearance was unsatisfactory. He selected several of the better looking units as standards of minimum appearance quality, and the reject rate started to skyrocket. So the divisional and plant staff, together with Hind's staff, studied the operation and added copper plating and buffing steps at the beginning of the manufacturing process and a hand-buffing operation at the end of the cycle.

Packer: I assume that this solved the quality problem, and at the same time created the pricing problem.

Frederick: Right. The appearance quality rejections dropped to under 1%, and the Chrome Products Division proposed to add the 40¢ per unit cost of the new operations to the price of the stove-top unit, as well as a 5¢ profit markup. That brought the price per unit from $5.00 ($4.50 was the outside supplier's price when the Chrome Products Division took over, plus 25¢ for design changes and 25¢ for price increases since then) to $5.45.

You can guess the rest: the Electric Stove Division objected to the proposed price increase (the wailing was audible for miles), and after three weeks of fruitless negotiations the dispute was submitted to us two weeks ago.

Packer: What's happened since then?

Frederick: Well, first we examined the arguments of each side. I've summarized them in this memorandum [Exhibit 9-2]. We also instituted a review of the added operation by the engineering department and the quality control department of the manufacturing staff. The former reported that the proposed costs were reasonable and represented efficient processing; the latter stated that the quality of the stove-top unit's appearance was definitely improved and that the new units were superior in quality to those purchased from outside sources 18 months ago.

Packer (reading through arguments): This sure looks like a tough one . . .

Frederick: . . . and either way, as it always is in these pricing disputes, someone's going to be plenty annoyed!

Exhibit 9-2. Arguments in Chrome Products–Electric Stove Dispute

Chrome Products Division believes it is entitled to the increased price:

1. We have been required by the manufacturing staff to add operations to our manufacturing processing at a cost of 40¢ a unit; we did not institute the change, and should not be forced to pay for it.

2. These operations have resulted in improved quality that could benefit only the Electric Stove Division. Since the payoff is in the marketplace, the Electric Stove Division should pay for these benefits.

3. The present price of $5 is based on old quality standards. Had the outside supplier been required to meet these new standards, its price would have been 45¢ higher.

Electric Stove Division believes it should not pay the increased price:

1. There was no change in engineering specifications, only a change in what was purported to be "acceptable appearance." This is a subjective matter which cannot be measured with any degree of precision.
Moreover, this case could establish a precedent: If we were to pay for any change in quality standards not accompanied by a change in engineering specifications, we would be opening up a Pandora's box. Every division would request higher prices because of giving us better quality based on some subjective standard. Every request by this division to a manufacturing division to improve quality would be accompanied by a price increase, even though we were requesting only that the quality be brought up to competitive levels. If we are to maintain control over costs, we cannot have every complaint about quality result in higher costs.

2. The Electric Stove Division did not request that quality be improved. In fact, we were *not even consulted* on the change. Thus, the division should not be responsible for paying for a so-called improvement which it neither reviewed nor approved.

3. Even if the division had been consulted, we probably would have rejected the change. It is doubtful that there is any improvement in quality *from the customer's viewpoint.* Perhaps to the highly trained eye of the quality control personnel there may have been an improvement. But the customer would not notice a significant difference between the appearance of the part before and after the change in quality standards.

4. Furthermore, even if there were an improvement in quality perceptible to the consumer, we believe strongly that it is not worth 45¢. For 45¢ per unit, we could add features that would be far more marketable than this quality improvement.

5. Any improvement in quality only brought the part up to the quality level that the former outside producer had provided. The cost of the improved quality, therefore, was already included in the $5 price.

10/ Crisis in Conscience at Quasar

THE CASE SETTING

Universal Nucleonics Company, the parent company for a number of wholly owned subsidiaries, suddenly found itself in the embarrassing position of having to report that its earnings for the year would be substantially lower than had been announced at the end of the previous quarter. Shortly thereafter, a statement appeared in the "Who's News" section of *The Wall Street Journal* reporting that Quasar Stellar Company, one of Universal's subsidiaries, had a new president and a new vice president of finance (replacing the former controller).

As time went on, the financial community learned that Universal had discovered that one of its subsidiaries had been withholding the truth, purposely distorting the facts, or otherwise misrepresenting the situation at hand in its monthly reports to corporate headquarters. By the time Universal had realized the actual condition of Quasar's financial situation, it was too late to correct it without affecting the reported year-end earnings of the parent company.

The two individuals most directly concerned at Quasar — John Kane, president, and Hugh Kay, controller — had both "resigned." It was generally agreed by the board of directors that there would be no public announcement as to the reasons for the resignations. Privately, however, one director stated flatly that out-and-out fraud was involved; another, more in tune with the times, said that the situation was directly attributable to the pressures to make good and the tendency to have a positive outlook on the outcome of all individual company problems.

Corporate headquarters was vitally interested in finding out why, given the organizational structure at Quasar, no feedback had been received independently of the president-controller monthly statement; whether any of the other executives were involved in the reports either knowingly or unknowingly, willingly or unwillingly; and, finally, what steps could be taken to prevent a recurrence of the situation in the future.

FACT-FINDING TEAM

To resolve these questions, Universal's executive committee decided that a direct approach should be taken. The executive vice president and the vice president of industrial relations for the corporation would conduct a series of interviews with the Quasar Stellar personnel who might have been involved. Both men were well qualified to appraise the situation. Jim Bowden, the executive vice president, was both an operating and a financial man, having spent a number of years in each area.

This case was prepared by John J. Fendrock and appeared in *Harvard Business Review* 46, no. 2 (March–April 1968): 112–20. Copyright © 1968 by the President and Fellows of Harvard College; all rights reserved. Reprinted by permission.

Hubert Clover, vice president of industrial relations, was a former professor of industrial psychology at one of the leading business schools.

It was further agreed that each executive would interview different men, compare notes, and then speak with each other's interviewees if the situation so warranted. After studying the organization chart (see Exhibit 10-1), and the company's "Manual of Responsibilities," they decided it would be best to talk to Peter Loomis, vice president-marketing; George Kessler, vice president-manufacturing; and William Heller, vice president-engineering.

LOOMIS' SESSION

The scene opens in a small conference room at Quasar Stellar Company. The first man to be interviewed is Peter Loomis, vice president-marketing, who is known to be outspoken, demanding, and intensely loyal. Loomis is greeted by Hubert Clover.

Clover: Pete, as you know, the purpose of our chat is to see if we can learn something from this unfortunate episode that can help to prevent such an occurrence in the future. I would like to get your version of what has happened and any suggestions you may be able to offer as to what can be done to help our planning.

Loomis (defensively): Well, Hubert, you know I thought very highly of John. I'm certain you are aware that he hired me for this job. I don't mind admitting that I think the decision to fire him was unwarranted and ill advised.

Clover: If there is one thing I am certain of, Pete, it is that there is no question of your loyalty to John. I hope that won't bias your outlook. As for John's resignation,

Exhibit 10-1. Quasar Stellar Corporation

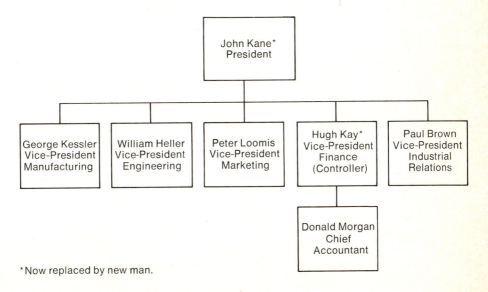

*Now replaced by new man.

perhaps the best I can say is that on the basis of all facts available, the board decided this was the only logical course of action. And if . . .

Loomis (interrupting): Let me set the record straight on two points. My loyalty to John was based on respect for his abilities — not on personal grounds. And I'm not disagreeing with you, either on the basis of the facts available at the time or on those turned up by the investigation, that the action was not warranted. But I also feel that there was too hasty a collection of facts and an overreaction resulting in his dismissal. What I'm saying is that had a more thorough and penetrating investigation been made, the conclusions would probably have been different.

Clover (attempting to lead the interview back): I understand your point, Pete, but what are some of the additional facts that you think could have influenced the decision differently?

Loomis: You are most likely aware that the failure to receive the Apollo and LEM contracts had significant effects on the overall picture. But when John informally notified headquarters that our chances of receiving these two jobs were less than 50-50, he was told he was just being pessimistic. It was quite evident to him that the board of directors felt these were two prestige jobs that we simply had to get. The trouble was that while we dissipated our efforts on trying to land these low-probability programs, a half-dozen other less known, but perhaps more lucrative, opportunities slipped by.

Clover: You say John told headquarters about this. Have you any idea why the so-so probabilities and the alternatives were not openly presented and discussed at the appropriate company board meeting?

Loomis: To be frank, the 50-50 chance was an after-the-fact estimate. When the decision was made to pursue the two jobs, because of the pressure from headquarters and knowing what the work could mean to Quasar, I was undoubtedly too optimistic myself. A staff meeting was held in which the two marketing efforts were reviewed in detail.

Clover: Who attended that meeting?

Loomis: As I recall, there was George Kessler, Bill Heller, Hugh Kay, John, and myself.

Clover: Was it unanimously agreed that you should go after the two contracts?

Loomis (shaking his head): Oh, no! Bill felt very strongly that we should. He thought that the engineering department could gain a heck of a lot by being involved — state-of-the-art stuff. George was against the effort. He argued that production would be severely affected, because these projects would require such a long-term engineering effort before production could start. He wanted more immediate work that would occupy his work force. Hugh was with George. Not only was he worried about overhead and profits, but he had a "gut feeling" that our chances were less than what I forecast. He was right, of course. John was in favor of pursuing the contracts only if we had about a 75% chance of capturing each. John tossed the ball to me when he asked what our chances of getting the jobs were. At the time, I indicated that while I couldn't stick my neck out to 75%, I was willing to guess it would be much closer to 75% than to, say, 50% or even 60%. Considering the attitude at headquarters, the stakes, and my projection, we finally decided to go after both.

Clover: Are you saying that you didn't really feel that your chances were as close to 75% as you indicated?

Loomis: I believe they weren't. But that isn't to say that I didn't feel they could or should have been.

Clover: How long had you been with the company when this meeting took place, Pete?

Loomis: Just about nine months. I'm quite sure I know the reason for your question. Actually, I was not as familiar with the company as I should have been to express so strong an opinion on such an important matter.

Clover: Obviously, you showed a good deal of enthusiasm . . .

Loomis (interrupting again): And, I'm afraid you'll have to agree, naiveté. Remember, however, that this is — or at least was — a gung-ho operation. I was anxious to earn my spurs. Those contracts would have put us on the map and made Quasar and Universal household words.

Clover: I can certainly understand your decision to go after the big fish, but, once you found that you were out of fishing water, why was headquarters not kept informed of the deteriorating market picture? Wouldn't that have been the logical thing to do?

Loomis: Logical, yes, but hardly practical. In retrospect, that is probably what we should have done, but let's go back six months. That's when our fears of a drop in production began to inject themselves. Hugh's warnings about profitability were proving to be only too accurate, and there was nothing that could be pulled in at the last minute to bridge the gap.

Clover: Yes, but you must have known very early that your odds were way off.

Loomis (after a pause): Well, perhaps I did not emphasize that fact strongly enough. I assure you, however, that both George and Hugh did, since their operations were directly and indirectly involved.

Clover (bothered by Loomis' evasiveness): How, then, was the decision reached not to inform headquarters of this situation? Didn't it bother you to think that there might be adverse effects on employment?

Loomis: Once the decision was made to go after the two projects, any reversal could only result in a loss of face and prestige. Like the gambler at the roulette wheel, we plunged deeper — with about the same odds — and lost. I must confess that I had my moments of doubt about our course of action. It was quite clear that people could get hurt, but that too is all part of the game. Frankly, at no time did it occur to me that I had a greater responsibility than the one I had to John. Perhaps this is wrong, but I have always felt that I owe more loyalty to my supervisor than to the company. And besides, I'm not certain to what degree personal morality should enter into business decisions.

Clover: Pete, let me ask you one final question. What do you think we might do to prevent this sort of thing from happening again in the future?

Loomis: Frankly, I feel that headquarters should give us more independence. For example, if headquarters had not exerted pressure on us to pursue these two contracts, we might have followed a different course. To me, what happened was that headquarters decided on a set course of action, passed the word down, and then — when it became impossible for us to follow through — they looked for scapegoats. Both John and Hugh were sacrificed because of poor headquarters policy.

Clover (rising): Thanks for a frank and open presentation of your thoughts on the situation, Pete. By the way, Jim Bowden may or may not wish to speak with you, depending on how things go in general. In any event, we'll let you know later. Once again, thanks for your ideas.

Loomis: Thanks for asking. I honestly thought this might just be allowed to die on the vine without anyone looking deeper into it.

FOLLOW-UP QUESTIONS

Hubert Clover brooded over his interview with Loomis, scanning his notes in a manner that suggested more sorrow and disappointment than thought. He then decided to summarize his observations and to recommend that Bowden not interview Loomis. But, after reviewing the results of Clover's conversation, Bowden concluded that there was one more thing he wanted resolved: Why had not Loomis, in routine fashion, been put in a position to send a report back to headquarters that would have been at variance with the official statement? Later that afternoon, the two men got together. After exchanging the usual pleasantries and engaging in small talk related to the previous interview, Bowden asked the specific question he had in mind.

Bowden: The one thing that puzzles me, Pete, is why you were not able to transmit your misgivings about the possibility of receiving the two contracts directly to the corporate vice president of marketing.

Loomis: Your question, Jim, implies that I was *unable* to do this. Actually, it was always possible, but I was not *required* to do it. However, I was expected to give my observations to John and to support him in any decision he made as to how the information was to be handled.

Bowden: Your answer implies to me that you were fully aware that two distorted monthly reports were sent to corporate headquarters. Am I correct in this assumption?

Loomis: From what I have said to both you and John, there is no doubt that your conclusion is correct. And, to be honest, I was completely aware of the distortions in the reports. I can only repeat what I said earlier this afternoon to Hubert: my loyalty is to my supervisor, and I always support him in his use of information in any way he sees fit.

KESSLER'S INTERROGATION

The next man to be interviewed was George Kessler, vice president-manufacturing, who was an old-timer by Quasar standards, having been at Quasar for 15 years. He was known for his outspokenness, integrity, and forcefulness. Clover and Bowden decided that Bowden should conduct the interview with Kessler because there existed a somewhat close relationship between them. As a former operations man, Bowden had taken a direct interest in manufacturing, and he had developed a healthy respect for Kessler. Bowden greeted Kessler, and the two exchanged a few pleasantries.

Bowden: I guess we could keep up the chitchat all day, George, but I'm afraid we've got to get down to business. A fellow in your position must have seen what was coming — how in hell could you let it happen?

Kessler: I would rather continue reminiscing about old times than get into this. To answer your question, Jim, I saw what was coming; but, to turn the question back to you, how could I possibly have prevented it?

Bowden: All right, George, you couldn't have stopped it. Really, what I am asking is this: Seeing what was happening, wasn't there something you could have done to raise the storm signals?

Kessler: You know me well enough to realize that I am not one of the gung-ho types. While I had tremendous respect for John's ability to analyze a situation, I always suspected that he had a streak of the gambler in him. Let's face it; if he had pulled those two jobs out of the hat, he would have been Universal's brightest star.

Bowden: Getting back to the point, George, wasn't there some way for you to signal headquarters of what was happening?

Kessler (frowning): You insist on pursuing this point, don't you? Jim, you know as well as I do that I answered directly to John. I'm not going to beat a dead horse; but, without going into details, I think I expressed my views strongly on the approach we were taking. Certainly, I was concerned about a number of things . . . the number of old-time employees who were going to take a beating if this thing fizzled, as it did; what might actually happen to the company overall; and what I owed to myself as well as to John. Taking all these points into consideration, I did what I thought was morally and managerially right, and I don't say that lightly. In expressing my doubts so forcefully, perhaps I did a disservice to everyone I tried to help.

Bowden: In what way do you think you performed a disservice?

Kessler: In short order, I found myself outside of the actual development of the monthly reports. The result was that any influence I might have exerted in determining what information was to be generated for headquarters was cancelled out.

Bowden (nodding): I appreciate your dilemma, George, and I also respect the position you took. But don't you feel that there might have been some way to get this back to our office?

Kessler: In weighing my responsibility to the company, corporate headquarters, employees, self, and supervisor, I may possibly have erred in following too narrow a path. It seemed to me at the time, and I feel the same way even now, that with the organizational structure we have, my only approach was to try to change things through the existing framework. My efforts failed. Perhaps I should have been more adventurous and requested — demanded, if you will — an audience with you fellows. But I am certain that if a similar situation arose again, I still would not do this.

Bowden: Then let me ask you what you think can be done to prevent this from happening in the future.

Kessler: To me, there must be an approach that will allow for greater communication between headquarters and the company office. Perhaps the answer lies in having an executive committee sign the monthly report; or possibly having each committee member prepare a short concurrence or dissent report of his own, after the pattern of the Supreme Court; or even a more direct approach of having each manager give an independent report to his respective staff contact at corporate headquarters. The fact is, so long as we have a characteristic line and staff organizational structure, we can only follow the channels of communication that the chief executive officer decides on. No self-respecting manager would consider surreptitiously reporting behind his superior's back.

Bowden (rising and extending a handshake): George, thanks for your observations. I like your suggestion of a concurrence or disagreement by an executive committee. I hope the next time we have a little get-together it can be under more pleasant circumstances.

HELLER'S INTERVIEW

To some extent, the interview had merely reinforced Bowden's estimation of Kessler. However, he couldn't help but feel a sense of frustration that a man of Kessler's caliber did not find a way to communicate his misgivings to those who could have done something about the developing Quasar problem.

After reading Bowden's notes, Clover concluded there was no need for him to talk with Kessler. Instead, he decided to carry on with the next interview. The final man singled out was William Heller, vice president-engineering, an intense, serious-minded, pipe-smoking engineer whose forte was considered to be R&D, not administrative work. He too was a long-term employee, having been with Quasar over ten years. Clover met him at the door of the conference room and, with a wave of his hand, motioned Heller to a chair.

Clover: I suppose the idea of sitting down to discuss this problem is not the most appealing thing to you, Bill. I hope it won't be as painful as realizing that an R&D project is going sour.

Heller: Since your call a few minutes ago was not completely unexpected, I prepared for this by fixing myself an extra tightly packed pipe of tobacco. It will give me more time to think about your questions.

Clover: What can you contribute to our understanding of the things that happened here, and do you have any suggestions as to how they might be prevented in the future?

Heller: I wonder if you could narrow your question somewhat. Exactly what would you like me to address myself to?

Clover: The specific problem, Bill, is this. Do you have an idea why Quasar's deteriorating condition was not reported back to headquarters? Of greatest interest, of course, is the overall condition of the plant operation, but the decline in engineering activity is something you can probably elaborate on in detail. Any light you can shed will be useful.

Heller: While you have become more specific, I still have a wide-open field. Probably I should first outline what happened to engineering, and from this we might then be able to work into the bigger picture. How does that appeal to you?

Clover (nodding): That would be a good start.

Heller: About a year ago, it became obvious that our engineering activity, including both research and development and general engineering, was going to decline. The decision was made that a joint effort with marketing would be undertaken. After a series of meetings, it was decided to pursue actively and aggressively two relatively large contracts.

Clover: Those would be the Apollo and LEM contracts. *(Heller nods assent).* When you say it was decided that those two contracts would be pursued, what did this imply?

Heller: It meant that a radically new — for us — course of action was decided on. Always in the past we had operated as a subcontractor to primes on large systems. However, John and Pete took the stand that we were in a position to enter the systems area itself. Frankly, while I had initial skepticism about this approach, John portrayed the picture in optimistic terms. He was convinced that the contracts would be awarded more on the basis of marketing activity than on the engineering proposal, and he was equally confident that Pete's personal contacts would help us in capturing this work. Apparently John knew, or he felt he knew, that Pete had influence with the right people where those two contracts were involved. Thus, while in the past we had been merely keeping our fingers in the pie and hoping to get a piece of the action, it was decided at that point we would go the whole hog after them.

Clover: And you agreed with this approach?

Heller: As I indicated, initially I was skeptical. Our organization is simply not capable of coping with proposals of this size. However, after John and Pete argued their case so persuasively, I was fully in favor of the decision. Actually, I knew it involved a lot of risk, but Quasar stood to benefit greatly if it worked out, and so I went along with them on it.

Clover: What did you think the chances were of getting those contracts, Bill?

Heller (pausing to light his pipe): To me, our chances were less than those expressed by Pete, who, as I recall, said he figured them to be closer to 75% than to 60% or so. Frankly, I would have guessed 60% to be the upper limit on our chances for each contract. However, even at that, it seemed like a good risk because, if we had captured but one of them, engineering would have benefited greatly.

Clover: And how about the rest of the plant operations?

Heller: Here, unfortunately, I was shortsighted. While the engineering activity would benefit, in retrospect the company as a whole could conceivably lose if only one, or perhaps even if both contracts were awarded to Quasar. I might add that this point was brought out strongly by George and Hugh. To offset this argument, however, it was pointed out that while a temporary downturn might occur, in about two years Quasar would be hard pressed to satisfy the requirements for the projects. In addition, Quasar would become so well known that interim work would be easy to come by.

Clover: Might it not also have worked to Quasar's disadvantage? How can you assume that other companies would be willing to give you work, knowing that it would be short-term and that you certainly would give attention to your own contracts once it was time to begin production?

Heller: Yes, it was an optimistic outlook and probably very shortsighted from a total company point of view.

Clover: Even assuming that the decision was a good one when made, why didn't someone recognize it was the wrong course before the entire operation went sour?

Heller (puffing on his pipe for a moment): Now you are in an area that is too deep for me. Once it was decided on to pursue those contracts, my group concentrated its efforts on the technical proposal. We are extremely thin in this area. Therefore, our R&D activity was almost totally devoted to the proposal. Let me add that for approximately a 3-month period, 10- to 12-hour days and 7-day weeks were common for my staff.

Clover: But this very activity reduced your effectiveness on current work, did it not, and resulted in costly overruns and delays on contracts already in the house?

Heller: Unfortunately, yes, but that was not totally unexpected. We attempted to minimize the overruns and delays, but some were certainly inevitable. Since we were trying to maintain our staff, a lot of the added cost went into overhead and project charges as we stockpiled personnel during the initial period when the decline began to manifest itself. Of course, we had to face facts later and let some people go when it became apparent that the plans were not working out.

Clover: At that point, why didn't the company reverse itself, abandon its course, and go after some short-term subcontract work? And why didn't you get back to headquarters with your problem?

Heller: At that point, both John and Pete felt retreat would be impossible. Frankly, I supported them against my better judgment, both because I could see no way to change their attitude, and because I had an obligation to do my utmost in attempting to rectify the situation. Now, then, your other question as to why headquarters was not informed is difficult for me to answer. What can I say?

Clover: I would like a frank comment on this point, Bill.

Heller (knocking the ashes from his pipe): Both John and Pete stood high in my book. I don't pretend to be a business manager; rather, I am an engineering manager. The tangibles of engineering are something I grasp and manipulate readily, but the intangibles of business are quite another thing. In retrospect, it's easy to criticize past decisions, but I respect the decisions that were made then. I personally felt there was an obligation to the parent company, but even though I disagreed with the principle of not reporting the situation to headquarters, I accepted it as a business decision.

Clover: Then you were aware, were you not, that the reports sent to headquarters distorted conditions at Quasar to such an extent that the status of projects was inaccurately reported, actual and projected earnings were blatantly inflated, and the entire status of the operation was totally misrepresented? How could you have accepted such a situation?

Heller: If only I could answer you in a manner that might express my feelings at the time. Was I aware of what was going on? Yes, of course, I was. But I didn't *want* to know about it. I will go so far now as to say that I tried *not to know* what was being done. Realistically, once I accepted the basic decision to ride the thing out, I felt stuck with the consequences. There was nothing, as I saw it, that I could do to alter the course taken.

Clover: Bill, did you have any opportunity to bring this to the attention of head-quarters?

Heller: Formally, no, of course not. No mechanism existed, or perhaps should ever exist, for circumventing top management. On a few occasions I might have had the opportunity to mention to the corporate vice president of engineering what was happening, but I certainly would not do that.

Clover (shaking his head slowly): I think you will agree such a situation should never be allowed to exist. Can you offer any suggestions as to how information of such importance to the welfare of both the company and the corporation could be made available to top management without violating any precepts — actual or imaginary?

Heller: I have given considerable thought to this point. I honestly feel that what gets reported back to headquarters can only reflect what the president sees fit. I would hit the ceiling if I found out one of my project managers was reporting directly or indirectly to the president. By the same token, the president shouldn't have to guard against insurgency in his ranks. The corporation might use an internal audit team composed of knowledgeable personnel to make frequent checks on various phases of the operation. Apart from that, I've no suggestion.

Clover: Bill, your pipe's been cold and empty long enough. Thanks for your comments. Hopefully, we won't need another one of these sessions with you.

MORGAN'S OPINIONS

Clover discussed his report with Bowden, and they agreed that another interview with Heller was unnecessary. Then they went over the results of all three interviews in depth. When they had finished, they decided to pursue two additional questions from two other specific areas: (a) Why did the accounting people not find a way to report to headquarters? (b) What was the quality of the morale of the personnel during this period?

Accordingly, Donald Morgan, chief accountant, and Paul Brown, vice president-industrial relations, were invited to sit down with Bowden and Clover, respectively, in two simultaneous sessions. Since both corporate fact finders felt that too much briefing might tend to "lead" the interviews and stifle response, they agreed that the only statement they would make at the start would be to the effect that efforts were being made to prevent a repetition of the Quasar situation in the future.

Bowden: Don, you certainly are aware of the upheaval here at Quasar, and I suspect you know pretty well the reasons for it.

Morgan: Yes, I have a good idea of what's what.

Bowden: I wonder if you would care to express your opinions on two specific points. First, why was it not possible to have the information fed back to corporate headquarters once the deteriorating situation began and, second, what might be done to prevent what happened from taking place again?

Morgan: As standard company policy on reports, we generate our financial statements from whatever information is given to us. Our statements, in turn, are sent to the controller's office, and he does what he sees fit with them. Should we receive instructions from his office to reorganize, let's say, or otherwise manipulate the reports, there is very little we can do but follow instructions. This is particularly true when matters of judgment are involved. Let me give you a for-instance: if a project is reported as being behind schedule by the program manager and, after review by the controller's office it is decided that it is not all that far behind, naturally adjustments are made. Or, say, an expected contract has not yet been received, but management decides to open up a project number anyway and begins accepting charges in anticipation of receiving the job; this too is done. So far as I can see, this is nothing more than exercising management prerogative. I will summarize my position by saying that I do pretty much what I am told. Sometimes I may not like it, but my job is not to set policy or to question decisions. Rather, it is to follow instructions.

BROWN'S OBSERVATIONS

At that point, Bowden decided that he had heard enough and abruptly ended the interview. Meanwhile, Clover was undertaking his interview with Paul Brown.

Clover: Paul, can you give any insight into the state of morale during the period when Quasar was apparently falsifying reports to the home office and after it became apparent that a serious problem existed?

Brown: For a while, everybody acted as if they were on "pot"; everyone was filled with high expectations. To be sure, there were a couple of exceptions. But, in rapid fashion, things began to settle down and disillusionment set in. Many people sensed that there was trouble ahead and that nothing was being done. After a month or two, the exodus began, and, as you know, it still hasn't ceased. I know that some of the managers tried their best to hang onto their key people, but as usual it was just this caliber of individual who could read the writing on the wall and got out while the getting was good. I'm equally certain that a number of the other top people would have left except for loyalty to the company and their fellow employees, their years of company service, and/or other factors. My only other observation on this is that I hope our new president and controller have been selected more for solid, long-range accomplishments than for flashy, short-term results.

The interviews having been concluded, Clover and Bowden are now faced with drafting a series of recommendations on the individuals interviewed and the steps to be taken by Universal Corporation.

11/ The Case of the Borderline Black

David Kimball stood by the window of his Philadelphia office, looking high out over the Schuylkill River Valley. He was waiting for his Design Engineering manager, Paul Kelley, to arrive for a 10:30 conference. In his hand was a memo Kelley had sent him after the meeting of section heads the day before. It read:

"I have considered the alternatives, and clearly LSI circuits is the program to cut back. I recommend letting two of our engineers on that project go. But I thought you ought to know that one of the two is Thomas Rawlins, the only black engineer we have in Design. What do we do about that?"

Kimball, a trim and athletic 51, was manager of the Engineering Department of Industrial Computer Products, the largest division of multinational International Business Systems, Inc. He had risen far in the company and hoped to go farther.

As he gazed out the window, Kimball thought back to his student debate-team days at Cornell, when he had spoken passionately about the race question in 1940, years before the general acceptance of civil rights causes. And he remembered his satisfaction three years ago when Tom Rawlins became his first black engineer.

The sight of a jet plane arching steeply up from the Philadelphia airport brought Kimball's thoughts back to the present. He lit a cigarette to clear his mind for the conference coming up with Paul Kelley. Systematically, he assembled and sorted out his thoughts about the meeting two days ago when his boss, Harold Page, vice president in charge of the division, had announced the cutback.

Page, 60 and a product of the Depression, was a hard driver with a brilliant mind, devoted to the rapid expansion of the industrial computer business. He demanded a lot from his managers. At the meeting Page had quoted part of a memo from the executive vice president, Louis Kagan, which read:

"The Automation Group of International Business Systems must take serious action. We have reviewed the rate of incoming orders and projected our expense levels from the last two quarters. I am convinced that for the balance of this year we are going to have to trim expenses throughout the Group. A 10% reduction is a reasonable target for the Industrial Computer Products Division."

The cutback was inevitable, of course, in light of the current recession, Kimball remembered thinking. IBS had grown into a successful company not only through its alertness in moving in on new technology, products, and markets, but also through its skill in controlling costs, adjusting to changing business conditions, and quickly trimming fat and eliminating unprofitable products.

This case was prepared by Theodore V. Purcell and appeared in *Harvard Business Review* 49, no. 6 (November–December 1971): 128–43. Considerable credit for the preparation of the case and its interpretation goes to the author's research assistant, Miss Irene E. Wylie. Copyright © 1971 by the President and Fellows of Harvard College; all rights reserved. Reprinted by permission.

But Page wanted to go further than Kagan. He had continued: "I've reviewed our incoming orders rate, our inventory, our backlog, and our cost structure, and I'm convinced that ICP can and should reduce costs 15%. I want each of our departments to take a long look at how we can cut back."

The department managers, although not surprised by Page's higher goal, had reacted negatively, for cost cutting is not easy and letting employees go is one of the hardest tasks a manager faces. Both Kimball and Toby Marotta, employee relations manager, had protested the 15% target. But Page had said, "We're determined to go beyond the demands of the New York office. I'm sorry, but you're going to have to cut your costs 15% for the next two quarters. Find ways and means to do it."

Later Kimball had called a meeting with the managers of his five sections — Software Applications, Design Engineering, Production Engineering, Drafting, and Model Shop — to inform them of Page's decision. He had talked to each about where the cost reductions should be made.

To Paul Kelley of Design Engineering he had suggested, "I think we might stretch out that LSI circuit program, Paul, don't you?" Kelley had said, "Well, I'll see what I can do about it, Dave. I think we can."

"But I didn't know," said Kimball now to himself, "that it would mean that Tom Rawlins has to go. Well, let's see what Kelley says."

"NOT SURE HE'S WORTH IT"

"Come in, Paul." Kelley strode in and eased his big frame into a chair by Kimball's desk. Just 40, likable, craggy-faced, he looked more like a football coach than an engineer.

"Thanks for your memo," said Kimball. "I'm asking Toby Marotta from Employee Relations to sit in with us. We need advice on this." Just then Marotta came in.

At 38, Marotta was young for an industrial relations manager, but he had had broad experience in three different locations of the IBS Automation Group, and was once in operating management.

"Thanks for coming, Toby," said Kimball. "Here's the problem. In order to meet that cutback, I've asked Paul Kelley to take two engineers out of Design Engineering. Paul and I agree that the program to slow down is large-scale integration circuits. LSI circuits is a development program for our next-generation computer, so we can slow it down without hurting any systems now in production or on the market.

"But Paul tells me that one of the two people who should be cut from that project is Tom Rawlins, who, you know, is the first black engineer we hired, a few years ago. I'd like to keep Rawlins, but we're in a tight spot. Think you can help?"

Marotta smiled and shrugged. "You know me. No miracles. Just difficult questions."

Kimball turned to Kelley. "Fill us in, Paul, on your reasons for recommending that Rawlins be laid off."

"Sure, Dave," said Kelley. "I hate to do it. I've gotten to like the guy myself, but I don't see any way around it. We have three men on the LSI program. One is Jack

Martin, a real hot-shot engineer. I can cut back on the program, but I can't cut back on Jack Martin. He's the center of it. The other two are Rawlins and a white fellow, Longworth Smith. Neither of them have been with us long, and neither are going to become really great engineers. And they couldn't keep LSI circuits going alone. Martin can."

"But you have about 35 engineers in Design," Marotta interjected, looking at the roster. Couldn't you let any of them go in place of Rawlins?"

"Hold on! It's 29, not 35; I've already lost 6 men and I'm pressed. But I did think of the alternatives. If I move Rawlins to another project, I'll have to take a more experienced man off it. I'm afraid Rawlins wouldn't be able to pull his own weight, and we can't afford to get behind in production now."

"Could you spell that out a bit, Paul?" asked Kimball. "What makes you think that Rawlins wouldn't cut it?"

"Let's face it," Kelley replied. "It's rough for any man to pick up a new job. It would take time before he knew it as well as someone who has been on the job nine months. I'm just not sure he would be able to catch on fast enough to maintain our schedules.

"And then there's the problem of backlash. If Rawlins bumps a white fellow, there's going to be talk of preferential treatment. As a matter of fact, there was some bad feeling several months ago among my engineers when there were rumors that some blacks over in the Manufacturing Department were favored during a layoff. If the men are resentful, they won't help Rawlins much. It would mean hours lost in poor morale."

"How do you think Rawlins would react to a situation like that?" asked Marotta.

"Well, he's a pleasant fellow — no chip on his shoulder," Kelley said. "And he's pretty well liked now. He might be able to win them around eventually, but you can't tell. It's a risk I don't feel I can take. And, frankly, I'm not sure Rawlins is really worth it. If he were white, I wouldn't even have brought it to your attention."

"HE'S DOING MUCH BETTER"

Kimball frowned and made a few notations on a pad. "We'd better have a look at Rawlins' background," he said.

"Rawlins is 34 years old," said Kelley, looking at his notes. "He got a B.S. in electrical engineering from Brooklyn Poly after a stint in the Army. His grades were fair. Let's see. . . . His previous job was an electrical engineering position with a construction company, and before that he did designing of telephone equipment.

"As you know, Dave, we hired him in 1968, and I was the one who did the hiring. As I think I told you then, he did seem marginally qualified for a job in this department. After all, our men are a cut above average. I'll be honest: if he'd been white, I don't think we'd have taken him on. But he seemed to have a good attitude and real potential."

"I remember," said Kimball. "That was about the time we began to ask, 'If a person isn't perfectly qualified now, is he qualifiable?' Black engineers were hard to come by, and '68 was a good year. We could afford to take a gamble on a man who might make it. But I seem to recall that there were some problems with Rawlins at first."

"Yes, there were," Kelley said. "Rawlins had some difficulty on a design. We had a complaint from the Manufacturing Department a couple of years ago on one of his projects. He was catching his mistakes late, Toby, and he had to send through quite a few alteration notices. Then Manufacturing was sore because it slowed down their production and raised their costs."

Marotta, looking up from the notebook on which he was doodling, asked, "What's your experience with other new engineers, Paul? Have other men had this kind of problem?"

"Well, even our experienced men send through alteration notices once in a while. But this was a bad case. Sure, I've had others that bad — some that eventually turned out well — but we worry about them."

"You were able to straighten Rawlins' problem out, as I recall," said Kimball.

"Well," Kelley went on, "he is doing much better now, but the situation got worse before it got better. Part of the problem was the Drafting and Model Shop men. You know what they're like — no engineering degrees, but they know an awful lot about their particular job, and once they find an engineer like Rawlins who isn't very sure of himself, they're going to give him a hard time. Then, of course, Rawlins being black didn't help matters.

"After that problem project, some of them didn't want to work for him at all. But I had a talk with Rawlins. I told him that when he is talking to these technicians, he should take a position and hold on to it. I spoke to the men too, and told them that no one is going to refuse to work for the man I assign him too."

Marotta broke in. "Let's go back to Dave's point about qualifiability, Paul. Do you think Rawlins really has the aptitude for an engineer's job in this unit? Were you able to do anything about his problem with design?"

Kimball looked up from his note pad and said, "I remember authorizing a two-week training program for Rawlins up in New York. That helped, didn't it?"

"It did," Kelley answered. "I also thought it would help to put him on this LSI project so that Jack Martin, the engineer I was telling you about, could kind of work along with Rawlins and bring him out a bit. He's been on LSI circuits ten months now and he's doing all right. He's developing, though slowly.

"But when I think how well he's responded to what we've demanded of him, it's gratifying. In the long run, Rawlins may be as good as some of the fellows I need to keep because of their experience on important jobs. But I have to remind myself that I'm not running a vocational training school; I'm managing a design unit in a highly competitive business. I really have no alternative but to recommend that he and Smith go."

"THAT CUT WILL BE NOTICED"

Kimball turned to Marotta. "Toby, your business is 'people business.' What are your reactions?"

"Just a few comments, Dave. Paul's right in hesitating to let Martin or any other really bright young guys go. You need to grow talent for Design Engineering. The service picture of these men doesn't help much, either. Rawlins has only been with IBS three years, and I doubt you have many other people with less service."

"I have a couple," said Kelley, "but they're in key positions. I can't do without them."

"Okay, let's try another tack," Marotta said. He turned to Kimball. "Could you use Rawlins in the Production Engineering Section, Dave?"

Kimball leaned back in his chair, lit a cigarette, and looked at Kelley and Marotta. "Well, fellows, of course I've thought of that, but it's impossible. I've asked the Production Engineering manager to cut back too, and I couldn't ask him to take on a new man who has no working knowledge of the products and isn't familiar with the factory end of it, not at a time like this."

Marotta nodded. "I can see that would be rough, Dave. But at the same time we've got to consider our affirmative action commitments. Let's look at the statistics. If you let Rawlins go, that means no blacks at all in the Design Engineering Section.

"But let's talk about the whole Engineering Department, which is your biggest concern, Dave. You supervise some 150 professionals and 90 nonprofessionals."

"That's right."

Marotta looked at his notebook. "Your nonprofessionals are 6.6% black. That's not too bad. But if you let Rawlins go, that brings your minority percentage for professionals down from 2.6% to 2%. That's low when you consider Philadelphia's large black population. That cut will certainly be noticed in our next federal contract compliance review."

"But it's not just a question of flak from the examiners, Toby," Kimball put in. "I personally feel that New York management was right in urging us to build up our black proportions in IBS, and I'd like to do what I can in our department."

"But at the same time, Dave," Kelley interrupted with some heat, "you're telling me I've got to cut two men to meet our cost reduction target. Now, the only two men I can see to let go, in all honesty, are Smith and Rawlins. We'll both be in trouble if we get our production schedules snared up."

"That's the key problem, isn't it?" said Marotta. He opened a small blue pamphlet. "Take another look at our IBS affirmative action policy: 'You should recognize that we are all expected to fulfill our Equal Employment Affirmative Action responsibilities while at the same time achieving our profitability goals. It's not an either/or situation, and one does not give relief from the other.' "

Kimball snorted. "Well, that helps a lot, doesn't it!"

"It does give you the parameters anyway, Dave," Marotta said. "Those aren't just empty words in that policy. Well, I guess the ball is in your court. It's your decision. I can't give you a pat answer."

Kimball snuffed out his cigarette and said with a sigh, "Well, thanks, fellows. I'll let you know tomorrow."

Kimball sat at his desk, solitary, concerned, puzzled. Mechanically he jotted down on a pad of paper the issues to be balanced, to be judged. The pros and the cons. The decision was his, all right.

He had to cut costs. LSI was the program to be cut in Design Engineering. He respected Kelley's judgment. He wanted to retain Rawlins, but he did not want to hurt Engineering's production by preferring Rawlins over some better qualified white engineer. He considered going to Page, but promptly rejected it because he knew that Page would be unsympathetic.

He thought of the excellent reputation of the Engineering Department. He thought of his own reputation and his future. Once you got soft on one decision, you could easily get soft on any decision. But was it really getting soft?

Kimball recalled the phrases of the IBS policy guide that Marotta had read: ". . . expected to fulfill our Equal Employment Affirmative Action responsibilities while at the same time achieving our profitability goals." Big help. "It's not an either/or situation." Big help. "One does not give relief from the other." Big help.

Yet what else could those policy makers in New York say? The decision was his.

For a strange moment he saw himself at the tiller of his ketch, plunging through waves off the Maine coast. Easier to sail a boat than manage a department under pressure. You could be pretty sure of the wind and the sea and a boat you knew.

Kimball got up from his desk. He walked over and stood alone by the window of his Philadelphia office, looking out over the Schuylkill River Valley.

12/ Brunswig Corporation

W ell, Martin, that's the twenty-sixth offer we've had to buy us out in five years. Why do we listen to all these people? I'm not sure this one is as sound as the last one from Allied Machinery Products Corporation. What do you think?"

"I'm surprised. Schneider Transmissions, Inc., must have heard about the Allied offer and cooked this deal up in a hurry. Even though they are just across town, they have never given us a hint before that they were interested in an acquisition. Well, let's think about it. The first thing I want to do is to check with some of the boys. Those who have worked at Schneider might have a few clues."

Martin Brunswig, Chairman of the Board and President of Brunswig Corporation, and Walter Brunswig, Executive Vice-President and Chairman of the Finance Committee, left the University Club — one for the main plant and the other for a family council at the Brunswig Country Club. This new, and unexpected, merger offer promised to delay the process of persuading 92 other family members to accept the brothers' opinion — that it would be only sensible to sell out to Allied Machinery Products Corporation.

Brunswig Corporation's principal business is the manufacture and the sale of a wide range of types and sizes of gears, gear drives, and shaft couplings for transmitting power in ranges of 1 to 30,000 horsepower or more. Brunswig's gears are found on tilting drives for basic oxygen steel furnaces, kiln drives for cement processing, paper machine drives, oil refinery compressors, as reduction gears for river towboats, mixer drives for penicillin manufacturing, and as equipment for satellite tracking and radar installations.

Brunswig produces a wide line of standard gear drives and speed reducers as well as special gears and shaft couplings made to order in sizes from 1 inch to 24 feet in diameter and from 1 pound to over 40 tons in weight. It sells directly through its own salesforce working out of 39 district sales offices in the principal industrial markets of the United States as well as through more than 250 distributors. Brunswig products are basic components of industrial machinery, do not have a seasonal sales pattern, and are not dependent on any one industry or industry grouping; but sales volume is affected by the general level of industrial activity.

The company's sales and distribution organization is widely recognized as among the most effective and efficient such networks in U.S. industry.

Brunswig is a leading producer in its lines. It has substantial competition for shaft couplings and smaller gears but very limited competition in the sale of large gears and very large couplings. Market share is as high as 40% to 60% in some lines. To maintain its position, Brunswig engages in sales engineering, applied product

Reprinted from William H. Newman and James P. Logan, *Strategy, Policy, and Central Management*, 6th ed. (Cincinnati: South-Western Publishing Co., 1971), pp. 341–48, by permission of South-Western Publishing Co.

Exhibit 12-1. Brunswig Corporation Statement of Income (000's Omitted)

	5 years ago	Preceding year	Preceding year	Last year	Current year
Net sales	$48,494	$58,837	$66,753	$63,621	$58,405
Cost of goods sold	33,013	38,671	43,251	41,294	38,300
Depreciation	1,850	2,093	2,213	2,609	1,943
Selling and administrative expense	8,455	9,724	10,978	11,101	10,766
Interest expense	326	366	200	283	414
Net income after taxes	2,399	3,906	5,069	4,372	3,396
Per share of common stock					
Net income	$2.47	$3.90	$4.88	$4.13	$3.18
Cash dividends paid	.825	1.05	1.20	1.25	1.40

engineering, and testing, together with some development work on methods of mechanical power transmissions. It has 100 engineers and machinery designers engaged principally in these programs on which it spent $2,500,000 last year. The firm has secured some patents, but it does not depend for its business on any one or a group of such patents.

About 2,800 employees work in three plants in the same southern Ohio city. None are represented by unions, and there has been no strike in the hundred-year history of the company. Hourly and salaried employees share in a trusted, noncontributory, incentive profit-sharing retirement plan to which Brunswig contributes a share of net income. Salaried employees also have a contributory pension plan.

Brunswig owns the three plants of varying ages and of cement and steel construction. Its buildings and machinery are well maintained and adequate for the presently anticipated volume of business.

Family members own a majority of Brunswig common stock and have administrative control over the corporation. Martin and Walter own 35,000 and 40,000 shares, respectively. Other directors who are family members own 50,000 shares among them. The over-the-counter price is currently $31 bid and $33 asked. The price range last year was $22–$30 and the year before was $26–$36. Pertinent financial data for Brunswig Corporation is given in Exhibits 12-1 and 12-2.

Schneider Transmissions' offer, in general terms, is to merge Brunswig Corporation into Schneider Transmissions, Inc., through Schneider's purchase of up to 49% of the outstanding shares of Brunswig common stock for $60 per share in cash and the exchange of 1.54 shares of Schneider Transmission common stock for each share of Brunswig common for the balance of the outstanding shares. The most recent closing price of Schneider common on the New York Stock Exchange was $40 per share. The stock is ranked A by Standard & Poor's.

Schneider Transmissions has three product groups:

1. mechanical components such as chains, sprockets, flexible couplings, gears, speed reducers, clutch plates, and pumps

Exhibit 12-2. Brunswig Corporation Balance Sheets (000's Omitted)

	Last year	Current year
Current assets	$29,397	$29,099
Investments	1,669	1,704
Net property and plants	19,380	19,946
Other assets	4,751	4,595
Total assets	$55,197	$55,344
Current liabilities	$ 9,617	$ 8,683
Deferred liabilities	2,509	2,644
Long-term debt	7,472	7,456
Common stock (authorized, 2,500,000 shares; issued 1,077,000 shares)	2,692	2,692
Additional contributed capital	4,611	4,621
Retained earnings	28,296	29,248
Total stockholders' equity	$35,599	$36,561
Total liabilities and equity	$55,197	$55,344

2. engineered systems, such as bulk materials handling equipment for mines, lumber and steel mills, and power plants, and equipment for the biological and mechanical treatment of sewage, refuse, and waste water

3. construction machinery such as concrete mixers, highway pavers, and maintenance equipment

Schneider Transmissions sells in the United States and Canada through company offices and local distributors. It has regional distribution centers in 11 cities. Abroad, the company has 11 sales offices as well as manufacturing and warehousing operations in Argentina, Australia, Brazil, England, France, Italy, Germany, and Japan. The main manufacturing facilities are in various southern Ohio cities.

Development engineering and sales engineering are the responsibility of each product group. The company spent about $4 million last year on this work.

Acquisitions in the past three years include two major manufacturers of quick-opening fasteners, a specialized gear manufacturer, a valve manufacturer, two sewage disposal manufacturers, and, recently, a medium-sized company that makes gears, speed reducers, clutch plates, and couplings. This latest acquisition, when combined with the firm's other gear manufacturing facilities, has allowed Schneider Transmissions to become a significant — but by no means the most important — factor in gear and coupling manufacturing. As it consolidates its organization in these lines and, above all, when it combines the sales work and develops a tested marketing capability, the company will be a very strong competitor in the mechanical power transmission industry. Market share in the gear and coupling lines may well increase to 15% — 18% if the marketing work is done effectively.

Selected financial data for Schneider Transmissions, Inc., are given in Exhibits 12-3 and 12-4.

Exhibit 12-3. Schneider Transmissions, Inc., Selected Financial Data

Year	Net sales	Net income	Times interest and preferred dividends earned	Dividend per share of common stock	Price range of common stock on NYSE
	(000's omitted)				
Current	$217,000	$ 9,610	3.36 times	$1.50	$44–40
Preceding	191,200	8,928	4.14 "	1.50	52–34
"	185,000	8,463	n.a.	1.50	55–30
"	165,400	10,843	n.a.	1.50	36–25
"	159,600	8,020	n.a.	1.20	36–24

Allied Machinery Products Corporation proposes that substantially all of the Brunswig assets and business be transferred to a wholly owned subsidiary (to be organized by Allied) in exchange for Allied preferred stock and common stock and the assumption by the subsidiary of substantially all the liabilities of Brunswig. Employees of Brunswig will become employees of the new subsidiary, which will continue to conduct Brunswig's business with Brunswig's name after the closing. The present Brunswig Corporation will be dissolved.

Allied's plan is to distribute 0.4921 of a share of Allied voting $3.50 cumulative convertible preferred stock and 0.32 of a share of Allied common for each share of Brunswig common stock.

Allied makes proprietary hydromechanical and electromechanical systems and components and proprietary machining systems. Its principal offices and plants are in a city about a hundred miles distant from the plants of Brunswig.

Exhibit 12-4. Schneider Transmissions, Inc., Balance Sheets (000's Omitted)

	Current year	Last year
Cash and marketable securities	$ 5,600	$ 7,000
Accounts receivable	41,100	37,000
Inventories	54,300	43,700
Total current assets	$101,000	$ 87,700
Net property	41,300	36,200
Other assets	7,700	5,500
Total assets	$150,000	$129,400
Total current liabilities	$ 35,900	$ 19,300
Long-term debt	14,800	14,500
$2.50 cumulative preferred stock (570,000 shares outstanding)	11,480	11,420
Common stock (2,992,000 shares)	29,992	29,453
Capital surplus	11,473	12,502
Retained earnings	46,355	42,225
Total liabilities and equity	$150,000	$129,400

The proprietary systems and the components are parts sold as original equipment to the aircraft and aerospace industries, the mobile equipment industry, the oil heating industry, and the petrochemical processing industry. These components account for about 82% of sales, while the balance is made up of machine tools and total machining systems sold to the general metalworking industry. Both the machine tools and the component parts require a high degree of research, development, engineering, and manufacturing competence. For all products, Allied has patents or some special processes and trade secrets that give it special property rights.

The components sold as original equipment include hydraulic pumps and motors, pneumatic starters, underwater power plants, hydrostatic transmissions, and constant speed drives that convert variable input speed from a jet or turbine engine to constant output speed to drive alternating current electrical generators. They also include electronic controls and instruments, oil burner fuel units, lubrication pumps, condensers, and evaporators for use in air-conditioning and refrigeration systems.

The numerically-controlled or direct-computer-controlled multi-operational machining systems perform a variety of metal-cutting operations and can change from one operation to another without interrupting the manufacturing process. The machines are highly accurate and are best suited for low-volume metalworking operations such as the production of prototypes and small-lot runs.

Allied exports from its own plants and has licensed other firms in all the major industrial countries in the world to produce its components and machining systems. It has three plants abroad in Sweden, Switzerland, and France.

A technically-trained salesforce and independent distributors sell the Allied line. Field engineers provide technical services to support sales effort. Other firms compete with Allied on one or more products, but none duplicates more than a small portion of its business.

Allied owns a large number of patents that are important in the aggregate to the conduct of its business. About 700 graduate engineers and engineering employees

Exhibit 12-5. Allied Machinery Products Corporation Selected Financial Data

Year	Net sales	Net income	Times interest and preferred dividends earned	Dividend per share of common stock	Price range of $3.50 preferred stock on NYSE	Price range of common stock[a] on NYSE
	(000's omitted)					
Current	$242,000	$14,300	4.3 times	$.80	$95–75	$91–64
Preceding	215,000	11,246	3.6 times	.80	83–71	87–29
"	152,000	8,020	n.a.	.60		30–18
"	122,000	5,253		.50		37–20
"	109,000	4,095		.50		24–18
"	108,000	2,581		.50		28–19

[a] This stock is ranked B+ by Standard & Poor's.

Exhibit 12-6. Allied Machinery Products Corporation Balance Sheets (000's Omitted)

	Current year	Last year
Cash and marketable securities	$ 4,657	$ 5,904
Accounts receivable	45,600	41,246
Inventories	91,023	87,690
Total current assets	$141,280	$134,840
Net property	80,087	74,339
Other assets	5,007	4,702
Total assets	$226,374	$213,881
Total current liabilities	$ 61,855	$ 84,270
Long-term debt	70,648	65,730
$3.50 cumulative convertible preferred stock (3,000,000 shares authorized)	200	197
Common stock, par value $1 (15,000,000 shares authorized)	4,853	4,124
Additional contributed capital	46,139	21,492
Retained earnings	42,679	38,068
Total liabilities and stockholders' equity	$226,374	$213,881

work on a wide range of applied research and product development programs that are conducted in addition to the regular product adaptation and testing work of the sales engineering group. Company policy is to spend about 5% of net sales on research and development work.

During the past two years, Allied has acquired eight small to medium-sized manufacturing firms that produce electronic systems and special alloy castings. For these it paid, in the aggregate, $6,400,000 in cash plus 612,000 newly issued shares of common stock and 252,400 shares of $3.50 cumulative convertible preferred stock.

Allied employs about 11,000 people, of whom 6,700 are production and maintenance employees. About 2,500 of these workers closed down two plants for 40 days and 40 nights earlier in the year as part of an effort to win a new 3-year contract. They succeeded. The company has various retirement plans, including pension, profitsharing, and money purchase plans covering most of the employees.

Selected financial data for Allied Machinery Products Corporation are given in Exhibits 12-5 and 12-6.

A week after the surprise visit and presentation by Schneider Transmissions executives, the Brunswigs — Martin and Walter — sat at lunch. Martin said:

"I believe what the Allied people told us. Their goal is to increase earnings per share of stock by increasing their market share, expanding their balance sheet leverage, and developing improved products to increase profits. They are clearly organized for action on mergers and, on the other hand, they are determined to avoid a take-over of their own company by making it too expensive. Their policy is to strive for a consistent improvement in earnings and, through this, to influence a high valuation of their stock by analysts as well as the general public.

"They have also defined their basic characteristics as being a 'mechanical engineering company' with interests in special market segments that have a relatively high growth potential. Of course, we know their special skills and advanced competence in aircraft and aerospace components and machine tools.

"But, in talking with them, I am impressed as much by their knowing all the financial moves — straight-line depreciation rather than sum-of-the-digits, smoothing profits through the development cost account, having high debt-leverage so that a raider can't buy you with your own money, diversifying to give a raider potential antitrust trouble, LIFO inventory, not amortizing goodwill, etc. — as by their knowing that our gears can be coupled with their hydrostatic equipment to develop a continuous speed device using an electric motor. This will expand the range of any electric motor well beyond the limited number of r.p.m.'s that it was originally built for. You and I know that our product lines are complementary and that there are many mutual development opportunities.

"How are we going to persuade the rest of the family? The yield on Allied common stock is very small (see Exhibit 12-7), but the use of both preferred and common stock will get dividends to them. And the preferred is not callable for the first five years. The exchange of stock with Allied is tax-free at present, and a capital gains tax would only have to be paid if the stock were sold some time in the future. But the

Exhibit 12-7. Comparative Per-Share Data

	Preceding year	Last year	Current year	Net book equity
1. To Brunswig shareholders				
A. Net earnings				
Actual	$4.88	$4.13	$3.18	$34
Pro forma, assuming merger with Allied Machinery				
Common stock	.79	.87	.90	
Preferred stock	1.72	1.72	1.72	
Total	$2.51	$2.59	$2.62	$48
B. Cash dividends				
Actual	$1.20	$1.25	$1.40	
Pro forma, assuming merger with Allied Machinery				
Common stock	.19	.26	.26	
Preferred stock	1.72	1.72	1.72	
Total	$1.91	$1.98	$1.98	
2. To Allied shareholders				
A. Earnings applicable to common stock				
Actual	$1.84	$2.38	$2.72	$16
Pro forma, assuming merger	2.46	2.72	2.84	$12
B. Cash dividends				
Common stock	.60	.80	.80	
Preferred stock	3.50	3.50	3.50	

Schneider proposal is nontaxable now only on the common stock part. Anyone who holds some of our original shares might have to pay capital gains on the cash portion. The maximum this would be per share would be $13.17 (25% of $60–$7.313).

"Allied management knows how to run a diversified company. Look at their proposal for a separate subsidiary. No one will be hurt by that move.

"And there is a final reason that I may have to pass up in public discussion. It will be a real pleasure to deal with stockholders who understand technically what this company is all about and to work with a technically-oriented management in a similar line of business.

"But what are the arguments in favor of Schneider Transmissions that we may have to meet? Schneider is local. We know the people and can trust them. And those whom we can't, we can keep a good eye on. Their asset size is closer to ours so we will be a more important part of the merged operation. Schneider is expanding, but not so rapidly as to destroy any sense of where we have been and where we are going. The people there are not trying to play any go-go conglomerate role. The money looks good. And certainly the products match. Schneider has no labor or union troubles. Why turn elsewhere for a partner when you've got the fellow down the street?

"Well, we'll have to persuade the others and then set up a special stockholders' meeting soon. It looks as if the Allied common stock will be close to $65 a share for awhile and the price of the preferred will be about $77 a share."

13/ Brazos Manufacturing, Inc.

INTRODUCTION

In 1946 Fred Brazos arrived in Virginia with a strong personality, a good background in electronics, a "beat-up" Chevrolet, and $300 in cash. Five years later he established Brazos Manufacturing, Inc., in Norfolk. In early 1960, at the age of forty-one, he was chief owner and president of an organization which in calendar 1959 did over $1.6 million of business.

Brazos Manufacturing, Inc., was a small firm in the part of the rapidly expanding electronics industry that was centered in eastern Virginia. The company's prime products were miniature potentiometers, which it designed, developed, and produced for the aviation, missiles and communications industries. Despite its title, Brazos Manufacturing, Inc., was primarily engaged in assembly operations. This fact, coupled with its size, presented the company with unique problems that it had to overcome.

The company relocated in Portsmouth, Virginia, and operated out of an attractive single-story, steel, ceramic tile, and glass plant built in 1956. Brazos employed about 175 workers, the majority of whom were women. A significant portion of these employees were highly skilled.

COMPANY ORGANIZATION AND OPERATION

Mr. Brazos invented many of the manufacturing techniques employed in the production of potentiometers, and was responsible for the development of other products in the line. This young president retained final authority on all production, sales, research, and financial decisions. In order to coordinate the different aspects of the business, Mr. Brazos met often with his top management group, among whom were Vice-president and Comptroller George Perkins, General Sales Manager Malcolm Ayers, and Production Manager John Wiley.

The six-man board of directors included two outside members, and a third who was the legal counsel. Mr. Brazos found that the board members were extremely active and hard working, and not at all of the "rubber stamp" character usually associated with one-man ownership and an inside controlled board.

Mr. Brazos' second-in-command and right hand man was the vice-president and comptroller, Mr. Perkins. Mr. Perkins, who had studied cost and system accounting at Babson Institute and Roosevelt University and attended night school at New York University, had been with the firm for about seven years and appeared very capable in his understanding and administration of the financial aspect of the company. In addition, his temperament made him a control for Mr. Brazos' great enthusiasm. To-

Reprinted from L. L. Waters, Wayne G. Broehl, Jr., Charles H. Spencer, and Ray M. Powell, *Administering the Going Concern: Cases in Business Policy,* © 1962, pp. 335–50, by permission of Prentice-Hall, Inc., Englewood Cliffs, N.J.

gether they made a talented team and their combined abilities were one of the definite assets of the company.

The lines of authority, as shown in Exhibit 13-1, ran from Mr. Brazos through Mr. Perkins to the sales, production, engineering, and accounting sections. Due to the size of the company, however, the actual functional lines of authority were not exactly as the formal organization chart showed them to be. Mr. Brazos was in direct contact with all aspects of his firm and was often out in the plant itself. He was primarily concerned with the forward product part of the business, both the engineering and production problems of these new products. He estimated that he spent more than half his time on future development, and maintained further that he tried to stay out of individual operating decisions as much as possible. Mr. Brazos also assumed a large share of the selling responsibility and spent considerable time on the road promoting new products, investigating new markets, and keeping in touch with present customers.

In summary, the company's president, who controlled 88 per cent of the stock, was also its chief supplier of ideas, its best salesman, and its most qualified engineer. Mr. Perkins and his knowledge of finance rounded out the functional management; he owned slightly more than two per cent of the company's shares.

PRODUCTION

Product Line

Brazos Manufacturing, Inc., produced precision potentiometers, "Torque Watch" gauges, small cathode ray oscilloscopes, and several other miscellaneous electronic products, mostly supplemental to the potentiometers.

Exhibit 13-1. Brazos Manufacturing, Inc.

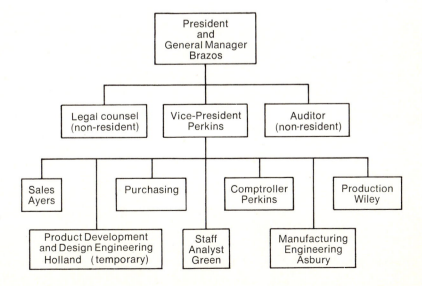

The main characteristic of the Brazos line was precision, and the company had an excellent reputation because of its high quality. The tiny potentiometers required highly skilled hands to produce the precision product required for such end uses as regulating the fins on a missile. Brazos rewarded and encouraged quality consciousness among its employees with a bonus plan figured on the basis of net shipments — shipments minus returns. The firm in turn benefited from an exceptionally low turnover rate among its employees, who often required three to six months for learning the necessary skills to assemble the potentiometers.

Precision potentiometers made up about 80 per cent of Brazos' product line. By far the major portion of the company's total potentiometer business was based upon government contracts. Potentiometers, or "pots" as they are called in the trade, are electronic devices which regulate the voltage level in a circuit. Pots serve a variety of purposes; for example, they are used in the tuning systems of radios and television sets and, as previously mentioned, in missiles to control such things as the fins while in flight. There are many styles and sizes of pots. Some can be mass produced in standard sizes, while others have special uses such as those for missiles and must be built to rigid specifications on a job-lot basis.

Brazos specialized in making the miniature precision specialized pots running in size from ½ to 1⅛ inches in diameter. Most of Brazos' pots were used in areas such as electronic weapons systems where quality and precision were vital.

High quality requirements, miniature size and variety of specifications required Brazos to produce on a job-lot basis, using highly skilled help and 100 per cent inspection. Some of the parts were so small that they had to be assembled and checked under a microscope.

The torque watch gauge comprised about 12 per cent of the Brazos product mix. The torque watch gauge, invented by Fred Brazos, is a device which measures rotary friction at low levels on small parts. Torque watches were of value to Brazos not only from a marketable product standpoint, but also as a useful instrument in measuring the torque on pots. Brazos enjoyed a dominant competitive position in regard to the torque watch gauge; the company held one patent and had several patent applications pending covering both the design and principles of operation of its gauges.

Cathode ray oscilloscopes made up from 4 to 6 per cent of Brazos' sales. They were of the small variety with a market demand just high enough to help Brazos cover some overhead and keep skilled employees busy during slack pot demand periods, but low enough to prevent large electronic firms from deriving profit from their manufacture. All of the parts for the oscilloscopes, including its necessary pots, were purchased from outside vendors; Brazos only assembled the scopes.

Several attempts had been made to add to this basic product line. A major effort was expended in trying to break into the cathode ray oscilloscope and the industrial meter markets, but the results were disappointing in relation to the expectations. Mr. Brazos found that his firm had difficulty producing a competitively priced item, and in those markets in which the company was able to obtain a foothold, there was not sufficient volume to justify the expenditure.

Despite this rather heavy reliance on potentiometers, Mr. Brazos remained confident of a continued demand and of the company's ability to satisfy it. Technical development was causing an almost daily change in the electronics industry, but he thought that even if some new item were to replace the potentiometer tomorrow, it would be ten or more years before a complete changeover could be made. The potentiometer had so many applications in the industry that replacement needs alone should keep demand alive for that long.

Plant Production Facilities

The Brazos plant provided excellent production facilities. The 23,200 square foot plant itself was constructed with an eye toward ease of expansion. The roof was supported by strategically placed columns. The walls did not support the roof and could be easily moved out to make additional production levels in 16,000 square feet of space, and the remaining 7,200 square feet was leased to another tenant on a short term basis. Lighting was excellent and the production area was well heated in winter and completely air-conditioned in summer. Maintenance was also easy and of a low cost nature in the plant. The plant had a thoroughly modern sprinkler system.

A complete model shop existed for making occasional special parts which were uneconomical to order from vendors, and to produce operating models of various new products developed by the engineering staff.

There were numerous jigs and fixtures for the various assembly operations for the pots, watches, and scopes. The manufacturing engineer was responsible for developing and improving production techniques. Between the manufacturing-engineering department under Mr. Asbury and the individual production line workers there developed an amazing number of work saving devices and methods, all of which helped to ease the job for the workers and cut costs for the company. Mr. Asbury's department was constantly occupied with improving production techniques with an eye on cutting costs, production time, and improving job comfort for the employees. The employees at Brazos were nonunionized. They appeared to show a great allegiance to the company and to be willing to make helpful suggestions.

Seasonal Fluctuations

The demand for Brazos pots was cyclical, with the peak period occuring from April to June and the trough occurring from November to January. Because of their hard-to-replace technical skills, every effort was made to keep the employees on the job during the slack periods. Production of oscilloscopes and torque watches combined with production of standardized pots and sub-assemblies for inventory were the methods used to keep the employees on the job.

Standardization

In an effort to produce job shop products on a mass production basis, Brazos began a three phase standardization program. Step one was the use of standard parts on as many products as possible. The pot shaft is a good example. Some customers wanted a slot, others wanted an O-ring, and still others wanted a mechanical stop pin. A new shaft was designed with machining for all these features, and had replaced the other three shafts. While the new shaft cost a few cents more, a net savings was realized through quantity purchasing and simplified inventory control.

Step two entailed the use of standard sub-assemblies. As an example, many different pots may use exactly the same shaft and bushing combination. Through the use of sales forecasts, these sub-assemblies could be produced for inventory. The advantages were quicker delivery on orders and a smoothing out of the production cycle.

Step three was the production of pots for inventory. Savings in production costs could be partially passed along to the customer, perhaps making it worth while for him to adjust his specifications to meet the standard pot. This would also help to smooth out the production cycle as well as provide for immediate delivery.

Brazos' officials anticipated that roughly 10 per cent of sales would be from inventoried pots, 25 per cent would utilize standard sub-assemblies, and an additional 50 per cent would contain standard parts. In this event, only 15 per cent of the pots would be produced on a pure job-shop basis.

Make or Buy

There was no definite make or buy policy, although most decisions were made by the Accounting Department. An example arose when an improved model of the torque watch required two flats milled on the aluminum body. The manufacturer quoted a price of 7.8 cents per piece. Because of a time lag, it was decided by Production to mill the flats in the present inventory within the plant. Using an obsolete and idle machine, direct costs were determined to be 5.8 cents per piece. When Production recommended that future purchases also be milled in the plant, they were turned down by Accounting on the grounds that overhead charges would make it more expensive than the manufacturer's price.

Purchasing

Purchasing was done through an agent under the comptroller. Production stated that its biggest problem was getting delivery of satisfactory materials on the promised dates. Rejections or late deliveries disrupted schedules, causing confusion in the plant and forcing Brazos to miss its own delivery dates. Delays of several months were not uncommon. When ordering for parts produced for inventory, extra long lead times were allowed, creating excess inventories when deliveries were made on time. For job order parts, Brazos was forced to allow a slack of weeks or even months on quoted delivery dates, and then just hope that enough time had been allowed.

Quality Control

Since Brazos was selling quality, control in this area was extremely important. Inspection was made through samples of all purchased materials. Sub-assemblies were also inspected, by sample or even 100 per cent in critical cases. Final products were also inspected, 100 per cent for all lots in which the quality of each piece was important.

Inventory Control

The max-min system was currently being used for all standard raw materials. These limits had been established through an analysis of economic lot size and reorder lead time. Contracts for standard materials were given as orders were received.

For cost accounting purposes, records were kept of every item as it went into production. Mr. Wiley would have preferred to set up a bin system for all minor parts, but so far had been overruled by the Accounting Department.

In some instances, vendor delays had been attributed directly to that vendor's inability to purchase key materials. For this reason, Brazos felt it worth while in several instances to guarantee a vendor's inventory. This, in effect, meant that the vendor would maintain his inventory of a specific material at a certain level. Brazos, in turn, guaranteed that the firm would buy this inventory in the event that it was no longer needed. One example of this was a special polyester resin inventory guaranteed with the Nonconducting Fabricators, Inc., of Newport News, Virginia.

Scheduling

Long range scheduling was done as orders were received by recording the item and quantity under the due date. Mr. Wiley was then able each week to schedule firmly the following week's work, taking into consideration the availability of raw materials as well as of plant capacity. In excess capacity situations he had to decide whether to advance future runs or cut back present production. In the reverse situation he had to weigh overtime costs against missed delivery dates.

Estimating the time required per lot per operation was still somewhat flexible. For repeat parts, records were available for this estimate. For new parts, estimates could be made only from similar standards. Whenever a standard proved to be out of line it was revised for future estimates. In this way, a library of accurate standard times was gradually being built. This library was useful not only for estimating production times, but also a reference if an individual incentive plan was ever established.

Daily bogies were established for each operation, and were used to measure the daily reports coming off the floor. In this way, bottlenecks were quickly pinpointed and relieved before the schedule was disrupted beyond repair. It also served as a follow-up device that showed where each lot was and where it may have been mislaid, if such were the case.

Standard Times

In the past, the Brazos management had felt hindered, primarily during the preparation of bids, by its inability to predict production times for new products. In an effort to solve this problem, Manufacturing-Engineering made a stop watch study of elemental operations. These times were thought to be valid regardless of the product involved and, in aggregate, were believed valid for providing standard times for most operations performed in the plant.

In practice, standard time estimates proved to be quite inaccurate, and the project was modified. The modification entailed the lumping of these element times into standard times for entire operations. These times were being modified by actual production data, forming a library of standard times which Mr. Wiley expected to use in future estimates.

MARKETING

Objectives

"We have two broad marketing objectives," stated Mr. Brazos. "One is the day-to-day job of increasing our share of the electronics market, and the other is to decrease our dependence on any one customer. Over 90 per cent of our business is associated with government contracts, and the potentiometer accounts for 80 per cent of our total sales. As long as defense work is such a big factor in the electronic and related industries, we have to expect a large sales dependence. But such a concentration of interests is dangerous. If a major demobilization program were put into effect, we would be forced to find new products and new markets in order to remain in business. A fifty-fifty split between government and industrial work would be much more desirable."

Market

The total market for the potentiometer was shared by 10 major companies and was estimated to be about $20 million, with miniature potentiometers accounting for roughly one half. In 1959 Brazos was able to capture 15 per cent of the small potentiometer business, rating second to Precision Instrument Corporation, which obtained approximately 40 per cent.

Brazos had sold to practically every aircraft and missile manufacturer in the country, and had over 750 accounts. By far the greatest portion of this business was split between the northeast and western parts of the country. The market potential in Southern California was increasing rapidly with over 35 per cent of Brazos' 1959 business being concentrated in and around Los Angeles. The largest single customer was a major aircraft company, accounting for slightly over 14 per cent of the firm's potentiometer business; two leading electrical appliance manufacturers were next in line with 10 per cent and 1 per cent, respectively.

Such a diversified list of accounts reflected the potentiometer's widespread application. However, its limited volume potential per company severely compounded the problem of maintaining customer contact, answering individual requirements, and providing adequate service.

Price

When Brazos entered the miniature potentiometer business in 1952, the firm was able to demand a price commensurate with the technical advantage that it held. In the following eight years, however, the number of competing firms expanded from two to twenty, with prices and profit margin dropping accordingly. In 1959, for example, unit sales increased but the dollar volume remained constant.

In most cases, sales were made on the basis of competitive bids, with each manufacturer submitting his respective prices, product specifications, and delivery dates. On several occasions, Brazos had been unable to meet the quoted price because of an adherence to higher quality standards than those demanded by the customer. Such a lowering of quality, it was felt, would cause extensive changes in the manufacturing process and have an adverse effect on the company's reputation.

Another significant change in the market had been brought about by the ease of copying a competitor's product and the relative lack of protection afforded by patents. This made it very difficult for a company such as Brazos to maintain any product differentiation, but it was to the advantage of the customer, providing him with the two or more sources of supply required in some contracts and assuring him of obtaining the lowest competitive bid.

Distribution

The major portion of Brazos' sales were made through manufacturer's representatives located in the various market centers. This provided the company with the necessary market experience and sales effort for a great deal less money than would have been required to maintain a permanent sales force with its large fixed costs independent of sales volume.

A great deal of technical knowledge and industry contact was needed in the sales effort to keep abreast of the general market demand and anticipate specific customer needs. It took time to develop the product design and manufacturing process behind a competitive bid. The salesman had to be constantly on the alert.

The company was almost entirely dependent upon the customer's engineering department for potential sales. The original contact was made with the purchasing agent, but the greatest problem was making sure that the engineer was aware of the product and its application. It was in the engineering departments that the product specifications originated. The closer they were to Brazos' product line and the earlier the company was able to come up with a satisfactory answer, the greater was its chance of obtaining the account.

DEVELOPMENT

The nature of the firm's products and their market made obsolescence the chief hazard. Consequently, the Brazos firm employed a relatively large staff of engineers who were constantly trying to improve the product line and add new items to it. Much of the research work resulted directly from Mr. Brazos' own ideas. Mr. Brazos noted that if potentiometers became obsolete his company would be out of business. Therefore, if something should eliminate a potentiometer he wanted to be very sure that the company made it. Consequently, the research could be characterized as developmental rather than basic. Exemplifying the emphasis on developmental research was the revolutionary kind of potentiometer which the Brazos engineering department had been working on for over a year. This new kind of potentiometer would take up much less space by utilizing a non-metallic film in place of the conventional wire-wound element.

Brazos recognized the importance of product development in maintaining a competitive position in the constantly changing electronics industry. In 1960 the firm had 20 to 25 new products waiting to be introduced into the market. All that was needed was a knowledge of possible markets and the sales force necessary to exploit them.

Not only was further diversification in the potentiometer field being undertaken by new product design and different applications, but the company also had designed and developed new products in the meter field. One of these was a transistorized contact meter relay controller to operate a transistorized switch capable of handling reliably and efficiently large amounts of power. Another new meter product would permit remote reading of water consumption by household users.

As would seem apparent from the growth record of Brazos Manufacturing, Inc., Mr. Brazos and his top aides expected considerable future expansion. They felt that this expansion should take several forms. First of all, they planned to expand the potentiometer business to meet the increased demands of the electronic industry for high quality potentiometers. Secondly, they sought product diversification in order to relieve the dependence upon a single product as the major source of revenue. Mr. Brazos was willing to consider the production of almost any high quality electronic component with the exception of consumer products. He believed that his company was not equipped to enter the consumer market as this was entirely foreign to the character of Brazos' operation. Thirdly, they planned to expand their sales to companies that were not dependent on defense contracts. All of these plans had two considerations involved: (1) Expansion potential; and (2) stability of income and earnings.

It was difficult to define any planned rate of growth for Brazos Manufacturing, Inc. This was due mainly to the personality of Mr. Brazos and the industry in which the company was involved. Although the company planned to expand its sales through its present operation, Mr. Brazos was also looking for another going concern to purchase. Any acquisition would be made with the intention of both expanding and complementing the present product line. This sort of transaction could be consummated on a moment's notice if Mr. Brazos felt that the time and circumstances were right. As a general goal for sales growth, including both internal and external expansion, Mr. Brazos and Mr. Perkins felt that a 10 to 15 per cent rate of growth would be reasonable.

FINANCIAL ASPECTS

Comparative operating and financial data of the company are presented in Exhibits 13-2, 13-3, 13-4, and 13-5. Footnotes to Exhibit 13-2 reveal that during 1959 the company absorbed three other corporations by merger: Fred Brazos, Inc., a dormant Virginia corporation formerly used as a manufacturer's representative; Expert Electrical Instrument Corporation, a New Jersey firm engaged in the manufacture of panel meters; and Aircraft Corporation, a Virginia firm which maintained an extensive testing laboratory directly across the street from the plant of Brazos Manufacturing, Inc. Mr. Brazos was the sole stockholder in the first two merged corporations, and he received 7,667 shares of Brazos Manufacturing, Inc., common stock as a result of the merger of these firms. Brazos Manufacturing, Inc., issued 54,202 shares of its common for all of the Aircraft stock and simultaneously acquired all of Aircraft's assets through a statutory merger. Mr. Brazos received 22,140 of these shares and Mr. Perkins and Mr. Holland each received 5,740 of these shares. Exhibit 13-5 presents Statements of Earned Surplus and Capital Surplus, including changes brought about by the mergers.

As of January 1, 1960, Mr. Brazos owned 210,125 shares of company stock and a trust of which his wife and children were the beneficiaries owned 9,020 shares; Mr. Perkins and Mr. Holland owned 5,740 shares each, and Mr. Ayers owned 820 shares.

The company's manufacturing and office building and laboratory were leased from a real estate trust of which Mr. Brazos was the beneficiary. The lease term was 5 years beginning January 1, 1960, with a renewal option for an additional 5 year period. The annual lease cost to the company was approximately $35,000.

As was brought out in previous discussion, Brazos management made strong efforts to hold down costs. Budgets were prepared on departmental levels. Because of the problems involved in the preparation of cost estimates, Production was given considerable latitude in preparation and submission of these estimates. Little attempt was made to control or account for variances between budget and actual results.

Since its bad debt losses between May 1, 1955, and January 1, 1960, had been only $664, the company provided no allowance for bad debts. Such losses were charged directly to expense as they arose. Inventory was valued at the lower of cost or market. Depreciation was provided by the straight line method over the estimated useful life of the asset involved.

As a result of the acquisition of Expert Electrical Instrument Corporation, a net operating carry-over of $230,000 became available to the company. Consequently the company made no provision for federal income taxes for the 9 month period ended January 31, 1960. See Exhibit 13-4. The net operating losses of Expert Electrical Instrument Corporation, per its tax returns, were as follows:

Fiscal year ended August 31, 1955	$74,500.00
Fiscal year ended August 31, 1956	69,400.00
Fiscal year ended August 31, 1957	53,200.00
Fiscal year ended August 31, 1958	29,700.00
Eight months ended April 30, 1959	3,200.00
	$230,000.00

Exhibit 13-2A. Balance Sheets, April 30, 1957, to October 31, 1959

Assets	4/30/57	4/30/58	4/30/59[a]	4/30/59[b]	10/31/59[c]	10/31/59[d]
Current assets						
Cash	$ 83,600	$173,500	$170,200	$173,400	$119,300	$153,700
Notes receivable	1,100	100	50	50		
Accounts receivable	158,900	109,300	131,900	131,900	204,300	210,700
Inventory	81,800	82,000	116,100	132,500	180,700	181,300
Prepaid expenses	300	4,100	6,700	7,100	4,200	5,100
Other current	1,900	2,700	2,300			
Total current assets	$327,600	$371,700	$427,250	$444,950	$508,500	$550,800
Fixed assets (net)						
Machinery and equipment	$ 23,300	$ 32,500	$ 35,200	$ 48,200	$ 47,900	$ 49,700
Furniture and fixtures	16,100	15,800	15,300	19,300	18,400	19,500
Laboratory equipment	6,000	5,100	8,900	9,000	10,000	30,400
Motor vehicles	8,900	22,900	15,900	18,100	16,900	17,400
Tools, dies, and molds				4,100	3,100	3,100
Patents				200	200	200
Total fixed assets	$ 54,300	$ 76,300	$ 75,300	$ 98,900	$ 96,500	$120,300
Other assets						
Notes receivable (non-current)	$ 16,200	$ 30,000	$ 30,000			
Deposits	15,500	15,400	15,400	$ 15,400	$ 15,400	$ 15,400
Cash surrender value of life insurance	7,300	9,600	12,200	12,200	12,600	13,400
Mortgage and interest received	21,000	21,000	21,000			
Goodwill (from consolidation)				93,100	93,100	
Total other assets	$ 60,000	$ 76,000	$ 78,600	$120,700	$121,100	$ 28,800
Total assets	$441,900	$524,000	$581,150	$664,550	$726,100	$699,900

[a] Prior to merger with Fred Brazos, Inc., and Expert Electrical Instrument Corporation.
[b] After merger with Fred Brazos, Inc., and Expert Electrical Instrument Corporation.
[c] Prior to merger with Aircraft Corporation.
[d] After merger with Aircraft Corporation.

Exhibit 13-2B. Balance Sheets, April 30, 1957, to October 31, 1959

Liabilities and capital	4/30/57	4/30/58	4/30/59[a]	4/30/59[b]	10/31/59[c]	10/31/59[d]
Current liabilities						
Notes payable			$ 4,350	$ 5,250	$ 5,400	
Accounts payable	$ 37,300	$ 23,500	24,800	27,800	28,600	$ 30,700
Accrued payroll	25,100	25,400	30,000	30,000	29,100	29,100
Accrued commissions	22,000	16,500	18,400	18,400	26,600	26,600
Accrued taxes	86,200	101,000	83,900	85,100	23,800	34,800
Engineering and science fee payable	7,200	14,600	21,000	21,000	45,400	
Accrued rent			400	500		
Other current	4,100	1,400	400	2,200	1,300	600
Total current liabilities	$181,900	$182,400	$183,250	$190,250	$160,200	$121,800
Other liabilities						
Notes payable			$ 48,000	$ 33,000	$ 30,800	
Mortgage payable				3,000	3,000	3,000
Total other liabilities			$ 48,000	$ 36,000	$ 33,800	$ 3,000
Total liabilities	$181,900	$182,400	$231,250	$226,250	$194,000	$124,800
Capital						
8% preferred	$ 35,000	$ 35,000	$ 35,000			
Common stock	15,000	180,000	180,000	$141,600	$141,600	$148,200
Capital surplus				112,900	112,900	149,300
Earned surplus	210,000	126,600	134,900	183,800	277,600	277,600
	$260,000	$341,600	$349,900	$438,300	$532,100	$575,100
Total liabilities and capital	$441,900	$524,000	$581,150	$664,550	$726,100	$699,900

[a] Prior to merger with Fred Brazos, Inc., and Expert Electrical Instrument Corporation.
[b] After merger with Fred Brazos, Inc., and Expert Electrical Instrument Corporation.
[c] Prior to merger with Aircraft Corporation.
[d] After merger with Aircraft Corporation.

Exhibit 13-3. Balance Sheet, January 31, 1960

Assets			
Current			
Cash			$229,700
Accounts receivable			192,600
Merchandise inventory			181,100
Prepaid expenses			3,100
Total current assets			$606,500
Fixed assets (at cost)			
Machinery and equipment			$ 93,000
Furniture and fixtures			35,100
Tool, dies, and molds			17,100
Laboratory equipment			50,900
Motor vehicles			39,700
Patents			300
Total			$236,100
Less: reserve for depreciation and amortization			118,200
Net fixed assets			$117,900
Other assets			
Deposits receivable			$ 15,400
Cash surrender value of life insurance			13,400
Total other assets			$ 28,800
Total assets			$753,200

Liabilities			
Current			
Accounts payable			$ 31,700
Payroll accrued			29,900
Commissions accrued			21,800
Rent, royalties, and miscellaneous accruals			90
Loans and exchange			600
Taxes accrued and payable			
Federal income			3,400
Social security, withholding, and unemployment			16,900
Other			12,500
Total current liabilities			$116,890
Total liabilities			$116,890

	Shares authorized	Shares outstanding	
Capital stock and surplus			
Common stock			
No par value	15,000	9,170	
$1 par value	1,000,000	249,740	$249,740
Capital surplus			67,070
Earned surplus			319,500
Total capital stock and surplus			$636,310
Total liabilities and capital			$753,200

Exhibit 13-4. Income Statements, April 30, 1955, to January 31, 1960

	4/30/55	4/30/56	4/30/57	4/30/58	4/30/59	1/31/60[a]
Net sales	$593,300	$950,600	$1,313,400	$1,515,700	$1,491,600	$1,288,400
Cost of goods sold						
Inventory, beginning	$110,000	$ 51,600	$ 76,800	$ 81,800	$ 82,000	$ 132,500
Purchases and freight	114,200	177,600	261,800	293,200	268,400	265,800
Direct labor	81,300	151,400	201,100	195,400	206,100	174,000
Factory overhead	130,400[b]	206,900	338,000	426,600	488,100	424,700
	$435,900	$587,500	$ 877,700	$ 997,000	$1,044,600	$ 997,000
Less: closing inventory	51,600	76,800	81,800	82,000	116,100	181,100
Total cost of goods sold	$384,300	$510,700	$ 795,900	$ 915,000	$ 928,500	$ 815,900
Gross profit	$209,000	$439,900	$ 517,500	$ 600,700	$ 563,100	$ 472,500
Operating expenses						
Selling	$ 73,900	$142,800	$ 239,900	$ 292,300	$ 276,000	$ 200,800
General administrative	89,500	128,300	147,300	153,600	162,700	134,600
	$163,400	$271,100	$ 387,200	$ 445,900	$ 438,700	$ 335,400
Operating profit	$ 45,600	$168,800	$ 130,300	$ 154,800	$ 124,400	$ 137,100
Other income	6,600	2,100	5,500	9,800	600	100
	$ 52,200	$170,900	$ 135,800	$ 164,600	$ 125,000	$ 137,200
Other deductions	19,500	10,000	400	—	2,100	1,500
Profit before taxes	$ 32,700	$160,900	$ 135,400	$ 164,600	$ 122,900	$ 135,700
Federal income tax	11,400	78,000	65,000	79,000	58,700	
Net profit	$ 21,300	$ 82,900	$ 70,400	$ 85,600	$ 64,200	$ 135,700

[a] Nine months unaudited.
[b] Includes royalties and license fees of $27,100.

Exhibit 13-5. Statements of Earned Surplus and Capital Surplus for the Fiscal Years Ended April 30, 1957, 1958, and 1959 and the Nine-Month Period Ended January 31, 1960

| | Fiscal year ended April 30 | | | Nine months ended January 30, 1960 |
	1957	1958	1959	(unaudited)
Statement of earned surplus				
Balance at beginning of year	$142,600	$210,000	$126,600	$183,800
Add: net income for the year	70,400	85,600	64,200	135,700
Deduct: dividends paid				
Common stock (cash)		1,000		
(stock)		165,000		
Preferred stock	3,000	3,000	3,000	
Premium paid on preferred redemption			4,000	
Balance at end of period	$210,000	$126,600	$183,800	$319,500
Statement of capital surplus				
Balance at beginning of year	$ -0-	$ -0-	$ -0-	$112,900
Acquired in merger with Fred Brazos, Inc., April 30, 1959 (excess of net assets at book value over stated value of capital stock issued)			112,900	
Acquired in merger with Aircraft Corporation, October 31, 1959 (excess of net assets at book value over stated value of capital stock issued)				96,600
Deduct: Goodwill due to acquisition of Expert Electrical Instrument Corp., April 30, 1959 (excess of liabilities over assets — transferred from goodwill account)				93,100
Sale of capital stock in excess of stated value ($15 per share) on December 30, 1959				13,360
Deduct: transfer to the capital stock account to reflect change from no par value to $1 par value for 249,740 common shares outstanding (unauthorized January 8, 1960)				62,800
Refund of federal income taxes on Fred Brazos, Inc. (merged April 30, 1959)				110
Balance at end of period	$ -0-	$ -0-	$112,900	$ 67,070

14/ Avalon Industries, Inc.

AVALON'S HISTORY

At the end of World War II officials of Mastercraft Tool Company, a well respected old line Philadelphia manufacturer of hand carpenter tools of many types, were eager to expand the company's lines and diversify into the manufacture of power tools for the general construction industry market. In the course of their investigation of the possibilities of such expansion, these company officials were in contact with officials of Erwin Electric Products, Inc., a family-owned Chicago maker of fractional horsepower electric motors, electric wiring, switches, fuse boxes, relays, and other electrical apparatus. This contact resulted in the merger in 1949 of the two firms into Avalon Industries, Incorporated.

The new company introduced a line of hand operated electric power tools for use in general construction work. Later, Avalon added a line of garden tools and lawn-mowers. Although the competition proved to be much more severe than had been anticipated, this line was enthusiastically received in the trade. Between 1955 and 1960 four minor concerns were purchased in order to fill in gaps and round out product lines. In 1965 Avalon took advantage of the opportunity to acquire, for cash, the Flufftex Corporation, a relatively small manufacturer of insulating materials for residential and commercial buildings. Flufftex was in serious operating difficulties. In fact, one of the most attractive features of the acquisition was the fact that Flufftex had net operating losses, available to Avalon as carryovers for 1965, 1966, and perhaps 1967, of approximately $5 million. These carryovers meant that the first $5 million of company profits after the acquisition would not be subject to the federal corporate income tax at the rate of 52 per cent. Aided considerably by this tax advantage, Avalon successfully rehabilitated the Flufftex Division in 1965 and 1966, in terms of both production and sales.

As of July 1, 1967, Avalon sales were at an annual rate of $60 million, divided approximately as follows:

	Millions of dollars
Hand Tool Division	$10
Power Tool Division	$15
Electric Components Division	$15
Garden Tool Division (includes lawn mowers)	$ 5
Flufftex Division	$15

After-tax profits for 1965 were $3.2 million; for 1966, after-tax profits reached $4 million. A condensed balance sheet for Avalon Industries is appended as Exhibit 14-1.

Reprinted from L. L. Waters, Wayne G. Broehl, Jr., Charles H. Spencer, and Ray M. Powell, *Administering the Going Concern: Cases in Business Policy,* © 1962, pp. 351–61, by permission of Prentice-Hall, Inc., Englewood Cliffs, N.J.

AVALON'S PRODUCTION AND MARKETING

In spite of the rapid rate at which properties had been acquired by Avalon, production facilities in all of its divisions were of equal or superior efficiency to those of competitors. The assets were not in such condition at the time the respective companies were acquired. Rather, the current productive efficiency was developed after the acquisitions by Avalon. Although Avalon's executives were marketing and promotion minded, they held the basic belief that product acceptability ultimately was based on efficient production facilities and continuing attention to technological innovation. All producing plants of Avalon were located in the United States east of the Mississippi River.

Avalon's production and marketing activities were divisionalized by product lines. Each division manager was responsible for producing and selling the goods of his division at a profit. With respect to selling, each division used salesmen and manufacturers' agents. The manufacturers' agents operated exclusively on the West Coast. In other parts of the country the company used salesmen each one of whom worked out of one of the numerous sales offices maintained by Avalon. Except in sparsely populated areas, a salesman was responsible only for the products of one division — although salesmen of two or more divisions might share the same physical facilities. In the sparsely populated areas, the salesmen pushed all lines of the company insofar as they were capable. Sales were made to wholesalers, building supply houses, large retail organizations, contractors, and industrial users.

Company officials saw an excellent opportunity for an increase of Avalon sales on the West Coast because of the home building and other construction activities. Avalon at the time had no production or marketing facilities in any foreign country. Top management, however, was not averse to this type of expansion. Two of the division managers were convinced that their lines would find ready markets outside the United States. No employees had been trained for foreign operations.

AVALON'S LEADERSHIP

Mr. Edward Bayne, President and Chairman of the Board of Avalon Industries and the chief stockholder in the corporation, owned 35 per cent of all of the company's outstanding stock. As Exhibit 14-1 indicates, only common stock was outstanding. Some 20 per cent of the stock was in the hands of four family trusts. These family trusts were organized in 1949 to hold stock in the newly formed Avalon Corporation. The remaining stock ownership was scattered, with no other stockholder owning more than 3 per cent of the total outstanding stock. The company's shares were listed on the Midwest Stock Exchange.

Mr. Bayne was 50 years of age and was the driving force behind the corporation's activities. In trade circles Avalon and Ed Bayne were inextricably identified as the same business operation. Mr. Bayne's goals and plans for the corporation, consequently, were significant. His chief goals for Avalon Industries were growth and diversification. Mr. Bayne stated:

Exhibit 14-1. Interim Balance Sheet ($000), June 30, 1967

Assets	
Current assets	
Cash	$ 6,328
Trade accounts and notes receivable (net)	6,978
Inventories	11,495
Prepaid items	320
Other current assets	242
Total current assets	$25,363
Other assets	
Miscellaneous advances	122
Investments	418
Total other assets	540
Property, plant, and equipment	
Land (at cost)	$ 1,341
Buildings (net of $2,970,000 accumulated depreciation)	6,510
Machinery and equipment (net of $5,940,000 accumulated depreciation)	10,152
Total property, plant, and equipment	18,003
Total assets	$43,906
Liabilities and shareholder equity	
Current liabilities	
Notes payable to banks	
Short term	$ 2,165
Serial notes, maturing within one year	500
Accounts payable	2,208
Accrued items	873
Dividend payable	382
Total current liabilities	$ 6,128
Long term debt	
Serial notes, payable $500,000 annually, interest 4 to 4½%	2,500
Shareholder equity	
Common stock — $10 per share par value	
Authorized 1,500,000 shares; reserved for sale to key employees, 75,000 shares; issued and outstanding 965,000 shares	9,650
Additional amount paid in	8,275
Preferred stock — 6% cumulative pfd., par value $100 per share; authorized, 75,000 shares; issued and outstanding	none
Earnings retained in the business	17,353
Total shareholder equity	35,278
Total liabilities and shareholder equity	$43,906

"In today's economy it has become a perilous adventure to operate a single, relatively small business. When it is expanding, this kind of business is vulnerable because it usually suffers from under-capitalization: if such a business is not growing, it cannot stay comfortable with its competition, because that competition will keep biting away at its business until there isn't any left for it. Operating any size of business is getting more involved and complex every day — so much so that it doesn't pay to be content with smallness. My $30 million ulcer pains me just as much as Mr. Donner's $3 billion ulcer. We just can't afford to take the risks which the big boys can in bringing out new products or entering new markets — and new markets and new products are what keep companies alive.

"In the last analysis, expanding a firm's profitability and size may be performed successfully in only two ways. First, the management can follow the route of internal growth and development. By this I mean a company can introduce new products or explore markets on its own hook and largely with its own funds. But this method, though important, is too slow and costly. Diversification, a necessary hedge against the ups and downs of the business cycle, is too difficult to attain in this manner.

"The preferred alternative — as I see it, to attain solid growth and diversification at the same time — is to acquire other businesses producing related products. This alternative assumes that your company has some reserve capacity in its management and marketing areas. When you acquire going companies you try to obtain only those with good trained staffs, accepted products, and markets you have not been in before. This procedure is much quicker and cheaper than trying to duplicate the facilities of such companies, and you can begin to cash in on your investment immediately, rather than waiting, perhaps for years, before you can develop an adequate return on the facilities you build yourself.

"The second method of achieving growth, and diversification at the same time, is to acquire businesses with related products — provided your company is capable of managing more and selling more than it has been doing. The advantage of buying another company is that you try to buy with it an accepted product and a trained staff and get into a new line and/or new markets the easy way. Usually a company can buy another company more quickly and cheaply than it can build its own facilities, and sometimes it is years before the company building its own facilities can realize on its investment, whereas the merger benefits flow in right away.

"Consequently, Avalon Industries is constantly on the lookout for acquisitions which will help us grow and diversify in the building materials, equipment, and supply fields. We want to round out our lines and expand our markets to get the full benefit of national advertising and product acceptance. We want to accomplish this without dilution of our stockholder equity in the business. This means that, as far as possible, we want to use cash for our acquisitions. We therefore want companies which have a high depreciation base and good profit probabilities or a favorable tax position which will help us generate cash in every conceivable way to use in acquiring more companies. . . .

"We want to develop or acquire a complete line of building materials, tools, and supplies to serve the areas of commercial and residential construction. We want our markets to be from coast to coast and international."

Bayne's operating philosophy included a firm belief in decentralization. He believed in developing good understudies for the various executive officers of the firm. As opportunities arose because of acquisitions and other expansion, he believed in giving these understudies primary executive authority and responsibility. Their effectiveness was checked through the results they achieved in their various divisional operations. Bayne liked to find submerged personnel in acquired companies who were more capable than their superiors. He sometimes remarked, "We look to see who is doing the work and not getting the credit." Executives were paid modest salaries but were allowed to participate in generous profit-sharing plans. Bayne had an informal executive development program, designed chiefly to give the budding executive the over-all point of view so essential in a well-rounded administrator. Selection of candidates for development depended upon demonstrated capacity. To a large extent, the choice was made because of technical qualifications. The system has been successful so far.

CONTACT WITH GATEWAY

In line with his goals, Bayne for some time had been interested in the expansion of his operations to include a complete commercial line of paints and varnishes. He investigated all the possibilities which occurred to him, but he could see no way to bring Avalon into the paint business on a national scale. The high cost of research and production facilities necessary to move into this line of business seemed prohibitive. The acquisition of a going paint concern seemed to him equally out of the question. All paint firms operating on a national basis appeared to be larger than Avalon could safely attempt to absorb.

Early in 1967, however, Mr. Bayne came into contact with the owners of Gateway Paint and Varnish Company of San Francisco, California. Gateway was a family-owned enterprise whose principal owner, Mr. Donald Wyatt, had become increasingly aware in the past few years of the perils facing small business, and who had wearied of the fast competitive pace in the paint business.

Discovering that Mr. Wyatt might be receptive to an offer from Avalon to buy the Gateway Company, Mr. Bayne entered into preliminary negotiations with the Wyatt family. Later Avalon was given a free rein to send in its investigative team of accountants, financial experts, legal talent, engineers, market analysts, appraisers, and chemists to draw up an extensive report on Gateway from the point of view of possible purchase. This team was comprised of certain members of the Avalon staff, heavily supplemented by personnel from Barker D. Small Associates, a widely known, highly respected research engineering firm. Mr. Wyatt displayed an extremely cooperative attitude toward the investigating team and appeared sincere in his desire to sell his interest in the Gateway Paint and Varnish Company. Industry rumors and the contacts of the investigating team with Donald Wyatt, suggested that a price acceptable to Wyatt might easily be one which Avalon *could* pay.

REPORT OF INVESTIGATING TEAM

A condensed version of the report submitted by the investigating team to Mr. Bayne on July 27, 1967, is presented in the following paragraphs:

Ownership

Gateway Paint and Varnish Company is a manufacturer of paints, varnishes, and shoe polish. The company has been in the business of manufacturing paints and varnishes since 1890 and in the shoe polish business since 1937. Of the 16,000 shares of Gateway common stock outstanding, Mr. Wyatt owns 8,500; his widowed sister, Mrs. Marie Townsend, owns 2,000; members of his father's brother's family own 4,000; and 1,500 shares are owned by key employees of Gateway. The entire 8,000 shares of 7 per cent cumulative preferred stock is owned by the Warner Robbins family of St. Louis. This stock was issued to the Robbins family in exchange for their stock in the shoe polish business which Gateway took over in 1937.

Accounting

Gateway's comparative balance sheet and income statements, certified by a small independent auditing firm whose senior partner is an old family friend of the Wyatts, are presented as Exhibits 14-2 and 14-3. Although the income statement does not reveal the fact, shoe polish accounted for about 17 per cent of Gateway's gross dollar sales in the fiscal year ending June 30, 1967.

Exhibit 14-2. Gateway Paint and Varnish Company: Comparative Balance Sheets ($000) as of June 30

		1967		1966
Assets				
Cash		$ 702		$ 610
Accounts receivable (net)		2,141		1,944
Prepaid items		142		192
Inventory		4,910		4,641
Total current assets		7,895		7,387
Plant and equipment at cost	$5,860		$5,842	
Less accumulated depreciation	3,327		2,977	
Net fixed assets		2,533		2,865
Intangible assets		10		10
Total assets		$10,438		$10,262
Liabilities and shareholder equity				
Due banks — current		$ 450		$ 390
Accounts payable		1,324		1,351
Accrued items		723		684
Total current liabilities		2,497		2,425
Due banks — 5% term loan (due July 1, 1969)		1,475		1,575
7% cumulative preferred stock ($100 par)		900		900
Common stock — ($100 par)		1,600		1,600
Retained earnings		3,966		3,762
		$10,438		$10,262

Exhibit 14-3. Gateway Paint and Varnish Company: Comparative Operating Statements ($000) for Fiscal Year Ended

		6/30/67		6/30/66
Sales (net)		$21,167		$22,385
Cost of sales		14,994		15,998
Gross profit		6,173		6,387
Selling expense	$4,595		$4,628	
Administrative expense	1,388	5,983	1,250	5,878
Operating profit		190		509
Other income or (loss)[a]		207		(63)
Net profit before income taxes		397		446
Provision for income taxes		140		213
Net earnings retained in business		$ 257		$ 233

[a] In fiscal 1967 this is accounted for chiefly by sale of almost fully depreciated idle plant at Los Angeles.

The company's formal pension plan is on a pay-as-you-go basis, with the cost of funding past service liability estimated at $150,000. Mr. Wyatt stated that the company could not afford "frills" in accounting and that Gateway therefore has no formalized budgeting or profit planning. The company's cost accounting system is minimal. There has been no analysis of profits by lines or territories. Gross profit margins, expressed as a percentage of sales, are approximately 10% under the industry average. Selling and administrative expenses are approximately 10% above the industry average.

An examination of Gateway's tax returns discloses that the returns of fiscal 1965 and fiscal 1966 have not been audited by the Internal Revenue Service. Avalon's tax experts feel that, if a claim were properly pressed, a refund of approximately $200,000 might be secured on these years' returns. All contracts of Gateway appear to be in order, with no allowances necessary on purchase or sales commitments.

Plants and Branches

The company has paint and varnish manufacturing plants in San Francisco, California, and in Seattle, Washington. The shoe polish manufacturing plant is located in St. Louis. Wholesale-retail paint branch operations are located in San Francisco, Oakland, Berkeley, Sacramento, Fresno, Santa Barbara, Hollywood, Huntington Park, and San Diego, California; Portland, Salem, and Klamath Falls, Oregon; Seattle, Spokane, and Tacoma, Washington; and in Victoria and Vancouver, British Columbia. Each branch is stocked with a complete line of paints and varnishes; branch salesmen, in addition to taking care of the walk-in trade, call on jobbers, large retail outlets, contractors, and industrial users.

Condition of Assets

Because of the obsolescence factor, inventories appear to be overvalued by about $600,000. Accounts receivable appear to be reasonably valued. The engineering and appraisal reports conclude that total book value probably represents a fair valuation of the total fixed assets. Striking differences exist, however, in the quality of the three productive facilities. The multi-floored building and the equipment of the Seattle plant are obsolete and dilapidated. The site, however, is a very desirable industrial location. At San Francisco the building is well adapted to operations; and the basic equipment, designed to produce Gateway's standard line of paints, is adequate for that purpose. Extensive alterations, however, would be required to produce "newer-type" lines of paints, such as latex wall paint, and special purpose paint for industrial machinery, and special colors and finishes used on some consumer durable goods. The entire plant at St. Louis is old, inefficient, and worn-out. The 25-acre site at St. Louis is in a very desirable industrial location; consequently, the land is quite valuable. The site contains more land than is needed for operations. Approximately 10 acres have been leased to a trucking company for terminal parking facilities; the lease has three more years to run.

The two principal patents, which Mr. Wyatt considers as important assets of the company, have 5 years to run. Since many companies in the paint industry apparently copy competing processes and formulas with impunity, the value of patent protection is dubious. The basic value of the patents and other intangibles would be difficult to estimate. They are believed, however, to be worth considerably more than book value.

Marketing

Paint is distributed via the sales branches previously described and through jobbers and dealers. Direct sales are made to large maintenance and industrial accounts. The company bids on industrial paint jobs, and furnishes all necessary labor to complete the contracts. In addition to the domestic marketing facilities for paints and varnishes on the West Coast, Gateway has an extensive distribution system for these products in Mexico, Argentina, Brazil, the Hawaiian Islands, and in the Philippines. Shoe polish is sold only in the United States. It is promoted and distributed on a national scale through wholesale houses, who, in turn, sell to shoe repair shops, limited price variety stores, and department stores. Many salesmen are used to call on the wholesale establishments.

Market analyses indicate that customer acceptance of Gateway's product lines is very good, considering that Gateway prices are slightly higher than competitors' and that the product line is badly unbalanced. Gateway is considered by the trade to be a quality manufacturer. The company consistently sells its larger quantity buyers, and customer services are considered satisfactory. Gateway is not well diversified in "new-type" lines. As an earlier part of the report brought out, it is weak on paints for special purposes. Also some branches are not well located. If the product line

were balanced, and if the advertising manager, who is paid handsomely, were producing aggressively, advertising might be more successful. Sales and advertising
policies appear uncoordinated and unrelated to production schedules. Product packaging is regarded as rather drab by the trade. Package sizes are regarded, however,
as adequate in Gateway's standard line of paints.

Avalon's marketing specialists made a preliminary analysis of the possibilities
of enlarging geographically the market for Gateway's products. The tentative conclusions were that, with present production facilities in San Franciso, (1) the areas
of Nevada, Arizona, and Utah could be serviced adequately; and (2) the prospects
of attracting a satisfactory share of the market in these states are fairly bright. The
specialists also believe that, if a new plant were located in a place such as Oklahoma
City, the booming market area of Texas, Oklahoma, Kansas, New Mexico, and Mis-
souri could be tapped. Use of a construction and leasing arrangement for the plant
might keep Avalon's capital investment for such an asset manageably low.

Market forecasts for paint sales on the West Coast and in foreign countries where
Gateway has been distributing look very favorable. Forecasts, however, indicate
little prospect of enlarging Gateway's share of the shoe polish market in the United
States.

The foreign operation was reported to be staffed with good talent which has produced very satisfactory sales at higher profit margins than have prevailed in domestic
markets. The foreign operation is the only decentralized, autonomous segment of the
Gateway business. Mr. Wyatt has allowed this segment of the business much more
independence than any other segment possesses.

Executives and Employee Benefits

Mr. Donald Wyatt, the 64-year-old president and principal owner of Gateway, has
spent his entire business life with the company. He is well-known and respected in
trade circles. Because of his feeling of having inadequate management personnel
under him, he has never delegated authority and responsibility when possible to
avoid such delegation. He conducts a highly centralized operation. Over-all management performance is spotty; however, it is hard to judge because of the lack of records of the type which would permit definite analysis of performance. Some management talent may be latent in the organization, but no formal management training
program has been used to develop it.

The company vice-president, Mr. Martin Bowden, age 59, has had four years'
service with the company. His prior business experience was largely confined to the
vice-presidency of a local beer manufacturer. He was in charge of sales. There is a
surplus of executives in many categories. Since most of this talent is perhaps only
average in ability, few of these executives could be absorbed into the Avalon company. The sales manager is not aggressive, but has good contacts. Avalon in 1966
considered hiring him, but turned him down because of his lack of "progressive-
ness." (At this point one ironic observation was made by the Barker D. Small Associates experts: Where Gateway is weakest in executive talent, Avalon has no surplus

available to plug the gaps. For example, Avalon has no surplus of top-flight cost accountants.) A tremendous duplication of office personnel exists in Gateway, with too many "high salaried office boys." Moreover, salaries paid management talent are inconsistent. These two conditions pose an integration problem in respect to Avalon's profit sharing system.

Personnel practices of Gateway are considered mediocre. In spite of poor hiring and firing practices, however, approximately 60 per cent of the production employees at all three plants may be considered very good. The fringe benefits of the company, including such things as pensions, vacations, life insurance, retirement, and other privileges are considered above average for the size of company involved. The reason for this is perhaps the powerful union which has successfully negotiated contracts more favorable to the employees than are the typical contracts of the industry. If Avalon were to absorb Gateway, relations with Avalon's union might become strained because of the disparity in benefits.

Research

Chemists' analysis of Gateway's product line shows that product quality is generally good. The engineers report that the product line is adaptable to improvement from the point of view of production techniques and quality. Probably the weakest link in the Gateway company is research. The company lacks an adequate research staff and has been riding along on the innovations of the chemist who originally developed the line. In recent years the research department has been content to copy the research of others, which policy forces the company to be in a position of following, not leading, the competition. Mr. Wyatt says, however, "Paint is paint, and Gateway is up there in the paint business."

Miscellaneous

The report also contained the following observations:

1. Certain management policies of the Wyatt family have drastically lowered the efficiency of Gateway. Wyatt's inability to delegate has bogged him down in detail and has contributed to a poorly integrated operation.

2. No open market exists for Gateway stock.

3. Wyatt is willing to serve on Avalon's board to add continuity to the Gateway operations until Avalon management has fully assimilated the business.

4. Gateway is about as large a company as Avalon can comfortably absorb.

5. The probability of Avalon's holding the bulk of Gateway's customers is "well above the point of a calculated risk."

6. In every acquisition which Avalon has made to date it has had to furnish or develop from within the newly acquired operation virtually all the management talent required by the new operation. The presumption is that this practice would have to be followed in the event that Avalon acquired Gateway.

7. The acquisition could include (1) the complete company; (2) the name, assets, liabilities, and "the going business" (but not the corporate shell), (3) the total assets and the "going business"; or (4) the net assets and the "going business." Payment could be made by (1) exchange of some of Avalon's unissued common or preferred stock for Gateway stock; (2) cash; (3) some cash and stock combination. The Warner Robbins' family has been contacted. The family is willing to sell for cash; a premium of approximately 20 per cent for its preferred shares was suggested. The family, however, would rather exchange its preferred for Avalon preferred at a ratio which would avoid reduction of the family's income.

8. Gateway "is a fine old company — dying on the vine."

Author Index

Subject Index